George Conroy

Occasional Sermons, Addresses and Essays

George Conroy

Occasional Sermons, Addresses and Essays

ISBN/EAN: 9783744742160

Printed in Europe, USA, Canada, Australia, Japan

Cover: Foto ©Lupo / pixelio.de

More available books at **www.hansebooks.com**

OCCASIONAL

SERMONS, ADDRESSES,

AND

ESSAYS

BY THE

RIGHT REV. GEORGE CONROY, D.D.

Late Bishop of Ardagh,

AND APOSTOLIC DELEGATE TO CANADA AND NEWFOUNDLAND.

New Edition.

DUBLIN

M. H. GILL AND SON

O'CONNELL STREET

1888

PREFACE.

A FEW of the Sermons, Addresses, and Essays of the late
Bishop of Ardagh are here given to the reader, in the hope
that they may be found useful and instructive, as well as
worthy of the Author's distinguished reputation. Some of them
have had the advantage of the author's own revision; some
of them were never intended for publication : but all of them
are fair specimens of the Author's opinions, style, and methods
of thought. It is for the reader to judge whether the work
now published deserves a place in Catholic literature. The
Author's memory will be entirely vindicated, and the highest
tribute paid to it, if this volume be instrumental in making
men of thought to recoil from the evils of our day—Pagan
Philosophy, drear Materialism, Religious Indifference, and contempt or heedlessness of the Apostolic teachings. It is con-
fidently hoped, in the words of the admirable preface to the
"Mystical Flora" of St. Francis de Sales, with whose gentle
spirit the late Bishop of Ardagh loved to act, that this book
"may bring pleasure to the lover of nature, as well as profit
to the seeker after grace."

FEAST OF ST. JOSEPH, 1884.

CONTENTS.

viii   CONTENTS.

ESSAYS.

MEMOIR.

George Michael Conroy was born, January 1, 1833, in the town of Dundalk, of parents whose piety and respectability are associated with the highest dignities of the Church of Armagh. At an early age he was marked out for the ecclesiastical state. He received his first instruction at Dromiskin, in the county Louth, and from this village he was moved in a short time to his native town, where he studied at an intermediate school kept by a classical teacher, whose name was Dunphy. Here he remained till the year 1848, when he entered the Diocesan School of Armagh. In Armagh he spent some two years.

A concursus was held in the year 1850, and at this concursus young George Conroy carried off first prize from all comers. The Archbishop, Dr. Cullen, who presided at the examination, saw that the young student showed considerable ability and cleverness, and he resolved to send him to the Propaganda College, Rome. In this college, which then, at least, counted amongst its professors the greatest theologians, canonists, and moral philsophers of the age, George Conroy studied for seven years—from 1850 to 1857—with marked success, gaining at least one gold medal, and almost always rising to first in his class. In his college he was esteemed learned, and pious, and

2

amiable. He easily gained the degrees of Bachelor of Philosophy and Doctor of Divinity. His health, however, suffered from his studies, and he returned to Ireland very much the worse of his labours, with a delicacy of constitution of which he never completely rid himself, and which many of his friends could not reconcile with his robust appearance. After a short time his native air restored him to better health; he then entered upon his useful career, for which his previous life was but the preparation.

Whilst he was still pursuing his studies in the Propaganda, his Archbishop had been translated to Dublin. This latter event occurred in 1852. Towards the end of the year 1857, the Archbishop of Dublin and the then President of the All-Hallows Missionary College, Drumcondra, Dr. Woodlock, the present learned, holy, and zealous Bishop of Ardagh, knowing the rare abilities of Dr. Conroy, and his fitness for a chair just then vacant at All-Hallows, determined to secure his services for the college. They soon obtained his acceptance of the post, and with the consent of Dr. Dixon, who then sat in the archiepiscopal chair of Armagh, Dr. Conroy became professor in All-Hallows in the latter part of the year 1857. As will be seen, his twofold duties now entered upon—of teacher and Dean—fitted him for the work that God was to impose upon him in the not distant future; and the life begun in the meritorious work of preparing the young missionary for his arduous and heroic work, was to be consumed in a foreign land in advancing the same holy interests which, in Propaganda, in All-Hallows, and in America, he had espoused, and held dear.

He had one other and most important duty given him in All-Hallows. The college was just then after surmounting the difficulties of early existence always felt by institutions that are destined for great good. He had, in common with his fellow-professors, to go through various parts of Ireland and England, during the summer months, to collect funds for the college, in order to enable it to give support and education to those who were destined for the poorer missions. He often afterwards, in modest language, spoke of this as the instrument which was intended to give him courage to address an audience—others would say, which was intended to make him an eloquent preacher. He never failed to convince his hearers that charity claimed and merited their support; and that those who came of the same race as St. Columbkille, and St. Columbanus, and St. Brendan, should help the young missionary to preach the Gospel of peace in distant America, and to the uncivilised tribes of Africa, and to the untaught populations of New Holland. Oftentimes at first badly received, sometimes looked upon with distrust by those who considered that Irishmen had quite enough to do for themselves for the first century after winning their religious freedom, he had to make the best case he could, and, by the sanctity of his cause, and the eloquence of his appeal, find a way to the heart of his hearers. And so he became skilled in the art of oratory, of which a few specimens will be found in this volume.

In the year 1866 he left All-Hallows and became Secretary to Cardinal Cullen. The mutual esteem that sprung up between the illustrious archbishop and the young schoolboy in Armagh, was ever gaining new strength, and proving itself in its growth. He had, together with this office of secretary—for which his elegant and agreeable manners, his bright disposition, and his solid and varied learning singularly fitted him—the chaplaincy of Mountjoy Prison, and certain missionary work in the Cathedral, Marlborough-street; and he was associated with the present learned Bishop of Ossory in the editorship of the *Ecclesiastical Record,* whose aim was so well expressed in its motto:—" *Ut Christiani ita et Romani sitis.*" In what home of Roman thought and Roman learning could this idea be woven into so many pleasing shapes, and its original purpose be so well attained, as in that house in Eccles-street where lived three of Rome's most distinguished sons !

In 1871, Dr. Conroy was raised to the Episcopacy. Some short time before this dignity seemed nearer to him than it did just now. During the last days of his cousin, Dr. Kieran, rumour had it, and those best competent to tell made it known, that Dr. Conroy was, by the almost unanimous consent of the ecclesiastical body of Armagh, destined to rule over his native diocese. There is a curious history in connection with this part of the present memoir, to which the future ecclesiastical historian may deem it right to refer, and which proves how inscrutable are God's ways. At present we shall only say that twice did Providence seem on the very point of entrusting great dignities to Dr. Conroy, which he was not destined to enjoy—one was the occasion just referred to, and the other was when, after having been raised to the rank of Apostolic Delegate, when everything occurring around him, and every one who witnessed his ability and success, promised him the highest favours the Pope could bestow, death put an end to his career.

His appointment to the See of Ardagh quite took him by surprise. But few, indeed, considered that he should succeed the late bishop, Dr. M'Cabe. He was at break-fast one morning, not thinking he should soon quit Dublin for ever, when the Cardinal made known to him that already the appointment had been made.

He was consecrated in St. Mel's Cathedral, Longford, on April 11th, 1871. The consecrating prelate was Cardinal Cullen. The cathedral was decorated in a most superb fashion. Appropriate flags and banners waved from the Ionic columns; the sanctuary was ablaze with all the ornamentation that could be procured. Never did that noble, severe Grecian temple look to such advantage, and never was it seen so gay and joyous and bright, and yet so ecclesiastical, as on that Easter Tuesday. Its young bishop, with his thirty-nine summers on his still fresh brow, his quick step, his bright, flashing eye, seemed destined to outlive his generation. And when one heard his well-attuned voice, and watched his graceful bearing, and took in his eloquent words at the evening's banquet, he was glad to think that now, indeed, was at hand the reversal of the story that Ardagh never gave to its spiritual rulers length of days. Few amongst that gathering—the flower of the diocese—could let in the thought that even in this case the story would receive but another confirmation.

For six years from that day till his appointment as Delegate Apostolic, he laboured zealously but unostentatiously for his flock. He appeared amongst his priests and people, ever guiding them with a strong hand, and yet in such a way as to seem rather their willing fellow-labourer than their chief. He believed in the maxim, that—

> "Man should be taught as if you taught him not,
> And things unknown proposed as things forgot."

His gentleness of character did not abandon him even in strained and tangled circumstances ; like the dew that in secret fertilizes whilst the rain-storm ruins, he spoke the mild word that breaketh wrath ; he loved to appeal to the inner heart ; he made his advice fatherly, and his intercourse genial, and his exhortation winning : and so, without ceasing to be the ruler that he was, he won the affections of his flock.

He used to say, that to a bishop his seminary was as the apple of his eye. To this, therefore, he applied himself with all the energy of his character. St. Mel's College, Longford, is a building not unworthy of a Catholic diocese. The great Dr. Kilduff, whose memory is still fresh in a grateful people, founded and endowed it. The former he did with the co-operation of priests and people, the latter he did from his own private means. Dr. Conroy saw that in the seminary of his diocese he had the materials in his hands of advancing Catholic and educational interests. It was for him who now inherited the riches which the toil of his predecessors had amassed, to carry out what had been so well begun. He accordingly spared no labour to make his seminary a flourishing institution. At first, whilst he lived in the college, and afterwards, when he might be seen to drive each day from the bishop's house in Newtownforbes, he was to be found continually in the class-halls, or amongst the students in the play-ground, or with the Professors—teaching, advising, consulting—showing by every word and act how dear the work was to him, and how he strove for its success. There were those, indeed, who considered his lofty views excessive, and who questioned the prudence of turning a diocesan seminary into a college of higher ecclesiastical studies. But he always maintained that the project was possible, that such was the mind of the Council of Trent, and that his views had favour with the authorities in Rome. Whatever may be thought of this reasoning it cannot be denied that his college was always full, that he was able to send to the Propaganda, and to Maynooth, and to the Catholic University, some of the most distinguished students they had ; and that there was a high standard of polite as well as ecclesiastical education maintained in its halls.

He established middle schools throughout the diocese, at Granard, at Ballymahon, and at Athlone, and over each he appointed a priest.

It is not generally known that when the Intermediate Act, which did and still does so much for intermediate education in Ireland, was being conceived, Dr. Conroy was the bishop with whom the minister, Sir Michael Hicks Beach, treated ; and that his scholarship and eloquent statement of Catholic claims made it clear to the government of Lord Beaconsfield that any interference with Catholic teaching would be unjust, and should not be tolerated.

He brought the Sisters of Mercy to Ballymahon, the Sisters of the Presentation to Granard, and the Marist Sisters to Carrick-on-Shannon ; and, in so doing, he brought education to the children of the poor, consolation to the sick and dying, peace to the afflicted, and an example of holiness to those who lived in the world. His greatest solicitude was shown to those who were engaged in this noble, heroic cause.

In the year 1876, Cardinal Franchi came to Dublin, as the guest of Cardinal Cullen, and took part in the blessing of Clonliffe College Chapel. During his short stay in Ireland he had many opportunities of making the acquaintance of the Bishop of Ardagh. A skilful discerner of character, the Prefect of the Propaganda was considered to be. He went back to Rome with the conviction that there was in the Ireland of that day, as well as in the Ireland of former times, the material out of which might be moulded the fitting representative of the Pope in foreign countries. He made known to his Eminence of Dublin that he would represent to the Holy Father, the heroic Pius IX., that Dr. Conroy was exactly such a prelate as should be despatched to Malabar to settle some difficulties that had existed there. This was kept secret from the principal persons concerned till the March of the following year, when a summons came for his presence in Rome. On his appearance there, Canada was given to him as his delegation, and he had no hesitation in selecting it : its climate, he thought, would better suit him than any to be found in the East.

On the 10th of April, 1877, after several interviews with the Holy Father, who in one of these audiences told him he was, no doubt, accepting office without having desired it, and even against his will, but yet that it was necessary sacrifices should be made for Holy Church; after receiving instructions from Cardinal Franchi, and the Cardinal's encouraging assurance that, notwithstanding his (Dr. Conroy's) diffidence, he must succeed, and that the Propaganda would give him all the assistance in its power, he took his departure from Rome, armed with the powers of Apostolic Delegate.

The following is a copy of his brief of appointment, and it will be seen that his powers and jurisdiction were most ample :

PIUS PP. IX.

VENERABILI FRATRI GEORGIO CONROY EPISCOPO ARDAGADENSI.

VENERABILIS FRATER, SALUTEM ET APOSTOLICAM BENEDICTIONEM.

Antiquissimi moris in Ecclesia est, ut Romani Pontifices, quo recte fungantur commissio sibi Apostolatus officio, habeant in dissitis locis, sub variis nominibus, Ecclesiasticos viros aut ex Provinciæ Episcopis selectos, aut ab hac Alma Urbe missos, qui ea qua par est jurisdictione muniti, suas illic vices obeant, et fidei incremento, morum puritati, canonum observantiæ, Cleri, Populique disciplinæ solerter advigilent. Itaque cum res Ecclesiasticæ in Canadæ regionibus eo in statu versentur, ut peculiarem Sanctæ hujus Sedis solicitudinem omnino expostulent, Nos cum Venerabilibus Fratribus Nostris S. R. E. Cardinalibus negotiis Propagandæ Fidei præpositis communicata re sedaloque perpensa, in eam sententiam devenimus, ut Delegatum Apostolicum in eas regiones mitteremus, qui earumdem statum cognoscere accurate valeat, controversias et quæstiones pro sua prudentia et arbitrio componere satagat, quæ vero praviora videantur, et medica Sanctæ hujus Sedis manu omnino egeant, ad Nos diligenter referre maturet. Quæ cum ita sint, ab quibusvis excommunicationis et interdicti, aliisque ecclesiasticis sententiis, censuris, et pœnis quovis modo vel quavis de causa latis quas si forte incurreris, hujus tantum rei gratia Te absolventes ac absolutum fore censentes, Te, Venerabilis Frater, qui religionis dilatandæ studio, pietate, doctrina, et in gerendis rebus prudentia egregie præter ceteros commendaris, de Venerbilium quos memoravimus Fratrum Nostrorum consilio, auctoritate Nostra Apostolica tenore præsentium Delegati Apostolici pro regione Canadensi ad Nostrum et Sanctæ hujus Sedis beneplacitum, titulo, juribus, honoribus, ac privilegiis augemus et decoramus ; itemque singulas atque universas Tibi facultates necessarias et opportunas tribuimus atque impertimus quibus præditus Ecclesiarum Canadæ, quas descripsimus, necessitatibus ac bono consulere possis et valeas. At enim volumus, ut officium Tuum exerceas juxta mandata, quæ corumdem Venerabilium Fratrum Nostrorum Congregatio Tibi dederit, ac non modo Diœcesibus Inferioris et Superioris Canadæ, sed etiam totius dominationis Canadæ, nec non Diœcesibus quæ in Insula Terræ Novæ sitæ sunt, Nostro et Sanctæ hujus Sedis nomine atque auctoritate præsis. Ceterum non dubitamus quin Venerabiles Fratres Archiepiscopi et Episcopi, item Clerus, Populusque earum regionum, Te Nostrum et Sanctæ hujus Sedis Delegatum debita reverentia et obsequio sint prosequnturi, atque in Delegato Delegantis auctoritatem suscipientes, illius consilio, monitis, mandatis, prompta animi voluntate obtemperaturi. Hæc volumus, mandamus, præcipimus ; decernentes præsentes Nostras Litteras firmas validas et efficaces existere et fore, suosque plenarios et integros effectus sortiri ac obtinere, et ab iis ad quos pertinent pertinerintve inviolabiliter observari, sicque in præmissis per quoscunque ludices et delegatos etiam causarum Palatii Apostolici Auditores judicari et definiri debere, atque irritum et inane, si secus super his a quoquam quavis auctoritate scienter vel ignoranter contigerit attentari. Non obstante, quatenus opus sit, Benedicti XIV. Prædecessoris Nostri rec. mem. super Divisione Matm., aliisque Apostolicis ac synodalibus, provincialibusque et universalibus conciliis editis generalibus vel specialibus Constitutionibus et ordinationibus, quibus omnibus et singulis, illorum tenores præsentibus pro plene et sufficienter expressis ac de verbo ad verbum insertis habentes, illis alias in suo robore permansuris, ad præmissorum effectum hac vice dumtaxant specialiter et expresse derogamus, ceteris contrariis quibuscunque. Volumus denique, ut præsentium Litterarum transumptis seu exemplis etiam impressis, manu alicujus Notarii publici subscriptis et sigillo viri in Ecclesiastica dignitate constituti munitis, eadem prorsus fides adhibeatur quæ adhiberetur ipis præsentibus. Datum Romæ apud S. Petrum sub Annulo Piscatoris die X. Aprilis, MDCCCLXXVII. Pontificatus Nostri Anno Trigesimo primo.

(Locus Sigilli.) F. CARD. ASQUINIUS.

On the 24th of April, Dr. Conroy returned to his diocese, not to enjoy the quiet of home, but rather *en route* for his distant mission. He received an affectionate address from his priests, in replying to which he was unusually sad and quite overcome with emotion, as if he had a presentiment that he was speaking to them for the last time and was parting with them for ever. He promulgated the decrees of the National Synod of Maynooth, in which he took a leading part as secretary. He entrusted the government of his diocese to his Vicar-General, Very Rev. N. O'Flanagan, who, he announced, had from the Pope the powers of an Apostolic Administrator. He procured the assistance of his esteemed and faithful friend, the present Bishop of Achonry, Most Rev. Dr. M'Cormack, for the Confirmations;—it was during these Confirmations the clergy became so conversant with the virtues, the learning, and general excellence of Dr. M'Cormack's life and character, that they afterwards sent forward his name to Rome for the appointment to the vacant See. He paid a hurried visit to his parents, whom he loved and honoured with the tenderest affection; he took with him, as secretary, the Rev. P. Reddy, at present the esteemed P.P. of Kilronan, and embarked at Queenstown on April 29th, 1877.

A remarkable story is told of him as he quitted Dublin for Queenstown. A number of relatives and attached friends accompanied him to the King's Bridge. As he entered the carriage, they offered him their sincere good wishes, and promised their prayers; and, as the whistle was sounded, and the train was on its way, he called to one of his friends and said: "Do you see all these kind, good friends, whose sympathy I have and of whose esteem and honour I am justly proud. They have come for my funeral."

The first act of the Delegate Apostolic was the consecration of the Archbishop, Most Rev. Dr. Hannon of Halifax; and the life of Dr. Conroy, from this period, belongs to the Ecclesiastical History of Canada and Newfoundland. He was well received everywhere, even from his landing, and as time went on, and the bishops became acquainted with his kind and conciliating disposition, he began to grow into his place as representative of the Pope. The people were charmed with his simple eloquence, and they seemed to recognise in his discourses new evidences of the Church's greatness. Addresses of welcome and loyalty were read to His Excellency, as he was now called, in every town through which he passed. The chief men of Canada, clerical and lay, came to offer homage to his person and his office. He presided at the sacred functions; as Delegate he had precedence of all the archbishops and bishops. It was a matter of wonder to all how he could have addressed, sometimes in Latin, sometimes in French, sometimes in English, the many deputations that waited on him. For each he had an immediate reply—at once elegant, solid, appropriate, and to the point—which proved him worthy of his new position. In Quebec and in Montreal, where he resided for a time, he was regarded with the utmost veneration, and even admiration; and every manifestation that the people could make of their respect and attachment to the man, and the bishop, and the Pope's representative, was right willingly resorted to. . From Canadian archbishops, who represented the old French noblesse; from Irishmen and Scotchmen, who boasted of Celtic blood and genius; from the Iroquois Indians, whose forefathers put to death the sons of Ignatius in their efforts to plant the cross amongst them; from the representative of English royalty who opened the banqueting-rooms of Government House to his illustrious fellow-countryman, from fellows of universities, from the outcast Magdalen, from prisoners in their cells, from the poor and wretched and forlorn, from all he received words of affectionate greeting at first, and then, as he was better known, assurances of grateful esteem and high approval.

It was well known that the Cardinal Prefect of the Propaganda was exceedingly pleased at his success. The Delegate wrote from Montreal in 1877 : " I received from the Holy See the most encouraging letters, in which the Holy Father condescends to manifest his sovereign satisfaction with what has been done since I came to Canada. Nothing can impair the completeness of the approval my poor labours have received." What was the precise benefit he had brought to the Church in Canada, or the changes he had made in its working, or the differences he had gently smoothed over, or whether the fruit he sowed still remains, we have no means of knowing; nor does the nature of his mission permit the veil to be rudely lifted. But history will record two facts—at present they do not require proof. First, no representative of a sovereign received a more cordial welcome, or more sincere congratulations, and (as time went on) more unmistakable proofs of success. Secondly, in all his negotiations, even those that were the most delicate and the most embarrassing, and in all his arrangements and judgments, he showed consummate tact, varied learning, undoubted prudence, even-handed justice, and the most painstaking concern for the interests entrusted to him. None other but a man of real ability could satisfy the demands that were made upon him. In satisfying them, he seemed only to have to draw upon an illimitable resource : certainly, none other but a cultured mind could have given the means to acquit himself as he did.

In the beginning of the following year, 1878, after spending eight months of incessant toil, he left Canada on a tour through the States. He had received from the Holy See several important commissions. In executing them, he proceeded slowly through the different cities, and as he went on his long journey towards the Pacific, he was beset with invitations to lecture and to preach. When any great charity was to be advanced, he willingly gave his advocacy. He was presented with addresses by the American priests who studied with him in Propaganda, and by those who studied under him in All-Hallows College at home. Receptions were given in his honour ; and he said that the costly banquets now organised to bid him welcome were more fatiguing than the hard work at Montreal. Except one week that he devoted to a spiritual retreat in Woodstock College, in the heart of the forest, where he put himself under the care of a Jesuit, for many years confessor to Leo XIII., his journey was full of labour.

At San Francisco he received a brilliant reception from Archbishop Allemani, his priests, and people, and from his former confrère at All-Hallows, Bishop O'Connell. The Delegate was greatly struck with the natural beauty of the country, the growing prosperity of the Catholic Church, and the results of Catholic education, as well as the teeming plenty that everywhere met his eye. He wrote to a friend: "This valley of Santa Clara is the most fertile spot on earth. Literally, it is overflowing with corn and wine. The sun is always bright, and the sky ever clear."

We must not omit to give here, as a specimen of some hundred others, an address presented to him by the Students of St. Mary's College, San Francisco, and the Delegate's reply. The latter, though made *impromptu*, is characteristic of his style; and the two great springs of thought that, with him, ever gushed into eloquence— Faith and Country—are availed of with profit, and are seen to advantage. A mind less keen than his could not help admiring the free religion and free education he found around him; how he did yearn to breathe the same in his own country these lines eloquently tell:

ADDRESS TO HIS EXCELLENCY.

MAY IT PLEASE YOUR EXCELLENCY,—We, the students of St. Mary's College, the pupils of the venerable De La Salle, beg leave to approach your Excellency in a spirit of the most profound respect and veneration for your sacred character, and to assure your Excellency that we regard your visit as the most distinguished honour that could be conferred upon us. Under any circumstances, the presence amongst us of a dignitary of our Holy Mother, the Church, would demand an expression of our reverence and homage; but in your Excellency we recognise not only the sacred character and high dignity of bishop, but the chosen counsellor of the Holy See, and the special envoy of the Vicar of Christ. We feel, in the presence of your Excellency, encouraged as we are by the approving smile of our dear and venerated Archbishop, the father of the Church in California, and in the presence of another distinguished bishop, and so many zealous pastors of the Church, that we are brought nearer the chair of Peter, and more under the direct influence of the paternal care of the Holy Father. Your Excellency is his mouthpiece, his messenger of peace and reconciliation, the executor of his mature deliberations and wise conclusions; and mindful as we are of the high esteem in which our late Holy Father held the American Church, and his tender solicitude for the welfare of Catholic youth and Catholic education, we cannot adequately express the reverence, gratification, and joy that fill our hearts in the presence of your Excellency, who *was* his confidant and is the angel of his love and good-will. There are other sentiments which bid us rejoice on this occasion. Your Excellency is a distinguished representative of the glorious hierarchy of that old nation which is the home of the love and the afflictions of the ancestors of most of us. Our mothers have breathed into our hearts, with their caresses, the same respect, reverence, and love for the Church and its ministers, that the labours, sacrifices, and sufferings of the priesthood of Ireland have made part of their nature; and they have committed us to the care of the sons of De La Salle, that while we acquire science, art, and literature, we may know their true inspiration, the principles that called them into being, and be able to give a reason for the faith that is in us. As Catholic students, and humble votaries of science, your Excellency is also endeared to us by your extensive knowledge of the laws of physics, and the happy facility with which you have moulded missiles aimed by so-called scientists for the destruction of religion, into an additional buttress of the Church of God. Your Excellency, the Catholic sons of the Golden West bid you welcome. Here, at America's uttermost bounds of the boundless kingdom of the Church, by the sun-set sea; within the hearing of the solemn throbs of the Pacific, which, in its immensity, grandeur, and calmness so well typifies the power your Excellency represents; here are young Catholic hearts true to the old faith, and to the traditions of their fathers : and we assure your Excellency that, in your travels throughout our vast country, none can greet you with a more heartfelt welcome than the students of St. Mary's.

May we ask your Excellency, in the deepest sincerity of our souls, to present to his Holiness Leo XIII. the offering of the love and attachment of the Catholic youth of California, whom we represent on this festive occasion.

And may it please your Excellency to say to his Holiness that in the Western world there are none more attached to his person, none more firmly connected with the light, truth, and unity, than the students of St. Mary's College.

Reply of Dr. Conroy.

My Students,—I receive with pleasure the address with which you welcome me to this College. While I thank his Grace the Archbishop for the kind thought of honouring in my humble person the supreme authority of the Apostolic See, I congratulate him on having been able to offer to-day to the Holy See a tribute of praise not unworthy of its majesty. In these days the reverence of all

Christendom is directed towards Rome, and the whole Catholic Church, like the wise men of the Gospel, is bringing forth from her "treasury old things and new," wherewith to honour Peter in the person of his latest successor, Leo. It is a pleasing sight to behold the bishops of countries made great by centuries of ancient civilisation, thanking the new-made Pontiff for the benefits conferred upon the nations by the beneficent power of which he is now the depositary. But I think a still more touching tribute is that which your bishop offers to-day in pledging to it, as he has done here to-day, the promise of the future. Since I have come to this country, I have observed with interest the various features of your national life, which, in a sufficiently extended survey, fell on my notice, and I was glad to read in them the promise of a greater destiny. I found it to be the noble characteristic of an American citizen that he loves not merely liberty, but a well-ordered liberty. Now, the very essence of well-ordered liberty consists in due respect for the rights of all, alike of the governors and of the governed, and the laws framed to make rights respected, find their best, I had almost said their only efficient, sanction in religion. The Christian theory in civil allegiance would have man obey, not from fear, but for conscience' sake. Now to us, who know that religion is not a vague sentiment, or a floating opinion, but a well-defined body of truth set forth by the living Church, built, as upon a rock, upon Peter and his successors, there can be no surer guarantee of the future strength of a nation than that its sons should be devoted by conviction and by affection to the centre of unity, the Apostolic See. No nobler tribute, therefore, could be offered to the Roman Pontificate than has been given to-day by this band of American youth, strong in their faith, and in their attachment to his person. For a richer offering cannot be made by youth to the Pontiff, and the homage of a cultured intellect, and of unfeigned affection nobler still, is this tribute when it comes from the growing city of San Francisco. For not Venice, when she became the centre of Eastern commerce, nor Genoa, when she rivalled her sister city, ever held in the history of the world a position of such importance as that created for San Francisco; for, seated on the highway of commerce, at the gate of the two worlds, she is destined to exercise an incalculable influence on both. You were pleased to address me also, as a representative of the Irish Catholic Church, and I confess that your words, most agreeable to me as they otherwise were, have awakened in me a feeling akin to sadness. I cannot help contrasting the scenes that I now witness with that which I have so often beheld in the capital of my beloved native land. There, as here, I have rejoiced to see the sons of Irish fathers, true to the best instincts of their race, throng the halls of the noble institutions which Catholic Ireland has created, and year by year endows, to be for her people a centre of intellectual life made perfect by religious truth. There, as here to-day, I have noted in the Irish student the flashing eye that tells of intellectual power; and I have felt how masterful in their eloquence and young voices they are when their theme is

God, or their country, or the truth of science. But at this point unhappily the parallel ceases. I know that this college, notwithstanding that it lifts on its summit high over the Pacific water the Cross of Christ; notwithstanding that its directors are men vowed to the religious life; is yet a chartered university, recognised by the State, and entitled to confer on its students those academic honours which are among the most precious rewards of scholarship. I know that its students can pass at once from its halls to make their way in the liberal professions, without first having been forced to wrest a degree from other universities whose office it is to kill the Church's faith in men's souls. There is no hateful monopoly here created by jealous statecraft to secure and perpetuate the ascendancy of a handful of citizens over the great mass of the nation. Not so in Ireland. There the State refuses to take any notice of the splendid efforts made in the cause of education by a people by no means rich in the substance of this world. There you may see the amazing spectacle of two parallel systems of education which absolutely ignore each other. One, the creation of the nation, the other the handicraft of the civil power, and the two divide everything between them, but in such wise that one possesses the confidence and affection of the masses of the people, while the other wields the patronage of the State. With you, when a student claims an academical degree, the State does not ask him where he has studied, or by what process he has been taught, but what he knows; and if it should find in him gifts and acquirements such as are calculated to make him eminently useful in his generation, it will not refuse to reward him for his years of study because he has chosen to add religion to his science by making a Catholic college his *alma mater*. But, if what I have seen here and in other similar institutions in America has somewhat saddened me, it has also taught me a lesson which I hope I shall never forget. It has given me fresh courage to fight, as becomes an Irish Catholic bishop, the battle of Catholic education in Ireland, and to strive to win for Irishmen at home what enlightened Governments have right willingly conceded to Irishmen abroad—facilities to educate their children in religion as well as in science. It has taught me not to brook the interference of the State between the parent and the soul of his child, and to resent as an outrage any attempt to dictate to a Catholic nation how it should educate its youth. I will tell my people what I have seen here, and in the noble Dominion of Canada. By the aid of a truly Catholic education in university, intermediate, and in primary schools, the Irish race at home and abroad shall become once again distinguished among the nations of the earth for its rarest gifts of genius, refined and strengthened by highest culture, yet, prouder than all its thought and its brilliancy is the satisfaction of being a willing captive to the faith of Christ.

Towards the end of April, 1878, he hurried back to Canada to assist at the Synod of Quebec. He hoped, after that, his mission would be completed. He had asked the Holy See for leave to return home, "but at Rome," as he said, "they lent a deaf ear." In a letter, written home from Chicago in May, he said: "I am somewhat tired now after my long journey from San Francisco to this city. Five days and nights of unbroken railway travelling is a little hard. In any other land, and among any other surroundings, it would have been intolerable."

A short time after assisting at the Synod he set out for Newfoundland. He was going from California, with its bright sun and its clear air, to the land of fogs, and damp, and chills, and, alas! for our fondest hopes and our grandest achievements, this journey was to close his earthly career. He was the guest of the Right Rev. Dr. Power, Bishop of St. John's, with whom he had been once associated in Holy Cross College, Dublin. The same joyous, glorious receptions were given to the Delegate Apostolic here as in Canada; in the same brilliant style did he acquit himself; and to the Catholic Church in that portion of the earth came the same peace and hope. The Delegate had run his course; the change of climate began to tell on a frame weakened by long travel, great anxiety, and hard work; congestion of the lungs attacked him; and, though doctors and everyone thought him seriously ill, no one feared that he would die. After battling with the disease for a fortnight, he was allowed to change his room for one that commanded a view of the sea; he was, in fact, considered convalescent. Two devoted Sisters of Mercy nursed him through his illness, and we have the following account of his last moments from one of them: "Everything promised well till Sunday, August 4th, when he seemed unusually strong. He talked and laughed. He sent me to assist the choir at the High Mass, the music of which was supplied by the nuns. When I returned, he was up. I said to him, 'My Lord, I think St. Dominick is continuing what St. Ignatius began?' It was on the Feast of St. Ignatius he began to recover. 'Yes,' he said, 'and St. Mary will crown all.' The day passed agreeably till 5.30, p.m., when I said he should have his dinner. He consented. Dinner was served by his servant, but before taking anything, he coughed a little, the breathing became quick and laboured, the extremities became cold and rigid. I lost no time in sending for his secretary, Father Ryan, S.J., his confessor, and the doctors. In one half hour after they came, the delegate had breathed his last." So, on the 4th of August, on the day that he was declared by the doctors convalescent, he died, uttering these memorable words : " My God, accept the sacrifice of my life." The people of St. John's, who loved him and reverenced him, who unharnessed his horses and drew his carriage amidst cheers and exultations six weeks before, now carried his corpse, by the pale light of the moon, and the flickering of torches, to the steamer Caspian. His diocese in far-off Ireland brought all that remained of him home, and laid him to rest in the spot he loved, where an Irish cross tells his life, and deeds, and death, and where sainted, loving hands make his grave ever fresh and radiant.

The universal gloom that was the result of his death, in Ireland and America, is understood, when one calls to mind that he died full of honours at the early age of forty-five, in the midst of a career of splendour unequalled by any bishop of his age, and with the prospect of reaching the highest dignities in the not-distant future : still more, when we consider that all his administrative and judicial arrangements in Canada and Newfoundland were likely to be overturned by his untimely death, and thus the same road would have to be travelled afresh by his successor.

His brothers in the Irish Episcopacy all can tell what a loss they sustained in his early death.

His learning and prudence, his quick discernment, his instinctive sense of Catholic truth, his far-reaching views, his skill in debate, and his facile pen at Synod or in council, have left a void that is hard to fill.

Only those who knew him can tell the happy, bright, cheerful, sunny character that shone in his social life.

3

Cheerful and gay himself, he suffered no one to be of gloomy disposition; kind, even to tenderness, he was the true type of the Christian father-of-the-family. He never patronised, he never assumed the role of the superior; all were charmed with his refined manners; all were delighted with his interesting conversation and his instructive remarks. With his priests around him, in his own immediate circle, he was the centre of playful humour, which was, by times, deep and sparkling, but never boisterous. When circumstances brought him into contact with the social life of men of repute in the world of letters, he was always able to make his influence prevail, and without in the smallest way lionising, he made himself revered. The very model of a Catholic bishop, whilst he continued the citizen of the world, with large views, and a big heart, and a deep sympathy, he won his way to the hearts of those who before thought him an ordinary man. Faults he had, as all the sons of men, but his excellences of character as a bishop, a scholar, and a friend, deserve a fitting recognition from all who love virtue, and truth, and charity.

SERMONS.

ST. KYRAN OF CLONMACNOIS.

"He that shall overcome, I will make him a pillar in the temple of my God; and he shall go out no more: and I will write upon him the name of my God."—APOC. iii. 12.

SOLEMN and touching is at all times the Catholic rite of dedicating churches to Almighty God, under the invocation of his saints. Especially solemn, however, and especially touching, is that rite as we have witnessed it here to-day, when, almost within sight of the gray towers of Clonmacnois, a church has been dedicated in honour of its founder, St. Kyran, patron of this ancient diocese. The spirit of the place has added to the majesty of the religious ceremony a significance peculiarly its own. As we stand here on this plain of Clonmacnois, the Christian life, as it was understood and practised by our fathers some thirteen centuries ago, comes back upon us, in the beauty of its almost unearthly perfection; and from the very foundations of this temple spring memories that find for themselves a voice in column and arch and altar, until the entire edifice becomes eloquent of the sacred glories of ancient Ireland. This is, in very truth, a temple of God; dowered, as the Church sings, with the Father's glory, espoused in love to the Royal Christ, radiant with the Spirit's gifts; but in it, as in that other temple of which my text speaks, Christ has set up a pillar which He Himself would have us admire. It is a mystic pillar, hewn of the living rock from out the kindly Irish earth; fashioned by God's hand, and the culture of Irish schools, into the sainted founder of Clonmacnois, whose heroic sanctity as monk, priest, and abbot, made him what Alcuin styles him: *the glory of the Irish race.*

Other churches in honour of St. Kyran have been raised before now in the favoured spots of Ireland where he had successively resided; but time and the spoiler's hand wasted them, and the church that we dedicate to-day is to take their vacant places. Their record, too, of the saint was but partial and fragmentary; for the direct purpose of each was to commemorate chiefly that single phase of his life of which its own site had been the scene: this new church will collect and revive the entire cycle of the memories that otherwise would perish with their crumbling walls. Two years ago these hands laid as its foundation a stone reverently gathered from the old walls of Clonmacnois, and bearing engraved upon it the mystic sign of the Holy Trinity, which our Celtic fathers loved to repeat in all their works. Springing thus from a sacred symbol, this church shall be a symbol itself, as a tree produces fruit after its kind; and its office shall be twofold. It shall address itself to men and to God. To men it shall proclaim Ireland's abiding reverence for St. Kyran's virtues; to God it shall speak Ireland's prayer for his intercession.

Such a monument, and at this time, was demanded by the piety of Catholic Ireland. That St. Kyran's virtues should never be without honour in Ireland was announced to himself thirteen centuries ago in Aran, when first he narrated to his beloved master, St. Enda, the vision that had been vouchsafed him of the future glories of Clonmacnois. He had seen the noble stream of Shannon flowing among these verdant plains, and on its banks a stately tree laden with leaves and fruits, and covering the land with its grateful shade. "That fruitful tree," explained St. Enda, "art thou thyself, for thou shalt be great before God and man, and shalt produce sweetest fruits of good works, and shalt be honoured throughout all Ireland." First fruits of these good works were the monastic virtues exercised by our saint in Aran. He entered that holy island in the bloom of his youth, and for the long years he sojourned there he was, as St. Enda described him, "the flower and strength of religious observance." His life was a pattern of humility. For seven years, well-born and scholarly as he was, he toiled with his hands at those labours which men commit to the least important of their servants. He would fain continue to the end in the practice of obedience; and even when at length he was compelled to become the master of others, he prayed that he and his charge might still continue under the guidance of St. Enda. His austerity was marvellous. Lashed by the Atlantic waves, swept by the Atlantic blasts, the island of Aran was the home of penance and mortification. Hundreds of Ireland's saints fled to it, as the anchorets had fled to the desert solitudes of the Thebaid. "Aran," says a recent writer,* "is no better than a wild rock. It is strewed over with the ruins, which may still

---

* Froude: "Short Studies," vol. ii., p. 216.

be seen, of the old hermitages; and, at their best, they could have been but such places as sheep would huddle under in a storm, and shiver in the cold and wet which would pierce through the chinks of the walls. . . . Yes, there on that wet soil, with that dripping roof above them, was the chosen home of these poor men. Through winter frost, through rain and storm, through summer sunshine, generation after generation of them, there they lived and prayed, and at last laid down and died." Most fervent among these austere men was our St. Kyran, who made of his innocent body a martyr of penance. As day followed after day, and week after week, and month after month, for seven long years, he ceased not to sacrifice his will by minutest obedience, his body by severe labour, his repose by incessant prayer; and this with the flinty rock for his bed, with coarse and scanty food, in poor attire, exposed to frost and sun, buffeted by wind and snow. And as he was a miracle of humility and of penance, so also was he a miracle of sweetest charity. As his penitential life tells eloquently of his love for God, so the story of his parting from his brethren, when he was called away from Aran to Clonmacnois, as related in the ancient Life of St. Enda, is a proof of his loving heart towards men. As the boat that was to carry him to the banks of the Shannon was spreading its sails to the breeze, St. Kyran came slowly down from his beloved cell, weeping and surrounded by his weeping brethren. Tenderly his gaze lingered on each familiar sanctuary as he passed onwards to the beach, and there, kneeling down, he asked for the last time the blessing of the father of his soul. In sign of the charity that filled their hearts, and of the brotherhood they had contracted between themselves and those who were to come after them, a cross was erected on the spot, and the two saints said: "Whosoever in after times shall break the loving bond of this our brotherhood, shall not have share in our love on earth, nor in our company in heaven." Near to where that cross stood, a church was erected to commemorate the virtues of St. Kyran as the perfect Religious. That church I have visited, and found a ruin. For centuries it told the history of St. Kyran's religious perfection; and now that its stones are scattered and its altar made desolate, would it not be a reproach to Irish Catholics if they were to allow to perish for ever the memories it was set up to record. From such a reproach the church we have dedicated to-day has saved us. These new walls take up the testimony of those old ones in their decay, and tell us of the perfect monk who toilsomely earned in Aran the merits that were to enrich Clonmacnois. Here to-day we set up once again the cross which Enda and Kyran erected in Aran, as a pledge of brotherhood between

themselves and those who were to come after them.   And by a
sweet providence of God, and as if to declare this church heir
to the office of that from which thirteen hundred years separate
it, the Bishop who dwells nearest to St. Enda's Aran has come
to Clonmacnois to-day, to join at the foot of that cross, in loving
brotherhood and communion of sacrifice, him who, most un-
worthily, holds there the place of St. Kyran.

From Aran, St. Kyran came to this part of the valley of the
Shannon, but not as yet to settle in Clonmacnois.   He was now
a priest, and on the island of Inis-Oenghin, in Lough Ree, he
practised for eight or nine years the virtues of the perfect
priest with as much fervour as he had practised on Aran those
of the perfect monk.   Surrounded now by disciples of his own,
constituted a teacher of the faith and a dispenser of the sacraments, it was no longer permitted to him to shun altogether the
concourse of men.   But he did all that he could to guard from
the world's tainted breath the gifts he had received and the
souls that had been entrusted to his charge.   St. Ambrose*
describes to us the attractions which islands such as those that
stud the noble expanse of Lough Ree possessed for the religious
men of that age.   They loved, he says, those islands " which,
as a necklace of pearls, God has set upon the bosom of the
waters, and in which those who would shun the pleasures of the
world may find a refuge wherein to practise austerity, and save
themselves from the snares of life.   The water that encompasses
them becomes, as it were, a veil to hide from mortal eye their
deeds of penance ; it aids them to acquire perfect continence ; it
feeds grave and sober thought ; it has the secret of peace ; it
repels the fierce passions of earth.   In it these faithful and
pious men find incentives to devotion.   The mysterious sounds
of the waves call for the answering sound of sacred psalmody ;
and the peaceful voices of holy men, mingled with the murmur
of the waters against the shore, rise harmonious to the heavens."
Here, then, did St. Kyran lead the life of the perfect priest.
Here did he practise the rule of a priest's life that had been
given to him at Aran, which his fellow-student, St. Carthage,
has written for us, and which tells of " the patience, humility,
prayer, fast, and cheerful abstinence ; of the steadiness, modesty,
calmness, that are due from a leader of religious men, whose
office it is to teach, in all truth, unity, forgiveness, purity, rectitude in all that is moral ; whose chief works are the constant
preaching of the Gospel for the instruction of all persons, and
the sacrifice of the Body of the great Lord upon the Holy
Altar !" (Rule of St. Carthage.)† Here did he reach the per-

---

* Hexæmeron : lib. 3, c. 5.   † " O'Curry's Lectures," vol. i., p. 376.

fection to which an ancient Irish treatise invites all priests : that "their hearts should be chaste and shining, and their minds like the foam of the wave, or the colour of the swan in the sunshine ; that is, without any particle of sin, great or small, resting in his heart!" And here another church was raised to perpetuate the memory of his virtues. Alas! that church also is in ruins. The wild briar grows in the place of sacrifice, and where saints expounded the mysteries of the faith few are ever seen, save, perhaps, thoughtless seekers after pleasure. But in this new St. Kyran's the memory of his priestly virtues shall find a new sanctuary. Right fittingly shall those years of teaching, of sanctification, and of sacrifice be represented at this altar where the same victim he offered is immolated, at these tribunals of penance where the same priestly power of loosing and binding is exercised, in this pulpit from which the same faith is preached!

At length the day came in which, about the year 544, he who was already the perfect monk and the perfect priest was to become also the perfect abbot, founder, and ruler of the glorious monastery of Clonmacnois. How splendid were the virtues that adorned St. Kyran as the perfect abbot, let Clonmacnois itself proclaim! It was long the most celebrated religious house in Ireland. It was the mother of countless saints. It was a treasure-house of graces. It became the chief seat of learning in Ireland. It was a school of art and literature. Kings esteemed it an honour to build its walls with their royal hands. The Emperor Charlemagne sent rich presents to it through Alcuin. The chieftains and princes of Erin bestowed their gifts upon it, until, in lands and treasures, in precious chalices and sparkling gems, in stately churches and rich crosses, it was the wonder of many lands. To be laid to rest beneath its earth, as near as might be to the relics of St. Kyran, was a privilege coveted by the noblest in the land. Bright with dew, and red-rosed, as it is styled in an old Irish poem, it was not its sunny meads or its bright flowers that won for it such esteem: it was Ireland's faith in the power of its founder's intercession. And yet he to whose merits all this was due ruled over the monastery he had founded for the short space of less than a single year. After seven months of labour there, he passed to his reward, and there beyond he rests, awaiting his glorious resurrection. There also, as was meet, arose a church in his honour. Among the churches that crown with their ruins the swelling hill, there is one named after the sainted abbot, and close to his venerable grave. But if it were painful to see the scattered walls of the church on Aran that told of the virtues of his youth—if it were painful to mark the desolation of the church on Inis-Oenghin, that once spoke of the virtues of his riper years—much more painful is it to see, not merely the ruin nor the desolation, but the desecration of the church that stands in Clonmacnois, to tell what its sainted abbot was, and point to where he lies! Far from me this day be the thought of wounding, by any words of mine, the religious sentiments of others; but I cannot refrain from lamenting in the bitterness of my soul that "our holy places are come into the hands of strangers; our temple is become as a man without honour" (1 Mach. ii. 12). What sin have his people done that their father's grave should have become the dishonoured temple of heresy? Some consolation, however, it is, that the ceremony of this morning has made atonement to the outraged honour of the saint of our hearts. Yes; there is joy in the thought that here in his own Clonmacnois, this beautiful temple has been raised under the invocation of his name. What if the Atlantic spray dashes unresisted over St. Kyran's ruined church in Aran; what if St. Kyran's church on Inis-Oenghin is roofless and desolate: what if even St. Kyran's church at Clonmacnois has been violated and degraded—have we not in this new St. Kyran's what will surpass the glories of the old? Blessed, then—a hundred times blessed—be the hands that built its walls and bade its stately arches rise! Blessings on you, first of all, O good pastor, with your helpers in the ministry! Blessings on you, faithful children of St. Kyran, who in the sweat of your brow, and by the toil of your hands—in the early dawn and when the sun was setting—added to your daily tasks, already heavy, the labour of bringing together materials for the building! Blessings on you, too, who, whether out of your poverty or out of your riches, provided means wherewith to carry on that good work! Proceed with courage till that work be gloriously completed. But if you would work successfully, remember what manner of men were those who preceded you in the task. The church you are building is to be the heir of all the glories that shone in the churches formerly raised to St. Kyran; if so, your souls must be pure as those saints of Aran, your hearts faithful to Catholic truth like those of the ecclesiastics in Inis-Oenghin, and your hands generous as those of the kings and nobles who built up Clonmacnois. These royal and illustrious patrons are gone; and you, their children, are servants where they once were lords. But their blood runs in your veins, and, better even than their princely blood, their faith glows in your hearts. They have bequeathed to you their work: be worthy of your sires, and let Ireland once more possess in Clonmacnois a monument worthy of her undying love for St. Kyran, the perfect monk, the perfect abbot!

And now let the solemn rite of Sacrifice proceed, and let the Pure, Holy, and Unspotted Host be offered up for the first time within these newly-hallowed walls. But as for us, let us bow our unworthy heads to the dust, while enters the shining company of saints and angels, who come hither to keep the high festival. They are coming, the saints of Aran—Enda, Finnian, and Columba—and with them they lead the white-robed crowd of religious men, among whom St. Kyran spent his youth. Coming are the sainted priests and holy Levites, whom he taught and sanctified in his island home in Lough Ree. And you, too, are here, you countless throng of the saints of Clonmacnois. Bishops and abbots, kings and chieftains, doctors and scholars, chaste youths and consecrated virgins. Coming, too, is the host of heaven, with glowing hearts and celestial song of triumph, encompassing Mary as she progresses to meet her Son. Enter then, O Lord Jesus Christ, enter then into this sanctuary which our hands have made, to crown and seal its dedication by the mystic outpouring of thy precious Blood upon this altar! And lead with Thee our patron, St. Kyran, who, for thy love, did overcome the world, and establish him, according to thy promise, as a pillar in this thy temple, that he may go out no more from among us. Write his name, together with thine own, O God, on the great heart of Ireland, as we have written them together to-day upon the face of this temple, and grant that when time shall have dissolved it in ruin like its predecessor's, thy name, and the names of the saints Thou hast given her, may be found imperishably united and living in her love. Amen.

THE PONTIFICAL JUBILEE OF PIUS IX.

"And Josue being now old, and far advanced in years, called for all Israel, and for the elders, and for the princes, and for the judges, and for the masters, and said to them : I am old, and far advanced in years ; and you see all that the Lord your God hath done to all the nations round about ; how he himself hath fought for you. . . . Only take courage, and be careful to observe all things that are written in the book of the law ; and turn not aside from them, neither to the right hand nor to the left ; lest after that you are come in among the Gentiles you should swear by the name of their gods, and serve them, and adore them : but cleave ye unto the Lord your God, and the Lord God will take away before your eyes nations that are great and very strong, and no man shall be able to resist you. "—JOSUE, xxiii, 1-9.

OF every man that is born of a woman it is written that he liveth for a short time, and that his life is fragile as that of the flower, and fleeting as the inconstant shadow. If, then, in its best estate, human life is thus brief and fragile, and insecure, how poor a thing is one single solitary day from among the few that remain at the close of a career already exceeding the common lot of man. And yet, one such day has just come in the life of an aged man who sits a prisoner in Rome, and it has made the hearts of more than two hundred millions of Catholics beat with joyous love.

The 16th June, which gave to Pius IX. alone among his predecessors, to equal, in the duration of his Pontificate, the years of St. Peter, rose upon millions who had prayed for its coming as men sigh for the dawning of the day of the joy of their hearts; its hours, as they ran their course, seemed to millions not long enough wherein to exult and rejoice in the day the Lord had made; and it set in a glorious burst of thanksgiving which, even yet, is mounting upwards from the whole earth, and our glad part in which we fain would take to-day. And why, beloved brethren, has the Catholic world thus made this day the beginning of its joy? Not, surely, as if we judged a shorter Pontificate to be a sign of God's disfavour, since we know that for Josias, whose memory was "sweet as honey in every mouth, and as music at a banquet of wine" (Eccles., xliv. 21), life was shortened as a reward; nor is it because we account a protracted life to be, of itself, a blessing singularly great; for have we not heard the patriarch Jacob, though bending beneath the weight of six score years and ten, declare that the days of the years of his life were few and evil; but because we feel that a singularly noble Pontificate, like that of Pius IX., could not be more fittingly crowned than by the singular privilege which preserved him that he might see the years of Peter. For what does that privilege, rightly considered, imply? It implies triumph! it implies victory! Not the base and vulgar triumph which marks the victory of stronger over weaker human passions, but the lofty, pure, serene triumph that fitly graces the victories won by the eternal truth of God!

For I need not remind you that in revolving ages the truth of God has had, and still has, its battle-fields, in which heavenly-appointed champions smite the dominant error of the time, and thereby win for the truth a victory, the glory of which is reflected on themselves. Therefore do we celebrate the Pontifical Jubilee of Pius IX. with exceeding great joy, because it has encircled his brow with the glory of a triumph bright as that which, fifteen hundred years ago, Athanasius won for himself by his successful defence of the Divinity of the Eternal Word. For God has two Words—one, the Eternal personal Word, who is the figure of His substance and the splendour of His glory—true God of true God; the other, the Word of that Eternal Word spoken to man in the Christian revelation, and living evermore in the Catholic Church. And, as to Athanasius was assigned the work of defending in his day the Divinity of the Eternal Word, so to Pius IX. has been assigned in our day the work of defending the Divinity of the Eternal Word's word and work in the Holy Catholic Church. The Arians, by denying that the Word was God, would make man's redemption impossible; those who deny the Divine power of the Catholic Church would render the scheme of redemption abortive and inoperative. And, as according to St. Athanasius himself, the battle in his day was against heretics, who, like new Pharisees, in sight of the very miracles of Christ, asked petulantly—how, being man, He claimed to be God; so, in our day, the battle is against those who, in sight of the thousand miracles which adorn the Catholic Church, ask how—being a human institution—she dares claim the possession of the very authority of God? And herein precisely consists the triumph of the Pontifical Jubilee of Pius IX.; that out of the materials and within the limits of his Pontificate, it supplies a most striking proof of the truth of his life-long teaching, that the Catholic Church speaks with the authority of God. I say a striking proof—for, as his Jubilee itself is a fact that stands out in solitary grandeur in the history of nineteen centuries, so also it is filled with events so extraordinary as to compel the wonder of all, and so certain that none may gainsay their truth. Such a proof, too, has all the weight attaching to those providential manifestations, to reject which is to exclude from history all trace of that imperfect sanction of the moral order which alone is permitted by the condition of this life. And if there be any one who is inclined to make light of such a proof, or to carp at it, as wanting in logical weight and dignity, let him explain how, in the text with which I commenced, Josue pursues a course of reasoning precisely similar to prove that the authority which he himself wielded was from God. Between the words of Josue to the princes and rulers of Israel, and those of the latest Encyclical of Pius IX. to the Bishops of the Christian Church, there runs a most remarkable parallel. It is full of sublime instruction to observe these two men—rulers, respectively, of God's people of the Old and of the New Testament—take their stand upon the height of years which they had painfully climbed, and trace for their flocks, in the struggles and victories of their own chequered career, a proof written by the finger of God Himself, that the authority exercised by them was from Him! Brighter days there may have been in the lives of both—days when their names were acclaimed by a thousand lips, and the great ones of the earth bent themselves before them; but, to my mind, the day of their rarest triumph was that upon which, in the history of their own lives, they could point to the triumph of the truth which it was given them to uphold. And such is the triumph which belongs to-day to Pius IX.

For, in truth, the twenty-five years of his Pontificate are luminous with the traces of three great characteristics which the instincts of enlightened faith unhesitatingly accept as evidence of the victory of the truth of God. These are : an endurance that no violence can overcome; a vigour which waxes stronger under hostile assaults; and the sanction of experience, whereby the truth of Catholic teaching is made wondrously manifest by the facts of history.

And see, first of all, how gloriously has he endured in his apostolical office of teaching truth. The truth of God, says Tertullian, has but one thing to fear upon earth, viz., lest it should be denied a hearing. Its enemies, guided by a diabolical instinct, are conscious of this, and use every exertion to stifle its voice, or to prevent it from reaching those to whom it is addressed. Hence, against the man whom God has chosen to be the mouthpiece of the truth which they hate, they exhaust all their power of persecution, if so they can succeed in hindering his Apostleship, by coercing him into silence. And thus, in such a struggle, the victory of the truth depends upon the endurance of its champion : as he endures, the truth endures— and by enduring conquers. And God, mindful of His own truth, is wont to give strength and endurance to him who has thus become its living and visible exponent among men. This providence was foreshadowed in that promise of a life stretching to a mysterious term which He made to the Apostle St. John; and it is clearly illustrated in the preservation of the Evangelist's life through the perils of a century of fiercest persecution, that so he might be a golden link between the ages to come, and the happy age that had seen the Lord. For one hundred years was he preserved that he might safely carry within his virginal breast, in the midst of the nascent heresies, the central truth of the Divinity of Christ. The same providence is especially seen in the history of that St. Athanasius, to whom I have ventured to compare Pius IX. Against him, as the defender of Catholic doctrine, the rage of angry sovereigns, and the unceasing hate of their Arian subjects, were pitilessly exercised. But throughout all, he endured, and with him and through him endured the truth of God. He was exiled by Constantine, and he endured ; he was proscribed by Constantius, and he endured ; he was persecuted by Julian, and he endured ; he was threatened under Valens, and he endured. Out of the forty years of his episcopate, he spent twenty far away from his see—now in the remote

Gaul, now amid the burning sands of the deserts, and at times even in his father's grave, and still he endured. Five times did he take the road to exile, and five times did he return ; and to his endurance do we owe it, under God, that the *Nicene Creed* is still on the lips and in the hearts of us all. And now, my brethren, if for the doctrine of the Divinity of Christ you substitute that of the Divine authority of the Church, what is the history of the twenty-five years' pontificate of Pius IX. but a reproduction of the History of Athanasius' trials, of his endurance, and of his victory.

Hardly had Pius IX. mounted the pontifical throne, when words of flattery and deceitful praises fell upon his ear. These were the treacherous beginnings of the storm that was soon to sweep across his life. The secret societies, which are the hands through which the evil spirit of this unbelieving age achieves its accursed works, singled out as the special object of their assaults the Pontiff, who claimed to control the minds and hearts of men, making them captive to the Divine authority of the Catholic Church. He was driven into exile ; he lived through it, and returned. Hardly had he resumed his place upon the throne, when his name was opprobriously dragged before the cabinets of Europe, and his kingdom denounced as the plague-spot of Europe ; he heard, and endured. And then imperial hands began to undermine his throne, removing one by one its bulwarks and its supports ; and, when the unholy work was done, imperial lips spoke the treacherous words that brought down upon the defenceless Pontiff the hordes of his foes. But he endured through all ; and he has lived to see the imperial hand paralysed, and to hear from the traitorous lips the sad cry— " I, too, have been betrayed." Then came the war of spoliation —stripping him year after year of his best provinces, of his towns, of his own Rome, of his churches, of his home, and finally, of his personal liberty. And throughout all this he has endured. Not for a single day did he flinch from upholding the Divine authority of the Church ; nor could flattery, nor threats, nor exile, nor calumny, nor brute force, nor the robber's violence, nor the loss of liberty, ever compel him to silence. By sheer endurance he has conquered his conquerors themselves, who in vain have prayed and hoped for his death. With eager eye they have been long watching for the approach of the shadow of death upon that august face ; with unholy joy they gloated over every fancied sign of infirmity; until weary at last and disappointed, they ask each other in dismay—" Is this old man never to die ? " Is not this marvellous endurance evidence of a present God who Himself is enduring because He is eternal, and of whose truth it is written that it remaineth for ever : *veritas Domini manet in eternum !*

But, besides the triumph of endurance, the authority of the Catholic Church has enjoyed, through Pius IX., another and yet nobler triumph in this—that the more it has been assailed, the more vigorous it has become. Two things combine to constitute the triumph of authority: first, that the title by which it claims the right to control its subjects should be clearly and forcibly set out; next, that this title should be recognised and obeyed by the subjects; and the more fully this double work has been achieved, the more full is the triumph of authority. Now, Pius IX. has, with signal success, rendered, throughout his Pontificate, these two most important services to the authority of the Holy See, as well with respect to its power of ruling and as to its power of teaching. Who has ever set forth more clearly than he the titles on which the Church rests her claim to rule the souls of men? and who has ever secured from the bishops and the people of God a more full recognition and a more loving reverence for these titles? He spoke the word, and immediately, in the north and in the south, where the sun rises and where he sets, new episcopal thrones arose in the Church, to become centres of sanctification and of civilisation to millions. He spoke again, and the Churches of two flourishing nations put off their mourning and forgot their secular sorrow in the joy of beholding once more the due order of the hierarchy re-established in their midst. At a sign from him the bishops of Christendom came from the ends of the earth, and gathered round the see of St. Peter, not once, but several times, and especially in the great Œcumenical Council of the Vatican. At his word again, the Catholic Universe paid to men whose names were obscure, and even a reproach, the honours of the altar, and, in the newly-canonised saints, heaven itself received new intercessors for the Church. And thus, at a period when every earthly throne was tottering, the Chair of Peter alone was vigorous and firm ; when every other power was scorned or despised, the power of the Pope commanded ever-growing reverence and love. But especially with regard to the Pontifical Magisterium, has Pius IX. won triumph for the authority for the Church. Christ, our Lord, when he had prayed for Peter's faith, that he might confirm his brethren, placed him and his successors high on the Pontifical Throne, that from them the world might learn what to believe, and that each one, by comparing his own faith with that of Peter, might know if he were walking in the paths of the Gospel. But it happened, a few centuries ago, that from the passions of men, there rose up here and there, over the world, a vague mist which came between the eyes of some few, and the face of the Apostolic Teacher, whom Christ had placed on his own throne. And these, to the

sorrow and scandal of their brethren, began to question the
Pontifical Infallibility, while courtier lawyers and heretics, each
to forward his own respective interests of evil, encouraged
and propagated the shameful error.   Early in his Pontificate,
Pius IX., by his dogmatic definition of the Immaculate Conception, exercised this high prerogative of his office, and he has
lived to confirm the decree of the Vatican Council, by which
the doctrine of the Pontifical Infallibility was declared an article
of Christian faith.   And thus, through him, have been cleared
away the clouds that intercepted from many the view of the
heavenly-appointed Chair of Truth ; so that, at this moment,
the entire Church of God looks with certain faith towards the
Holy Roman See, as towards the very pillar and ground of
Catholic faith.   And when we reflect upon the difficulties that
beset the close of many of the general councils; when we
recall the long and weary period over which the sessions of the
Council of Trent itself were extended ; when we consider the
vigour and audacity of that handful of men who have dared to
call in question the authority of the Vatican Council, we begin
to see how great is the blessing which the Providence of God
has drawn even from the evils which have rendered necessary a
temporary suspension of its sessions.   For, behold ! the entire
Church has had time to profess its faith in the doctrinal decrees
of the Vatican Council, as in the very word of God Himself ;
and, at the close of his twenty-fifth year's pontificate, Pius IX.
has had the consolation of beholding, from the height of his
Apostolic Throne, two hundred millions of human souls trust-
ing themselves in peaceful confidence to the guidance of one
teacher, whose faith is never to fail.   In the presence of this
sublime spectacle of triumphant authority, how poor becomes
even the world-wide empire of ancient Rome—that *immensa
Romanæ pacis Majestas*—the vision of which seemed to the
imperial statesmen something too majestic to belong to earth !
   But there is yet more.   As Josue, now old and advanced in
years, could appeal to the testimony of history for a sanction of
the truth of his teaching, so can Pius IX. point to the unparalleled events of the last few months, as to a convincing
proof that his words of instruction were inspired by the spirit
of divine wisdom.   Like Josue, he warned his people that they
should not be led away by the errors of the nations that dwell
among them, nor swear by the names of their gods, nor serve
them, nor adore them, for that speedy destruction would come
upon these nations, however great and mighty and strong they
might appear ; and the very month that brings to him the day
of his jubilee, enables him to appeal, like Josue, to his hearers'
experience of the awful accuracy with which his predictions have

been fulfilled. "I am old and far advanced in years, and you *see* all that the Lord your God hath done to the nations round about; how He Himself hath fought for you." Who are the gods of those nations which, with a civilisation of their own, surround the Catholic Church in this age? How are they adored? What manner of service is offered to them? These questions have been answered by Pius IX. in that Syllabus which will mark to future ages the moment when the advancing waves of naturalism were first stayed in their destructive course. In it he has held up before the faithful the gods of the modern Gentile world, unmasking the hideous idols of pantheism, and naturalism, and rationalism; in it he has described the fashion after which these monsters are adored—indifferentism, and that false liberalism which practically degrades the truth to the level of error; in it he has unfolded how these gods, themselves the creatures of man's evil passions, are served by irreligious education, by unbridled lust of pleasure, by a licentious press, by public immorality, by the tyranny of the mob; in it he reveals the turpitude of the attempts made to. banish God from the marriage contract, from the family, from the school, from the cabinet, from the whole range of social and civil life. And whereas these things were set forth as essential conditions of the only true and lasting progress, without which nor public property, nor stable government, nor security at home, nor peace abroad, nor riches, nor liberty, nor public virtue could ever be hoped for; again and again did the Sovereign Pontiff warn the faithful that they should not be seduced by these brilliant promises, for that these idols would bring sure and speedy destruction on the nations who worshipped them as the source and cause of their own greatness and strength. This truth did he speak in love; but many received not the love of the truth that they might be saved: therefore, God sent them the operation of error (2 Thess. ii. 10). And now that he has lived to celebrate his jubilee, he has lived long enough to see the sad experience of history confirm his words to the fullest extent. His teaching can no longer be considered as a theological abstraction, which men may contemptuously reject as too subtle for the wear and tear of busy life; for he now can point to facts that startle the least observant by the complete justification of his teachings which they contain. "See," he says, "what has come of the attempts to exclude the supernatural influences of religion from the life of man. Learn from the horrors of the last few months what Godless education has made of the young! The hands which you would not allow to make the sign of the cross are red with innocent blood, most cruelly spilled. See what your non-religious training has made of woman!—the gentle and loving being whom the Catholic Church would have formed upon the type of the Holy Mother of God, has become in your hands a fiend, scattering fire and death on every side! See what education without religion has made of your soldiers, of your citizens, of your statesmen! See its fruits in the school-room, the threshold of which is strewn with the shattered fragments of the image of Him whom impious hands have cast out from among the little ones whom He loves! See its fruits in the barbarism into which society has fallen, in murder, in conflagration, in the denial of property, of the soul, of God Himself! 'Amen, amen, I say to you, this generation shall not pass away until all these things shall be fulfilled!' "

This is the triumph, my brethren, which his jubilee sheds upon Pius IX., a triumph all the more glorious because it finds him in a prison. Beyond all doubt, the final issue of that imprisonment shall be victory; for the God who has guarded him from his youth will surely not abandon him now that the evening of his life has come, and his day fast inclining to its close. But of what sort shall that victory be? Shall it be the crown of martyrdom? Oh! deliver us from blood, O God, the God of our salvation, and our tongue shall announce thy praise. But if it be thy will that this trial should come, I know of one at least who evermore sayeth from out his prison: "My heart is ready, O Lord, my heart is ready!" and who would gladly crown the glory that has been vouchsafed to him of St. Peter's years, by imitating St. Peter's death for his Master's name. But whatever the blessed Providence of God may decree— whether the remaining days of our Father's life are to be days of blood, or of tears, or of joy—in the triumph of to-day we have a solemn pledge that they shall end at last in triumph, and in such a triumph as will announce, even in this life, the dawn of that imperishable triumph wherein the elect, for whose sanctification the Church exists under its visible head, will sing to thy name, O Lord, and will praise with one accord thy victorious hand!

THE ECCLESIASTICAL SEMINARY.

IT is fitting that this corner-stone should be lowered to its place with solemn religious rite, to the sound of sacred psalmody, by the hand of one of the Princes of the Church; for it marks a spot that henceforth shall be blessed in the land. The edifice that will soon rise above it is designed for no profane or common

purpose, but rather in its fair and stately proportions it will crown
this noble hill as with a Sacred Tabernacle, within which the
Catholic Church may securely achieve a work of incomparable
holiness and dignity. Here will she gather to her maternal
bosom youthful Levites in the fresh bloom of their early innocence; here, with patient love, day by day, and year by year,
will she pour out upon them those tender and gracious influences
of which she alone possesses the secret; here will she fit them
to the hand of Christ, her spouse, as instruments to sanctify the
souls of men. This is the office, this the work of an Ecclesiastical
Seminary, such as that which the Diocese of Kilmore has commenced to-day; and when I consider the loftiness of the purpose
which this new seminary is to serve; when I consider the
magnificent completeness with which it is designed that it should
serve them; when I consider the splendid results that may be
hoped from its service, I can well understand the deep and holy
joy which fills the heart of all here present, and of which even
this jubilant ceremonial is scarcely the adequate expression.

The purposes of Christian education, under any circumstances,
are simply among the grandest that can stir the energies of man,
for they aim at leading, to its highest perfection, the noblest of
God's works on earth—the human soul. Beautiful as is the
universe with a thousand types of loveliness; teeming as it is
with uncounted forms of wealth; wondrous as are the powers
with which it is equipped; its beauty, and riches, and forces
fade into insignificance before the dignity of man. And in man
himself the perishable frame is of little account compared with
the immortal soul, which, with its two imperial faculties of
intellect and will, as with two outstretched arms of yearning,
evermore seeks the Supreme Truth and the Sovereign Good,
which is God. And since our faculties then reach their perfection, when they are united with the object for which they are
formed, how glorious is the purpose of a Christian education,
which not only strengthens, purifies, and exercises the faculties
of mind and heart, but, furthermore, unfolds to them the blessed
vision of the God of Truth and of Goodness, who has made them
for himself, that he may make them happy with himself for
ever. Now, the Catholic Church alone possesses, in its completeness, this beneficent power of education. Others, who undertake
the task, aim merely at developing intellectual power, forgetful
that, in our corrupt nature, intellect is too often the slave, not
the controller of passion; or they seek to direct the wayward
will by the cold and uncertain light of moral philosophy alone;
or, after having cultivated the soul's faculties to the highest,
they declare themselves incapable of satisfying the cravings
they have encouraged, and can only ask with Pilate, *What is*

truth? or with the Athenian, point to the altar of the *unknown God.* But it is not so with the Catholic Church. She trains the intellect and disciplines the will, but at the same time with authority, with clearness, without the risk of error, she sets before the former what truths are to be believed, and before the latter what laws are to be observed, while by the grace, of which her sacraments are the channels, Faith and Virtue are made both possible and meritorious. The Catholic notion of the purposes of education is then the only complete one, for it alone embraces the whole of human nature, and consults at once for the temporal and for the eternal interests of man. It alone is the answer to the prayer of St. Paul for his disciples (1 Thess. v. 23), that their whole spirit and soul and body might be preserved blameless unto the coming of our Lord Jesus Christ. If, then, the purposes of education rank among the highest; if the conception of education prevailing in the Catholic Church be the most complete and the most perfect, how surpassingly noble must be the purposes of an Ecclesiastical Seminary, in which not only the blessings of education will be conferred, and that through the Church, who will lavish all her love and energies on the task, but in which those to be educated constitute, among the youth of the land, a class of special importance. Even to the pagan mind youth was an object of reverence for its candour, its innocence, its glowing hopes, and the bright promises of its future; but to us, who know that the Eternal High Priest has condescended to become a child, and to rest in the arms of a Mother chosen amongst the daughters of men, the child whom He has called, like Aaron, to his altar, appears invested with a new sanctity. The ecclesiastical vocation makes his young life bright with a secret glory, like that which shone in the hidden life of the Divine Child, who grew up in wisdom and in grace before God and man. He is the object of a special Providence which encompasses him and caresses him—a Providence that prepares him for his high destiny, by shaping to favourable issues the external circumstances of his life; a Providence that invites him by filling his young soul with holy thoughts, sanctifying the early aspirations of his heart, and hushing the turmoil of nascent passion that would drown the voice of the spirit. As with Job, in the days of his youth, God is secretly with him in his tabernacle; His lamp shines over his head, and he walks by his light in darkness (Job, xxix. 3, 4). The angels of heaven, conscious of the secrets of the Most High, behold with awe how the destiny of many souls is linked in the divine decrees with the future of a fragile creature, through whose ministry they are to be brought to salvation. How many souls are there throughout Ireland in whom, at this very hour, the Spirit of God is thus sweetly working out his purpose? And how many of them will come to this spot at no distant future, meek of eye, and gentle in face and speech, as were the Kevins and Kierans of old, bearing beneath a modest, perhaps even an humble exterior, the richest graces of God, and the dearest hopes of souls and of the Church. And when they shall have come hither, oh! how will they raise to heaven their pure hands to bless him by whom these walls were bidden to rise to shelter them, while, like olive branches, they surround the altar of God, preparing for the day when, in the sacrament of Orders, the Holy Spirit shall be enthroned in power in their hearts, wherein He had so long dwelt in love! This is the purpose for which the new seminary is to be built, and is it given to the thought of man to conceive of one more sublime?

But since, as the Scripture tells us, the thoughts of mortals are timid and uncertain, it often happens that the noblest purposes are marred in their execution by means that were honestly and seriously meant to promote them. It is not so in this case. When the Bishop of Kilmore set himself to draw up the plan of his new seminary, he took into his council, not the capricious fancy of an individual, nor the views of a party, nor the half-wisdom of local or partial experience; but, like a new Bezeleel, having undertaken to make things necessary for the uses of the sanctuary, he resolved that they should be made only according to the pattern pleasing to God, and set forth by the Church herself in the Council of Trent, where it treats of Ecclesiastical Seminaries. I am speaking his mind when I say it to be his solemn purpose, that in this new Seminary of St. Patrick, from the corner-stone that has just been laid, to the cross that shall surmount the building, there shall not be one single detail which will not fully accord with the prescriptions of the Council of Trent. I cannot follow out so large a plan in each of its particulars; I must be content to single out four of the leading principles, which, being recognised as essential, are to regulate the entire details both of the material and moral construction. These fundamental principles are—1st, that this seminary shall be a centre of loving obedience to the Holy See of St. Peter; 2nd, this seminary shall be free from the trammels of State control; 3rd, that for its students it shall make provision for an intellectual culture, the highest in kind, and the widest in range that can be compassed; and 4th, that it shall neglect nothing by which the ecclesiastical spirit may be preserved and developed in the hearts of its *alumni*.

To be fruitful of good, ecclesiastical training must be inspired by the principle of loving obedience to the Holy See. As in the natural, so in the supernatural order, union with their head is

the condition of growth in the members. And, as in our spiritual life, according to the apostle, we grow up in him who is the
head, even Christ, from whom the whole body, being compacted
and fitly joined together, maketh increase; so also it is in him
who is her visible head, and through whom, as the centre of her
unity, her whole body is compacted and fitly joined together,
that the Catholic Church maketh increase unto the edifying of
herself in charity. Whenever, therefore, you hear that in this
or that Catholic country faith is languishing and virtue dead,
or that the priesthood has saddened the Holy Spirit of God, you
may be sure, my brethren, that this has come to pass because
the seminaries of that country have fallen under the curse that
fell upon the mountains of Gelboe, inasmuch as, being cut off
from the fertilising influence of Rome, nor dew nor rain from
heaven has come upon them, and that, for this reason, they have
ceased to be the field of first-fruits. And if to-day the Catholic
Church mourns with a mother's sorrow over the apostasy of a
few proud professors in the centre of Europe, it should not be
forgotten that one of the early steps taken by the leader of these
unhappy men upon the road that has led him to the precipice,
was the uttering of disrespectful words against the teaching of
Rome. He boasted, in his conceit, that the candlestick of
Catholic theology had been transferred from Italy to Germany,
whither alone the Catholic schools should henceforth look for
their enlightenment. To-day we see the dreadful punishment
of his presumption and disloyalty; for he who, out of contempt
for Rome, had claimed for himself and his handful of pupils to
be the source of theological learning, has miserably lost even the
light of faith, without which it is impossible to please God.

After union with the Holy See, I have placed next among the
conditions for the due training of ecclesiastics, that the clerical
seminary should be independent of control on the part of the
civil power. The Catholic Church, from her constitution as a
divinely-founded religious society, is and must be independent
of the civil power. This independence has ever been viewed
with a jealous eye on the part of the State. At all periods of
the Church's history statesmen have attempted, under one form
or another, to possess themselves of ecclesiastical influence, or at
least to control the Church's power, by employing it for their
own purposes. The entire history of the Church is but a recital
of the struggles made by her, especially by the Roman Pontiffs,
against these encroachments, and for the multiplied victories she
has achieved in this perennial warfare. But, I think, not one
of the many attempts made upon the Church's liberty has ever
been more dangerous than that which aims at controlling the
training of the priesthood. It is against such attempts, even

when they claim for the civil power merely a right to direct the method of studies in seminaries, that the forty-sixth proposition of the immortal Syllabus is directed. Such interference on the part of the State is fatal to the working of an ecclesiastical seminary. The formation of the priestly character is too sacred a work to be entrusted to any agent other than the Church herself. The growth of the sacerdotal virtues in the soul under the mysterious action of the grace of the Holy Spirit, is a process too exquisitely delicate to bear the inspection of profane eyes, or the rough handling of profane hands. The figure of this world is passing away ; and each of its passing phases brings into fashion new principles of action, new theories of morals, new models in literature and art, to which, as to the idols of the hour, the tyranny of public opinion would have everything to bow down. What misery, then, would it be if the ever-changing passions of the day were to be allowed to form the ministers of a religion that never changes, because it is the truth of Christ. No ! Between the Catholic Church and the soul of the young Levite no power on earth must be allowed to stand, to counteract her blessed influences, or to call evil what she calls good, or good what she calls evil.

Besides, the Church, far from discouraging, as her enemies assert, counsels and prescribes to her ministers the highest intellectual culture. As the spouse of that God who rejected the imperfect victim, because unworthy of his acceptance, she loves to present at his altar, in her priests, the choicest fruits of cultivated intellect. Indeed, it is not too much to say, that in the present age, it is only in her schools that we behold faith and science, each in the fulness of its own proper dignity, meet together in unity. With regard to the faculties of the modern Trivium, viz., letters, philosophy, and theology, it would be easy to adduce a catena of forcible exhortations repeatedly addressed by the Holy See to the rulers of ecclesiastical seminaries, in which the fullest and most complete development of each subject is inculcated with an anxious earnestness. Thus, in his Encyclical *Inter Multiplices* to the Bishops of France (21st March, 1852), Pius IX. defends the use of the classics against some who would remove them from the schools, and prescribes that ecclesiastical students should be carefully trained in literature, and taught to acquire elegance of style and eloquence from the writings of the Holy Fathers and from the classical authors, purged from the indecencies of Paganism. And whilst, in our day, the growing school of Positivism openly and unequivocally condemns metaphysical studies, as tending to lift men above the region of the senses, it is remarkable that the Catholic Church has exerted herself to the utmost to protect and promote them.

In the Syllabus and in the decrees of the Vatican Council the rights and dignity of the human reason are powerfully defended; and in its communication with the bishops, the Holy See has again and again urged that at least two years of the students' course should be devoted to the study of metaphysics and moral philosophy; and such studies have never been more necessary than in this age, which directs its attacks rather against the natural truths which constitute the preamble to faith, than against the doctrines of faith themselves.

I need not say a word about theology, since, indeed, our enemies charge us with narrow-mindedness, on account of a too exclusive devotion to its study. But, in thus accusing us, they do not see what even Prudhon, the father of the modern Commune saw, when he declared that behind every great political and social question there lurks a question of theology. They forget, also, that to master any one science as thoroughly as the priest is trained to master his theology, is, in itself, an education such as never can be imparted by that discursive study of many various subjects now in fashion, and which scatters and weakens the energies of the mind; and finally, they forget that the volumes of theology placed in the student's hands contain the treasures of thought that for nineteen centuries the kings of the intellectual world have been storing up, and that to despise them is to despise all that is wise and noble in the history of human intelligence.

The preservation and increase of the ecclesiastical spirit is the very secret of the success of a clerical seminary. The world mocks at what it styles the gloomy virtues of the priesthood, and is indignant that its own principles, its literature, its heroes, its fashions, its amusements, are not accepted in places of ecclesiastical education. I hope that it shall never have reason to withdraw or to soften that accusation. In this new seminary, at least, the priceless blessing of the ecclesiastical spirit will be protected by the sweet and vigorous discipline, traditional in the Catholic Church, of which the habit of prayer, meditation on the eternal truths, repeated retreats, frequentation of sacraments, the study of ascetic and pastoral theology, are the integral parts. By these means will be formed that sacerdotal character, which, with its grave and solemn principles of duty, of self-denial, of patient courage, of gentleness, is a joy to the faithful Catholic, and which not unfrequently conquers even the hostility of the enemies of the Church. These four principles, faithfully carried out in the new Seminary of St. Patrick, will place in the hands of the Church, for the education of her ministers, all that is sanctifying in religion, all that is profound in science, all that is graceful in literature, all that is vigorous in discipline, all that is gentle in charity, and thus will make it a perfect expression of the Church's plan of a house of ecclesiastical education.

And from such a realisation of such a plan, what splendid results may you not expect. I wish it were in my power adequately to describe to you the wonderful influences upon society and religion which must flow from the ministrations of priests trained according to the spirit of the Council of Trent. "What is a priest?" asks Balmez. "What his character and functions? What is the mission he is to discharge upon earth? The priest is, as it were, a mediator between God and man; it is his to offer to the Almighty incense and sacrifice; to carry before the throne of infinite mercy the prayers of mortals, to appease the Divine Justice unceasingly provoked by their crimes; and, receiving in return from the hands of the Eternal, gifts most precious and necessary, he scatters them upon the world as unfailing treasures of consolation and hope. Look upon him when engaged in his august functions; surrounded by his entire people, who, in the spirit of profound humility, bow low before the Holy of Holies; clothed in symbolical and mysterious robes, standing before the altar in the glow of lights, enveloped in the sweet and fragrant cloud that rises from his hands towards the throne of the Eternal God, he pronounces with faltering lips the universal prayer, he entones the majestic hymn to the God of Sabaoth, he lifts up, with trembling hand, the Host of Salvation, and presents for the adoration of the people the Lamb without stain, whose blood has redeemed the world. Does not this sublime spectacle move to transport your entire soul? Are you not penetrated with a religious feeling which humbles you before the majesty of the Most High; and, at the same time, is not your heart filled with profound respect for the dignity of his minister?" These are eloquent and noble words, and powerfully depict the exalted idea of the priestly dignity cherished by that great man. But eloquent and noble as they are, in my heart I believe them weak and colourless when compared with that majestic conception of the priesthood which faith and love have impressed on the mind of the simple Irish Catholic. Among all the nations of the earth there is not one which more correctly appreciates the dignity of the priesthood, or more lovingly reverences it, than the Irish. Men say that this devotion of the Irish to their priest is but a bigoted superstition. No! but it is the outcome of faith in a high-souled nation, clean enough of heart to look upon the face of Christ to whom sorrow has brought them close, and quick enough to recognise in their priests the very traits they have adored in Him! They say that it is the growth of ignorance! No, but it is the enlightened homage which the intellect of a believing nation pays willingly to the sacerdotal virtues of humility, chastity, love of learning, the spirit of labour, union with God ! They say that it is the result of fear! No, but it is the outpouring of a love that has been growing in the heart of Ireland for the last fifteen centuries, fed year after year, as the sea by the inflowing rivers, by the active service of a priesthood whom gold could not corrupt, nor prosperity alter, nor sorrow crush, nor the fear of death itself sever from the people whom God had given them! And chief among the good results which will flow from this seminary upon society do I account this, that through it the religious influence of the priest upon the people will be deepened, strengthened, purified, and intensified. Through it will be renewed those brilliant virtues of the Irish priesthood, the history of which, handed down by the tradition of ages, has enkindled the love of the Irish for the minister of God. At this moment two classes of enemies conspire to weaken this love ; first, the *doctrinaire* statesmen, who seek to revenge upon the clergy the failure of their own insolent educational experiments upon the faith and morals of our people ; and next, the enemies of order, who gnash their teeth, because in Ireland religion has been found stronger than revolution. These are our two most dangerous enemies at this hour, but the fruits of the work that has been undertaken to-day shall make us secure against both ; for, upon the heart of Catholic Ireland the influence of the man on whose brow she beholds the triple glory of learning, virtue, and the sacerdotal character, will ever be simply irresistible. And what shall I say of the influence of the good priest upon the interests of religion? When the young priest leaves the threshold of the seminary, with the unction of sacerdotal grace yet fresh upon him, to begin his journey in the midst of the sorrows and the sins of men, we know that he does not go alone. With him there goes One, who, as He took upon Himself the sins of the world, that He might expiate them, so also He took upon Himself the sorrows of men, that He might console them. How many sorrowing hearts daily call out to the priest of God for comfort in their sore agony ? How many sinful heads are bowed before him, asking that their load of guilt may be lifted off from them ? Nor in vain do they cry ; for in the hands of the priest the Redeemer and Consoler of men has deposited His own beneficent power ; or rather through his minister, He uses that power, even as He used it when, in the days of his flesh, he went about doing good. And thus, to the other results of the seminary, we may without presumption add this one, which in itself includes the various excellences of all the rest, that in the life of every priest sent forth from it shall be renewed the infinitely loving and infinitely beneficent action of Him who is the Lamb of God taking away the sins of the world. O happy bishop! to whom God has given it to unseal for your people these fresh streams of gladness and salvation. O happy clergy! who will soon behold within these walls heirs of your virtues and learning, and helpers for your weakness in your hour of need. O happy people! for whose sake God has filled the heart of your pastor with such glorious purposes, to be so magnificently carried out to such splendid results. May He in whose name the beginning has been made to-day, be unto the work increase and growth, until, in his own good time, He bring it to the desired perfection. Amen.

ST. PATRICK AND HIS WORK.

"Arise, arise, put on thy strength, O Sion, put on the garments of thy glory, O Jerusalem. . . . Shake thyself from the dust, arise, sit up, O Jerusalem: loose the bonds from off thy neck, O captive daughter of Sion. . . . How beautiful upon the mountains are the feet of him that bringeth good tidings, and that preacheth peace: of him that showeth forth good, that preacheth salvation, that saith to Sion: Thy God shall reign! . . . Rejoice, and give praise together, O ye deserts of Jerusalem: for the Lord hath comforted his people."—ISAIAS, lii., 1-9.

SELDOM has the sternness of the prophets unbent to joyous exhortations more thrilling than those here addressed to the afflicted people of Israel. And since our human heart is so fashioned that it will not pass from sorrow to joy merely at the bidding of another, and without its proper motive, Isaias is careful to set before his hearers a reason powerful enough to lift them from their depth of woe to the rejoicing to which he invites them. He knew well how bitter the sorrow that had fallen on the prostrate daughter of Sion; he knew that for very grief her songs were hushed in the strange land; but he knew, also, that captive, sorrow-stricken, and mute as she was, she could not but find a beginning of joy in the clear and distinct vision of him who was to come to conduct her, rescued from her woes, to the full light of God's best blessings. Therefore, he bids her contemplate how beautiful upon the mountains are the feet of him that bringeth good tidings, that preacheth peace—of him that showeth forth good, that preacheth salvation—that in this contemplation the deserts of Jerusalem might rejoice and give praise together.

These same words of the prophet are applied by the Apostle St. Paul, to the preachers of the Gospel of Christ, and especially

to those who, like St. Patrick in Ireland, were the first to preach
the faith to nations sitting in darkness and in the shadow of
death. They have, therefore, a special fitness on this occasion
of the dedication of a Church which has been raised almost over
St. Patrick's tomb, to be a memorial of his apostolate in this
land. The more so, because Catholic Ireland, like the daughter
of Sion, to whom they were first addressed, has had, and still
has, so much cause to mourn. Her lot, like that of Jerusalem,
has been the sad lot of the oppressed ; her strength has gone out
from her ; for ages her robe has been moist with the tears, and
too often, alas ! with the blood of the children of her love. But
some rays of purest joy shall ever come to brighten the gloom
of her sorrows, as long as the memories of which this church is
the visible shrine shall survive throughout the land. In the
hour of her anguish she has but to fix her eyes on the noble
and majestic figure of her Apostle, and, as in the dawn of her
history he was the first to bring her good tidings, so to the last
will he be to her a source of peace and of rejoicing, because
through him the Lord hath comforted his people.

St. Paul compares the preachers of the Gospel to the starry
orbs that announce God's glory to the ends of the earth ; and,
as star differs from star in brightness, so apostle differs from
apostle in the characteristic glories of his mission. Some there
are to whom, as the scene of their labours, vast regions are assigned, teeming with a busy population, and rich in cities,
conspicuous as seats of empire or marts of commerce ; and by
the labours of such as these is garnered a harvest as vast as the
field on which it is reaped. Others there are to whom a scanty
corner of earth is made over, where, unknown and obscure, they
may earn for themselves an apostle's crown, not the less brilliant because the triumphs it rewards are unseen by human eye.
Either of these apostolates is glorious ; but the apostolate of St.
Patrick has this peculiarity—that it combines in itself the
united excellences of both. Of himself as compared with the
other apostles of modern nations, St. Patrick might well say,
although in a sense different from St. Paul's : " I am the least
of the apostles, and I have laboured more abundantly than all ; "
for it is the special characteristic of his work, and although
confined within scantiest limits, it has produced colossal results,
compassing within a narrow sphere, and with slenderest materials, as much as others have hardly achieved in the widest
field and under the most favourable circumstances. It is this
union of lowly resources with splendid success which distinguishes beyond that of others the apostolate of St. Patrick,
imparting to it a characteristic glory which for ages has shone
with unimpaired, and to-day shines with renewed lustre around
his tomb.

To the mind of the youthful Patrick, the mission to which he was called must needs have presented itself under the most uninviting aspect. To a man of his time and nation, Ireland was but a far-off island, lying beneath the wintry cold, and inhabited by a race of men removed from all peaceful intercourse with the civilised world. It formed no portion of the Roman Empire, for it possessed nothing to tempt the greed, or to attract the political sagacity of the Imperial statesmen. It was not a seat of learning like Gaul, whose schools were famous even in the Eternal City. There were other peoples in Europe, cultivated and influential, among whom an apostle might hope to win by his labours brilliant victories for God; but between Ireland and the nations around there appeared no community of feeling which, after the conversion of the country, might become the vehicle of Christian influences. Nay, more, he knew well that the Irish had already refused to hear the preaching of Palladius, and that this holy man abandoned their land as an unfruitful field of labour. Besides, he himself had had to suffer at the hands of the Irish people the greatest outrage that man can suffer from his fellow-man—the loss of his personal liberty. In his fifteenth year he was taken captive and brought to Ireland, where he was employed in tending sheep, and exposed to the storms of snow, and rain, and wind, that break with such violence on the hills of the north. And yet it was to these men that his thoughts and heart ever turned in love, when, after escaping from captivity, he found himself once more in the midst of his friends in his own France. For such as these he gave up his free birth; for the sake of such as these he left his home and kindred; for the sake of such as these he steeled his heart as well against the tears of those he loved, as against the brilliant prospects that were displayed invitingly before his eyes; and, what was harder still for him to bear, for the sake of these he incurred even the displeasure of his elders. But he feared none of these things, neither did he count his life more precious than himself, so that he might consummate his course and the ministry of the Word which he received from the Lord Jesus, to testify to the Gospel of the grace of God.—(Acts, xx. 24). With what deliberate fulness of purpose, and with what conscious self-sacrifice he did so, we may learn from his own words in his Confessions:—From heaven, he tells us, it was given him "to know and love God, and also that I should give up my home and parents. And many offers were made to me with weeping and tears, and I incurred displeasure there from some of my elders, contrary to my wish; but, under the guidance of God, I in no way consented nor gave in to them; yet not I, but the grace of God prevailed in me, and resisted them all, that I might come

to preach the Gospel to the people of Ireland, and bear with the
ill-treatment of the unbelieving, and that I should be reproached
as a foreigner, and have to endure many persecutions, even to
bonds, and that I should give up my free birth for the good of
others."

And what manner of man was he who thus sacrificed the
familiar usages of country, home, kindred, liberty, to take instead
the ill-treatment of the unbelieving, insults, persecutions, bonds,
and life-long servitude? He speaks of his own attainments in
language of the deepest humility, but a single glance at his personal history will show how well fitted he was, by the gifts of
nature and grace, for the apostleship of the most illustrious
nations. His youth was spent in closest intimacy with St.
Martin of Tours—a man of incomparable merit, whether we
view him in the camp or court, or in perils of exile borne for the
faith, or on the desert rocks of the Mediterranean coast, or on the
episcopal throne. In his riper years he lived in Lerins—that
island sanctuary which was made a paradise not only by the
gushing streams, the luxuriant wealth of vines, the fair valleys,
and the fragrant scents so lovingly described by St. Eucherius,
but still more by reason of the angelic life of its inhabitants.
There he found the seat of all the knowledge of the age; for
thither had flocked all that was learned, and noble, and saintly
in France, and from this glorious band the most illustrious
Sees of Europe received their bishops. But to St. German of
Auxerre, perhaps more than to all the rest, was St. Patrick indebted for the qualities that best adorn the man of God. At
his feet, as Gamaliel at the feet of the Apostle Paul, he grew
into the perfect ecclesiastic, rich in all learning, and richest of
all in the best learning of the saints. The best spur to learning
is, we are told, the excellence of the master; what treasures,
then, did not St. Patrick store up in mind and heart under the
instructions of this great man, who, after having been distinguished for his skill in the conduct of the most important
affairs of the empire, continued, as bishop, to enjoy in a singular
degree the respect and admiration of the emperor himself.
When St. German visited Britain as a delegate of the Holy See
to crush the Pelagian heresy, St. Patrick went with him; by
him our saint was guided through Italy to the court of the emperor, and, better than all, to the steps of St. Peter's chair in
the Apostolic City. St. Patrick's, therefore, was a mind which,
first fed in solitude with all the learning of the age, had afterwards been strengthened and polished by continual intercourse
with men of affairs and by all the advantages of travel; and
though these are but human gifts, a virtue less solid than his
might easily have been led astray by the thought that, after so

elaborate a training, it would be better to choose as his sphere of labour some country less remote and wild than Ireland, and less unworthy of such masters. But hardest of all was it to him to feel that, if he should go to Ireland, he should be cut off for ever from those saints whom he loved as the fathers of his soul, and reverenced as models of sanctity, and organs of the Holy Spirit. In his Confessions he testifies how gladly he would return to Gaul, "that I might visit my brethren, and look once again upon the face of the saints of my Lord, and it is known to that Lord how earnestly I long to do so." But between him and all this happiness there stood the souls of his Irish children, among whom he was to labour—the lowliest of apostles.

And yet, how magnificent in their vastness were the results which he achieved! What wonders did he not work, first in his own soul, and next in that Irish Church, towards which, as towards our mother, our hearts turn in love! During a long life, with unabated diligence, he toiled to make his soul a sanctuary of the highest virtues. What are the qualities that make men saints? The fear of the Lord is the beginning of their wisdom; the condition of their progress is faith, for the just man liveth by faith; and the crown of their sanctity is the love of God. Now that these three virtues were the characteristic virtues of the soul of St. Patrick, his own confession affords the clearest proof. Again and again does he speak therein of the love and faith with which he regarded Him:—" I confess to my Lord, and do not blush before Him, because I tell the truth, that from the time I knew Him in my youth, the love of God and his fear increased within me, and until now, by the favour of the Lord, I have kept the faith." And again:—"I cannot and ought not be silent concerning the benefits and graces which the Lord has bestowed on me in the land of my captivity. . . . . After I had come to Ireland I was daily tending sheep, and prayed fervently during the day, and the love of God, and his faith and fear, increased in me more and more, and the spirit was stirred, so that in a single day I have said as many as a hundred prayers, and in the night nearly the same, so that I remained in the woods; and on the mountain, even before dawn, I was roused to prayer in snow, and ice, and rain. . . . . I pray God, therefore, that He may give me perseverance, and that He may vouchsafe to permit me to give Him faithful testimony for my God, even until my death; and if I have done anything good for my God, whom I love, I beseech Him to grant me that I may pour out my blood for his name." And these three virtues found their fitting expression in the wonderful austerities, in the ardent love for the souls of the Irish, and in the complete sacrifice of self that pre-eminently distinguished his life. His austerities renewed on our island the wonders of Thebaid, where, under the training of St. Anthony, men had learned to die to this earth by the practice of the most rigid penances. Kneeling at the feet of the Vicar of Christ at Rome, his heart was filled towards Ireland with that almost passionate love for souls of which the Apostolic See has at all times been the furnace: " so that," as he tells us, in his Confessions, "with fear and reverence, and without murmuring, I should faithfully serve the nation to whom the charity of Christ hath transferred me, and given me for my life, as long as I shall survive, and that with humility and truth, I should serve them. I am bound in the spirit, and He who witnesseth will account me guilty if I leave them, and I fear to lose the labour which I have commenced, and not I, but the Lord Christ who commanded me to come and be with them for the rest of my life." . . . . And, again, in his letter to Coroticus:—" Did I come to Ireland according to God or according to the flesh ? Who compelled me ? I was led by the spirit that I should see my relatives no more. Have I not a pious mercy towards that nation which formerly took me captive? According to the flesh I am of noble birth; but I do not regret or blush for having bartered my nobility for the good of others. I am a servant of Christ unto a foreign people for the ineffable glory of eternal life, which is in Jesus Christ my Lord. Christ it was who has raised me up from my neighbours and sons, for whom I have forsaken my country and parents, and would give up even life itself if I were worthy." Finally, his entire life of sublime sacrifice was but the faithful fulfilment of the vow he had made, that of his soul and all his aspirations he would make a living victim to his God.

All this he did accomplish in his own soul, the grace of God aiding him in his constant labour, and, in addition, how marvellous were the successes that crowned his apostolate in this land! The conversion of Ireland to the Catholic faith stands alone in the history of the Church on account of the exceptional circumstances that attended it. The day-star of faith rose upon her, not in storm, but mildly springing. Unlike Jerusalem, Ireland killed not the prophets who came to bring her to God's admirable light, nor did she stone those who were sent to her. Along the roads, painfully traversed by other nations in their progress to the Church, you may trace the frequent stains of martyr-blood shed by the first heralds of the Gospel, and by their earliest converts. Ireland's path to Christ is strewn only with the garlands of the peaceful triumphs of grace. In the glorious company of saints who, at St. Patrick's bidding, went through the land to evangelise our pagan fathers, there is not one who carried off, save in his heart's desire, the martyr's palm. They preached the word on a good ground, to a people who, in a good and very good heart, heard it and kept it, and brought forth fruit in patience, (Luke viii. 15). There is an Irish legend embalmed by one of our poets in his exquisite verse, which tells how the daughter of Lir, whom some evil power had constrained to wander, imprisoned within the snow-white plumage of a swan, over the lonely waters of Moyle, was freed from the dread spell by the first sound of the Mass-bell that ever broke upon the silent solitudes wherein she had languished for ages. Hardly had the first solemn peal floated past her, like a wave of heavenly melody, when, her durance ended, the royal lady rose not only in the full grace and bloom of her earthly beauty, but with her soul purified and brightened by heavenly influences of faith and love. This is but the history of the conversion of Ireland to Christianity. No tedious and painful process of transformation was required ; and long as she had lain fascinated by a strangely masterful superstition, at the first sound of St. Patrick's voice proclaiming one God, the living and the true, she turned quickly away from her idols, and submitted to the law of Christ the strength of her arm, the fire of her intellect, and the love of her heart. And not only did she submit to what Christ commanded, but she rose at once to the height of the evangelical counsels. St. Patrick's converts became not only Christians but saints, passing, without resting in any intermediate stage, from the vileness of paganism to the sanctity of the religious profession. St Patrick himself was forcibly struck by this special feature :—" Wherefore, behold ! " he cries, " behold how in Ireland they who never had the knowledge of God, and hitherto only worshipped unclean idols, have lately become the people of the Lord, and are called the sons of God. The sons of the Scoti and the daughters of princes are seen to be monks and virgins of Christ . . . . and of those born again in this way we know not even the number." Now, if the measure of honour paid to the monastic profession by any nation be, as it undoubtedly is, a safe standard by which to estimate the degree of religious life that prevails therein, how glorious must have been the spiritual fecundity of the early Irish Church thus beauteously flowering forth in this vigorous bloom of virginal youths and maidens !

Among them all there are two, St. Brigid and St. Columba, whose names, even in death, have not been disassociated from that of St. Patrick, and of whose precious relics, as of his, the very earth upon which we stand has been the shrine. From the spotless soul of St. Brigid—the Mary of Ireland, as our fathers loved to style her—there has ever since streamed out on Ireland such a radiance of chastity as alone would be sufficient argument of the glory of him whom she reverenced as the father of her soul. And in St. Columba we have the type of these scholar-apostles peculiar to the Irish Church, representing, on the one hand, sacred learning of which its schools were the chief sanctuary in the west, and on the other, the devouring zeal for the glory of God and the salvation of souls, which St. Patrick had bequeathed to his children. So abundant was the fruit brought forth to God in these monastic schools, that St. Bernard, speaking of your own Bangor, applies to the period in which it flourished the words of David : " Thou visitest the earth and waterest it, Thou greatly enrichest it ; the river of God is filled with water. Thou preparest their corn ; Thou makest it soft with showers ; Thou blessest the springing thereof." From these schools issued forth, year after year, bands of holy men, who, to use the expression of the same St. Bernard, passed over Europe like the following waves of the sea. This is not the place to dwell upon what Scotland owes to St. Columba ; and England to St. Aidan ; and Burgundy, Germany, and Italy, to Columbanus ; and Switzerland to Gallus and Fridolin ; and Thuringia to Kilian. Let it be enough to say that England in a great part, Scotland, Belgium, Switzerland, the chief parts of France and Germany, and many places of Italy, in a word, almost all the countries that go to make up Western Europe, owe to Irish missionaries their conversion to the Catholic faith : and is not the glory of all this reflected back again upon the man whose labours had made of Ireland not only a nation of saints, but also a nation of doctors !

But soon, too soon, there came a change—that dreadful settling down of darkness upon Ireland, foreseen by our Saint in vision ; and even the horrors of that change could not dim the glory of the Apostle of Ireland. Even in his own lifetime a foreign foe had visited with persecution the Catholics of Ireland. His fatherly heart was torn at the sight of his suffering flock ; and, in his letter to the ferocious Coroticus, he thus cries out in grief and sorrow : " O beautiful and well-beloved brethren and children, whom I have brought forth in Christ in such multitudes, what shall I do for you ? The wicked have prevailed over us. We have become outcasts. It would seem that they do not think we have one baptism, and one Father, God. They think it an indignity that we have been born in Ireland. . . . . Therefore, I grieve for you, O my beloved ones! But, on the other hand, I congratulate myself I have not laboured for nothing—my journey has not been in vain. This horrible and amazing crime has been permitted to take place. Thanks be to God, ye who have believed and have been baptised, have gone from earth to paradise. Certainly, ye have begun to migrate where there is no night, nor death, nor sorrow ; but ye shall exult, ye shall

5

reign with the apostles, and prophets, and martyrs, and obtain
the eternal kingdom.": These words sound like a prophetic
anticipation of the condition of Irish Catholics under the penal
laws. The brutal prevalence of force over right, with the fire
and bloodshed it brings in its train ; the proscription that placed
the Catholic outside the reign of the law ; the refusal to consider
him as a Christian, or even as a member of the human family,
with the natural rights and duties wherewith God has bound
man to man ; the insults heaped upon Irishmen in their own
Catholic land—are not all these things painted in the glowing
words of the afflicted Saint ? But, thanks be to God, these
efforts were utterly useless ; neither craft nor cruelty could move
Ireland from the solidity of her faith ; and in the white-robed
army that he beheld ascending from earth to heaven, to take
their places with the apostles, and prophets, and martyrs, St.
Patrick saw yet another of the glorious results of his own
labours, through which Ireland, that had been the nation of
Saints and of Doctors, had now become the nation of Martyrs
and Confessors.

Once again there has come a change over the face of the land.
The patient endurance of the faithful people has worn out the
malignity of their persecutors, and the fair form of the Catholic
Church once more moves among us in her heavenly majesty.
And this very change is in itself another striking proof of the
success of St. Patrick's apostolate. For, be it remembered, the
so-called Reformation was much more a political than a religious
movement. Its successes were not due to the uprising of men's
consciences to attest their conviction of the truth of the new
doctrines ; but, on the contrary, the movement was the result of
plots laid by politicians against the religion of the masses, and
executed by help of brute force. But, as a political instrument,
Protestantism was equipped with terrible power, and Ireland,
bleeding, bruised, and chained for three hundred years, is a
proof of the intolerant ferocity with which that power was employed. And yet, in the blessed providence of God, it has come
to pass that the first blow dealt since the Reformation against
the social and political fabric of established Protestantism in
Europe, has been inflicted by the living faith of Catholic Ireland.
The tide of success that has carried Protestantism in triumph
for three hundred years has at length commenced to ebb, and
the first shore to beat back its waters has been the shore of St.
Patrick's Ireland !

But there is still more : there are other fruits of the faith of
Ireland deserving of our consideration. To the Catholic faith
do we owe it, that the domestic virtues—the true vigour of a
nation—bloom so luxuriantly beneath the humble roof-tree of

the Irish peasant's cottage. In all the weary days of his cease-less, and often thankless, toil, his faith still puts before him that Holy Family at Nazareth, in which One whom he adores as his God took upon Himself, and upon those He loved, the poor man's lot of poverty and hardship, that he might teach the lowliest how to sanctify their lives. Hence come the spirit of unceasing prayer and of resignation, the purity of morals, the tender charity and the other Christian virtues of highest order which, in a society perishing from the dissolution of the bonds of the family, undoubtedly adorn the Irish household. And those who carp at the faults into which at times the Irish peasant is betrayed, should bear in mind that in the conditions which have hitherto surrounded his life, no virtue could have survived unless in hearts subdued by the strongest power of religion.

It almost passes belief that a people who, a few generations ago, were shut out from all secure and valuable property should, out of their very poverty, have covered the face of the land with the thousand noble edifices their faith has raised to the honour of God, for the relief of the suffering, and for the spread of know-ledge! And while this was doing at home, the Irish race was pouring itself out all over the globe, bearing, whithersoever it went, the faith of St. Patrick, to become the foundation-stone of new churches in lands beyond the seas. In Australia, in North and South America, in India, in Africa, in the islands of the great oceans, from where the sun rises to where he sets, the poor exiles of Erin have built up the Catholic Church, giving to the embrace of the Mother of Souls more children by millions than all the guilt of the Reformers had torn from her arms. Going out from their native land, they took their journey along the highways opened by commerce or war—*euntes ibant*. It was hard to leave the loved ones that were sleeping in the quiet graveyard. It was hard to leave the mother who bore them—and so they went in sorrow, sorrow so deep, that God's pitying angels could trace their course by their tears. *Euentes ibant et flebant.* They lived among those hard taskmasters, who used them and then scorned them; but in the heart of the great cities, and in the forest clearing; in the gloom of the mine, and in the furnace's fierce glare; in the name of Mary, the Mother of God, and of the successor of St. Peter, Christ's vicar on earth, they were ever casting the seed of the Catholic Faith: *euntes ibant et flebant, mittentes semina sua.* Already that seed has multiplied a hundred-fold, but no tongue can tell how vast the harvest to be reaped from it in no distant future, when in that upheaval of society, which everything pre-sages, the empire of the world shall have passed to nations deriving from Ireland the pure freshness of their faith, as well as the generous strength of their youth. And as each fresh sheaf of the mighty harvest gathered by this nation of apostles is carried before God and presented as the fruits of our Saint's labours on earth, St. Patrick's lips will repeat the prayer he had so often uttered when on earth, that through the mercy of the Lord he may never at any time lose that people whom God has given into his hands.

That prayer shall be heard, and Ireland's perseverance in the faith delivered to her by St. Patrick shall be the crowning glory of the marvellous work achieved by the lowliest among the Apostles! If any man doubt it, let this Church rebuke him by the memories with which it is peopled. It is in very truth a Memorial Church. Placed here by Catholic Ireland, near the tomb of her Patron, its stones will ever cry to God: Be mindful, O Lord, of our David, and of all his meekness. . . . . How he swore to the Lord, that he would give no sleep to his eyes, and no rest to his temples, until he should build up among us a tabernacle to the God of Jacob. For the sake, then, of David thy servant, let not the face of thy Christ be ever turned away from us. . . But here, in this Ireland, let thy rest be for ever and ever : here mayest thou dwell, for it is the place of thy choice. Blessing, thou shalt bless her widows, and her poor ones—for they are many—thou shalt fill with bread ; thou shalt clothe her priests with salvation, and her enemies with confusion, and may thy sanctification shine forth for ever upon this people of whom he has made a nation of saints, of doctors, of martyrs, and of apostles !

IRELAND'S OFFERING TO THE SACRED HEART.

"Stude sapientiæ, fili mi, et lætifica cor meum ut possis exprobranti respondere sermonem,"

"Study wisdom, my son, and make my heart joyful, that thou mayest give an answer to him that reproacheth."—PROV. xxvii. 11.

FROM all eternity the Almighty Father found his ineffable delight in the co-eternal wisdom which He possessed in the beginning of his ways of old, before the earth was made. * Afterwards, when in the fulness of time, that wisdom of the Father was seen upon earth, † He, in turn found his delight, and found it

----

* Proverbs, viii. 22, 23.   † Baruch, iii. 38.

in being with the children of men. * And as the Father delighted in his Son, because He was the brightness of his glory
and the figure of his substance, so the Incarnate Word finds
his chief delight on earth in his rational creatures, because they
image forth his own distinctive quality of wisdom. Hence, the
Sacred Scriptures declare that " He loveth none but him that
dwelleth with wisdom." † And He Himself, speaking through
the author of the Proverbs, in the text I have recited, tells us
that his love for souls in which wisdom shines is more than love,
for it is love in its most beauteous form—joyous love—love
mingled with delight. Nay, more, He there describes this his joyful love as caused in his breast not merely by the beauty of wisdom in itself, but also by the efforts made by the human soul to
attain to the possession of it. And therefore, as a father
might tenderly plead with a child, He pleads with man that,
by skilful culture of his faculties, and by earnest striving after
wisdom, he would make joyful his heart. And thus the entire
process of man's spiritual and intellectual training in true wisdom is set before us, as an object invested with a solemn and
almost awful power over the Heart of God. " Study wisdom,
my son, and make joyful my heart ! "

Wisdom is described as the knowledge of things human and
divine, and of their causes. Now, since, as the Vatican Council
teaches, there is a twofold order of knowledge, one being by
natural reason, the other by divine faith—one including the
things which natural reason can reach, the other the truths of
revelation—a Catholic University, being a place of teaching
universal knowledge, is the natural home of both, and is, therefore, in a sense most true, the seat of wisdom. It is the place
wherein men are taught how best to comply with the divine
exhortation of studying wisdom in its widest range ; and therefore, without presumption, we may believe and hope that it is a
place precious beyond others in the sight of that God who alone,
as Job tells us, rightly understandeth the way of wisdom, and
knoweth the place thereof.‡ It is in this faith and in this hope
that it behoves us to assist at the ceremony of to-day, by which
Catholic Ireland consecrates her University to the Sacred Heart
of Jesus Christ.

Some there are to whom this ceremony is simply void of
rational meaning ; others, again, will deride it as an extrava-
gance of childish piety, or resent it as an exhibition of unen-
lightened fanaticism. But, in sober truth, it is an act of surpassing dignity and loftiest significance ; for it is the act of a
nation ; and a nation's act, in the cause of truth and justice,

* Proverbs, viii. 31.   † Wisdom, viii. 28.   ‡ Job, xxviii. 23.

ever possesses an indisputable grandeur of its own.   And it is
a national act of the highest order; for it is a solemn renewal
of the profession of faith by which Ireland long ago dedicated
her intellect to Jesus Christ.   And she has chosen to give to
this act the form of consecration to the Sacred Heart of Jesus,
guided rightly by love's delicate instinct to believe that this
choice would give to the Heart of Jesus the greatest joy, and to
the souls of her children the richest graces to help them in their
season of need.   Besides, the Sacred Heart enables her, in the
words of the text, to give an answer to those who reproach her,
for it contains at once the noblest defence of her past struggles,
and the sure grounds of her hopes for the future.   No element
of true grandeur, then, is wanting to this ceremony, which thus
unites in closest ties the mind and heart of a believing nation
with the mind and heart of the Incarnate Word.

And, in the first place, it is a nation's act; for it is the
direct outcome of a principle that has distinctively marked at
all periods the genius of the Irish people.   The whole history
of Ireland moves on two lines representing two of the master
passions of our race—the love of religion and the love of learning.   But in our history these two lines never run apart; rather,
like the mystic lines in the tracery that adorns the Celtic crosses,
they are bound to each other at so many points, and by ties so
fine and close, that no power can sunder between them.   The
Irish have ever loved scholarship, but they would never have it
separated from religion.   No man can be the child of science,
it was said in a Celtic monastery of the sixth century, who does
not love truth and justice, and there is no truth and justice
without the knowledge of God.   And as it was in the sixth
century, so has it been ever since, and so it is now in the nineteenth century.   And if any were to gainsay it in spite of the
express declaration of the Irish people, from the highest to the
humblest class, in spite of these countless religious schools
throughout the land, crowded with a joyous throng, while the
godless institutions are as barren mothers without children, the
very walls of this University would cry out against them.   No
royal munificence has bidden it to rise; no imperial treasury has
subsidised it; no wealthy noble, no merchant prince has endowed
it.   It is the creation of the nation.   There is not a stone in it
but has a voice, and cries out its witness to the faith of the men
of the Irish race, who, from Ireland and England and Scotland, from America and India and Africa, and the islands of
the sea, have sent their painfully earned money to build up in
this, the heart of their native land, a shrine wherein fullest
science and simplest faith may dwell together in amity.   And
the hands that raised this University rested not until they had

raised likewise this stately church ; and high over the altar they
enthroned her who is the seat of wisdom, that so the generations
of students, who were to come hither to seek for science, might
ever find the Light of the World, as the Wise Men of the East
found Him, resting on the lap of Mary. Now, what is to-day's
ceremony—by which Ireland's highest seat of intellectual culture is reverently placed within the very sanctuary of divine
love—but a magnificent outward expression of the principle
which has thus ever been the very life of Irish thought, that
education and religion should be inseparable. This consecration
of the University to the Sacred Heart is, therefore, an act belonging to the whole Irish race. We are not alone here to-day.
We are here the representatives of the millions of our nation
now scattered over the earth ; and hither, too, has come a shining
cloud of witnesses stretching from every period of our past history to mingle their voices with ours—from the venerable founders
of great schools, like Armagh and Clonard, to the felon priest
who taught grammar in the heart of the morass, bringing with
them the glorious traditions that are Ireland's conquests from
the ages, to swell Ireland's antiphon, with which she prays
to-day that God may sanctify this house which she has built for
science, and that He may put his name there for ever, and that
his eyes and his heart may be there always.* How glorious for
Ireland, and how impresssive this spectacle of millions of minds
swayed by a single thought, and of millions of wills knit together in one resolve, not to secure any questionable material
or political triumph, but for an object the noblest that can stir
the pulses of a high-souled nation, the intellectual and moral
and religious progress of its sons. No wonder that, like David's,
the heart of the Catholic Church in Ireland is filled to-day with
great joy as she beholds her faithful people make these their
offerings ! No wonder that with him she, too, should cry out :
" Oh, Lord God of our fathers, keep for ever this will of their
heart, and let this mind remain always for the worship of
Thee " †
    And next, to-day's ceremony is the noblest of all national
acts, for it is a national act of faith in Jesus Christ. The habit
of faith, St. Thomas tells us, ‡ works by a double process. It
inclines us to believe what we are bound to believe, and it re-
strains us from assenting in any way to those things which we
ought not to believe. This double fruit of the supernatural
habit of faith has been splendidly illustrated in Ireland's action
with reference to education during the last three hundred years

---

* 3 Kings, ix. 31.   † 1 Paralip. xxix. 18.
    ‡ In Lib. iii. Sent. Dist. xxiii., q. iii., art. iii

With unerring accuracy of judgment, and with invincible vigour of will, she ever turned away from systems and institutions that were hostile to faith, while she as unvaringly recognised and cherished those that were favourable to it. And this is especially true of university education.

An eloquent voice has described,[*] in touching language, how across the sanguinary scene of war and turbulence and bloodshed that followed the English occupation of this country, there flitted from time to time the graceful vision of a university appearing to-day, disappearing to-morrow, reappearing on an after day, but unhappily never able to root itself on a firm foundation in the soil. Alas! this picture is but too true, even to-day; but the fault is not Ireland's. It is true that with the failure of the university schemes, with reference to which these words were first spoken, faith had little to do, for as yet the unity of religion was unbroken in the two countries. Nevertheless, there were then at work other causes of failure besides war and the turbulence of the times, and of these causes due account has not always been taken. No matter how fair the outward seeming of each university that then presented itself, its success was hindered by one serious drawback. The language on its lips was not the language of Ireland—it wore the mien and air of a stranger; it was not warm with Irish blood—it had no kindred with the Celtic millions. And therefore, though Ireland pined with longing for the stores of learning it had brought, she could not cherish it as her child, and it disappeared. But when the vision that had disappeared in the Catholic times reappeared in the reign of Elizabeth, the Faith of Ireland rose indignant against it. For, this time its ornaments were the plunder of God's altars and of the shrines of the saints—its dowry, the spoils taken from the weak—its doctrines the condemnation of all that her children reverenced. It was the daughter of the stranger come back again, flaunting, in the face of a Catholic nation, the strange creed she had learned during her period of absence. What could Ireland do but close heart and ears against her wiles, and pray for patience to endure her pitiless tyranny? Again, however, a change has come. The power which created that University has risen up against her, and lo! in its turn the Protestant University has disappeared, and, in its stead, a new University, as unblushingly godless as the worst creations of infidelity, is presented for acceptance by Ireland. And if Ireland turned coldly away from the stranger in the Reformation period—if she rejected the Protestant

* Speech on moving for leave to bring in a Bill relating to University Education in Ireland, by the Right Hon. W. E. Gladstone, M.P. London: Murray, 1873, page 25.

University because it was the foe of the religion she loved—with what scorn does she not look upon the University that has cast off its baptism to secure for itself a few more years of existence? But, at length another fair and graceful vision of an University meets the gaze of Ireland! No stranger this one, but the bone of our bone, and the flesh of our flesh ; no follower of false religions, but beautiful with the beauty of the holiness of the Sacraments, keeping, amid the fullest treasures of Science, the true Faith ; with the blessing of Peter on her brow, and the sweet name of Mary, the Seat of Wisdom, engraven upon her heart; no slave of infidelity, but with the faith and love of Jesus Christ glowing in her soul, and boldly proclaiming to the world, that though now-a-days Christ is to some a stumbling-block, and to others foolishness, to her He is the power of God and the wisdom of God.* Like some royal bride bearing in her bosom the hopes of empires, this Catholic University carries within it the best—I had almost said the only—hopes of Catholic Ireland. It is the visible symbol of principles without which Christian liberty is impossible in this land. It is a protest against the tyranny which would violate the sacred rights of parents to control the education of their children. It is a protest against the tyranny that would refuse to the Church the exercise of her heaven-given prerogative of guarding the Faith of those who call her the mother of their souls. It is a protest against the mutilation of education by banishing from the schools the knowledge of God and of the supernatural order. And it does more than protest against what is wrong and false; it asserts what is right and true. It asserts that Faith and Reason are not necessarily foes, but rather twin lights of various orders to conduct man to the knowledge of truth. It asserts, with the Vatican Council, that the Catholic Church, far from opposing the highest culture in human arts and learning, promotes it and helps it on. It asserts, with the same Council, that the Church does not forbid the sciences to follow, each in its sphere, its own proper principles and its own proper method ; that she holds the liberty of so doing to be one of the just liberties of science ; but that this liberty must not be abused for the destruction of Christian faith. It asserts the just claims of the Irish Catholic to all the educational privileges and helps that are given to others. On it depends the future of Ireland, for the education given to this generation of Irishmen will colour for centuries the history of our country. Towards this University Ireland's spirit of Faith turns in love ; and this is the offering which on this day she humbly presents to Jesus Christ.

* 1 Cor. i. 23, 24.

Can we conceive a nobler act of national Faith? The Catholic University is the fruit of Ireland's Faith, gathering up in itself all of good that has been purchased by the sufferings of three hundred years. By solemnly devoting it to-day to the Sacred Heart of Jesus Christ, Ireland declares that the continuity of that profession of Faith shall be unbroken. By it she proclaims that she has given and will preserve her intellect captive to the Incarnate Word, and that neither death, nor life, nor things present, nor things to come, nor might, nor height, nor depth, nor any other creature, shall be able to separate her from the love of God, which is in Christ Jesus our Lord.*

Nor has her love been at fault in choosing to address her offering to the Sacred Heart, since no other devotion could be more consoling to Christ, none more fruitful of graces to her children. For what is the object of this devotion to the Sacred Heart of Jesus Christ? Pius VI. tells us that "the substance of this devotion consists herein, that under the symbolical image of his Heart we should meditate on the boundless charity and outpoured love of our Divine Redeemer." The Heart of Jesus, then, is the symbol of his love, and, like every other real symbol, it invites our consideration to the three distinct elements that go to make up its symbolic character: firstly, to the *sign* itself, which is the real Heart of Jesus inseparably united to the person of the Word, and therefore adored by the faithful without separation or abstraction from the Divinity; secondly, to *that of which it is the sign*, namely, our Divine Redeemer's love; thirdly, to the *reason* why the Heart of Jesus is the symbol of his love, namely, because of the intimate connexion naturally existing between the human heart and the affections of the soul. Now, from our consideration of these three points, there springs up in the devout soul a triple act of love—of adoring love, due to the Sacred Heart of Jesus, inseparably united with the Godhead; of grateful love, awakened by our Redeemer's immense love for us; and of penitent love, answering with its poor sympathy the sorrows with which that Sacred Heart was racked for our sins. This triple love is the proper fruit of the devotion to the Sacred Heart; and happy, thrice happy, those pure souls who taste of it in its fulness, and are filled with the blessings of its sweetness! And these three loves answer, each to each, to the three solitary joys which, as the Holy Scriptures tells us, belonged to the Heart of Jesus. The first was his joy in the simple faith of his followers, by which they believed in his Father and in his own Divine nature. St. Luke (x. 21) tells us how in that same hour He rejoiced in the Holy Ghost, and said: "I confess

* Rom. viii. 38, 39.

to Thee, O Father, Lord of heaven and earth, because Thou hast
hidden these things from the wise and prudent, and hast revealed them to the little ones. All things are delivered to me
by my Father, and no one knoweth who the Son is but the
Father, and who the Father is but the Son, and to whom the
Son will reveal Him." And may we not hope that the
adoring love which springs from the contemplation of the Sacred
Heart will renew this joy of our Lord. His second joy was in
the consciousness of being beloved by his own : "These things,"
He told them (John, x. 11) " have I spoken to you, that my joy
may be in you." And of what else did He then speak except of
that furnace of his love which ever glows in the Sacred Heart ?
It was just after the institution of the Eucharist, and just before
the agony in the garden, and yet in the midst of the sorrow of
separation from his own, and in the very shadow of death, the
Sacred Heart found joy in the thought of the grateful love of
his children. And what else is the Sacred Heart ever repeating
to us but these same things that Jesus spoke of on that saddest
night ? And when our hearts are warmed by its silent eloquence
does not our grateful love give fresh joy to our Lord ? His
third joy was that joy of heart which He felt on the day He was
crowned for our sake with the crown of thorns, to which allusion is made in the Canticles, when we are called on* " to go
forth, and see Our King with the diadem wherewith his Mother
had crowned him on the day of the joy of his heart." That
crown of thorns He yet wears on his Heart, and the penitent
love it must needs excite in our souls will, indeed, bring back
to Him the day of his joy. And thus the triple stream of love
that flows into our hearts from the Heart of Jesus is allowed to
return in waves of gladness to its Divine source. Blessed, then,
be that Heart, which teaches to our cold souls so many happy
secrets of love ! And thrice blessed be it in this time and place,
for nowhere are its life-giving graces more needed to-day than
in the great seats of learning. There, more than elsewhere,
men have forgotten how to adore and how to love ; the name of
Christ has been cast out from academic halls as if it were an unclean thing ; and in every avenue to every science the professors
of infidelity have laid snares for thoughtless youth, that so they
may slay in their unwary souls the faith of Christ. Not that in
the beginning, at least in our country, those men openly dishonour Christ or his doctrines ; but, rather, like the destroying
angels that smote the first-born in Egypt, they set themselves
to their work under cover of darkness—the darkness caused by
the systematic exclusion of Christian knowledge. They know
well that he who knows not Christ will not adore him ; and

* Cant. of Cant., iii. 11.

therefore do they forbid in the schools the language of Catholic
theology, each term of which, St. Gregory of Nyssa tells us,
is as a perfumed vase breathing the fragrance of God. Now,
the Sacred Heart is in itself a compendium of all Christian
Doctrine. The unity of God's essence and the distinction of the
Divine Persons ; the Incarnation of the Son, the Reality of his
adorable Humanity ; the inseparable union of the two natures
in one Divine Person, with all the gracious and tender mysteries
flowing from these, are to be read therein. Fixing on this
Heart the gaze of an enlightened faith, Catholic students will
find in it a treasure of religious knowledge. And the adoring love that shall spring from this saving knowledge will be to
them in the fire of the daily temptation that meets them, as the
angel of the Lord who went down with Azarias and his companions into the furnace, and made the midst of the furnace
like the blowing of a wind bringing dew, and the fire will not
touch them, nor trouble them, nor do them any harm.*

Nor is grateful love less needful. It would seem as if a
poisoned breath had passed over modern science, blasting its
high aspirations, and killing its sympathies with whatever is
noble and elevated in the destiny of man and of the world. It
positively cannot, or will not, see in man anything but the brute
animal, owing such better qualities as it has to a process of
natural development, without an immortal soul, without free-
will, without a true moral sense, without the image of God.
It cannot, or will not, see even the possibility of a supernatural
revelation opening out before man the surpassingly fair vision of
a supernatural order, in which his place is little less than that of
the angels, so tenderly and so fully is his life encompassed by
God's loving care, and so glorious the end towards which his
existence is directed. And accordingly, its whole study is to
sap the natural truths that are the preamble to Faith, and to
subject to a solvent criticism the records of revelation, in order
to degrade them to the rank of old-world legends. All in vain
does nature, and history, and the insatiable cravings of man's
soul panting after the living God, plead with this brutalised
science in favour of a recognition of our matchless dignity ; no
sursum corda can rouse it from the depths of materialism and
sensuality in which it buried itself. Alas! in losing its faith in
God's love, it has lost the key to the mysteries of the universe.
But whosoever contemplates that abyss of wisdom and of love
which is the Sacred Heart of Jesus, will find all these mysteries
made clear in the light of the ineffable love that glows therein.
Who shall dare, even in thought, to question the dignity of that
creature for whose elevation God's love bridged over the space

* Dan., iii. 49, 59.

between heaven and earth in the Incarnation—for whom the Eucharist was instituted—for whose dear sake the pains of the Passion were borne! And who will find even the Incarnation, the Sacraments, the Passion, too much for the infinite love of the Heart of Jesus? Ah, surely, at the sight of that open wound in the Sacred Heart, the *non credam*—the *I will not believe*—of unbelieving Science will be changed, as on the lips of Thomas, into the cry of grateful love: *My Lord and God!* For who that reflects constantly on the boundless love of which it is the symbol, can marvel at any place of dignity assigned to man by that Divine Goodness which recognises as man's best claim upon it man's own littleness and misery!

And then the need of penitent love! The sense of sin seems as if it would die out of the world. How heinous it is to transgress the law must needs be forgotten by minds upon which the law itself has little hold, and the law whose sanction is not remembered is a law that is dead. And if this be true of all ages and of all places, how much more is it true in case of those who in great centres of learning, in the flush of youthful passion, set out to voyage over strange seas of thought alone, or in the current of evil example. But who that habitually looks upon the Sacred Heart of Jesus, ever crowned with its crown of sorrow, can forget how tremendous the sanction of that law, whose Author did not spare even His own Son because He had taken on Himself the iniquities of us all. And as the thought of the enormity of sin grows upon him he will seek in the Sacred Heart itself a means by which he may cleanse his soul from its foul stains. Borrowing of its sorrow for the offences against God, he will humbly confess his guilt in the Sacrament of Penance, and sprinkled with hyssop he shall be cleansed, and washed in the blood of the Lamb he shall be made whiter than snow.

Most fittingly, then, does Ireland to-day consecrate her University to the Sacred Heart of Jesus, commending to the love of the Incarnate Wisdom the cause of religious education in this country. The Sacred Heart is her sufficient answer to those that reproach her. Men marvel at our obstinacy in clinging to the principle that religion and education must not be separated. To shrink from that principle is to renounce our part in the Sacred Heart of Jesus Christ, for now the question has been narrowed to this, education with and for Christ or—Paganism? Men say that we are unwise advocates, and imperil by our rashness the causes we love. If so, let us place it in the hands of the best of advocates. It is a just cause; and is not the Heart of Jesus the Throne of Eternal Justice! It is a holy cause; and is not the Sacred Heart the Sanctuary of Holiness!

But, just and holy as it is, this cause is, humanly speaking, a weak one, as the cause of justice too often is on earth. It has been tossed to and fro as suited the calculations of politicians; it has had arrayed against it the power of bitter foes, and the treachery of dishonest or weak advocates. But did not Pilate and Herod chaffer in petty political intrigues over his stricken Heart, smarting from the violence of enemies, and the shame of betrayal by friends! Let the world say that success is beyond our strength to achieve, at any rate it is not beyond the strength of Almighty God. That strength we here suppliantly implore to-day. "Now, therefore, arise, O Lord God, into Thy resting-place, Thou and the ark of Thy strength."* "See what things the enemy hath done in the Sanctuary . . . they have defiled the dwelling-place of thy name on earth. They said in their heart, the whole kindred of them together: Let us abolish all the festival days of God from the land. . . How long, O God, shall the enemy reproach: is the adversary to provoke Thy name for ever? . . . Deliver not up to beasts the souls that confess to Thee: and forget not to the end the souls of thy poor. . . . Arise, O God! O God! arise and judge thine own cause."†

THE HOUSE OF THE GOOD SHEPHERD.

"And, behold, a woman that was in the city, a sinner, when she knew that Jesus sat at meat in the Pharisee's house, brought an alabaster box of ointment: and, standing behind at his feet, she began to wash his feet, with tears, and wiped them with the hairs of her head, and kissed his feet, and anointed them with the ointment. And the Pharisee, who had invited him, seeing it, spoke within himself, saying: This man, if he were a prophet, would know surely who and what manner of woman this is that toucheth him, that she is a sinner. And Jesus, turning to the woman, said to Simon: Dost thou see this woman? Many sins are forgiven her, because she hath loved much. And he said to her, Thy sins are forgive thee. Thy faith hath made thee safe. Go in peace."— LUKE, vii. 37-50.

I AM here to-day, dearly beloved brethren, to appeal to your charity on behalf of the most wretched of God's creatures on earth—fallen, but repentant women. And had I no arguments to urge in their favour other than these two, that they are in sore distress, and that they are your fellow-creatures, governed by the good Providence of God, how could you remain indifferent to my pleading? For the spectacle of a human heart racked by suffering under the eye of a merciful God, although it may tempt those of little faith to blaspheme the divine goodness, or wisdom, or power, is for the Christian an intimation of the duty of almsgiving. The Christian knows that the creature's

---

* 2 Paralip. vi. 41.   † Psalm lxiii.

pain was not part of the divine plan in the beginning; but, rather, an after-stroke of man's malice that came to mar the tender beauty of the Creator's original design. He knows, too, that the Creator, even after his design had thus been marred, did not regard with cold indifference the sufferings wayward man had brought upon himself, but directly assumed the office of relieving the misery from which He wished his creation to have remained for ever exempt. The Supreme Being has willed to become the consoler of his afflicted creatures, and, while He proclaims Himself King of kings and Lord of lords, He loves also to style Himself Father of the poor, Protector of the widow, and Avenger of the wronged orphans' tears. Now, by what process does the Providence of God set itself to fulfil towards the distressed the office of mercy to which it has thus pledged itself? I know He could command the heavens to rain down food for the hungry, as the manna fell for the Israelites in the desert. I know He could bid the birds of the air bring sustenance to the widow, as the ravens brought bread to the prophet in the wilderness; and that He could make the corn to spring forth at the touch of the orphan's hand, or on the place whereon his feet had stood. But continually to have recourse to means such as these would be to supersede his ordinary by an extraordinary Providence, to destroy the reign of law in nature, and make of the miraculous the rule and not the exception. This He has not wished to do. Since, therefore, on the one hand, He has pledged Himself to give his creatures meat in the season, and since, on the other hand, He will not usually have recourse to supernatural methods of providing for them the promised support, does it not plainly follow that He has made their maintenance a charge upon the good things with which his ordinary Providence blesses the earth from year to year? No matter, therefore, into what hands God's bounteous gifts to the world may pass; no matter who among men may become their proprietor, there clings evermore to the possession of them the obligation of succouring God's afflicted creatures. And when the cry of the homeless, famished, forlorn outcasts, for whom I plead to-day, rises to heaven and penetrates to the Creator's heart, He refers its prayer back to earth to those whom He has constituted owners of what the Apostle calls the substance of this world, the good gifts which at his bidding bounteous nature produces for the support of man. To-day, through my words, He addresses to you the petition of fallen women who have cried to Him from the depths of their distress, and from you He asks in their behalf the succour without which they must perish, body and soul. How many squander whole fortunes to compass frail woman's degradation; and shall it be possible that while the world's

Aspatias revel in luxury you will allow Christ's Magdalens to starve? Especially since in return for your almsgiving God promises you spiritual blessings beyond all price. We are too apt to forget that in God's universe things material and things spiritual fit into each other, and work together as parts of one harmonious whole. The order of grace does not circle in distant space round the sensible creation, as a planet of larger might course round one of narrower orbit, without contact or commingling. On the contrary, God has chosen material elements to be the vehicles of spiritual benefits to man. Thus, words spoken by human lips to human ears convey to the hearer's soul the doctrines of that faith without which it is impossible to please God. Sensible matter duly wedded to sensible form in the sacraments becomes the channel of sacramental grace. And so, in a remarkable degree, does it happen with almsgiving. The material act of bestowing material gifts, in obedience to the law of charity, has for its effect not merely to please God, as He is pleased by any other act of virtue, but to cause Him to confer in return upon the almsgiver certain spiritual benefits of sovereign importance. So explicit are his promises to this effect, so clearly has He set forth the connection established between man's act of charity and his own outpouring of supernatural blessings, that it would almost seem as if the latter were bartered for the former. "For alms delivereth from death : and the same is that which purgeth away sins, and maketh to find mercy and life everlasting" (Tob. xii., 9). Therefore, my brethren, I will say to each of you to-day, with an ancient father : *Da panem, accipe Paradisum !* Give to these sufferers a morsel of bread, and take in exchange the kingdom of heaven ! You could not refuse it to them, my brethren, even if their lot were merely on a level in misery with that of the other homeless and forlorn poor. But it is not so ; for the lot of the fallen but repentant woman has a bitterness peculiarly its own. Other shelterless creatures are wretched in the knowledge that they are homeless ; in her misery the most poignant element is to know that she is not without a home. Her mind is haunted, first of all, by the thought of the home of her innocent childhood. As she walks in her desolation, exposed to the pitiless pelting of the storm, ever and anon there rises before her the vision of the humble cottage in which her early years were passed in sinless peace. In spirit she stands once more upon the well-remembered threshold, and gazes upon those whom throughout all her vileness she has never ceased to love. Once more she sees the father whose grey hairs she has dishonoured ; the mother in whose heart her daughter's shame has killed joy for ever ; the brothers and sisters, once her playmates in infancy, but who now shrink as from a blow at the chance mention of her name. She sees her own place vacant in the household, and, with irresistible yearning her heart goes out towards her home, exclaiming with Job in his misery, "Who will grant me, that I might be according to the months past, according to the days in which God kept me ? When his lamp shined over my head, and I walked by his light in darkness? As I was in the days of my youth, when God was secretly in my tabernacle ? " (Job, xxix. 2-4.) But suddenly there flashes upon her soul the knowledge that her place shall know her no more ; that between her and the home of innocence her sin has dug a mighty gulf which never, never can be bridged over ; and that she is forever excluded from her paradise, as hopelessly as if, like Eden, it were guarded against her by a stern angel and a flaming sword turning every way. And so, with a wild despairing cry she rushes away through the night, homeless at the very threshold of her home. Cast out from the home of her innocence she next finds herself at the door of another home, the home of her sin. She is starving, and she knows that there she will find shelter, and raiment, and food, and warmth, and light; she is forlorn, and she knows that there wanton companions await her and joyous revelry and the intoxication of guilty delight. Oh ! may God help her now, poor fragile creature, as she stands trembling between sin and starvation ! In such a moment the strength of the most seasoned virtue becomes as the ashes of tow, and to guard their weakness against a trial such as this, the best and holiest unceasingly pray : " Lord ! lead us not into temptation." If the cedars of Lebanon fall before the fierce breath of temptation, how shall the broken reed be strong enough to endure?

It was but a few days ago that the fallen woman began to repent; her good resolutions are hardly formed ; her soul is still sick with the dregs of sin ; not yet has she found strength in the arms of the Good Shepherd. But, nevertheless, in the pauses of the conflict she hears his voice calling to her to come to Him, and she turns resolutely away from the home of sin, determined to follow after her Saviour, no matter how rugged the way or how toilsome the journey that will lead her to his feet. She flies from the accursed place, and sternly nerves herself to fight her waning life by toiling for a morsel of bread as only the despairing can toil. And so once again she looks out for another shelter, this time in the home of honest labour. When Adam sinned God condemned him, in punishment of his offence, to work in the sweat of his brow. To what a depth of misery has she fallen when the life of grinding toil that was Adam's curse by her is regarded as a blessing, to be sought for with hungry desire anywhere and everywhere. To be sought for, but not

6

to be found! In the very hour of his divine anger God set a mark upon Cain, but it was a token of mercy, that whosoever found the guilty fratricide should not kill him. Too soon does she discover that she also has had a mark set upon her, but not in mercy! Her sin has branded her with a mark so loathsome that barely to see it dries up in all the very fountains of human sympathy. "This man, if he were a prophet," said, within himself, the Pharisee when he saw the Magdalen anoint our Saviour's feet, "would know surely who and what kind of woman this is that toucheth him : for she is a sinner." No prophetic gift is needed in the present organisation of society, to detect who and what is the cowering female form that comes without recommendation or friendly testimony to solicit the meanest employment. And once it is known who and what she is every door is shut in her face. Whatever she touches is accounted unclean. Nothing short of divine charity itself is brave enough, I do not say to defend or comfort her as Christ defended and comforted the Magdalen, but even to brook that she should enter beneath an honest roof. Excluded thus from the home of labour, loathing, through God's grace, again to enter into the home of sin, cast out for ever from the home of her innocent childhood, where shall the hunted creature lay her wearied head? Is it any wonder, my brethren, if, in this drear hour of her complete outlawry from her kind, there comes to her the thought of the one home which she is free to enter at will, in which so many of her forlorn sisters have sought rest before her, the home of despair beneath the waters of the deep, dark, rushing river? Well may we shudder as we see her standing on the brink, holding as it were her life in the palm of her hand, and weighing, in her agony, whether it be not less bitter to die than to live! Our sense is too dull to conceive and our language too cold to describe the wild, intense anguish of the soul, that on account of its sins feels itself forsaken by God and man. Enough to say that this feeling of desolation was the last drop in the chalice of suffering, which in his passion the Redeemer wished to drain even to the dregs. He came not only to redeem man, but to console him ; therefore, He willed to take on Himself every form of pain of body and of mind, so that among the generations that were to suffer on the earth not one individual should have to bear a pang which He had not first sanctified by carrying it in his own heart. And in the procession of sorrows that came upon Him, the greatest came last : and the last was the desolation. He felt when hanging upon the cross He found the sins of the world laid upon his innocent shoulders, and Himself substituted for us as the object of his Father's abhorrence. He had borne in silence the insults of the soldiery, the scourging at the pillar, the burden of the heavy cross, the sharp nails, the thorny crown ; it was only when he felt Himself abandoned that He cried out in awful words :—" My God, my God, why hast Thou forsaken me !" Even such in kind though not in degree is the appalling sense of desolation that pierces the soul of the fallen woman when remorse forces on her the conviction that for her sins God's mercy and man's compassion have quitted her for evermore. " O all ye that pass by the way attend, and see if there be any sorrow like to my sorrow: for he hath made a vintage of me, as the Lord spoke in the day of his fierce anger. From above He hath sent fire into my bones, and hath chastised me: he hath turned me back: He hath me desolate all the day long. The yoke of my iniquities hath watched: they are folded together in his hand and put upon my neck: the Lord hath delivered me into a hand out of which I am not able to rise " (Lament, i., 12-14).

She is not able to rise from her despair, but you, my brethren, are able to set her free. For, although all other homes deny her shelter, there yet remains one home better than all the rest, which it is in your power to open for her to-day—the home of the Good Shepherd. Its foundations were laid in the very day and hour in which, on Calvary, Christ for our sins was forsaken by his Father, that through his dereliction all desolate souls might find comfort. In that hour, St. John tells us, there stood by the cross of Jesus, Mary his Mother, and Mary Magdalen (John, xix. 25). How unspeakably solemn this meeting, in tender companionship at the foot of the cross, of Mary the purest of virgins with Mary the penitent sinner! Surely this was no chance encounter, but rather a revelation of the new relationship the Good Shepherd was establishing in his Church between the virginal life of which Mary was the type, and the penitent fallen ones, of whose conversion the Magdalen's was the prophecy. It was the reversal by the Sacred Heart of Jesus of the cruel sentence of perpetual scorn enforced by the world against degraded womanhood even in its repentance. It was a proclamation of the irresistible power of penance to repair the wreck made in the soul by sin, and of the sinner's restoration to the privileges of innocence effected by true contrition. It is this teaching that has created in the Catholic Church the convents of the Good Shepherd, in which tender and delicate ladies, virgins consecrated to Christ, live as in one united household with those who have been the vilest of the vile outcasts of society. Far different is this sacred companionship from the selfish charity that is satisfied with purchasing from others for the afflicted services it is too dainty to

render in its own person and from the fitful outpourings of
sentimental benevolence; it is a true, living, and working love,
and, like all true love, it has its foundation in the amiable
qualities of its object. And if you ask me what titles to their
love do the Nuns of the Good Shepherd discover in their penitent sisters, I answer, the same that Mary the Mother of God
recognised in Mary Magdalen. In the Magdalen, kneeling before Jesus, pouring out her precious ointment on the feet that
had so often grown weary in search of her soul, and washing
them with her tears, Mary recognised a soul that loved her
Son, and loved Him with an exceeding love. In the Magdalen,
defended by Christ against the cruel Pharisee, Mary recognised
a soul whom her Son loved, and loved much, for the measure
of the divine pardon is the measure of the divine love, and
much was forgiven her because she was loved much as well as
for her own exceeding love. In the Magdalen clasping the
foot of the cross and glistening with the priceless drops of the
sacrificial blood that had fallen upon her from the Saviour's
wounds, Mary reverenced the first-fruits of her Son's bitter
passion. And ever since, to pure hearts like Mary's, the vilest
and meanest among penitent women appear, shining with a
triple beauty, as loving Christ, as loved by Christ, and as the
dear fruit of his sufferings. There is not one among the fallen
ones for whom I plead to-day who, in the call she has received
to penance, does not possess a sure pledge of these three privileges of the Magdalen, but it is in the home of the Good
Shepherd alone that this pledge can be fully redeemed. It is
for you to introduce her there. If it is your duty to be generous
towards her because she is one of God's suffering creatures,
miserable even among the miserable, does not your obligation
become the stronger when you remember that this miserable
being has capabilities of noblest spiritual excellence which
without your aid must be lost and with your aid can be brought
to marvellous perfection. If at all times it is a duty to relieve
physical suffering, much more is it a duty when the relief of
physical suffering puts a stop to moral evil, and, most of all,
when together with removing physical and moral evil the help
you give has power to repair the havoc both had made in God's
creature, and to sanctify to God a soul and a body that had long
been desecrated. To assist the House of the Good Shepherd it
is therefore to perform a work of manifold charity, and such as
raises you to become in a singular degree, fellow-workers with
God. When through it you supply shelter and food to the
homeless, starving penitent, you co-operate with God the Father,
the Creator, who gives and maintains in his creatures the gift
of life. When you snatch her from the occasions of sin so fatal

to her frailty, you co-operate with God the Son, who came to redeem us from guilt. When you place her within the convent walls, within daily reach of the grace that flows from the sacraments as from never-failing fountains of mercy, you co-operate with the Holy Ghost, the Sanctifier of Souls. Of those who were fellow-workers with the apostle in his sacred ministry, St. Paul declared that their names were written in the Book of Life. How great, then, the assurance of salvation that belongs to those who have become fellow-workers with God Himself!

And now, dearly beloved brethren, I conclude by addressing to each of you the words addressed by our Saviour to the Pharisee, concerning the Magdalen: "Dost thou see this woman?" Look at her as homeless, tempted, cast out, despairing, she approaches the door of the home of the Good Shepherd that stands in the midst of your houses. Like Magdalen she is attracted by the Saviour's influence, but, unlike Magdalen, she has no beautiful vase fragrant with costly unguents wherewith to honour Him. She has only a wasted life and a broken heart to bring to Him, but yet her soul tells her He will not reject her. For her, on this side of the portal is pain, and shame, and remorse, and cruel agony, on the other peace, love, pardon, and the Good Shepherd. But of herself she is not able to open the door; without your help she must remain shut out from the blessings that are almost within her grasp and go back to her despair. She looks to you for help; God wishes that you should help her. "Dost thou see this woman?" There was a day when men looked on her as David looked on Bethsabee, and their look brought shame and ruin upon her. For the honour of humanity, is there no one now who will look on her with a look of compassion that shall undo the curse of that look of lust and save her from death? "Dost thou see this woman?" Often before to-day have her fellow-creatures looked upon her as the Pharisee looked upon the Magdalen, and her heart is cut with their unkind glances, and still bleeds from their more unkind words and acts. Is there no one who, like our Saviour, will take account of the change wrought in her heart, and count her tears as they fall, and bid her broken spirit take courage? And you, my brethren, how will you look upon her? Will you see her with the eyes of the Pharisee or with the eyes of Christ? "Dost thou see this woman?" The spouses of Christ have seen her coming, and they left father and mother, and all the golden joys of life, that their hearts, emptied of all other love, might be entirely for her, and they toil their strength away, and starve within the convent walls that they may have a crust wherewith to satisfy her hunger. Is there no one to help them to keep a roof over their heads, and to rescue them from being cast out with their wretched charges upon the highway? "Dost thou see this woman?" Mary the Mother of God sees her, and in her recognises the companion who clung to her in love when even apostles fled in the dark hour of the Passion. And shall the companion in whose caresses Mary the Mother of Sorrows found comfort, be left to perish unheeded in her distress? Shall she be entitled to a place on Calvary, and be cast out from the house that God has built for her among you? "Dost thou see this woman?" Jesus Christ sees her. In the Magdalen standing at the foot of his cross He saw each and every one of the sinful sisterhood who in the course of ages after having imitated her in her own sin was to imitate her likewise in her repentance; and to receive each of them the Good Shepherd opened wide his arms in the embrace of his cross. These arms are open still: they are open to-day; they are open in this place. Now, may the God of mercy inspire you to make such a sacrifice as shall securely place within the arms of the Good Shepherd the sheep that has gone astray and has been recovered, the soul that had been lost and has been found, the woman who had sinned much but to whom much has been forgiven!

THE CRY FROM THE WILDERNESS.

"And this is the testimony of John, when the Jews sent from Jerusalem priests and Levites to ask him, Who art thou? . . . They said therefore unto him, Who art thou, that we may give an answer to them that sent us. What sayest thou of thyself? He said, I am the voice of one crying in the wilderness: Make straight the way of the Lord, as said the Prophet Isaias."— JOHN, i. 19-23.

THE office discharged by the precursor of Christ, St. John the Baptist, whose feast we celebrate to-day, is a type of the office belonging to the Catholic Church as the teacher of men. His it was to point to the Lamb of God who had come to take away the sins of the world; hers it is to continue to the end to preach the same Christ, and Him crucified. Born in mystery, brought up in desert solitudes, marvellously austere in mien and garb and speech, he came upon a luxurious generation as an apparition, perplexing it with wonder and dismay. Who is this? men asked in their astonishment; who is this who dares thus sternly to rebuke our pleasant vices, and to disturb our cultured ease with his harsh summons to penance, and his threats of future punishment? Even so has it been with the Catholic Church. For now nineteen centuries she has traversed the

earth, unearthly in her origin, in her power, in the beauty of
her holiness, and in every age she has been confronted by men
asking her, now in anger, now in love, now in hatred, as the
Jews asked John, " Who art thou? what sayest thou of
thyself?" And, like John, she has ever answered, " I am the
voice of one crying in the wilderness, Make straight the way of
the Lord." No two words are less becoming on human lips
than these two words, *I am.* God alone has the right to say,
" I am who am." The history of man's greatness, man's glory,
must be told in other speech. *Fuit Troja, et ingens gloria.*
Alone among all institutions on earth the Catholic Church can
say, " I am;" for the " I am" of her priesthood is contained in the
eternal " Thou art a priest for ever," spoken by God to his Son,
her Founder. With this simple assertion of her existence she
has triumphed over the enemies that have ever beset her path.
When Pagan emperors arose with sword in hand and every
implement of torture to crush her for daring to dispute their
tyranny, she answered, " I am;" and the successor of the
pontiffs whom they slaughtered took his seat upon their vacant
throne. When Arianism came forth to deny the divinity of
Christ, and make the only-begotten Son of the Father that
Father's creature, and when the entire world, seduced by its
wiles, shuddered at finding itself almost enveloped by its hateful
doctrine, the Church said, " I am," and Arianism with its
baneful power became a thing of the past. When savage
nations and savage hatreds were in the ascendant, and Christian
civilisation was on the point of being extinguished in blood,
once more the Church asserted herself, and Attila retired before
Leo. And later on, when the empires she herself had raised
would have laid impious hands upon her liberties, she broke
their bonds by declaring that she was the spouse of Christ, and
triumphantly exercised the freedom He had given her; and
later still, when at the so-called Reformation the nations of
Europe rose up against their Mother, and when a thousand
voices re-echoed Luther's boast that he was the death of the
papacy, once more she said, " I am;" and, lo! she finds in the
new world more children by millions than she had lost in
the old. Whilst Protestantism is crumbling around her she
lives victorious and triumphant. What, then, if to-day the
Governments of the earth have broken with her? what if in
their Cabinets statesmen are busy weaving bonds wherewith
to cripple her liberty? As wax is wont to melt before the sun,
so shall their bonds disappear and they themselves perish, whilst
she shall endure. Already this terrible truth is being recognised
in that Germany which has taken the first rank amongst the
persecutors of the Church. "This struggle must cease," cries

one of the official organs of public opinion in that country.
" Under the banner of the Kultur Kanuff, all the elements
hostile to religion and to Christianity have for many years
exercised their work of destruction, and the consequences are
too evident and acknowledged by the most liberal. The State,
the school, the family—our whole life is falling to pieces
without religion and its support. Unless we wish to fall into
the evils of socialism and become the prey of revolution, it is
absolutely necessary once more to establish education on the
basis of religion, impose silence upon the so-called struggle for
civilisation, and raise the siege that has been proclaimed for so
many years against the Catholic Church." They begin to see
that without the Pope there is no Christianity, and without
Christianity there is no hope for society. " But where Peter
is," cried out St. Ambrose, some fourteen hundred years ago,
" there is the Church, and where the Church is no death shall
come, but life unfailing." *Ubi Petrus ibi ecclesia et ubi ecclesia
ibi nulla mors sed vita sempiterna.* And what does the Church
say that she is ? There lived a barbarian king who said he was
the scourge of God. The impious Mahomet loved to call himself
the sword of the Most High. The Catholic Church says of
herself that she is but a voice. There exists on earth nothing
weaker than a human voice ; the summer winds scatter it, and
man himself rifles it of what strength they spare, by deeds that
belie his promises ; and yet, weak as it is, it is by divine institution the link that unites the temporal with the eternal—man
with God ; " for how shall men be saved unless they believe,
and how shall they believe unless they hear, and how shall they
hear unless it be preached unto them ?" So that it is strictly
true that the means established by God for the accomplishment
of his designs of mercy towards man is none other than the
voice of the Church's teaching ; for how shall they preach unless
they be sent ? Nor is there any other means more worthy of
man or more noble. For, as man himself is the noblest of God's
creatures, so man's highest nobility resides in his reason, and
language is the very flower of his rational gifts. In making,
therefore, his Church a voice, God proclaims his respect for the
free will He Himself has created in man, and declares that He
would reach man's will only through man's intellect, his own
grace aiding. And hence the Church is not, as her foes assert,
the enslaver of the human intellect, but simply the highest form
of intellectual force. Consult all that her voice has uttered,
from the first Council of Nice, when she defended the divinity
of the Eternal Word, to her last Council of the Vatican, where
she vindicated the just liberties of human science, and you will
not find a syllable disrespectful to man's reason, or opposed to

the right use thereof. It was this voice, noble in its weakness, which, speaking first through twelve poor fishermen, and ever since through a mighty army of preachers, has shaken the pagan world, brought nations to the faith, and created Christian civilisation. And its power was not human, for it was the voice, not of a mere man, but of one crying in the wilderness who was both God and man. The Holy Scriptures tell us of three mysterious cries uttered by our Lord during his mortal life. These three cries we find reproduced in the Catholic Church, and in her alone. The first was the cry of healing, of which we read in St. Luke (ix. 54), when He took the dead girl's hand in his and cried out, " Maid, arise," and her spirit returned and she arose immediately. There is no healing for the sins and sorrows of men, whether in the individual, or in the family, or in the commonwealth, save in the life-giving touch of Christ and in the sound of his creative voice. In vain do philanthropists construct schemes of beneficence; in vain does political economy seek remedies for the ills that harass men; there is a depth in human sorrow and an unfathomable abyss of woe which no science can reach, and which demands a divine comforter. That divine comforter speaks only in the Catholic Church. Where else save in the Catholic Church do you find the tribunal of penance, in which, over heads bowed low with sin, the Redeemer's absolving words are spoken, and what is loosed on earth is loosed in heaven? Is there a single form of human suffering, of physical misery, for which the Church has not established some religious order in which the virtue of Christ's restoring touch lives and operates? The second of Christ's mysterious cries is the cry of faith with which, as we read in John (vii. 38), " Jesus stood and cried, saying, If any man thirst let him come to Me and drink." Where else save in the Catholic Church is faith to be found to-day? Faith is a belief, not upon human, but upon divine authority, and is it not a simple fact that no other religious body claims to speak with divine authority? Nay, do they not repudiate for themselves and for their rivals any share in the gift of infallibility, without which there is no certainty of faith even for the inspiration of God's written Word? Except the Catholic Church, then, who can say with confidence to men thirsting after the truth, "If any man thirst, let him come to Me and drink?" As a matter of history, she alone has converted Pagan nations, and in the great upheaving of modern thought she alone offers a rational basis for faith. Compared with the unity and harmony of her creed, how discordant the jarring sounds of the conflicting opinions that ceaselessly rend and tear other religious communions, until their followers in their despair declare positive doctrines to be unnecessary, and

seek refuge in the weaknesses of an emotional religion. The
third of Christ's solemn cries was the cry of sacrifice uttered
upon the cross, when, crying with a loud voice, He yielded up
his spirit. Is it not again a fact of history that throughout the
length and breadth of the earth, from the rising of the sun to
the going down thereof, no sacrifice is offered to the living and
true God save in the Catholic Church? She alone dares utter
the dread sacrificial words; she alone lifts up to heaven the pure
Host, the holy Host, the unspotted Host, the true bread of life
eternal, and the chalice of perpetual salvation. And as Christ
was at once priest and victim in his own sacrifice, so she and
she alone would have her priests sacrifice first themselves and
then the body of the Lord. Before she pours out upon the
youthful Levite the unction that makes him a priest for ever,
she bids him turn away from the cares and the pleasures of life,
and become, like St. Paul, crucified to the world, as the world
is to be crucified to him. She alone preaches the sanctity of
poverty, of chastity, and of obedience, and for her alone, as St.
Augustine says, "flowers forth the beauteous bloom of chaste
youths and maidens whom she consecrates to the Lord." With
a voice thus one with the voice of Christ, how truly does she
claim as addressed to herself the words of Christ, "He that
heareth you heareth Me." It is true that to-day, more, perhaps,
than at any period of her existence in the past, the Church cries
in the wilderness. In the political world the atmosphere is dark
with the cloud of war, and the earth begins to tremble beneath
the shock of conflicting armies; fear is seizing upon the nations,
and men are uncertain whether they have more to fear from the
enemy that marches against them from without or from the
secret societies that darkly conspire against society in her own
bosom. In the world of thought disorder has reached its
highest materialism, has penetrated into every avenue of every
science; and free-thinking, after upsetting the fundamental
truths of the natural order, now boldly denies to man the very
power of thought. Men would fain blot out the eternal moral
distinction between right and wrong, and cynically mock at
what their fathers reverenced as virtues. Christianity is openly
assailed; the Divine Author of our Faith openly blasphemed;
his teaching not merely set aside, but derided; the whole supernatural order impugned; and if a God be permitted to exist,
He must be a God unknown to and unknowable by man. The
moral universe is shaken to its centre, and the Catholic Church
alone stands firm in the universal dissolution of principles and
of institutions. She cries out in the wilderness, "Prepare ye
the way of the Lord," and her words are at once a prophecy
and an exhortation—a prophecy addressed to the enemies of

religion, and an exhortation addressed to us. She has lived long enough to know by experience that there is no counsel, no power, no wisdom against the Lord; she knows that He who out of the evil of the first sin drew the priceless blessings of redemption—He who made the hands of guilty Jews open the fountains of the Precious Blood—He who bent the empire alike of Cæsar and of savage to the purposes of his Church, will, in his all-wise Providence, know how to bring salvation from out the ills that are now let loose upon the world. She sees that the destructive agencies now at work are destroying the evils of the past as well as the good, and secure in her immortal existence, confident in the power that sustains her, she can afford to wait. The future is hers, for it is God's, and God has given it to her, and therefore does she prophecy to her foes that they are but clearing the ground for her operations and preparing the way of the Lord. But to us her words are words of exhortation. She would have us prepare the way of the Lord in our own hearts, and make straight his paths by the holiness of our lives, and united to Him, resting upon Him, she bids us be without fear. (Ps. xxviii.) "What though the waters are rising and the surges are threatening to engulf the Church, let us not fear, for the voice of the Lord is upon the waters; what though, like cedars on Lebanon, the mighty of the world stand against us, the voice of the Lord breaketh the cedars and reduces them to pieces; what though the flames appear and threaten death, the voice of the Lord divideth the flames of fire; what though the world become a desert, the voice of the Lord shall shake the desert of Cades, and the Lord shall sit King for ever and will give strength to his people, and the Lord will bless his people with peace." Ages after the present danger, when the very names of her enemies shall be forgotten, the Church will be chanting her eternal "I am;" and with her voice, weak and noble as now, yet strong as the voice of Christ, she will speak words of healing, and of faith, and of sacrifice to generations to come; and out of the desert of man's crimes and man's weaknesses she " will prepare the way of the Lord and make straight his paths."

FOR AN ORPHANAGE.

"Take this child, and nurse him for me: I will give thee thy wages."—
EXOD. ii. 9.

UNDER the trees that overshadow the Nile, in the presence of a brilliant court, from the lips of a royal lady, did the mother of Moses receive, in the words I have just quoted for you, the

charge to bring up and educate her child.   Not by the streams
of the Nile, but by the life-giving waters of the baptismal font;
not in presence of the great ones of the earth, but in sight of
the angels of heaven ; not from an earthly sovereign, but from
the lips of Jesus Christ, King of kings and Lord of lords, a similar
charge is given to each of you to-day touching the orphan
children whose cause it is my duty to plead before you on
this occasion.   " Take this child," said the Egyptian Princess to
the Hebrew woman, " this forlorn and castaway child which
I have snatched from the waters of death, and for which I feel
all a mother's tenderness and a mother's love : take it and
bring it up—not for yourself, not for others, but for me, for
having adopted it as my own I claim for myself all its duty
and its service."   " Take this child," says Christ to each of you
here present, this homeless and fatherless orphan whom I have
saved from eternal death by the waters of baptism ; take it and
bring it up—not for the world, not for yourself, but for Me
who have bought it at the price of my blood."   This was the
infant Moses, as he drifted, a helpless waif, amid the rush of the
mighty river-waters, not in nearer peril of death than is the un-
protected orphan girl who is tossed to and fro upon the billows
of a cruel world.   She is in daily peril of death both of body and
soul ; in peril for want of food, and raiment, and shelter ; in
peril from the malice of others, from the malice of her own
heart ; in peril from ignorance and from false teachers ; and
her hope of escaping from all these dangers without that help
which Christ asks from you to-day on her behalf is as slender
and as frail as the fragile ark of rushes which hardly divides
the Hebrew infant from the waters of death.   Allow me to ask
you, beloved brethren, and would that my words could reach
the innermost heart of each one here present, allow me to ask
you, how are you disposed to receive the request made to you
to-day by our Divine Lord ?   Will you imitate the Hebrew
mother by a cheerful and generous compliance, or rather, by
a contemptuous or indifferent refusal, will you follow the example set by the Pharisees on the occasion of a similar request ?
Once before our Lord gave to the Pharisees a charge similar to
the one He gives you to-day, that they should make to themselves friends out of the mammon of iniquity by devoting some
of their wealth to the relief of the poor.   But they refused, and
being covetous, as the Sacred Scriptures tell us, they derided
Him.   But bear in mind, beloved brethren, that if you imitate
them in their refusal you shall be sharers in their scorn of
Christ, for such is the character of Him who imposes on you
the obligation of charity, that to refuse to fulfil his charge is to
scorn Him.   The duty of obedience follows close upon the right

to command, and can no more be separated from it than the shadow can be disjoined from the sunshine it follows after; and to refuse obedience when the right to command is admitted to exist is to make a scorn of authority. Now *all authority is centred in God.* He is the King of kings and Lord of lords. He holds the keys of the universe, and whatever He opens no man may shut, whatever He shuts no man may open. "Who," asks the apostle, "who resists his will?" Throughout all creation his word is law. He spoke the word and they were made; He commanded and they sprang into being. The sun may not swerve from the course He hath marked out; the stars of heaven shine out in their appointed place; the seasons, succeeding each other in the due order He has traced, crown the full year. He hath placed bounds to the deep, and the swelling billows touch them and are checked. He commands the winds and the waves, and they are hushed before his voice. And among all creatures shall man, formed before all others to obey, alone be exempt from that duty? No. He is our Master, we are his servants, and whatsoever is pleasing in his eyes that we are bound to do. Now it is beyond all doubt that He calls upon you to take care of the poor and of the orphan;— how, then, can you refuse? His authority to command you is unquestionable; the expression of his will in this case is beyond doubt; beyond doubt also is your duty to obey.

The more so that what He asks from you is not so much yours as his own. Is there a blade of the corn which is now springing from the earth for the food of man which his hand has not formed? Is there one grain of your gold and silver which He has not given you? "Gold is mine," saith the Lord, "and mine is the silver." Is there one hero, no matter how wide his acres, or great his wealth of gold or brain upon whose lips God does not every day place the same prayer that He places on the lips of the poorest, "Give us this day our daily bread?" If, then, all, all that you have is from God—if in yourselves there was nothing—why, you rather than your neighbour should be blessed with wealth; if what you possess is yours because He has given it to you, and if He has reserved rights over such portions of it as are required for his designs of mercy towards the poor, would it not be wrong in the extreme if you hardened your hearts against the request He makes from you to-day?

Especially since what He asks from you is so little. If He asked from you every moment of your lives every shilling you possess, your entire service, your health, your very life, you could not find a reasonable excuse for not complying with his request—so boundless, so universal is God's right over his creatures. And yet He leaves you your time, your health,

your life, to employ at will; He leaves you your wealth to be
spent for the necessaries, the comforts, and even the amusements of life, and is it too much to ask from you for the
helpless orphan the superfluity that remains when all the real
wants of your state of life have been satisfied?

*And while He asks you to give but little to Him in the person of
his poor, how royal is his own munificence to you; how much does
He Himself give to you, and with what liberality?* His hand is
never wearied in heaping gifts upon you. What have you
which you have not received?—Your soul with its faculties,
your body with its wondrous powers, your position in the
world, your family, the children of your love, your many
friends. And, as if all this was nothing, He has given you
his grace, his true faith, his sacraments, his Church, his Mother,
Himself to be your stay in this life and your abiding joy and
crown for ever. And what is more, He has given these in such
a way that the gift of them has cost Him personal labours,
personal suffering beyond all that love has ever made one man
suffer for another: for greater love than this no man hath,
that a man should lay down his life for his friends. And, in
face of this unparalleled devotion to you, will you hesitate, and
dole out grudgingly to Him a miserable pittance, less than you
spend upon one of your pleasures, and which you would feel
ashamed to offer to a servant.

*And yet you yourselves, every day and every moment, ask for
favours from Him.* Upon God all creatures over wait, that He
may give them food in due season. He opens his hand and
fills them with benediction. And what motive has brought
you all here to-day but to ask for mercy from God. But if in
the very act of asking Him to give you what you require, and
have no right to, you refuse to give Him what He requires, and
has a right to, how can you presume to expect a favourable answer
to your prayer? Do you not know that the law He has laid
down for Himself is: "Give and it shall be given unto you?"

If, then, my brethren, you admit that God has an unquestionable right to command you; if you admit that in asking
your alms for the poor He is only asking what is his own; if
you admit that He asks you for less than He might; if you
admit that He has in his own person set you the example of
liberality, and at immense personal cost; if, finally, you admit
that even while you refuse Him what He asks from you, you
will go on asking Him to give gifts to you: if you admit all
this—and you must admit it—is it not true that if you refuse to
be generous to-day to the orphans of God, that you are disrespectful to his Divine Majesty? If the refusal of the
Pharisees was a mockery, can it be true that a similar refusal
on your part is an act of respect?

But even if you were to forget all you owe to God, still, such is the nature of the charge laid upon you by Him, that you cannot refuse to accept it. Nothing is more precious than the object therein confided to your care. Childhood is a thing so winning, so graceful, so tender, so confiding—with a future so fair, an innocence so fresh, so lovely, and, alas! so fragile—that it claims not only all our love, but our deepest reverence. It was so even before Christ came ; but since He was born on earth, since the Lord of glory condescended to rest in the blessed arms of a Mother chosen from the daughters of men, infancy and childhood have been sanctified for evermore. And even for Him, the Man-God, the innocence of childhood has special attraction : He wished them to come to Him, his choicest blessings were for them, He declared them to be the type of those whom He would love.

Now, it is this precious object, this childhood, that is given over to your care to-day. And precious as childhood is in itself, it is equally precious in that it is the passage to something beyond. So closely do the cords of Adam bind our race together, that every human being, no matter how mean and humble, exercises influence for good or for evil upon others of his kind. How much more so the mother of the family ! But especially precious is childhood, touched by the sorrow of when it is joined with orphanhood, for then it gains a new value from the intimate relations the majesty of God has been pleased to contract with it. It is the express teaching of Holy Scripture that God is the Father of the orphan. The God who is King of kings and Lord of lords, whose power breaks the sceptres of rulers, who holds the sea in the hollow of his hand, before whom all the earth is a grain of dust, or a drop of morning dew upon grass—the Almighty God has been pleased to take to Himself the special title of Father and Protector of the orphan child, and the office of avenging his wrongs. And is it not an honour, my brethren, that God should invite you to be sharers with Him in this noblest work of his mercy ? Is it not an honour to be fellow-workers with God? " Is it a little thing," asks David, " to be son-in-law of a king ?" And is it a little thing, I ask, to have confided to your care the wards of the Eternal God ?

And wards though they be of God, they challenge your compassion, for they are the very type of sorrow and of weakness. There are some sufferings that are only of the heart, but they are terrible indeed. They are powerful to rob life of all its charm, to dim even the splendour of a crown, and to make drear and dark what once was brightest. Other sufferings there are of the body : cold and hunger, and poverty and disease, and the thousand ills born of these. Not always, not often, does the

Ruler of the world permit both classes of suffering to press with
united weight upon the same subject, but in the case of the
orphan He does permit it; in the heart of the orphan both
streams of sorrow are allowed to meet and mingle their waters
of bitterness almost unto death. What one of earthly blessings is
it either of heart or body which the orphan does not lose with its
parents? What single joy is there which it does not bury in
their graves? With them it loses home—that sacred spot
dearer than a palace ; it loses a father's tender care, a mother's
love—that love no one can adequately describe : all its affections
were bound up in these in a thousand ways, and all are now
snapped violently asunder; it is cast forlorn upon the cold
world, like Moses on the dark waters. What wonder, then, that
when the prophet would describe the extreme wretchedness of
the condition of the captive Jews, he could find no expression
more apt than to liken them to orphans: "We are become
orphans without a father!" What wonder that one of the
most extreme punishments threatened by God against the
enemies of his people was that the children should become
orphans? What wonder that the crowning sorrow which our
Lord would taste—the last drop in his bitter chalice of affliction
—was that of orphanhood, when on the cross He cried out to
his Father: "My God! my God! why hast Thou forsaken me?"
Would it not, then, be cruel in you, my beloved brethren, to
whom God has given so much happiness, to pass by in cool indifference, and leave the orphan's heart to break in silence? If
in the sight of this unutterable woe we should be niggardly in
endeavouring to assuage and relieve it, can we claim to have
the hearts of Christian men?

And if the weakness of the orphan will not move us, at least
let us be moved by the consideration of their power. Weak
in themselves, as I have described, in their very weakness lies
their strength. The orphan's tears, beloved brethren, are all-
powerful with God. Woe to the man who by his wickedness
makes one of them fall to the ground! Woe to the man who
despises it or slights it as it falls! That poor, wasted orphan
hand that is held out to you to-day for alms wields the very
power of God Himself! That voice, so plaintive and weak,
has an echo in the courts of heaven, and is powerful to
bar or to open its blessed portals for you. The cry of the
orphan, like the blood of Abel, ascends on high, and will not
depart until God shall have heard. Make, then, to yourselves
friends of the orphan, that their powerful help may lead you in
turn to the heavenly tabernacles.

And how noble is the work you are called upon to perform
with regard to the orphans thus confided to your care. *You*

are called upon, first of all, *to preserve a human life*. Without
Christian care the orphan must either starve, or drag out a
miserable existence, which latter is rather a penalty than a boon.
What can be more noble than to preserve a human life—that
heavenly spark of the gift of life which came originally from
the breath of God, and which links together in wonderful harmony the body and the soul of man? It is one of the noblest
of human sciences, that which devotes itself to save and to prolong life when attacked by disease, and men who devote to it
their young years, and waste the midnight oil, and expose themselves to fatigues and plagues to advance it, are true martyrs of
humanity, and deserve to be reckoned among the noblest of men.
But surely it is not less glorious to anticipate and prevent the
inroads of disease and death than to combat them directly when
they have already delivered their assault?

*You are called upon to do the very work which at the Last Day
shall win for you a favourable sentence.* By contributing to the
support of the orphan you feed the hungry, you give drink to
the thirsty, you clothe the naked, all together : your one deed
of charity is like a diamond which, though solitary, yet sparkles
with various light, and in itself embraces all. You have brought
back home and happiness, you have given education, you have
rescued from vice ; and amen I say to you, what you have done
for the least of these orphans, you have done for Christ.

*You are called to do the very work that brought Christ down
from heaven to earth.* He came that men should have life, and
should have it more abundantly ; and this is eternal life, that
men should know the one true God, and Jesus Christ whom He
sent. Now, this is the very work you are called upon to perform on behalf of the orphans, by enabling them to receive a
Christian education. You are to teach them the God who made
them, the Saviour who died for them, the Holy Ghost who
sanctifies them ; you are to enlighten their ignorance by instruction, to correct their corrupt will by the sweet influences
of grace. This was the fire Christ came on earth to scatter
among men, and He has no desire more vivid than that it
should be everywhere enkindled. How many martyrs and mis-
sioners have spent their lives in labouring to effect this, and
yet you can effect it at a slight sacrifice, indeed. The daughters
of St. Francis are there to take on themselves all that is really
severe in the work : they will instruct, they will devote their
lives, their strength to this work ; they only ask your help to
enable them to do so, and they will share with you their
reward.

Whether, then, you consider, beloved brethren, the claims
of Him who has given you the charge I have set before you, or

7

the nature of the object confided to your care, or the character of the work you are called upon to perform, you cannot refuse your generous co-operation; but should any further motive be wanting, think of the reward you will receive. St. Paul tells us that the pagan philosophers were inexcusable, because, whereas every creature spoke to them of God, they did not glorify Him as they ought. The heavens told them of his glory: each day that died published it to the day that rose; and the silence of the night was eloquent with the theme. They were inexcusable because of the cloud of witnesses whom God had sent to speak to them of Himself. And so shall you be without excuse, beloved brethren, if you refuse to be generous in your charity, for God has raised up a similar cloud of every kind of witnesses to tell you of the rewards of almsgiving. Ages before Christianity, and even among those outside the pale of the Jewish religion, from the land of Uris, Job raises his plaintive voice to tell you how blessings followed him because he had delivered the fatherless. If from the sad spectacle of the sufferings of Job you turn to the glories of the people of God, and, like the Queen of Sheba, visit the royal palace of Israel, in its golden courts you will hear the voice of the King Prophet declaring how blessed is the man who taketh thought for the needy and the poor, and how in the evil day God will deliver him. Follow the Jewish people to captivity, and though their harps hang silent on the willows, and their songs are hushed in the strange land, yet not hushed is the voice of the good Tobias, who tells you that alms deliver from all sin and from death, and will not suffer the soul to go into darkness. Even the angels of God join their voices in praise of charity with the voices of earth; and Raphael, one of the seven who stand before God, announces that alms deliver from death, and maketh to find mercy and life everlasting. Do you desire more? To the voices of sage and saint, and prophet and angel, the Eternal Wisdom, the Word made Flesh, unites his majestic utterance, and the voice that made the world proclaims to you that what remaineth give as alms, and behold all things are clean unto you!

Give charity, then, this morning, copiously and generously, to the orphans of St. Clare; take these children of Christ, bring them up for Him, and He, the faithful and true, will give you your reward.

FOR AN ORPHANAGE.

'And when He had fasted forty days and forty nights, afterwards He was hungry."—Matt. iv. 2.

"Not in bread alone doth man live, but in every word that proceedeth from the mouth of God."—Matt. iv. 4.

THE cunning which ever prompts the Evil One to seize on any opportunity likely to further man's spiritual ruin, is nowhere more plainly displayed than in the Gospel history I have just read. This cunning taught him to detect in our Lord's hunger an occasion which would point out and strengthen the temptation he was about to urge; for he knew well that among frail men, such as he believed our Lord to be, the want of the necessaries of life is a sower of rebellious thoughts against the blessed majesty of God's providence. And, indeed, beloved brethren, it is difficult, at first sight, to justify that providence to the eye of the starving and naked wretch. If you tell him of our Heavenly Father, who clothes the lily in array fair beyond the king's glory; if you speak to him of the Being who encompasses with tender care the commonest of his beings, how will he hear you as long as he feels that the clothing bestowed on the grass of the field, and the tenderness lavished upon the birds of the air, are denied to him, though he be the so-called lord of that earth of which these creatures are but the rude furnishing? If you tell him of the Almighty hand which love causes evermore to open, and which, when it opens, gives food in fitting season to every creature waiting upon it—nay, even if you tell him that the very same Almighty hand that feeds all creatures has been nailed to the cross for him, through love—what impression will you make on his heart, hardened by the thought that all this love has passed him by, pitying all but him, unpitying for him alone, without warming or cherishing him in its passage? This is a great difficulty, indeed, to face, my brethren; but there is even a still more complicated form of it. The Psalmist tells us (Ps. cxlvi. 9) that it is God who giveth food to the young ravens that call upon Him; but by what means does He feed them? He Himself tells us in Job (xxviii. 41) that it is by providing food for their mother when her young ones cry to God, wandering about because they have no meat. That is to say, my brethren, it is the mother that feeds the brood, and yet even so it is God who feeds them, for it is God who has placed

in her heart the unerring, inscrutable instinct of love that urges
her to seek and find and bring food to her little ones. And
as it is with the young of the raven, so is it with the children
of men : they, too, call to God's providence for food, and God
provideth it for them by means of their parents, whose love and
labour are the means He has established to feed his little ones.
And yet, my brethren, we see that God frequently takes
away from over these little ones the parents who gave them
birth—that is to say, God's providence deliberately denies
to the orphan those very means of existence which that same
providence had established as the instruments of his bounty
towards them. God forbid, my brethren, that the dark thought
should enter your mind that by sending death to the parents
God wishes that the orphans should all perish off the earth !
Reason recoils from believing such cruelty of the God who
spareth all because He loveth souls : our heart refuses to accept
it, and makes room instead for the words of the Psalmist,
" *Patris orphanorum et judicis reduarum* " (Ps. lxvii. 6).
God Himself proclaims it to be false by declaring Himself
in an especial manner the Father of the orphan. On the
contrary, my brethren, it would appear as if the removal of
the parents did but draw the orphan closer to the heart of
God, as if the chain that binds God to man is shortened
by the dropping out of some of its links. In the genealogy
of our Saviour, Adam only is called the son of God, the
other generations each being attributed to their respective
progenitors ; and so in the case of the orphan, God wishes him
to be called his son : " I am the Father of the orphan." It
would be blasphemy, then, my brethren, to think that God
ceases to wish to preserve those whom He has made orphans ;
but this truth, so plain and so certain, does but increase our
difficulty. If God's providence has charged itself with the
sustenance of its creatures ; if it habitually fulfils this charge by
certain ordinary means adapted to the end ; if it deliberately
remove these means in the case of orphans and others, without
ceasing to wish to attain the end proposed, what are we to say ?
How does it happen that while He deliberately wishes the poor
orphan to live, He with equal deliberation removes the means
by which only this wish can be accomplished ? You have heard
the only answer that can be given, and you have heard it from
the divine lips of Jesus Christ Himself. It is not by bread
alone that man lives, that is, it is not only by ordinary means
that God can attain his end, but by whatever means He pleases.
All means are alike to Him.

All the means in God's hands may be roughly reduced to
two classes—the supernatural and the natural. God had recourse

to supernatural means when, having led out the Israelites into the desert, away from the flesh-pots of Egypt and the Egyptian plains of waving corn, He fed them for forty years with manna sent down from heaven; and it was with respect to this miraculous interposition of Providence that the words quoted by our Lord were originally used. I know, my brethren, that God could have recourse to similar means to feed his orphans; that He could send the ravens to bring them bread, as He did to Eliseus the Prophet; that He could rain manna upon them from heaven, or bid the corn spring up at the touch of orphan feet, or the earth supply them with rich metals from its bosom. I know He could do all this, but I know that He has been pleased not to do it. To expect these miraculous interpositions of God on behalf of his little ones is to expect that what is only an exception should become a rule; nay, more, it is to say what the Evil One said: "Let these stones become bread." God, then, does not wish to realise his plan, to fulfil his wish, by supernatural means: natural means He has removed. How, then, are God's orphans to be fed? They must be supported either by their own toil, or by the help of those to whom God has given in greater or less abundance the riches of this world. To say that they are to support themselves is a mockery; therefore, very beloved brethren, we are inevitably brought to the conclusion that either God has pledged Himself to do what is impossible and is false to his pledges, or that it is his clear and positive will that you are to be the instruments of his providence with regard to these little ones whom He loves. As truly, then, as that God does not undertake impossibilities, or break his pledges, so truly you are called upon by Him to be fellow-workers with Him on behalf of the orphans. Do not fret, my brethren, or impatiently regard the burden of this duty; for the hand that lays it upon you is the same which gives you your worldly substance; nay, it is one of your titles to what you possess. Before you close your heart against the call God makes on you on behalf of his orphans, let us consider that we have got all things from the bounty of God. He could ask you for your time, your life, your health, &c.: will you refuse Him the little He does ask in reality? It is said that when God crowns our good works He does but crown the merits He Himself has given us; and, in like manner, we may say that when He imposes a duty on us it is but a way of conferring some fresh favour upon us. When He imposes on you the duty of helping Him to feed the orphan, He is but conferring a boon upon you. If we examine in Sacred Scripture the dealings of God with man, we shall see that He has ever followed this rule: whenever He avails Himself of the

assistance of any man in any one work He Himself is most
liberal towards his fellow-worker in the gifts analogous to the
work on which He has employed him. Thus He called on
Moses to be his instrument in a deed of might, and so largely
did he bestow on his creature the gift of power that He said:
"*Ecce constitui te Deum Pharaonis*" (Exod. vii. 1). He called
on the widow to feed his Prophet Elias, and He rewarded her
with an abundance because she had been liberal in her poverty.
He called on Mary to help in the sanctification of the world,
and He was most liberal to her in gifts of grace and sanctity.
He called on Cyrus to effect his will in deeds of arms, and He
made him the anointed among strong persons. When, therefore, He calls on you to be his sharers in a work of mercy, He
will be liberal in many ways towards you.

And now, my brethren, see what this co-operation with God
brings with it. It is a rule of his Providence that whenever
He asks man to assist Him in any undertaking, He communicates to his chosen helpers such abundant graces and favours as
to prove them to be his assistants: He, as it were, hands over
to them his attributes. See, then, that you have become by
this the representatives of the mercy of God to man. "For
He shall deliver the poor from the mighty : and the needy that
had no helper. He shall spare the poor and needy: and He
shall save the souls of the poor" (Ps. lxxi. 12, 13). The cry of
the orphan comes to Him, and He sets you out as his representative to clothe, and feed, and nurture his desolate ones. They cry
to you, you must hear them ; they ask for you, you must grant
what they ask ; they are placed in your hands, you must be
kind, and tender, and loving, and generous to them. Your
pleasures day by day ask from you, and you give to them,
and yet you are not to them the representatives of God's mercy.
If you accept a trust, you must be ready to carry out its require-
ments ; if you assume a position, you must fulfil its duties ; if
you undertake to stand for another, you must do what he would
do if you had not taken his place. If you deliberately contracted the obligation of providing for some weak and poor
person, and pledged yourself to act the part of a parent towards
him, you would be unjust and cruel if you proved false to your
word. Now, beloved brethren, you must accept the position
God has assigned you with respect to the orphan. That position
is a privilege to you, but its acceptance is compulsory ; you
are compelled to accept it, and shall be condemned for its
omission. This is what is most wonderful about your case.
Justice and charity, your duty and your interest, alike forbid
you to refuse to accept the duty laid upon you. Charity to
yourself forbids it, for it is the highest privilege God could

bestow upon you. It is that image that is reflected in man, which moves God to love him; that image is impressed more plainly and fully in baptism; and if, faint or faded by sin, it has turned away God's love from you, by this privilege it is restored and refreshed, and being refreshed, God's love for you is refreshed in like manner. If, then, you would hide the sins of your soul, clothe yourself in the image of God. Besides, in warfare it sometimes happens that men escape death by wearing the uniform of their foe. You have armed against you the justice of God : save yourself from it, my brethren, by putting on the badge of mercy. I do believe, my brethren, that to be asked to feed God's orphans is a proof of God's intensest love towards you and your own inheritance. He will show mercy to the merciful; and the more merciful are his creatures, the more mercy shall they find at his hands. Now the work of mercy increases in proportion to the intensity of the misery which it heals; greater is the mercy which meets the greater need. Now, I deliberately assert that in the whole band of sorrow that preys on men there is none more bitter, more crushing, than falls to the share of the orphan. The orphan is either conscious or he is unconscious of his loss. If he be un-conscious of it, my brethren, his case appears to me still more pitiable and melancholy. Or if the child be haply conscious of its loss, I will not attempt to describe its sorrow; but rather I will ask you, oh, parents who have lost the child of your love, or have trembled at the thought of losing him, I will ask you to tell us the bitterness of that moment of separation. From what you have suffered we may know what a bereft child does suffer ; for parental and filial love are but equal strands of the self-same cords of Adam that bind men together, and when they break they exhibit cor-responding firmness. But I will say this much: Happiness is the state of gratified desire ; as long as a desire remains un-satisfied we are never happy ; the more desires unsatisfied, the more our unhappiness increases. Give the child the fond look, the loving smile of father or mother, and you gratify his heart's desire ; take them away, and you cause the pang that constitutes the unhappiness of the orphan.

But, last of all, if you would understand the depth of the sorrow you are called upon to heal, call to mind that Jesus Christ came on earth not only to save us, but to console us : He is not only Christ the Saviour, but Christ the Consoler. To this end He wished to suffer every pang, to bare his heart to every wound that poor human nature can suffer ; He wished to drain every drop of the bitter chalice of suffering any of his children should ever suffer. But in the procession of sorrows that invaded Him, the greatest came last; the last days of his passion were the days of his greatest pains, and among those of his passion the most intense were still the last. The betrayal by Judas was a bitter pain, but He gave no sign of his sorrow; the scourging, the blow on the face, the crucifixion, brought no tear or expression of sorrow from Him; but the moment of his supreme agony was come when He felt Himself bereft of his Father, and his sorrow wrung forth the awful cry, amid the darkness that overhung Calvary, "My God, my God, why hast Thou forsaken me?" The sorrow that He reserved to the last, the last drop in the chalice of woe, was to become an orphan.

And this is the infinite sorrow He calls on you to heal, this is the infinite mercy He wishes you to perform, that He may be infinitely merciful to you.

FOR THE WIDOWS' HOME.

" Honour widows, that are widows indeed."—1 TIM. v. 3.

FINDING myself here to-day, dearly beloved brethren, filling the place of the distinguished prelate whose unavoidable absence we all regret, I cannot but confess that I experience a feeling of apprehension and anxiety. I know I have no reason to be apprehensive on the score of your charity, which, as these walls can witness, has never been found wanting to any good cause; but I am anxious that the interests of the widow may not suffer by being confided to my charge. Indeed I look upon these good widows for whom I am about to plead as doubly widowed—widowed first, long since, of that help which a husband's arm brings, and widowed now of the powerful advocacy so often and so successfully exerted for them here by the respected voice we miss to-day. However, the pressure of my anxiety is considerably lightened when I consider the vantage ground supplied to the cause I am to-day pleading by the admonition directed by St. Paul to his disciple, the beloved Timothy. Emboldened by the teaching of the apostle, I am not content to have your compassionate assistance for their virtuous Christian widowhood: I furthermore call upon you to pay towards it respect and honour. I cry out with the apostle: "Honour widows, that are widows indeed."

No doubt it may be a matter of surprise to you that whereas you came here to show mercy, and pity, and tender compassion, you should hear yourselves called upon, in addition, to pay a tribute of respect and honour. It may startle you a little to find those whom you are prepared to hear described as objects of compassion raised upon a pedestal and elevated into objects that demand to be honoured also at your hands. Your surprise is, perhaps, natural, beloved brethren, and it is right that you should be cautious, seeing that in the daily life of the world you are so often called upon to honour what is really and truly deserving of all your contempt. You make a purchase because the merchant affirms his wares to be genuine, and you find they turn out worthless; you receive into your confidence a person who is recommended as trustworthy, and on closer acquaintance you find him dishonest; you give your esteem to a man who wears the garb and mien of virtue and respectability, and you soon find his good qualities did but cover a multitude of defects. But, notwithstanding all this, you can and ought to believe that Christian widowhood is entitled to your respect. Men may deceive you when they invite you to pay honour, but God cannot and will not. It is the voice of an inspired Apostle— it is the counsel of Holy Scripture, it is the word of God itself that calls upon you to honour their widowhood; therefore, beyond all gainsay, without any doubt, Christian widowhood is de- serving of being honoured by you. It is the infallible teaching of God that honour should be paid where honour is due, and therefore, whenever we are commanded to pay honour it is infallibly certain that the honour is really due. Are you a husband or a wife? You claim respect and honour from the partner of your life;—and why? Is it not because God com- mands the husband to love and honour his wife, and the wife to love and honour her husband? Are you a parent? You claim respect and honour from your children;—and why? Is it not because God has said to children, "Honour thy father and thy mother?" Are you an employer or a master? You expect to be obeyed and respected by them under you;—and why? Is it not because God has commanded inferiors to respect their betters? The groundwork of society consists in the mutual observance of relative duties imposed by God on all, and to exact this observance you have constant recourse to God's command. And you are right, beloved brethren; but if you are wise and just in exacting the honour due to yourselves, because God has given you a right to it, am I wrong when to-day, on the self-same authority, I call upon you to enlarge your hearts and pay to Christian widowhood the honour God asks for it: "Honour widows, that are widows indeed" (1 Tim. v. 3).

If I ask too much, so do you; if you do not ask too much, then I have a right to be heard. I call upon you, therefore, to honour the widow to-day; and I say that God expects from you that you will not slight their petition, or remain cold and indifferent to their cause. How can you be said to honour the widow if you grudge to bestow upon their cause the attention and the interest you so lavishly bestow on other things?

And now, beloved brethren, I wish you to penetrate the full meaning of what is understood by the command to honour Christian widows. The Holy Scriptures contain several such precepts: thus, we are commanded to honour God, to honour the king, to honour our parents, to honour our brethren in Christ. Now, honour is nothing else than a testimony we freely render to the excellent qualities of him we honour: thus, we honour God when we acknowledge his infinite perfections; we honour our superiors when we recognise in them the authority which God has given them over us; we honour our brethren when we bear witness to the bonds that unite us all together in Christ. Is it not wonderful then that, as we are told to honour God and our superiors, so we should also be told to honour Christian widowhood? What is there in this last that it should exact our respect? What are the excellent qualities in it to which we are to bear testimony? My brethren, I will not now delay to set forth the manifold excellent qualities of the state of Christian widowhood. I will not delay to tell you how, in the Sacred Scriptures, it ranks in dignity close after the holy state of virginity; how St. Paul himself has given special rules in its regard; how many virtues it develops; how much merit it stores up. But rather I will claim your respect for widowhood because of this, that God has established most intimate relations between those afflicted ones and his Divine Majesty. The virtuous widow is in a most especial manner a ward of Divine Providence. The God who is from all eternity, who claims to Himself the titles of King of kings and Lord of lords, whose power breaks the sceptres of kings, and who holds the sea in his hand, this Omnipotent God has given Himself the title of Judge of the widow, Father of the orphan: He has taken upon Himself the task of avenging her wrongs; and among the woes which He denounces against the Levites and Pharisees there is a dreadful woe to these because they injure the widow. The widow is in an especial manner the hand of God. Now, let me ask you, by what means does God exercise this guardianship, this protectorate? Does He, in person, interfere in the case of every single one of the widows from whom He has removed the husband, the means of support He Himself had given her? I know very well that He could, if He pleased, send ravens to feed them as He did Eliseus, or multiply miraculously their little store, or bid the earth produce fruits and food when watered with a widow's tears. He could do all this; but I know also that He does not do so. It is not his wisdom to alter the whole scheme of creation, and make miracles the rule and not the exception. If, then, it be true that God is in an especial manner the guardian of the widow—and it is undeniable—if it be true that He has been pleased not to exercise his guardianship in person by miraculous intervention, it follows most clearly that He has left it to you, to whom He has entrusted the goods of this world, to take his place towards the desolate widow. There is no other way by which it can be done, and therefore it is the will of God that you should honour Him in his ward by becoming the channel of his love to the desolate and afflicted. It is God's intention to provide for the widow through your alms.

This was well understood in the very earliest ages of the Church. During the lifetime of the Apostles all the faithful contributed their money, and the fund was especially intended for the support of the widows. Hence, St. Paul exhorts such as had widows relations, and were able to support them, to do so at home, in order that the Church might be relieved, and that enough might be left for the other widows. Hence we read that the Apostles themselves looked after the maintenance and support of the widows among their flocks. Not a single widow was left uncared for, not one was friendless, not one houseless. What matter if God had stricken her with sorrow?—she had her fellow-Christians to console her. What matter if God had removed her stay and her support?—she found in the charity of her brother the support she required. What matter if her home was broken up, and her children orphans?—she found a home and a father with and in the Apostles themselves. Suppose, then, I say, suppose that we who are here to-day were carried back at this moment eighteen hundred years, the widow for whom I am pleading would find in the faithful who fill the church those who recognised it to be their duty to contribute to their support. There would be no hesitation : everyone here would contribute ; an apostle or another Timothy would call upon them to honour widows. Now, I ask, why should we not here to-day do the very same thing that we would have done if instead of being Catholics of the nineteenth century we were Catholics of the first century? Why should the widows of to-day be neglected

by us, and the widows of that day be supported and nourished?
Is the God of our fathers not our God also? Is the Church of
the Apostles not the Church to which we belong? Is the
command of God different for them and for us? Has charity
ceased to be an obligation? Most certainly not. Are we not
bound, then, to deal literally with the widows? And will you
not imitate this morning the charity of those who were your
fathers in the faith? Behold, you are gathered round the same
altar as they were. The blood of the same Victim was offered
up for you to-day that was offered up for them. A successor
of the Apostles, one who came down in an unbroken line from
the priest who offered sacrifice for the early Christians, has
offered sacrifice for you. You have the same faith, the same
hope, the same obligations, the same God—why should you
not have the same charity?

And no wonder, beloved brethren, that God should take
such care of the widow ; for among the many forms of misfortune that have saddened and still sadden the world there is not
one, perhaps, so dark or mournful as that of widowhood—at all
events, there is none which so thoroughly and effectually pros-
trates the heart and makes such awful havoc in the life of the
sufferer. There are in the forest many trees of various strength
and firmness. Some there are that cast out their roots on every
side, and shoot up their tall and sturdy stems, and stretch out
wide their branches. Others, again, cannot grow but by the
aid of their stronger neighbours ; to these they cling, to these
they attach themselves, borrowing from them all the strength
they have, all the vigour they feel. Should the woodman's axe
or the storm lay prostrate their support, they fall with it,
crushed and torn ; and even though their own roots are still in
the earth, even though they make a feeble effort to live, they
that were once so fair, and fresh, and blooming lie there the
very type of weakness and prostration. So among men the
widow is the very type of desolation and distress. It is the
will of God and of nature that the wife should cling to her
husband, as the tender plant to the strong tree. God cuts off,
as it were, all other supports from her ; she is to leave father, and
mother, and home, and cling to her husband ; man and woman
are no longer two, but one, and one by so holy and close a bond
that it has been made fast by God Himself, so that no earthly
power can ever sunder it: no man can sunder what God
hath joined. When, therefore, God Himself withdraws the
husband, He withdraws the only support on which the life and
strength of that frail creature rested, and the blow that deprives
her of her spouse deprives her at once of love and help, and
almost of hope. What wonder, then, that when God wished to

describe the utter desolation of Jerusalem, He said that she had become a widow? What wonder that among the punishments wherewith the Royal Prophet threatens the wicked it is said that their wives shall be made widows? What is it of earthly blessing a wife does not lose with her husband, the partner of her love, the father of her children, the sharer of her sorrows, the confidant of her cares, the breadwinner whose arm kept plenty in her humble home, the stay and support of her home, her guide and her adviser? If there be any sorrow which demands and requires charity, it is the sorrow of the widow. And would it not be selfish in us, to whom God has given so much happiness, to pass over in silence this breaking heart? There are some sorrows that are of the heart only, and they are often more poignant than mere physical distress; there are others who feel physical distress, while they are spared that of the mind. But in the poor widow the sorrow of the heart is felt together with the distress. Every arrow is directed against her; she is wounded everywhere; and if it be an angelic work to cheer the afflicted, what work is it to heal this doubly broken heart?

If in sight of such woe unutterable, of such weakness, we should be unmoved—if we should be deaf and niggardly in endeavouring to assuage it—can we claim to have the hearts of men? Not so did holy Job; not so did Eliseus, who fed the widow; not so did the tender heart of our Lord, who made the grave give back its dead, that He might restore her only son to a broken-hearted woman who was a widow! And if this should not move us, ought we not at least to fear for ourselves?

And yet, beloved brethren, if you ought to assist the widow because she is weak, I think you ought to assist her the more because she is strong. Weak in herself, in her very weakness lies her strength. The widow's tears are all-powerful with God. Woe to the man who causes one of them to fall to the earth by his injustice and cruelty! Woe to him who slights them as they fall! The cry of the poor ascends to the Lord, and will not depart until it shall be heard. And blessed is he that shall dry up these tears; blessed is he for whom the widow and the orphan shall raise their hands in prayer!

FEAR OF DIVINE JUSTICE.

"For because sentence is not speedily pronounced against the evil, the children of men commit evils without any fear."—Eccles. viii. 11.

In that wonderful dialogue in the Book of Job, wherein God condescends to justify his own conduct before his creature, the Almighty explains the want of foresight and the recklessness of consequences apparent in some of the brute creation, by saying that He had deprived them of reason, and that neither did He give them understanding. Only to man did He vouchsafe this gift of reason and understanding, and only in the children of men, therefore, may we expect to find the faculty of comparing one thing with another, of tracing the relation of cause and effect, of forecasting the consequences of present actions, and of estimating their present actions according to the consequences that are to follow them. Elevated by the possession of reason above the level of the rest of creation, man gazes down upon the vast network of cause and effect that girdles and keeps together the universe; and it is at once the title and the privilege of his sovereignty that he can follow out its various threads, as they bind together in various relations being with being, and action with action. Ask of the metaphysician, and he will tell you that the highest function of the mind is nothing higher than this faculty of comparison of relations. Inquire from the philosopher, and you will find that he reserves his praise for that system which teaches us to arrive at general laws by a calm and patient study of particular cases. Listen to the views of a great statesman, and you will find them valuable because they give correctly the bearings of one public act upon another. We should expect that to happen which we really find by experience, that for the reasoning man no act stands by itself, but that it leans on some other, or is the result of some other, or has in itself the virtue to produce some other. But to this rule is it not strange that there should be an exception? And is it not stranger still that this exception should occur in the matter which, of all others, by its transcendent importance demanded the strictest and most careful attention : I mean the commission of mortal sin. The children of men, says the text I have quoted for you, commit evils without any fear. And why? Because they ignore the connection between sin and the punishment of sin ; because they separate the crime from its penalty ; because they make sin stand by itself, and then draw a curtain between it and the vengeance that follows after it, deliberately banishing that fear which would stir the veil. They teach themselves to think of sin without thinking of its punishment; they say to themselves, "I have sinned, and what harm has befallen me?" And so they go on losing that holy fear which is the beginning of wisdom, until at length they drink in iniquity like water. And how does this come to pass, my brethren? If we analyse the passion of fear we shall find that two distinct ideas go to form it—the apprehension of evil, and the persuasion that such danger threatens ourselves. To destroy fear of God's punishment for sin we must teach ourselves either to believe that there is no such thing, or at least we must have no apprehension of its being likely to overtake us. Now, the Catholic who sins without any fear does not, my brethren, abandon his faith in the existence of punishment for sin. For a man in such a state of sin has no terrors ; he feels no fear in offending God ; and, beloved brethren, the man who feels no fear in offending God, the man for whom sin is a mere pastime, a thing of nothing, that man does not, at least consciously, believe that there is no punishment for sin. How could he? A God who does not punish evil is a God who shows Himself to be indifferent to evil, and a God who shows Himself indifferent to evil is a God who is regardless of the truth ; for what is sin but a lie which falsely proclaims the creature to be more than the Creator, and a God regardless of the truth is no God at all. No! they admit that sin is to be punished. How, then, do they kill this salutary fear? Because they do not see God baring his arm for immediate vengeance after sin, because they do not see the punishment tread close on the sin, they persuade themselves that they have nothing to apprehend, that they may continue to drink in iniquity like water ; and so without fear the wicked children of men commit evils against the Most High God. If the murderer's arm should fall powerless before his victim's blood was yet dry upon it ; if the blasphemer was stricken dumb before the sound of his evil words had died away ; if a foul leprosy should suddenly fall upon the man who should be guilty of those abominations which the apostle says should be unnamed among us, the sinner could not think of sin as separate from its punishment. But after his sin he finds himself as sound as before ; the sun is made to rise as bright for the sinner as for the just ; the rains of heaven fertilise the earth for him as well as for the saint ; the world's beauty is as fair to his eye as to that of the holiest ; in a word, he says: "I have sinned, and what am I the worse for it?" This is, indeed, a delusion, a most fatal delusion, but one for which there is no excuse.

Holy Job exclaims: "O that a man might so be judged with God, as the son of man is judged with his companion!" (Job, xvi. 22.) If this privilege, which Job sighed for in vain, were granted to such a man as the one we are just considering; if against God's accusation he were allowed to enter a defence of his state of mind, as one man does when engaged in a lawsuit with another, think you, my brethren, that he could find any pretext which could serve to excuse him? To form an accurate judgment on this point, recall to mind the decision given in similar cases in Holy Scripture. "Behold, among his saints none is unchangeable, and the heavens are not pure in his sight. How much more is man abominable, and unprofitable, who drinketh iniquity like water (Job, xv. 15, 16). "Now they have no excuse for their sin," says our Lord, of the world;—and why? "Because I have come and spoken to them." "They are inexcusable," says St. Paul of the pagan philosophers. And why? Because the things that are made testified and showed forth that divinity which they denied. That is to say, according to God's views, the more numerous the witnesses and the clearer their testimony to any truth, the more inexcusable he who refuses to believe it. If, then, the pagan philosophers were without excuse because they closed their ears to the testimony of earth and sky, of night and day, of the starry firmament, as they mutely witness to the existence of God, how much more sins the bad Catholic who hardens his heart against the cloud of witnesses that give evidence of the immediate vengeance taken by God on sinners!—I say a cloud of witnesses, my brethren, for it is a most remarkable fact that God has given examples of speedy vengeance on sin in every class of reasonable beings, in every dispensation with which He has been pleased to visit man, in every class of society, in every age, in every kind of sin, in every country, in every profession in every state of life. Do you want a witness to God's speedy vengeance from the very sunlight of the world's history? Before the blood of Abel was yet dried upon the earth its cry had drawn from the lips of God a deadly curse on the murderer Cain. And Cain himself lifts up his voice: "Behold Thou dost cast me out this day, this very day of my sin, from the face of the earth."

In the patriarchal age the iniquities of a corrupt world rose up before God in the days of Noah, and in the days of Noah the Deluge bears witnesses as numerous as are the corpses of young and old that are dashed among the waves of its shoreless sea; among pagan populations the unbelieving men of Sodom are

struck blind in the very hour of their iniquity, and their city
becomes a prey to the flames; in the Jewish dispensation, Core,
Dathan, and Abiron, the blasphemers and Sabbath breakers, are
stoned without the camp. In the New Testament, Ananias lies
to the Holy Ghost, and immediately falls dead to the ground;
Sapphira lies, and the feet of them who have buried her husband
are at the door to carry her away. Herod is arrayed in king's
apparel, and sitting in the judgment-seat, and the people make
exclamation, saying : " It is the voice of a god not of a man "
(Acts, xii.) And forthwith an angel of the Lord struck him,
because he had not given the honour to God, and being eaten up
with worms he gave up the ghost. One such example in each
of these dispensations was enough to inspire fear into the men
of that time, how is he to be excused who is deaf to their
cumulative testimony ? Is it not madness to imagine that God
will deliberately depart in his case from the law which He followed in the beginning, in the days of the patriarchs, under
the law of Moses, in the early days of the Christian Church ?
We do not dread a repetition of the Deluge, because God has
promised that it should not be, and has attested the memory of
this promise by the bow that spans the heavens. But is there
any promise, any rainbow of hope that he will not punish at once,
immediately, irresistibly, the sins we may be guilty of ? He has
left us no loophole of excuse for so thinking ? Do we flatter
ourselves that our sins are not such as theirs were who were
punished so promptly ? But what kind of sin has he left not
punished with instant chastisement : in Adam a simple disobedience, in Cain a deed of blood, in Sodom a sin of lust, in David
a sin of vanity, in Aman a sin of words, and in his angels a sin
of thought ? Do we flatter ourselves that our position will in
some measure secure us ;—but what station in society has He left
without an example. Are we as high as the angels ?—and yet
He crushed the angels in an instant. Are we as low as the
Sodomites ?—and yet He slew them immediately ? Are we in a
position of worldly greatness ? Herod was so great that he was
called a god, and yet he was struck down. Are we rich ?—
so was Herod ; are we poor ?—so were Ananias and Sapphira ;
are we old ?—so was Heli ; are we young ?—so was Cain.

In view of these terrible judgments of God, how can the
sinner persuade himself that his punishment is only in the long
future ? How can the soul now stained with sin flatter itself that
it will have time to enjoy sin now, and leisure to repent hereafter ? How can a Catholic surrender his heart to temptation,
with the idea that the punishment is so remote? Not so
did David : " *Confige timore tuo carnes meas ;*" and why ?
" *A judiciis enim tuis timui.*" Then, there can be no ex-

8

cuse for such a frame of mind; it is unreasonable, inexcusable. That men should sin at all is inexcusable; but that they should perpetrate evils without any fear, because they refuse to think of the punishment of sin, is most inexcusable. But here it may be said that my argument has been one-sided, and therefore not to be trusted. No doubt, it will be urged, God has in all ages and in all circumstances given many and terrible proofs of his prompt justice; but in relating the history of such examples we should not exclude the many instances of patient endurance, and of long suffering with sinners which He has exhibited. And perhaps the words of the apostle may be quoted against us, "Despisest thou the riches of his goodness, and patience, and long suffering? Knowest thou not that the benignity of God leads thee to penance?" (Rom. ii. 4). And do not the very words of the text suppose that at least now and then the interval between the sin and its punishment is 'not of the shortest, that sentence is not speedily pronounced against evil?

I know, my brethren, that God is long-suffering with sinners, and that He waiteth patiently to have mercy on them. If I were cruel enough to deny it, the history of our own lives would rise in witness against me. Yes, my brethren, it is true and I admit it, we sin, and yet the arrows of the divine punishments of which David speaks do not reach us. But why?—Is it because those arrows have not been aimed at us? Is it because having been aimed they have not flown? Is it because having been aimed and having flown they have not known how to hit the guilty breast? No; for none of these reasons; but because, between avenging heaven and sinful earth, the sinner and his judge, uprose the pure and holy figure of Jesus Christ, baring his breast so as to intercept the shaft in its flight towards us, receiving the bruises that were to punish our iniquities, and mangled with the wounds that were to avenge our sins. We are in peace because He took upon Himself the chastisement which was to bring us peace; in one word, my brethren, we have escaped thus long from the punishment of our sins, only because, as Isaias says, Jesus Christ on the cross hath borne the sins of many, and hath prayed for the transgressors. And is it upon long-suffering such as this, which Mercy has purchased from Justice at so fearful a price as the Blood of the Son of God, that you would reckon in order to be able to sin without any fear? Oh, the unspeakable meanness, the incredible selfishness of the man who says to himself, "I will sin without fear, because another has undertaken to bear the first brunt of the punishment; I will sin without fear, because Christ has prayed for pardon for me, because He has died to obtain for me time for repentance." " Father, forgive them, for they know not what they do."

Such a one, my brethren, would efface these tender and loving words from the millions of hearts in which they are inspired, and would substitute in their stead words so blasphemous, so hideous, that I can hardly bear to repeat them. " Father," he would force the dying lips of Jesus to utter, " Father, these men know that I am dying for them ; they know that this crown of thorns, these cruel nails, these cruel wounds, are the marks of punishment due to their sins; they know that thy justice will be appeased by my sufferings ; they know that thy right hand is disarmed by my death, and for this reason do they sin without any fear; do Thou, therefore, Father, forgive them, because, knowing all this, they nevertheless sin against Thee. Father, forgive them, because they know not what they do ! "

The delay of punishment, therefore, because it is a proof of love, and because through it God endeavours to win the sinner to justice, should not destroy fear in his heart. Nor, my brethren, have you any right to think that such delay is a delay of love ; it is in itself the most terrible sign of God's wrath. There is a long-suffering on the part of God, which, the apostle tells us, is intended for penance ; but there is a long-suffering which, the same apostle declares, is intended to show wrath. God, willing to show his wrath, and make known his power, did what ? —did He judge the nations, did He fill up ruin, did He crush the heads of his foes ? No, but He did what was far more terrible, " He endured with much patience vessels of wrath fitted for destruction." "God has been patient with you in your sins,' I would say to the man whom this very patience makes courageous, " but has He shown you a patience of love, or a patience of vengeance ? Am I to congratulate you as being the object of the unspeakable love of God, or am I to weep over you as the victim of his most deadly vengeance ? " This is a question of the greatest importance to you, and it is a question you can answer in some measure for yourselves. As light differs from darkness, as day from night, so does the patience born of mercy differ in its effects from the patience born of the wrath of God. The Magdalen was waited for and she came not as yet ; He still waited for her and she laid aside her sin, and grace superabounded where sin had abounded before. The philosophers of ancient Greece and Rome were waited for, and they came not ; God ordered them, and they came not ; and then He left them to the desire of their own hearts, to a life filled with all iniquity, and malice, and fornication, and avarice, and wickedness, while they gilded over all these with the name of wisdom, of good common sense ; for professing to be wise, they became fools.

In which of these two ways does God's patience affect your life? Is yours the life of a Christian who, crying out to God from the depths, keeps up a daily, steady warfare against the sins and temptations of the world, the flesh, and the devil; or do you live only to gratify all the desires of your own hearts, forgetful of the evil past? Do you, like Magdalen, draw near to Jesus Christ, to look for the forgiveness you feel you do not deserve, or do you keep away weeks and months, and perhaps years from the sacraments of the Catholic Church, where you may find Him and His grace? Do you give the reasonable service of love and obedience to the faith and the practices of the Church, or do you form the judgment which the world passes on the supernatural, becoming fools when you profess to be most wise. These are questions, this an investigation I have neither the power nor the will to pursue further : but if you find that your life is similar to that of the philosopher, must you not fear that the patience God is certain to show you is the patience of vengeance? Must you not doubt that while you become fearless at what you think delays punishment, that supposed delay was itself punishment of the most terrible order ?—and is it possible that anyone can close his heart against the fear of God for such a delay of punishment ?.

This, then, my brethren, is the case I make : the Holy Scripture complains that men sin without any fear, and that they are without fear because they do not see sentence immediately pronounced upon evil. Now, no man, in view of the numberless instances of prompt vengeance, can with any security believe for a moment that God will not punish him at once ; and if he have any apparent reason to think that God is waiting for him in mercy, he is surely not warranted by such reason to exclude fear from his heart, especially as he cannot be certain that the very delay of punishment is not in itself a most terrible punishment. What, then, are we to do? We are to identify in our minds the thought of sin and of its punishment, we are not to think of sin without thinking of its penalty, we are to work out our salvation with fear and trembling. Should our memory recall the thoughts of the past, we are to think of it as having entailed on us a punishment which penance only can remove ; should sin present itself in the present or future, let us remember that, however seductive its beauty, it has infallibly, inseparably connected with it the avenging punishment of God.

Yet our fear must not be a grossly servile fear : it must not be that cowardly fear which checks only the hand from the evil deed which the heart continues to desire; but that rational fear, which while it checks the hand from doing, teaches the heart not to lose itself in guilty desires. *"Bonus est,"* says

St. Augustine, "*iste timor utilis est.*" Nor, my brethren, are you to rest at this : you are to love God as well as to fear Him. God calls for your love, for a deep, tender, personal, supreme love. Perhaps as yet this love for God is but a tender, fragile seedling springing up in your hearts ; if so, then, let fear be its prop and its support, and when your love has grown to ripeness, fear shall fall away and leave your love alone. You shall be alone with God ; for God is love, and loving Him and loved by Him, you will taste for ever the unspeakable sweetness of the saying of St. John, "perfect charity casteth out fear."

ON ROSARY SUNDAY.

THE festival of the Rosary of the Blessed Virgin, which is this day celebrated, must be my excuse for not observing the order I had established. And yet, what do I say ? Is anything that relates to Mary out of place or extraneous to the mysteries of the Christian faith ? No ; I am not afraid that in speaking of the Rosary I shall be faithless to the duty assigned me of confirming your faith in these doctrines ; on the contrary, I am convinced that I shall be promoting in an admirable manner that happy result. I cannot but remember that when, first of all God intimated to the sin-stricken pair in Eden that the ruin which had been so foully accomplished in them was to be repaired by a Redeemer to come, He coupled with the mention of that Redeemer the mention of his Mother : "I will place enmity between thee and the woman, between thy seed and hers." And at a later period, when the Spirit of God spoke through the fire-purified lips of Isaias, the Virgin who was to bear the Emmanuel was the object of his prophecy almost quite as much as the birth of the Redeemer. Taught by God, therefore, I need not fear to draw off your attention from Christian doctrine and from revealed truth by speaking to you of Mary, of whom the Church declares that she alone has put an end to all heresies in the entire world.

Let us, then, console our hearts by speaking of our Mother and our Queen, and, entering into the spirit of the Church, let us speak of her Rosary. I do not intend to show you how right it is, how pleasing to God to venerate and pray to Mary. Of this you are as well persuaded as I am. It is your joy to do so, and your best consolation. But, taking for granted that it is right and agreeable to God, and useful to us, to venerate and pray to Mary, I propose to show you that of all the devotions in her honour the Rosary is the best and most appropriate. I propose to excite in your hearts an esteem and a reverence for this holy prayer as being the one most calculated to promote her glory and your own good. Yes, we must love the Rosary, because it is the best of devotions; but we must esteem it because it is the best of devotions in the effects it produces.

And to begin with considering the kind of devotion the Rosary is, I remind you, in the first place, that its object is to honour the Incarnation of the Eternal Word by repeating the salutation addressed to Our Blessed Lady by the Angel Gabriel at the time of the Annunciation. Now, the Incarnation is the one event on which the world turns. The ages before it exhibit to us a long procession of patriarchs and prophets looking forward to it sadly and earnestly, a religion of symbol and figure which was to find reality in its accomplishment, and all true sincere men look back upon it as the source of life, and hope, and happiness. Before it took place the holy ones of God longed to see its day, and the vision of it vouchsafed to them, although distant and almost evanescent, filled them with joy. Since it has happened, how can we sufficiently testify our joy and gratitude? What shall we render unto the Lord for all He has rendered unto us? Now, the Rosary has for its especial object to keep fresh before our minds the Incarnation. In it we repeat over and over again the great words of the angel to Mary, which contain all that is great and wonderful in the mystery. And here we see how true that is which I said before, that Jesus and Mary cannot be separated. We set out with the intention of praising Jesus for the infinite condescension of his Incarnation, and we find ourselves naturally repeating the praises of Mary: we begin to bless Jesus, and our heart and our lips instinctively salute Mary as the Blessed among women. And this instinct is a true one. For Our Lady in the economy of the mystery of the Incarnation was such as to fill us with wonder and admiration. That the Son of God should resolve to become man, that He should have foretold this excess of love in a thousand prophecies, that He should have established a religion of symbols and figures to foreshadow the kingdom He was to found, is strange, indeed, and a wonderful condescension; but that, after his resolve, and the prophecies, and the figures, He should ask and wait for the consent of a poor maiden before effecting it, this, indeed, is beyond all comprehension. For, when the Scripture tells that the Angel Gabriel was sent from God to Mary, what message do we find him bring? Is it a sovereign, inviolable command to receive and guard in her womb the Divine Pledge God had decreed to confide to her? No, my brethren. The bright angel bows down before the inexperienced Virgin, and proclaims her full of grace, and united in a singular manner to the Lord. He proposes to her the great mystery of the Incarnation, and reverently awaits from her the decisive answer. Mary, aware of the awful mystery to which her co-operation is requested, examines, reflects, objects. Oh, moment of moments on which the fate of the world hangs! It is true a God is waiting for the free, full consent of his creature, to become her Son; a world's destiny depends on the words of a poor maid. God, who could have done it otherwise, wished that it should be so; and on the full, free consent of Mary, the redemption of the world is dependent. And that full, free consent is not long delayed: with full knowledge of what she was doing, Our Lady gives her consent. "Be it done unto me according to thy word." O blessed lips! O blessed words! O holy Mary, cause of our joy! how can we thy children better recall to our minds the mystery of the Incarnation than by recalling the share that thou hadst in its accomplishment? Can we ever grow tired of calling thee blessed, and blessed the fruit of thy chaste womb? Thus, the Rosary is the legitimate, full expression of our love and devotion to the Incarnation. But the Incarnation is the highest, the most glorious of the truths of the Christian religion; therefore, the Rosary, which is the devotion of the Incarnation, is the highest, the best, the dearest devotion we can practise.

Again, let us see what kind of devotion is the Rosary, considering the prayers of which it is composed. It is called the Rosary or the Chaplet, because it is, as it were, a crown of roses woven of the choicest flowers of prayer to grace Our Lady's pure brow. Now, a wreath is not composed altogether of the same kind of flowers; there is in it a variety of hues, and forms, and perfumes. And so, in the Rosary we have the Hail Mary, and the Lord's Prayer, and the Glory be to the Father, and the Creed, all garlanded together in fair order. We have seen already how great should be our veneration and love for the Apostles' Creed; and as to the Lord's Prayer, what need have we of seeking points in its praise beyond its very name? Is it not the prayer which Jesus Himself has taught us? Is it not the prayer which He has recommended to us? "When you pray, saying our Father," &c.; and then the Glory be to the Father, is it not an echo, as it were, of the voices that ring perpetually through the bright courts of heaven, proceeding from the choirs of angels singing with one accord glory and honour to the Eternal Trinity? Is it not the very expression of our dearest Lord's rule of action: "I seek the glory of God that sent me?"

Is it not the formula which expresses the ends for which we have
been created, i. e., the glory of God? Does it not cast over
every act of our lives the brightness and holy light of God's
presence? Is it not a solemn protestation of our belief in the
Trinity, of that Catholic belief for which the saints and martyrs of old shed their blood, and which all who are outside the
Catholic Church are now fast losing? What, then, are we to
think of the excellence of a devotion which is composed of the
words of our Lord Himself, of the Angel Gabriel, and of the
whole Church of God? Has it not about it the very breath and
odour of heaven? Ought it not to be dear to every Catholic
heart? And if we are convinced of its excellence by considering its kind and its nature, such conviction will be strengthened
by reflecting on the effects it has produced and will produce.

My dear brethren, the Rosary has been an arm of power from
its very first institution. In the days of St. Dominic, in the
13th century, there arose a sect of wild and cruel heretics, who
laid waste the plains of the South of France, and kindled war
wherever they went. The Catholics were on the point of being
overwhelmed by this savage foe, when Our Blessed Lady herself
revealed to St. Dominic that in the Rosary he would find a sure
help and defence against the enemies of the Church; and so it
was. By help of the Rosary the Albigenses were overcome,
and the faith of Christ was saved from destruction in France.
Ever since that time it has been the favourite devotion of all
Catholics, rich and poor, learned and ignorant, saints and poor
struggling souls, all, all have found the Rosary a tower of
strength, a source of grace. But if it was ever productive of
good, it is especially calculated to produce it in our age and in
the country in which we live. It is a sad thought and an awful
one, that outside the Catholic Church the belief that Christ
is God is fast disappearing. Men who are not Catholics are saying now more loudly than ever, either that the Second Person of
the Blessed Trinity is not really and truly God, or that the Son
of Mary is not also really and truly the Son of God. In either
case the whole supernatural order is destroyed. The spirit of
the age is against the supernatural; men proudly refuse to
believe that God has condescended to become man; they are
satisfied with man as they find him, and refuse to attend to the
supernatural virtues God wishes him to possess. Riches and
honours, delights of the sense, and success—these are the aims
of man, these are the end of life. And these doctrines come
upon the Catholic in a thousand ways—some open and undisguised, others secret and insidious. From books and newspapers, in conversation and in lectures, in coarse jokes and in
refined sensuality, in the worship of the natural, in extravagant

and sentimental love of nature, from every quarter and in every way this poison is breathed on him. And how shall he be able to defend himself against all these?—where shall he be able to obtain strength to resist it all? Is he not likely to be hurried away, to begin to think with less respect of Christianity, which requires him to submit his intellect to mysteries, and to train his will to detachment from the world and its goods? Is there not danger lest the incessantly repeated maxims of the world may out-influence the teachings of his faith, and that he, too, may begin to be pagan? No, my brethren, there is no danger as long as he is devout to the Rosary. As long as he recalls each day to his mind and meditates upon some of the scenes of the life of our Lord and his Blessed Mother he need not fear the contagion of the age. As long as he repeats the salutation once delivered by the angel to Mary, and recalls tenderly and lovingly the glory of the Incarnation, he is safe. From the manger and the presentation altar in the temple, and the Olive Garden, and the hall of Pilate, and from Calvary, there will come forth influences so sweet, so holy, so divine, so supernatural as to have power against all the world has effected, or can effect. And as he thinks on Mary, and her part in the scenes of Re-demption, and as her name and praises linger on his lips, the fresh fragrance of her virtues will strengthen him and bear him up. No, the Catholic who is devout to the Rosary is armed against the world. Let the world be as strong as it likes—let fashion, and wealth, and intellect be abused, and success be all on its side—let the world be a very giant in its strength, each bead of his Rosary will be as the little polished stone of the brook, with which, like another David, he will lay it low and triumph over it.

Again, my brethren, see the effects it produces in the spiri-tual life. You all know that prayer is essential to us. "Watch and pray," said our Lord; we must pray always and never fail; "ask and ye shall receive." You know that mental prayer has its own excellences, and vocal prayer its own. But in the Rosary the advantages of both are united. In reflecting on the mystery proposed in each decade we engage in the highest kind of mental prayer. In repeating the Our Father, Hail Mary, and Glory be to the Father, we are praying vocally. Thus it was that Mary prayed; for we read of her that she laid up all she heard about Jesus and his birth, pondering upon them in her heart. Thus did Jesus pray in the sad night of his agony in the garden, saying the self-same thing. If mental prayer, then, be productive of good to the soul, if vocal prayer be a source of benediction and grace, what should be our esteem of the Rosary, which contains the perfection of both?

FIRST SUNDAY OF LENT.

"Remember, man, that thou art dust, and unto dust thou shalt return."

AFTER many days' wandering in the desert of Bersabee, the forlorn Agar perceived at length that the hand of death was upon her son Ismael. With keenest grief she laid him down in the shade of "one of the trees that were there, and she went her way, and sat over-against him a great way off, as far as a bow can carry, for she said: I will not see the boy die: and sitting over-against, she lifted up her voice and wept" (Gen. xxi. 15, 16). This mother, my brethren, could not endure to witness the agony which death was about to bring upon her child; she fled from the sight of the sorrow and desolation which death in its approach casts like a shadow upon the soul. Far different is the conduct of our mother, the Church, towards us at the commencement of this holy season of Lent. Not only does she bear to look upon the sorrow that settles on our heart at the thought of death, but she deliberately sets herself to produce that sorrow. Unlike Agar, she bursts into no passionate wailing over our coming doom, but she makes her voice stern enough to tell us herself of the sentence passed against us; far from shunning what would remind her of our death, she realises it by a most striking symbol, when with her own hand she strews with ashes each proudest, and noblest, and fairest brow of the children of men; ashes to ashes, dust to dust; mingling the ashes that are dead with the ashes yet alive, that the lifeless clay may remind its kindred clay, so soon to be lifeless, that man is dust, and unto dust fated to return. How is this, my brethren? Why is it that the mother who bears man into this world weeps to see death's sadness on him, while the mother who brings man forth for heaven seems to be glad that he should thus sorrow? Why is it that the one cannot bear to look upon his anguish, while the other herself bids his tears to flow, and would fain by her stern message have him taste all the bitterness of the memory of death? And yet, my brethren, in that stern message there is an undertone of love, with which the Church seems to say to us what the apostle said to the Corinthians: "Although I made you sorrowful by my words, I do not repent: and if I did repent, seeing that the same (though but for a time) did make you sorrowful, now I am glad: not because you are made sorrowful, but because you are made sorrowful unto penance . . . for the sorrow that is according to God worketh penance unto salvation" (2 Cor. vii. 8-10). In awakening in us at this time the thoughts of our coming death, the Church intends not to fill us with melancholy, but to lead us to penance. The memory of death scatters broadcast the seeds of sorrow, but upon the growing sorrow the Church would engraft what will bring forth fruits worthy of penance. Death is our punishment, she would make it our remedy; death is the penalty of sin, she would teach us, by the message of the text to-day, how to change it into an incentive to virtue.

And, first of all, observe, my brethren, that she does not present herself as if announcing some new truth hitherto unknown to you; she does but exhort you to remember, to recall to your mind what you have had occasion to learn before now. She would have you bring before your mind that scene on the threshold of Eden, when first this dread sentence was pronounced, when an angry God disclosed to guilty man : " In the sweat of thy face shalt thou eat bread till thou return to the earth, out of which thou wast taken : for dust thou art, and unto dust thou shalt return " (Gen. iii. 19). Such recollections cannot fail to lead us to penance. Remember that this so much dreaded death is but the punishment of sin, and that sin is the cause of death. Had there been no sin, then there had been no death, for God would have hedged in man from its inroads. By one man sin came into the world, and by sin death. How, then, can man go on cherishing and loving that very sin which has brought upon us an evil we so much fear ? Let sin be ever so attractive, let it be decked with all that is bright, and fascinating, and winning, we can never approach it without approaching at the same time that death which ever follows it as closely as shadow follows upon sunshine. The honey on which Jonathan feasted was luscious and delightful; but, think you, would he have enjoyed its sweetness had he known, as later he knew, that under its sweetness lurked the bitterness of death ? " Fasting, I have tasted a little honey, and so I must die." If death be an evil, then sin must be an evil; if death be no evil, why does the Church's message of to-day cast gloom upon our souls ?

Remember, besides, who it is that inflicts death as the punishment of sin. It is God : that is to say, a Being so just that He cannot exceed in the severity of his punishments, a Being so holy that He cannot harbour thoughts of undue resentment, a Being so merciful that all his works are tempered with tenderest compassion. And yet this just, and holy, and merciful God has judged that death, the greatest of earthly evils ; death, that has brought upon man woes innumerable, is but part of the fitting punishment deserved by sin. Sin, therefore, must be an evil so great that the death we dread is scarcely its equivalent; and remembering this, how are we not moved to detest the blindness which has taught us to prize what we should most abhor? Remember, again, how strangely sin has affected the almighty power of God. What could be more loving and tender than what God's power did, before his anger was stirred by sin, for his creature man? How fair the earth God had created for his use! how pleasant the paradise planted for his enjoyment! how light the command laid upon him to be the source of merit! how joyous the life He gave him! how beautiful the soul, rich in a thousand gifts of nature and of grace! All God's power seems to have been busied about him, to bless him and make him happy; and yet, such was the poison of one sin, that this power, hitherto omnipotent to bless, became omnipotent to punish. Paradise was lost, God's graces and gifts were forfeited, the earth became a place of misery, man's life a weary struggle with sorrow, and disease, and toil, to end at last in the grand defeat of death. Is it not madness, then, on the part of sinners, to go on deliberately to outrage that God whose power to punish sin is so mighty? God gave Adam a command; Adam broke it and sinned; and swift upon his sin came punishment with all the might of an angry God. God gave us commands; we break them and sin: upon what grounds dare we hope to escape?

And if the circumstances under which this message had been first delivered dispose us to penance, much more so does the substance of the message itself, by what it tells both of our present state and of what one day is to happen to us. "Remember, man, that thou art dust." This is said to each one of us in particular. When we think of death, we generally think of it as it affects others, or we reason about it as about a question of philosophy in the abstract; but with the thoughts of our own death we do what we do with the dead themselves, we hurry to hide them and bury them deep out of sight. Death in connection with ourselves we see only in the long future, and by aid of this convenient abstraction we are enabled to give ourselves up to seek for our happiness among the sensible goods of this earth. But the recollection that we are dust must perforce detach us from that inordinate love of pleasures, and riches, and honours which makes up all the sin of our lives. It is because we implicitly promise ourselves many years of life, that with the infidels in the Scripture, we seek so keenly for pleasure, saying with them: "Come, therefore, and let us enjoy the good things that are present, and let us speedily use the creatures as in youth. Let us fill ourselves with costly wine, and ointments, and let not the flower of the time pass by us: let us crown ourselves with roses before they be withered: let no meadow escape our riot: let none of us go without his part in luxury." (Wisd. ii.) But even while these words are on our lips we are warned that we are but dust, and that we are to die we know not how soon. If we resolve upon sinful enjoyment of the good things that are present, death may smite us down in their midst; the time we destine for delight may be the hour of our agony; we may die before the roses are withered which we gather for our revels; the meadow we select for our joyous riot may be our grave. This unbridled lust of pleasure, this life of mere enjoyment on the part of men, who are but dust, is called by the Holy Ghost blindness and malice, even in those infidels who knew not the secrets of God, nor hoped for the wages of justice. And yet to these men death meant simply annihilation. "Our body shall be ashes," said they, "and our spirit shall be poured abroad as the soft air . . . like a mist which is driven away by the beams of the sun." And if even in those darkened souls the lust of pleasure was blindness and malice, what is it in us who know the secrets of God, who believe that the wages of our deeds await us beyond the grave, who are certain that when our bodies die our souls shall live for evermore? We know death is to the sinner the beginning of endless misery; we know that between sinful pleasures and the awful anger of the living God there is but the barrier of the moment of death; and since we are but dust, that death may come upon us at any moment. Is it not, then, almost incredible audacity to persevere in sin, since the very God we outrage is He who holds in his hands our life and our death? Daniel had no language to depict the folly of the hapless king more forcible than this: "The God who hath thy breath in his hand, and all thy ways, thou hast not glorified." With the lust of pleasure mingles the fever of struggle for success, of money-making, of business, of achieving position—things good enough in their way, but which, through our own fault, overmaster us by the hold they have upon us.

And, again, we complacently recite to our own hearts the list of the honours we have achieved and the riches we have accumulated, and we say, like the rich man in the Gospel: "My soul, thou hast many good things laid up for many years' enjoyment; take thy rest, eat, drink, and make good cheer." The worldly goods to which we cling are, no doubt, enough for the enjoyment of many years, but who will promise us the many years wherein to enjoy them? The announcement made to that rich man: "Thou fool, this night do they require thy soul of thee, and whose shall those things be which thou hast provided?" is re-echoed in the message delivered to us to-day—that we are dust. Give a man the best position that even his greedy heart can desire; let him enjoy all that makes the prizes of life, the struggle for which absorbs us so often to the forgetfulness of our souls' concerns; give him wealth, and reputation, and honoured name; and when he shall have become what Job was in the bloom of his prosperity, great among all the people of his country, what is he, after all, but a passing stranger in the midst of all his greatness? Should he call himself owner of those goods, ask him to prove his title by retaining them as his own for ever; and if, being dust, he cannot retain them, if he is to go out from amongst them stripped of all his riches, then he is but a sojourner, and not a master. And if so, shall we neglect for those things, which in spite of ourselves we must leave, the care of our souls, and thereby forfeit the riches that remain for ever?

Finally, my brethren, we are warned to-day of something which is one day to happen to us, and in this warning we are once more exhorted to penance: "Into dust thou shalt return." These words tell us of a sore affliction coming upon us which can find no consolation but in God. God has been so merciful towards us as to hide from us the day in which our dissolution shall take place; but we are here reminded that it is inevitable, and that one dreadful moment shall come for each one of us, in which others will tell us, or we shall tell ourselves, "For me life is over; I must die." My brethren, who but God alone can soften the bitter agony of that awful moment? All the goods of earth, all the science, all the love of our nearest and dearest, all the strength of our own manhood—of what avail will they be to lighten that supreme sorrow? Ezechias was a sovereign whose life had been spent amid all that makes life sweet; and yet, upon hearing the words, "thou shalt die and shalt not live," he wept with much weeping. Saul had a daring spirit, and yet when he heard from Samuel that on the morrow he should die, he fell forthwith on the ground, for he was frightened with the words. Even to those who have lost all, that moment is full of anguish. Agag, deprived of crown, country, friends, liberty, yet cried out at the approach of death, Oh! bitter death, "doth bitter death separate in this manner?" Darker than the gloom that encompassed him, wilder than the passionate hate of his foes, was the fear that rushed in upon him at the sight of his coming death. But if we would learn how weak and panic-stricken one feels in the awful presence of death, look in the Garden of Olives, at the prostrate figure of Him in whom our human nature existed in its highest and most perfect form. And if He found no consolation in his sorrow save in this, that He was doing the will of his Father, if the comfort that came to Him came only from the angels of God, where shall we turn for our comfort and consolation except to that same God? But if, through neglect of penance, we have made that God our enemy, how will it add to our desolation to think that we are about to fall into the hands of the living, outraged God ? But if before that moment we shall have done penance, if we shall have bewailed our sins and made God's will the rule of our life, oh ! how sweet it will be to return to dust in those same hands that once from the dust had moulded us, those very hands which for us, penitent sinners, were crucified for love ! What though at that moment our poor nature cannot unlearn its life-long fear of death ; what though death appears to claim victory over us, his love will mingle with our fear, as in the dawn light mingles with the darkness ; and we shall know that He has wrested from the grave its victory, from death its sting. No ; the torment of death shall not touch the souls of the just, since through death Christ hath destroyed him who had the empire of death, and delivered them who through the fear of death were all their lifetime subject to servitude (Heb. ii. 14, 15). But all this happiness, all this consolation, belongs only to those who shall have done penance.

Remember, then, my brethren, that you are dust, and that into dust you shall return, and let the remembrance serve to excite within you the spirit of penance ; let it teach you to abhor the sin which has been the cause of your death, the sin of whose malignity its woes are but the faint expression, the sin whose poison changed life into death ; let the thought that you are dust detach you from all inordinate love of the pleasures, and riches, and honours of this world, so that in seeking them and using them you may not neglect the eternal welfare of your souls. Let the thought of your coming dissolution move you to lay up treasures of consolation for the suffering of the day of affliction. But lest in these thoughts you may be overwhelmed with too great sadness, bear in mind that if the thought that you are dust stirs up terror in your heart, that self-same thought that you are dust awakens in God's heart an inexpressible tenderness and compassion towards you. "He knoweth our frame," saith the Psalmist ; "he remembereth that we are dust" (Ps. cii. 13, 14). And therefore "as a father hath compassion on his children, so hath the Lord compassion on them that fear Him." Your very terror of death may thus be made an argument of confidence. The more terrible it is, the more tender and compassionate towards you becomes the heart of your Father who is in heaven. Even in the very moment of our death, when at last that punishment of sin shall have overtaken us trembling, we have the right to call upon God no longer by the name of Judge, but by the meet name of Father, and into that Father's hands we may with confidence commend our spirit. Thus did the Church, by her sanctifying touch, convert our natural sorrow for death into a sorrow according to the Lord which worketh penance unto salvation. And thus by the almost omnipotent efficacy of penance the Justice and the Mercy of God are made to meet over the head of the dying penitent Christian; and if Justice exacts death as the punishment of sin, Mercy makes out of the punishment itself a stronger claim to pardon. And thus by virtue of penance in death are blended together God's forgiveness and man's sorrow, like light and darkness in the twilight when the dawn is breaking in the East; and thus, through penance, is the sadness of death evermore swallowed up in the joy of victory.

STATIONS OF THE CROSS.

IF external honour rendered to the Passion of Christ is all that Christ asks from us Christians, then, my brethren, you have every reason to hope that your Saviour looks down upon you to-day with eyes of satisfaction and love. As a Christian is known by the sign of the cross, so the very situation of your town is made manifest to the traveller, when still [far from it, by this beautiful church which, crowning this height, is raised, as it were, between your homes and the heavens, a link between both, through which your prayers, ascend, to descend in a thousand graces from God upon you. And what feeling has raised this church but a desire to do honour to that altar on which day after day the death of the Lord is shown forth? God has been lavish to your native spot, and has poured over its hills and valleys a wealth of beauty, of which only rare drops are bestowed elsewhere; and you have in return remembered Him. If his hand has crowded beauties about you, for your benefit, your hands have not been slack in crowding beauties about his cross for the honour of that same. And to-day, my brethren, you are here to add another work of heaven to his Passion by erecting here the Stations of the Cross, whereby you may be enabled ever to keep before your eyes the thought of all that your Redeemer has suffered for you. To honour the Passion you have searched the bosom [of the earth for the hard rock which you moulded into springing columns, and clustering arches; to honour the Passion you have sought for trees in the forest which you might shape into goodly forms of use and beauty for this edifice; to honour the Passion you have brought from nature the wax of the teeming bee, from industry the labours of the loom to adorn the altar, the fairest flowers of the garden to perfume the sanctuary; you have made even the sunlight of heaven tributary to your reverence, since you will not allow its rays to fall upon the tabernacle, but across rich colours, from which you teach it to burn new glory and new beauty; and to-day you have assembled in crowds to put up another and most explicit testimony of the honour in which you hold your Redeemer's sufferings. If, then, external honour is all that is required by God, never did people better fulfil their duty than you; but you know well, my brethren, that the God who complained of the Jews that they honoured Him with their lips, whilst their hearts were far from Him, does not stand in need of our goods, but of our hearts; that all we do for Him is unprofitable unless it be the type of the homage of our heart. The external honour we pay Him should be like an impression on wax, of which the seal is the love of our hearts. And, to speak more especially of what we are doing to-day, do you think that God would value your offerings if they were nothing more than simple ornaments such as men set up in their homes? Do you think that He would esteem them unless as the expression of the feelings excited in you by Him for his sorrows? He certainly would not: He wants not our images, nor our paintings, who made all things. Those paintings, therefore, are for each one of you an act by which you express the feelings that our Saviour's sufferings have excited in you. Now I would have you to remember, my brethren, that the events of the Passion, when they really occurred, were seen by very different people, and excited very different feelings in them according to their different dispositions. The Jews saw the Passion, and Mary saw the Passion; the same persons were under the eyes of both, the same words fell upon their ears. But, oh, how far different were the judgments and the feelings that were borne by each! The one consented to the suffering, the other's heart was rent by it. Now, my brethren, in the same way the events of the cross are represented on these pictures, and, as we said, God accepts from each of you these pictures as an expression of the feelings his sufferings have awakened in your hearts: the figures are the same, but the feelings may be different; if so, my brethren, in the eyes of God to-day these stations have as many different meanings as your hearts have thoughts about Christ. A picture is but a painted word, and a word is but the expression of a thought; these pictures, then, represent Christ as you conceive of Him in your hearts. Such, then, as Christ is in your thoughts, such shall He be before God in the pictures you present to Him. It is necessary, therefore,

9

my brethren, that you should carefully inspect and examine
what kind of feelings are those which fill your hearts to-day
about the sufferings of Jesus Christ.

My brethren, I would do an unjustice to you if even for a
moment I could suspect that among you there is even one who
in the devotion of this day does not wish to pay a tribute of respect and tender affection to our Saviour. I will be your spokesman. "Yes, O my Saviour, my outraged, insulted Lord, elsewhere, indeed, this morning ungrateful men may insult Thee
and spurn Thee, elsewhere men may heap contumely on thy
holy person ; but here, here at least, there is a faithful people,
each one of whom is anxious, in the devotion of this day, to
salute Thee with honour, and reverence, and respect. Elsewhere men may turn their backs upon Thee, but there is not
one here who does not long to approach near to Thee, to press
his sinful lips to the hem of thy garment, for we hardly dare to
touch thy divine face ; elsewhere let men revile Thee in words ;
of all those present there is not one who will not bid Thee hail a
thousand times." But even while I speak, my brethren, a cold
chill falls across my soul, and a terrible thought checks my utterances. Did not Judas say as much to Jesus as I have now said
for you ? Did he not approach our Lord with downcast, reverent
eyes as you have done ? Did he not come close to Him, did he
not open his accursed arms to embrace Him, did he not press the
Lamb to his perjured heart, did he not fix upon the countenance of
the Holy of Holies a kiss of tender salutation as warm as yours ?
Could it be possible, then, my brethren, that there is anyone
among you whose devotion to-day is only an act of treachery
and hypocrisy as was that of Judas ? Can it be possible that
there is any one to whom at this moment our Lord is saying, as
He sees him before Him taking part in worship, "Judas, wouldst
thou then betray the Son of Man with a kiss ? Dost thou come
here to betray me by joining in devotion to my honour ?" Oh, my
brethren, I am compelled to believe that it is possible! Judas
was an apostle, you are not so high ; Judas was the chosen
friend of Christ, you have not had that grace ; what Judas
did, you may do. Perhaps the mark of Judas is on some of your
souls to-day ;—and what is in this mark ? Avarice, my brethren,
and greed of unjust gain. If there be anyone here to-day
who for the sake of gaining a few shillings, or less, would not
hesitate to commit sins, and sell his God ; if there be anyone who
has laid up to himself the property of another ;—that man has
the mark of Judas upon him ; and to-day, my brethren, whilst
he is here pretending to pay respect to his God, he is betraying
his Saviour with a kiss.

Did Judas honour Christ, although he kissed him so reve-

rently? No, no, but he insulted Him by his pretended devotion far more than if he had struck Him a blow. Think of
these two things—Judas devout to Christ, and Judas selling Him
for thirty pieces—and answer me, could Christ accept his
homage? Then say of yourself: I am here to-day to venerate the Passion of Christ, when I know that I have sold
Him for a little unjust gain : and answer, can Christ accept
your devotion to-day? Oh, no, my brethren, if you would
please Christ to-day you must have all the respect of Judas
without any of his hypocrisy ; you must not only show but feel
love for Christ under all circumstances.

I ask you, then, to-day, do your hearts glow with love
for your suffering Lord? I do not mean apparent love,
superficial love, but that love of which Augustine says, *vera
devotio imitare quod colimus*—a love not of words but of deeds,
a love of the crucifix which crucifies the world to you, and you
to the world : a love which makes you mortify your passions
because Christ is suffering for you, which makes you given to
penance because Christ is hanging on the cross, which teaches
you to keep in check every desire. My question, then,
means, do you love suffering, denial of self-gratification, penance,
abstaining from the pleasures of the world, because Christ is
overwhelmed with such? I will not conceal from myself, my
brethren, that it is hard for our hearts to love Christ's suffering
in this way. Our hearts are so fond of pleasure, of indulging in
what is gay, and bright, and happy, that they find great difficulty
in loving a Saviour whose soul is one sea of sorrow and tenderness, whose body is one mass of bruises, whose very sight
puts to flight the follies and the pleasures we love in the
world. But if you have not this in some measure, how can you
say that you sympathise with Jesus?—for sympathy means fellowship in suffering, and if you love not such suffering as Christ
bears, how can you say you share it with Him? It would not
be so hard, you think, to love Him as He was when a tender
infant, or when He healed the sick, and gave sight to the blind,
and made the lame to walk, and raised the dead to life; but it is
hard to love Him bruised, melancholy, sombre, and grieving. My
brethren, it is for that very reason we ought to love Him ; it is
because He is filled with suffering that you ought to love Him.

You might have some excuse for not loving Him,
suffering as He is, if, when He began to love you, He found
you exposed to no suffering or saddened by no calamity.
If He came to you and found you happy, cheerful, a source of
joy, not condemned to any punishment, and if He loved you as
such ;—then, perhaps, you might refuse Him your love because
He was not so happy as you, but rather covered with woe. Now,

in what condition did our Saviour find you? Can there be any state imagined more full of suffering than ours? In our soul —in our body—in our sickness – death—hell? Call to mind all the punishments due to sin, multiply them as often as sin has been committed in the world, then say these sufferings were to be undergone by me when my Saviour first loved me; if, then, Christ so loved you, although condemned to such punishments as these, ought you not in return love Him, although He is filled with suffering, as you see?

You should share his sufferings, then, my brethren, even although they were altogether his own. But, O my God, are these sufferings—the very sight of which often saddens us—are they his, or not rather ours? Surely He had no suffering of his own, that is, none that He did not endure for our salvation. "Surely He hath borne our infirmities, and carried our sorrows: and we have thought Him, as it were, a leper, and as one struck by God and afflicted. But He was wounded for our iniquities, He was bruised for our sins: the chastisement of our peace was upon Him, and by his bruises we are healed" (Isaias, liii. 4, 5). Whence, then, came this sea of suffering? for as man, Christ's body was sinless, and, if sinless, therefore painless. Add up all that He endured : poverty, neglect, insult, scorn, the crown of thorns, the scourge, the crucifixion;—they are yours, not his. And shall we not love Him the more for the very reason that He is so afflicted, so bruised; seeing, too, that He most deliberately accepted them all for our sake.

Not only are they our sufferings, but He shows Himself most loving when He is most covered with wounds. We should then love Christ most when He is most loving to us. But He is then most loving to us when He is most covered with wounds. His whole life is an act of love towards us; but there are times when his love surged up in waves of greater strength, glowed in flames of greater intensity. What are the occasions when this so happened? When He speaks of his Passion. Hear the words of burning love He then addresses to us : "I have a baptism wherewith I am to be baptised, and how I am straitened till it be accomplished" (Luke, xii. 50). "The chalice that my Father gave me, shall I not drink it?" (John, xviii. 11.) "Having loved those that were in the world, He loved them to the end" (John, xiii. 1). Nay, He Himself, like a true lover, has insisted that we should remember Him, that we should ever keep his memory green in our hearts. When we wish to live in the memory of our friends, my brethren, do we not desire to be remembered in the most agreeable light, with most love and greatest affection. Well, then, "this do ye in commemoration of me." He might have wished to be remembered as an infant, as an obedient child, as a benefactor of our race, as a king, as a wonder-worker; but no, He wished rather to live in our memories as suffering for us. Would it not, then, be the blackest ingratitude on our part to love Him less for that very reason by which He proves that He loves us most? But it is hard to love suffering with a heart that is inclined to love pleasure. It is hard to forego present pleasures and present honours out of love for a suffering Redeemer who is *not* present, and whom we do not see. Company, jests, amusements, gain, take a great hold on the heart, and it is hard to banish them all to go share the sufferings of the Crucified. Is it so, my brethren, is it so? Is it difficult to forget present pleasure for future good; if so, then, how do you spend your days in hard toil and not in pleasure? Is it hard to forego present gain? If so, why do you commit to the ground so much seed with the hope of future harvest? How do men spend time, money, pains, health, life, were fatigue ever unbearable and future joy of no value? Is it possible that only where Christ is concerned difficulties will spring up; only when sin is to be avoided that future enjoyment will be valueless.

But granted that it is so difficult, that the heart dreads pain and suffering; for that very reason we ought to be devout to the Passion of Christ. You say that the heart is made for enjoyment; I say that it is made for sorrow and suffering. Sin and sorrow may tarry apart for a while, but in the end they come together. Everyone must suffer sorrow and pain in life or death. If so, my brethren, is it not better so to live as to have in our day of need comfort, alleviation, succour in our distress? The question is answered by being asked. But where can the heart find such so truly as in the Passion of Christ. In our distress, and especially in our death, it will be our refuge in fear, our comfort in pain.

Well then, my brethren, I will ask you once more before I present in your name these Stations, do your hearts glow with love for the Passion of Christ? He found you suffering and still loved you;—would you refuse to love Him because He suffered? His sufferings were not his, but yours; will you not love Him who did this for you? He suffered to show his love for you; will you fear to love Him? Will you refuse to do for Him what you do for the world? Will you deprive yourself of all the help of his Passion? No; behold, then, O Saviour, the people devout to thy person; let these Stations be a pledge of their love.

PASTORAL LETTER ON THE JUBILEE OF 1875.

GEORGE, BY THE GRACE OF GOD AND FAVOUR OF THE APOSTOLIC
SEE, BISHOP OF ARDAGH AND CLONMACNOIS, TO THE FAITHFUL
OF HIS DIOCESE.

DEARLY BELOVED IN CHRIST,

While Daniel the prophet " was praying and confessing
his sins and the sins of his people, and presenting his supplica-
tions in the sight of his God" (Dan. ix. 20-24), the Angel
Gabriel, flying swiftly, touched him at the time of the evening
sacrifice, and revealed to him the speedy accomplishment of
God's merciful designs, "that transgression might be finished,
and sin might have an end, and iniquity might be abolished,
and everlasting justice might be brought." How beautiful in
the sight of the man of desires were the feet of the angelic
messenger, thus bringing good tidings to the sinful people, and
preaching peace and salvation. How sweet to him the assurance
that, even from the beginning of his prayer, the answering
word had gone forth from the heart of God, and that the Lord
was at length about to show his face upon his sanctuary that
had lain desolate so long. It is our pleasing duty to convey to
you to-day, beloved brethren, a similar message of mercy on the
part of God. Our Holy Father, Pius IX.—the angel of the
Catholic Church, who in these days of trial is to his children as
Gabriel, the *Strength of God*—has charged us to announce to
you that for the exaltation of the Church, for the sanctification
of the people of Christ, and for the glory of God, he has granted
a universal and great Jubilee for the entire year 1875. For this
year he has opened wide to you, and to all the faithful, the
heavenly treasure of the merits, and sufferings, and virtues of
Christ our Lord, of his Virgin Mother, and of all the saints,
which has been entrusted to him by the Author of man's salvation. Once, and once only, during the year all those who
comply with the prescribed conditions can obtain the great Indulgence of the Holy Year of Jubilee, and full remission and
pardon of all their sins. "And thou shalt sanctify the fiftieth
year, and shalt proclaim remission to all the inhabitants of thy
land: for it is the year of Jubilee" (Levit. xxv. 10).

And that we may be enabled to profit fully by the great
grace thus extended to us, the same Holy Father exhorts us to
send up public prayers to the God of clemency, that He would
fill with his light and grace the minds and hearts of all, that

they may know this the day of their salvation, and may not despise the riches of his goodness, and patience, and long-suffering. For this purpose, therefore, beloved brethren, we invite you to join with faith, humility and perseverance in those prayers which we have appointed to be recited in the churches, to obtain from God for the faithful of this diocese the grace of making good use of the blessings of the Jubilee. Such prayers are the most fitting and necessary preparation for the Holy Year. We have hitherto abused many and many of God's graces; ought we not, then, tremble lest our past ingratitude should render us unworthy of this latest and crowning favour? Our sins have risen up like a wall, "and have divded between us and our God" (Isai. lix. 2); and now no effort of ours will avail to undo their dreadful work, "that hides his face from us that He should not hear," unless we are helped by Him "who is our peace, who hath made both one, breaking down the middle wall of partition . . . for by Him alone we have access to the Father" (Ephes. ii. 14, 18). The work we are about to undertake is difficult in the extreme, for it involves nothing less than the thorough cleansing of our corrupt, weak, and perverse hearts, the sundering of the chains of sin, the denying of ourselves, and the newness of the supernatural life. How, then, can we expect success save through Him, without whom we can do nothing, but in whom, when we are strengthened, we can do all things? Let us, therefore, approach the holy work of the Jubilee in the spirit of humility and with a contrite heart, but also with David's confidence, saying: "Send forth, O God, thy light and thy truth: they have conducted me and brought me to thy holy hill, and into thy tabernacles. Why art thou sad, O my soul, and why dost thou disquiet me? Hope in God, for I will still give praise to Him, the salvation of my countenance and my God" (Ps. xlii. 1).

Our Holy Father next reminds us of our obligation of instructing you concerning the Jubilee itself, its nature, its advantages, and the steps you are to take to secure these advantages for your souls. What, then, is the Jubilee? What are the benefits which it brings? And what are the conditions upon which these benefits are to be gained?

The Christian Jubilee contains within itself, by the power of our Lord Jesus Christ, in a spiritual manner, and with superabundant excellence, all those benefits which the Old Law, figurative of the future, had provided for the Jewish people at the return of each fiftieth year. Among the Jews, as each period of seven days, of seven months, and of seven years was closed by a sacred festival to which special obligations were attached by God, so also each period of seven times seven years was followed by a sacred year, called the year of Jubilee. This year, beginning on the day of expiation, and ushered in to the sound of trumpets, was a year of complete rest and renovation of all things. The land was allowed to rest from tillage; each family received back its absent members and the property that had been estranged from it; the payment of debts was not exacted; bondsmen regained their liberty. Chief, then, among the benefits brought by the Jewish Jubilee were these : expiation of guilt, refreshing rest, restoration of lost advantages, forgiveness of debts, emancipation of slaves; and these same benefits, transferred to the spiritual order and splendidly enlarged, are reproduced in the year of the Christian Jubilee.

It is a year of expiation and redemption : of it the Saviour spoke when coming in his Passion with apparel red, and garments like theirs that tread in the wine press. He said : " I that speak justice, and am a defender to save . . . the year of my redemption is come " (Isai. lxiii. 4). It is a year of refreshing rest; for in it the Prince of peace invites to his heart all those who labour and are heavy burdened, that He may refresh them, that they may find rest for their souls. It is a year of renovation, in which we are allowed to redeem our misspent time, to recover our lost graces, to restore our wasted strength, to revive our perished merits. In it God tells us : " He will make the early and the latter rain come down to us, as in the beginning . . . and I will restore to you the years which the locust and the mildew have eaten; and you shall praise the name of the Lord your God, who hath done wonders with you " (Joel, ii. 23-25). It is a year of mercy and pardon. The periods of the world's history are rapidly passing, and each year as it follows after year carries before the judgment-seat its own dark record of sin, by which man unceasingly provokes the anger of the God of justice. But at length, in the midst of all those sin-stained years, a white year of pardon has come, in which God's work upon earth is no longer that of the anger that slays, but of the mercy that gives life : " O Lord, thy work in the midst of years bring it to life ; in the midst of years Thou shalt make it known; when Thou art angry Thou wilt remember mercy " (Hab. iii. 2, 3). It is a year of emancipation from bondage. Our Lord has applied to Himself and to his mission the words in which the Scripture describes the Jewish year of liberation : " The Spirit of the Lord is upon me, wherefore He hath anointed me, to preach the Gospel to the poor He hath sent me, to heal the contrite of heart, to preach deliverance to the captive, to set at liberty them that are bruised, to preach the acceptable year of the Lord " (Luke, iv. 18, 19). Most truly, indeed, may it be styled the acceptable year of the Lord, for it brings to us "those times of refreshment, those times of the restitution of all things," of which, St. Peter says, God has spoken by the mouth of his prophets from the beginning of the world, "which shall come from the presence of the Lord, and He shall send Him who hath been preached unto you, Jesus Christ" (Acts, xi. 20, 21).

And as the Jewish Jubilee was instituted by God chiefly that it might be, at constantly recurring periods, a sensible proof of God's supreme dominion over men, and a practical lesson of confidence in his Divine Providence, so, too, the Christian Jubilee returns at determined intervals to exhibit to a world but too apt to forget such truths a living memorial of God's mercy, and of the copious redemption that is with Him. The unwritten tradition of Christendom had long celebrated this season of grace at intervals of a hundred years; Boniface VIII., however, in 1295, was the first to establish by the authority of a decree that it should be held at the beginning of each century. In 1345, Clement V. reduced to fifty years the interval between each Jubilee, and this term was still further reduced to thirty years by Urban VI. in 1389, and to its present duration of twenty-five years by Paul II. in 1470. The un-happy circumstances of the times did not allow the celebration of the Jubilee in 1850; and even to-day, far from being come to an end, these same obstacles exist in an aggravated form. "Notwithstanding this," writes our most Holy Father, "taking into consideration the many evils that afflict the Church, the many hostile efforts directed to uproot the Christian Faith, to corrupt sound doctrine, and to diffuse the poison of impiety; the many scandals that everywhere beset the faithful; the in-crease of immorality; the violation of all rights, human and divine, so widespread, so ruinous, and so destructive of every sentiment of rectitude; and considering that in so great an abyss of evil we are the more strictly bound by our Apostolic office to procure that faith, religion, and piety be the better strengthened and revived; that the spirit of prayer be cherished and everywhere increased; that the fallen be excited to heartfelt penance and amendment; that the sins which justly kindle the anger of God be redeemed with holy actions; results to obtain which the celebration of the greater Jubilee is principally directed: We have determined, as far as circumstances permit, not to allow the people of Christ to be deprived on this occasion of so salutary a benefit, in order that, strengthened in spirit, they may daily advance in the paths of justice, and cleansed from all sin, may the more easily and fully obtain mercy and pardon from God." *

* Encyclical, 24th December, 1874.

The Encyclical requires also that on this occasion of the promulgation of the Jubilee the faithful should be instructed concerning the nature of indulgences.

Thanks be to God, the accurate knowledge, dearly beloved, which you possess of the doctrines of our holy religion happily renders this part of our duty easy of discharge. Wherefore, abstaining from any lengthened explanation of what is already well known to all, we shall merely repeat for your benefit the summary of instruction which, on occasion of the Jubilee of 1750, the learned Pontiff, Benedict XIV., held to be sufficient for the faithful people: "It will be enough for the faithful people to know, that through the Sacrament of Penance, if properly received, the guilt and eternal punishment of sin are taken away, while the debt of temporal punishment is very rarely taken away, but remains to be discharged by works of satisfaction in this life, or by the fire of Purgatory. It will be enough for the Christian people, likewise, to know that there is in the Church an unfailing treasure consisting of the infinite merits of Christ, to which are added the other merits of the saints; that the administration of this treasure has been confided by the same Christ our Lord to his vicar on earth, the Roman Pontiff; and that, consequently, according to the prudent discretion of the Roman Pontiff, and for just reasons, these merits may be applied more or less amply for the benefit of the faithful; for the living, by way of absolution; for the dead, by way of suffrage: on condition, however, that the living shall, by penance, have cancelled their guilt and the eternal punishment due thereon, and that the dead shall have departed this life united to God by charity. This application of merits is called an Indulgence, and whosoever gains it is freed from the temporal punishment of his sins, according to the measure of the application which the legitimate dispenser of the same had determined to grant. Hence it follows that the use of Indulgences is most advantageous to the Christian people, and that the erroneous doctrine which holds Indulgences to be of no avail, or the Church not to have the power of conferring them, is to be altogether condemned. Finally, the faithful are to be instructed that the Indulgence of the year of the Jubilee is Plenary, and that it is to be distinguished from all other Plenary Indulgences, even if granted by way of Jubilee, in this, that in the Holy Jubilee year confessors receive more ample powers, as well to absolve from sins as to dispense from certain obligations and impediments by which the consciences of penitents are sometimes constrained." *

---

* In Bullario Bened. xiv.

From the consideration of the origin and nature of the Jubilee, let us now pass to consider the excellence of the advantages which it brings to us. How great that excellence will easily be understood by those who reflect on what the Jubilee really is. The Jubilee is a merciful offer of unlimited forgiveness made by God to sinful man on conditions most easy of fulfilment. Ponder well these words, beloved brethren, and you will find in each one of them a fresh proof of the value of the advantages now offered for your acceptance. The Jubilee is, in the first place, a signal exercise of the mercy of God. God's mercy is the one universal need of man, recognised as such by the human conscience, and yearned after with inexpressible longing by the human heart in every circumstance of time and place, but most of all in the hour of remorse, when the evil that sin is makes itself more keenly felt. Now the Jubilee brings God's mercy down, and places it within the reach even of the most sinful amongst us. Recall to your minds, beloved brethren, all that you have ever learned concerning the unspeakable mercy of God. Measure its irresistible power by what it has done in the Incarnation, in which it brought down the Eternal Word from heaven to earth to be the Light and the Life of the world. Estimate its ineffable sweetness by what it has done for individual souls, as when it cleansed the penitent thief at his life's close, or when to meet the flowing tears of the Magdalen it gushed from the Good Shepherd's heart, a fountain of water springing up into life everlasting. And when the contemplation of the strong and sweet mercy of God shall have filled your soul with mingled longing and fainting—with longing to hide your wretchedness in its embrace, and with fainting through the consciousness of your own unworthiness ; then remember that the Jubilee is the outstretched arm of mercy itself. In it is reproduced for each one of us that touching scene described in the Gospel, in which the sinful woman was left by her accusers in silent shame at the feet of Jesus, "and there remained alone," as St. Augustine says, "these two : Mercy and Misery." Blessed, then, be this year of Jubilee, which will bring face to face our misery and God's mercy !—that mercy which grows more tender the greater the misery that appeals to it, and that misery which sin has made so drear and so utterly helpless !

Nor is God's mercy content, in this season of the Jubilee, with simply waiting to receive the sinner, should he come : it goes so far as to invite him most earnestly to repentance. To be at last admitted to pardon, after many prayers and tears and protracted penance, would be a blessing beyond all our deserts ; how much greater, then, the blessing when God anticipates us by offering pardon of his own accord ! And yet, not

only does He offer it, but He lovingly goes in search of the
wanderer, tracking him through all his waywardness; and when
He has found him, constraining him by loving violence to be
reconciled with his only Good. "All we like sheep have gone
astray, every one hath turned aside into his own way" (Isai.
liii. 6); and now the Good Shepherd leaves the ninety-nine
sheep that have been faithful, and sets out after that which was
lost until He find it, and when He hath found it lays it upon
his shoulders, rejoicing. Now, more than at any other time, is
it verified of Him that He is "come to call not the just but
sinners to repentance." Now does his voice sound sweeter than
ever in the ear of the sinner, no matter how dark his guilt or
how seared his conscience: "Come to me, all you that labour
and are burdened, and I will refresh you" (Matt. xi. 28). No
matter, then, how far we have strayed away, nor how devious
the paths which we have followed; no matter how sadly torn
by sin our soul, or weakened by worldliness, or held fast by
chains of evil habits, the proclamation of this Jubilee is
nothing less than the voice of God's mercy calling to each
individual soul—nay, crying out to us to accept his pardon
and peace.

And what manner of pardon is now offered to us? A
pardon the most generous and the most complete that can be
desired or even conceived. The pardon offered during the
Jubilee is a pardon absolutely without limits or restrictions. It
includes the remission of the dreadful guilt of mortal sin. It
includes the remission of the eternal punishment which is due
for mortal sin. It includes the remission of the guilt of venial
sin. It includes the remission of the temporal punishment due
for sins whether mortal or venial. It is the fullest exercise
practised by the Church of that amplest power of binding and
loosing which has been placed in her hands by the Saviour of
men for the destruction of sin. It is her largest use of that
sublime power of the keys of the kingdom of heaven which has
been entrusted to her for the sanctification of souls. During
these days of mercy confessors are invested with powers altogether extraordinary, and not granted at other seasons, to
absolve from sins, even the most heinous, and to loosen the
bonds of excommunication and of other ecclesiastical censures.
The treasury of the Church's Indulgences is flung open wide,
and a Plenary Indulgence of the fullest kind is granted to all
who comply with the prescribed conditions. What more can
man ask from God? What more can God do for man? Well,
indeed, may He ask us at this season: "What is there that I
ought to do more to my vineyard, that I have not done to it?"
(Isai. v. 4.) And in this season of Jubilee well may we answer,

with St. Paul, that absolutely "there is now no condemnation to them that are in Christ Jesus" (Rom. viii. 1). The Lamb of God has come to us and has taken away our sins; what was red as scarlet He has made white as snow; He has bound up that which was broken, and has strengthened that which was weak; our Beloved to us, and we to Him; our God all in all. No darkness of sin is there, nor fear of sentence in this happy hour of completest pardon, to cast a shadow between the soul and the bright light of his face; the grace of the Jubilee, to its thrice blessed possessors, is as the prelude of the peace of heaven, and the foretaste of the Beatific Vision of God.

And, next, the priceless grace of this unlimited pardon is to be obtained upon most easy conditions. "How easily all men may become sharers in its riches," writes Leo XII., speaking of the Jubilee, "may be learned both from those amplest powers of remitting sin which are granted to confessors, and from the nature of the works imposed for the expiation of sins."* To gain the Indulgence of the Jubilee it is no longer necessary, as it was in the olden time, to perform works of great difficulty, such as the pilgrimage for the liberation of the Holy Land, which, as blessed Cardinal Thomasius observes, "by reason of the expenses, inconveniences, most toilsome journeys, and imminent peril of life that attended it, was a commutation rather than a remission of penance." So easy, indeed, are the conditions required by the modern discipline of the Church for the gaining of so great a favour, that Leo XII. thought it necessary to warn Christians against a danger to which they might be exposed of making too light of their sins, and thereby falling more readily into graver excesses, treasuring for themselves wrath in the day of wrath. The works enjoined for the gaining of the present Jubilee in this diocese are as follows: First, to receive with the due dispositions the Holy Sacraments of Penance and the Eucharist; second, to visit three times the Parish or District Church; and, third, there to offer pious prayers for the prosperity and exaltation of the Catholic Church, and of the Apostolic See; for the extirpation of heresies and the conversion of all who are in error; for the peace and unity of the entire people of Christ, and according to the intention of our Holy Father the Pope.

See, then, beloved brethren, how slender the service which is asked for so rich a reward. From whom could we dare expect so much for so little, save from that infinitely good God, who knows the clay of which we are formed, and whose merciful rule it is to set over great things in the joy of their Lord

---

* Jubilee Encyclical of 1825

those servants who in little things have been faithful to Him. Is not this a fresh reason why we should serve Him the better and hope in Him the more? "Preserve me, O Lord, for I have put my trust in Thee. I have said to the Lord, Thou art my God, for Thou hast no need of my goods" (Ps. xv. 1).

"Moreover," adds the Sovereign Pontiff, Pius IX., in the Jubilee Encyclical, "nothing is more worthy of the time of the Holy Jubilee than the unwearied exercise of every work of charity; wherefore, it will be likewise part of your duty to procure with all zeal that the poor be relieved, and that sins be ransomed by almsgiving, of which the Holy Scriptures contain so many praises; and in order that the fruits of charity may be more widely diffused, and be made more permanent, it will be very fitting to devote the charitable contributions to the maintenance or establishment of those pious institutions which are considered at present most conducive to the welfare of soul and body."

And here, dearly beloved, we are encouraged by these words of the Pope to recommend to you the collection which is to be made throughout this diocese on next Sunday, the third Sunday of Lent, for the necessary repairs of the magnificent Cathedral of St. Mel. Many and powerful reasons combine to favour this appeal. The Cathedral Church of each diocese has been specially designated by the Pope as first among the churches to be visited, when possible, by the faithful who seek to gain the benefits of the Jubilee. And why? To teach the faithful that their Mother Church ought to be in an especial manner the object of their pious veneration. The Cathedral in each diocese is the visible expression of Catholic unity of Faith. It takes its name from the Episcopal Chair, of which it is the appointed seat, and from which bishop after bishop, from the first to the last, preaches with authority to successive generations of the flock of Christ, one and the same Catholic doctrine. It is also the expression of the unity of communion with which God has bound together the members of his Church. As it is the mark of the heretic to set up altar against altar, and of the schismatic to set up chair against chair, so it is the sign of the good Catholic to reverence the one altar and the one chair, which make the Cathedral the centre of the religious life of the diocese of which he is the child. From the Cathedral goes forth the authoritative word of the Chief Pastor, to bind and loose according to the power confided to him by the Holy Church. Within its venerable sanctuary the young Levite receives with the imposition of hands the ample power of the priesthood, and thence he goes forth with jurisdiction to bless, and absolve, and teach. Before its altar the Holy Oils are blessed, which are to sanctify the newly baptised, to strengthen the young in con-

firmation, to consecrate the hands of the priest, and refresh
and purify the senses of the dying Christians. All over the
world, in these days of the Jubilee, each Cathedral Church,
like an exulting mother of many children, will be filled with
a pious throng of the faithful coming in obedience to the voice
of the Vicar of Christ to pay their due reverence. If you
cannot imitate their example by visiting the cathedral of your
diocese, you can at least prove your piety by contributing to
maintain it in honour such as befits the holy purposes for which
it was erected. It is, in truth, a glorious thing for this diocese
to have offered to God a temple so beautiful in its majesty; is
it not equally glorious to preserve it from injury, now that it
has been for so many years the resting-place of the Lord, consecrated to his service, and chief seat of his mercy amongst us?
Nothing is more afflicting to the pious soul than to behold the
House of God dishonoured by the traces of decay. Hence it
was that Mathathias, rending his garments at the sight of the
dismantled Temple, cried out in sorrow: "And behold our
sanctuary, and our beauty, and our glory is laid waste!" (Mach.
ii. 12.) Let, then, your exertions on next Sunday on behalf
of the restoration of our cathedral be not unworthy of those
which you made for its erection, lest it be said of us that we
have grudgingly repented of our gift to God. Be mindful,
also, that it is incumbent on you to be liberal in almsgiving
during Lent, so as to make some compensation to God for the
indulgent relaxation which, through compassion for the infirmities of her children, the Church has permitted in the
rigour of her law of fasting. Finally, calling to mind that
almsgiving is one of the virtues that have been specially recommended to you for the Jubilee by our Holy Father the Pope,
endeavour to satisfy by one generous effort on next Sunday this
threefold call of charity. "Give, and it shall be given to you:
good measure and pressed down and shaken together and running over shall they give unto your bosom. For with the same
measure that you shall mete withal, it shall be measured unto
you again" (Luke, vi. 38).

But, although the conditions for gaining the Jubilee are thus
easy, yet they require for their due fulfilment no inconsiderable
care, attention, and watchfulness on our part. It is not enough
to simply perform the works enjoined, we should do our utmost
to perform them with devotion. St. Catharine of Genoa used to
say that if Christians did but know how difficult it is to gain indulgences, the knowledge would fill them with fear. The pious
and learned Dr. Hay, whose works ought to be found and read in
every Catholic family, thus explains what things are necessary
for gaining a plenary indulgence:

(1). "That a person be in the state of grace, and in friendship with God ; for while one continues in sin, at enmity with God, and deserving eternal punishment, he is incapable of receiving an indulgence. On this account, in all grants of plenary indulgences the general condition required for gaining them is that the person apply first to the sacrament of penance in order to put his soul in the state of grace, without which he cannot receive that benefit.

2. "That the conditions required in the grant of the indulgence be exactly performed; for indulgences are always granted on certain conditions, to be performed on our part, such as approaching to the Holy Sacraments, works of charity and mercy, exercises of piety and religion, prayers for the necessities of the Church, and the like. If these conditions be not complied with we cannot gain the benefit of the indulgence granted.

3. "In order to gain the full benefit of a plenary indulgence, it is also necessary to have a perfect repentance and sincere detestation of all our sins, even the least venial sin ; because, as the punishment of sin will never be forgiven while the guilt of it remains in the soul, and as a sincere repentance is absolutely required for the remission of the guilt, therefore this sincere repentance must precede the remission of the punishment.

"Hence, we may see how few there are who gain the full effect of a plenary indulgence, as there are few who have a sincere and efficacious repentance for every venial sin, and a firm resolution of avoiding every sin, great or small, with all the occasions of sin. Still, this ought not to hinder us from endeavouring to gain a plenary indulgence when occasion offers; for though we should not gain the whole effect of it, the more we endeavour, and the better our dispositions are, the more ample benefit will we reap. We can never, indeed, be certain to what extent we gain this benefit, and from our imperfect dispositions have too much reason to fear that we have yet a great debt to pay.

"Our endeavouring to gain an indulgence, therefore, ought not to render us remiss, but rather encourage us to lead a penitential life; for the more we strive by works worthy of penance to satisfy the divine Justice, the better shall we be disposed for gaining the more abundant fruits of an indulgence when the opportunity offers. When we have done our best, it is little to what we ought to have done. Indulgences supply the deficiencies of human infirmity, but can never be supposed to encourage negligence or sloth."[*]

"Finally, we address ourselves," these are the holy father's concluding words, "to all you who are children of the Catholic Church, and with fatherly love we exhort each and every one

[*] Dr. Hay's " Sincere Christian," On Indulgence.

of you, to make such use of this opportunity of pardon presented
by the Jubilee as a true regard for your salvation demands from
you." It has ever been, and now is, most necessary to cleanse
your conscience from dead works, to offer sacrifices of justice,
to do fruits worthy of penance, and to sow in tears that you may
reap in joy. The Divine Majesty has made manifest what He
expects from us, for, by reason of our guilt, we are long suffering beneath his threats, and beneath the breath of the spirit of
his anger."* "When men are straitened by some hard necessity, they are wont to despatch ambassadors to the neighbouring
nations in search of help. Let us do better, and send an embassy
to God;" from Him let us ask aid, towards Him let us turn
with our heart, with prayers, and fasting, and alms-deeds.
" The nearer we approach to God, the farther shall our enemies
be repelled from us." But you, above all others, do you listen
to our Apostolic voice, speaking in the name of Christ; you
who labour and are burdened, and straying from the paths of
salvation, are oppressed by the yoke of evil lusts, and of the
slavery of the devil. Do not despise the riches of the goodness,
the patience, and the long-suffering of God; and while so easy
and wide a road of safety lies open before you, do not by your
obstinacy render yourselves inexcusable before the Divine
Judge, nor treasure up for yourselves wrath in the day of
wrath, and of the revealing of the just judgment of God.
Return, therefore, O sinners, return to the Heart, make your
peace with God; the world and its concupiscences are passing
away; put away the works of darkness, and put on the armour
of light; be no longer the enemies of your own souls, that so at
length you may merit peace in this world, and in the next the
eternal joys of the just. These are our prayers; this we shall
ask from our most merciful Lord; and this, in union of prayer
with all the children of the Catholic Church, we trust fully to
obtain from the Father of mercies.

And may the grace of our Lord Jesus Christ be with you
all. Amen.

✠ GEORGE CONROY,
Bishop of Ardagh and Clonmacnois.

St. Mel's, Longford, 16*th February,* 1875.

---

* S. Maximus Taur. Hom. xci.

10

LECTURES.

LECTURES.

THE MIXED SYSTEM OF EDUCATION IN IRELAND.

OUR demand that our rights in the matter of education shall be respected could not be addressed to our rulers from a more fitting spot than this splendid Cathedral, which you have raised to be a proof of your own respect for the sovereign rights of God, and a school of respect for the rights of others. The spirit of the place will breathe into the words that shall be spoken here to-day the two qualities that are the glory and the strength of a just man's claim—firmness and moderation : a firmness that forbids us to palter with wrong done to our Faith, and a moderation that, while we unflinchingly demand our own rights, shall check us from compassing the slightest violation of the rights of others. These qualities are most conspicuous in the Catholic movement that is now taking place throughout Ireland ; and I know of nothing more honourable to our beloved country than the noble spectacle which, in these days of a wild and debauched democracy, she alone affords, of a believing nation assembling in its peaceful thousands under the shadow of the cross, to strive, with no other weapons than those of truth and justice, against those who would deny to Catholics the blessings of a religious education. It is to be regretted that the conduct of our adversaries has not displayed like fairness and temper ; on the contrary, the Non-Conformists in England and the Presbyterians in Ireland and Scotland have conspired, in language bristling with insult and menace, to force upon the Government a system of godless education for Ireland, not on the ground that it alone is just, or because it is plainly the best for the country, but avowedly because it is pernicious to Catholic interests. And it is still more to be regretted that these bigots have found a mouthpiece in the Secretary for Ireland, who, with unhappy dexterity, has succeeded in gathering into one sentence all their insolence and injustice when he declared, *" We will never allow education in Ireland to be handed over to the priests.*" This little sentence, so bitterly scornful in its tone, does in truth contain the two false principles from which, as from a double root, the whole system of godless education springs, and from which it derives the radical injustice that incurably infects it. The first of these principles asserts that education is a civil function, and not a domestic or religious office ; that the State has the right to pass the threshold of the house of each father of a family with a compulsory educational code in hand, to be administered as a department of politics, without regard to the conscience of the parents. The second principle asserts that education may safely and wisely be divorced from religion ; nay, that religious influences ought to be excluded from the school. The cry, *no priests in education !* is but the practical application of these two principles ; and before I attempt to show how unjust they are in themselves and in their application, I wish to draw your attention to the fact, that the utterers of that hateful cry find themselves in very bad company indeed. It is the cry of all the enemies of Christianity and of social order throughout the world. The mixed school, giving a godless education, is distinctly the creation of the spirit of infidelity ; and you will find that in proportion to the decay of faith in Europe its advocates have grown bolder and still bolder. In the happy days before religious unity was broken, and when from the temples of a united Christendom there went up to God one harmonious hymn of praise, the idea of education without religion was too monstrous even to enter into the minds of men. With unfailing regularity, under the shadow of the stately cathedral, rose the university, and in the country hamlet the village school ever stood near the humble church. Among the canons, which one of the earliest synods declares, " ought to be guarded by the bishops as the apple of their eye," there is one to remind them " that every church which has not its scholars clustering round it is like a barren woman who hath no children." And in Ireland, so little has the lapse of ages changed this Catholic conception of the union between human and divine learning, that when we of to-day seek to clothe with words our ideal of what education ought to be, we find it expressed to the life in the maxims current in the old Celtic monasteries of the sixth century—that no man can be the child of science who does not love truth and justice, and that there is no truth or justice without the knowledge of God. But when Protestantism appeared, the happy union between faith and science was rudely sundered. Luther declared that the high schools were " an invention of the devil, destined to obscure Christianity, if not to overthrow it completely ; " and that the four soldiers who crucified our Saviour

were but symbolical representations of the universities with
their four faculties. And among the propositions condemned
in John Wicliff, by Pope Martin V., the twenty-ninth is, that
" universities, places of study, colleges, degrees, and masterships in the same, have been introduced by vain paganism, and
are of as much service to the church as the devil is."

But the movement which began by thus sacrificing education in the supposed interest of religion, finally ended in sacrificing religion in the supposed interests of education. As one
dogma after another melted away before the newly acquired
right of private judgment, the school faithfully reflected the
decay of religious influence on the individual, domestic, social
life of the people, until to be godless became its normal type,
and education was at last degraded to be the vile handmaid of
infidelity. For the infidelity of our day is not merely a speculative opinion lurking in the hearts and minds of its professors;
it has a public policy of its own, in pursuance of which it aims
at the destruction of Christian civilisation, that instead it may
build up a new society, without God, without authority, without
property. Now, the great obstacle to the success of this scheme
has been found to exist in the Catholic school, through which,
mainly, the Christian idea continues to strike deep its roots in
the hearts of the people. It was resolved, therefore, that education should be secularised; that the crucifix should be cast
out from the school, and the image of the chaste and tender
Mother of God should be expelled, lest the children by looking
upon the face of their Christ or of her who bore Him should
learn how to live and to die as the Christian faith prescribes.
And this is the avowed motive of that passionate declamation
against the presence of the priest in the school, which issuing
from the dens of the secret societies, through the infidel press,
through the parliamentary tribune and the popular platform,
has overspread all the countries of Europe. Now, have we not
a right to grow indignant with the men who, through sheer
anti-catholic bigotry, would force the government of this country
to take, as the principle of their educational policy, the very
watchword of those ruffianly infidels and revolutionists? Will
it be wise in our rulers to present themselves to this Christian
nation as the accomplices or the dupes of the enemies of religion
and of social order? Will its avowed resolution of unbaptising
the intelligence of the Catholic youth of Ireland, win for authority that respect which is for society the very breath of life?
But we are told, forsooth, that the spirit of the age cries out
against the priest, and that the statesman must be in harmony
with his time. So reasoned the statesmen who encouraged Voltaire to attack the priest; but there soon arose Rousseau, who

proceeded to attack the state, and prepare the revolution which swept all that could perish of the Church, and all the institutions of civil society. And, to-day, that Europe is tossing uneasily under the fever of these same principles of '89, and that religion is toiling to calm the perilous unrest that fearfully presages dissolution, is it not pitiable to find men in authority join, from their place of power, in the ribald shout against the ministers of religion; to the scandal of believers, to the loss of the cause of order, and to the clear gain of their own sworn enemies! For, be it remembered, the priest, although he disdains to wear the livery of this or of that political party—for he is the servant, not of man, but of the living God—really wields the only conservative force that exists, because he alone will have the courage to rebuke excesses of power in those who govern, and he alone can teach those who are governed how to obey for conscience' sake!

The first principle on which the godless system is based asserts, that education is a function of the State. This is a false assertion. The assumption of the educational office by the State constitutes in reality a grave violation of the natural rights of parents, of their civil liberties, and of that religious equality which the law has sanctioned for all. Nature herself unequivocally designates the parent as the divinely appointed educator of the child. The infant, incapable of thought or action of its own, is given, at first, absolutely into the hands of its parents, upon whose intelligence and love it instinctively depends for succour and maintenance. As infancy ripens into childhood the same relations of absolute dependence continue to appear. Towards the parent the budding faculties of reason turn for training, as unerringly as towards the sun the opening petals of the flower, and their demands, be they ever so incessant, can never exhaust the treasure of unwearied love that is stored up in the parent's heart. Who has so strong an interest in the task of educating as the parent, who knows that on his child's training depends the honour and happiness of his family, and the support of his own hoary age? And deep down in the recesses of the human conscience is there not written in burning words a law, which even the savage tribes acknowledge in their wildest deserts, ceaselessly intimating to the parent that it is his to form the mind and heart of the child, and to the child that he is bound to listen with reverence to his father's voice? Thus, to secure the due discharge of the parental office of educating, the Author of Nature has put in motion the three most powerful motives that can sway the heart of man—love, interest, and duty—and yet we are told that the parent has no right to educate! Nay, more, according to Bentham, the natural element

of indissolubility in the marriage tie itself is built on this right
and duty of the parent to provide for the education of the child.
To usurp, therefore, the right to educate, is really to aim a
blow at the very foundation of society, which is the family.
Nor is it less a violation of the civil rights of the parent. For
what tyranny can be more hateful than that of a government
which arrogates to itself the power of moulding, according to
its own petty interests or caprice, the very thought of a nation?
Pharao complacently described the completeness of his sway
over a nation of slaves, by saying that, save at his beck, no
man in the land of Egypt would dare to move hand or foot;
but the lust of power of our new Pharaos is not satisfied until
they have fitted to each of the intellectual faculties of freemen
fetters marked with their brand! Is not such a control of
national education more dangerous to the true liberty and moral
dignity of a people than a standing army? There are cases in
which the State can and ought interpose its authority, and stand
between the parent's action and the soul of his child, and for
these cases the law of the land makes exceptional provision.
These are cases in which the parent has been proved to be grossly
unfit for his charge, and in which the child's interests require
that the formation of his character should not be subjected to
sceptical or immoral influences, even when these are set in
motion and directed by a father's hands. To such monsters of
parents the State may well declare : Your parental rights have
been given to you that you may edify, and not that you may
destroy your child. We will not allow the education of your
child to be handed over to those who would sap its faith or corrupt its morals. These cases of interference with the rights
recognised in the parents by law, are happily exceptional ; but
the foes of religious education would make them the rule !—
and they would make them the rule, not as against a few
wretches in whom preternatural malice has overpowered the
natural love of their children's innocence, but as against the
parents of this entire kingdom whose homes, even if humble,
are admitted to be very shrines of faith and virtue !—and this
not to rescue the children from what might injure their religious
belief, but avowedly to withdraw them from the teaching that
would make them strong in faith!—not to throw protection
around their frailty, but to expose them to the rude shocks of
undisciplined passions, without the religious safeguards which
even the strongest virtue dare not forego ! And is this no in-
vasion of the civil rights of the parent?

Nor less grave is the violation of religious equality, which
results from the usurpation by the State of the office of educator.
A Catholic parent, by the very fact that he professes to be a

Catholic, publicly proclaims his conviction of two cardinal truths. He proclaims, firstly, that he feels it to be his conscientious duty to obey the Catholic Church, as the infallible teacher of Christian truth ; and, secondly, that he is bound to form the minds and hearts of his children in all things in accordance with that teaching, upon which he stakes the salvation of his own immortal soul. This twofold declaration is essentially contained in the profession of the Catholic faith ; and in this country, where religious equality prevails by law, each citizen has a perfect right to demand that he shall suffer no penalty by reason of that profession. Now, is it not a gross violation of this right to say to him : We will not allow you to surround your children's education with those safeguards, which we admit you have a right to consider as indispensable for the due discharge of your parental obligations. We will force you to pay taxes to be expended for educational purposes, but we will provide no other means of education for you except such as are repugnant to the religious convictions, in the professing of which the law declares you have a perfect right to the protection of the State. In spite of religious equality, you shall be placed in this dilemma : either sacrifice your conscience by surrendering the child of your love to influences which your religion condemns, or sacrifice the educational advantages which the State provides, and thereby blast his career in this life. Is not this a violation of religious equality, is not this to impose penalties for religious opinions ? And yet into this inconsistency men who profess to be the apostles of religious freedom are betrayed by the theory that education belongs of right to the State.

But although we deny that the State can usurp the office of educating without violating the rights of the parent, yet we admit it to be one of the highest functions of Government to promote the advancement of learning, and to provide for the enlightenment of its citizens. In discharging this duty, however, it must always be content to take the place of assistant, and not aspire to that of principal. Its sole claim to interfere in education is to advance the public good by assisting parents to discharge with greater ease and efficiency the duty imposed upon them of educating their children according to their own conscientious convictions. From this spring several consequences of considerable importance—First: the State has an undoubted right to assure itself that the public money devoted to education shall be properly spent in providing such sound secular instruction as the peculiar circumstances of time, place, and persons seem to point out as necessary. Second : that the State has no powers of compulsion in the matter of education,

unless in default of the parent or of the religious body to which
the child belongs. Third : that the State cannot justly establish
a monopoly in education, either directly by prohibiting the
establishment of schools other than its own, or indirectly, by
bestowing state patronage exclusively on educational establishments created by itself.   Fourth : that in a community consisting of members of various religious bodies it shall observe
rigorous impartiality, by checking proselytism on the one hand,
and on the other by abstaining from undermining all religion
by spreading indifferentism or infidelity.   And this brings me
to the second of the false principles by which our adversaries
defend the mixed system, viz., that religious training may and
ought to be separated from secular instruction.

The object of the mixed system is to afford united literary
and separate religious instruction to children of all persuasions
in the same school, upon the fundamental principle that no attempt shall be made to interfere with the peculiar religious
tenets of any description of Christian pupils.   Whatever might
be the intrinsic merits of such a system, one should have thought
that the peculiar circumstances of Ireland would have at once
pointed out how unsuited it was to the wants of this country.
If the system were designed for the use of a country answering
the description given of the United States of America by a
distinguished Prussian, that it was a land with two thousand
religions, and nobody believing in a God, it would, indeed, still
remain a most pernicious system ; but its founders might point
to this very multiplicity of sects as a plausible apology for their
experiment.   But to establish such a system in Ireland, where
the overwhelming majority of the nation was Catholic and poor,
and where the non-Catholic minority, though extremely scanty
in numbers, was bloated by centuries of ascendency, was a proceeding which, to say the least, cannot be regarded as demanded
by the necessity of the case.   How much money would have
been saved to the country, how much religious discord abated,
how many sore controversies would have been prevented, how
many tens of thousands better educated, if a system of denominational education had been given to Ireland instead of the
mixed system, which, when applied to a Catholic nation, is
necessarily self-contradicting, and which, under any circumstances, must, from the very nature of things, fail in fulfilling
its promises.   I say that the mixed system in a Catholic nation
is self-contradicting, for its fundamental principle is at variance
with its method.   Its fundamental principle is that it shall in
nowise interfere with the peculiar religious tenets of any
description of Christian pupils; and, on the other hand, its
method is to separate religious from secular instruction, thus

canonising the principle of education without religion. Now, the profession of this very principle constitutes a distinct inter- ference with the religious tenets of Catholics. For, surely, it must be allowed that the Sovereign Pontiff and the entire body of bishops of the Catholic Church are authentic interpreters of the religious tenets of Catholics, and in the face of their autho- ritative statements no one can doubt that the exclusion of religion from education is condemned by Catholic teaching. A system which, on the one hand, professes that it will not interfere with the peculiar religious doctrines of Catholics, and, on the other, proceeds essentially on a principle condemned in express terms by the Catholic Church, is, surely, a self-contradicting system. In the famous letter of Lord Stanley, which is the original charter of the National Board, we find the following remarks with reference to the educational shortcomings of the Kildare- street Society : "While they (the Government) do full justice to the liberal views with which that society was originally insti- tuted, they cannot but be sensible that one of its leading prin- ciples was calculated to defeat its avowed objects, as experience has subsequently proved that it has. The determination to en- force in all their schools the reading of the Holy Scriptures without note or comment was undoubtedly taken with the purest motive. . . . . But it seems to have been overlooked that the principles of the Roman Catholic Church (to which, in any system intended for general diffusion throughout Ireland, the bulk of the pupils must necessarily belong), were totally at variance with this principle ; and that the *indiscriminate* reading of the Holy Scriptures, without note or comment, by children, must be peculiarly obnoxious to a Church which denies even to adults the right of unaided private interpretation of the Sacred Volume with respect to articles of religious belief. Shortly after its institution, although the society prospered and extended its operations under the fostering care of the legislature, this vital defect began to be noticed, and the Roman Catholic clergy began to exert themselves, with energy and success, against a system to which they were on principle opposed, and which they feared might lead in its results to proselytism, even although no such object were contemplated by its promoters. When this opposition arose, founded on such grounds, it soon became manifest that the system could not become one of national edu- cation." In its stead arose the mixed system ; and if Lord Stanley's reasons for establishing it are of any weight ; if to be at variance with the principles of the Catholic Church be as he declares, a vital defect which must hinder the success of any educational system in Ireland, I contend that the same reason- ing must hold good against the present National System, so far as it is based on the principle of teaching with the indiscriminate reading of the Bible. On his showing, there is precisely the same necessity at present for reforming the National System in Ireland as there was in 1831 for establishing it; and if the Mr. Stanley of that day was wise in correcting the defects of a system, even although it had prospered and extended its operations under the fostering care of the legislature, can Mr. Gladstone be condemned as indiscreet, if, in the same statesmanlike spirit, he modifies the existing system so as to bring it into harmony with the feeling of the people for whose benefit it has been founded?

Nor is this the only point in which the present system is at variance with Catholic teaching. It is, as every Catholic child knows, a fundamental doctrine of the Catholic Church that the Apostles and their successors, the bishops of the Church, have been divinely commissioned to teach all nations. In virtue of this commission the bishops are bound by an obligation imposed exclusively on their body to teach all divine truth, and, therefore, they are empowered to condemn and banish from the flocks entrusted to their charge whatever, in their pastoral vigilance, they shall judge to be injurious to the purity of the Catholic faith and the sanctity of Catholic morality. Now the National System in Ireland radically and unequivocally refuses to the bishops the exercise of this prerogative; and not only does it refuse it to the bishops, whom Catholics regard as holding it by divine right, but it arrogates it to the Commissioners, who, in the minds of Catholics, have no claim to it at all. Take, for example, one of the most important elements of any educational system, the books which are to form the mind of the nation: " It must be borne in mind," says the Report of the Royal Commissioners (page 38), " that the Commissioners have at all times laid down and acted on their rule of exercising the most complete control over all the books used in the schools; that no books are permitted to be used but those sanctioned by the Board, and that no relaxation has ever been acceded to." Again, the Board took on itself the training of the masters and· mistresses, who were to form the entire Catholic population, on the rules which they had learned in godless model schools under the absolute control of the Board. Again, when the bishops of Ireland felt it to be their duty to remonstrate, from time to time, against arrangements which they believed to be injurious to the spiritual welfare of the Catholic scholars, how were their letters received? Have their wishes and their reasons been attended to? In 1866 the entire Irish hierarchy addressed to the Home Secretary, Sir George Grey, a letter unsurpassed for clearness and for the moderation with which it pointed out cer-

tain necessary changes in the National System. When this
document was referred to the Commissioners, what attention did
they pay to it? They simply declined all discussion on the
points referred to therein, and, on the ground that it was "inexpedient and undesirable," they beg to be relieved from the
necessity of making observations on the memorial of the Roman
Catholic prelates! How different was the conduct of the Board
with regard to Presbyterian remonstrances! Mr. Carlisle, the
resident Commissioner, did not think it inexpedient or undesirable to open negotiations with the Synod of Ulster, nay, he
so far forgot what was due to his position that he, the resident
Commissioner of a Board professing to care for educational
interests to the exclusion of all religious feelings, consented to
act on the Presbyterian Committee, formed to defend, as against
the Board, the special religious interests of that body. And the
result of these scandalous negotiations is pithily described in the
Report, page 54: "The course of these negotiations demands
close attention. In May, 1833, the Government rejected three
propositions offered by the Presbyterians, because they considered them to strike entirely at the principle of the system.
Upon this, the Synod of Ulster appointed a committee of
ministers, including Mr. Carlisle, the resident Commissioner,
and 'they changed the three propositions, without changing
their principle, into four.' The four propositions, though identical in principle with the three propositions which had been
rejected in May, as 'striking entirely at the principle of the
system,' were accepted in August as in perfect accordance with
the general principles on which the new system of education is
founded." Whatever may be the true key to these proceedings,
justly qualified in the report as "inconsistent and contradictory," one conclusion may at least be safely drawn from their
history, viz., the Commissioners who refused even to consider
the temperate remonstrances of the Catholic bishops, did not
hesitate to give a scandalously partial attention to the objections
of the Presbyterians, Surely the bishops had good reason to ask
Mr. Cardwell, in their letter of March, 1860, "In what instance
are our rights practically admitted? Have the heads of the
Catholic Church been consulted about the appointment of Catholic Commissioners and Inspectors who are supposed to be
charged with Catholic interests? Are they, in a word, simply
as bishops, practically admitted by Government or the Board to
do any one thing in the control or administration of the National
System?" Now, I ask you, is it not the grossest contradiction
to say: We demand the confidence of Catholics for the National
System, on the ground that it will never interfere with the
peculiar tenets of the Catholic Church; and yet we profess to

build that system on the practical denial of two from among the fundamental doctrines of the Catholic religion ! We hear much of the intolerant claims of the hierarchy, and of the despotic control over human thought, to secure which is supposed to be the one master passion of what is called Ultramontane Prelates. I ask, did the bishops ever, even where, in the fulness of their sacerdotal power, they held undisputed sway—even among nations who recognised their divine commission and the infallible authority of the Church, in whose name they spoke—did they ever put forward claims to control the moral and the material elements of education as sweeping as those arrogated over a Catholic nation by the National Board of Ireland? What liberty has been spared by these men ? They claim to control the liberty of reading, for they must compile or sanction the books ; the liberty of teaching, for they must be allowed to train the masters ; the father's liberty of choosing a place of education for his child, for they heap disabilities upon religious teachers ; the liberty of religious profession, for they banish all signs of Christianity from the school ; the very liberty of the soul to turn to God, for they make prayer a penal act ! And all this tyranny in the name of liberty ! And all this done by a Board which officially describes its own function to be " to act and not to argue," and which excuses itself from attending to the statement of Catholic grievances because " any attempt at controversy, conducted by them as a body, would demand an impossible identity of opinion."—(Letter of Board to Sir George Grey, 11th April, 1866.) Is it possible to conceive of an exercise of power more high-handed and more despotic than that of a body which thus refuses to listen to the remonstrances of those whom its action chiefly concerns, and which, on its own showing, acts without arguing, because discussion would reveal the discord necessarily prevailing in its own body. After this, it is easy to understand how Mr. Carlyle could have become the head and hand of such a Board ; but the knowledge does not conduce to give more confidence in the system to the Catholics of Ireland !

But besides being self-contradicting, the mixed question of education applied to Catholics must necessarily fail in fulfilling its promise of not interfering with their religious tenets. Survey for a moment the entire domain of human thought, and especially such portions of it as constitute the material of higher education, and tell me if you can find therein a single province upon which you may enter without being driven to cross the boundaries of theology, and thereby violate the principle of religious neutrality which the system so solemnly promises to maintain. Theology, as such, must, of course, be altogether excluded, and this, in itself, constitutes an interference with Catholic doctrines. As well might you pretend than an astronomer, in his study of the planetary system, should take no account of the sun, as that a Catholic, from his study of the sciences, should exclude theology, upon which, in his system, they all absolutely depend. And how can you deal with history without speaking of that One Life towards which, with ever-unfolding purpose, the world's course has progressed from the beginning, and which, for the last two thousand years, has changed the face of the earth. And if you speak of Him, how will you describe Him? Unless you speak of Him adoringly, as true God of true God, you must perforce either merely give Him a place among Oriental masters who have founded religions, or leave open the questions as to what He was, as to what was his work on earth, what the nature of his Church, and what its place in the world? Now these are questions that compel an answer, and cannot be left open; you must be with Him, or you are against Him; you must gather with Him, or you scatter his glory to the winds. I say nothing of the dangers to faith contained in the physical sciences as they are handled in this materialistic age; but, I ask, how can the Christian religion be more effectually combated than by subverting the metaphysical truths which constitute the preamble to faith, and thereby rendering its demonstration impossible? The existence of God, the spirituality and immortality of the soul, the free will of man, the nature of rational certitude, the power and limits of the reason, the principle of causation, all these are questions which it is not possible to avoid, and of each one of them the prevalent philosophy of the day has made a vehicle for the conveyance of error or of doubt such as must slay the faith of the unsuspecting student. This result may not be apparent at once, for the soul is not always conscious of the wounds she receives in this warfare; but at length the day comes when, in some hour of supreme temptation, the young Catholic, trained in this godless philosophy, finds, to his cost, that, like Sampson, he had been robbed of his strength as he slept in fancied security. Nor is the case of primary education any better.

I have frequently heard it answered to those who insisted on the necessity of a religious education, that there was no need of being always at prayer, and that religious exercises were not required for the demonstration of a proposition in Euclid or the working of a sum in algebra. No doubt this is true. But, I would ask in reply, if there be no need of being always at prayer, is there any need of excluding prayer, as if it were an infection, from the school? and if religious exercises minister no direct help towards the solution of geometrical or algebraical problems, what help is derived from the prohibition of such exercises? Has the absence of the Cross, or of the figure of the Mother of God, some sacramental efficacy by which the difficulties of primary education are smoothed down for the young Catholic? Besides, those who employ this argument forget that Catholics do not object to the absence of religion from one or another of the scholastic exercises taken by itself, but to the enforced absence of religion from the continuous series of the acts which go to make up the education of the young. An individual act, when not openly irreligious, will not offend Catholic feeling, merely because it is not decidedly religious; but when there is a question of a series of acts spread over months and years, the absence of religion becomes the denial of religion, especially in the case of the youthful mind, which, like a sheet of virgin paper, so drinks in the first impressions traced upon it, that never again can they be entirely effaced. The impossibility of giving united secular and separate religious instruction without interfering with the faith of Catholic pupils is apparent also from this, that the influence exercised by the teacher over his disciples is morally irresistible. Our adversaries are so well aware of this that their exertions are principally directed to achieve the expulsion of priests and religious from the schools, although their skill in teaching, their entire devotedness to the young, the cheapness of their service, and the affection of the people, naturally designate them as the fittest persons to train the young. "We must protect the young," said M. Pauer, of Meine, chairman of the Committee of Education in the Frankford National Assembly of 1848, "against the influence of the Church, and against any influence whatever of an opinion imposed by the State. Away with the pretensions of the school to direct the child. Let it be allowed to go whither it is led by the breath of life moving within its soul. The clergyman carries about with him in his dress, in his mien, and in his countenance a character of restraint, which proves him to be unfit for the task of guiding the young towards that unrestrained development which is the end of education. A teacher beyond all else must represent feeling emancipated from all control."

It is useless to say that the master is not allowed to give expression to his own religious sentiments, for he cannot avoid doing so as long as the world of thought and the world of action are brought so close in man. In our nature intellect and will are so wed together that the convictions felt by the former are invariably answered by sympathetic feelings in the latter, and in the long run feeling will force its way into expression, all the more violently for having been long pent up and repressed; and if this be true of warm feeling of any kind, how much

11

more true is it of religious or irreligious feeling, which sways
the soul with surpassing vehemence. To say, therefore, that
the teacher will not have any feeling in religious matters, or
that, having them, he will strictly repress all expression of
them, is to claim that the laws of human nature have been suspended in favour of the mixed system of education. One of
the chief glories of the mixed system is that it was to produce
the most cordial feeling between pupils of different religions,
whom it was to bind in perpetual amity *ex opere operato* through
what has been pleasantly called the new sacrament of juxta-
position on the same school benches. It was to have been the
rainbow appearing in the stormy sky of Ireland, blending in
peace the many colours that reflect the religious discord which
divides her sons. Has it done so? Were the Presbyterians of
the North ever more rampantly fanatical than they are now,
when they profess themselves so satisfied with the working of
the system? Is there peace between them and the Catholic
Church in this very matter of education, from which the mixed
system was to banish disunion "for ever and a day?" Its best
admirers cannot say that it has brought peace to Ireland; but
we may all hope that it will not bring to us the sad fruits that
it has brought elsewhere. What these fruits are let us learn
from the bishops of the United States, assembled in their Plenary
Synod of Baltimore, 1866:—"Familiar intercourse with those
of false religion, or of no religion; the daily use of authors
who assail with calumny and sarcasm our holy religion, its
practices, and even its saints: these gradually impair, in the
minds of Catholic children, the vigour and influence of the true
religion. Besides, the morals and examples of their fellow-
scholars are generally so corrupt, and so great their licence in
word and deed, that through continual contact with them the
modesty and piety of our children, even of those who have been
best trained at home, disappear like wax before the fire."
Since then, on the part of the sciences to be taught, on
the part of the teachers themselves, and on the part of the
companionship to which it exposes, the mixed system deals
deadly blows at the faith and morals of Catholics; since
the attempt to enforce such a system upon Ireland is a
gross violation of the rights of parents and of the civil and
religious liberties belonging to all the subjects of the kingdom; since the system is in itself the direct creation of infidelity and the most powerful agent of revolution, are we not
justified in demanding that it be removed from among us? Are
we not justified in declaring that, come what may, we will never
rest satisfied as long as this unjust thing is in our midst? As
long as there shall remain a Catholic bishop or priest in Ireland

so long shall the opposition to this evil system be sustained. As long as Catholic Ireland shall retain the lessons taught to her by centuries of persecution for her faith, so long shall she continue to drive the godless system far from her, in the same spirit in which the high-souled maiden in the poem drove from her the sacrilegious wretch—

> "Whom her soul was hourly taught
> To loathe, as some foul fiend of sin,
> Some minister, whom Hell had sent
> To spread its blast, where'er he went,
> And fling, as o'er our earth he trod,
> His shadow betwixt man and God."

THE CHURCH AND CIVILISATION.

On the 8th day of October, 1670, the Cardinal Prefect of the Sacred Congregation *De Propaganda Fide* submitted for the approbation of the Sovereign Pontiff the choice that had just been made of Francis de Laval as the first Bishop of Quebec. On the 8th day of October, 1877, the Cardinal Prefect of the same Sacred Congregation is acclaimed Protector of a Catholic University in Quebec bearing the honoured name of Laval. How different, however, is the Quebec that engaged the attention of the Cardinal Prefect some two hundred years ago, from the Quebec that holds so large a place in the thoughts of his distinguished successor in office. It is true that the natural features of the place have remained unaltered in their lines of beauty. Then, as to-day, the forests that clothe the mountains were ablaze with the gold and crimson of the autumn; then, as now, the majestic river broadened out to mirror a sky clear and blue as the sky of Italy itself; then, as now, the frowning rock, not yet an historic fortress, uplifted its front in stern contrast with the soft lines of wooded slope and yielding shore with which yonder island divides the rapid stream. All else, however, has undergone a change. Where, then, a handful of noble colonists found a precarious resting-place, now stands a noble city, the capital of a wide and fertile province, teeming with a happy population. Where, then, the savagery of Huron and Algonquin pressed close upon a feeble civilisation struggling to

root itself in the uncongenial soil to which it had been trans-
planted from France, a University now rises, a *Mater Studi-
orum* so magnificent in its completeness that divine and human
learning find in it a home not unworthy of their excellence. At
that time, when the rare ship carried at long intervals news from
Canada to Rome, the record was generally one of privations, and
sufferings, and heroic endurance. At present, the speed and ease
with which science has endowed modern means of communication
are tasked in the effort to chronicle the continual advance of a
people faithful to their God, loyal to their sovereign, and blessed
in the well-ordered freedom of their institutions.

As truly as the abundance of the harvest is contained in the
seed committed to earth in spring, so truly were the present
splendours of your moral and material prosperity involved in
the act which, on this day two hundred and seven years ago,
gave its first bishop to Quebec. For that bishop carried hither
in his consecrated hand the power which alone is able to create
true civilisation, namely, the Faith of the Catholic Church.
Now, I hold that a Catholic university, as being the place
wherein faith and science, spiritual and intellectual culture,
meet in harmony, is at once the outcome and the highest expression of true civilisation. Right fitting is it, therefore, that
as a Cardinal Prefect of the Propaganda first laid the foundations of your social edifice, so a Cardinal Prefect of the Propaganda should now assume the office of protecting what so nobly
crowns the finished work. Right fitting is it, that as it was a
Cardinal Prefect who first gave to Canada a place among the
established churches of Christendom, so also a Cardinal Prefect
should maintain Canada's University in the place of honour
which the supreme authorities in the Church and in the State
have accorded to it among the chartered seats of learning in the
republic of letters. And it is especially fitting that the ceremony which this evening brings the University face to face, so
to speak, with its protector, should be witnessed not only by the
illustrious Archbishop who so worthily fills the throne first filled
by De Laval, but also by the venerable bishops of the province,
as representing the sixty episcopal sees which, during the course
of two centuries, have been formed out of the single see of
Quebec, making this once solitary diocese to become the joyful
mother of children. The same act of Pontifical authority that
gave to the University its distinguished protector, gave to it
likewise these prelates to be its guardians in things pertaining
to faith and morals; and well may the University exult not
only on account of the honour that has thus been bestowed
upon it, but also in the thought of the solid advantages which
that honour brings in its train.

To inspire his hearers with confidence amid the perils of their mortal pilgrimage, St. Bernard bade them consider the lofty attributes of the heavenly spirits whom God has appointed to be their protectors. " Why," he asks, " why should we fear? Our protectors are faithful, they are prudent, they are strong: *Fideles sunt, prudentes sunt, potentes sunt. Quid ergo trepidamus ?*" It would seem to be the lot of Catholic Universities beyond other institutions to have to pass through many tribulations. Of them more than of others, it is true that they must sow in tears what they are to reap in joy. Witness the Catholic Universities of France, which after half a century of struggle, are even now barely allowed to lift up their head in the land of St. Louis. Witness the Catholic University of my native land, which after more than twenty-five years of constant effort and of painful sacrifice has recently seen the cup of hope once again dashed from its lips. And this University of Laval, has it too not experienced its trials? has its path always been strewn with flowers? —have there been no dangers to beset its footsteps ? But the ceremony of this evening speaks to its heart words of encouragement as sweet and tender as the utterances of St. Bernard's gentle voice. Consider, it seems to say, consider what manner of power this is, which God has given to be your protector. Behold, it is faithful, it is prudent, it is strong. Why, then, should you be anxious? Why should you be afraid ?

And truly it is a faithful power. Among the titles given in Holy Writ to our Saviour there is one, the very mention of which in the midst of the world's hollowness falls upon the ear like a strain of heavenly melody. It is the title which describes Him as the Faithful Witness to the truth. As He has given to his Church his Truth, so has He given to it his faithful heart. And as Rome possesses in St. Peter's chair the seat of his truth, so likewise she possesses, through the same, his prerogative of faithfulness. What afflicted Church ever trusted to Rome and was disappointed ? None; but yours least of all. For two hundred years and more your race has borne here the burden and the heat of the day. Many and sore have been your trials, and painful your sufferings: tell me even of one in which you or your fathers found Rome indifferent to your anguish ?

Besides, it is a prudent power. Even in man's best estate, our thoughts are timid and our foresight uncertain : *Cogitationes mortalium timidæ, et incertæ providentiæ eorum* (Sap. 9, 14). But, in the present time, when truths have been diminished among the children of men, it behoves us to walk more circumspectly than ever, for truly the days are evil. Now, the wicked are stronger in their wickedness than before, and the weak more feeble in their weakness. Great and lofty natures are rare, the type of

men's souls has become frivolous and degraded. In too many
instances, alas! the most precious things on earth—the liberty of
the Church and the truths of the faith—are of necessity entrusted
to earthen vessels, and how much prudence is needed to save the
treasure from being spilled in the shock of human passion! We
are told by the Holy Ghost, there is a time for speech and a time
for silence; but in the actual condition of society when the world's
might is arrayed against the Church's right, who will lightly
undertake to decide when it becomes a duty to speak in her defence, and when to be silent? If we speak out of season, may
we not in our imprudence expose the Spouse of Christ to insults,
and her tender face to the blows of those who hate her? Again,
if we keep silent when it becomes us to raise our voice, may we
not in our guilty cowardice palter with the wrong by sacrificing
to some imaginary necessity the liberty without which she cannot
live? Happy you, therefore, who in the harassing perplexities
that swarm around you, possess a most sure guide in the Protector whom God has assigned you! No matter if in your partial
and defective knowledge of the varying phases of the battle that
is going on between truth and error, justice and iniquity, you
are forced at times to hesitate how and when to act. From the
heights whereon your Protector is placed, his larger vision takes
in the entire field, and he will counsel you. He will tell you
where your own lines are weakest, and those of your foe strongest.
He will warn you of the coming attack; he will put you on your
guard against feints; he will check you, if necessary, in the indiscreet vehemence of your onset. And thus in the protecting
power extended to you by Rome, you shall find not alone a helper
in tribulation, but a helper whose prudence is a grace in seasonable aid.

And this faithful and prudent power is also strong. It is
urged against the Catholic Church that the vigour of the scientific
spirit becomes paralysed at her touch. Any connection, we are
told, between her and the physical sciences can be maintained
only by holding the latter in a bondage of misery and shame.
The iron circle of ecclesiastical dogma is too rigid and narrow to
permit of independent research, experiment, or proof; and without these science must needs languish and die. These charges
are false. It would, indeed, be idle, within the walls of a Catholic
University and in this presence, to ransack history for proofs to
show that the Catholic Church has not been hostile to learning
in the past. This topic I will, therefore, abandon to the schoolboys; and, rather, I will invite your attention to an argument
lying somewhat deeper, suggested by some of the characteristics
of modern scientific development.

The masters of modern science may be divided into two schools, perhaps equally brilliant in scientific attainments, but strikingly dissimilar in their method of applying their knowledge. For example, the Newtons and the Secchis are certainly not less distinguished in discovery than the Comtes and the Tyndals, and yet how widely different is the general spirit of their respective teaching. The former as well as the latter devote themselves to the study of the phenomena of the physical world, and seek by patient and skilful research to establish the course of Nature's laws; but at this point their methods diverge. The former do not refuse to take account of the existence of sources of knowledge other than the science which is their own proper pursuit. They are willing to admit that outside the physical order with which they occupy themselves, and independent of it, there exist other orders of metaphysical, moral, and theological truth which cannot be ignored. The latter, on the contrary, practically canonise physical science as the sole criterion of truths and single source of human knowledge, and proceed to fashion, exclusively from its data, a philosophy and a cosmogony of their own. Now, I ask, which of these methods affords the better evidence of a strong scientific spirit? Is not the whole attitude of the latter towards the circle of human knowledge narrow, arrogant, and fanatical, while that of the former is broad, liberal, and catholic?

It is the office of physical science to establish facts, not to construct theories. The fabric of the material universe has, indeed, many and marvellous secrets to unfold concerning itself. In the phenomena it presents, the man of science may surely read the history of the stupendous changes wrought, and to be wrought, in its condition by mighty cosmical forces; but there is one secret concerning which, by the very necessity of the case, these phenomena can furnish no information. They are silent and must forever be silent as to the origin of matter. It is true that, from the consideration of visible creation, the right mind straightway ascends to the Creator; but this is an argument of an order other than the physical, and, as such, it is contemptuously rejected by modern science. And yet, this same modern science insists upon extorting from the physical phenomena around us, and from facts, however rightly they have been established, the one secret these facts can never reveal. They declare the verdict of science to be that matter is eternal. It is a patent fact that the school of science which follows the latter of the methods described above, has sooner or later everywhere ended in materialism. In Germany, in France, in Italy, and in England its leaders have become the prophets and apostles of materialistic doctrines. Now, if we inquire into the cause of this painful and scandalous result, we shall find it to lie in the

principle from which the infidel scientific movement takes its
start; it is the principle which asserts that there exists but a
single order of knowledge, namely, the natural.   It will not
brook the existence of a metaphysical order of knowledge with a
domain of truth peculiarly its own.   It refuses to notice the
spiritual phenomena presented by man's nature in the facts of
human history; it sneers at the soul's yearnings after God, and
its ineradicable faith in a world to come.   And, above all, it rejects the supernatural, nay, it arrogates to itself the honours of
the divinity itself. "In the arid deserts of the desolate Olympus,"
said Terenzio Mamiani, a few years ago, "there now reigns no
god but science."   It is seriously maintained by the later philosophers that science is the last end of man; that the relations it
reveals are the only moral law; that man is to order his life not
to God and a world to come, but to a vague and shadowy happiness to be won for humanity through science.   Like Herod, it
demands that men shall receive its dicta as the voice of God, and
that the objects of man's faith and hope and love shall be cast
down for ever at its bidding; but in the very moment of its
blasphemy it begins, like Herod, to give birth within itself to
the loathsome instruments of its own dissolution.   To deny the
spiritual order is to deny God; and the science that denies God
inevitably develops a dark and drear materialism, which degrades
thought to a mere function of matter, and reduces man to the
level of a brute.   And is this the evidence of the strength of the
scientific spirit which, we are told, comes of the emancipation of
science from religion?   Is it not rather a proof that there is no
security and no strength for science but in the assertion of a
twofold order of truth human and divine; and that the human
science which refuses to walk in due companionship with its
heavenly sister, will soon lose even the earthly comeliness on
which it prides itself, and sink far below the level of human
dignity?

The Catholic Church alone is able to avert this calamity from
science.   In the present day, while the halls of infidel science
are littered with a wreck of incoherent systems, she alone exhibits a theory of knowledge complete in itself, harmonious and
consistent.   In the Vatican Council she lays down that there
exists a twofold order of knowledge, of which the one is by
natural reason, the other by divine faith.   She refuses to believe
that the one can contradict the other, for she knows that both
are from God.   She holds that each has its own sphere and its
own domain, and while she encourages science to establish facts,
which is its proper function, she forbids it to transgress its limits
and invade the province of faith.   But she unmistakably pro-

claims that each of the human sciences in its sphere may make use of its own principles and follow its own method : and this she holds to be among the just liberties of science. She forbids not research however deep ; she puts no limit to the range of experiment ; she refuses to recognise no fact. And lest you should be disconcerted as you pursue your studies by the appearance of a seeming contradiction between so-called scientific discoveries and the teachings of Faith, she explains that this false appearance of contradiction is mainly due either to the dogmas of Faith not having been sufficiently understood and expounded according to the mind of the Church, or to the fact that what is a mere hypothesis or what rests on insufficient proof has been rashly accepted as the truth. These are the principles that create and foster, rather than weaken, the scientific spirit, and these are the principles upon which a Catholic University rests. It is because these principles have been unhappily abandoned in so many of the modern schools of science that the Catholic Church seeks to draw off her children from the dangerous sources that are opened to them in infidel colleges, and to gather them into universities where religion shall have its due part in their education. According to the mind of the Church, science as cultivated in a Catholic University should be as large and wide and deep and thorough as in the most favoured and illustrious seats of learning ; but she can never forget that not by physical science alone does man's soul live, but by every word that cometh from the mouth of God. In placing your studies under the protection of Rome you are therefore securing for them a perpetual source of strength.

Thus cherished, guided, and invigorated by a protecting power at once faithful, prudent, and strong, the Catholic University of Laval shall flourish apace. Under the happy influence of that power, all that is profound in knowledge, all that is graceful in literature, whatever there is of beautiful or of true shall be hers, securely, and without taint of error. And nobler even than the highest culture of their intellects shall be the culture she will impart to the hearts of her children, teaching them to find in the fear of the Lord the beginning of wisdom, and its fulness in Him in whom alone are hidden all the treasures of knowledge.

REPLY TO AN ADDRESS.—SEMINARY OF OUR LADY OF ANGELS, NIAGARA FALLS.

I AM very grateful for the cordial reception you have given me on this occasion, and my gratitude becomes all the greater when I reflect that the rapid stream which courses by your door has been fixed as the limit beyond which I am not at liberty to exercise the exalted office you wish to honour in my person. Your Catholic instincts, however, are too strong to brook that any barrier, even though it be the awful wall of Niagara itself, shall hinder you from expressing your loving devotion to our Holy Father, Pius IX. It is not for me certainly to gainsay your decision. Indeed I think I may be allowed to claim that some portion at least of my office has followed me from the other side of the river. For Pius IX. is the heir not only of St. Peter's supreme power, but also of St. Peter's love for the entire Church; and although he communicates his authority to his delegates only within certain limits and with such reservations as seem fit to his sovereign wisdom, he desires that at least his paternal affection for the faithful shall be represented by them throughout the Church without measure or restriction.

If, then, every representative of Pius IX. may claim to exercise a general though unofficial jurisdiction of love, I surely have sufficient warrant for doing so in a house of education, where young minds are formed to the truth; for the truth, in its fulness, is the heritage of the Apostolic See alone. The more so because this house is a house of clerical education, the purpose of which is to send out year after year into the world young Levites upon whose brows, after patient years of prayer and study, shall have been placed the triple aureola of the priestly power, holiness of life, and learning. But most of all have I a right to do so in this seminary, in the case of which Pius IX., by an unusual favour, has exercised the prized prerogative of father—that of giving a name to the child of his affection. For it was the Pontiff himself who gave to this house its beautiful title of St. Mary of the Angels.

I confess I am not a little impressed by the many memories called forth by the occasion that has brought us together to-day. An Irish bishop from that Clonmacnoise to which Charlemagne sent gifts, and from which he obtained teachers, delegated by the Roman Pontiff to the noble Church of Canada, whose two centuries of existence embrace the lowliness of the Indian mission and the glory like that of the Church of France in its best estate, passes from the territory of the mighty sovereign of England to one of the States of this wonderful Republic, along yon wooded heights that within this century ran with the blood of brave men spilled in fight. And what is he come to do ? He comes for a purpose of peace, and not unworthy of Rome, that he may give to virtue and to learning their due rewards. There is no portion of the field of science which the Catholic Church would withdraw from cultivation by her children. The great Chancellor of England reduced all the objects of knowledge under three heads : God, nature, man. It is one of the characteristic defects of our time that one or other of these three is made the exclusive pursuit of scholars, to the general detriment of learning. The undue preference shown for the physical sciences at the expense of mental and moral philosophy and of theology, but too often ends in a dreary materialism and in the denial of the spiritual and supernatural orders. The Catholic Church has never approved of this unnatural and unscientific sundering between the various parts of man's intellectual kingdom. She bids her children search deeply and fearlessly into the secrets of nature ; she bids them shrink not from any discovery of physical laws, nor dread to acknowledge any fact that has been tested and proved by research. But she bids them at the same time remember that the material creature is but a small portion of the universe, that there is a spiritual and a moral world to which the material is ordered, and that above all worlds there is God, the ever-living source whence Truth proceeds. Hence to-day she has prepared rewards not merely for proficiency in physical, mathematical, and classical science, but also for success in metaphysical and ethical studies, and, above all, for the knowledge of the truth that is in Christ Jesus our Lord. I rejoice that it has fallen to my lot to take part in the distribution of these rewards, and I pray that the Seminary of St. Mary of the Angels may grow daily in prosperity, and that every blessing may attend the students it so successfully trains for their country and for God.

REPLY TO THE ADDRESS OF THE LAITY OF BUFFALO.

I THANK you very sincerely for the warm welcome you have given me this evening. I know I am indebted for the greater portion of the honour you have been pleased to show me to the exalted office which, by the sovereign command of the Holy Father, I exercise in the neighbouring dominion of Canada. You are well aware that I am here this evening, not as one of the crowd of visitors whom the fame of your splendid city every year attracts to the shores of Lake Erie; but your illustrious bishop and you have wished to prove that the man whose privilege it is to represent Pius IX., no matter in what country, can never be a stranger to you, but rather your most honoured guest. I bless God that this deep reverence for the Holy See prevails so strongly in the Catholic youth of this great Republic. The homage it suggests is no common homage. As the gladiators entered the amphitheatre where they were to be butchered to make a Roman holiday, they were wont to salute the cruel Cæsar who bade them die with the exclamation : *Morituri te salutant* Cæsar ! the dying hail thee ! What more fitting tribute to the most deadly tyranny that had ever cursed the earth than this cry coming from the jaws of death ! And what more fitting tribute to the chair of Peter, established by Christ to be the bulwark of the liberty of our consciences, than the acclamation of a generous youth, rich in the promise of life, and bearing in their hearts the hopes of the future of America ! There was a day when the sovereigns of kingdoms claimed to protect the Church, of which they styled themselves the First-born Sons. But never in their proudest estate did they offer to the Spouse of Christ service as chivalrous, as pure, or as powerful as that contained in the love for the Holy See which dwells in the young men of a nation such as this, where Faith is free to ally itself with the highest enlightenment and the noblest aims.

Some part, however, of the honour you have paid me to-night has been suggested by another motive. You have wished to honour in me not only the delegate of Pius IX., but also the Irish Bishop. The diocese that God has given me to govern is styled from its position the Heart of Ireland ; and, believe me, in that great heart all Ireland's children have a place, whether they are here beyond the ocean, or still nestling in the old home. And though Ireland is a loving mother she is also a wise one. She knows that by the disposition of Providence and by nature's

sacred laws the children who have gone out from her have contracted new ties and are bound by new associations in their
adopted country ; and far from being jealous of the new love
they have formed, she gives to it her blessing and her sympathy.
But she is jealous about two things : one, lest you should ever
forget the lessons of faith you learned at her knee ; the other,
lest in your loyalty to America you should altogether cease to
cherish affection for herself. You have honoured me as representing here this evening Pius IX., and Ireland ; allow me, in
turn, to consider myself your representative to them. To Pius
IX. I will speak of your affection to his sacred person, and to
the holy Catholic Church. To Ireland I will speak of your undying love of the green isle which gave your fathers birth.
What nobler office can a Catholic Bishop desire than this, which
constitutes him a link of union between Rome, Ireland, and
America ?

REPLY TO THE ADDRESS OF THE UNIVERSITY OF
LAVAL.

I RECEIVE with great pleasure the address in which the Catholic
University of Laval welcomes to its halls the delegate of the
Apostolic See.

The history of the great ancient universities of Europe shows
that they are indebted for their origin and growth to the fostering care of the Roman Pontiffs. Unhappily, however, many, if
not all of them, have departed from the plan on which they
were first established, and, following the irreligious tendencies
of the age, have abandoned the Christian traditions of the schools
that created European civilisation.

The results of this change have been most injurious to the
interests of learning, of morality, and, consequently, to the best
interests of society at large.

Through it the domain of science has been arbitrarily cur-
tailed. The science of Theology, which treats of God, and the
science of Philosophy, which deals with the intellectual and
ethical sides of man's nature, have been altogether expelled from
the Academy, or at best degraded from their high estate to a
place of inferiority, while the purely material sciences have been
unduly exalted as the sole object worthy of attention. Or, if
metaphysical studies have been, in some instances, retained, they

seem to have been retained for the purpose of sapping the foundations of Christianity by destroying those truths of the natural order which constitute what St. Thomas calls the *Preambles to Faith*, and without which a rational demonstration of the doctrines and facts of Revelation becomes impossible.

From this to the subversion of the moral order there is but a single step. It has been well said that the speculative theories of one generation become the ethics of the second, and the popular practice of the third. Hence it is that the corruption of the universities affects the entire body of society. Hence, too, the pernicious idea now so prevalent that science and faith are antagonistic, and that eminence in the various professions open to educated men is incompatible with sincere devotion to religion.

To remedy this evil it was necessary to return to the old type of the university and to reconstruct places of general study on the large and free plan conceived by the Church. This nineteenth century has beheld with surprise splendid universities start into being at the bidding of the Roman Pontiff wherever liberty of education was permitted to exist. And with still greater surprise it has seen their halls thronged by the generous youth of the rising generation.

It shall ever be ranked among the imperishable glories of Catholic Canada that she has created a Catholic University worthy of the name, in which the fulness of religious truth shall ever be happily united with the unfettered pursuit of knowledge. I cannot refrain from expressing here my admiration of the ecclesiastical corporation of the Seminary of Quebec, which, instead of employing its resources in securing for its members the luxuries of a life of learned ease, such as that which has rendered some of the older universities a byword among scholars, has expended them in erecting, endowing, and equipping, with all its necessary appliances, a seat of learning that would do honour to a king's munificence.

With the blessing of the Sovereign Pontiff, under the guidance and loving care of the illustrious Episcopate of this Province, with the confidence and support of this Catholic population, the University of Laval shall undoubtedly become a source of true blessing to Canada and to the Church of North America. Already many colleges and seminaries have been affiliated to it, to the great benefit of education, and the circle of its affiliates will become larger from year to year. I shall account it an honour and a happiness to be allowed to serve its interests, and I pray that it may abound in every good and perfect gift that cometh down from the Father of Light.

REPLY TO ADDRESS OF WELCOME, BROOKLYN, U. S.

I RECEIVE with much pleasure this address in which you desire, as students of All Hallows College to welcome your former professor, as priests of Irish origin to do honour to the Bishop of an Irish see, and, as devoted Catholics, to reverence the representative of the Sovereign Pontiff in the dominion of Canada. The work of All Hallows in your regard may fittingly be described in the words employed by St. Eucherius in praise of the island sanctuary of Lerins, in which many of the apostolic men of the fifth century, and among them our own St. Patrick, were formed to virtue and to learning : *Quos suscipit filios, efficit patres.* That College received you as its children, and trained you to be spiritual fathers of men's souls. I account myself singularly fortunate in that after having known you in your years of study, after having been permitted to take some share in your ecclesiastical education, I now enjoy an opportunity of witnessing for myself the fruits of your missionary work in this great country. I have often heard it said, by men of experience, that the success with which God blesses a priest's ministry is proportionate to the love with which the priest himself cherishes the *Alma Mater* where, under the influences of the sweet but firm discipline of the Catholic Church, his soul has been prepared for the grace of Holy Orders. I am not surprised, therefore, at seeing that the fruits of your labours in the sacred ministry are, under God's blessing, so large, so varied, and so rich. When I recall to mind the fervour with which, in those early days, you laid deep-set in humility and obedience and prayerful industry the foundation of your ecclesiastical life, I thank the Eternal High Priest that He has been pleased to build thereon so fair a superstructure of priestly virtue and of priestly merits. Like the patriarch of old, in the hour of his unhoped-for meeting with the son of his love, whom God had made great in a foreign land, I feel to-day a double joy. Not only do I look once more upon the face of friends to whom I had said good-bye, as I thought, for ever, but I behold with my own eyes the spiritual increase their zeal has given to the holy Catholic Church. " And he said to his son : I am not deprived of seeing thee ; moreover, God hath shown me thy seed. *Non sum fraudatus aspectu tuo ; insuper ostendit mihi Dominus semen tuum*" (Gen. xlviii. 11).

As bishop of an Irish see, I delight to hear the loving words your lips have uttered in praise of the mother Church of our

beloved native land.   The see of Ardagh and Clonmacnoise is
rich indeed in the splendid inheritance that has come down to it
from the ages.   To it belong the faith and merits of a long line
of sainted bishops, reaching back in unbroken succession to St.
Mel, who received the episcopal unction from the hand of St.
Patrick.   To it belong, too, the sanctity and learning of a second
line of saints, beginning in Clonmacnoise with that St. Kiaran
whom Alcuin styled "the honour of the Irish race."   However
unworthy the present occupant of that venerable see may be, he
feels that the glories of those in whose place he stands are too
brilliant to be obscured by his demerits.   And therefore I think
that without presumption I may thank you for what you have
said in praise of the diocese which God has given me to rule,
and for the loving admiration with which you linger upon the
services rendered by Irish bishops to religion and civilisation.
And allow me to remind you that to you also there comes down
from these olden times an inheritance peculiarly your own.   The
bishops who went out from Ireland to evangelise the nations
which now constitute the Western Christendom in the old world,
did not go forth to their holy task alone.   With them went
bands of venerable priests, of whom St. Bernard says that they
passed across Europe like the following waves of the sea.   I have
read in a Norseman's chronicle, written at the close of the tenth
century, how the son of one of the noblest among the writer's
contemporaries was driven by stress of weather to lands beyond
the western sea, and there, in a district called Greater Ireland,
received the sacrament of baptism at the hands of an Irish
priest.   I will not stay to discuss the historical value of this
document, which would go to show that in the far-off past men
of your race were your predecessors in the work of preaching
the Gospel in this portion of the American continent.   Whether
in the past there existed in this country a Christian Ireland may
—nay, in the nature of things must—be mere matter of conjecture.   But there is no doubt that in our day a Christian Ireland,
among the pastors of which you hold no inconsiderable place,
does exist in North America.   And from what I have seen of
this great nation, in which so many millions of the Irish race
have found a home and a prosperity that have been denied to
them in the land of their birth, I think I may congratulate you
that your lot has been cast in this portion of God's vineyard.
In the American people I reverence the natural and social
virtues that indicate the good, and very good heart, which,
according to Holy Scripture, disposes men to hear God's word
and to keep it, and keeping it, to bring forth fruit in patience.

As delegate of the Holy See in the dominion of Canada, I
thank you for your professions of attachment to St. Peter's Chair.

The welfare alike of individuals and of society depends on religion, and we know that the Holy See is the centre of unity,
and the divinely appointed seal of that fullest ecclesiastical
authority without which religion cannot survive amid the shock
of human passions and the vicissitudes of the world's history.
The dignity and independence of the Holy See are the supreme
religious necessity of the age, for they are the only safeguard of
the liberty of men's consciences.   Without the Papacy religion
becomes either a political engine, a mere human opinion, or a
vague unstable sentiment.   It shall be my pleasing duty to lay
at the feet of Pius IX. this expression of your attachment, and
to assure him that the Catholics of America, sprung as they are
from many and various nations, are thoroughly united in love of
religion and of their country, and that their devotion to the
Holy See, while retaining all the strength of an ancient faith,
is marked in addition by the freshness, energy, and thoroughness
that are characteristic of the American nation.

ADDRESS DELIVERED IN OMAHA.

WHEN brothers meet together in a foreign land the first word
that rises unbidden to their lips is the name of their mother.
And if among them there be one whose privilege it is to have
looked latest of them all upon that mother's face, and to have
been called to devote his life more unreservedly than the rest to
that mother's service, he is sure to be questioned with all the
eagerness of love concerning her welfare and the state in which
he left her.   You and I are here this evening, for the first time,
face to face, and yet we meet as brothers, for we are all children
of the same holy Catholic Church.   And since we are brothers,
I feel that your hearts interrogate mine, asking from me how
fares it with the mother of our souls?   The more so because
you have heard that powerful enemies have arisen against her,
and that violent hands have been laid upon her, and her cries
and lamentations in her distress have reached your ears.   Perplexed by the inroad of so many evils, you fain would cry to
me as the Idumeans cried to the prophet out of Seir: "Watchman, what of the night!   Watchman, what of the night!
Think you that the dark night of persecution that has come
down upon the Catholic Church will last over long.   Can you
12

discern any sign of peace appearing as yet amid the storm ?" To this questioning I would, in words like those employed by the prophet, yet coming from one who speaks with more than a prophet's authority, say, "The morning cometh, also the night" (Isai. xxi. 11). Without doubt, Christendom is passing at present through a crisis dark and drear as the night. "We are dismayed," says Leo XIII., in his noble allocution of 28th March, "we are dismayed by the most sad condition to which has been reduced almost everywhere, not merely the civil society of the world, but also the Catholic Church, and especially this Apostolic See." But though they may be dismayed, Catholics are not to be discouraged at the gloomy prospect before them. Although the night is there, the morning cometh, and already the first gracious harbingers of the dawn may be seen in the brightening sky. Hope is the life of Christian prayer, and our Holy Father bids us join our prayers with his to " that God who is rich in mercy, that He may always assist us by his kindly grace, guide towards good our counsels and acts, render happy the years of his Pontificate, and finally subduing the storms and calming the angry billows, conduct the bark of Peter to its wished-for haven of tranquillity and peace." It is not necessary for me to remind you that the Catholic's confidence in the indestructibility of the Church is not based on any trust in human power however mighty, but on the teachings of faith. On the one hand we have been forewarned that in this world the Church is never to enjoy absolute repose from the persecution of men. " If," says Christ, " they have persecuted Me, they will also persecute you" (John, xv. 20), and " in the world you shall have distress ; but have confidence, I have overcome the world" (John, xvi. 33); and on the other hand we are assured that "the gates of hell shall not prevail against the Church," and that Christ Himself will be with her " all days, even to the consummation of the world." It is sweet and consoling to mark in the course of history the working of this law, which in the Church has wed together weakness and strength in a union so wonderful that, like the apostle, when she is weak then she is most strong. And it is specially sweet and specially consoling in the very crisis of a persecution such as that which now weighs her down, to contemplate the tokens of unexpected strength she exhibits at the moment in which, humanly speaking, her strength would seem to have departed from her. To some of these tokens of this supernatural strength in weakness I would invite your attention this evening. And, first of all, it is impossible not to be struck with the favourable position the Catholic Church holds to-day in the world of modern thought, notwithstanding the attacks to which she has long been exposed, both from religious bodies outside her own pale, and from the schools of scientific unbelief. As far as religious bodies not Catholic are concerned, they may for our present purpose be conveniently distributed into three classes: first, established or national churches; second, churches not established, and retaining some fragments, more or less considerable of Catholic doctrine, while rejecting the rest; and third, churches which consider religion to be a matter of sentiment or emotion rather than of precise or definite doctrine. It was from the side of established or national churches that the Catholic Church, for a long time, incurred the greatest dangers and suffered the greatest evils. In them were embodied the principles of the so-called Reformation of the sixteenth century, which, as it was itself chiefly due to political rather than to religious causes, so had for its fruit political rather than religious results. According to the Catholic conception, the Church was an universal worldwide society, free from the trammels of the State, and in its own sphere independent of all control not strictly ecclesiastical. According to the new doctrines, the Church in each country was the slave of the civil power—"*cujus est regio, illius et religio.*" For many decades of years the national churches established by the State lorded it over the persecuted Catholic Church. But time has at length wrought a remarkable change. The national churches of the day have become, all of them, merely political institutions, without life or influence on the souls of men, while some of them have sunk to the lowest depths of moral and social degradation, like the Russian Church, and others, like the Anglican, have become nests of foulest simony, through which they have lost all dignity and spiritual vigour. We have even begun to see the hand of disestablishment applied by the State to these cumbrous and noxious parasites of its power, and the case of the Protestant Church in Ireland seems to be a type and forerunner of a reaction against established churches, even on the part of the governments whose creatures and slaves they have hitherto been. Not so with the Catholic Church. While her proud rivals are falling, stricken by the poison of State control, her youth is being renewed as of an eagle. In Holland, in England, and in other countries she has restored her ancient hierarchy, while in the virgin fields of the new world she has found millions of children to comfort her for those who had been torn from her in Europe.

Nor is the condition of the non-established churches that have retained some fragments of the old faith better than that of the established Protestant Churches. The age in which we live is an age of critical, solvent scepticism. There is no man outside the Catholic Church whose soul has not been thrown in upon itself and forced to test the grounds of his religious belief by asking himself the awful question, "What reasons have I for my faith in the supernatural? Why do I believe this and reject that doctrine?" This stern investigation must result in one or other of these issues: either he finds that he believes on divine authority, and then he has the seeds of Catholicism sown deep in his heart, or he discovers that his faith rests on historical or æsthetical arguments which have no other than a human value. In the first case, the grace of God, rightly corresponded with and made fruitful by prayer, will lead him to the fulness of Catholic truth, as we have seen the kindly light lead on some of the imperial intellects of our age. In the second case he passes insensibly to the ranks of the infidels. Not so with the Catholic. He knows who it is whom he has believed. Built on the rock of Peter, secure in possession of God's gift of faith, which satisfies at once intellect and heart, he rests secure in the one unvarying teaching of a Church which, while it speaks with authority, carries with it, as if in its hand, the motives of credibility that win for it the homage of the mind. He halts not in his belief, choosing to profess this portion of revelation and to reject that according to his own capricious fancy. He holds fast by the entire body of revealed truth, because God has revealed it in its integrity, and the Church proclaims it without mutilation or change. Nor is he shaken by the teachings of the unbelieving science of the age.

It is distressing to every believing mind to observe how the science of the age, as taught in such universities as are not Catholic, has become absolutely sceptical or materialistic. For one who is not a Catholic it is next to impossible to resist the current of modern infidel thought, because nowhere outside of the Catholic Church is it held that there is any other order of knowledge save that which is purely human in origin as well as in object. Now, whoever starts from the principle that there is no second order of truth divine in its origin and in its object, and under this conviction undertakes to voyage over strange seas of thought alone, must inevitably end in materialism. This is precisely the course of the hostility to revelation that is characteristic of modern science. It is only the Catholic who can unite his faith in God with the fullest and freest study of the natural sciences. For he knows from his Faith that there are two orders of truth, one divine, the other human, and he knows that the God who is the Author of revealed truth is the same who is the Lord of sciences. He can read securely the two books in which our Heavenly Master has written his thoughts, and to Him the pages of the one are but a supplement to the contents of the other. Hence it happens that to-day, by the very force of logic, science sinks into unbelief wherever it has been removed from the influences of Catholic discipline. I think it is plain, therefore, that we Catholics have no reason to be discouraged by the place the Catholic Church holds in the world of modern thought. In the next place, I think that, considered in herself and in her internal life, the Catholic Church has never been stronger at any period of her history than she is to-day. When St. Cyprian would describe in what the Church's vitality consisted, he defined her to be "a people made one with its priest; a flock closely clinging to its shepherd" (Ep. 49). Never before in the entire range of the Church's history has this marvellous unity been more complete, or more splendidly conspicuous than at present. Never before was the laity, united in itself, more thoroughly and heartily one with the general body of the clergy than it is to-day. Never was the general body of the clergy more united with the Episcopate; never was the Episcopate more united with the Pope; and never, so far as the Church's members are concerned, was the authority of the Apostolic See, as centre of unity, more clearly asserted or more loyally sustained than at present. Each separate element of this complex unity is in truth a magnificent exhibition of power. That more than 200,000,000 of believing men, differing in age, in country, in habits, in language, and in interests, should freely continue, century after century, bound together as members of one great corporation, submitting to the same laws, and calling each other brothers, is in itself an historical marvel.

The empire of ancient Rome, because it held together some 120,000,000 of men by the force of stern laws, and strong legions, and by the inducement of incalculably valuable privileges of citizenship, has been ever regarded as perhaps the grandest expression of human power the earth has seen. And yet, after a few centuries, it was ground into the dust beneath the heel of the barbarians, while the Catholic Church, century after century, has but waxed stronger in the ever-increasing number of her united children. The foul spirit of revolution is now abroad in the modern world, setting class against class, and stirring up between labour and capital, between the rich and the poor, between the masses and the civil authority, dissensions which, in their mad outbursts, will shake modern civilisation to its centre, and endanger the very existence of society. No organisation but that of the Church has shown itself possessed of strength sufficient to meet these mighty influences of disunion, and to repel from itself their destructive force. She alone panders not to the passions of the rich or of the poor, she alone condemns unjust acts, whether they be committed by the holders of capital or by labourers' organisations. She alone rebukes the excesses of rulers, and teaches subjects to obey for conscience' sake. She will not allow her children to belong to those secret societies, which usurp to themselves, over their wretched adepts, the dread functions of supreme power; and it is well for the world to-day, and it will be well for the world in the near future, that her hold upon the consciences of two hundred millions of men, instead of being weakened, grows stronger in this period of social crisis. And if the strength of her unity be great, the secret by which she created and by which she maintains it, reveal a strength more glorious still. The secret of the unity of the Catholic masses lies in the frequentation of the holy sacraments of God's Church ; for, as the Apostle says, " They are one body all that partake of one bread " (1 Cor. x. 17). Now, never perhaps, since the early ages of faith, have the sacraments been more generally or more worthily approached by the faithful than at present.

The spiritual reformation inaugurated by the Council of Trent has now reached its almost full development, and if we contrast what we read in the episcopal acts of St. Charles Borromeo with the details of the daily life of the Catholic masses that continually fall under our own notice, we shall find reason to bless God for the change that has taken place ; and when we remember that the frequentation of the sacraments is but another name for the habitual, close, and loving union between the faithful and the spiritual Head of the Church, Jesus Christ Himself, by virtue of which the Christian man clings more tenderly to this Saviour, thinking the thoughts of Christ, loving what Christ loved, hating the evil that Christ hated ; who would not rejoice at the sight of that marvellous strength of the Catholic Church which I have attempted to describe? Who would not salute and bless her as the most powerful agent that lives and works to-day in the midst of a world rotting and perishing in its materialism ?

And as the frequentation of the sacraments binds the Catholic laymen in the closest union among themselves, so the administration of the same sacraments binds the clergy to them, and them in their turn to the clergy. The Catholic naturally, and without effort, complies with the Apostle's exhortation : " Let a man so account of us as the ministers of Christ, and the dispensers of the mysteries of God " (1 Cor. iv. 1). " What is a priest ?" asks Balmez. " What his character and functions ? What is the mission he has to discharge on earth ? The priest is, as it were, a mediator between God and man. It is his to offer to the Almighty sacrifice and incense, to carry before the throne of infinite mercy the prayers of mortals, to appease the

Divine Justice, incessantly provoked by their crimes, and receiving from the hands of the Eternal gifts most necessary and precious, to scatter them upon the world as unfailing treasures of consolation and of hope. Look at him when he is occupied in the discharge of his august functions, surrounded by his flock bowing low in the spirit of humility before the Holy of Holies, clothed in symbolical and mysterious robes, standing before the altar in the glow of lights, enveloped in the sweet and fragrant cloud that rises from his hand towards the throne of the Eternal, he pronounces with faltering accents the universal prayer; he intones the majestic hymn to the God of Sabaoth; he lifts up, with trembling hand, the host of salvation, and presents, for the adoration of the people, the Lamb without stain, whose blood has redeemed the world. Does not this sublime spectacle move to transports your entire soul? Are you not penetrated by a religious feeling that humbles you before the Most High, and, at the same time, is not your heart filled with profound respect for the dignity of his minister?" These are eloquent and noble words, and powerfully depict the lofty conception of the priesthood, which faith and love impress upon the minds of the Catholic masses, and which binds them to their clergymen in bonds of affection altogether unparalleled in any other religious body. Men say that their devotion to the priest is but a bigoted superstition. No! it is the outcome of faith in the great heart of the people, who, after looking on the face of their Christ, are quick enough to recognise in the priesthood the traits they have adored in Him. Men say it is a growth of ignorance. No! it is the enlightened homage which millions of intellects pay willingly to the sacerdotal virtues of humility, chastity, love of learning, zeal for man's salvation, the spirit of labour, union with God. They say that it is the result of fear. No! but it is the outpouring of a love that has been growing in the hearts of the faithful laity for eighteen centuries, fed year after year as the sea by the inflowing rivers, by the service of a priesthood whom gold could not corrupt, nor prosperity alter, nor persecution crush, nor labour tire, nor the fear of death itself sever from the flocks which God had committed to their charge! And, blessed be God, never at any other period of the Church's history has the clergy been more worthy of their people's love than in these days of ours, and never has their people's love and confidence been more unreservedly theirs. It is not too much to say that this wonderful union between the laity and the clergy is one of the most powerful elements of that heaven-given strength which sustains the Catholic Church under the pressure of the persecution which now so furiously assails her.

And as the laity is united in itself and with its immediate pastors, so the pastors in turn are united among themselves and with their bishops. Those who have seen the inner life of the Catholic clergy can bear witness how fully the Psalmist's conception of what is good and pleasing is realised by the spirit and practice of brotherly love that prevails among them : "Behold how good and how pleasant it is for brethren to dwell together in unity" (Ps. cxxxii. 1). And those who witness how faithfully and unreservedly the Catholic priest carries out the promise made by him to his bishop in the solemn hour of his ordination, at once recognises in this union of the two orders of the clergy the fulfilment of the counsel given by St. Ignatius in the first century of Christianity : "Let all follow the bishop, as Christ follows his Father." In one word, the relations between the priests and bishops in the Catholic Church exhibit the latter as the living centre of an authority respected by all, and, as in very deed, "placed by the Holy Ghost to rule the Church of God." So true is this that the efforts that are now being made to shatter the organisation of the Catholic Church in several of the European States, are avowedly based upon this principle : that unless the clergy can be brought to break with the bishops, all the violence of the persecution will spend itself in vain. "We must give to the inferior clergy," wrote an Italian politician on a recent occasion, "such a position of material independence as will secure for them dignity, strength of character, moral independence and liberty in the face of the episcopate and of the Papacy. . . . This would serve to transform the Church, which now belongs to the Pope, into a Church which would belong to the nation." And another politician of the same school wrote a few years ago : "There is no other way to fight the Papacy than by destroying its influence, by emancipating the masses and the inferior clergy from its tyranny."— (*Gazzetta della Capitale*, 12th Aug., 1878). And, touching the same subject, a few months ago another writer, holding similar views, distinctly declared that measures such as these, useful in other countries, are necessary in Italy, which, as he says, is the "centre of the great struggle against Catholic reaction."

But, notwithstanding all the efforts of these men, sustained as they have been for some years by an unbridled press, encouraged by the favours and stimulated by the patronage of successive governments, the Catholic clergy has remained absolutely united with the episcopate, and, through the episcopate, with the Pope. In Italy alone, *out of more than forty thousand parishes, but two were found* in which the clergy proved false to the teachings of the Church, by accepting an uncanonical election. Before this sacerdotal firmness the mighty Kulturkampf itself has failed. And not Catholics alone, but all who profess the Christian religion, have reason to admire the strength of Catholic unity as exhibited in the Catholic priesthood; for the enemy that has been vanquished by it is the sworn foe not only of the Catholic Church, but of all churches professing the Christian religion. This is candidly acknowledged by a recent German writer, Hartmann, in his work on "The Religion of the Future." "The true meaning of this struggle"—he is speaking of the persecution of the Church in Prussia—" is the answer to the following question : " Will mankind, as it is to-day, assign the first place to the next life or to the present life ; to the spiritual or to the temporal ; to eternity or to the things of this world ? Which of these interests must prevail—those of Christianity or those of civilisation ? We shall now be in a position to measure how much of true Christian spirit remains in the Protestant sects by observing what degree of resistance Protestantism will offer to the State, and how far it will consider the interests of Christianity identified with those of Catholicism. Should the Ultramontanes win, their victory will involve victory also for the evangelical orthodox Protestants ; but, on the other hand, the triumph of the State over Catholicism would scatter their pigmy hosts as a puff scatters the dust on an old book." Since then the most terrible persecution that has been unchained for centuries against the Christian religion has been guided by the keen instincts of hatred to deliver its most furious blows against the Church's armour in the place where the two orders of her clergy meet in union; and since, with a firm, constant, unyielding spirit, the priesthood of the Catholic Church remains to-day more than ever steadfast in due and canonical accord with the Episcopate, we have reason surely to bless the Lord God of Sabaoth for the strength He has herein bestowed upon his Church.

It is not necessary that I should dwell here at any length upon the union that binds the members of the Episcopate together, and with the Sovereign Pontiff. All that could be said to describe the most perfect form of ecclesiastical unity is summed up in the mention of the results of the Vatican Council. The union which at the present time prevails between the entire episcopate of the Catholic Church and the Sovereign Pontiff is absolutely without a flaw. There is not a single member of a hierarchy that girdles the whole earth, and counts in its members men, leaders in the world of thought and of action in a hundred different countries, but teaches his flock to-day, as the very word of divine truth, each and every definition issued from the mystic assembly of the Church's latest Council. There is not one of that illustrious throng who does not venerate the

Roman Pontiff as the infallible teacher of Christians, and as the supreme ruler of the entire Christian Church. From a thousand episcopal thrones in the old world and the new, from the Oriental Churches in the mystic East, from the great European centres of modern civilisation, from the bustling and prosperous cities of this American Republic, from the islands of the sea there rises up as one voice the same cry of greeting and of homage to the newly-elected Pontiff. As St. Bernard asked, concerning the Pope of his day, they ask Leo XIII., "Who art thou?" and then they themselves, speaking for their flocks, reply with one accent, "Thou art the Great Priest; the Sovereign Pontiff, the Prince of Bishops, the heir of the apostles; thou art Abel, in primacy; in government, Noe; in patriarchate, Abraham; in order, Melchisedech; in judgment, Samuel; in power, Peter; in unction, Christ" (De Cons. 1, 2). And from the height of his pontifical throne, Leo answers with Gregory and with Pius, "My honour is the solid strength of my brethren. Then am I duly honoured, when to each and every one of you his due honour is not denied" (St. Greg. ep. ad eulog. Alex.) How surpassingly beautiful is this vision of perfect unity in the midst of the world's dissensions and strifes! Surely it is of no earthly forging, the bond that links, in full and perfect accord, so many millions of men with each other and with their respective pastors; that gives one heart and one soul to so many pastors and to their bishops; that unites these bishops to Leo, and Leo to them; and Leo and bishops and priests are faithful to the Sacred Heart of Christ! Can we conceive of a more perfect fulfilment of the prayer of Christ to his Father, that his followers should be one, even as He and his Father are one? Is not the Catholic Church to-day, in the living strength of its internal unity, the one fold and the one Shepherd which our Saviour promised to create?

REPLY DELIVERED AT QUEBEC.

I THANK you very sincerely for having invited me to visit this evening the *Cercle Catholique* of Quebec, and for the cordial welcome with which you have treated me.

I accepted your invitation the more willingly because you assured me in your address that your society does not in any way take an active part in politics. As a delegate of the Holy See, I could not but view with satisfaction an association which proclaims that the purpose of its existence is the intellectual and moral culture of its members, in order that, as you have so well expressed it, they may become "faithful subjects of their sovereign and good Christians before all." I congratulate you on these noble aims of your society, and on the Catholic spirit you have shown by placing under the guidance of your illustrious archbishop the efforts you are making to realise them. As long as those efforts continue to deserve the blessing and patronage of your Ordinary, they cannot fail to be successful. Not by books alone, but by the stronger power of your good example you will ground yourselves and others in that "sincere devotion and unlimited obedience to Holy Church and your pastors," which you justly prize as the distinctive characteristics of all Catholic associations worthy of the name. It is the spirit of the Catholic Church to respect the rights of all men while she most strenuously defends her own; and, guided by her, her children, in their dealings with their fellow-men, ever imitate her example of forbearance and charity towards others, while they themselves cling with unfailing devotion to the truths of which she is the infallible teacher.

I desire also to congratulate you, and through you, the citizens of Quebec and the French-Canadian population of the whole Dominion, on the touching ceremony of the interment of the remains of Mgr. de Laval, at which it was my happiness to assist. No one could fail to be impressed by the majesty of the sacred rite within the walls of your venerable Basilica; no one could witness unmoved the religious pageant in the streets, which, in its grandeur, would have well become a Montmorency in the days when a Montmorency mated with kings; no one could behold with indifference the serried thousands that followed from church to church, from monastery to monastery, the remains of the great bishop whose prescient love, two centuries ago, had bidden these edifices to rise for their and for their children's benefit; no one could listen without a thrill to the eloquent episcopal voice that spoke so nobly the praise of the mighty dead. But I confess that what most of all stirred my inmost soul was the thought that I was standing in the presence of an entire Christian people honouring the ashes of the father of their country! I felt my whole heart beat in sympathy with the great heart of that Canadian race I have learned to love so well; and, Celt as I am, I was proud to be there to join my Celtic kinsmen—kinsmen in faith even more than in blood—in the outpouring of their love and gratitude towards the man who had built up their nation.

It was my lot some twenty years ago to stand by the side of another grave that had just been opened, to give back for a moment to the world's homage the ashes of a great man who had reposed for some centuries in its embrace. The place was on the slope of the Roman Janiculum, from which the eye of the traveller follows the winding Tiber, and passes over the countless domes of the Holy City to where, beyond the solemn Campagna, the blue Latin Hills stand against the sky. The re-opened grave was the grave of Torquato Tasso. The dust before me was all that remained of the earthly tabernacle of the poetic soul that had sung of Jerusalem Delivered, and of the hero whose pious arms had won back from Paynim hordes the sepulchre of Christ. Contrasting in my thoughts the several glories of these two illustrious graves, I said within myself that what the poet had dreamed of, Mgr. de Laval had in great part accomplished. Tasso sang of a new kingdom founded on faith, planned in minds of knightly mould, built up by deeds of knightly valour, whose citizens were to be men of Christian courage and endurance, and gentleness, and truth, and loving kindness. Alas! that fair visions such as these should prove to be visions and nothing more. It is the glory of Mgr. de Laval that here, on the banks of the St. Lawrence, he built up a people fashioned, in a large measure, after so lofty an ideal, a people whose polity is based on Catholic truth; whose courage has been tested by severest trials; whose charity reaches all form of suffering; whose genius, at once refined and strong, has already created a literature of its own; whose aspirations after liberty consist with sincerest loyalty to the constitution that protects them; in a word, a people which, in the various phases of its domestic, civil, and political life, never loses sight of its spiritual destinies, and refuses to be dragged down by the degraded materialistic tendencies of the age.

May God's blessing long preserve such a people! may it grow in every gift of the dew of heaven and of the fulness of the earth! and may its sons, living in harmony with their fellow-citizens of every class, protected in their own rights by the law, and respecting scrupulously the rights of others, advance in moral and material prosperity, and continue to add strength to the Confederation of Canada!

ESSAYS.

ESSAYS.

INTRODUCTION TO "THE ECCLESIASTICAL RECORD."

"CHRISTIAN is my name, Catholic my surname," said one of the early Fathers, when he wished to give an adequate description of his religious belief. In the same way, the name and surname of this publication sufficiently indicate its character and scope. First of all, it is Ecclesiastical, by reason of its subject-matter, of the class which it addresses, and of the sanction under which it appears. Next, it is Irish, because, to the best of its humble ability, it is intended to serve the Catholic Church of our native country. Father Segneri tells us in one of his sermons, that in his day men used to flock to the religious houses in Italy, eagerly asking: "What news from Ireland?" Those were the stormy days of the latter half of the seventeenth century. How often, on such occasions, in the cool cloisters of Roman colleges, where he had spent so much of his blameless life, was the name of Archbishop Plunket pronounced by the old friends to whom his worth was so well known ! How many a listener went straight out from such conferences to pray for his stricken brethren of the suffering Irish Church ! At that time the trials, the wounds, the sorrows, the triumphs, the hopes of Irish Catholics were the subject of many a discourse, the anxious care of many a heart. To-day all this is changed in great part. No foreign preacher now-a-days would allude to his hearers' widespread interest about the Irish Church, as one of the signs of the times. And why ? Not because—due allowance made for changes—our country has become less interesting ; for surely our Catholicity, in the bloom of its second spring, is not less remarkable than it was when torn and beaten to the ground by persecution. And if fraternal love made our distant brethren look sorrowfully over the sea upon our Church when in ruins, surely the same love would teach them not to turn away their eyes from

13

us now that we are once more setting in fair order the stones that had been displaced. Brothers share each other's joys as well as each other's sorrows. The reason of the change is, that Irish Catholic intelligence does not find its way abroad. There is much to be said about the Church in Ireland, there are many anxious to hear it, but there is no messenger to bear the news. It is not, perhaps, too much to say that there is less known abroad about the state of the Irish Church in these days of telegraph and railway than there was when Dr. Plunket had to borrow a name under cover of which to write to the inter-nuncio, and when Irish news was not thought out of place among the *Epistolæ Indicæ et Japonicæ* of the Jesuit Fathers. The *Irish Ecclesiastical Record* will endeavour to meet this want. It will give some account of the necessities, the progress, the efforts of the Irish Church. Facts of ecclesiastical administra-tion, episcopal letters of general interest, various documents that go to make up the history of a Church, shall find their place in its pages. By these means we shall have at hand a ready answer when we are asked what are we doing in Ireland. Other-wise, our silence is likely to be taken as an admission that we have nothing to show worthy of the *Insula Sanctorum et Doctorum.*

Besides, as the world goes on, history is ever repeating itself, but with a difference. In Father Segneri's time the Catholics of Italy asked after the news from Ireland ; now it is our turn to ask, "What news from Rome?" Then the Head was ten-derly solicitous about the suffering members ; now the members are troubled for the perils of the Head. This being the case, it is intolerable that modern journalism, with its lies, clumsy or clever, should be teachers of Pontifical history to the Irish clergy. The sheep should hear the very voice of the Chief Shepherd, and not the distorted echo of that voice. We want no unfriendly medium between us and our Holy Father's words as they run in his Allocutions, Briefs, Decisions, or in the responses of the Sacred Congregations. It will be the privilege of the *Record* to publish from genuine copies those documents, which, if left to hostile or indifferent channels, might otherwise either be cast away as useless or mutilated in the carrying. In addition, we shall give from time to time Roman intelligence of general interest to the clergy.

A distinguished German scholar has lately said that the candlestick of theological science has been moved in our days from its primitive seats, and that upon the German mind has devolved the charge of becoming the principal support and guardian of theological knowledge. We do not share this view. The science of theology being supernatural in its nature, al-

though at a given date it may flourish more in one country than
another, can never become the special property of any. In
Rome, above all, and in Italy generally, in Belgium, in France,
in Spain, in America, as well as in Germany, much is being
done for Theology. The literary and scientific labours of Catholics in all these countries ought to be better known amongst us.
Surrounded by a literature which, non-Catholic at its best, is
fast losing all colour of Christianity, we have need to profit by
all that modern research has anywhere contributed to the Catholic solution of the great questions of which the age has been so
fertile. Nor is Catholic Ireland without her own proper treasures to give in exchange for what she receives from abroad.
Not to speak of the actual labours of Irish divines in Theology
and History, it may be said that few Churches are so rich as
ours in remains of ecclesiastical antiquity of the highest importance. A catena could be formed from the unpublished writings
of Irish Fathers so complete and so full that scarcely a single
dogma of faith or practice of religious life would be left outside
the circle. Fresh researches will every day bring new treasures
to light, and the application of sound critical principles will
teach us to estimate at their true value those already in our possession. These remains have been scattered over many countries,
but pious hands are even now bringing them together once
more. The *Record* will tell how the work of restoration progresses, and give from time to time some of the more valuable
documents to the light.

The *Record* would thus be, in some degree, a link between
the clergy of Ireland and their foreign brethren. It would likewise serve as an organ for direct communication between the
priests of Ireland themselves. We have, no doubt, many excellent Catholic newspapers and periodicals which are of material
service to our holy religion. But it is quite true, nevertheless,
that ecclesiastical subjects cannot well be treated of in publications devoted to general literature. Liturgical decisions, rubri-
cal questions, remarkable cases, points of theology, notices of
books treating of clerical or pastoral duties, Christian archæology,
if they can gain admission to their pages at all, look strangely
out of place in the midst of an indiscriminate gathering of the
changing topics of the day. Besides, the general reader might
complain, were too much space given in such works to the discussion of new phases of Protestantism or infidelity, to accounts
from the Foreign Missions, to the claims of Catholic education;
whilst the clergyman would regret to find his letter or paper on
some ecclesiastical matter cut down to a size altogether out of
keeping with its importance. In one word, the Catholic clerical
body requires a special organ for itself. This want has been

felt in Italy, in France, in Belgium, in Bavaria; and in all these
countries the clergy now have a publication exclusively devoted
to what concerns their sacred calling.   We have abundant
assurance from many quarters that these periodicals are esteemed
as of great advantage to the clergy.   To-day the *Irish Ecclesiastical Record* takes an humble place among them, content to do
even a little in so great a work.   We are confident that it will
receive the sympathy and support of our brother priests of this
country; for the feeling that has called it into existence is a
feeling that lies close to the heart of everyone amongst us,
namely, a true love for the Catholic Church of Ireland.

A RECENT PROTESTANT VIEW OF THE CHURCH OF THE MIDDLE AGES.

THE history of the Church in the Middle Ages has ever forced
upon Protestant minds a difficulty which they have met by many
various methods of solution.   The Middle Age exhibits so much
of precious side by side with so much of base, so much of the
beauty of holiness in the midst of ungodliness, so much of what
all Christians admit as truth with what Protestants call fatal
error, that the character of the whole cannot readily be taken
in at first sight from the Protestant point of view.   Some there
are who dwell so long on the shadows that they close their eyes
to the light, and these declare the mediæval Church to have been
a scene of unmitigated evil.   To their minds the whole theology
of the period is useless, or worse than useless, harmful.   They
connect the Middle Ages with wickedness as thoroughly as the
Manichæans connected matter with the evil principle.
    Others there are who honestly admit that these Ages, especi-
ally their earlier part, are not Protestant, but at the same time
contend that neither are they favourable to Roman doctrine.
These believe that facts abundantly prove that in the bosom of
the Church which was then, the two Churches were to be found,
which afterwards disengaged themselves from one another at
the Reformation.   This is the philosophy of mediæval history
which, as we learn from the preface to his collection of *Sacred
Latin Poetry*,* has recommended itself to Dr. Trench, the present

* *Sacred Latin Poetry*, selected and arranged by R. C. Trench, D.D., Archbishop of Dublin, &c.   Macmillan & Co., London and Cambridge.   1864.

Protestant Archbishop of Dublin. "In Romanism we have the residuum of the Middle-Age Church and theology, the lees, after all, or well-nigh all, the wine was drained away. But in the mediæval Church we have the wine and lees together—the truth and the error, the false observance, and yet, at the same time, the divine truth which should one day be fatal to it—side by side." For such thinkers the sum of all the history of that period amounts to this: a long struggle between two Churches —one a Church of truth, the other a Church of error—a struggle which, however, ended happily in the triumph of the Church of truth by the Reformation, in which the truth was purified from its contact with error.

It is not without its advantages to know what views the occupant of an Irish see so distinguished is led to take of the Church to which seventy-seven out of every hundred Irishmen belong, with all the convictions of their intellects, and all the love of their hearts. It seems to us that his theory is not likely to satisfy any party; it goes too far to please some, and stops short too soon to be agreeable to others. But what strikes us most of all in it is the fatal inconsistency of its parts. Of this the very book to which it serves as preface is proof enough. Dr. Trench's position is this: he tells his Protestant readers that whereas in the mediæval Church there was a good church, and an evil, all the good has found its resting-place in Protestantism, all the evil in tyrannical Rome. Whatever of good, of holy, of pure, has ever been said or done within the Church, Protestants are the rightful inheritors of it all. From the treasury of the Church before the Reformation he proposes to draw, and to collect in this work what his readers may live on and love, and what he is confident will prove wholesome nourishment for their souls. He would set before them the feelings of the Church during these thousand years of her existence, and would summon from afar, from remote ages, "voices in which they may utter and embody the deepest things of their hearts." Such, he assures them, are the voices of the writers whose poems have found a place in his book. Now, if we are to understand that the two ante-Reformation Churches stood out quite distinctly, one from the other, in open antagonism, like Jerusalem and Babylon, each having its own position more or less clearly defined, we should naturally expect to find in Dr. Trench's book the thoughts and words only of the Reformers before the Reformation, of the men, that is, who never bent the knee to Baal, but ever cherished in their hearts the true doctrine of salvation. If his own theory be worth anything, he must have recourse for his present purposes to that one of the two Churches which alone has been perpetuated, victorious after conflict, in Protes-

tantism.   Where else shall he find sympathies that answer to
those of Protestants ?   But he does not do so.   For in the beginning of his preface he tells us that he has not admitted each
and all of the works of the authors whose productions he inserts.
He tells us that he has carefully excluded from his collection
"all hymns which in any way imply the Romish doctrine of
transubstantiation," or, "which involve any creature-worship,
or speak of the Mother of our Lord in any other language than
that which Scripture has sanctioned, and our Church adopted,"
or which "ask of the suffrages of the saints ?"   These certainly
are not the doctrines which have been perpetuated in Protestantism.

His own practice, therefore, is inconsistent with his theory,
if that theory means to assert the existence of two Churches in
the Middle Age, distinctly antagonistic one to the other.

The only escape from this tangle is to reply that Dr. Trench,
although he may find two Churches in the bosom of the Middle
Age Church, does not, however, place between them a separation
so sharp as to suppose the Church of good absolutely without
evil, nor the Church of evil altogether destitute of good.   In
each there is good, and some mixture of evil: error relieved by
a vein of truth.   His favourite authors, by whose labours he
wishes to make his readers profit, are, in this last hypothesis,
men who are subject to the influence of both Churches : men
who belong partly to each in turn, whose doctrines are a pitiable
admixture of truth with falsehood—who, in one word, are
visited both by "airs from heaven and blasts from hell."   At
times they say what all, even Protestants, may treasure up in
their hearts, to live on and love ; at times, again, they are made
to utter what all should reject and condemn, as so many snares
for unwary feet.   We shall say nothing of the difficulty the
mind feels in accepting such a description of the position of
these writers, nor of the task we have to persuade ourselves that
those who teach belief in deadly heresies to be essential to salvation, can be, at the same time, the chosen tabernacles wherein
the pure spirit of real piety can ever take up its abode.   Such
was not the feeling of the ancient Church.   We ask, instead,
who are the men upon whose writings Dr. Trench would sit in
judgment, " to sunder between the holy and profane," to distinguish between the errors and the truth, to decide what we
are " to take warning from and to shun, what to live upon and
love."   With the exception of the two, Alard and Buttmann,
all are men highly honoured by the whole Catholic world, and
all, without exception, are praised for their excelling virtues by
Dr. Trench himself.   Among the twenty-three names we read
with reverence those of St. Ambrose, St. Bonaventure, Venerable

Bede, St. Bernard, St. Peter Damian, Thomas à Kempis, Peter the Venerable, Jacopone, and others of great reputation for sanctity and learning. These are the men whose writings Dr. Trench is to parcel out into two portions; this to be venerated as sacred, that to be condemned as profane. It needs great faith in the censor to accept readily his decision in such a case. What test does he undertake to apply? what criterion is to influence his choice? Why does he cast away the poems which celebrate St. Peter as Prince of the Apostles, and approve of those that extol St. Paul? Why should he style Adam of St. Victor's hymn on the Blessed Virgin an exaggeration, and quote as edifying his *Laus S. Scripturæ?* Why are St. Bonaventure's pieces in honour of Mary visited with censure, and his lines, *In Passione Domini* made the theme of praise? Dr. Trench gives us his reasons very plainly. " If our position mean anything," says he (page x.), " we are bound to believe that to us, having the Word and the Spirit, the power has been given to distinguish things which differ. . . . It is our duty to believe that to us, that to each generation which humbly and earnestly seeks, will be given that enlightening Spirit, by whose aid it shall be enabled to read aright the past realisations of God's divine idea in the wise and historic Church of successive ages, and to distinguish the human imperfections, blemishes, and errors, from the divine truth which they obscured and overlaid, but which they could not destroy, being one day rather to be destroyed by it." That is to say, we, as Protestants, in virtue of our position as such, are able by the light of the Holy Spirit to discern true from false doctrine, the fruits of the good Church from the fruits of the evil Church. This enlightening Spirit will be given to each generation which humbly and earnestly seeks it. But, we ask, what are we to believe concerning the working of the same enlightening Spirit in the hearts of the holy men whose exquisitely devotional writings Dr. Trench sets before us? Were they men of humility and earnestness? If they were not, Dr. Trench's book appears under false colours, and is not a book of edification. And if they were, as they certainly were, who is Dr. Trench that he should take it on himself to condemn those who enjoyed the very same light which he claims for himself? And why should we not the rather believe that as these holy men had, on his own showing, the Spirit of God, Dr. Trench, in condemning their doctrine, does in truth condemn what is the doctrine of the Church of the Holy Spirit.

The theory is therefore as inconsistent as on historical grounds it is false. Such as it is, however, the conclusions we may draw from it are of great importance.

    1. Dr. Trench declares that, both by omitting **and** by

thinning, he has carefully removed from his selection all doctrine implying transubstantiation, the cultus of the Blessed Virgin, the invocation of saints, and the veneration of the cross. Now, as the great bulk of the poems he publishes belong to the Middle Ages, strictly so called, it follows, on Dr. Trench's authority, that these doctrines of the Roman Catholic Church were held long before the Reformation, and that the Church was already in possession when Luther came.

2. Since he tells us (page vi.) that he has counted inadmissible poems which breathe a spirit foreign to that tone of piety which the English Church desires to cherish in her children, it follows that the spirit of piety in the Church of old is not the same as that in the present Church of England. Now in such cases the presumption is against novelty.

3. Dr. Trench (page vii.) reminds his readers that it is unfair to try the theological language of the Middle Ages by the greater strictness and accuracy rendered necessary by the struggle of the Reformation. A man who holds a doctrine *implicitly* and in a confused manner, is likely to use words which he would correct if the doctrine were put before him in accurate form. This is a sound principle, and one constantly employed by Catholic theologians when they have to deal with an objection urged by Protestants from some obscure or equivocal passage of a Father. It is satisfactory to be able for the future to claim for its use the high authority of Dr. Trench.

4. A special assistance of the Holy Spirit is claimed for all those who humbly and earnestly invoke Him. This assistance is to enable those blessed with it to distinguish between error and divine truth. Is this happy privilege to be exercised either independently, without the direction of the ministers of the Church, or is it one of the graces peculiar to the pastoral office? In the former case, every fanatical sectary may judge in matters of religion as securely as if he had the whole world on his side. In the latter case, it would be interesting to know how much does this privilege differ from the infallibility claimed by the Catholic Church.

5. Finally, the contradictions inherent to the whole theory are most clearly to be seen in the following passage about the noble lines which Hildebert, Archbishop of Tours, in the beginning of the twelfth century, places on the lip of the city of Rome :—

" I have not inserted these lines," says Dr. Trench, " in the body of this collection, lest I might seem to claim for them that entire sympathy which I am very far from doing. Yet, believing as we may, and to give any meaning to a large period of Church history, we must, that Papal Rome of the Middle Ages had a work of God to accomplish for the taming of a violent and brutal

world, in the midst of which she often lifted up the only voice which was anywhere heard in behalf of righteousness and truth—all of which we may believe,
with the fullest sense that her dominion was an unrighteous usurpation, however overruled for good to Christendom, which could then take no higher blessing—believing this, we may freely admire these lines, so nobly telling of that
true strength of spiritual power, which may be perfected in the utmost weakness of all other power. It is the city of Rome which speaks :

> " ' Dum simulacra mihi, dum numina vana placerent,
> Militiâ, populo, mœnibus alta fui :
> At simul effigies, arasque superstitiosas
> Dejiciens, uni sum famulata Deo ;
> Cesserunt arces, cecidere palatia divum,
> Servivit populis, degeneravit eques.
> Vix scio quæ fuerim : vix Romæ Roma recordor ;
> Vix sinit occasus vel meminisse mei.
> Gratior hæc jactura mihi successibus illis,
> Major sum pauper divite, stante jacens.
> Plus aquilis vexilla crucis, plus Cæsare Petrus,
> Plus cinctis ducibus vulgus inerme dedit.
> Stans domui terras ; infernum diruta pulso ;
> Corpora stans, animas fracta jacensque rego.
> Tunc miseræ plebi, nunc principibus tenebrarum
> Impero ; tunc urbes, nunc mea regna polus.
> Quod ne Cæsaribus videar debere vel armis,
> Et species rerum meque meosque trahat,
> Armorum vis illa perit, ruit alta Senatûs
> Gloria, procumbunt templa, theatra jacent.
> Rostra vacant, edicta silent, sua præmia desunt
> Emeritis, populo jura, colonus agris.
> Ista jacent, ne forte meus spem ponat in illis
> Civis, et evacuet spemque bonumque crucis.' "

THE IRISH CHURCH ESTABLISHMENT.*

AUTUMN leaves do not fall in Vallombrosa more frequent than
the invectives which, for the last thirty years, have been constantly directed against the Irish Church Establishment. Men
of views the most unlike have contributed their share to this
hostile literature. Lord Normanby and Count Cavour present
very dissimilar types of mind and feeling, and yet both are of
accord in condemning the Establishment in Ireland. Lord
Palmerston and Mr. Disraeli see things from opposite stand-
points, and yet neither of them has praise to bestow upon it.
Every species of composition which could be employed as a
weapon of offence has been made to tell the wrath of men against

* *Is Good News from Ireland True? Remarks on the position and prospects
of the Irish Church Establishment.* By H. S. Cunningham, of the Inner Temple,
Barrister-at-Law. London : Longman, 1864 ; pp. 45.

the monster grievance.   This rich variety of arguments against the Establishment has its advantage and its disadvantage.   It is, no doubt, an advantage that light should be poured in upon every side of a question so important.   But it is a disadvantage to discover the question to have so many sides, that it becomes a task to master them all.   It is not our present purpose to increase the literature of this subject by adding another to the already large list of attacks of which we have spoken above. Our object is rather to set forth the one argument against the Establishment, which, upon an analysis of that literature, is found to underlie all the others.   If we consider the various charges against the Law-Church in Ireland mainly in reference to what they have in common, we discover that they are, generally speaking, modifications of this one objection, viz., that the Irish Establishment is an unjust application of State funds.   No doubt there are other and more solemn reasons to be urged against it.   No Catholic can be indifferent to the presence within it of that poison of error which robs the Church of so many children, and heaven of so many souls.   Judged upon grounds such as these, it is already condemned.   But the struggle is now mainly transferred to a field other than that of religious principles.   We base our objections against the Establishment on this—that it is a political and social injustice.   We cannot expect all to agree with us in believing the Establishment to be a fountain of erroneous doctrine ; but Mr. Cunningham's little work, named at the head of this article, is an excellent proof that right-minded men, of whatever creed, will join us in protesting against it as a political and social wrong.   The proof that the Established Church is an unjust application of State funds may be stated thus :—

The State has some six hundred thousand pounds to administer every year in the religious interests of the population of Ireland.   Of that population seventy-seven per cent. are Catholics, the remainder belonging to various sects of Protestantism.   The State, when it does not persecute, at least completely ignores the religion of the seventy-seven per cent., and gives that enormous sum of the public money of the country to the religion of the remaining fraction of the population.   Can any injustice be more flagrant than this ?

The force of this argument rests on two assertions : one, that the Catholics have an immense numerical majority over the Protestants ; the other, that an enormous sum of public money is squandered upon the Establishment.   If these assertions can be once proved, the argument is simply crushing in its conclusiveness.   Now, the proof of these assertions is easy, and cannot be too often repeated to the Catholics of Ireland.

On the 17th of April, 1861, the resident population of Ireland were taken as follows :—

Members of the Established Church,	11.9	per cent.
Roman Catholics, . . .	77.7	,,
Presbyterians, . . .	9.0	,,
Methodists, ...	0.8	,,
Independents, Baptists, and Quakers,	0.1	,,
All other persuasions, . .	0.3	,,

Thus out of a total population of 5,798,900, there were in round numbers, Catholics, four millions and a half; Protestants of all denominations, rather more than a million and a quarter. In Connaught the Catholics are 94.8 per cent. of the inhabitants ; in Munster, 93 ; in Leinster, 85 ; in Ulster, 50 per cent. The Presbyterians in Ulster are 26.3 per cent. of the whole population. In none of the other provinces do they reach one per cent.

"The Established Church ranges from 38.4 per cent in the county of Fermanagh, its highest level, to 2 per cent. in Clare. In Armagh it numbers 30 per cent.; in the suburbs of Dublin, 35 per cent.; in the counties of Dublin, Wicklow, Antrim, and Londonderry, between 15 and 20 per cent. ; in King's and Queen's counties, Cavan, Carlow, Kildare, Donegal, Monaghan, and the city of Cork, between 10 and 15 ; in the counties of Longford, Louth, Meath, Westmeath, Wexford, Cork, Tipperary (North Riding), Leitrim, and Sligo, and in the cities of Kilkenny, Limerick, and Waterford, members of the Establishment are between 5 and 10 per cent. ; in the counties of Kilkenny, Limerick, the South Riding of Tipperary, Kerry, Roscommon, and the town of Galway, the percentage is between 3 and 5 ; while in the counties of Waterford, Galway, and Mayo it is between 2 and 3, sinking at last to 2 per cent. in Clare.

"The Roman Catholic population has decreased by very nearly two millions, from 6,430,000 to 4,500,000. The dioceses where the loss has been greatest have been those of Tuam, Killaloe, Meath, Elphin, and Cloyne, each of which has lost something more than one-third of its Catholic inhabitants. Achonry has escaped with the loss of one-thirtieth. Waterford of that of one-eleventh, while the two dioceses of Dublin and Connor have the rare distinction of showing a slight increase in numbers. In nine dioceses Roman Catholics are between 95 and 99 per cent. of the total population ; in ten they range between 90 and 95 ; in four, between 85 and 90 ; in one, between 80 and 85 ; in two, between 75 and 80 ; while in three their numbers fall as low as between 26 and 35 per cent.

"Turning to the classification of parishes, we find that there are at present 199 parishes—5 less than in 1834—containing no member of the Established Church ; 575—nearly one-fourth of the entire number—containing more than 1 and less than 20 members; 416 containing more than 20 and less than 50 members ; 349 where there are between 50 and 100 ; and 270 with between 100 and 200 members ; 309 between 200 and 300 ; 141 between 500 and 1,000 ; 106 between 1,000 and 2,000 ; 53 between 2,000 and 5,000 ; 8 parishes only range as high as 5,000 to 10,000, and 2 between 20,000 and 30,000.

"The Roman Catholics have 532 parishes to set against 53 Protestant, in which their numbers range between 2,000 and 5,000 ; 133 parishes with from 5,000 to 10,000 members ; 32 in which the numbers lie between 10,000 to 20,000 ; and 3 ranging from 20,000 to 30,000. Of landed proprietors, 4,000 are

registered as Protestant Episcopalians, 3.500 as Roman Catholics, which seems
to prove that a considerable area of land has now passed into the hands of
Catholic owners, who have accordingly a good right to be heard as to the employment of State funds, with which the soil is primarily chargeable."

In face of these statistics there can be no doubt but that the
first assertion is abundantly proved.

As to the second, all the State aid granted to Catholics is
involved in the grant to Maynooth. The Presbyterians have the
" *Regium Donum*," first given by Charles II., who allowed them
£600 secret service money. William III. made it £1,200 per
annum. In 1752 it amounted to £5,000. To-day it amounts
very nearly to £40,000, and is capable of extension on very
easy terms.

The funds of the Established Church, in round numbers, may
be stated as follows :—

Annual net income of episcopal sees, .	£63,000
Revenues of suppressed sees and benefices, now held and administered by the Ecclesiastical Commissioners, . . .	117,000
Tithe rent-charge, payable to Ecclesiastical persons, ...	400,000
	£580,000

These figures give an inadequate idea of the real riches of
the Church. The *Dublin University Magazine*, quoted by Mr.
Cunningham, says :—

"We have before us a letter from a dignitary, whose statement is, that his
predecessor was twenty years in possession, that he leased severally to one relation after another, as each dropped off, the lands from which came the emoluments of his office ; and, finally, to his son, who for twenty years after his death
is to hold the land for one-sixth of Griffith's valuation, which, as everyone
knows is, as a general rule, twenty-five per cent. under the rental, with a small
renewal fine. So that though this dignitary did not preach in any of his
parishes, for he was a pluralist also, for nearly thirty years, and died leaving a
very large sum of money, he managed to impoverish his successor for the benefit
of his heirs for twenty years after his death. *Qualis artifex perco!* must, we
should imagine, have been the reflection of this successor of the Apostles, as he
lay on his bed of death and reflected complacently on his literal fulfilment of
the Scriptural mandate, to provide 'for them of his own household' no less than
for the interests of 'the Church of God.'"

Besides this pilfering on the part of the prelates, we must
not forget the enormous sums sent into this country to help the
proselytising societies in their work. Let Mr. Cunningham give
us a few examples from which we may gain a fair idea of the
working of the rest :—

"'The Hibernian Bible Society, established for diffusing copies of the Scriptures, of course in a Protestant interest, has, since 1806. spent £80,000 in this way, and has given away more than 3,000,000 copies. The Primitive Wesleyan Methodist Home Missionary Society has for its object 'the propagation of the Gospel in Ireland,' and employs fifty missionary agents and upwards of fifty circuit preachers. The Hibernian Wesleyan Methodist Missionary Society has an income of £137,000, 849 missionaries, 1,000 paid, and 15,000 unpaid agents, of whom 25 missionaries, 54 day-school teachers, and 166 Sunday-school teachers are employed in Ireland. Besides these there are the Irish Evangelical Society, 'for promoting the evangelisation of Ireland, by the agency of ministers, evangelists, town missionaries, schools, &c.; the Parochial Visitors' Society, for enabling the clergy near Dublin to 'have the assistance of fit persons to act under their direction in matters which the spirit and constitution of the United Church of England and Ireland allow its clergy to depute to such agents; the Scripture Readers' Society for Ireland, with sixty-four readers, each with a regular district; the Incorporated Society for promoting English Protestant Schools in Ireland; the Islands and Coast Society, 'for promoting the Scriptural education of the inhabitants of the islands and coast;' the Irish branch of the Evangelical Alliance, under the presidency of the Earl of Roden; the Society for promoting the Education of the poor in Ireland, which has educated at its Model Schools in Kildare-street, 43,000 children, trained 3,000 teachers, and issued a million and a half of cheap school books; the Church Education Society, maintained in distinct antagonism to the National System, and to all appearance a very formidable rival; it has 1,500 schools in connection with it, and 74,000 children on its rolls, of whom, be it observed, no less than 10,000 are Catholics, receiving 'Scriptural instruction' at the hands of Protestant teachers, and consequently the objects of as distinct proselytism as can be well imagined. Then, under the presidency of the Dowager Duchess of Beaufort, there is the Ladies' Hibernian Female School Society, for 'combining a Scriptural education with instruction in plain needlework;' Gardiner's Charity for apprenticing Protestant boys; the Sunday School Society, with 2,700 schools on its books, 21,000 gratuitous teachers, and 228,000 scholars; the Irish Society for promoting the 'Scriptural education of Irish Roman Catholics;' the Ladies' Irish Association, with a similar object; Morgan's Endowed School, 'for forty boys of respectable Protestant parentage;' Mercer's Endowed School, 'for forty girls of respectable Protestant parentage;' the Protestant Society, with 430 orphans; the Charitable Protestant Orphan Union, for 'orphans who, having had only one Protestant parent, are therefore ineligible for the Protestant Orphan Society;' and last, though not least, on the imposing catalogue, the Society for Irish Church Missions to Roman Catholics, and the West Connaught Endowment Fund Society.''

In addition, then, to six hundred thousand pounds of public money, all this enormous income is yearly spent to uphold in Ireland the religion of a fraction of the population! It would take us too far out of our way to follow the author in his investigation of the results obtained by these powerful resources, especially in the west of Ireland. Let it be enough to say that he rejects the current stories about wholesale conversions to Protestantism among the peasants of the west. But we cannot pass over the following remarks made by Mr. Cunningham on the handbill method of controversy adopted by the proselytisers :—

"After politely requesting the reader not to 'be offended on receiving this,' the handbill goes on to state that the invocations of the Madonna and saints are 'pronounced by the Bible to be the awful sin of idolatry, and that all

idolators have their place in the lake that burneth with fire and brimstone. Do
not be hurt,' continues this agreeable mentor, 'at this strong statement, but
think! is it true?' Do not be hurt! And this, after a summary statement that
the religion of three-fourths of the Christian world, the creed of whole generations of the best, purest, and most devoted of mankind, the hope and joy in
life and death of millions of humble and faithful saints, is pronounced by the
Bible to be punishable with the everlasting torments of hell fire! Verily, if
this be the 'spirit and manner' of these 'true Christian pastors,' the less we
hear of this new Reformation the better!"

The charge of being a political and social injustice, which we
have brought against the Establishment, is fully proved by what
has hitherto been said. Even if there were no other arguments
on which to rest our case, save the single one which we have
developed above, it must be admitted that we have made good
our accusation. "I hold," said Lord Palmerston, in 1845, "that
the revenues of the Church of Ireland were destined primarily
for the religious instruction of the people of Ireland. . . . It
is impossible, in my opinion, that the present state of things in
Ireland, in regard to the establishment of the two sects, can be
permanent." But there is more. Evil is ever the parent of
evil; and in one comprehensive injustice like the Irish Establishment are involved a thousand minor wrongs. The effects of
these wrongs in Ireland, and the mischief wrought by them on
our people, we daily see with our own eyes, and hear with our
own ears. But to Mr. Cunningham we are indebted for a
striking and rather novel view of the Establishment, as a source
of mischief to England also. The very guilt she has incurred
by the perpetration of so great an injustice is, in Mr. Cunningham's opinion, the greatest of misfortunes. "To do wrong is a
far greater misfortune than to endure it. No man enjoys a
wrongful privilege, tramples on his fellow-citizens, or violates
fair play without forthwith incurring a moral loss, compared
with which, any external advantage is a bauble indeed." Noble
words these: and most refreshingly do they fall upon Catholic
ears, wearied with the noisy utilitarian philosophy of the day.
Nor does the Establishment confer any external or material
advantage on England. On the contrary, it is preparing for
her some grievous and humiliating calamity. Who sows the
wind must expect to reap the whirlwind; and no other harvest
but calamity can possibly be gathered from the evil seed of disaffection on one side, and of tyranny on the other, which the
Establishment has sown in Ireland. Mr. Cunningham thus describes how the chronic disaffection of Irishmen is produced:—

"The church funds of Ireland belong, without the possibility of a cavil, to
the Irish nation; that nation has, from one reason or another, persistently refused to follow us in deserting the general creed of Christendom. They have
clung and still cling to their faith with that desperate tenacity which persecu-

tion best engenders. . . . But the gradual abandonment of the atrocious penal code—as one by one its provisions became revolting to the increased humanity of the age—was a virtual confession that we gave up all hope of driving the Irish Catholics within the pale of our Church. . . . Angry at resistance, the English Government, co-operating with English fanaticism, set itself delibe- rately to persecute, degrade, almost destroy those whom it could not succeed in converting. All has been tried, and the Establishment remains, as of old, the privilege of a powerful minority, the badge of conquest upon a prostrate race, a perpetual source of irritation, and nothing more. So far from being Protestantised, the Irish are already the hottest Ultramontanes in Europe, and are assuming more and more the triumphant air to which their numerical ascen- dancy entitles them. There is not the ghost of a chance of Ireland becoming other than she is, or of the Establishment making such strides as might render her present position less transparently absurd. The one question is this, whether we choose to perpetuate a state of things condemned by all statesmen as vicious in principle, and proved by long experience to be productive of no- thing but a tyrannising temper on the one hand, and chronic disaffection on the other. Every Irish peasant has sense enough to appreciate the injustice of the arrangement which obliges him to build his chapel, pay the priest, and gives his landlord a church and parson for nothing. He may be excused, too, for a feeling of annoyance, as he trudges past the empty parish church, supported at the public expense, to some remote chapel crowded with peasants, out of whose abject poverty the necessary funds for its support have to be wrung. He may be excused if his notions of fair play, equal rights, and political loyalty, are somewhat indistinct, and that where the law is from the outset a manifest wrong-doer, it should be sometimes superseded by rougher and more effective expedients. He is naturally a rebel, because the State proclaims herself his enemy. He naturally thinks it monstrous that any proprietor of the soil should have it in his power to refuse the inhabitants a spot of ground on which to cele- brate their religious rites; that men, women, and children should be obliged to walk five, six, and even ten miles to the nearest place of worship; that edu- cation should be constantly refused, except coupled with open and systematic proselytism; that terrorism and coercion, the mean contrivances of bigotry, should be suffered to do their worst, without the strong hand of Government intervening to lighten the blow, or provide means of protection" (pp. 28, 29).

All this is well said: nor is the author less happy in his description of the tyrannising temper which it fosters on the part of the Protestants.

"And if the Establishment works ill as regards the Catholic masses, its effects on the privileged minority seem to us scarcely less disastrous. It en- genders a tone of arrogant, violent, uncharitable bigotry, which happily is un- known in this country beyond the precincts of Exeter Hall and the columns of the 'religious' newspapers. Indeed, we have only to turn to *Good News from Ireland* to assure ourselves of the detestable temper in which these modern Reformers set about the process of evangelisation, and of the extraordinary hardihood of assertion by which their ministrations are characterised. The creed of an Irish peasant may be superstitious—where is the peasant whose creed is anything else?—but religion in Ireland has at any rate, in the true spirit of Christianity, found its way to the wretched, the degraded, the despair- ing: it has refined, comforted, ennobled those whom external circumstances seemed expressly designed to crush into absolute brutality. The Irish peasant is never the mere animal that for centuries English legislators tried to make him. He is a troublesome subject, indeed, and has a code of his own as to the 'wild justice' to which the oppressed may, in the last instance, resort; but in the domestic virtues, chastity, kindliness, hospitality, he stands, at least, as well as English or Scotch of the same condition in life. As regards domestic purity, indeed, Ireland, by universal confession, rises as much above the ordi-

nary standard as Scotland falls below it : and, as regards intemperance, there
has been in Ireland of late years a marked improvement, for which, unhappily,
no counterpart is to be found in any other part of the United Kingdom. Yet
we are gravely invited to believe, on the testimony of a few hot-brained fana-
tics, that the whole Catholic system in Ireland is one vast conspiracy against
piety, happiness, and civilisation. . . .

"That Protestants are perfectly well aware of the mortification entailed upon
their Catholic fellow-subjects by the existing state of things, and regard it with
complacent acquiescence, is not the least painful feature of the case. The Irish
Church is bad, not only in itself, but as being the last of a long series of oppres-
sions which fear, passion, or necessity have at various times led the English to
inflict upon their feeble neighbour. There have been periods when the deliberate idea of even intelligent politicians was, that the one population should
exterminate the other ; and Burke has pointed out how the religious animosi-
ties, which seem now the great cause of dispute, are in reality only a new phase
of far earlier hostility, grounded originally on conquest, and strengthened by
the cruelties which conquest involved. It is to some such fierce mood, tradi-
tionally familiar to the ruling race, that an institution so unjust in principle,
so troublesome in practice, so incurably barren of all useful result, can appeal
for sanction and support. The blind and almost ferocious bigotry of Irish
Presbyterians is owing, one would fain hope, less to personal temperament than
to the tastes and convictions of a ruder age, embodied in evil customs and a
conventionally violent phraseology. And the same is more or less true of
their Episcopalian brethren. It is from the calmer feelings and more discrimi-
nating judgment of the English nation that any remedial measure is expected "
(pp. 33-37).

We have nothing to add to this. Every Catholic will recognise the truth of the picture thus ably drawn. Our obligations
to Mr. Cunningham do not, however, end here. There is still
another lesson which, although he does not mean to teach it, we
are glad to learn from him. It is this. Speaking of the paid
clergy of the Establishment, he says :—

"So far from assisting the Government in its schemes, they are often among
its bitterest opponents. Dr. Cullen himself is hardly more hostile to the National Education System than these paid officials of the State, for whom the
one possible excuse would be an unflinching support of State measures. The
Church Education Society numbers something like two-thirds of the Established clergy among its adherents, and is one of the most serious difficulties
with which at present the cause of National Education has to contend. What
shall be done with these spaniels that forget to cringe, but bark and snap at the
hand that feeds them? Might they not, at any rate, be scourged and starved
into a more submissive mood ?" (p. 43.)

These words reveal to us the position which men of the world
would expect a clergy paid by the State to assume towards the
State. From being ministers of God, they are to become paid
officials of the State; from being the stewards of things divine,
they are to recommend themselves to their masters by an unflinching support of the State measures. And if conscience
should at any time call upon them to refuse the support demanded at their hands, the Government has the power and the
will to scourge and starve them into a more submissive mood.
What a practical commentary does Mr. Cunningham here offer

on the words used by Mgr. Brancadoro,* in declining the pension
offered by the British Government in 1805 ! Better, far better,
poverty with the liberty of the sanctuary, than rich endowments
with slavery. We demand the abolition of the Establishment
on the broad grounds of social equality and justice, and not
because we wish to enrich ourselves with its spoils. We are
rich enough in the love of that noble Irish race, than which
none other ever gave more blessed consolation to the ministers
of Christ.

CARDINAL CONSALVI AND NAPOLEON BONAPARTE.

The concordat signed at Paris on the 15th July, 1801, between
Pius VII. and Napoleon, is one of the most important facts of
modern history. The magnitude of its results may best be
learned from the contrast between the present state of religion
in France and that which existed during, and for long after, the
Revolution. " There is no negotiation," says M. Thiers, "which
is more deserving of serious meditation than that of the Concordat ;" but up to the present day the materials for such a study
have been wanting. At length the full light of history has
been let in upon the secret conferences in which the articles of
that treaty were prepared ; and the hand which has traced for
us their history is the same which signed the Concordat itself.
The memoirs of Cardinal Consalvi, who took part in the negotiations as the plenipotentiary of the Roman Pontiff, penned by
him during the days of his exile, have at length been given to
the world.† Since the Cardinal's death, in 1824, these memoirs
have been religiously left in the obscurity to which their author
condemned them, and which he willed should last as long as the
life of the principal personages of whom he has made mention
in his pages. But when at length, in 1858, there appeared no
reason for further silence, they were handed over by Consalvi's
executors to M. Cretineau-Joly, who has published, not the
original text, but what he assures us is a faithful version of

* *Irish Ecclesiastical Record*, No. II., pp. 50-55.
† *Mémoires du Cardinal Consalvi, secrétaire d'Etat du Papa Pio VII., avec
un introduction et des notes, par J. Crétineau-Joly.* Paris : Henri Plon, Rue
Garencière, 8, 1864. 2 vols., 8vo, pp. 454-488.

14

it. We propose to give our readers a sketch of the history of the Concordat as it is recorded in these memoirs, and, in doing so, we shall make use as often as we can of the Cardinal's own words.

The victory of Marengo, gained June 14, 1800, made the First Consul master of Italy. Five days after the battle, passing through Vercelli at the head of his army, he charged Cardinal Martiniana, bishop of that city, to communicate to the Pope his desire of negotiating a settlement of the religious affairs of France, and for this purpose he requested that Mgr. Spina, archbishop of Corinth, might be sent to him to Turin. His request was gladly complied with. But scarcely had that prelate entered Turin than he was ordered to set out at once for Paris, where Napoleon awaited his arrival. It needed but a short stay in that capital to convince Mgr. Spina that the projects of concordat proposed by the consul were absolutely inadmissible, as being founded on a basis completely at variance with the laws of the Church. In vain did the Pope, in his anxiety to promote the good of religion, forward to Paris an amended plan of concordat, in which he made every concession permitted by his duty as head of the Church. The only answer he received was an intimation from M. Cacault, the French agent at Rome, that unless within five days the proposals made by Napoleon were accepted without the slightest change, the least restriction or correction, he, Cacault, should declare a rupture between the Holy See and France, and immediately leave Rome to join General Murat at Florence. To all these threats, and to the menace of the loss of his temporal power, the Pope had but one reply, that same reply which we have heard from Pius IX. in our own day—that *non possumus* against which all the assaults of the masters of legions have ever failed, and evermore shall fail.

M. Cacault, not daring to disobey the orders he had received, prepared at once for his departure; but his excellent heart and his affection for Rome suggested to him a means of preventing the mischief that was sure to follow from the anger of Napoleon if once kindled against the Holy See. He proposed that Cardinal Consalvi, the Pope's secretary of state, should at once set out for Paris, to lay before the First Consul the imperious reasons by which the Holy Father was forced to refuse the proffered concordat. The French agent felt confident that, whilst it would flatter Napoleon's pride to be able to exhibit to the Parisians a Cardinal prime minister in waiting upon his will, the presence of Consalvi would also be a proof of the Pope's anxious desire to come to a favourable understanding on the affairs of the French Church. After mature deliberation this

plan was adopted. The Cardinal took care that to the creden-
tials usually given in cases of treaties, the Pope should add a
most precise command that his envoy was to consider the project
of concordat which had been corrected at Rome, and hitherto
rejected at Paris, not only as the basis of the future treaty, but
as the concordat itself. Powers were granted, however, to make
such changes as did not alter the substance of the document.
" I thought it necessary," says the Cardinal, " to have my hands
tied in this way, because I foresaw that, unless I were in a position to show the French Government how limited were my powers,
they would soon force my entrenchments."

Leaving Rome in company with M. Cacault, Cardinal Consalvi arrived at Paris at night, after a tedious journey of fifteen
days, and took up his abode with Mgr. Spina and his theologian,
P. Caselli, afterwards cardinal. Early in the morning he sent
to acquaint Bonaparte of his arrival, and to learn at what hour
he could have the honour of seeing the First Consul. He in-
quired also in what costume he should present himself, as at that
period the ecclesiastical dress had been abandoned by the French
clergy. These communications were made through the Abbé
Bernier, who, from having been one of the leaders in the war of
La Vendée against the Republic, had taken a great part in the
pacification of these provinces upon the terms offered by the
consular government, and had thereby secured for himself the
favour of Bonaparte. He was appointed negotiator on the part
of the Government, and brought to his task much theological
knowledge, diplomatic skill, and the advantage of being agreeable to both the contracting parties. This ecclesiastic soon
returned to Consalvi with the intimation that the First Consul
would receive him that same morning at two o'clock, and that
he was to come in the fullest possible cardinalitial costume. The
Cardinal, however, did not gratify him in this latter particular,
believing it to be his duty to present himself in the dress usually
worn out of doors by cardinals when not in function. He was
introduced to Napoleon under circumstances well calculated to
embarrass a less evenly poised mind than his own. " I know,"
said the First Consul, "why you have come to France. I wish
the conferences to be opened without delay. I allow you five
days' time, and I warn you that if on the fifth day the negotiations are not concluded, you must go back to Rome, as I have
already decided what to do in such a case." Consalvi replied
with calm dignity, and was soon afterwards conducted to his
hotel. On the same day the Abbé Bernier came again to Consalvi, and asked him for a memorial setting forth the reasons
which had constrained the Pope to reject the project which had
been presented at Rome by M. Cacault. Although wearied by

his long journey, the Cardinal spent the watches of the night in drawing up the memorial, which, on the following day, was communicated by the Abbé Bernier to Talleyrand, who, in turn, was to report upon it and lay it before the First Consul. The design of the memorial was to justify the refusal of the Concordat in the terms in which it had been drawn up by the French Government, and to show how reasonable and just were the modifications insisted on by the Pope. This design was not attained. Talleyrand wrote on the margin of the first page of the memorial these words, well calculated to confirm Napoleon in his idea that the Pope's minister was actuated by personal enmity towards the French Government: " Cardinal Consalvi's memorial does more to throw back the negotiations than all that has hitherto been written on the subject." These words, although they produced an unfavourable impression on the First Consul, did not, however, retard the negotiations. The fatigue of these negotiations was very great. Twice each day for many days beyond the five granted by Bonaparte, the Cardinal held conferences with the Abbé Bernier, always in the presence of Mgr. Spina and P. Caselli. The nights were frequently spent in drawing up and correcting memorials to be presented to the Government. It was at this period in the negotiations that the limit which the Pope had placed to the Cardinal's powers was found to be of the greatest practical advantage. The Abbé Bernier, when any difficulty occurred, incessantly declared that, however strong his own convictions, he could decide nothing of himself without referring the matter to the First Consul. On the contrary, the Cardinal was never allowed to despatch a courier to consult the Pope and receive his commands. The pretext for this prohibition was, that the Concordat should absolutely be finished the next day. Under these circumstances, his limited powers were the only means left to Consalvi by which he might resist the pressure brought to bear against him. The orders he had received from the Pope were, not to break off the negotiations and refuse the Concordat because he could not make it as favourable as might be; but, on the other hand, not to sign it by overstepping those instructions given him before he left Rome, of which we have spoken above. For twenty-five days the conferences continued. Every nerve was strained to avert a rupture on the one hand, and undue concessions on the other. The consequences of a rupture were frequently laid before the Cardinal during these days, which he calls "days of anguish," by the Count de Cobenzel, Austrian ambassador at Paris. He was asked to consider that if the First Consul should break with Rome, and definitely separate from the head of the Catholic Church, he would, as he had often threatened, force Germany, Spain, Italy, Switzerland, and Holland, to become the accomplices of his apostasy.

Finally, after incredible fatigue, after sufferings and anguish of every kind, the day came which brought with it the long-looked-for conclusion of their task. The Abbé Bernier, who reported every evening to Bonaparte the results of the daily conferences, at length announced that the First Consul accepted all the disputed articles, and that on the following day they should proceed to sign two authentic copies of the treaty, one copy to remain in the hands of each of the contracting parties. The project thus accepted was substantially the same as the one which, having been amended at Rome, had been rejected by the French Government before the Cardinal's journey, and which had led to M. Cacault's withdrawal from Rome within five days. It was arranged that the signatures should be six, three on each side. The Cardinal, Mgr. Spina, and P. Caselli, were to sign on behalf of the Holy See; Joseph Bonaparte, brother of the First Consul, Cretet, Councillor of State, and the Abbé Bernier, on behalf of the French Government. It was further arranged that the Abbé Bernier should call for the three ecclesiastics at a little before four o'clock on the following day, 14th July, and conduct them to the residence of Joseph Bonaparte, where the solemn act was to be completed.

"There," said Bernier, "we shall be able to do all in a quarter of an hour, as we have only to write six names, and this, including the congratulations, will not take even so long." He also showed them the *Moniteur* of the day, in which the Government officially announced the conclusion of the negotiations. He added that on the next day, anniversary of the taking of the Bastile, the First Consul intended to proclaim, at a grand dinner of more than three hundred guests, that the Concordat was signed, and a treaty concluded between the Holy See and the Government of far more importance than even the Concordat between Francis I. and Leo X.

Shortly before four o'clock the next day the Abbé Bernier made his appearance, having in his hand a roll of paper, which he said was the copy of the Concordat to be signed. On their arrival at Joseph Bonaparte's, they took their places at a table, and after a short discussion as to who should be the first to sign, Joseph yielded that honour to the claims of the Cardinal. He took the pen in his hand, and then followed a scene which must be described in his own words: "What was my surprise when I saw the Abbé Bernier place before me the copy which he took from his roll, as if to make me sign without reading it, and when on running my eye over it, I found that it was not the treaty which had been agreed on by the respective commissioners and

accepted by the First Consul himself, but one altogether different! The difference I perceived in the first lines led me to
examine the rest with the most scrupulous care, and I satisfied
myself that this copy not only contained the project which the
Pope had refused to accept, but that it moreover included certain
points which had been rejected as inadmissible before the project
had been forwarded to Rome at all. This occurrence, incredible,
but true, paralysed my hand when about to sign my name. I
gave expression to my surprise, and declared in plain language
that on no account could I accept such a document. The First
Consul's brother appeared equally astonished at hearing me
speak so. He said that he did not know what to think of what
he saw. He added that he had heard from the First Consul
himself that everything had been arranged, and that there was
nothing for him to do but affix his signature. As the other
official, the state councillor, Cretet, made the same declaration,
protesting his total ignorance, and refusing to believe my statement about the change of documents, until I had proved it by
confronting the two copies, I could not restrain myself from
turning rather sharply towards the Abbé Bernier. I told him
that no one could confirm the truth of my assertion better than
he could; that I was exceedingly astonished at the studied silence
which I observed him to keep in the matter; and that I expressly
called upon him to communicate to us what he had such good
reason to know.

"With a confused air, and in an embarrassed tone, he stuttered
out that he could not deny the truth of my words and the difference between the copies of the Concordat, but that the First
Consul had given orders to that effect, affirming that changes
were allowable so long as the document was not signed. 'And
so,' added Bernier, 'he insists on these changes, because upon
mature deliberation he is not satisfied with the stipulations we
have agreed upon.'

"I will not here relate what I said in answer to a discourse
so strange. . . . I spoke warmly of this attempt to succeed by
surprise; I resolutely protested that I would never accept such
an act, expressly contrary to the Pope's will. I therefore declared that if, on their part, they either could not or would not
sign the document we had agreed upon, the sitting must come
to an end."

Joseph Bonaparte then spoke. He depicted the fatal consequences which would result to religion and to the State from
breaking off the negotiations; he exhorted them to use every
means in their power to come to some understanding between
themselves on that very day, seeing that the conclusion of the
treaty had been announced in the newspapers, and that the news

of its having been signed was to be proclaimed at to-morrow's
grand banquet. It was easy, added he, to imagine the indignation and fury of one so headstrong as his brother, when he
should have to appear before the public as having published in
his own journals false news on a matter of such importance.
But no arguments could persuade the Cardinal to negotiate on
the basis of the substituted project of Concordat. He consented,
however, to discuss once more the articles of the treaty on which
they had agreed before. The discussion commenced about five
o'clock in the evening. " To understand how serious it was,
how exact, what warm debates it gave rise to on both sides, how
laborious, how painful, it will be enough to say that it lasted,
without any interruption or repose, for nineteen consecutive
hours, that is to say, to noon on the following day. We spent
the entire night at it, without dismissing our servants or carriages, like men who hope every hour to finish the business on
which they are engaged. At mid-day we had come to an understanding on all the articles, with one single exception." This
one article, of which we shall speak later, appeared to the Cardinal to be a substantial question, and to involve a principle
which, as has often been the case, the Holy See might tolerate
as a fact, but which it could never sanction (*canonizzare*) as an
express article of a treaty. The hour when Joseph Bonaparte
must leave to appear before the First Consul was at hand, and
" it would be impossible," says the Cardinal, " to enumerate the
assaults made on me at that moment to induce me to yield on
this point, that he might not have to carry to his brother the
fatal news of a rupture." But nothing could shake the resolution of the Papal minister or lead him to act contrary to his
most sacred duties. He yielded so far, however, as to propose
that they should omit the disputed article, and draw out a copy
of the Concordat in which it should not appear, and that this
copy should be brought to Bonaparte. Meantime the Holy See
could be consulted on the subject of the article under debate,
and the difficulty could be settled before the ratification of the
Concordat. This plan was adopted. In less than an hour
Joseph returned from the Tuilleries with sorrow depicted on his
countenance. He announced that the First Consul, on hearing
his report, had given himself up to a fit of extreme fury ; in the
violence of his passion he had torn in a hundred pieces the
paper on which the Concordat was written ; but finally, after a
world of entreaties and arguments, he had consented, with indescribable repugnance, to admit all the articles that had been
agreed on ; but, with respect to the one article which had been
left unsettled, he was inflexible. Joseph was commanded to
tell the Cardinal that he, Bonaparte, absolutely insisted on that

article just as it was couched in the Abbé Bernier's paper, and that only two courses were open to the Pope's minister, either to sign the Concordat with that article inserted as it stood, or to break off the negotiation altogether. It was the Consul's unalterable determination to announce at the banquet that very day either the signing of the Concordat, or the rupture between the parties.

"It is easy to imagine the consternation into which we were thrown by this message. It still wanted three hours to five o'clock, the time fixed for the banquet at which we were all to assist. It is impossible to repeat all that was said by the brother of the First Consul, and by the other two, to urge me to yield to his will. The consequences of the rupture were of the most gloomy kind. They represented to me that I was about to make myself responsible for these evils, both to France and Europe, and to my own sovereign and Rome. They told me that at Rome I should be charged with untimely obstinacy, and that the blame of having provoked the results of my refusal would be laid at my door. I began to taste the bitterness of death. All that was terrible in the future they described to me rose up vividly before my mind. I shared at that moment (if I may venture so to speak) the anguish of the Man of Sorrows. But, by the help of heaven, duty carried the day. I did not betray it. During the two hours of that struggle I persisted in my refusal, and the negotiation was broken off.

"This was the end of that gloomy sitting which had lasted full twenty-four hours, from four o'clock of the preceding evening to four of that unhappy day, with much bodily suffering, as may be supposed, but with much more terrible mental anguish, which can be appreciated only by those who have experienced it.

"I was condemned, and this I felt to be the most cruel inconvenience of my position, to appear within an hour at the splendid banquet of the day. It was my fate to bear in public the first shock of the violent passion which the news of the failure of the negotiations were sure to rouse in the breast of the First Consul. My two companions and I returned for a few minutes to our hotel, and, after making some hasty preparations, we proceeded to the Tuilleries.

"The First Consul was present in a saloon, which was thronged by a crowd of magistrates, officers, state dignitaries, ministers, ambassadors, and strangers of the highest rank, who had been invited to the banquet. He had already seen his brother; and it is easy to imagine the reception he gave us as soon as we had entered the apartment. The moment he perceived me, with a flushed face and in a loud and disdainful voice, he cried out:

" 'Well, M. le Cardinal, it is, then, your wish to quarrel! So be it. I have no need of Rome. I will manage for myself. If Henry VIII., without the twentieth part of my power, succeeded in changing the religion of his country, much more shall I be able to do the like. By changing religion in France, I will change it throughout almost the whole of Europe, wherever my power extends. Rome shall look on at her losses; she shall weep over them; but there will be no help for it then. You may be gone; it is the best thing left for you to do. You have wished to quarrel; well, then, be it so, since you have wished it. When do you leave, I say?' "

"After dinner, General," calmly replied the Cardinal.

This laconic answer produced on Napoleon an extraordinary effect. He started, and fixed on the Cardinal a long and searching look. The man of iron will felt that he had to deal with another will, which, while it matched his own for firmness, surpassed it in the power that ever springs from self-control. Taking advantage of the Consul's surprise, Consalvi went on to say that he could not exceed his powers, nor could he agree to terms in opposition to the principles of the Holy See; that it was not possible in ecclesiastical matters to act as freely as was allowable in urgent cases wherein only temporal matters were concerned. Besides, in fairness, the rupture could not be laid to the Pope's charge, seeing that his minister had agreed to all the articles with one single exception, and that even this one had not been definitely rejected, but merely referred to the judgment of his Holiness.

Somewhat calmed, the Consul interrupted, saying that he did not wish to leave after him unfinished works: he would have all or none. The Cardinal having replied that he had no power to negotiate on the article in question as long as it remained in its present shape, Napoleon's former excitement flashed out once more as he repeated with fire his resolution to insist on it just as it was, without a syllable more or less. "Then I will never sign it," replied the Cardinal, "for I have no power to do so." "And that is the very reason," cried the other, "why I say that you wished to break off the negotiations, and that I look on the business as settled, and that Rome shall open her eyes, and shall shed tears of blood for this rupture." Then, almost rudely pushing his way through the company, he went about in every direction declaring that he would change the religion of Europe; that no power could resist him; that he would not be alone in getting rid of the Pope, but would throw the whole of Europe into confusion: it was all the Pope's fault, and the Pope should pay the penalty.

The Austrian minister, the Count de Cobenzel, full of consternation at the scene, ran at once towards the Cardinal, and, with warm entreaty, implored of him to find some means of averting so dreadful a calamity.   Once more had the Cardinal to hear from lips, to which fear lent most earnest eloquence, the harrowing description of the evils in store for religion and for Europe.   "But what can be done," he replied, " in the face of the obstinate determination of the First Consul to resist all change in the form of the article?"   The conversation was here interrupted by the summons to dinner.   The meal was short, and was the most bitter the Cardinal had ever tasted in his life. When they returned to the saloon the Count resumed his ex-postulations.   Bonaparte, seeing them in conversation, came up to the Count and said that it was a loss of time to try to over-come the obstinacy of the Pope's minister; and then, with his usual vivacity and energy, he repeated his former threats.   The Count respectfully answered that, on the contrary, he found the Pope's minister sincerely anxious to come to terms, and full of regret at the rupture ; no one but the First Consul himself could lead the way to a reconciliation.   " In what manner ?" asked Bonaparte, with great interest.   " By authorising the commis-sioners to hold another sitting," replied the Count, " and to endeavour to introduce some such modification of the contested point as might satisfy both parties."   These and other remarks of the Count were urged with such tact and grace that, after some resistance, Napoleon at last yielded.   " Well, then," cried he, " to prove to you that it is not I who seek to quarrel, I con-sent that the commissioners shall meet on to-morrow for the last time.   Let them see if there be any possibility of an agree-ment ; but, if they separate without coming to terms, the rupture may be looked on as final, and the Cardinal may go.   I declare, likewise, that I insist on this article just as it stands, and I will allow no change to be made in it."   And so saying, he abruptly turned his back on the two ministers.

These words, ungracious and contradictory as they were, nevertheless contained the promise of a respite.   It was resolved at once to hold a sitting the next day at noon in the usual place, in the hope that, having come to some agreement between them-selves, they might win the First Consul's consent through the influence of his brother Joseph, who had a great regard for De Cobenzel, and who was desirous of peace.

That night, following a day of such anxiety, and preceding a day of dreadful struggle, brought but little repose to Cardinal Consalvi.   But, when the morning came, a circumstance occurred which filled to overflowing the cup of bitterness he had been condemned to drain.   At an early hour Mgr. Spina came into his room with sorrow and embarrassment in his countenance, to report that the theologian, P. Caselli, had just left him, after having announced that he had spent the night in reflecting on the incalculable mischief likely to follow from such a rupture; that its consequences would be most fatal to religion, and, as the case of England proved, without a remedy; that, seeing the First Consul inflexibly bent on refusing any modification of the disputed article, he had come to the determination of signing it as it stood; that, in his opinion, it did not touch doctrine, and the unparalleled character of the circumstances would justify the Pope's condescendence in such a case. Mgr. Spina added that since this was the opinion of P. Caselli, who was so much better a theologian than he himself, he had not courage enough to assume the responsibility of consequences so fatal to religion, and that he, too, had made up his mind to receive the article and sign it as it was. In case the Cardinal believed that it was not competent for them to sign without him, they would be under the necessity of protesting their acceptation of the article, thereby to save themselves from being responsible for the consequences of the rupture.

This declaration, coupled with the thought that he was now alone in the conflict, deeply affected the Cardinal. But it did not shake his resolution nor take away his courage. He set himself to the task of persuading his two friends of their mistake, but his endeavours were in vain. Perceiving that all his arguments were counterbalanced by the dread entertained of the consequences, he ended by saying that he was by no means convinced by their reasons, and even single-handed he was resolved to persevere in the conflict. He therefore requested them to defer the announcement of their having accepted the article until the conference was at an end, if it should be necessary to break off negotiations. They willingly assented, and promised to give their support to his arguments in the course of the debate, although they were resolved not to go as far as a rupture.

Precisely at noon the sitting was opened at the residence of Joseph Bonaparte. It lasted twelve hours, the clock having struck midnight as they arose from the table. Eleven hours were devoted to the discussion of the article of the Concordat which had been the cause of so many disputes. It is now time to redeem our promise to enter somewhat into detail concerning this famous question.

At Rome two things were considered as absolutely essential to the Concordat, of which they were declared to be conditions *sine quibus non*. One of these was the free exercise of the Catholic religion; the other, that this exercise of religion should be public. The Head of the Church felt it indispensable that these two points should be proclaimed in the Concordat, not only because it was necessary to secure for religion some solid advantage which might justify the extraordinary concessions made by the Holy See, but also because the spirit of the secular Governments both before, and much more after, the French Revolution, ever tended to enslave and fetter the Church. Besides, it had become quite evident, in the earlier stage of the negotiations, that the Government of France was obstinately opposed to the recognition of the Catholic religion as the religion of the State. That Government had ever met the exertions made by Rome to gain this point by reciting the fundamental principle of the constitution, which asserted the complete equality of rights, of persons, of religions, and of everything else. Hence it was looked upon as a great victory, and one for which Cardinal Consalvi deserved high praise, when he succeeded in extorting the admission that stands at the head of the Concordat, to the effect that the Catholic religion in France was the religion of the majority of the citizens. Another reason there was to insist upon these two points: that universal toleration, which is one of the leading principles of the *jus novum*, had long been proved by experience to mean toleration for all sects, but not for the true Church. The Cardinal had not much difficulty in obtaining the recognition of the free exercise of the Catholic religion. Perhaps the Government already had thought of the famous organic laws which it afterwards published, and which effectually neutralised all its concessions on this point. But a whole host of invincible difficulties was marshalled against the demand made for public exercise of the Catholic worship. It was urged with some reason, and no doubt in a good measure with sincerity, that circumstances had made it impossible to carry out in public, with safety to the general peace, all the ceremonies of religion, especially in places where the Catholics were outnumbered by infidels and non-Catholics. These latter would be sure to insult and disturb the processions and other public functions performed outside the churches; and it was not to be expected that the Catholics would bear these outrages with patience. Hence, not being willing to sanction an indefinite right of publicity, the Government expressed its views in these terms:* "The Roman Catholic Apostolic religion shall be freely exercised in France : *its worship shall be public, regard being had, however, to police regulations.*" This is the article the discussion of which had occasioned so much labour and anxiety.

Cardinal Consalvi discovered in the article thus worded two fatal defects : firstly, it tended to enslave the Church by placing

* Art. i. §. 6. Religio Catholica Apostolica Romana libere in Gallia exercebitur : cultus publicus erit, habita tamen ratione ordinationum quoad politiam.

her at the mercy of the civil power ; and, secondly, it implied on
the part of the Church a sanction of the principle which would
serve to legalise such enslavement. For many years court
lawyers had spoken but too plainly concerning the supposed
right of the crown to regulate external worship ; and so far had
this right been extended in practice that the Church found herself almost, or even altogether, the slave of the civil power.
" I had good reason, therefore," says the Cardinal, " to entertain
a sovereign dread of that indefinite and elastic phrase, ' regard
being had to' (*en se conformant*)." Besides, many things pointed
to the probability that in virtue of such a convention signed by
the Holy See, the police, or rather the Government, would interfere in everything, and submit everything to its own will and
pleasure, without the Church being able to object, her liberty
being tied up by the expression in the treaty. No doubt the
Church frequently finds herself in such circumstances as lead
her to tolerate *de facto* violations of her rights and laws, such
toleration being recommended either by prudence, or by charity,
or by lack of power, or by other just motives. But she never
can authorise by a solemn engagement the principle from which
such violations spring.

Whilst fully decided never to accept at any risk an article
so fraught with mischief to the Church, Consalvi was too loyal
and too honest to deny the force of some of the arguments
brought into the field by the French commissioners. Hence he
proposed various expedients by help of which the dreaded
dangers to the public peace might be turned away. One of these
expedients was a Papal Bull to the French clergy, commanding
them to abstain for some time from certain public ceremonies in
places where those hostile to Catholicism were numerous or intolerant ; another was to insert an additional article limiting the
duration of the proposed exception, and determining the cases
in which the police might interfere : but all was in vain ; the
Government obstinately clung to its idea. The Cardinal tells us
that he would have preferred to omit all mention of the right to
publicity of worship, and thus cut the knot it was so troublesome to unravel ; but his orders from Rome to include that
point were too decided, and he was not allowed to send a courier
to solicit fresh instructions from the Holy Father on the subject. He felt, therefore, that, even at the cost of a rupture
between the two contending parties, he was bound by his most
solemn and sacred duty to refuse his sanction to the obnoxious
proposition.

With these convictions, Consalvi took his place at the meeting, on the result of which hung the spiritual interests of so
many millions of souls. We shall not follow out in detail the

shifting phases of the negotiation, but we will come at once to
its closing passage. The French commissioners declared that
the State had no wish to enslave the Church; that the word
police did not mean the Government, but simply that department
of the executive charged with the maintenance of public order,
which order was as much desired by the Church as by the State.
Now it was absolutely necessary to preserve public order, and
no law could stand in the way of such a result. *Salus populi
suprema lex.* It was impossible, they said, for public order to
last throughout parts of France if unrestricted publicity were
once permitted in religious ceremonies; and as no other power
save the Government could judge where such publicity might be
safe, and where dangerous, it should be left to the discretion of
the Government to impose, for the sake of peace, such restrictions as the general good required. The Cardinal admitted that
public tranquillity was by all means to be preserved, but he contended that the article did not restrict, either in point of object
or of time, the power it assigned to the Government; that such
unrestricted power was dangerous to the Church; and therefore
some clause should be added to determine more plainly the
precise nature and bearing of the authority to be given to the
police to regulate public worship. At length he urged a dilemma
which completely vanquished the commissioners. "I objected,"
says he, "thus: either the Government is in good faith when it
declares the motive which forces it to subject religious worship
to police regulations to be the necessary maintenance of public
tranquillity, and in that case it cannot and ought not refuse to
assert so much in the article itself; or the Government refuses
to insert such an explanation; and then it is not in good faith,
and clearly reveals that its object in imposing this restriction on
religion is to enslave the Church."

Caught between the horns of this dilemma, the commissioners
could only say that the explanation required was already contained in the word *police*, police regulations being in their very
nature regulations directed to secure public order. "I replied,"
continues the Cardinal, "that this was not true, at least in every
language; but even supposing it to be true," said I, "where is
the harm in explaining it more clearly, so as to remove any mistaken interpretation which may be prejudicial to the liberty of
the Church? If you are in good faith you can have no difficulty
about this; if you have difficulty, it is a sign you are not in
good faith." Pressed more and more by the force of this
dilemma, and unable to extricate themselves, they asked me
"what advantage do you find in this repetition you propose?"
(for they continued to hold that the word *police* expressed it
sufficiently). "I find in it a very signal advantage," replied I;

" for by the very fact of restricting in clear and express terms
the obligation of making public worship conform to the police
regulation, we exclude restriction in every other case, for *inclusio
unius est exclusio alterius.*   Thus the Church is not made the
slave of the lay power, and no principle is sacrificed by the Pope,
who, in that case, sanctions only what cannot be helped, for
necessitas non habet legem."

This reasoning overcame the commissioners, who had no
further answer to make.   It was resolved to add to the article
an explanatory phrase which should narrow its meaning, and
preclude the possibility of unfair interpretations in after days.
The amended article read as follows: "The Roman Catholic
Apostolic religion shall be freely exercised in France : its worship shall be public, regard being had, however, to such police
arrangements *as the Government shall judge necessary for the preservation of the public peace*" (*quas gubernium pro publica tran-
quilitate necessarias existimabit*).   The Concordat was thus finally
agreed to by the commissioners of the two contracting parties;
and although Bonaparte had declared himself determined to
allow no change to be made, his representatives resolved to sign
the document, modified as it was.   To this step they were
strongly urged by Joseph Bonaparte, who, with keen insight
into his brother's character, declared that if before signing they
should again consult Napoleon, he would refuse to accept the
amendment, whereas, if the Concordat were brought to him
already completed, he would be reluctant to undo what had been
done.   Joseph charged himself with the task of endeavouring
to secure the First Consul's consent.   On the stroke of midnight
the six commissioners placed their signatures to the important
document.   Not a word was said about any other articles save
those contained in the Concordat itself.

Another anxious night followed.   In the morning Cardinal
Consalvi learned from Joseph Bonaparte that the First Consul
had been at first extremely indignant at the change which had
been made, and had refused for a long time to approve of it;
but that at length, thanks to his brother's entreaties and reasons,
after protracted meditation and a long silence, which later events
sufficiently explained, he had accepted the Concordat, and
ordered that the Pope's minister should be at once informed of
his consent.

Universal joy followed the announcement of the signing of
the Concordat.   The foreign ambassadors, and especially the
Count de Cobenzel, came to congratulate the Cardinal and offer
their thanks as for a service rendered to their respective countries.
On the following day Bonaparte received the six commissioners
with marked courtesy.   Ever true to his duty, the Cardinal took

care on this occasion to make Napoleon observe that the Holy
See had not uttered a single word about its temporal concerns
throughout the whole course of the negotiations. "His Holiness
has wished to prove to France, and to the world, that it is a
calumny to accuse the Holy See of being influenced by temporal
motives." He also announced his own speedy departure within
a few days.

Next day he was suddenly summoned to an audience of the
First Consul. For some time he could not detect the object
Napoleon had in view in engaging him in conversation; but at
length he was able to perceive that it was the Consul's intention
to appoint some of the constitutional bishops to the new sees.
With much difficulty the Cardinal convinced him that the appointments of these men would never receive the sanction of
the Holy See unless they made a formal declaration of having
accepted the Pontifical decision on the civil constitution of the
clergy.

During the ensuing three or four days the Cardinal had no
private audience. On the eve of his departure from Paris he
saw Napoleon at a review at which he and the rest of the diplomatic body assisted according to custom.

It was his intention to address, by way of leave-taking, a
few words to the First Consul before they left the saloon; but
when that personage proceeded to make the round of the room,
and began by conversing with the members of the diplomatic
body, at the head of which stood Consalvi, he looked for a moment
fixedly at this latter, and passed on without taking the slightest
notice of him, or sending a word of acknowledgment to the Holy
Father. It was probably his intention to show by this public
slight how little he cared for a Cardinal and for the Holy See,
now that he had obtained all he required from them ; and to
make this insult the more remarkable, he delayed for a considerable time to converse on indifferent topics with the Count de
Cobenzel, who came next after Cardinal Consalvi, and then with
the other ambassadors in turn. The Cardinal retired without
awaiting his return from the review. When he had just finished
his preparations for his departure, which had been fixed for that
evening, the Abbé Bernier made his appearance at the hotel to
announce that it was the will of the First Consul that between
them they should come to some understanding about the Bull
which, according to custom, was to accompany the treaty. It
was in vain to refuse, and this new labour imposed on the Cardinal another sitting of eight hours. He rose from the table to
enter his carriage, and, after travelling day and night, he reached
the Eternal City on the 6th August, more dead than alive,
overcome by fatigue, and with his legs so swollen that they were

unable to support him. The Pope received him with indescribable tenderness, and expressed his perfect satisfaction with all
that had been done. A special consistory of all the cardinals in
Rome approved of the Concordat, which was solemnly ratified
thirty-five days after it had been signed at Paris.

Thus was completed the great act which has been fruitful of
so many blessings to Europe, and for which, under God, the
Church is indebted to the wisdom of Pius VII. and the firmness
of Cardinal Consalvi.

It was long before the Concordat was published at Paris,
and when at length it did appear, what was the pain of the
Holy Father to find, together with the treaty and under the
same date, a compilation of the so-called *organic laws*, which were
put forth as forming part of the Concordat, and included in the
approbation of the Holy See! Of the organic laws it is enough
to say that they almost entirely overthrew the new edifice which
Cardinal Consalvi had found so difficult to erect. In spite of
the solemn protestations of the Popes, these laws still remain,
but they remain as a standing proof of the dishonesty which
Cardinal Consalvi has shown to have marked the entire conduct
of Napoleon Bonaparte in the negotiations for the Concordat.

MEMOIRS OF MY MINISTRY BY CARDINAL
CONSALVI.

In the lonely hours of his exile at Rheims, whither he had been
banished by Napoleon for having refused to assist at the imperial
marriage with Maria Louisa, Cardinal Consalvi found employment in tracing from memory an outline of the great affairs
which had occupied him during his ministry as Secretary of
State. It was no self-love nor mean desire of praise that induced the man of action thus to become the historian of his own
deeds. To the same zeal which had nerved him in his conflicts
for the cause of the Church do we owe the truthful record he
has left us of the fortunes of these conflicts in which the Holy
See was so audaciously attacked and so successfully defended.
The thought that, perhaps, one day his words might be of advantage to the interests of religion, or might supply weapons

15

for its defence, was a motive strong enough to influence him to
undertake the task under circumstances the most unfavourable
that can well be imagined.   "I have drawn up these memoirs,"
he writes, "at most critical moments; how critical may well be
imagined when I mention that as soon as I have finished a page
I must hide it at once in a safe place, so as to secure it from the
unforeseen perquisitions to which at all times we are exposed.
. . . I am without notes either to guide or to confirm my re-
miniscences.   I have not the leisure, nor the tranquillity, nor
the security, nor the liberty which I require if I would enrich
my narrative with comments and becoming ornaments. . . . If
God grant me life and better days, I hope to give to my work
all that perfection of form and style which is at present beyond
my power."

But, whatever the narrative may lack in perfection of form
and style is abundantly compensated by the interest attaching
to the events it describes.   It sets before us a picture of the
movement of European society during the stirring period of the
Cardinal's administration.   The intrigues, and schemes, and
falsehoods of diplomacy ; the art of masking ambitious designs
under generous language, and laying snares for a rival's unwary
feet ; the dishonourable selfishness ; the detestable hypocrisy ; in
a word, all that goes to make up the strategy of modern statecraft, is laid bare in its pages by a master hand.   And what
lends fresh interest to the subject is the contrast it offers between
the baseness of courts and the loyal rectitude of the Holy See,
between the plotting which, on the world's side, exhibits nought
but the cunning of the serpent, and the honourable prudence on
the part of the Church which tells also of the simplicity of the
dove.   On the one hand we have a web of intrigue, each thread
of which is meant to secure some perhaps undue advantage ;
on the other, a straightforward policy placing religion above
everything, and worthy of the Pontiff who is vicar on earth of
that Lord who loves souls.   That the voice of such a policy
should be heard at all is due, under Providence, to the temporal
sovereignty of the Holy See.   The folly of those who would
wish, for the sake of religion, to see the Pope a subject rather
than a sovereign, cannot be better shown than by the history of
the relations between the Holy See and the courts of Europe
during Consalvi's administration.   During that period Naples,
Spain, Portugal, Austria, Russia, Malta, and France had each
of them separate negotiations to conduct with the Holy See on
matters affecting the liberty of the Church and the interests of
religion.   It was a time when the interests of different states
crossed each other in a thousand ways, and if the Pope had been
the subject of any one of these kingdoms, it would have been

simply impossible, humanly speaking, to carry on the government of the Church. Statesmen would have at their hand the ready pretext that the decisions of the Holy Father were coloured by undue national prejudices, and this pretext would serve to excuse their own encroachments upon the liberties of the Church in their own territories. Besides, that jealousy of the Church which has ever impelled statesmen to fetter its action, would certainly influence the sovereign who might claim the Pope as his subject to interfere with the liberty of so formidable a rival. The success which followed Cardinal Consalvi's management of affairs was due, no doubt, in great part, to his surpassing abilities; but these abilities required, as the condition of their exercise, the vantage-ground of independence. Speaking from the steps of a throne, with all the liberty which that position secured to him, the Cardinal Secretary had an influence which could never belong to the mere ecclesiastic raising a suppliant voice at the footstool of some haughty sovereign.

The relations of France with the Holy See in the beginning of this century were such as to demand the unceasing attention of the Papal minister. We have already given the history of the negotiations concerning the Concordat with the First Consul; we are sure that the Cardinal's narrative of other transactions between Napoleon and the Pope will prove not less interesting to our readers.

It is not a little singular that the earliest negotiation between Pius VII. and France was precisely similar to the latest, and that the name of England held a prominent place in both. It is not at all singular, however, that the Pope followed in the latest the self-same principles of conduct which he professed in the earliest, even though this faithful adherence to his duty cost him his throne and his liberty. Soon after his arrival in Rome from Venice, there was some reason to fear lest the French army might proclaim once more the Roman Republic, and thus deprive the Holy Father of his dominions. All anxiety was soon dispelled by the proclamation issued by Murat to his troops, then about to march upon Naples through the Pontifical territory. In this proclamation he commanded his soldiers to observe strict discipline in passing through the friendly territory of the Holy See. This recognition of the papal sovereignty was a joyful surprise to all those who heard of it. But among those who did not hear of it was a Mgr. Caleppi, just named as Nuncio to the Brazils, who had become acquainted with Murat at Florence. Filled with zeal for the Pope, Mgr. Caleppi, without having received any orders from Rome, hurried after the general and overtook him at Florence. He there induced Murat to agree to a treaty, securing the integrity of the Papal territory on cer-

tain conditions, which he promised would be at once carried to
Rome and gladly accepted by his Holiness. The treaty was
short, but contained one article which plunged the Holy Father
into a most embarrassing position. This article declared that
the Pope would close his ports against the English and all other
enemies of France. Nothing could be more opposed than this
to the view the Pope took of the duties of his position as common
Father of the faithful and minister of peace. He had resolved
to maintain a strict neutrality in the great struggle that was
going on, hoping by this conduct to preserve the free exercise
of his spiritual sovereignty, even in the countries against whose
sovereigns France was waging war. The indiscreet zeal of
Mgr. Caleppi placed him in the alternative of either breaking
through his fixed rule of conduct, or of making a declaration of
neutrality at a time when such a declaration was sure to be
attended with the most disastrous consequences. He resolved
not to ratify the treaty. In a short time Murat came to Rome,
and, by his frank and loyal character, won for himself the
esteem of Consalvi. When they came to treat of the convention, and when the Cardinal disavowed the proceedings of Mgr.
Caleppi, Murat gave a signal proof of his affection for Pius VII.
It was in his power to insist on the ratification of the treaty, and
to inform Bonaparte of the Pope's refusal; but he preferred to
lose the credit he could have won for himself by such an act, and,
after employing many arguments to shake the Pope's resolution,
he at length exclaimed: "Well, then, since this treaty is a
source of so much trouble to the Holy Father and to you, let us
throw it into the fire, and say no more about it."

Soon after this occurrence Consalvi went to Paris to negotiate
the Concordat. After the ratification of the French Concordat
came the discussion of the Italian Concordat for the kingdom of
Italy. What the organic laws were to the French Concordat
the decrees of the President Melzi became to the Italian one.
The Emperor's decrees—which, while they appeared to revoke
those of Melzi in deference to the Pope's opposition, in reality
confirmed them—completely frustrated the good effects of the
Concordat. The difficulties of these two negotiations were hardly
over when the marriage of the Emperor's brother, Jerome, was
a source of fresh trouble to the Holy See. Napoleon urged the
Pope to declare null the marriage his brother had contracted in
America without the consent of his mother or his brother.
Cardinal Fesch, the Emperor's uncle, was charged with the
management of this affair, and spared no importunities to extort
from the Pope the desired decision. The whole question hinged
on this: could the Emperor prove that the decrees of the Council
of Trent had been published at Baltimore, where the marriage

was contracted? If proof of this were forthcoming, the Pope
would at once decla.e the marriage null and void; but if it
could not be proved, then the marriage was perfectly valid,
seeing that the defect of the consent of the parents was not an
impedimentum dirimens, but only a civil disability in the eyes of
the French law. The Cardinal relates that in the many letters
written by the Emperor to the Pope during the course of this
affair, he frequently insisted, and with extreme energy, on the
fact that his brother's spouse was a Protestant, and he censured
in the most abusive language the Pontiff, who, as he said, was
desirous of maintaining a heretic in a family every member of
which was destined to mount a throne. The Pope's reply was,
that although this difference of religion rendered the marriage
unlawful, yet it did not make it invalid. After these letters,
who could believe that as soon as the ecclesiastical authorities at
Paris had declared the American marriage null and void, the
Emperor would make Jerome marry another Protestant, the
daughter of the King of Wurtemberg, and afterwards Queen of
Westphalia?

Next came the great event of the journey of Pius VII. to
Paris, to officiate at the coronation of the Emperor. One day a
letter came to Rome from the Cardinal Caprera, then Legate at
Paris, containing an announcement as unexpected as it was important. The Legate stated that the Emperor had summoned
him to an audience, and had represented to him that all orders
of the State, and the best friends of the Church, believed it
likely to be of service to religion that he should be crowned by
the Pope under his new title of Emperor of the French; that
this was also his own opinion; that the State of France made it
impossible for him to go to Rome to receive the diadem there,
and that consequently the ceremony could not be performed
unless the Pontiff should consent to come to Paris for the purpose, as some of his predecessors had done; that, by reason of
the advantages which would accrue from it to religion, the Pope
would remain satisfied with his journey beyond all his hopes;
that the matter should be laid at once before the Holy Father;
and, in case he consented, that the Government would forward
a formal invitation with all the solemnity and pomp befitting
such a guest and such a host.

The imperial representations were backed by the Cardinal
Legate's own remarks. He added that he was in a position to
declare that great benefits would follow the Pope's compliance,
whilst the worst consequences might be speedily expected from
a refusal; that a refusal would be felt very much, and would
never be forgiven; that excuses based on the health or the advanced age of the Pope, on the inconveniences of the journey,

&c., would be looked upon as mere pretexts; that a tardy reply would be equivalent to a refusal; and that it was idle to raise objections on the etiquette of the reception and sojourn at Paris, for the writer knew, on the best authority, that the reception of the Holy Father would equal, and even surpass, in magnificence all former occasions; but the Emperor was not willing to undergo the humiliation of binding himself by a formal treaty to do that to which his own heart naturally inclined him.

This proposal was of a nature to require the most careful consideration. The impetuous character of Napoleon made it easy to foresee what disastrous consequences might spring from a refusal; and, on the other hand, the state of European feeling towards the Emperor was such as to convince anyone that to accept the invitation was to provoke the indignation both of governments and of individuals. What was the Holy Father to do in such a crisis? He did what the Popes have ever done: calling to mind that human wisdom is weak at its best—*cogitationes mortalium timidæ et incertæ*, as he expressed it in his allocution—he implored from God light and help, to the end that he might discover which of the two courses would better promote the honour and the interests of religion. He set aside all earthly influences, and refused to take counsel from human motives. He convoked the Sacred College, and laid before it the letters of the Cardinal Legate and of Cardinal Fesch, who, as French Ambassador at Rome, had been charged by his Government with the negotiation. The Cardinals gave their opinion in writing, and by a majority declared that the invitation should be accepted. The Emperor had formally pledged his word that the journey would be productive of much good to religion, and it was thought the Pope could not refuse an invitation so expressed. A refusal would throw all the blame of the consequences on the Holy See, and it was of the last importance that no pretext for these calumnies should be afforded to the enemies of that See. Besides, all the Catholic powers of Europe, and many besides, had already recognised the new empire. In addition to these general reasons, there were two to which special weight was attached. The organic laws, and the installation of constitutional bishops, who had not retracted their errors, were two outrages upon religion in France, which caused perpetual grief to the Holy Father. The formal promises of Napoleon, coupled with the advantage of the Pope's presence in Paris, gave good grounds to hope that these two evils could be remedied if the Emperor's invitation were accepted. It was not thought prudent, however, to accept the invitation in the dark, as it were; nor did the Emperor's verbal promises to the Legate, nor Cardinal Fesch's vague generalities on the good of religion, inspire confidence

enough. Before the Pope would give his final consent, he determined to reduce to something tangible and obligatory these
vague, indefinite promises of the French Government. Cardinal
Fesch advised that the Pope should exact, as a condition of his
consent, the restitution of the three Legations which France had
torn from the States of the Church. But the pure soul of Pius
VII. revolted against the idea of admitting any thought of temporal advantages: not only did he reject the Cardinal's well-
meant suggestion, but positively forbade him ever again to
make mention of it. He refused to give his consent unless the
French Government would promise to withdraw the organic
laws, and to abandon those of the constitutional bishops who
should refuse to make a public and sincere retractation. It took
four or five months of negotiation to extort these promises from
Napoleon. During that period Consalvi had daily conferences
with Cardinal Fesch, whose warm temper frequently led to
lively debates. At length M. de Talleyrand addressed an official
note to the Cardinal Legate, in which it was expressly declared
that, as to the organic laws, the Emperor would treat directly
with the Holy Father, whose representations should be attended
to in such a way as to give his Holiness the most complete
satisfaction. The Emperor was ready to do even more than the
Pope had asked; and it was insinuated that he would be happy
to listen with favour to any requests the Pope should make
concerning his temporal interests. Touching the intruded
bishops, M. de Talleyrand made large promises, but their tenor
was so vague that the Holy Father did not remain satisfied until
he held in his hand a written promise that the constitutional
bishops should make their retractation in the Pope's hands in
the form prescribed by him, and that any who might refuse to
do so should be forced to resign his see. This point having
been arranged, it was thought that the due regard for the
majesty of the pontifical dignity demanded some other precautions. The Holy Father felt that he ought not to expose his
high office to insult or irreverence, and this consideration urged
him to request some information as to the manner in which he
was to be received at Paris by the Emperor. In his reply to
the inquiries made on this point, Talleyrand employed these
remarkable words: "Between Pius the Seventh's journey to
France, his reception there, his treatment, and the results which
are to spring from it, and Pius the Sixth's journey to Vienna,
there shall be as much difference as there is between Napoleon I.
and Joseph II." Another precaution judged necessary by Consalvi regarded the coronation itself. The later notes of Cardinal
Fesch were remarkable for a strange variety of expression.
Instead of the word *coronation* (*incoronazione*), employed in the

original invitation presented by the Cardinal Legate in the Emperor's name, the Cardinal Fesch had commenced to use the word *consecration* (*consecrazione*). Consalvi at once demanded the reason of this change, and Cardinal Fesch replied: "Beyond all doubt, the Pope is to crown the Emperor; but I believe there is to be a double coronation: one in the Church by the Pope, the other in the Champ de Mars by the Senate." The Pope at once sent a despatch to the Legate at Paris commanding him to signify to the Emperor that the Holy Father could not allow his Majesty to be crowned by other hands after he had been crowned by the Pope; that a second coronation would be an insult to the dignity of the Head of the Church; and that, consequently, if it were intended that the Emperor should be twice crowned, the Holy Father would not go to Paris at all. Talleyrand replied in an official note that the Emperor set too high a value on his coronation by the Pope to wish to receive a second diadem from the hands of others.

The choice of those who were to form the suite of the Pontiff next came under discussion. The French Government was anxious that the Pope should take with him twelve cardinals and a corresponding number of prelates and of Roman nobles. The Holy Father resolved to bring only four cardinals and four bishops, besides the prelates attached to his immediate service, such as his *maggiordomo* and his *maestro di camera*. The two Roman princes who commanded the noble guard were to follow him. However, in deference to Cardinal Fesch's requests, he added to this little court the two cardinal deacons, Braschi and de Bayane. The other four cardinals were Antonelli, de Pietro, Borgia, and Caselli.

To conduct these negotiations to a happy issue was a task of immense difficulty. The Cardinal writes that while they were proceeding he had to bear what was almost intolerable, and what only his zeal for the interests of the Holy See could have made him brook. At length the decisive *yes* was spoken, at first confidentially, because no formal invitation was to be delivered until such time as all arrangements were completed. The French Government at once announced the Pope's intended visit, in order that the publicity thus given to his promise might make any change of purpose impossible or very difficult. Having thus made himself sure of the presence of the Roman Pontiff at his coronation, Napoleon all at once changed his tone, and made the Pope feel how little respect he really had for the Head of the Church. Indeed, it was Cardinal Consalvi's deliberate opinion—and after events show that he was correct in his judgment—that the French Government was fully determined never to carry out the promises which the Pope's minister had extorted

from it. The formal invitation was couched in language that
fell far short of the ancient formula used on similar occasions,
and which the Government had promised to employ. Then,
instead of deputing ecclesiastics or great dignitaries to present
the Emperor's letter to Pius VII., Napoleon sent through
Brigadier-General Caffarelli a note so mean in every respect
that the Holy Father was inclined to refuse to accept it. But
as he had undertaken the journey for the good of the Church,
he resolved to bear with calmness and patience whatever slights
might be put upon him. He soon found abundant occasions for
the exercise of these virtues. In the first place he was forced
to set out on his journey with a precipitate speed that was
equally unbecoming his dignity and injurious to his health. He
left Rome on 2nd November, 1802, in order to arrive at Paris
on the 27th or 28th; and during this long journey he was
allowed to rest only twice—once at Florence for a day or two,
and again a day at Turin—a few hours of repose being with
difficulty permitted him at other places on the road. Besides,
he was not even consulted about the day to be fixed for the
ceremony, although common politeness should have· suggested
this mark of deference. " I will say nothing," says Consalvi,
" of all the Pope had to suffer from the disrespect shown him in
the capital ; I will not speak of the manner in which Napoleon
made his first appearance before his Holiness at Fontainebleau,
in the midst of a pack of fifty hounds, as if going to or returning from the chase ; I will not tell how the Pope was made to
enter Paris by night, and in silence, in order that no eye might
see the Emperor at the Pontiff's left, for, being in his own carriage, he was forced to yield the right to his guest. I will be
silent as to how and why, on the day of the consecration, Napoleon made his Holiness wait a full hour and a half seated on the
throne near the altar, and how all the arrangements which had
been agreed on for the ceremony were set aside ; I will not tell
how the Emperor himself placed the crown on his own head,
having rudely snatched it from the altar before the Pope
stretched out his hand to take it up ; I will not tell how, at the
imperial banquet on that day, the Pontiff was made to sit in the
third place at the table where sat the Emperor, the Empress,
and the Prince Elector of Ratisbon ; nor will I say a word of
the second coronation which, contrary to solemn pledges, took
place in the Champ de Mars, nor of the way in which Napoleon
although, as it were, in his own house, took the right of his
Holiness on all occasions when they made their appearance together in public, nor of the little respect he showed him. He
never paid him those marks of veneration which so many great
kings and emperors have been proud to pay to the Sovereign

Pontiffs.   Finally, I will be silent about the humiliations which Pius VII. was made to undergo during the whole period of his sojourn.   I have but enumerated these sufferings to the end that all may understand how much virtue, moderation, and goodness the Pope had need of to follow the magnificent examples of self-abasement which the God, whose vicar he was here below, has bequeathed to the world.   I have wished, likewise, to expose conduct on which I will not allow myself to pass judgment, for I could not do so with becoming coolness and self-respect."

These insults would have been more sweet to the Holy Father if he had been able to realise all the good he had promised himself to achieve for religion at the price of his condescension. But here, too, he was disappointed.   After many memorials on the subject to the Emperor, and after many interviews, he was forced to surrender all hopes of seeing the organic laws abolished. Napoleon was simply false to his solemn promises.   Nor would the government fulfil its engagement to force the constitutional bishops to a retractation.   But what the power of the State would not do the force of the Pope's gentle virtues happily effected.   He called the bishops several times to an audience ; and his affectionate manners, his kind language, and the charm of his goodness made such an impression on their minds, that they avowed their schism, and made a solemn retractation in the form prescribed by the Holy See.   Nor did any one of them ever afterwards, by word or deed, give sign of their ancient errors.   The Pope thus had the unspeakable delight of having, by his journey, extinguished that dangerous schism, to effect the destruction of which he had before agreed to the Concordat.

We must pass over the other indignities which the Pope had to endure before he could effect his departure from Paris.   It was while the Pope was his guest that the Emperor changed the Italian republic into the kingdom of Italy, taking formal possession of the three Legations, and adding the pontifical keys to his coat-of-arms.   He was also disrespectful enough to neglect his duties as host by setting out for Italy before the Pope left his palace.   He even compelled his Holiness to follow him, and wait at every post for the use of the horses which had been employed to draw the imperial carriages.   He was too jealous to allow the Pope to officiate in public at any religious ceremony, even on Christmas Day, on which festival the Sovereign Pontiff had to go to the parish church to say a low Mass.   Even the presents which he gave in return for the magnificent gifts which Pius VII. had brought from Rome, where Canova had selected them, were disgracefully mean, with the exception of a costly tiara, of which, however, the most precious jewel was a diamond taken from the pontifical tiaras under Pius VI., to pay the exactions of Tolentino. The newspapers were filled with the description of a wonderful altar, two rich carriages, and other splendid presents; but these objects never found their way to the Pope.

On his way home Pius VII. had the consolation of receiving back into the Church the famous Mgr. Ricci, whose name is so well known in connection with the Synod of Pistoia. This prelate made before the Pope a full and sincere retractation of all his errors. At length the Holy Father arrived at Rome amidst the enthusiasm of his subjects, who so soon were to be torn from him by the very man to do honour to whom he had undertaken and suffered so much.

' THE HISTORY OF A CONVERSION.

THE department of religious literature, which is made up of histories of individual conversions to the faith, has received of late years many remarkable additions. This class of literature is regulated in its growth by very peculiar conditions, and must be judged according to exceptional laws. Its subject—the mysterious workings of grace in the soul—is such as rather to impose a reverent silence than to invite fulness of description; and so well do elevated souls appreciate the sacredness of such silence, that, except for interests of religion or justice, they are unwilling to bring before men those inner secrets of their hearts. But when the interests of religion or justice have convinced them that silence is no longer a duty, the history they consent to unfold can rarely be other than attractive and profitable, seeing that it describes a human soul's toilsome journey from error to truth. The very minuteness of personal detail, which in any other composition would be a blot, in this becomes a merit and a charm. Among the religious motives that not unfrequently dictate such a history, a spirit of thankfulness for the blessing of faith has its fitting place. The favoured soul looks out from the shelter of its Father's house upon the perilous path it has just traversed, and gratefully traces the Providence by which its wayward feet were guided where so many strayed

to their ruin ; just as the rescued mariner hangs up *ex voto* a
sketch of his frail bark in the moment of her peril, when, but
for heaven's help, she would have foundered in the raging
waves.   Fruit of this pious gratitude is the narrative* we are
now engaged upon : a narrative which will interest every
Catholic, not only because it is the history of a remarkable conversion, but because of the light it incidentally throws on the
present condition and future prospects of German Protestantism.
But before we set ourselves to trace the steps of the process
which led Dr. Laemmer from a many-faced Protestantism to
the Catholic Church, it will be useful to make a few preliminary
remarks.

In Dr. Laemmer we have a witness who has had rare opportunities of becoming acquainted with the very highest and best
forms which Protestantism has been enabled to assume in the
country of its birth.   He is, above all things, the child of the
German Protestant universities.   Of the twenty-six universities of which the learned nation is so proud, six or eight are
Catholic,† four are mixed,‡ and the remaining fourteen are exclusively Protestant.§

Now, Dr. Laemmer was student successively at Kœnigsberg,
Leipsic, and Berlin universities, that is to say, at the very universities which at the present time are the chief seats of Protestant thought, both in philosophy and in theology.   The leading
Protestant schools in Germany are at present three in number,
called respectively the neo-Lutheran, the Mediation, and the
Tübingen, or historico-critical school ; of these‖ the neo-Lutheran, or Lutheran reaction school, has specially existed in Berlin
and Leipsic ; the so-called Mediation theology at Berlin ; and
the Tübingen school (now almost extinct in its native home, and
renewed by Hilgenfeld at Jena), has made its influence felt
throughout.   Besides, at Kœnigsberg, he came, as we shall see,
under the influence of one of the ablest defenders of Hegelianism.   We should exceed our limits were we to enter upon a
statement of the principles of these schools.   Be it enough to

---

* *Misericordias Domini:* Histoire de ma conversion au Catholicisme. Par
le Doct. Hug. Laemmer, Pretre du diocese d'Ermland, Traduit de l'allemand,
pp. 206.   Casterman, Tournai, 1863.

† 1, Prague; 2, Vienna ; 3, Friburg ; 4, Munich; 5, Olmutz ; 6, Graetz ; 7,
Würzburg ; 8, Munster.

‡ 1, Tübingen ; 2, Innspruck ; 3, Breslau ; 4, Bonn.   These are called *pari-
tarian* universities : with the exception of the Faculty of Theology, all the
other faculties are Protestant.   There are two Faculties of Theology, one
Catholic and the other Protestant.

§ 1, Heidelberg ; 2, Leipsic ; 3, Rostock ; 4, Greifswald ; 5, Marburg ; 6,
Kœnigsburg ; 7, Jena ; 8, Kiel ; 9, Halle ; 10, Göttingen ; 11, Erlangen; 12,
Stutgardt ; 13, Giesen ; and 14, Berlin.

‖ See Farrar's *Critical History of Free Thought,* p. 390.

say that the first-named school, by defending the authority and credibility of the Scriptures, aims at reconstructing the historical basis of Christianity, and insists on a return to the Lutheran Confessions of the sixteenth century. Since the political troubles of 1848, an ultra-conservative party, called the Hyper-Lutheran, has arisen within this school, which goes back beyond the Reformation, and insists on the principle of a visible authoritative church, a rigid sacramental theory, and the doctrine of consubstantiation. Stahl, and Leo of Halle, to whom Dr. Laemmer makes an important allusion, to be hereafter quoted, belong to the most advanced of this party. Among the representatives of this school, with whom Dr. Laemmer was brought into direct contact, were Hengstenberg and Kahnis.*

The Mediation school takes its stand between the Lutheran party on the one hand, and the school of criticism on the other, and without going back to the principle of authority, or forward to that of discovery, proposes to unite the use of reason with belief in Scripture, and to understand what it believes. Of the members of this very numerous school Dr. Laemmer had intercourse with Twesten and Nitzch. The Tübingen school had for its leader Christian Baur, and, starting from the principle that the only portions of the New Testament undoubtedly genuine are four of St. Paul's Epistles, viz.: to the Romans, to the Galatians, and the two to the Corinthians, it comes to the conclusion that Christianity in its present form is the result of the controversy between the Jewish, or Petrine, and the Pauline Christianity of the apostolic and following ages. All the other books of the New Testament it attributes to some one or other of the contending schools. That this school, extravagant as its conclusions may appear to us, is every day gaining ground in France with a very numerous party, we have been lately assured by competent authority.† That it has many advocates in England is well known.‡ A critic in the *Home and Foreign Review*§ speaks of "the importance of those inquiries of Dr. Baur and his followers into primitive Christianity, which have in some way modified the views of almost everyone who has become acquainted with them."

These are thy gods, O Israel! These are the shapes of Protestantism that wander to and fro in the various universities of Germany. Dr. Laemmer, speaking with full knowledge of the

---

* The *Kirchen-Zeitung* and the *Kreuz-Zeitung* are the organs of this body.

† Father F. Mertian, of the Society of Jesus: *Etudes, etc. par les Peres de la Compagne de Jesus.* No. 32, May, p. 59.

‡ *The Tübingen School and its Antecedents: A Review of the History and Present Condition of Modern Theology.* By R. W. Mackay, M.A. London: Williams and Norgate.

§ No. 5, July, 1863, p. 235.

subject, sums up in one word the result of all this unhealthy movement, and that word is—*chaos*. And what heightens the confusion is, that although the systems which form this chaos are in absolute and perpetual conflict with each other, yet does each professor claim for himself the exclusive possession of truth, as if he, and he alone, had been gifted with infallibility.

The special feature of Dr. Laemmer's conversion appears to us to consist in this, under the grace of God, that he approached faith through its historic side. Sound and conscientious historical research has been the means of his deliverance from bondage. His mind from boyhood inclined towards things grave; the details he communicates concerning his choice of authors reveal that sobriety of judgment which is the first quality of a student of history. The bent of his mind in this direction was strengthened by study of the Fathers, of the history of the Papacy, and of the Catholic theology of the Reformation period. We invite special attention to the happy result of historical studies in his case, because we see in it a promise of much future good for Catholic truth in Germany. The broad distinction between the German method of the present century and that of the past lies in this, that the nineteenth century is the age of historical inquiry, whereas the last century was that of critical thought. Even the Tübingen school is an improvement on the destructiveness of Strauss, for it admits and calls attention to the historical value of at least some portion of the Scriptures. In the other schools above described this tendency is of course still more marked. The modern spirit tends not so much to examine the ontological value of an opinion as to investigate how men came to hold that opinion. It was this spirit which suggested the questions of concursus which, as we shall see, changed the current of Dr. Laemmer's life. Now, we hold it very probable that as this spirit becomes more extended its fruits will be these: men will become familiar with the teachings of Christian antiquity; and although this knowledge may be sought not for the sake of the doctrine itself, but as a preliminary to other studies, still such is the divine power of truth, that, once revealed to the soul, it creates therein a wondrous craving after itself which will dispose the soul for the grace of faith. There must be at this moment many thoughtful men in Germany who, in virtue of this spirit, are engaged in the examination of the fathers and of the theologians of the Catholic Church, and who, finding themselves, like Dr. Laemmer, between the ruins caused by Protestantism and the unbroken strength of Catholic teaching, are even now turning their eyes towards Rome, therein to seek her who was their mother of old.

Hugh Laemmer was born of a Protestant father and a Catholic mother, at Allenstein, in Eastern Prussia, on 25th January, 1835. His mother was a woman of most fervent piety, who, in almost unceasing prayer, sought and found consolation under her many severe afflictions. It was not given her to exercise much influence over the mind of her son, who, long before her death, had gone to reside with his father's relatives, by whom he was brought up as a Protestant. The lad, nevertheless, had a tender love for his mother, and from his earliest years was conscious of an indescribable leaning towards his Catholic friends in preference to his Protestant kindred. This feeling was the natural growth of observations made by the quick-witted boy regarding the piety, firm principles, and good conduct of the Catholics. At the same time, the devotion of the faithful in their processions and pilgrimages served to put him on his guard against the bigoted prejudices which his Lutheran cousins ever sought to instil into his mind against their Catholic neighbours. When, with the other schoolboys, he went to church on Sunday, the sermon made no impression on him, and no wonder, for the preacher carried with him into the pulpit the chilling rationalistic principles he had imbibed at the university. Even in those early years the boy's heart tended towards the beautiful and spacious Catholic Church of his native town. Once, when his father took him to Heiligenlind (a famous resort of pilgrims), and the old sacristan showed him the rare treasures of the church, he experienced an emotion so strong that it survived even the rude trials of his after life.

In 1844 he entered the gymnasium of Kœnigsberg. He brought with him from home a good stock of elementary and grammatical knowledge, and soon discovered that his tastes inclined him to the study of literature more than to that of science. Ellendt, then rector of the gymnasium, was a man who possessed, in a remarkable degree, the power of making his lectures interesting to his pupils. Explained by such a master, Homer and Herodotus became in a short time the favourite authors of M. Laemmer, who, on the other hand, had no taste for what he calls "the tedious narratives of the Anabasis, and the pedantic tirades of the Cyropædia." He preferred Cæsar and Livy to Cicero, whose philosophy especially he found to be commonplace. Modern French literature had no attractions for such a mind as his; the contemporary romance writers of that nation excited even his disgust. As Germany is considered by many to be the very home of perfection in classical studies, it will be interesting to hear the opinion Dr. Laemmer's experience has led him to form concerning the special dangers which beset middle school education at the present day :—

"I believe it to be a mistake," he says, "to make modern languages, mathematics, and the physical sciences occupy very much of the time appointed for the study of the classics ; and, as far as middle class instruction is concerned, we have reason to be grateful to the Raumer ministry for the prominence it has given in the new educational plan to the wise principle, *non muita, sed mullum.* It is highly dangerous to the young to distribute their faculties simultaneously over many heterogeneous branches of knowledge. *Ubique hospes, nusquam domi:* such a system is the sure path to that half-learning which, without giving a thorough knowledge of anything, encourages young men to talk presumptuously of a host of subjects of which they have but the barest surface knowledge. What happens when the examination papers exact from students a knowledge of science as well as of literature, physics, chemistry, natural history, and the different branches of mathematics? It is a well-known fact that, with the exception of a few intended for certain professions, young men are careful to forget as soon after examination as they can the information it has cost them so much labour to acquire. Against this it is vain to urge the importance which the natural sciences have nowadays attained to, an importance so great that no one, save at his peril, can remain a stranger to them ; for on no account should we furnish new weapons to materialism. At most, it is required that students should be supplied with such elementary information as may enable them in the future to keep in sight the true bearings of things, and in creatures recognise Him who is proclaimed in the first article of the Creed. That extravagant cultivation of the natural sciences, so often substituted by our ministers in place of the lessors of Holy Writ, is as perilous as is the undue exaltation of man and of man's pretended victories over nature. The laws of nature have never acknowledged any master save one—our Lord Jesus Christ —and in Him the saints with whom it has pleased Him to share his sovereignty" (p. 13).

Whether the authorities at the gymnasium shared these views or not we are not in a position to state. One thing, however, is certain : much attention was paid there to the study of the German language and literature; much of our student's time was passed in the excellent library of German authors provided for the use of the scholars. What an eventful moment that is in which a youth, in the flush of the early vigour of his mind, finds himself for the first time in a library where the treasures of human thought are gathered before him clothed in the language he has learned from his mother's lips ! Then begins for him that daily contact of mind with the mind of others, which will infallibly colour for good or evil the history of his future. He who, without an enlightened and friendly guide, adventures inexperienced upon this commerce,

"Voyaging through strange seas of thought alone,"

runs no little risk of being caught unawares by error where his generous ardour looked only for truth. In the world of books as in the world of men, evil lies very close to good, and wears its garb and mien ; and how shall the inexperience of youth be able to see through the disguise, or how avoid becoming captive to its snares? And from such captivity, how harassing the toil of escape! Of that toil let him make light who has never had experience of the almost ceaseless influence erroneous principles exercise on the mind with whose growth they have grown. From reading Newton on the Prophecies in 1816, Dr. Newman, then a boy of fifteen, became convinced that the Pope was Antichrist; and his imagination was stained by the effects of this doctrine up to the year 1843.* Nor did M. Laemmer come away safe. His random reading brought him both good and evil, so intermingled each with each, that his unripe judgment could no more discern between them than the hand can disjoin the sunshine from the shadow that follows after it. After ransacking the bulk of German literature, he selected from out the rest certain writers to be his prime favourites. The choice he made reveals at once the bent of his mind, and the dangers to which that very bent exposed him. The schools of German poetry and taste are divided, in Vilmar's *History of German Literature*, into five classes. First, that which preceded Lessing, subdivided into the Saxon school, and the Swiss school of Wieland in his early manner, to which was akin the Göttingen school of Klopstock and Voss; second, that of Lessing and the writers influenced by him; third, the Weimar school, with its three great names, Herder, Göethe, and Schiller; fourth, the later schools, the romantic, represented by the two Schlegels, Novalis, and the patriotic; fifth, the modern school of reaction against absolute government, headed by H. Heine. Of these schools only the second and third gave M. Laemmer delight. There was a hidden sympathy between the qualities of his own mind and the exquisite critical genius and reasoning power of Lessing, which made him find the writers of the first class insipid and trivial. He came under the influence of Lessing to a remarkable degree; and if to that influence he owes the gain of an important truth, to it must be attributed also his acceptance of a most fatal error. That remarkable man, author, or, as it now appears, editor of the *Wolfenbüttel Fragments*, in consequence of that publication, had a warm controversy with the Lutheran pastor, Göze, in which he forcibly showed, by historical arguments chiefly, that the principle of *the Bible and nothing but the Bible*, was illogical and false. M. Laemmer followed the course of the controversy, and found to his dismay that the arguments of Lessing had brought home to him the conviction that Lutheranism rested on a false basis. This was a great gain; but it was counterbalanced by a great loss. The ardour of his youthful admiration blinded him to the dangerous prin-

* *Apologia*, p. 63.

16

ciples of indifferentism and doubt contained in his master's works, and particularly in his *Education of the World.* The third Fragment sets it forth as impossible that all men should be brought to believe revelation on rational grounds. These principles, destructive of all faith and certainty in belief, were adopted by the young student, and warmly defended by him in a special dissertation.

Towards the end of his course he devoted himself to the study of Herder; and here again vague reading brought to him gain and loss, truth and falsehood together. He learned from this writer to believe in the mysterious action of Providence in the world; but the view he was led to form of the divine plan was confined, superficial, and vague. He also gave much time to the reading of Schiller, in whose works he found an assault on the frigid deism then predominant in Germany. But the deity which that poet brought so near to men was not the Blessed Trinity, but the gods of Olympus; and whilst his strains rebuked the philosophy which never rose above the laws of gravity, he himself did but serve the cause of epicureanism by his praises of the pleasures of the earth.

From Goethe M. Laemmer learned to appreciate, in some measure, the Sacraments of the Church, and to think kindly of the Church itself. But what solid advantage could he gain from the man who wrote to Lavater of the chief gospel miracles that " he held them for blasphemies against the great God and his revelation in nature?"

The reader will have observed that this course of reading made several important additions to M. Laemmer's religious views. And yet the books among which his reading lay were either not at all, or not directly religious. We are now to inquire how far his ideas were modified by any directly religious training. The answer to this question opens up such a view of the condition of Protestantism in the country of its birth as well deserves our careful study. Let M. Laemmer tell us what fruits it has produced at Kœnigsberg. First of all, in the various schools where he resided during his stay in that town there was no common practice of religion: the religious exercises of the gymnasium were limited to the singing of a few stereotyped chants. The religious instruction of the students was attended to by an aged professor, who was one of the leaders of the Freemasons, and whose religion was the religion of pure reason. He was assisted in the religious training of the students by a younger man, whose doctrines were kindred with his own, and whose lectures, though erudite, were arid. Fortunately for himself, M. Laemmer had learned from his mother the habit of night and morning prayer. This habit he retained, although for want of fixed principles it became a work of mere routine. Such was the state of religion in the gymnasium. In the city itself things were still worse. From the orthodox Lutheranism of Superintendent Sartorius down to the absolute Rationalism of Rupp, every intermediate stage of error had its exponents and followers in the city of Kant. In the eyes of Sartorius, Catholicism, which he knew only from Luther's caricatures, stood on the same level with Rationalism; he assigned to the Confession of Augsburg almost the same authority which Catholics claim for tradition, and, together with Baur, Nitsch, and Winer, made an unsuccessful attempt to refute Moehler's *Symbolism*. Rupp, on the other hand, denounced all symbols, even that of St. Athanasius, which he declared to be incompatible with Christian doctrine; his system was based on Indifferentism of the lowest kind, and conceded to women as well as to men the right of deliberating and of teaching in religious matters. And yet these two men, so diametrically opposed to each other in doctrine, preached for a time in the same church and from the same pulpit. And, whilst Sartorius, who revered Luther as a man of God, preached to empty benches, Rupp found assembled around him a crowded audience, composed of the highest as well as the lowest in the land. The different churches at Kœnigsberg had preachers of every shade of doctrine. During the course of his studies M. Laemmer made trial of them all, but found not satisfaction in any. At length, in the midst of this Babel, he became acquainted with the man who was destined to exercise a most salutary influence on his life. That man was Lehnerdt, Superintendent-General of the province of Saxony. Born in Brandenburg, and educated at Berlin, in the school of Schleiermacher and Hegel, he escaped the pernicious influence of his masters by a profound course of historical studies. On the one hand, he combated the rationalistic exegesis of Paulus, and, on the other, devoted himself with all his might to the study of the Fathers. He was a man of great piety; and, in preparing M. Laemmer for confirmation, spoke with such unction of God and the world, man and sin, Christ and salvation, that his words wrought in the young student's soul a blessed reaction. An intimate and affectionate relationship sprang up between the two which was interrupted in the middle of 1851 by Lehnerdt's departure for Berlin, where he succeeded Neander as professor of history, but was resumed again at a later period in that city.

M. Laemmer passed from the gymnasium to the university of Kœnigsberg at Easter, 1852. He remained there but one year, during which time he acted as secretary to Voigt, whose able *History of Gregory VII.* was the beginning of a new epoch for ecclesiastical history in Germany. One of the professors of philosophy was Rosenkranz, the pupil and biographer of Hegel. This able man was an eloquent partisan of Hegelianism, and, by the poetic colouring he contrived to throw around its doctrines, exercised an extraordinary influence over the youth of the university. M. Laemmer tells us that, during a fever which at this time brought him to death's door, one of his keenest regrets was his inability to attend Rosenkranz's lectures. He made up for his absence from lecture by a careful study of his professor's writings, and completely adopted the views expressed therein. It was long before he was able to shake off the yoke of Hegelianism which he then assumed. In the university Biblical literature was treated altogether from the rationalistic point of view. One of the fruits of this method is the isolated and independent study of various parts of Sacred Scripture. " It was reserved for Protestantism," says M. Laemmer, " to cultivate in minute detail what is called Biblical Theology, and to write volumes upon the doctrine of such and such an apostle in particular. . . . This anatomical process, this study of atoms, has led many to apply those fine theories to various periods of Church history, and, like certain heretics of the Middle Ages, to speak of the Christianity of St. Peter, and of the Christianity of St. Paul, not excluding by any means that of St. John " (pp. 47, 48).

At the Easter of 1853, M. Laemmer passed from the university of Kœnigsberg to that of Leipsic, on a burse founded in the old Catholic times by a Catholic priest of his native town. His departure from Kœnigsberg marks the close of the first period of his university career, and it will be interesting to stop and take a comprehensive view of the phases of thought through which he passed during that time. As far as religious opinions are concerned, this first stage of his life may be subdivided into two periods : one of demolition, the other of reconstruction. In the former he lost his belief in Lutheranism and its central doctrine of the *Bible and nothing but the Bible ;* that is to say, he lost hold of the only dogmatic principle he held. Being thus deprived of a fixed belief, he was more open to the action of Lessing's principles of universal tolerance, which amounted to the coldest indifferentism and doubt. These principles he made his own for a season. The spectacle of division and discord which was exhibited daily under his eyes at Kœnigsberg helped to complete the work of destruction. Even his very prayer became a dry form, lacking all influence for good. The period of reconstruction commenced with the friendship that bound him to Lehnerdt, by whose influence were sown in his mind the seeds of a reaction, which, by the play of intellectual

as well as moral causes, was afterwards developed into the fulness of Catholic belief. The intellectual cause that led to this
happy result was, as we said before, the spirit of historical inquiry; the moral cause, under God's grace, was the deep religious
sentiment which formed part of his original character, and which,
once aroused by Lehnerdt's words about justice and the judgment to come, never allowed any antagonism of feeling to stand
long in the way of his acceptance of the truth. Not that the
action of these causes was at all times unimpeded. The
Hegelianism which he imbibed from Rosenkranz for a long time
seriously crippled his mind in its exertions after truth.

In these dispositions M. Laemmer came to the University of
Leipsic.

Among the professors at Leipsic Winer was, beyond doubt,
the most remarkable. His labours on the idioms of the New
Testament Greek, his lexicological and bibliographical works,
and even his reply to Moehler's *Symbolism*, with all their defects,
give proof of solid study. But he permitted himself in his
lectures to launch sarcasms against the rites of the Catholic
Church. Indirectly he was the occasion of much good to M.
Laemmer, who read Moehler's and other Catholics' works, in
order to test the statements advanced by Winer. It was Winer,
too, who first suggested to him the idea of devoting himself to
teaching in the university. Tischendorf, so famous for his
studies on the Bible texts, and Wachsmuth, who has rendered
immense services to truth by his Roman history, written in refutation of Niebuhr, were among the professors whose courses
he followed at Leipsic. Two resolutions taken at this period
by M. Laemmer reveal the gradual change which was taking
place in his convictions owing to the action of the causes mentioned above. First, he determined to assist no longer at the
lectures of Theile, on account of his grossly rationalistic treatment of the doctrine of the Word in the Epistles of St. John.
Theile died shortly after. "He was a man of rectitude," says
M. Laemmer, "and conscientious; I cannot think of him without a feeling of deep sorrow. You might read on his brow the
painful and fruitless efforts he had made to attain to the fulness
of truth and to that peace which the world cannot give" (p. 65).
Daily more and more disgusted with rationalism, and wearied
with ineffectual efforts to reconcile the contradictions which
everywhere appeared in theology, he now began to entertain
serious thoughts of confining himself exclusively to philosophical
studies. But these thoughts were put to flight on occasion of
his first sermon, which he preached in a suburban village where
one of his friends was pastor. The subject of the sermon was
charity, as described by St. Paul; and its treatment had the

effect of reviving in the preacher's heart his old love for religious questions. He was now approaching the crisis of his life. While he was bewildered by the endless variations of Protestantism, and endeavouring to form out of them a religious system such as would satisfy his reason and conscience, the first rays of the grace of faith began to dawn more nearly upon his soul. In what manner this came to pass we shall allow himself to tell :—

"I said before that during my stay at Leipsic the study of a question proposed for concursus exercised a powerful influence on my religious views, and that to it is to be attributed my first step towards Catholicism. The subject chosen for the concursus of 1854, by the Leipsic Faculty of Theology, was the exposition of the doctrine of Clement of Alexandria on the Word. This theme made upon me a most vivid impression. At once, and with great joy, I resolved to become a candidate. I will now state the motives of this resolve. The conflicting theological systems which I had observed, both in books and in oral instructions, occasioned me extreme torture. I was too independent to follow the example of so many others by attaching myself blindly to a party; I wished to examine for myself the successive phases undergone by the Protestant principle, and, with full knowledge of the subject, to make my own selection. All those systems, whether confessional or non-confessional, could not satisfy me long; on the other hand, the distraction caused by philological and philosophical studies could not give peace to my heart, which only in God could find an end to its unrest. *Inquietum est cor nostrum, donec requiescat in te.* I felt I must escape from the chaos of modern theology, and I most eagerly availed myself of this opportunity to draw from the spring of Christian antiquity. I procured a copy of Klotz's portable edition, and set myself to the study of my author. Pen in hand, I began my task by reading him through and through before I took any account of what others had written about him.

"A new world opened on my sight as I read the earliest master of the Alexandrian Catechetical School—the teacher of Origen. What treasures lie hid in these three works, the *Exhortatio ad Græcos*, the *Pædagogus*, and the *Stromata!* The *Exhortatio ad Græcos* is a masterpiece of Christian controversy against Paganism, considered in its popular mythology, its poetry, and its philosophy. The *Pædagogus*, written for catechumens, sets before them a magnificent portrait of the true and only Master—the Eternal Word of the Father—who has created man to his own image; who alone can provide a fitting remedy for fallen and guilty humanity; who, though man had become of the earth, earthly, yet enables him to attain to his heavenly destiny; who, in fine, confides him to the maternal yet virginal love of the Church. Then came the eight books of the *Stromata*, an unpretending mosaic, in which the loftiest problems of philosophy and theology are treated with great learning and rare penetration. These three works were, without doubt, connected together in the author's mind. The idea of the Word is the central point of Clement's entire demonstration; and in that idea we must seek the essential unity of his system. It is the Word which tenderly invites man; which instructs him; which guides him to his end by leading him to see the things of God in their profundity; and thus the idea of the Word embraces in one same circle all philosophy, dogmatic as well as moral" (pp. 85, 88).

The monograph on Clement of Alexandria was prefaced by prolegomena, containing a sketch of Clement's life, an analysis of his doctrine, and an inquiry into the historical sources of his doctrine on the Word. For this the author had to examine the relation in which Clement stood in philosophy and theology towards classical antiquity, Alexandrine Judaism, the Apostolic

Fathers, and the first Christian apologists. The subject proper of the essay was divided into two parts: the first treated of the relations of the Word with God; the second considered the Word as the Revealer. The work was well received by the faculty of theology, and its author was declared the successful candidate, 31st of October, 1854. By the advice of Winer and others, and by the kindness of Tischendorf, it was published in March, 1855. Wacksmuth, dean of the faculty of philosophy, advised M. Laemmer to stand his examination for the doctor- ship in philosophy, and backed his advice by the offer of a burse to enable him to meet the expenses. The young student ob- tained this degree after having presented a dissertation on the religious philosophy of Clement of Alexandria, and having passed a successful examination.

We have seen that M. Laemmer qualifies this episode in his studies as the first step he made towards Catholicity. It may be asked, what was the special fruit derived by him from these patristic studies? The answer is, that it enabled him to shake off the influence of the Tübingen theories, which had hitherto held sway over his mind. The whole work of that school simply amounts to an attempt to submit to the all-powerful action of critical caprice the canon of Scripture and the most remarkable works of Christian antiquity, and to affirm all their own theories as indisputable facts, while they treat as fables the most authentic facts of history. Now, the more clearly it is proved that the historical origin of Christianity is able to resist the crucial tests to which it has been submitted, the more shadowy and incon- sistent do these capricious theories become. Hence, the study undertaken by M. Laemmer did in reality, by occupying him with the objective side of patristic teaching, most powerfully contribute to destroy in his mind the authority of Baur, Hilgen- feld, and the others of the Tübingen school.

Soon after the publication of his work, M. Laemmer was in- vited to the University of Berlin by his kind friend Lehnerdt, who had never lost sight of his promising pupil, and now wished him to prepare himself for a professor's chair by a solid course of theologico-historical studies. On arriving at Berlin the youth- ful doctor of philosophy was appointed to hold for two years the Evangelical Centenary Burse, founded by the city of Berlin in commemoration of the three hundredth anniversary of the Refor- mation. After his conversion many persons demanded that he should make restitution to the burse fund, which, according to them, he had employed against the intentions of the founders.

"But (asks Mr. Laémmer), for what reasons was I chosen in preference to the other candidates? I contented myself with presenting my memoir on the Alexandrine Clement's doctrine on the Word; the examiners of the Leipsic faculty of philosophy testified that I had successfully passed the examination : the faculty of theology of the same city said, amongst other flattering things, that I had applied myself to the studies of theology with equal ardour and success. As to the two memoirs presented for the concursus of 1853 and 1854, it was said that in them I had given proof of solid classical studies, of a remarkable knowledge of theology, of sound judgment, and penetrating mind, and that my work on the Word showed great aptitude for historical investigations. These were, beyond doubt, the reasons why the committee preferred me to the other candidates ; and the sole condition imposed upon me, namely, that of becoming a licentiate, I complied with within the appointed time. Why, then, all this outcry ? Why these demands for restitution, with which even a Hengstenberg has been associated ? Herein consists the head and front of my offending, that the use of private judgment, or, to speak accurately, the secret inspirations of God's grace, led me to see the truth and to betake myself to the bosom of the true Church. If instead I had become an unbeliever, the slightest murmur of complaint would not have been heard ; but when there is question of Catholicism, pietism the most honeyed often makes common cause with the grossest infidelity : the great point then is to form a compact body against the mighty foe " (pp. 105, 106).

We cannot linger over the account given by M. Laemmer of the different tendencies he found in the theological faculty of Berlin, nor on the present state or future prospects of the Union.* But the name of Hengstenberg† is so well known to most Catholics that the description given of him by one who has known him so well is sure to excite interest.

" The reputation which Hengstenberg had acquired by his numerous works brought him frequently before my mind. The impression he made on me when I saw him at Berlin did not modify the notion I had long formed of him. It is well known that he passed through many phases of doctrine before he reached the point at which, for some years, he has remained stationary. He left the University full of the pietism of the day, and was immediately appointed professor at Berlin, where, as professor and author, he bent all his energies against the rationalistic criticism, the application of which to the Holy Scriptures had produced such disastrous consequences. It must be admitted that, in this respect, he has brought back to better ways a certain number of his contemporaries ; that he has arrested the progress of extravagant criticism; that, in his works on the Pentateuch, the Psalms, and the Messianic Prophecies, he has won for sound views the consideration long refused them. But it was impossible that his ablest scholars should not see the weak side of his hermeneutical and theological principles ; hence many of them have abandoned his method for one altogether different. His *Commentary on the Apocalypse* is assuredly his most characteristic work. To comprehend his standpoint in this work we must remember that he composed it in 1848 and 1849. In it he frequently and unreservedly favours the chiliastic tendencies of Irving. . . . He has endeavoured to remove some of the Protestant prejudices against the Catholic Church, such as Luther's blasphemy of the Roman Antichrist. He admits (as Luther did when under the influence of the Christian idea) that Catholicism is in possession of the word of God, the true sacraments, and the power of the keys. He is clearer and more straightforward than his predecessor, Bengel, in the *Gnomon Novi Testamenti.* But he halts in his march,

---

* On the condition of the Protestant Church in Germany, see Döllinger's *The Church and the Churches*, p. 267 ; M'Cabe's translation, 1842.

† Father Perrone makes frequent reference to Hengstenberg's Biblical labours, especially in tract. *De Incarnatione*, Part I.

laying himself open to the charge of Catholic tendencies, and could but be silent when reproached by Schenkel, who told him that Romanism was more honourable than the vacillating and intermediate position he had assumed. He resembles Stehl, Kliefoth, and others, who would wish to place in the same setting the jewels of Catholicism and those of Wittemberg; who rank together the theory *nothing but the Bible* and the principle of authority; who are but half acquainted with Luther, and almost ignorant of Rome; who, in spite of their pretended adhesion to principle, would be disposed to all kinds of compromises; who lack the courage and the humility requisite to comprehend that the fragments of truth possessed by Luther have been borrowed from the immense and indivisible treasure of the Church. The Church has nothing to hope from men of this class: they lack a thorough and absolute thirst for truth; they are self-complacent; they imagine themselves to have received from heaven an extraordinary mission like the prophets; they assume the right to dictate to the infallible authority of the Church; to satisfy them we must become syncretists, and ask them what is it their pleasure that the Catholic Church should modify in its doctrines, its ceremonies, and its discipline; men of fine phrases, and not of action; more of show than of reality" (p. 117).

During his residence at Berlin M. Laemmer entered upon a careful preparation for the degree of doctor of divinity. He devoted himself more and more to the study of the Fathers; the works of St. Hilary of Poitiers on the Trinity left him an humble and firm believer in that august mystery. In 1856, his mind received a fresh and more decided impulse in the direction of the Church. In that year the Berlin faculty of theology gave as the subject of the concursus, *Give an exposition (from the documents) of the Roman Catholic doctrine contained in the memorial presented to Charles V. at the Diet of Augsburg, in as far as it appears to throw light on the true Evangelical doctrine set forth in the Augsburg Confession.* This subject was chosen for the concursus by Lehnerdt, who felt that Catholic theology, from the beginning of the Reformation to the Council of Trent, was almost entirely unknown. M. Laemmer, having resolved to become one of the competitors, at once set about the necessary study. He first examined the Protestant confessional books in order to fix the points at issue between them and their adversaries. If he were to trust these authorities, nothing could be clearer than the stupid ignorance of the Catholics, and the wisdom of the Protestants. But the declamation with which this was urged appeared to him to be the language of passion. He determined to learn from their own writings the character of the Catholic theologians so soundly abused by their opponents. He first examined the *Official refutation of the Augsburg Confession*, the joint work of the flower of the Catholic theologians, Eck, Faber, Wimpina, &c.; next he came to the various works published by them, before and after 1530, against the various successive developments of Protestantism; then came the German theology of Berthold Chiemsie; the Confession of Cardinal Hosius; Erasmus; Tetzel; Henry VIII.; Fisher, Bishop of

Rochester; Ambrosius Catharinus; the Sorbonne; Sadoletus; Contarini; the minutes of the conferences held at that epoch in Germany and Switzerland; the pontifical instructions in Rainaldi and Leplat; and last, the acts of the Imperial Diet, as far as they touched on religious and ecclesiastical questions. In all he had to study seventy Catholic works of the period.

"God knows," he tells us, "how I was moved as I read them, and how violent were the struggles in which I was engaged. I endeavoured to resist the force of the arguments before me, but I could not. I would not permit myself to call in question that great axiom of Protestants, that the Reformation was right and necessary. The humility required to correspond with the motions of grace was wanting to me; scientific pride still insisted on its pretended rights. I had only arrived so far as to understand that the opinions pronounced by the reformers on their adversaries were frequently partial, erroneous, and malevolent; that the intellectual power of these latter was not so contemptible as it had been represented; and finally, that their principles had been frequently travestied at the pleasure of the fathers of Protestantism " (p. 139).

Having completed his study of these sources, he arranged his materials in the following order: the first chapter treated of the Church, the Primacy, the Scripture, Tradition, the Councils; the second, of the state of innocence, of the fall, of original sin and its consequences; the third, of free-will and grace; the fourth, of justification, of the fulfilment of the law, and of the evangelical counsels; then came the sacraments *in genere et in specie*; finally, the saints and the worship due to them. The title of his manuscript was *De Theologia Romano-Catholica quæ Reformatorum ætate viguit, ante-Tridentina*. The work was successful, and received high praise from the faculty of theology. It was said, however, that the author was too impartial—*nimis justus*—towards Catholicism. This qualification was added at the request of Hengstenberg, who did not like too well the favourable notice given of Catholic writers. And yet, notwithstanding all this, Dr. Laemmer was still far from being a Catholic. He himself tells us that at most he had arrived at the position held by Leo. On the 3rd of August, 1856, he received the prize, and had the satisfaction of learning at the same time that his memoir was accepted as the dissertation required for the licence. In a few days he passed the *rigorosum*, and in the same month made his public disputation, taking for the theme of his introductory discourse St. Bernard's work, *De Consideratione*. He received his licence, and immediately left Berlin for the country to recruit his shattered health. In the country he preached frequently, wrote an analysis of G. Voigt's *Pius II. and his Age*, and a dissertation on the doctrine of justification held by the Catholic theologian, Contarini, in which he now admits he was mistaken as to his estimate of the sentiments of that divine. Returning to Berlin with renewed health, he was

appointed to give religious instruction, and to teach Hebrew in
the Frederic Gymnasium. It must have been a difficult task
for one perplexed in mind, as M. Laemmer was, to undertake
the religious instruction of a body of young men at the very
doors of the University of Berlin. Among his youthful hearers
he found open infidelity, rationalism, the doctrines of Schleiermacher, pietism, confessionalism, in one word, each class was a
miniature copy of the Protestant world around. But he did not
swerve from the path of duty. He boldly set before them, as
the central truth of religion, the Man-God dying on the cross
for the world. In vain did his hearers bring forward the pretended results of modern criticism, and natural explanations of
supernatural facts; M. Laemmer insisted with energy upon the
credibility and the inspiration of Sacred Scriptures, and on the
miracles and prophecies narrated in them. He also made it his
duty to lead his charge to love and practise prayer. In spite of
their resistance, he obliged even the higher classes to recite the
Decalogue and the Apostles' Creed; and he was consoled by
seeing his firmness rewarded by the happiest results. At Easter,
1857, he passed his examination for the doctor's degree, having
chosen for the subject of his theme Pope Nicholas I. and the
Court of Byzantium. Again he was successful: Lehnerdt, to
whom he had dedicated his thesis, observed to him with great
gentleness that he was not far from Hurter's idea of the Papacy.
And in truth this last labour had brought him much nearer to
the Church by reason of the brilliant light it cast on the character and office of the Papacy in Christianity. In 1857 he
found time to publish a new edition of St. Anselm's *Cur Deus
Homo*, and to write a paper on the conversion of Herman of Kap-
penburg. In June, 1858, he revised for the press his treatise
on the ante-Tridentine theology. In preparing the revision he
made a study of modern Catholic works on history, dogma,
moral and canon law. He became familiar with the Roman
Breviary, to which his attention had been called by the attempt
made by a Protestant minister to form a Lutheran Breviary.
He also read and admired Cardinal Wiseman's *Fabiola*.

"I now understood the *Memorare* and the *Sub tuum*; I began to recite the
Ave Maria, to salute together with the angel the Mother of my God, to seek
her compassion, that she might obtain for me grace to be completely enlightened, and to enter into the Saviour's one fold. The sting of doubt tormented
me unceasingly; on my knees, before my crucifix in my lonely chamber, I experienced the most painful struggles. As I had ever preserved such fragments
of Christian truth as the Reformers had spared, and as for many long years I
had occupied myself with the solution of the leading questions in philosophy
and theology, it appeared to me very hard to submit my reason to the yoke of
faith. But prayer removed all these obstacles, and when, soon after, I came to
knock at the door of the Church, I found it easy to assent to all the truths that
were proposed to my belief" (p. 163).

With many other Protestants, he assisted at the exercises of a mission given at Berlin by the Jesuit Fathers, and reaped therefrom much benefit. In July, 1858, he received permission from the minister of worship to explore the libraries of Germany and northern Italy, to collect such manuscripts of Eusebius as might be found, with a view to a new revision of the text of that historian. He visited Leipsic, Dresden, Vienna, Venice, Padua, Milan, and Munich. At Dresden, Wolfgang de Goethe took him to be a Catholic priest. At Venice he met with F. Ignazio Mozzoni, of the Order of St. John of God, author of a remarkable history of the Church, and was edified by the piety and the literary activity of the Melchitansts. The intercourse he had with Catholic ecclesiastics, and the sight of Catholic ceremonies and rites, were of signal service to him by removing unfavourable impressions. Among other details he tells us :—

"I shall never forget a certain Irish Dominican, the very type of a perfect religious, who aroused in me profound emotions by the account he gave me of the sad condition of his fellow-countrymen, crushed by English rule " (p. 191).

His scientific mission was finished at Munich, whither he returned from his long journey still a Protestant. But the end was at hand, and we must allow him to describe it in his own words :—

"After leaving Munich I continued for some weeks to suffer great anguish of mind. At length the decisive hour came, and the sun of grace had completed the work of my enlightenment. I decided to become a Catholic on the 14th of October, 1858, the feast of St. Theresa, whose powerful intercession strengthened my weakness. I communicated my resolutions to the minister of worship, and to the Faculty of Theology of Berlin, and I requested my bishop —the Bishop of Ermland—to receive me into the bosom of the Roman Catholic Church, in which, after long and painful struggles, I had at length recognised the depositary of the truth, and the legitimate spouse of the Son of God; thus would my heart be at peace. 'Glory and praise,' said my letter, 'to our Lord Jesus Christ, who has enabled me to surmount all obstacles, who has graciously heard my prayers, who has had pity on me, who has broken my chains, who has scattered the darkness that hung over me, who has shown me the path to the fold. Since conscientious investigations have proved to me that the so-called Reformation of the sixteenth century has but disfigured the type of the true Church of Jesus Christ, and that its principles, far from being salutary, are essentially destructive and the necessary cause of the effects which history has registered during three centuries, that the Protestant confessions and their apologists, instead of attacking the Church's genuine teaching, do but distort it to insure an easy victory; since I am convinced that the Reformers had neither the duty nor the right to attempt a reform apart from and against the head of the Church and the episcopate; that the religious divisions of our age are caused by the refusal to submit to the Church and return to the centre whence we departed in the sixteenth century; since the historical development of the Church has been proved to me unbroken down to the present day; since I have learned to justify and love her doctrine, her morality, and her worship; from the day on which the grace of God has permitted me to be convinced of

these truths, my return to the Catholic Church has become a matter of necessity, and it is only by a public confession of my faith that I can hope to regain
tranquillity of conscience, that peace of the heart which the world cannot give,
nor yet, in spite of all its fraud and anger, can ever take away.' "

It is needless to add that the Bishop of Ermland acceded to
this touching request. On St. Catherine's Day, during the
Jubilee of 1858, Dr. Laemmer made his profession of Catholic
faith, and received the sacraments of baptism and the Eucharist.
Towards the end of the same year he was admitted to the diocesan seminary of Ermland, where he received confirmation,
tonsure, and holy orders. Soon after his ordination he was sent
to Rome. Several valuable works on subjects of ecclesiastical
history have since appeared from him, and much is still expected at his hands.* In the bosom of the Catholic Church, his
doubts dispelled, his heart at peace, well indeed may he love to
repeat with joy and gratitude—*Misericordias Domini in æternum
cantabo !*—(Ps. xxxii. 21).

---

* The following are some of the works published by Dr. Laemmer since his
conversion :—

1. Εὐσεβίου τοῦ Παμφίλου 'Εκκλησιαστιῆς 'Ιστορίας Βίβλοι Δέκα. Euselii
Pamphili Historiæ Ecclesiasticæ libri decem. Græcum textum collatis qui in
Germaniæ et Italiæ bibliothecis asservantur Codicibus et adhibitis præstantis-
simis editionibus recensuit atque emendavit, latinam Henrici Valesii versionem
passim correctam subjunxit, apparatum criticum apposuit, fontes annotavit,
prolegomena et indices adjecit D. Hugo Laemmer, Presbyter Varmiensis. Fasc.
I. Cum tabulis duabus Specimina Codicum septem continentibus. Scaphusiæ
sumtibus librariæ Hurterianæ. MDCCCLIX.

2. De Codicibus Recensionibusque Historiæ Ecclesiasticæ Eusebii Cæsari-
ensisi scripsit D. Hugo Laemmer, 1860.

3. Ancedota Baroniana, ex codd. MSS. collegit, selectaque specimina edidit
D. Hugo Laemmer. Rome, 1860.

4. Monumenta Vaticana, historiam ecclesiasticam sæculi XVI. illustrantia.
Ex tabulariis S. Sedis Apostolicæ secretis excerpsit, digessit, recensuit, prole-
gomenisque et indicibus instruxit Hugo Laemmer. Una cum fragmentis Nea-
politanis ac Florentinis, 8vo.

RICHARD FITZ-RALPH, ARCHBISHOP OF ARMAGH.

"Many a mile have I gone, and many did I walk,
But never saw a holier man than Richard of Dundalk."
Old Couplet. *

§ I.—INTRODUCTION.

In all the habits of social life many of the early English settlers in Ireland soon became more Irish than the Irish themselves. In the vigorous tenacity of their attachment to the Catholic religion some of these families have ever remained as Irish as the Irish themselves. Having made our people their people, they became sharers in our grace of faith, so as to keep ever since our God their God. To the Talbots and the Plunkets we owe two great archbishops, whose figures stand out prominently even among the illustrious band of prelates who fought the good fight in the days of the persecutors. And as our Church reckons Anglo-Irish bishops among her martyrs, so among her doctors, who guarded and enriched the sacred deposit of faith, we may count Anglo-Irish prelates equally illustrious : and of these the subject of the present notice offers a distinguished example. A variety of great qualities, rarely united in one individual, gives a singular attractiveness to the history of Richard Fitz-Ralph, Archbishop of Armagh. Extraordinary holiness of life, of which proof remains not only in the popular couplet at the head of this paper, and in the appellation of St. Richard of Dundalk, by which he was known for centuries, but in the stronger evidence of a Pontifical commission, issued by Boniface IX., to examine into his miracles with a view to his canonisation ; rare intellectual power exhibited in every branch of theology—erudition both various and profound—eloquence of a high order, to which his sermons still extant bear testimony ; all these are qualities which, especially when exercised under the trying vicissitudes of a great controversy within the Church, could not fail to constitute a remarkable career. Of this career we now propose to lay before our readers an outline as perfect as the

* This couplet is quoted by Prince in his *Worthies of Devon* from *Paul* Harris, c. 5, p. 88, who thus introduces it, "of whose (Fitz-Ralph's) sanctity the common people of Ireland, by ancient tradition, were wont to chant this distich." In the loose papers prefixed to the *Martyrology of Donegal*, the verses are quoted from *Henry* Harris in *Apolu.* This false reference has led Dr. Todd into a slight mistake, vide *Martyr. of Donegal,* App. to Int., p. xlii.

materials within our reach will allow us to sketch. We do so with the hope that others, in whom better skill is backed by richer materials, may be led to supplement from their store our slender contribution to the history of an illustrious successor of St. Patrick.

§ II.—THE FITZ-RALPH FAMILY: RICHARD'S PARENTAGE.

Ralph, founder of the Fitz-Ralph family, held forty-nine lordships in England in the reign of William the Conqueror. From this stem various branches issued, and several families of Fitz-Ralphs were to be found in the twelfth and thirteenth centuries. To which of these Richard belongs is a matter of uncertainty. Prince, in his anxiety to enrol him among the worthies of Devonshire, refers him to the Fitz-Ralphs of Wide-comb-in-the-Moor, who, about the time of Edward I., changed their names and residence, henceforth calling themselves Stil-lingford, from their new abode near Exeter. But this is mere guess work. It is far more probable, in our opinion, that he belonged to the Derbyshire Fitz-Ralphs, of which family the Frechevilles and Musards of Staveley* became in after times the representatives. Our reasons are these : Ralph (Musard) Baron Staveley, a direct descendant of Ralph, the founder of the family, had a daughter Margaret, who, on his death, became co-heir with her brother Nicholas and her sister Isabella. Mar-garet married an Irishman, named in the pedigree Joannes de Hibernia, and died in the year 1308. Three children were born of this marriage—John de Hibernia, Ralph, and Alicia. Thus we actually have the heir of the Fitz-Ralphs born of an Irish father. As his mother's heir, John de Hibernia was owner of the third part of the manor of Staveley, and this property he gave and granted to Ralph de Frecheville. The evidence taken at an inquisition held at Staveley, in 1316, asserts that the said John "had no other lands in England." This would lead us to conjecture that he had lands in Ireland ; and after this time the pedigree no longer adds the words *de Hibernia* to any of the Fitz-Ralphs. Now, it is certain that Richard must have been born about this time ; and, although the precise year of his birth is not known, the date of his promotion to Armagh would allow him to have been the son of this John, or of his brother, Ralph. But, setting conjecture aside, one thing is proved beyond a doubt, viz., that about the time of Richard's birth the Fitz-Ralphs of Staveley had a close connection with Ireland.

---

* *Collectanea Topographica et Genealogica*, vol. iv. London, 1847. Pedigree of the Frechevilles and Musards.

§ III.—HIS BIRTHPLACE.

An almost universal tradition fixes his birthplace at Dundalk. According to Wadding, the tradition was that his parents came to Dundalk from the well-known territory in the north of Ireland called *Ruta*, or the Route. Wood states that almost all writers—*auctores pene omnes*—make him an Irishman. This tradition is also clearly expressed in the appellation of Richard of Dundalk, by which he was universally known. It was the custom of the age to designate men by the name of their native place. Of this we have an excellent example in the name of John Baconthorpius, or of Baconthorpe, who, as we shall see, was Fitz-Ralph's professor at Oxford. Cotton, in his *Fasti*, tells us that "it has been contended, with some appearance of truth, that this prelate was born in England." He here alludes to the opinion maintained by Rev. John Prince,* who considers it probable that our prelate was born in Devonshire, adding, "Some tell us that he was an Irishman, and born in the town of Dundalk in that kingdom, and hence called by the name of Richard of Dundalk. Whereas it is possible he might be so denominated, not from his birth, but from his long residence, or his doing some eminent exploit there, or from some other like occasion there. Others say he was an Englishman, which is not improbable, for these reasons : that he had his education at Oxford ; that he was chosen commissary of that university ; that he was made archdeacon of Lichfield ; and that he was encouraged against the friars by English bishops."

These are the only arguments alleged to prove that Archbishop Fitz-Ralph was born in England. They are of no weight whatever when compared with the mass of testimony on the other side. 1. The name of Richard of Dundalk could not have arisen from the primate's long residence in that town, for he resided in his diocese only for about nine years, and certainly did not spend all his time in Dundalk. 2. Nor is it told in history that he performed any eminent exploit here. 3. It does not make against the Irish origin of Archbishop Fitz-Ralph that he had his education at Oxford, It is well known that at the beginning of the fourteenth century there were very many Irishmen at Oxford. Bale gives the names of several most distinguished Irishmen who flourished there at that period—in 1310, Malachias Minorita ; in 1320, David O'Buge of Kildare ; in 1330, Gilbert Urgalius, who, *consueto Hibernorum hominum more*, went to Oxford after completing his rudimentary studies. Besides, among the *nations* whose contests in the thirteenth and

* *Danmonii Orientales Illustres ; or, The Worthies of Devon.*

fourteenth centuries so often made Oxford anything but a quiet
abode of learning, the Irish had their place, and generally went
with the Southern men.   And the Archbishop himself, in his
discourse at Avignon, relates how he had sent to Oxford four
priests of the diocese of Armagh.   4. That the appointment of
Richard as chancellor or vice-chancellor of Oxford does not
necessarily suppose him to have been an Englishman, will appear
from what we have to say farther on concerning this office.
5. Nor was it strange that an Irish ecclesiastic should hold
benefices in England.   Clement VI., in 1351, granted to John
do Briane, Dean of St. Patrick's at Dublin, who held at the
same time the parish of Hatfield in Lincoln, permission to retain
his benefices during his five years' course at a university.*
   Summing up the evidence, we have, on the one hand, the
almost universal tradition that our prelate was born in Dundalk;
we have an established connexion between the Derbyshire Fitz-
Ralphs and Ireland about the time of his birth.   On the other
hand, against his Irish origin we have no argument stronger
than mere probabilities which, when examined, are found to
have no substance.   We conclude, therefore, that Richard Fitz-
Ralph was born in Dundalk.   This conclusion receives some
confirmation from a narrative in Fox,† where we are told that
a copy of the entire Bible, translated into Irish by Archbishop
Fitz-Ralph, was found, many years after his death, in the walls
of his cathedral.   Now, if this story be true, and it is indirectly
confirmed by Ussher, it is plain that the Archbishop must have
been born in Ireland.   It is hard to believe that nine years,
broken as they were by provincial visitations and other labours,
would have been sufficient to make an English prelate master of
a language so difficult as the Irish, and that to the degree of
perfection requisite for a translation of the sacred text.

§ IV.—HIS STUDIES AND UNIVERSITY CAREER.

   Richard Fitz-Ralph went to Oxford, and was entered of
Balliol College (then recently founded), where he remained until
he had taken his degree of Master of Arts.   The statutes in
force at that time required him to leave Balliol.   As soon as he
received his degree in Arts he accordingly passed to what is
now known as University College, but which, after 1332, was
called *Magna Aula Universitatis*, and which owed its origin to
the liberality of William de Durham, who, dying in 1249, bequeathed a sum of money for the benefit of ten or twelve poor

* Theiner, *Monumenta*, pp. 296-594.   † *Martyrol. Angl.*, tom. i., p. 296.

17

masters. By a decision of congregation in 1280, four masters, "whoever might be considered fittest for promotion in Holy Church," were to be chosen to enjoy these funds, each master being entitled to fifty shillings sterling yearly for his maintenance. The same document enjoins that the above-mentioned masters, living together, shall attend lectures on theology, and shall be able, at the same time, to hear lectures on the decrees and decretals. As to their way of living and learning, they shall behave as they are directed by some fit and experienced men appointed by the Chancellor.*

His residence at Balliol gave him special opportunities to become proficient in arts. The college had been endowed to enable sixteen scholars to study in arts, each scholar receiving a yearly revenue of twenty-seven marks. His residence in University College enabled him to cultivate theology. Thus all the materials of knowledge then existing were brought within his reach. At that date the course of studies had changed a good deal from the ancient narrow limits of the Trivium† and Quadrivium.‡ Out of the logic of the Trivium the new philosophy was developed, and the sciences of the Quadrivium became mere preparatory studies to the Facultas Artium.§ It is mentioned by Tanner and others that Richard Fitz-Ralph attended the theological lectures of the famous Carmelite, John Baconthorpe. This remarkable man was one of the most illustrious scholars of the day, and exercised a powerful influence on the mind of his pupil. It has been observed that when the latter had become Archbishop of Armagh, and had entered upon his controversy with the friars, he ever showed a marked affection for the Carmelites.

The early half of the fourteenth century was a season of much agitation in philosophical and theological opinions. The ancient struggle between the Nominalists and the Realists entered at this time upon a new phase. The Realism of St. Thomas of Aquin was opposed by the Nominalism of Occam, and Fitz-Ralph found Oxford still agitated by the controversies that master had excited. The Franciscans were generally Nominalists; the secular clergy, as a body, were Realists. The entire university was divided into two opposite camps. The "Northern men" declared for Realism, the "Southern men" for Nominalism.‖ Fitz-Ralph became a leading Realist, and the marked divergence between his views and those of the Franciscans was

* Huber, *English Universities*, vol. i., p. 438 ; Newman's edition.
† Grammar, logic, and rhetoric.
‡ Arithmetic, geometry, astronomy, and music.
§ Huber, *English Universities*, vol. i., p. 53.
‖ *Ibid.*, note xx., p. 408, vol. i.

probably not without its influence on the controversy to which hereafter we shall have occasion to refer.

How deep and how extensive were the studies of Fitz-Ralph shall best be learned from the list of his works at the conclusion of this notice. It will be enough for our present purpose to state here that his labours cover almost the entire field of Catholic controversy with the Greeks and Armenians, as well as (by anticipation) with the Reformers. A remarkable element in his writings, and one the presence of which reveals the form of scepticism current in his age, is the contribution he has made to the literature of the Christian Demonstration. He defends the Christian religion against the Jews by contrasting the sacraments and ceremonies of the New Law with those of the Jewish dispensation. This line of defence was called for by the altered method of attack which the Jews, about the twelfth century, began to employ against the Church. In the early ages the controversy turned upon the question whether our Lord was the Messiah. In the middle ages they had recourse to the scriptural defence of their own position and calumnious attacks on Christianity. It is not strange that he should have combated Mahometanism. It should be borne in mind that the age of Frederic II. had witnessed the birth of a strange admiration for Mahometan literature; that Pope Gregory IX. had fought against this novel danger; that against the Arabian Averroes and his philosophy St. Thomas of Aquin himself had entered the lists. It is not surprising, therefore, that the archbishop's zeal urged him to provide a remedy for the evil by proving that the Saracenic law itself confirmed the authority of the books of the Old and New Testament.

Before 1333 he proceeded to his degree of Doctor of Theology.

§ V.—HIS PREFERMENTS IN ENGLAND.

Ware* declares that Dr. Fitz-Ralph was made Chancellor of Oxford University in 1333. On the other hand, Wood asserts in his history that no record of this chancellorship exists either in the University or the Episcopal archives. However, the same Wood admits him to have been *Commissarius* of the university in that year, or, as we may describe it, vice-chancellor. Is there any way by which these different statements may be reconciled? It appears to us that an attentive consideration of the various phases through which the office of chancellor of Oxford has passed will supply a very probable solution of the difficulty.

* *De Presulibus Hib.*, pp. 20-21.

First of all, we must bear in mind that Oxford was not at that time the seat of a bishop, but was included within the diocese of Lincoln. Next, we should consider that even during the course of the fourteenth century the chancellor was an episcopal officer, not an academical one ; he represented the ordinary of the diocese, and from him drew all his jurisdiction and authority. As the university grew in importance and extent, the position of the chancellor, as a power extern to the university, became untenable, and by degrees the nomination to the office passed from the hands of the bishop to those of the academicians.* For a time the bishop struggled to retain at least the right of confirming the election ; but in the course of the fourteenth century even this claim was abandoned. The period 1330-1350 forms, therefore, a peculiar epoch in the history of the Oxford chancellors, marking as it does the transition period between the chancellors who were episcopal officers and the chancellors elected by and out of the university. Now this transition was not effected suddenly, but almost by way of compromise : there was no sharp separation between the two classes of chancellors ; the one gradually merged into the other. We should therefore expect to find some confusion in the list of chancellors ; the bishop's chancellor being considered as the legitimate chancellor by those who sided with the bishop, whereas the academicians would naturally look up to their own nominee. Now it is quite certain that Richard Fitz-Ralph, master of theology, was appointed Chancellor of Lincoln on the 6th of July, 1333, for the appointment is entered under that date on the register of Bishop Burghers. We may conclude, therefore, either that as Chancellor of Lincoln he was Chancellor of the University, as the episcopal officers before him had been, or that his appointment having fallen upon a time of some dispute about the nomination of the chancellor, he was styled *Commissarius* only, or that the story of his Oxford chancellorship took its rise from the fact that he was chancellor of the bishop in whose diocese Oxford was situated. According to some authors, he was also Archdeacon of Chester. But he was certainly Dean of Lichfield, at least from 1337, and held this office until his appointment to Armagh. Wood relates that shortly before his own time the first window on the northern side of the choir of Lichfield cathedral contained a picture of Richard Fitz-Ralph clothed in his sacerdotal vestments, and above the following inscription : *Richardus Radulphi filius, Armachanus, Hujus Ecclesiæ Decanus.*

---

* Huber, vol. i., p. 132.

§ VI.—HIS NOMINATION TO THE SEE OF ARMAGH.

The see of Armagh became vacant by the death of David O'Hiraghty, which took place, according to the *Annales Nenagh-tenses*, on the 16th May, 1346. Dr. O'Hiraghty had been Dean of Armagh, and was elected by the chapter of Armagh, *quasi per inspirationem divinam*, as John XXII. mentions in the bull by which, on July 4th, 1334, he ratified the election.* He was consecrated at Avignon, and, having ruled his diocese for nearly twelve years, died in 1346. On the 31st July, 1346, Clement VI., *jure provisionis*, appointed to the vacant see Richard Fitz-Ralph, then Dean of Lichfield. The bull of nomination contains that the chapter of Armagh had already unanimously elected the same Richard, and that he had given his consent to the election.† The Four Masters place, in the year 1356, the death of Farrell (son of Jeffrey) Mac Rannall, Primate of Armagh and representative of St. Patrick. This, as Dr. O'Donovan remarks, is evidently a mistake of the Four Masters, as Richard Fitz-Ralph was certainly not one of the Mac Rannalls. We may say that besides the mistake in the names there is also a mistake in the dates. It was precisely in 1356 that Archbishop Fitz-Ralph set out upon that visit to London which was the occasion of his controversy with the Franciscans. The mistake made by the Four Masters is all the more incomprehensible, for this reason, that of all the primates who sat at Armagh since the days of St. Francis of Assisi, no one was more likely to be remembered by the Franciscans than Archbishop Fitz-Ralph.

Dr. Fitz-Ralph was consecrated at Exeter on the 8th of July, 1347, by John Grandison, Bishop of Exeter, and three other bishops.‡ If this date be correct, the Primate found himself engaged in the onerous duties of his new office even before his consecration. On the 10th of April, 1347, Clement VI. appointed him, together with the Archbishop of Cashel, to make inquiry, on the part of the Holy See, into some charges brought against the Archbishop of Dublin by the Bishop of Ossory.§ On the 12th of July of the same year he received faculties from the Holy See to dispense, in a case of invalid marriage, the parties belonging to the diocese of Armagh.‖ The bishops of Ardagh and Cloyne were appointed, on the 29th August, 1347, to give him the pallium.¶

---

* Theiner's *Vetera Monumenta*, n. 517, p. 263.
† *Ibid.*, n. 270, p. 286.
‡ *Annal. MSS.*, in Bibl. Cotton.
§ *Vet. Monum.*, n. 271, pp. 286-7.
‖ *Ibid.*, n. 272.   ¶ *Ibid.*, n. 273.

§ VII.—THE ACTS OF HIS EPISCOPATE.

One of the most striking characteristics of Archbishop Fitz-Ralph's pastoral life was his assiduity in preaching the word of God to his people. His sermons on the principal festivals, still extant in MS. in the university libraries of Dublin, Oxford, and Cambridge, and in the British Museum, would fill a large volume. Already, as Dean of Lichfield, he had been remarkable for his fervour in preaching; but, as successor of St. Patrick in the see of Armagh, he seemed to have received a double spirit of zeal and diligence. A volume of his sermons, once in the possession of Ware, and lately purchased for the Britism Museum at the sale of the Tennison library, includes sermons preached at Avignon, London, Drogheda, Dundalk, Trim, and other places of the province of Armagh. The fame of his eloquence preceded him to the Holy See, and, when at Avignon, he was frequently admitted to the high honour of preaching before the Holy Father and the cardinals and prelates of his court. He loved to make our Blessed Lady's virtues the subject of his discourse. *De Laudibus S. Deiparæ* is the title of many of his sermons. There are also special sermons on her Conception, Visitation, and Assumption. His sermons are generally constructed on a uniform plan. After quoting his text it was his custom to begin with some short prayer like the following, which occurs in a sermon preached at Avignon on the Feast of All Saints, 1358: *Pro edificandi gratia impetranda, devote, si placet, matrem gratiæ salutemus, dicentes Ave Maria.* And in a sermon preached before Innocent VI., on the feast of the Epiphany, after the text *Videntes stellam Magi,* he begins with the invocation, *O Maria stella Maris, Mater stellæ solaris.* After the introductory prayer he repeats the text in the vernacular, and then proceeds with the division of the subject. In dividing his discourse he generally employs the rigour of the scholastic method; each member of the division being complete in itself, and forming, as it stands, a finished whole. Hence, the great feature of his style is its singular clearness: a clearness which, however, never becomes hard or cold, so tender is the unction that pervades the entire. He appears to have had a singular devotion to St. Catherine the Martyr and to St. Thomas of Canterbury, among the saints; three or four different sermons are to be found in the collection in honour of each. It is much to be regretted that those beautiful sermons have never been printed.

Anxious to secure efficient pastors for his flock, he took care that his clergy should have the benefit of the highest literary and ecclesiastical training it was within his power to procure.

With this view he sent four of his priests to the University of Oxford, where he himself had spent so many happy years of profitable study. He also acquired for his diocese from the Benedictines of St. Mary of Lenley's in Normandy, the priory and houses of St. Andrew in the Ardes, belonging to that order. Besides this he was diligent in visiting every portion of his province. Among the rolls of Edward III. there is a letter, of 28th April, 1356,* addressed by that King to the Archbishop, at a moment that the latter has actually engaged in his visitation of the diocese of Meath. Edward calls upon the Primate to return with all speed to Dundalk to treat with Odo O'Neill, who was advancing upon that town with a considerable army of Irish. Nor was it the first time that the Archbishop's virtues enabled him to discharge the blessed office of peace-maker in the disturbed state of society in which his lot was cast. As far back as 1348, he had received from the King full powers to treat for peace between the English and Irish.†

While careful of the spiritual interests of his diocese, Archbishop Fitz-Ralph did not neglect to take care of its temporal concerns. He justified to the letter the description given of him in the bull which made him Archbishop: *in spiritualibus providum, in temporalibus circumspectum.*

On January 11th, 1351, he received from Clement VI. a favourable answer to his petition that he might be allowed to incorporate with the mensal funds of his see the income of four churches with care of souls, provided the ordinaries consented, and that the sum did not exceed the annual value of one hundred marks. The petition of the Archbishop set forth that the entire income of his see did not reach four hundred pounds sterling per annum. On the same day the Pontiff issued letters requiring the Abbot of St. Mary's in Dynelek (Duleek), the Prior of St. Leonard's in Dundalk, and the Archdeacon of Armagh, together with the chapter of the cathedral, to examine how far it would be useful to exchange certain church lands, rents, and other immovable property for others which the Primate judged more likely to be advantageous to the see of Armagh.

Two documents preserved by Rymer show how careful Dr. Fitz-Ralph was not to sanction by any act of his the claims made to the primacy by the Archbishop of Dublin, to the detriment of Armagh. The first is dated 8th December, 1350, and is an order, from Edward III., that the Archbishop of Armagh should not have his cross carried before him within the limits of the province of Dublin. Archbishop Fitz-Ralph was unwilling to cause disturbance by refusing to obey this order ; but, on the

* *Claus.* 29, 30, Ed. III.   † *Pat.* 29, Ed. III.

other hand, he felt that to comply with it fully would be to prejudice the legitimate claims of his see.

He resolved, in consequence, simply to absent himself from Dublin. He procured a royal license, which excused him from personal attendance at the parliaments held at Dublin, on the ground that within the province of Dublin he was not permitted to have his cross borne before him. In 1349, he was charged by the same king to plead in the royal name before the Sovereign Pontiff, Clement VI., for the grace of a jubilee on behalf of the people subject to the English crown. In Oxford there is a MS. entitled, *Propositio ejusden* (*Ric. Rad. sive Fitz-Ralph Archiepiscopi Armachani*) *ex parte Regis Angliæ Edwardi III. in consistorio Domini Papæ, Avinione pro gratia jubilæi ejus Domino Regis populo obtinenda, anno* 1349. A similar heading is prefixed to another *propositio* of the same prelate, which, as we shall see, he urged in person at Avignon in 1357. Pope Clement VI. was engaged in anxious efforts to restore the Oriental churches to union with Rome. The Armenians were, in an especial manner, the objects of his paternal solicitude. The remarkable series of questions which the Pope proposed to the bishops of that church are well known in ecclesiastical history. It was, probably, during this visit to the Holy See that Archbishop Fitz-Ralph became acquainted with the two Armenian prelates, Nerses or Narses of Manasgarda, and John, Bishop-elect of Clata, in Greater Armenia. These Oriental bishops had long and earnest conferences with their Irish brother on the sad state of their once flourishing church, and, at their earnest and oft-repeated requests, the Primate resolved to contribute his aid to the great work of bringing back the Armenians to unity. One circumstance connected with the occasion, though it narrowed his field of argument for the time, has given, nevertheless, to his writings a character which makes them valuable in modern controversy. In his *Questiones Armenorum* he was forced to defend the Catholic doctrine almost exclusively from the Holy Scriptures, seeing that his adversaries did not admit the authority of the Roman Church. Hence his position as a controversial writer does not differ from that which the Reformation has imposed upon modern theologians since the time of Bellarmine.

Before the publication of Theiner's *Vetera Monumenta* there was but a single writer, Raphael of Volterra,* to assert that Archbishop Fitz-Ralph had been created Cardinal. This solitary testimony, though positive, was not considered by Ware and others strong enough to counterbalance the negative argument

* *Commentar. Urbanor,* lib. 3.

drawn from the silence of all other writers on the subject, and
especially from the fact that upon the elaborate catalogue of
cardinals, drawn up by Panvinio and Ciacconia, the name of
Fitz-Ralph is not to be found. Among the documents published by Theiner there is a consistorial process drawn up, in
1517, on occasion of a vacancy in the see of Ardagh,* in which
mention is made, among other glories of Ireland, of the Cardinal
of Armagh, who flourished in the year 1353. This is no other
than our Archbishop Fitz-Ralph. It is curious that the statement in this process is made in words almost identical with those
used by Raphael of Volterra. So close is the likeness between
the two statements that one is clearly copied from the other. It
is also to be observed that in the Papal documents he is never
styled Cardinal, and that even as late as October, 1358, Archbishop Fitz-Ralph is styled by Innocent VI. simply Archbishop
of Armagh, although in the same letter the Pontiff makes mention of the cardinals appointed to examine into the questions at
issue between our prelate and the Mendicant Orders. However
this may be explained, we have the weighty authority of an
official document, drawn up at Rome, and accepted by the Holy
Father himself, for believing that the see of Armagh was
honoured by the Roman purple in the person of Richard Fitz-
Ralph.

§ VIII.—HIS CONTROVERSY WITH THE MENDICANT ORDERS.

We now approach the grave controversy which was carried
on for years between our Archbishop and the Mendicant Religious Orders. Even if the space at our disposal permitted it, we
would not be willing to enter here into a detailed account of the
dispute.

Had it been given to Archbishop Fitz-Ralph to see as clearly
as history has enabled us to see, the blessings which our Church
owes to the heroism of the religious orders in the days of persecution, far from opposing, he would have been the first to
enlarge their privileges in Ireland. But, as it was, it is quite
clear that in his opposition to them he was influenced solely by
motives of an elevated nature. The whole struggle was simply
a domestic misunderstanding, and of such character as that one
may and must feel deep respect for both parties. We cannot
do better than lay before our readers the explanation of his object and motives offered by the Archbishop himself to Pope
Innocent VI. in person, at Avignon, 8th November, 1357.†

* Vet. Mon., p. 521.   † Defensorium Curatorum.

"In the name of the Father, and of the Son, and of the Holy Ghost. Amen. 'Nolite judicare secundum faciem sed justum judicium judicate' (*Joan.*, cap. 7).

"Most Holy Father, I protest, at the very beginning of my discourse, that I do not intend to assert or rashly to affirm anything which may clash with Christian faith or Catholic doctrine, and that it is not my intention to solicit, or even to advise, the abolition or retrenchment of the mendicant orders approved by the Church or confirmed by the Sovereign Pontiffs. But rather it is my desire that these same orders be brought back to the purity of their original institution, and in this also I am ever ready to submit to the correction of your Holiness. And, to approach my subject without delay, coming to London, Most Holy Father, about certain matters connected with my Church of Armagh, I found a dispute going on between certain learned doctors concerning the mendicant state and the mendicity of Christ our Lord and Saviour. After repeated invitations to preach to the people, I there delivered, in the vernacular, seven or eight discourses, and, always under the above-made protest, I defended in public nine conclusions, on account of which, and for what else, I then said, the friars have appealed, though without reason, to this Holy See."

The visit to London here alluded to took place in 1356, and, as we have seen, in 1357 the case was already under judgment at Avignon. For three whole years the archbishop remained at the Holy See, while a congregation of cardinals, specially appointed for the purpose, took cognisance of the dispute. No official decision was given; but as the privileges of the mendicant orders were confirmed, and a letter sent to the English bishops commanding them not to interfere with the friars, it may be said that the Archbishop failed to make good his cause.

§ IX.—HIS DEATH.

On the 16th November, 1360, according to Henry of Malmesbury, Richard Fitz-Ralph slept in the Lord at Avignon. "Of whom," says Fox,[*] "a certain cardinal, hearing of his death, openly protested that the same day a mighty pillar of the Church was fallen."

In Wadding's *Annals* it is told that towards the end of his life, seeing it was not likely he could succeed in his struggle, he withdrew to Belgium, and there died in the mountains of Hannonia. The same account appears in the Camden Annals of Ireland. But Ware[†] tells us that the Armagh copy of these annals agrees with other histories in placing the death at Avignon. In 1370 his remains were removed by Stephanus de Valle (who, from the see of Limerick, was translated to that of Meath by Urban V., in 1369), and brought back to his native town of Dundalk, where they were deposited in the church of St. Nicholas. The memory of his extraordinary merits soon

---

* *Acts and Monuments*, i., p. 465, seq.
† *De Scriptoribus*, lib. i., p. 10.

attracted to his tomb crowds of the faithful. The usage of styling him St. Richard of Dundalk became quite general, and many miracles were ascribed to his intercession. Moved by the report of these prodigies, Pope Boniface IX. appointed John Cotton, Archbishop of Armagh, Richard Young, Bishop-elect of Bangor, and the Abbot of Osney, near Oxford, as commissioners to institute a judicial examination of the miracles. The result of their labours is not known. Stewart, in his *History of Armagh*, mentions,* that in a synod held at Drogheda, in 1545, it was ordered that the feast of St. Richard of Dundalk should be celebrated in the diocese of Armagh with nine lessons, *in crastino Joannis et Pauli.*

§ X.—THE WORKS OF ARCHBISHOP FITZ-RALPH.

(A.) Printed works:—

1. (*a*) *Richardi Archiepiscopi Armachani, Hyberniæ Primatis, Defensorium Curatorum, adversus eos qui Privilegiatos se esse dicunt*, habitum Avinione in consistorio coram D. Papa Innocentio VI. et D.D. Cardinalibus et Prelatis, anno Christi 1357, nunc recens excusum juxta vetus exemplar et ex fide codicis MS. diligentissime castigatum. Parisiis apud Joan. Libert, via D. Joan. Lateranens. e regione Auditorii Regii, MDCXXI., pp. 1-136.

(*b*) The same is printed in the *Appendix ad Fasciculum Rerum expetendarum et fugiendarum* opera et studio ed. Brown Parochi Sandrigiæ in agro Cantiano. London : Chiswell, MDCXC., vol. ii., pp. 466-486.

(*c*) The same in Goldast's *Monumenta S. Romani Imperii*, vol. ii., pp. 1391-1410.

2. *Summa Domini Armachani in quæstionibus Armenorum*, noviter impressa et correcta a magistro nostro Joanne Sudoris, cum aliquibus sermonibus ejusdem de Christi Dominio. Jehan Petit, venales habentur in vico Divi Jacobi sub lilio aureo . . . quinsiène jour de Juillet mil cinq cens et douse, fol. clxxvii.

As this is the most important of all the writings of Dr. Fitz-Ralph, and as the printed book is very rare, it will please our readers to have a more detailed account of its object and contents. The work forms a real encyclopædia of theological learning, and reveals the vast extent of the author's studies and acquirements. The introduction runs as follows:—

"Reverendis in Christo patribus, Versi Manasgardensi, ac fratri Joanni electo Clatensi Majoris Armeniæ, Richardus Radulphus Archiepiscopus Armachanus, Hiberniæ Primas, per gratiam sitire justitiam donec hauriatis aquas in gaudio de fontibus Salvatoris. Ex revelatione Vestræ sanctæ devotionis accepi, ob defectum exercitii in Sacris Scripturis antiquas quasdam hereses a Sanctis Patribus reprobatas, et nonnullas contra S. Scripturas novellas assertiones erroneas in vestris partibus pullulasse, propter quas per doctores Latinos ex sacris Literis resecandas, eo quia earum patroni auctoritatem Ecclesiæ Romanæ non admittunt estimantes ejus auctoritatem ex Sacris Literis probari non posse,

---

* *Dowdall Register.*

ad Romanam curiam zelus domus Dei et Christi charitas vos adduxit. Cum vero super ipsis erroribus vobis cum ibidem aliquoties contulissem, meam exilitatem devotius stimulastis ut super quæstionibus vestris illud vobis scriberem quod mihi dignaretur Dominus aperire. Cui Vestro tam accepto Deo desiderio resistere non audebam, exactiones spiritualis usuræ formidans, si de bonis ad Domino acceptis officium negligerem institoris, et juxta ipsius promissa *qui evangelizantibus dat verba virtute multa* ardenter desideratis ampliora ob hoc recipite ut abundem magis. Nec debent indignari mihi majores, ex quo ipsi per quos melius perfici potuit illud penitus neglexerunt, et ego cum vidua evangelica cupiam minuta quæ habeo in Domini domum offerre, ipso teste confidens humilis orationis suffragio amplius quam subtilitate ingenii deficilia penetrare. Nec majorum correctionem renuo sed affecto, et ipsum opus (cujus titulem volui esse *De quæstionibus Armenorum* quod in xix. particulas sive libros distinxi, singulis libris materiam fidei et ipsius causam premittendo), approbationi et reprobationi nostri Papæ Patris Clementis VI. universalis Ecclesiæ Summi Pontificis in toto et in parte committo. In primis quinque libris illa principalis quæstio Armenorum pertractabitur : numquid Christus habuit in se duas plenas naturas, scilicet, divinam et humanam ita quod propter unionem illarum duarum naturarum in ipso fuit Dominus IESVS Christus veraciter suppositum, persona, sive hypostasis in utraque natura verus Deus et verus homo.

Primus itaque liber contra heresim Nestorianam, a quodam Nestorio introductam, affirmantem in Christo naturam humanam duntaxat, ita ut Christus homo fuerit et non Deus; quam heresim secuti sunt Cherintus, Armerintus, Theodocio, et etiam excæcati Judæi, et multæ Orientalium nationum usque in prasens, patefacto primitus quis sensus sit literalis Sacræ Scripturæ censendus, ex Scriptura N. T. juxta sensum literalem ipsius ostendit Christum quem colimus esse Deum. Secundus liber contra Judæos specialiter ex V. T. juxta literalem sensum ipsius, probat Christum sive Messiam in sua Scriptura promissum Deum esse debere.

Tertius liber ex eadem V. Scriptura ostendit Christum nostrum quem colimus esse sive fuisse illum qui erat Judaico populo in ipsa Scriptura promissus.

In quarto libro tractantur objectus Judaici populi contra ostensa in lib 2° et 3° et dantur et probantur in ipso regulæ certæ istos objectus, et omnes alios objectus Judaicos dissolvendi.

In quarto libro contra heresim Arii et Apollinarii affirmantem quod in Christo anima humana non fuit, divinitas loco animæ in Christo erat : ad hoc, contra heresim Manichæi dicentis Christum non verum corpus humanum sed corpus fantasticum habuisse Scripturæ testimonia adducuntur, et consequenter contra heresim ponentem corpus humanum in Christo fuisse et divinitas veluti indumentum ac vestem sicut in angelis cum corpora humana assumunt; et contra heresim Dioscori affirmantis naturam humanam in Christo in divinam fuisse mutatam ex utroque Testamento testimonia proferuntur.

Sextus liber ex Scripturis utriusque Testamenti ostendit Spiritum Sanctum a Filio sicut a Patre procedere, quod a Grecis et ab Armenis plerisque negatur.

Septimus liber probat ex Scriptura quod Romana Ecclesia sit caput totius Ecclesiæ Christianæ.

Octavus liber de Sacramento baptismi et ejus forma plures Armenorum quæstiones absolvit.

Nonus liber de Sacramentis Corporis Christi et Sanguinis Confirmationis et Unctionis plures quæstiones eorum tractat.

Decimus liber de modis illicitis conferendi et acquirendi et detinendi dona Dei gratuita ac præposituras Ecclesiæ quæstiones eorum pertractat, et an requiratur gratia Dei ad habendum dominium.

Undecimus* liber de potestate absolvendi simplicis sacerdotis, et de punitione animarum hominum impiorum ante finale judicium quæstiones ipsorum dissolvit.

---

* Cardinal Bellarmine warns his readers that our author is *caute legendus* in the 4th cap. of the 10th and the 4th cap. of the 11th books. The Cardinal does not approve of his doctrine, *de potestate presbyterorum*, nor of his teaching on the mendicant state.

Duodecimus liber quæstiones Armenorum pertractat de beatitudine animarum quorumdam justorum et de purgatione aliquarum animarum ante finale
judicium.

Liber decimus-tertius, quem propter Athanasium Græcum qui negat Purga-
torium adjeci, quatuor pertractat articulos, de satisfactione, debita pro peccatis
in vita et etiam post hanc vitam.

Liber decimus-quartus tractat quæstiones Græcorum et Armenorum de
visione nuda atque clara divinæ essentiæ a vere beatis quam negant plerique
eorum.

Liber decimus-quintus objicit contra auctoritatem nostræ Scripturæ per
contingentiam futurorum prænuntiatorum in ipsa quæ possint non fore, et occa-
sione cujusdam novelli erroris asserentis omnia futura ex necessitate sive inevi-
tabiliter evenire, quare offendit libertatem contradictionis in voluntate humana
tam ex physicis scripturis quam ex divinis in multiplici ratione, et contingentiam futurorum.

Liber decimus-sextus ponit tres de pretactis objectionibus acceptis de infalli-
bilitate scripturæ divinæ, a divina præscientia immutabili, a voluntate divina
omnipotente invincibili. et etiam efficaci ; et solvit eosdem ex propriis principiis
evidenter ostendens contingentiam futurorum et libertatem contradictionis
voluntatis divinæ et humanæ.

Liber decimus-septimus residuos sex ponit objectus de Dei co-operatione
speciali cum voluntate hominum operante ; de sustentatione rerum intrinseca
ab omnipotenti divina potentia ; de divina coöperatione generali eum omni
agente creato ; de necessitate eventus actuum intrinsecorum nostrorum, etc.

Liber decimus-octavus ostendit auctoritatem Legis Antiquæ et Novæ, et
probat utrumque Testamentum ex lege Saracenorum firmari ; et cum in multiplici ratione affirmat Legem nostram traditam in suis majoribus articulis non
fuisse aut esse corruptam.

Liber decimus-nonus comparat Legem nostram quoad sacramenta et cere-
monias cum lege Judæorum. Pertractat etiam de miraculis Apostolorum, et
ostendit Legem nostram robur amplius habere quam ratio naturalis, aut aliqua
secta gentilium et hoc totum opus consummat.

Quia vero per interrogationem et responsionem modus tradendi videtur
multis facilior, licet sit aliquantulum prolixior, unum de nostris, mihi discipu-
lum predilectum, quasi mecum disputantem accepi. Ita ut Joannes vicem
gerere quærentis, et Richardus intelligatur vicem gerere docentis licet potius
respondentis. Vos igitur, Reverendi Patres, opus accipite quod petistis, orationis si placet mercedem mihi pensantes pro labore hoc.

(B.) Works in manuscript :—

1. (a) *Summa contra Armenos*, lib. xx., fol. 126, xc. New College, Oxford.
(b) *Responsio de Armenorum Heresi*, fol. 218, xviii. Lincoln Coll., Oxford.
(c) *Armachanus de Questionibus Armenorum*, Cod. 250, n. 4. St. Benedict,
Cambridge.
(d) *Scriptum Armachani de Questionibus Armenorum*, Cod. 224. Pembroke,
Cambridge.
(e) *Richardi Armachani*, lib. xix., *Questionum adversus Armenos*. Trin.
Coll., Dublin.

2. *Ricardi Radulphi Armachani Opus in P. Lomdardi sententias* in questiones xxix. distributum, prævio sermone super idem. xv. Oriel College,
Oxford.

3. (a) *Ricardi Rad. Armachani, Propositio facta in consistorio coram Domino
Papa et Cardinalibus ac Prelatis super materia mendicitatis ac privilegiorum mendicantium contra Fratres de ordinibus quibuscunque, apud Avinion. Die 8
mensis Novemb. Anno Domini MCCCLVIII.*, fol. 54, xxxviii. Magdal. Coll.,
Oxford.

(b) *Propositio ejusdem facta in consistorio coram Papa, Cardinalibus et Prelatis ad utilitatem cleri ac populi Christiani super materia mendicitatis ac privilegiorum contra fratres de ordinibus mendicantium quibuscunque apud Avinion.*
8 *Nov.*, 1357, fol. 184. St. Johu Bapt., Oxford.

(*c*) *Ric. Filii Radulphi, Archiep. Cantaur.* (sic) *sermo habitus Avinionæ viii. die mensis Novembris A.D.* 1357. *in istud Nolite judicare secundum faciem, etc.,* fol. 53. Corpus Christi Coll., clxxxii., Oxford.

4. *Propositio Ric. Armachani ex parte Regis Angliæ Edwardi III., in consistorio D. Papa Avinione pro gratia jubilæi ejus D. Regis populo obtinenda, anno* 1349, fol. 177. St. John Bapt., Oxford.

5. *Rich. Fil. Rad. Armachani de paupertate Christi* libri septem, cum prologo ad Innocentium Papam VI. et titulo capitulorum cuique libro prævio, fol. 143. King's Coll., Oxford, cxviii.

6. *Objectiones ejusdem contra seipsum in Materia de Mendicitate et aliis cum suis solutionibus,* fol. 196, S. Q. B., lxv. Oxford.

7. *Responsio ad Objectiones Mendicantium.* British Museum.

8. *Excerpta varia ex Ricardo Fitz-Rauf;* (a) *excerpta ex testamento S. Francisci contra fratres Minores;* (b) *excerpta notabilia ex quodam libro qui vocatur Summa Summarum;* (c) *excerpta ex libro Copiosæ charitatis.* Bodl.

9. *Rich. Radulphi Armachani Primatis Dialogus vel Disputatio de Rebus ad S. Scripturam pertinentibus.* Lincoln, 75.

10. (a) *Sermones Domini Richardi Dei gratia Archiep. Armach. Hiberniæ, habiti Avinione et aliis locis quampluribus de diversis Sanctis et temporibus.* St. John Bapt., lxv., Oxford.

(*b*) *Ric. Rad. sive Fitz.Ralph, Archiep. Armach. sermones de tempore et de sanctis, per totum annum.* New Coll., xc.

(*c*) *Sermones tam de tempore quam de sanctis.* Trin. Coll., Dublin.

(*d*) *Sermones V. ad crucem Londonensim,* an 1356, et *alii de laudibus S. Deiparæ.* Ibid.

(*e*) *Sermones Richardi filii Radulphi de Dundalk, Archiepiscop. Armachani.* Ibid.

RELIGIOUS TOLERATION AS APPLIED TO CATHOLICS.

1. THE intolerance that wears the mask of liberality is especially hard to bear. And yet this is the special characteristic of the intolerance exhibited by a large class of the modern assailants of the Catholic Church. There is not a weapon in their armoury they do not wield against her; not an attack which their strength can compass do they spare her; and all this time they complacently exhibit themselves as very models of toleration, and of forbearance, and of fair play. They are almost angry with us Catholics when we refuse to praise them for their magnanimity towards us. The Irish Catholic finds this state of things exemplified every day at his own door. Leaving outside of our consideration that portion of the Protestants of these realms who hold any concession to Catholic claims to be a national sin, it is really surprising how intolerant even those are who affect to be the most tolerant of men. Illustrating our

remarks from a recent essay on toleration,* by a writer of this school, we propose in this paper to point out how that Protestant toleration, of which we hear so much, and for which so much gratitude is expected from us, means, as far as Catholics are concerned, intolerance in its most repulsive form.

2. With the most charming modesty the writer in question apologises even for the use of the word toleration. He is careful to explain that it implies no proud consciousness of superiority on his part, no feeling of thankfulness that he is not as other men, especially as those publicans who live around him. He feels it presumptuous to tolerate anybody or anything, and it requires some reasoning to bring his shrinking spirit to believe that there must be limits to his benevolence. Differences of race, of religion, of philosophy, of moral development, differences even in codes of morality, are as nothing in his eyes. Whether a man be an Athanasian or an Arian Christian is to him a question parallel to the one that asks whether he be an allopathist or a homeopathist. This is surely the very flower of benevolence. Who would expect that its fruit was to be bitter as this :—

"Our course, therefore, seems plain, totally to refuse to Catholics their postulate, that religious freedom means freedom to carry out whatever their Church calls religious action" (p. 221).

Never did conclusion spring from premises more unexpectedly than this. What is there in the Irish Catholic that this all-tolerating man, who consents to overthrow the domination of the Irish Established Church, who wishes to apply ecclesiastical funds to the moral and intellectual training even of Catholics, refuses to give him full freedom of religious action? What is there in the Irish Catholic that, whereas for other men, religious freedom means freedom to do what their religion prescribes, for him it means the absence of such freedom? Why is it that, whereas toleration is conceded to others as a boon, it is to be given to Catholics only as a poisoned gift in order to destroy them?

"The right mode of fighting against Romish error is to give Romanists *full equality*; insist on free press, free speech, and popular education, and tear out the roots of Popery from the Anglican Church. By these methods it will infallibly be destroyed" (p. 219).

3. Why is it that universal toleration in the case of the Church becomes downright intolerance? The solution of this problem is of the highest importance to him who would under-

* "Religious Toleration" in *Frazer's Magazine*, No. cccxxviii. for Aug., 1865.

stand aright the position held by the Church in the social and political questions of the day. The conditions of the problem have not their origin in the theological differences between the two Churches. The *odium theologicum* has very little to do with their existence. Our essayist explicitly declares that whether a man be an Athanasian or an Arian, whether he look upon our Lord as the Eternal Word made flesh, or as a mere creature, his opinions ought to be respected, or at least tolerated. It is only when from the sphere of speculative doctrine we pass to practical duties that we hear of any limits to toleration:—

"When a form of worship, *a cultus*, assumes a character which is widely different from scientific research or opinion, it cannot claim the immunities of science. If it persist in public practices which are incentives of foul vices or encroachments on public right, it exposes itself to the attack of the law and to proportionate penalties. And even when it is not legally punished, it may deserve executive discouragement, and be barely *tolerated*" (p. 206).

If, then, to the Catholic body of these countries, though tolerated, the State is to refuse permission to carry out what their religion prescribes as religious action, it must be because the Catholic religion sanctions public practices which are incentives of foul vices or encroachments on public right. Now, no sane person pretends for a moment that the Catholics of Ireland, as such, are trained up in foul vices. It remains, therefore, to conclude that they are to be discouraged because their practical principles constitute an encroachment on public right, and this is, in fact, our essayist's plea for his opinion.

"The main fact is, that the Church is a formidable organisation, stretching over many lands, proved by long experience to be fierce and tyrannical, and upholding a *political morality* essentially opposed to our own" (p. 219).

In other words, Protestant toleration is intolerant of the Catholic Church, because that Church is an organisation independent of the State, because the Pontiff and bishops who form that organisation claim the right to control their flocks on principles of morality opposed at times to the political morality of the age, and have an unpleasant habit of saying *non licet* at inconvenient times. In a word, the Catholic Church is a living organisation, and not a spiritual principle only; it stands between the tyranny of the State and the souls of men; it is the only impediment to the realisation of that slavish formula invented by Protestantism, *cujus regio, illius et religio;* and therefore it is to be discouraged, or if to be tolerated, to be tolerated only for its destruction. It is the old story: the State is jealous of the influence and power of the Church, and would therefore wish to destroy it. Unable to overcome its divine vitality, it would at least fetter it in the name of toleration. Protestant toleration, therefore, is reduced to this : absolute indifference on the part of the State to truth or falsehood in points of mere belief, but resolute opposition to the Church as an organisation which will not become the slave of the civil power. Believe what you please, but do not dare to follow advice other than mine : this is the meaning of the toleration for which we are called upon to glorify the Protestant State.

4. Now, this toleration, upon analysis, is no toleration at all, but the grossest tyranny. The relations between the Roman emperors and the early Christians were certainly not those dictated by toleration. But, on what principle did the ancient Roman emperors persecute the early Christians? Was it zeal for purity of doctrine that urged Nero, or Diocletian, or Decius, to crush out the Christian superstition? Certainly not. If they were asked to put into a form of words the rule of statecraft that inspired their edicts, they would have said* that they opposed the Christian Church *as a powerful organisation upholding a political morality essentially opposed to their own.* In fact our essayist admits this, and rather sympathises with their views on the subject :—

"Looking, as Protestants do, on Christianity as a spiritual principle only, we are apt to forget that a Roman emperor saw it as a dangerous and illicit organisation; while to the very freest spiritual research, and public preaching of the results, he had absolutely no objection " (p. 206).

What, then, is the difference between the pagan idea of persecution and the modern Protestant idea of toleration? The former had no objection to the freest spiritual research, the latter has no objection to any form of spiritual error; the former persecuted the Church because it considered the sacerdotal power a rival to its own sway, the latter wishes to check it because it is a *formidable organisation*, with a *political morality opposed to its own.* Wherein, then, do the two systems differ? We can see no shade of diversity between them save this one: The Pagan honestly styled himself the foe of the Church, and erected monuments in his own honour as the destroyer of the Christian superstition; the Protestant glories in his religious toleration, and, at the same time, does his best to destroy those whom he tolerates. If the action of the former was tyranny of the darkest dye, is that of the latter less harsh because honoured with the sacred name of liberty?

* St. Cyprian, *Epist. lii.* (ed. Maur.) *ad Antonianum,* has preserved for us the words used by Decius when he heard that St. Cornelius was made Pope : " *Cum multo patientius audiret levari adversum se æmulum principem, quam constitui Romæ Dei sacerdotem.*"

5. Besides, this organisation, which is objected to, is the very life of the Church. The religion founded by Christ is not a spiritual principle only, as modern Protestantism is described to be by our essayist; it is not merely a national institution to be maintained by the State "in order to banish heathenism from our minds and hearts, and impart religious sanction to our mutual duties;" it is a humano-divine society which, as a moral body, has a complete organisation of its own, and in that organisation its life. Of the advantages this organisation brings with it we have a proof in our own day. At this moment the Protestant churches of North and South in the United States are almost completely severed one from the other; the divisions which have disappeared from the body politic continue to rage fiercely in the ecclesiastical corporation. In vain have anxious efforts been undertaken to bridge over the chasm; the unity of that church is lost. Side by side with these fragments the Catholic Church of America possesses her soul in unbroken peace; the Northern Bishop admits the Southern Bishop into his church, they celebrate at the same altar, and preach the same doctrine from the chair of truth. What has enabled the Catholic episcopate to preserve one heart and one soul in the general disruption? The organisation of the Church—the fact that the Church has rules of conduct directly opposite to the ever-changing political morality of the day. To pretend, therefore, to tolerate the Church, and in the same breath to object to her organisation, is simply dishonest. Our essayist's ideal of a church appears to be realised in Roumania, where, according to what we read in the Bucharest journal, the *Voix de la Roumanie*, the modern theory of toleration has its full influence on the Greek Church of that country. A few months ago the Minister of Worship conducted to the palace of the reigning Prince the Primate of Roumania and the Bishops Athanasus, Denis, Melchisedech, and Gennadius. The Primate was presented to the sovereign by the minister, and, as he made his appearance before the throne, was clothed by the minister *with the episcopal cope*. The other bishops were then introduced with the same ceremonial. The reigning Prince then conferred upon each of the prelates the pastoral cross *in token of investiture*. This is the result of the toleration which objects to the organisation of the Church; but this result is nothing less than death to the liberty of the Church. If, like those unfortunate Greek bishops, the Catholic episcopate were to consent to obey men rather than God; if they would but receive from the hand of an infidel statesman the robe that clothes them before God's altar, and the cross, which is the sign of their spiritual jurisdiction, we should hear very little about the necessity of discouraging them as a

formidable organisation. But they would have abrogated their own title to the obedience of men; they would be the tools of cabinets, and no longer those whom the Holy Ghost has placed as bishops to govern the Church of God. The toleration which avowedly aims at this result, is it toleration or tyranny ?

6. But our essayist's remarks on toleration are not intended by him to remain in the air. They are of immediate application, and, what adds to their importance, of application to Ireland. The main logical strength of the opposition made against admitting Irish Catholics to political equality with Protestants lay, he thinks, in this fact that, owing to various causes, the national spirit of Ireland was built upon the Church, which was the only native organ left to the people. Catholicism being thus intimately connected with national feeling, gave new strength to the disaffection which arose when that national feeling was wounded. If, then, the national feeling could be separated from the religious, if the Irishman could be brought to be less the Catholic and more the citizen, it was argued that the difficulties of the case would be considerably lessened. This was to be done by emancipating the Catholics. Besides, it was said, Catholicism had changed, and was no longer the monster of bigotry it had been in the dark ages. But the result of emancipation has not corresponded with these hopes. The Irish Catholics are as discontented as ever, and the problem now comes back nearly as it did in 1828 :

"It is difficult to measure the immensity of the mischief to England from a disaffected Ireland. The first and most obvious evil is, that an army of not less than thirty thousand men is to be kept there against the chances of insurrection and tumult. The expense of this in men and money is its least mischief. It exhibits us to the world as only encamped in Ireland, as Russia in Poland, as Turkey in Thessaly, or in Servia. Conscience makes cowards of our statesmen when they desire to speak truth concerning foreign despotism. But let us forget the much boasted foreign influence of England—indeed its credit has of late run down to zero—for which our great and expensive embassies are said to be maintained. While Ireland is disaffected, not only does English capital not flow in, but Irish capital is rather hoarded than allowed to fructify. Under our half measures the Catholic laity are not and cannot be satisfied any more than the clergy ; hence their increased power does but make them aspire to more ; and the Protestant laity, frightened at the prospect, is susceptible of dangerous fanaticism as a supposed necessary self-defence" (p. 211).

Many causes have contributed, according to our author, to keep up this unhappy condition of things. Among them he places the Irish Church Establishment, which he denounces as a grievance which meets the Irish Catholic at every turn, and which ought to have been removed before the question of admitting Catholics into Parliament was moved. We will not follow him into this topic, but will confine ourselves to what has a direct bearing upon the subject of this paper. He draws attention to two mistakes made by the Government in dealing with the Catholic question, and suggests remedies to illustrate more and more clearly the nature of the Protestant idea of toleration towards Catholics. The first mistake was that of assimilating Catholics to Protestant dissenters, and this he pronounces to have been a most mischievous error. According to our essayist, Protestants differ from one another, not in kind, but in degree. Hence a Protestant national church should embrace all Protestant sects, and exclude none. But this argument holds only with Protestants, "for they alone stand side by side as brethren, equal in right, and separate in responsibility to a higher tribunal."

Catholics can never take their place on the same level with Protestants :

"A wall of partition always remains between them : a gulf which cannot be passed by gradual steps. We may, on the whole, believe that the moral benefit of the Catholic clergy is greater than the drawbacks. We may be willing to sanction the appropriation of public funds to support them, as at Maynooth, or as in a Prussian university. We may maintain that Maynooth ought to be forced to migrate into Dublin University. We may wish the Catholic priests of Ireland, as of France, to receive payment direct from the State. But two facts would remain unchangeable : first, their Church would still be an uncongenial, hostile, arrogating system, with no common ground of science on which we and they could stand ; secondly, we, on our side, could not be in frank unsuspicious amity with them, but must ever be on the watch as against an encroaching foe " (p. 216).

These remarks will at once remind our readers of the system of toleration proposed by John Milton.* In his scheme all religious sects were to be tolerated with one exception, the exception being the Roman Catholic Church.

The system of our essayist is not dissimilar, and the essayist is the exponent of modern Protestant feeling. But is this a toleration for which we are to be thankful ? When will Catholics learn not to be deceived with fine words? How long will they admire the liberality of Protestants, and endeavour to win their esteem by advances and compromises which only degrade their religion, while they rivet its chains? When will they begin to see that the glitter of liberality which Protestantism so boastfully exhibits is not all pure gold ?

The second mistake made by the Government in dealing with Catholics is still more to the point :

"The policy of England to Romanism from the day of Elizabeth's accession to the English throne has erred in this capital point, that it has tended to

---

* See *Record*, vol. i., p. 456.

throw the Catholic laity into the interests of the clergy, and unite both against us. None can effectually bridle the clergy of that Church but its own laity" (p. 221).

And how is this to be remedied? By detaching the laity from the clergy. This is open and advised speaking. But let us see what is the position assigned in this plan to the laity of Ireland? Our essayist has asserted in so many words that the only way to destroy the Catholic Church was *to tolerate* it in the true sense of the word. He now lays down just as distinctly that the true plan of toleration is to separate the laity from the clergy, and use them as against the clergy. Therefore, the honourable office assigned to the favoured portion of our laity— to those among them who have received power and influence in the country—is that of destroyers of the Church which they believe to be the work of God. Again, the main difficulty in the way of full toleration of the Catholic Church is its organi- sation, which means its independence. The Protestant State has tried every means of violence to break down that organisa- tion and crush that independence. But violence was vain. It now has recourse to another means, and that is to make the Catholic laity the destroying power. This is the toleration which is offered so ostentatiously. And does not such toleration mean simply destruction?

Such is the insulting estimate formed of our Catholic laity, whom, our author says, "it could never really offend to follow the precedents of France or Austria, though such of them as owed their seats in parliament to clerical influences might talk as ultramontanes" (p. 221).

But there is one charge brought against the Church to jus- tify this system, namely, her doctrine of persecution.

THE FREEMASONS PAINTED BY THEMSELVES.

THE Count de Maistre has left it written of sovereign power that, like the river Nile, it endeavours to hide, as far as possible, the source whence it first issued. The same may be said of Freemasonry, which would conceal not only the source whence it has sprung, but the course it follows and the point it seeks to reach. But, in our days, the mysterious Egyptian river has been forced to yield up its long-guarded secret. The patient toil of skilful travellers has been at length rewarded with the

sight of those springs of Nile which so many had sought in vain
to behold.   Freemasonry must be content to submit to a similar
destiny.   It must endure the scrutiny of profane eyes keen
enough to search its very depth of mystery.   It must be satisfied
to have its organisation laid bare before the world.   And, what
is harder still, it must endure to hear its own condemnation in
the cry of horror which breaks from every honest man at the
sight that meets his gaze once the veil is removed from off its
face.

The hand that has struck away the veil is none other than
the consecrated hand of the Roman Pontiff.   Never raised but
to bless—never blessing without effect—that hand has been to
Europe, and to the world, the source of true civilisation.   And
yet at times, for the hardness of their hearts, men turn away
from its gifts.   Like Noah, the Roman Pontiff foretells the
coming deluge, and, like Noah, he is sometimes slighted by a
perverse and thoughtless generation.   This has happened to
some extent in the case of the denunciations which the Holy See
has so often issued against Freemasonry.   Had those in power
been more attentive to the words of the Sovereign Pontiffs, and
more docile to their teachings with respect to secret societies,
how many evils might have been averted from European society!
In his latest allocution, Pius IX. complains that the efforts of
the Apostolic See against Freemasonry have not been followed
by the due result.   Far from being crushed, the Masonic body
every day boasts of larger and larger increase.   Even some of
those whose duty it is to be first in carrying out the Pontiffs'
decrees have proved sluggish and negligent of their task.   Many
Catholics who judge of Masonry only from what they read in
newspapers friendly to the body, or from the good qualities of
individual Freemasons of their acquaintance, are reluctant to
believe what they find so solemnly asserted by the Sovereign
Pontiffs.   In their eyes Freemasonry is but a benevolent or a
convivial society, without any aims beyond those of charity, or
any thought of conspiracy except to promote brotherly union
between the members of different classes in society.   They cannot persuade themselves that so many estimable men, whom they
know to be Freemasons, are really those monsters of iniquity so
darkly described in the allocution.

To such as these, and to all who consider the Catholic view
of Freemasonry to be extravagant and unreasonable, we address
ourselves to-day.   We assure them that the portrait of Masonry
presented to the world in the allocution is a faithful copy of the
portrait which Masonry, with its own hand, has drawn of itself.
We wish to justify the Pope by the help of Freemasons themselves.   Descending in detail to the charges made against them

by the Holy Father, we are able to substantiate them one by one, not from mere hearsay reports, nor from the evidence of credulous or hostile witnesses, but from the free admissions of the accused. Our argument is this. You hesitate to believe that Freemasonry is wicked, because you consider the Holy See to be misinformed. Be it so. But you cannot hesitate to give credence to the Freemasons themselves. *Habemus confitentem reum.* Why delay any longer to believe him guilty ?

The documents we are about to quote in evidence are unquestionably authentic.* The sources whence they have been collected are the official records of Masonry, published under the approval of the Masonic superiors. For, it is worthy of remark, that among the very men who so loudly condemn the Catholic censorship of the press, liberty of the press is not tolerated. Nothing may be printed concerning the body without the permission of the superiors. In case of each document herein quoted, references are given to the source whence it has been drawn, so that anyone may verify it at will.

Before entering upon our subject, we wish to remark here that not every individual Freemason† is at all cognisant of the plans entertained by the society to which he belongs. We declare at once that we do not presume to judge individuals. There are many grades in the body, and thousands never pass beyond the lowest. Besides, it is generally said that in England, Scotland, and Ireland, Masonry has preserved a character comparatively innocuous. But, even when this is granted, it does not follow that all Masons in these countries are to be held exempt from blame. Men who elect to remain in close and practical brotherhood with a society which, as such, is elsewhere notoriously irreligious and anti-social, run the risk of being considered as accomplices in the evil deeds of their fellows. In a mercantile community no honest man can allow swindlers to use his name, and expect to preserve his reputation immaculate. The same holds good in the case of any other voluntary association. But we are compelled to believe that Masonry in England is something more serious than a gay heresy, as it has been charitably called. In a speech delivered in 1863, at a grand Masonic banquet, M. Hayman took occasion to review the operations of Masonry in the various countries of Europe. He drew attention to the great spread of Masonry in England, which he

---

*For these documents see *La Franc Maçonnerie soumise a la publicité a l'aide de documents authentiques.* Amand. Neut. Gand., 1865.

† " The number of exceptions to be made for upright Masons is beyond the conception of those who are not thoroughly acquainted with the principles and the proceedings of the sect." *Barruel, Memoirs of Jacobinism,* tom. ii, pp. 273-5.

attributed to this, that Masonry supplied a want long felt by
the Anglo-Saxon heart, namely, the want of a religious worship :
" Those whose reason and good sense do not find satisfaction in
the ancient dogmas flock in crowds to the Masonic temple, where
reason, good sense, morality, and philosophy are represented
under a touching symbolism."*

From this it would appear that, according to the Masons
themselves, Masonry is considered in England as a substitute
for Christianity, upon which it is an improvement.   Again, M.
Goffin, in his *Histoire Populaire de la Franc-Maçonnerie* (p. 468),
states that the lodge of Freethinkers founded by him at Verviers,
on 1st September, 1862, received its authorisation (*lettres de
constitution*) from the grand lodge of Memphis of London. Now
this lodge of Freethinkers, as its founder tells us, has made it
a rule to admit no one as member " who will not make a formal
engagement, in writing, never to have recourse to the ministry
of the Church in case of having to contract marriage, and who
will not oblige himself never to consent to receive religious
burial after death ; to that effect signing a masonic will, by
which the fulfilment of this obligation may be secured." How
far this anti-Christian spirit represents the feelings of the lodge
which granted letters of institution to the Verviers Masons we
have no means of judging.   This much, at least, appears certain, that the relationship between the London and Verviers
lodges is as close as that subsisting between mother and daughter.
We need say no more.

The allocution asserts that Freemasonry is a society (1) of
obscure origin and widespread organisation, which (2), under a
specious appearance of harmlessness, entertains designs subversive of religion and of civil society.   The irreligious and guilty
character of the association is made plain (3) from the fact that
it is common ground for men of every form of belief, (4) from
the secrecy that shrouds its meetings, (5) from the rigorous oath
taken by its members never to reveal anything concerning the
body, and from the severe punishments they subject themselves
to in case they became false to their obligations.   We proceed
to justify these charges by the authority of the Freemasons
themselves :—

1. Upon the origin of Masonry a thick cloud ever rests,
which even the Masons themselves are not able fully to raise.
In a discourse pronounced on 8th of August, 1839, in the lodge
of the Chevaliers of the Cross, Orient of Paris, M. de Branville,
ex-officer of the Grand Orient of France, inclines to the belief
that the religious doctrines of Masonry are the continuation of

* *Monde Maçonnique*, tom. iv., pp. 742-749.

the Egyptian mysteries preserved in the Temple of Isis, and transmitted by the Templars, who, to escape persecution, established the Masonic Association. The history* of the Order of the Templars, and of the execution of James Molay, their master, is represented in Masonry under the double allegory of the Temple of Solomon and of the story of Hiram (*Le Globe*, Masonic Journal, t. i., pp. 294-297). But, however obscure its origin, Freemasonry has attained an extraordinary development. The *Tableau Général des loges*, drawn up by a distinguished Mason, M. Rebold, sets forth the number of lodges in existence throughout the world in 1850. We give this remarkable document in full :—

GEOGRAPHICAL TABLE OF FREEMASONRY,

INDICATING ALL THE GRAND LODGES, ETC., EXISTING IN 1850.

States, Islands, or Countries.	Names of the Grand Lodges.	At the Orient of	Year of foundation.	No. of Lodges.
	EUROPE.			
England,	Grand Lodge of England,	London,	1813	820
Scotland,	„ „ St. John of Scotland,	Edinburgh,	1736	730
Ireland,	„ „ Ireland,	Dublin,	1729	632
France,	„ Orient of France,	Paris,	1772	314
„	„ Lodge or Sup. Council for France,		1804	50
„	„ „ or Mother Lodge of the Misraim rite,	Paris,	1816	4
„	„ National Lodge of France,		1848	8
Prussia,	„ Lodge of Three Globes,	Berlin,	1740	111
„	„ „ Royal York of Friendship,		1798	31
„	„ National Lodge of Germany,		1773	69
Saxony,	„ Lodge of Saxony,	Dresden,	1755	13
Hamburg,	„ „ Hamburg,	Hamburg,	1737	19
Holland,	„ „ Holland,	The Hague,	1770	83
Sweden,	„ „ Sweden,	Stockholm,	1754	25
Denmark,	„ National Lodge of Denmark,	Copenhagen,	1747	15
Belgium,	„ Orient of Belgium,	Brussels,	1832	25
	„ Lodge or Supreme Council,		1817	11
Switzerland,	„ Alpine Lodge,	Zurich,	1844	14
Bavaria,	„ Lodge of the Sun,	Bayreuth,	1742	9
Hesse Darmstadt,	„ „ Onion,	Darmstadt,		3
Francfort on Maine	„ „ „	Frankfort,	1783	14
Hanover,	„ „ Hanover,	Hanover,	1841	16
Portugal,	„ Orient of Lusitania,	Lisbon,	1805	
Greece,	„ Lodge of Corfu,	Corfu,		
Turkey,	Independent Lodges,	Belgrade,		
	NORTH AMERICA.			
United States,	Grand Lodge of New York,	New York,	1787	130
„	„ „ Louisiana,	New Orleans,	1812	24
„	„ „ Massachusetts,	Boston,	1777	32
„	„ „ Pennsylvania,	Philadelphia,	1786	47
„	„ „ Virginia,	Richmond,	1778	77
„	„ „ Maryland,	Baltimore,	1783	28
„	„ „ North Carolina,	Raleigh,	1778	46
„	„ „ South Carolina,	Charleston,	1787	17

* For further information on the origin of Freemasonry see Professor Robertson's excellent *Lectures on Modern History and Biography*, p. 407 sqq.

States, Islands, or Countries.	Names of the Grand Lodges.	At the Orient of	Year of foundation.	No. of Lodges.
United States,	Grand Lodge of Kentucky,	Louisville,	1810	123
,,	,, ,, Colombia,	Washington,		22
,,	,, ,, Missouri,	St. Louis,		23
,,	,, ,, Ohio,	Lancaster,		170
,,	,, ,, Maine,	Augusta,		63
,,	,, ,, Mississippi,	Natchez,		65
,,	,, ,, Connecticut,	New Haven,	792	38
,,	,, ,, Georgia,	Milledgeville,	1786	77
,,	,, ,, Florida,	Tallchassa,		13
,,	,, ,, New Hampshire,	Concord,	1790	26
,,	,, ,, Rhode Island,	Providence,	1791	18
,,	,, ,, New Jersey,	Trenton,	1786	10
,,	,, ,, Indiana,	Indianopolis,		18
,,	,, ,, Tennessee,	Nashville,		100
,,	,, ,, Delaware,	Douores,	1806	4
,,	,, ,, Alabama,	Tuscaloosa,		42
,,	,, ,, Illinois,	Rushville,		10
,,	,, ,, Iowa,	Bloomington,	1842	10
,,	,, ,, Vermont,	Montpellier,	1774	34
,,	,, ,, Wisconsin,	Moriral Point,		25
,,	,, ,, Arkansas,	Little Rock,		22
,,	,, ,, Michigan,	Detroit,		8
Canada,	,, Provincial Lodge of Upper Canada,	Kingston,		31
,,	,, ,, ,, Lower Canada,	Quebec and Montreal,	1792	14
Mexico,	,, ,, ,, Mexico,	Mexico,	1825	
Texas,	,, ,, ,, Texas,	Austin (Houston),	1837	45
New Brunswick,	,, ,, ,, New Brunswick,	Frederickstown,		9
Acadia,	,, ,, ,, New Scotland,	Yarmouth,		20
California,	,, ,, ,, California,	San Francisco,		3
Newfoundland,	,, ,, St. John, dep. on England,	St. John's,		3
Cape Hulon,		Sydney,		1
	SOUTH AMERICA.			
Brazil,	Grand Lodge of Brazil,	Rio Janeiro,	1822	22
Venezuela,	,, ,, Caracas,	Caracas,		7
Peru,	,, ,, St. John,	Lima,		
Bolivia,		La Plata,		
British Guyana,		Strabock,		1
French ,,		Cayenne,		
Dutch ,,		Paraweribo,		
La Plata,		Buenos Ayres,		
Colombia,	Lodge of St. John,	Panama,		
Uruguay,		Maracaibo,		
Paraguay,		Monte Video, Assumption,		
Haiti,	Grand Lodge of Haiti,	Prince's Gate,	1823	15
Dominica,	,, ,, St. John,	San Domingo,		6
Cuba,		Havanna,		1
Porto Rico,		St. Jean de Porto Rico,		2
Jamaica,		Kingston,		12
Martinique,	Lodge of St. Jean,	Port Royal and St. Peter,		5
Guadaloupe,		Basseterre,		4
Dominick,		Roseau,		3
Barbadoes,		Bridgetown,		3
Bermuda,		Bermuda,		2
Curacoa,		Williamstadt,		
St. Bartholomy,		The Carenayl,		
St. Cruise,		Christianstadt,		
St. Thomas,		St. Thomas,		
St. Eustachius,		St. Eustachius,		1
St. Martin,		Philisburg,		1
Trinidad,		Port of Spain,		2
St. Christopher,		Basseterre,		1
St. Vincent,		Kingston,		1
Antigua,		St. John,		
Grenada,		St. George,		2
Demerara,		Demerara,		
Bahama,		St. Salvador,		

States, Islands, or Counties.	Names of the Grand Lodges.	At the Orient of	Year of foundation.	No. of Lodges.
	AFRICA.			
Algiers,	Grand Lodge of St. John,	Algiers,		4
		Constantine,		11
Canary Isles,	,, ,, St. John,	Teneriffe,		
Upper Guinea,		Cape of Sierra Leone,		3
Senegambia,		Bathurst,	1735	2
Cape of Good Hope,		Capetown,	1736	6
St. Helena,		Jamestown,		1
Isle of Bourbon,		St. Denis,		4
Mauritius,		Port Louis,		3
Marquesas,		St. Peter,		1
Senegal,		St. Louis,		4
Mozambique,		Mozambique,		
	ASIA.			
Hindoostan,	Grand Orient of Bengal,	Agra,		6
	Lodge of St. John, dep. on various G. O.,	Pondicherry, Allahabad, Goa, Bombay, Carneatic, Barrilly, Concam, Dejepour, Chezepoor, Futtesgur, Torres de Vedras,		57
China,	L. of St. John, dep. on G. O. of England,	Canton,		12
		Hong Kong,		
Ceylon,		Colombo,		2
Prince of Wales' Isle,		Georgetown,		2
Turkey,		Pera,	1738	
,,		Smyrna,		
	OCEANICA.			
Sumatra,	Lodge of St. John, dep. on various G. O.,	Palembang,		
Java,		Batavia,	1730	3
New Holland,		Port Jackson,		2
New South Wales,		Sydney, Paramatta	1828	3
New Zealand,		Bay of Islands,	1840	
Van Diemen's Land		Hobartown.		

According to M. Rebold there are five hundred thousand Masons who take an active part in the labours of their lodge, and from eight to nine millions who, though accepted members, take no direct part in the Masonic operations. Since 1850 the number has increased still more. In 1858 the list of English lodges amounted to 880; in 1862 it had grown to be 996. In 1862 fourteen lodges in Europe, outside the United Kingdom, were dependent upon the Grand Lodge of London, of which three were at Malta, two in the Ionian Islands, two at Constantinople; in Asia ninety-seven were similarly dependent, thirty-seven of which were in Bengal, twenty in Madras, eight at Bombay, three in China; in Africa twenty, of which fourteen were at the Cape of Good Hope, one at St. Helena; in America 126, of which eighty-two were in Canada and Nova Scotia, thirty-four in Central America, eight in South America, and two in the Bahamas. In 1860 the United States had 4,841 lodges, and 213,056 members. In Italy, since 1859, no less than seventy-seven regular lodges have been erected. Nothing, therefore, can be more true than the words of the allocution, wherein it is said that the masonic corporation is spread far and wide over the earth, that at this most critical period of the world's history it raises its head in every nation, and exhibits itself with ever increasing audacity.

2. A corporation so widespread must necessarily wield an enormous influence for good or for evil. No one who has the interests of society at heart can look with indifference upon this gigantic association, which has enmeshed, as with a net, the entire world. Such an association, for the very sake of public peace, ought to be above suspicion. Far from being so, it is quite certain that within it lurk doctrines absolutely irreconcilable with Christian revelation; that in its social action it aims at displacing Christian in favour of a purely pagan civilisation; and that its method is irreligious and anti-social.

In order to gain an accurate idea of the religious doctrines of Masonry we cannot do better than examine a Masonic profession of faith by the aid of a Masonic commentary. The Italian lodges, having drawn up their constitution, lately published some few copies of the document for the exclusive use of the higher officers of the body. One of the copies fell into the hands of the editor of the excellent journal, the *Unità Cattolica*, who printed it in the issue of his paper of 21st and 22nd July. Its authenticity has never been called in question. We make from it the following extracts, which embody religious principles:—

"Art. 4. Masonry recognises its God in the principle of the natural and moral order, under the symbol of the Greek Architect of the universe."
"Art. 5. It prescribes no particular profession of religious faith, and excludes only the beliefs which require intolerance of the belief of others.
"Art. 8. It proposes to itself as its final object to unite all free men in one vast family, which may and ought to take the place of all churches founded on blind faith and theocratic authority, and of all kinds of superstitious worship, thereby to constitute the true and only Church of Humanity."

It requires but a slight analysis to show that the doctrine contained in these articles is anti-Christian by reason of what it excludes, by reason of what it asserts, by reason of its effects, and by reason of its leading principle and method. And first by reason of what it excludes.

Historically considered, the phrase "the Great Architect of the universe" appears to have been the leading principle of the secret doctrines which, through the Templars, have been handed down to the Freemasons from remote antiquity. M. Juge, one of the very highest officers in the French Masonry, describes a

Gnosticism which admits the existence of one only God, co-
eternal with being itself, not divisible into several persons, not
subject to human misery, and who consequently never died nor
can die. If to this, he says, be added the belief that Christ was
not God, but merely a philosopher, that miracles are an impossible violation of eternal and immutable laws, and that God has
no need of such means of procuring obedience to his will, " are
not," he asks, " these doctrines, which are taken entirely from
Gnosticism, the very fundamental doctrines of Masonry ? Does
the Mason divide the incomprehensible Being whom he calls the
Great Architect of the Universe? Does he believe that He died,
or can ever, and that his sole will is not law for all men ?" (*Le
Globe*, t. iii., pp. 307-310.) It follows, therefore, that the phrase
Grand Architect of the Universe implies the denial of the Trinity
and of the whole supernatural order of Christianity. These
are declared to be the fundamental doctrines of Masonry by M.
Juge, who, among other offices, held that of Grand Inspector-
General, 33rd degree, and who must be supposed to be acquainted
with the nature of Freemasonry. Next, by reason of what it
asserts.

Quite recently several of the French lodges came to the
determination of omitting from their constitution all mention
of the existence of God and of the immortality of the soul.
M. Rebold thereupon addressed to Marshal Magnan, the Grand
Master, a protest, dated 3rd November, 1864, in which he declares that a belief in the existence of God and in the immortality of the soul is the basis of Masonry. He adds that the
general formula, *Grand Architect of the Universe*, was adopted
from ancient times by the Masons, and accepted by men of all
religious persuasions. And M. Hayman (*Monde Maçonnique*,
t. iv., p. 657) explains it to be a " generic denomination of God,
which everyone may accept for the God he adores ; even those
who do not believe in a God." At best, then, Freemasonry
asserts a frigid deism. It admits of no mediator between God
and man ; no order but the natural order ; no relation between
the Deity and man save natural ones such as they suppose
existed at the beginning.

It is anti-Christian by reason of its effects. We do not see
how Art. 4 can be reconciled with Art. 5. If the former be
true, Masonry has a definite religion of its own which makes it
impossible for anyone to become a true Mason and at the same
time retain his own faith. This is candidly admitted by the
more advanced of the fraternity. " When Masonry," says M.
Goffin,* " opens its temples to a Jew, a Mahometan, a Catholic,

* *Histoire Populaire de la F.-Mason.*, p. 517.

or a Protestant, it is upon condition that he will become a new man, that he will abjure his past errors, that he will lay down the prejudices and the superstitions of his youth. Without this what business has he in our Masonic meetings? what ideas is he likely to acquire there?"

Another direct result of this fifth article is an appalling religious indifferentism which is made one of the conditions of admission. Besides, open war is here declared against Catholicism, which, of necessity, cannot tolerate error, although it may and does tolerate the erring. No Catholic who recites the creed with faith can possibly become a good Freemason. Finally, notwithstanding all its disclaimers of wishing to impose a religious system, notwithstanding its repeated promises to respect and admit all forms of religious belief, Freemasonry deliberately asserts that it aims at supplanting all Churches founded on revelation, and establishing on their ruins the Church of Humanity. Its leading principle and method are anti-Christian, by reason of their utter rationalism. "Masonry addresses itself to the reason as the basis of conviction and of certitude; it addresses itself to the reason as the foundation of universal morality; it binds man to God, not by the mediation of an usurping theocracy, but through the sentiments and ideas that God Himself has placed in the heart of man, made to his own image, to communicate immediately with Him. It is thus that it is willing and able to explain the great mystery of humanity."* After this admission there can be no need of further evidence to show that Freemasonry is absolutely incompatible with supernatural Christian revelation.

The social action of Freemasonry is exerted to procure the substitution of pagan instead of the Christian civilisation. On this subject we shall say nothing from ourselves. We invite our readers to follow a distinguished Mason in the account given by him of the present labours and tendencies of Masonry in Italy, Germany, England, America, Asia, and Belgium. His discourse was addressed to his brother Masons on occasion of the grand festival of the Order in 1863, and is to be found in full in the *Monde Maçonnique*, t. iv., pp. 742-749.

"In the Italian peninsula Masonry looks on the past as one of its least important cares; it has adopted a programme which expresses in the most accurate and precise manner the wants of the nations of our epoch. Raising aloft the immortal device of our institution, it deduces from it all its natural consequences—complete and unrestricted manifestations of thought; the union of all nations by means of the Masonic bond, and by the development of that idea of solidarity which is the result of Liberty, Equality, and Fraternity. . . .

---

* Discourse of M. Frantz Faider at the Fidelity Lodge, Ghent, 2nd July, 1846.

Not only do our Italian brethren look after working men's associations and public instruction, but they devote even to agriculture a share of their time and their efforts. . . . They proclaim their aversion for everything like monopoly, beginning with the worst of all monopolies, the *National Banks*. . . . The religious question likewise forms the most considerable part of the programme of our Italian brethren; but, I hasten to say, not that religious question which tends to sunder men by differences of rites, forms, and revelations; but the sole and only religious question which Masonry has raised in all times and in all ages, by proclaiming all beliefs to be equal, without caring for the exterior form, and by fostering a worship of the Great Architect of the Universe, an ideal superior to and earlier than every revelation and every professed dogma. . . .

" In the north of Europe Masonry follows a course more easy and less perilous; it mixes but little with the practical life of nations. More speculative than practical, it is content to sow in the hearts of its members seeds which sooner or later end by coming to the surface. . . . The dominant idea in the minds of these, our brethren, is the search after that social equality which we, children of 1789, do not lack, but which is wanting to our brethren beyond the Rhine, among whom birth, religions, and professions are impassable barriers in certain states, and which only Masonry helps to suppress."

As to English Masonry, we have already quoted some of the remarks of M. Hayman. He adds :—

" In spite of the reclamations often uttered against our brethren in England by the French Masons, who look upon the English temples as something like churches, our institution plays an important part in England and America, because it has proclaimed love in the heart of a society that worships the individual, and because it has bestowed a worship upon those who before had but a cold enthusiasm. Nor is this all. The off-shoots of Anglo-Saxon Masonry bear their fruits among the least civilized of men. In America there are lodges which affirm that all creatures have equal rights. . . . On the banks of the Ganges Masonry achieves what the political labours of centuries have not been able to accomplish. . . . The Indians are becoming Masons; in the lodge they hear it proclaimed as a principle—all men are equal—rajahs and pariahs are brethren. This is the work of that English Masonry, the efforts of which we sometimes hear slightingly spoken of.

" Coming nearer home, I am glad to look towards Belgium, that happy land, where our Order prospers and thrives. Our brethren there have concentrated their efforts upon one point, which in itself includes much of the mission of the progressive humanity of our day : that point is the complete, absolute, and unlimited assertion of liberty of conscience. And what labours, what attempts, what means have they not had recourse to ! Discourses, lectures, publications, everything has supplied opportunities to their activity, which exerts itself in all ways and in all places. Disputes, municipal interests, election struggles—each day has brought them new cares. . . . Brother Verhaegen, the Grand Master of Belgium, has lately passed to a better world, filled with the thought of two things worthy of such a soul—the free university which he had founded, and Masonry, which is the refuge of freethinkers, the place where they gain fresh strength, and where, like the wrestlers of old, they anoint themselves with that oil of truth that makes them strong.

" Masonry—if I have sufficiently described the labours of our brethren, and I have duly sketched the picture I had in view—Masonry is the ideal of nations as well as of individuals, in which each one occupies himself according to the measure of his capacity and of his wants. Here affecting a political action, there a social character, elsewhere simply economical, everywhere moral, Masonry has one scope, that of setting men free from the physical and moral obstacles that hinder their development."

From this sketch, drawn by a friendly hand of the work

undertaken by contemporary Masonry all over Europe, we can
safely conclude that Masonry addresses itself to solve all the
great social and religious problems that can occupy men upon
this earth.   What region of human activity does it leave untouched ?   Religion, education, administration, social and political economy, agriculture, industrial training, working men's
associations— all are made the field of its labours. What channel
of influence does it leave unused ?   The press, the lecture-hall,
the popular instructor, the university, the primary school, the
domestic hearth, are all turned to account.   For every problem
raised it has a solution ready, based on the Masonic ideal. That
ideal is not Christian, for it professes to rise superior to all
dogmas ; it is an ideal of the earth, earthy.   It rejects the work
of centuries of Christian civilisation, it ignores the Church, it
takes no account of the Incarnation of the Divine Word, who
came to be the way, the truth, and the life of the world.   As if
Christ had never redeemed man, as if He had never left behind
Him a Church to continue this work, as if there were no sacramental channels of divine grace to strengthen humanity when
it faints by the way on its journey towards eternity, these men
undertake to conduct society to a perfect civilisation upon principles of their own, and independently of all revelation.   Is it
not clear, therefore, by their own admission, that they are not
the friends of Christian civilisation ?

  Of the anti-social character of its method we shall here furnish but one direct proof. The Freemasons aim at the possession
of political power.   From a document issued by the Grand
Orient of Belgium to regulate the action of the brotherhood in
case of elections,* we learn how the success of the Masonic candidate is secured.   First of all, " a Mason is proposed· in the
lodge ; and, having been there elected by the members, subject
to the approval of the Grand Orient, he is *forced* upon the
brethren obedient to the lodge.   Whether the election be national,
provincial, or municipal, the approval of the elect by the Grand
Orient is indispensable.   Each Mason shall *swear* to use all his
influence to secure the election of the adopted candidate." The
person elected by the Freemasons shall be compelled to make in
the lodge a profession of faith, of which act a formal account
shall be drawn up.   He is requested to avail himself of the
wisdom of this lodge, or of the Grand Orient, in such important
events as may occur during his time of service. The non-observ-
ance of his engagements will expose him to severe penalties,
even to expulsion from the Order ; the application of these
rigorous measures shall be left to the discretion of the Grand

* *Neut.* p. 235, App. 12.

Orient. Any lodge which judges publicity to be of use may make its own arrangements to procure a notice in the news-papers; but the Grand Orient reserves to itself the right of re-commending such journals as are in its confidence.

When once their candidate is returned, he is become their bondsman for evermore.

As usual, we shall bring proofs from their own documents. A circular letter from the Grand Orient of Belgium, dated 1st March, 1856, contains a reply to the following question: *Has a lodge the right to demand from one of its members, who has entered into politics, explanations concerning his political acts?* The answer declares that " the lodge has not only the right, but the duty of watching the political acts of such of its members as it has sent into political life; the duty of asking explanations whenever one or more of these acts do not tend to enlighten society with the torch of truth; the duty of accepting these ex-planations when they are satisfactory, of expressing censure when they are not forthcoming, and even of cutting off from the Masonic body the members who deliberately have failed in the duties which their quality of Mason imposes upon them, especi-ally in their public life."

Now, is it not plain that all this is a serious injury to the rest of the community? What can be more fatal to the best interests of society than that public men should be deprived of the liberty of following that line of political conduct which appears to them best calculated to advance the well-being of their country? What can be more injurious to society than that men who hold political positions of trust should be subject to the authority of an irresponsible and unknown tribunal, claim-ing the right to sit in judgment upon their conduct, and to bind them to a course which, perhaps, their conscience condemns? It is especially dangerous when Freemasons occupy the first places in the State. Is there not every reason to fear lest even the public authority might, in such a case, be made use of to forward the views of the Order? Are Freemasons so perfect that they are above the temptation of employing their power for their own purposes? And this danger increases a thousand-fold when the education of the country is allowed to exist in the hands of a Government which may be under Masonic control. It is sad to think of a Catholic people, whose innocent little ones, born again of water and of the Holy Ghost, children of our Holy Mother the Church, are handed over to be educated by men to whom the Catholic faith is a mockery and an abomination. What system will be followed in schools and universities under influ-ences such as these men obey? How many tempting baits held out to the young to lead them astray?

19

It now remains for us briefly to examine the special charges urged in detail by the allocution.

The Holy Father asks, " What means that banding together of men, whatever may be their religion and their faith ?"

Catholic and Protestant and Jew and Rationalist and Buddhist all meet upon common ground in the Masonic Lodge. Can they become good Masons and preserve their own religion intact ? Certainly not. We have seen above that the more candid Masons believe that they cannot. All moral is founded upon dogma, and Masonry has moral principles of its own which are founded upon its own special doctrinal principles. If men meet to put these moral principles into practice they must take them as they find them, that is to say, rooted in and springing from the doctrinal treating proper to Masonry. Their doctrines on God, man, and nature necessarily colour their practical rules of action, and these in turn reflect the doctrines by which they have been detailed. Masonry is operative, and its practice hinges upon its theories. The mingling of different religions in the lodges must necessarily end either in a cynical indifferentism to all religion, or to the adoption of the Masonic religion as it has been described above.

4. The secret that shrouds the meetings and working of the society at once stamps it as objectionable. That this secrecy is considered essential to the well-being of Masonry, and even to its very existence, we are assured by a very high authority. M. Defrenne, an experienced and trusted Mason, in a discourse delivered on occasion of the opening of a new Belgian lodge, on 17th August, 1840, declared to the assembled novices that the duration of their existence as Masons depended on the rigorous custody of their secrets.* And M. Thory† says that the publication of the works of the Abbé Barruel and Professor Robison so discouraged English Masonry that it did not recover from the blow until after many years.

Now, secrecy is the hiding-place of moral evil. " In the actual condition of civilisation, is it possible," asks M. Faider,‡ " to make public our doctrines and preach them to the world ? I think not, unfortunately. Too much ignorance, too many prejudices, too much resistance would arise to oppose our efforts, and to crush them." We reply, in our turn, that body of doctrines against which the moral sense of society would rise in rebellion cannot be pure or honest. If pure and honest, why conceal them ? The Freemasons complain that Catholic intolerance has denounced them unjustly and without cause. If

* *Journal Hist. et Litt. de M. Kersten,* tom. viii., pp. 535-545.
† *Acta Latomorum,* tom. i., pp. 205 and 224.
‡ Discourse at Ghent, 2nd July, 1846. Neut, p. 120.

so, why not lay bare to the whole world their entire system, organisation and method, and thereby prove the Roman Pontiffs to be false accusers ? According to its own statement, Masonry is but a benevolent society ; so is the Society of St. Vincent de Paul. If the former be as innocent and as useful as the latter, why not imitate the latter in its frankness and openness ? As long as it loves the dark, right-thinking men will condemn it as the home of deeds of darkness.

Besides, it is highly immoral and dishonourable in a man to pledge himself solemnly, and that by oath, to obey unknown and irresponsible leaders, and to do whatever they should be pleased to command him. It is hard to imagine human liberty reduced to a more degraded condition than this. There is no man who feels the dignity of manhood, and is conscious that he is responsible for his actions to a most wise Judge, who would not feel repugnance at the idea of binding himself to take part in deeds of which he knows nothing, and which, therefore, may be wicked. And this, above all, in the matter of politics, wherein men's views differ so broadly, one from another, as to what is just or unjust, honest or dishonest, useful or noxious.

5. The consciousness of the vital importance of this secrecy has dictated the atrocious oath which has to be taken by a candidate for admission, and which is specially mentioned in the allocution as a proof of the evil character of Masonry. "If I violate my obligation," thus runs the oath, "I allow my tongue to be torn away, my heart to be dragged out, my body to be burned, reduced to ashes, and flung to the winds, so that no memory of me remain among men." This hideous oath is admitted to be the Masonic oath by M. Branville, ex-officer of the Grand Orient of Paris, in a discourse delivered by him in the Lodge of the *Chevalier de la Croix*, on 8th August, 1839.* It is also to be found in the Masonic Ritual corrected in 1856. The iniquity of such an oath is patent to all. Either it is taken by the candidate seriously, or as a piece of mock solemnity in keeping with the character of the trials to which the neophyte's nerves are subjected on his entrance into the Order. If in the latter sense, how black the sin that solemnly calls upon the Creator of all things to be witness to a ridiculous and childish farce ! But if it be taken in serious earnest, as the source of an obligation to make binding certain relations between man and man, it is simply abominable. Whence does this society claim the right to punish its disobedient sons with death ? Is it from God ? Let them produce the authorisation. Is it from the State ? On the contrary, every well-ordered Government has

* *Le Globe*, t. i., pp. 294, 297, § 3.

interdicted the Freemasons, and no Government has made them lords of life and death. Is it from the individual who has taken the oath? But is it not beyond a doubt that no individual is master of his own existence? and how could the neophyte make over to another a right he never could claim as his own?

We have followed thus far the Sovereign Pontiff in the accusations he has brought against Freemasonry, and, with the Masonic documents in our hands, without setting down in malice aught from ourselves, we have seen that each and every charge has its full justification in the teachings of the Masonic Order itself. It may be said that these documents do not convey the real Masonic doctrine; that they are the creation of individuals whose heated fancy has distorted the stern and simple truths of the lodges. If so, why do not the Freemasons repudiate such sentiments, professed, as they were, in the very sanctuary of the temple, before young and inexperienced novices who were to be formed by the speakers to all Masonic virtue? Or, perhaps it may be said, these are the theories of some individual lodges, fruits of exceptional circumstances, and confined to special districts. If so, we say again, why not repudiate them? Why, on the contrary, are the very men who profess such theories treated as brothers? why are they allowed to claim all the practical advantages that Masons so often share with each other to the detriment of distributive justice and to the injury of non-Masonic citizens? Or, it may be urged, these are the unreal dreams of impractical foreigners, and treated by English and Irish Masons as unreal dreams, deserve to be treated as such. Even if it were so, and we have shown why we cannot believe that it is so, is not Freemasonry hereby most fully condemned, in that it is a society in which the best of men meet side by side with the worst, pledged to the same principles with them, with a vague atmosphere of incredulity overhead, and most flagrant and unmistakable wickedness around them, and yet absolutely powerless to exorcise the hidden evil of the principles or to check the patent wickedness of the deeds? If Freemasonry be wholly bad, the case is proved against the Order; if it be wholly good, then many of its best and highest are deceivers and false teachers, for, as we have seen, their own words bear witness against them; if some be good and some wicked, how long will the good bear the yoke of the wicked; how long will they endure that their own light should be mingled with the darkness? "*Faxit dives in misericordia Deus ut redeant insipientes ad cor!*" *

* *Vide* the Allocution.

THE CONGRESS OF STUDENTS AT LIEGE.

"MAY you be enabled some day to behold in us the best and happiest work of your hands, when, children of 1830, with the cross of Christ on our country's banner, we shall march to conquer the future, under the shelter of constitutional liberty, under the guidance of our venerated and beloved dynasty, in the name of Faith."

These words were addressed on the 27th November, 1857, by the students of the Catholic University of Louvain to the Rector and Professors of their Alma Mater. They breathe the generous and hopeful ardour of youth, but an ardour chastened and perfected by religion. Who will say that the future steps of these young men were less manly because made in the name of Faith? or that they loved their country the less for having been taught to ennoble their patriotism by uniting with their country's flag the cross of Christ? Freedom from restraint is the passion of youth; but these young men avow that they can distinguish between liberty and licence. Will they serve the cause of liberty the worse for having been taught to serve it only by lawful means? If in their address they recall the memories of 1830, it is that their religious and civil rights may be respected by their rulers; and they speak dutifully of their sovereign lest their loyalty should be called in question. Thus all that makes youth the season of promise in them is purified and exalted, without being weakened. Piety without fanaticism, patriotism without narrowness, independence without audacity, loyalty without servility, are the gems of which their words are the setting.

The system of education which produces such results as these has fulfilled all the conditions required in the best interests of religion and society. Now, that system is the system which makes religion the groundwork of education. The noble sentiments we are admiring are the proper fruits of a Catholic University.

Let us now turn our attention to a very different set of speakers. They belong to the same country as those we have been listening to; they live under the same Government with them, and are subject to the same laws. They are taken from the same ranks of life as the students of Louvain, and are destined to fill in society positions similar to theirs—as lawyers, physicians, merchants, men of letters, or of property. Most of them have been baptised in the Catholic Church, and brought up in the Catholic faith. At present they are students of the godless universities of Belgium, and the basis of the system which has trained them is that the Catholic Church shall have no control over education. Their instructors proclaim that the Church is incompetent to teach; that her formulas of faith dwarf and narrow the intellect, while her repressive system destroys all the nobler energies of the will; that her action upon education makes it the nurse of fanatical sectarianism; that the civic and natural virtues are stifled under an unscientific theocracy; that she teaches youth to divide its allegiance. For some time back the State has taken upon itself the work of education. It banished religion far from the academic halls in which it assembled crowds of young men, lured by the fascination of bright promises and solid rewards. This godless system has had time to carry out its theories, and to contemplate at length the work of its hands. Wise men never doubted for a moment what that work would be. But to-day not even the unwise or the careless can hesitate to condemn it, and to judge the tree to be evil which has borne fruit so undoubtedly pernicious. The students themselves have met in congress at Liege, and, with all the impudent shamelessness of corrupt hearts, have revealed themselves to the world such as godless education has made them. Three terrible words suffice to describe the abyss into which they have been led: Atheism, or infidelity in religion, materialism in philosophy, and socialism in politics. Terrible words these in any case, and under any circumstances; but they become absolutely appalling when uttered by lips which Catholic mothers once taught to lisp with infant love the holy name of God. It is not possible to repress a cry of indignation against that treacherous system which has seized upon so many innocent souls, to rob them not only of the natural virtues which are so fair in youth, but of their hope in this life and of their God.

The sessions of the students' congress were scenes of frightful confusion. We have had, even here in Ireland, a sample of what an unbridled mob of students, trained by the godless system, can achieve in the way of disorder. But their brethren in Belgium—perhaps because trained more fully in the spirit of that system—have far surpassed all we have as yet been condemned to witness in this country. We willingly abstain from describing the abominable scene. After all, its accidental horrors sink into insignificance before the hideous doctrines asserted, defended, and applauded to the echo by the congress. Nor shall we attempt to follow the order of the discussions, for logical order there hardly can be said to have been. One merit, must, how·

ever, be conceded to the speakers. They cannot be accused of want of precision in their statements, or blamed for reticence or equivocation. Hence we need only collect their testimonies, and arrange them for clearness' sake under the three heads mentioned above. We have chosen these heads because we believe that there can be no more searching test of the godless system than an examination of its results affecting respectively the central truths in Religion, Philosophy, and Social Science.

And first as to Religion.

At the morning session of the 31st October, M. Leon Fontaine of Brussels thus categorically expressed the objects his party sought to achieve in the religious order:—

"We seek the physical development of man, and this cannot be attained without bread. As to man's intellectual and moral development, that is a secondary question (c' est un côtè secondaire). As socialists, we desire in the religious order the annihilation of every religion and of every church, and we seek to arrive at the denial of God, and to the freedom of private judgment."*

And the same speaker again says:—

"We have no liberty of conscience. If a certain sect to which belong that of the solidaires, wished to establish a religion called Atheism, would the State grant us a subsidy?
"A Member—Atheism is a negation.
"M. Fontaine—No; it is an affirmation. (Applause.) They would give us no subsidy, but would hinder us from practising that worship. If a thousand of us Atheists were to meet in any town, and if I were appointed by them a bishop of Atheism, I would get no palace, nor even a little church, nor even the smallest pulpit."

M. Cas, of Paris, in the same session, spoke as follows:—

"I propose a resolution to the effect that the Catholic religion must be allowed no part in education, and I demand the complete exclusion of every individual who represents the idea of religion. When I hear men speak of God I think of my spine; when I hear men speak of liberty, I think of Napoleon. . . . I recognise no authority in the State, since I do not recognise the only real authority, that of God."

These utterances are plainly and unmistakably atheistic. We now pass to others which, though equally destructive of belief in God, are veiled under forms fortunately hitherto generally unknown to the bulk of our populations, but which now require to be unmasked. We allude to the doctrines of Positivism. This is not the occasion to point out the place held by Comte, the founder of the Positivist school, in the history of infidel philosophy. We must be satisfied with drawing attention to the atheistic tendencies of his teaching. Be it enough, there-

* La Patrie, Nos. 310, 311; 6th and 7th Nov., 1865.

fore, to say that the extract given below from M. Burque's speech is but the application of the general law which Comte declares to preside over the progress of knowledge. This law, according to Comte, has three stages through which each science passes onwards towards its perfection. The first, or the theological, is that in which the mind examines into final causes, and refers phenomena to special providence; the second, or metaphysical, discards supernatural or personal causes, and seeks for abstract essences; in the third, or *positive* stage, it is content with facts, and does not ask for causes. The first stage may be called theistic, the second pantheistic, the third atheistic. The third is the stage of perfection. It admits of no facts but such as are presented by sensation. Hence Positivism is altogether silent about the existence of a God; it refuses to conclude from the order visible in nature to the existence of a designing Mind; it knows nothing of spirit, or personal immortality of the soul; it excludes Providence, and substitutes for it a network of stern immutable laws. With this explanation we shall be better able to understand M. Burque:

" The radical reform of education consists in declaring Positivism to be the only rational method. To apprehend truth we require a brain, a soul, a something or other. Education has been first theological, then metaphysical or mathematical, at present it is and ought to be Positivist. For example: For a long time it was believed that the astronomical world was guided by a sovereign hand. Science has discovered that this harmony resulted from the ponderable qualities of bodies. We must educate the boy after the fashion in which humanity itself has been educated, and we must bring the same system to bear on his brain. . . . To enable him to understand complex phenomena we must first prepare his organisation. When it becomes clear that there is no defect in his brain, we can unfold to him the reason of man. . . . Positivism has an art and a morality of its own. I venture to say, and I say it from my conscience, that a young man thus trained will be able to comprehend his own dignity."*

M. Burque found an opponent in M. Foucher de Careil, who, while he attacked theology, defended the spiritualist thesis. To him a M. Armengo replied: " Positivism is neither deism nor atheism : it altogether declines to occupy itself with the question." This remark, which contains the very pith and definition of the entire godless system of education, was received with general applause.

M. Regnaud throws still more light on the atheistic tendencies of Positivism. " M. Foucher de Careil proclaims the idea of God; I attach myself to Positivism. There are two methods of education, but only one is correct, namely, the Positivist or experimental or materialist. . . . There are two

* *La Patrie*, No. 309, 5th Nov., 1865.

standards : one, that of God and of the reaction ; the other, that of Positivism."

We have put in evidence abundant enough to show that atheism and infidelity are among the results of godless education. In olden times there were men who said there is no God, but they said it in their hearts, in the dark recesses of their own guilty consciences. Those who say it at present glory in their shame, and meet in the midst of populous cities to make boast of their unbelief, and to insult to his face the God that made them. Why this difference? Let those answer the question who established it as a principle that religion must be banished from education.

Materialism in philosophy ever follows close upon atheism, or immediately precedes it. The congress of students declares itself to be materialist by the very fact that it avows its partiality for Positivism. But explicit assertions of materialism are to be found in abundance. M. Regnaud declares that " the word *materialism* must not be rejected on account of the attacks of which it has been made the object. As for me, I frankly declare that I am a materialist (applause). Comte was a great man, and a follower of Diderot, our great Diderot. The middle age was a period of darkness, wherein only funeral piles gave light to the world. If Julian the Apostate had been successful, perhaps the fifth century would have had the noble institutions of the French Republic. . . . To-day every man of progress is for materialism. On our banner you may read the device, progress by means of science."

M. Laforge also undertook the defence of materialism :

" There are two systems of education, the purely materialistic system which rejects God, and what is more, does not concern itself about Him, and spiritualism, which leads straight to absolutism. With spiritualism there is no morality. Catholicism is the most powerful engine that has ever been constructed from the idea of God, and, unfortunately, it is still powerful. After four thousand years of struggle (?) it is still standing. Listen to what Catholic morality teaches : there is a God who directs the universe by his absolute and efficacious will. Is not this fatalism? God from all eternity has fixed the number of the predestined. . . . According to Catholic morality we can do nothing to gain heaven."

M. Jacqlart said :

" Thus far the question has been clearly put. In fact, the question is between God and man. We wish to determine whether we ought to retain in education the spirit of religion, or exclude it altogether. Let us see what has Catholicism done for morality, for art, for letters, for philosophy, for science. Morality ! how beautiful was that of the ancients ! It had for its motto, *Potius mori quam fœdari :* Death before dishonour. This was the morality of a Cato, of a Lucretia. . . . Catholicism condemns this morality. Catholic morality is contained in these words : *Initium sapientiæ timor Domini.* Is that a point of view worthy of us ? Is the motive of our actions to be the fear of punishment, or the hope of a boundless enjoyment like to that of the saints?" . . .

As to socialism, almost all the speakers on the 20th October professed the doctrines of the France of 1793. Almost all attacked the right of property, authority, and, in general, the bonds that keep society together. Almost all invoked brute force—the terrible force of the Reign of Terror—as the regenerating principle of modern society. We shall be content with a few as quotations. M. Fontaine, after proving to his own satisfaction that in Belgium they had no liberty of any kind, goes on to say :—

"We have therefore no liberty. Who will give us liberty? and how? Revolution means equality and the abolition of all privileges. . . . In the political order, by realising republican ideas, we wish to arrive at the federation of all nations, and the solidarity of individuals. In the social order, we demand the suppression of the right of property, the abolition of heritage."

M. Janson said :—

" We must suppress all privileges of race and birth, all distinctions of orders and castes ; we must proclaim the government of the nation itself ; in one word, we must create the republic. In my opinion, there is but one thing deserving the attention of young men—the republic and socialism."

To crown our extracts we give the words of M. Robert of Brussels, in which is contained the sum of all that had been said by his compeers : —

"It is idle to talk of materialism and of spiritualism. As for me, I hate all authority; I hate authority in religion, authority in politics, authority in social reform. Authority is the weight that crushes us. As long as science is not able to rise to heaven, to rise above heaven, to rend the vault of heaven as if it were a ceiling of paper, there is no such thing as science."

We conclude by making two observations. The first regards the bearing of the scene we have here described upon the educational question now debated in Ireland. In the words of one of the speakers at Liege, we say that in Ireland, as in Belgium, " the question has been put clearly enough." Are we to maintain the religious spirit in education, or are we to exclude it peremptorily and altogether? We will not now enter upon the merits of this question. We will merely remark that those who hold that religion ought to be excluded from education must take their places side by side with the blasphemous students of the congress of Liege. Their views are but the echo of the views of these misguided young men. And why have the members of the congress so emphatically proclaimed the necessity of excluding religion from education? They do not attempt to conceal their motives. It is because they believe such education to be the best means of propagating the anti-Christian views entertained by them in matters of religion, philosophy, and social science. The proficiency they have already made under the system has given them a right to speak with authority on this subject. And thus it comes to pass that what the Holy See has long since authoritatively declared, is now confirmed and proved by the testimony of this congress, namely, that education without religion is a source of indifferentism, infidelity, and rebellion. Let us hope that this witness rising from the dead, this voice crying out from the dead hopes and blighted promises of a wasted youth, may be listened to by those who have refused to hear Moses and the prophets.

In the next place, we wish to draw attention to a coincidence which appears to us eminently suggestive, and of great importance in the present matter. Whosoever examines the Liege discourses must be struck at once with the central place which Positivism holds in the minds of the speakers. It suggested to them a plan of studies; from it they borrowed epithets in need; its method is their method; it pervades and colours their entire spirit. There were, it is true, even among them some few who have not bent the knee to Comte and Littré. But they were few in number, and the remedy they would apply was little better than the disease. Almost at the same time that Positivism was thus enthroned in the congress of Liege, here in Dublin, in Trinity College, a distinguished Catholic student, in an address read by him before the College Historical Society, took occasion to heap praises on that very Positivism and its author. While he admitted that Comte has fallen a prey to the silliest and most ridiculous fancies when laying down laws for the new community of which he was to be the author, the speaker expressed his belief, nevertheless, that his philosophy will, "perhaps, modify the convictions of every thinking mind." He commends to his hearers Comte's Science of History as suggesting hopes of a splendid future.

And yet the Positivism thus commended is a system which is without God in this world, which knows not the spirituality and immortality of the soul, and which logically destroys Christianity by making all proof of it impossible! If in Belgium they are reaping the whirlwind, in Ireland we are sowing the wind.

POSITIVISM.

I.

EARLY in 1828 a handful of men assembled in a modest lodging, in a quiet street in Paris, to hear a youthful teacher of mathematics explain a new system of philosophy of the Sciences. The system then first proposed rose above the philosophical horizon, like a cloud no bigger than a man's hand, and, apparently, with little to distinguish it from the many systems that daily rise only to disappear. Thirty-eight years have since elapsed, and each succeeding year has seen that cloud grow larger and blacker, until at length it threatens to hide from the sight of men all that is bright in the entire arch of heaven. The influence of the Positive Philosophy has gone on, ever steadily increasing, since the day on which it was inaugurated by its founder, Auguste Comte; and day by day its influence still increases. That influence is deadly beyond all example. Whatsoever it touches it breaks to pieces. Other systems of philosophy have been a revolt on the part of reason, as against religion; Positivism makes war on both religion and reason. Other philosophies have set forth solutions of the great problem of man's destiny: solutions, no doubt, various, false, and contradictory in themselves, yet each sincerely professing to be a solution. Positivism declares any attempt at a solution to be delusion or audacity. The existence of a personal and living God, the immortal soul, free will, faith, prayer, Providence, conscience, truth—all that makes the moral life of nations and of individuals—must disappear before its corroding negations. It would ruthlessly tear man from every hope in the divine promises, and would check the outpourings of the heart towards our Heavenly Father. To be without God in this world is the highest wisdom it sets itself to teach.

We propose, in this paper, to give some account of the members of the Positivist school in France and in England. It is the misfortune of our time and position, as Irish Catholics, that if we would read the current literature at all we must expose ourselves to the influence of writers whose thoughts and language are coloured, without our knowing it, by the spirit of some pagan system. Reviews, magazines, journals, histories, even the very novels that circulate in thousands among Catholics, are often so many channels of insidious influence established in the interests of a most pernicious naturalism. It is a sore scandal that Catholic journals should admit into their columns praise and recommendations of such works. It would be a useful undertaking if one were to set forth in plain language the various doctrines which inspire the leading periodicals habitually read by millions. How many would be surprised to find their favourite writer or review to be in reality the apostle of some system subversive not only of all that the reader holds as sacred in religion, but even of the principles upon which he unhesitatingly rests his theories of right and duty as towards society ! How many would be astonished to learn that the scientific, or poetical, or tenderly emotional writing concerning God, upon which their simple piety is wont to rest with delight, is nothing else than a roundabout way of denying altogether the existence of a personal God !

The first place in our notice is due to Auguste Comte, the founder of the Positivist philosophy and religion. The sources whence we have drawn our information are eminently favourable to him, seeing that they are the writings of those who are personal friends of his own, and devoted adherents of his system. Mr. George Henry Lewes (*Fortnightly Review*, No. xvi., 1866, pp. 385-410), lately published a sketch of M. Comte, based on the writer's personal knowledge of the man, and on the statements of M. Littré and of Dr. Robinet, the philosopher's physician. No man in England has done more for Positivism than Mr. Lewes; no man is more thoroughly penetrated with the spirit of the new philosophy. In following him as closely as we can, in the sketch he has drawn of the master, we are safe from being unjust to the memory of Comte.

Auguste Comte was born of Catholic parents, at Montpellier, on the 19th of January, 1798. When nine years of age he became a boarder in the Montpellier Lycée, where he soon became remarkable alike for talent and resistance to discipline. At the age of twelve, having exhausted the course of studies usual at the Lycée, he was allowed to begin mathematics. In these he made such proficiency that in his sixteenth year he had already gained a first place at the Polytechnique. At the age of seventeen he was admitted to the École Polytechnique, and there fully sustained the brilliant reputation for capacity he had acquired in his earlier years. In a short time, however, his rebellious spirit showed itself by an act of insubordination of a grave character. This led to his expulsion, and to his being placed for a time under the surveillance of the police.

Long before this event he had cast off both the religious belief and the royalist tendencies in which his parents would have trained him. At fourteen he is supposed to have been a complete infidel. He was deeply read in the irreligious and revolutionary literature for which the eighteenth century was remarkable. It may be easily imagined that his pious parents were deeply afflicted at the sad change that had been wrought in their son, and that they became intensely anxious about his future career. Their anxiety was deepened when he announced to them his fixed intention of proceeding to Paris. They remonstrated and threatened, but remonstrances and threats were equally powerless against his obstinacy. He went to Paris, and, by the aid of a few friends, earned for himself a scanty subsistence by giving private lessons in mathematics. For the space of three weeks he acted as private secretary to Casimir Périer ; from Périer he passed, in 1818, to St. Simon, with whom he lived for six years. His intimacy with this man began in enthusiasm on Comte's part, and ended in a violent rupture, which was the result of difference in opinion between the old philosopher and his younger friend.

According to Mr. Lewes, Comte owes to St. Simon's influence only this : a conviction that the revolutionary work of the eighteenth century was complete, and that the work of the nineteenth century should be towards a reconstruction of society on a new basis. However this may be, it was in 1822, about four years after his first meeting with St. Simon, that Comte laid the foundations of the new philosophy, " which he called *positive*, because it was the generalisation of the method which each positive science had employed in particular " (p. 388). In that year he published his *Plan des travaux nécessaires pour reorganiser la Société*. In 1825 he published in the *Producteur, Considerations Philosophiques sur les Sciences et les Savants*, and *Considerations sur le nouveau Pouvoir Spirituel*. These essays contain an outline of the Positive Philosophy :—

"There it is shown (1) that all phenomena, even those of politics, are subject to invariable laws ; (2) that the human mind passes from initial to theological conceptions to final positive conceptions ; (3) that human activity, in like manner, passes through industrial *régime*, through the transitional state of a defensive military *régime* ; (4) that everywhere, and at all times, the state of opinions and manners determines the institutions, and that the nature of the general beliefs determines a corresponding political scheme ; (5) that philosophy (or general beliefs) in passing from the theological to the positive stage, must bring about the substitution of the industrial for the military *régime*; and, finally, that the spiritual reorganisation, which is the necessary condition of all social reorganisation, must repose upon the authority of demonstration, it must be based upon science, with a priesthood properly constituted out of the regenerated scientific classes. In other words, the spiritual authority must issue from a philosophy which can be demonstrated, not from a philosophy which is imagined " (pp. 389, 390).

This year is remarkable also for his marriage with Caroline Massin, an event which exercised a pernicious influence on his

after life. The marriage was singularly unhappy. He absolutely declined all religious ceremony in contracting it. After
years of vexatious quarrels, the parties separated in 1842. We
may here add that in 1845, whilst his wife was yet living, he
first met Madame Clotilde de Vaux, whose husband also was
living, but condemned to the galleys for life. Mr. Lewes remarks that each of them, though morally free, was legally
bound. "Marriage being thus impossible," says our author,
"they had only the imperfect yet inestimable consolation of a
pure and passionate friendship." She died the next year.
"The remainder of his life was a perpetual hymn to her memory.
Every week he visited her tomb. Every day he prayed to her,
and invoked her continual assistance" (p. 401). The extruva-
gant nonsense which Comte has written about this woman is
almost incredible. To her influence he attributes whatever of
tenderness his system exhibits. She was the Beatrice of the
new Dante, and, had she lived, was destined to become the
priestess, or rather the goddess of the new religion.

At the time of his marriage Comte had but one pupil in
mathematics: that pupil afterwards became General Lamoricière.
By the month of April, 1826, he had sufficiently matured his
system for a dogmatic exposition, which he announced in a
course of seventy-two lectures in his private rooms. It may well
surprise us to find among his auditors men like Humboldt and
Poinsot. After the third or fourth lecture the philosopher became insane. On Friday, 24th April, he went out and did not
return. On Monday a letter came from Saint Denis, whither
his wife hastened, but found him no longer there. She found
him, however, at Montmorency, in a most alarming state. When
he grew calmer he expressed a wish to go out for a walk with
his wife. "As they came to the edge of the lake of Enghien,
he suddenly declared that, although he could not swim, he
should not be drowned if he walked into the lake, and he began
to drag his wife with him. She was young and strong, struggled,
and caught hold of a tree, and saved them both" (p. 392). He
was placed in an asylum, but his recovery was slow. His poor
mother hurried from Montpellier to Paris to attend on him. On
the day he quitted the asylum for his home his mother, aided by
M. de Lamennais, succeeded in inducing him to contract marriage before the Church. At home, at the end of a week his
recovery began, and in three weeks he was left alone with his
wife. More than once during this period he threw his knife at
Madame Comte, to frighten her into compliance with his wishes.
At the end of six weeks all danger was over. But such was the
melancholy that overwhelmed him at the idea that he could no
longer study as he had done before, that he resolved upon

suicide. He slipped out one day and threw himself into the
Seine, but was rescued from death by a soldier, who plunged in
after him. He expressed great regret for this attempt, and in
July was well enough to visit his parents at Montpellier.

In 1828 he commenced his lectures, and this time was able
to complete his course. In 1830 he published the first volume
of his course; the second, in 1835; the sixth and last in 1842.
These twelve years were years of incessant toil. In 1833 he
obtained an office in the Ecole Polytechnique, which, with other
engagements, gave him an income of ten thousand francs. The
publication of his work raised a storm against him which soon
became so violent as to drive him from his official position.
Once more he had to toil for his daily bread as teacher of
mathematics. This change of circumstances developed the pre-
posterous self-conceit of the man. We shall let Mr. Lewes
tell how :—

"With the publication of the *Philosophie Positive* he assumed his place
among the great thinkers of all ages, but drew upon himself the bitter hatred
of rivals and humiliated professors, which, being supported by the indignation
of theologians, metaphysicians, and journalists, who were irritated at his dangerous doctrines and sweeping scorn, ended in driving him from his official
position. He was turned adrift once more to seek a laborious existence as a
teacher of mathematics. The story is told by him in his preface to the sixth
volume of the *Philosophie Positive*, and in fuller detail by M. Littré. It need
not be repeated here ; the sad result is enough. To mitigate the blow, three
Englishmen, Mr. Grote, Mr. Raikes Currie, and Sir W. Molesworth, through
the intervention of Mr. John Mill, offered to replace the official salary for one
year, understanding that at the end of the year Comte would be either rein-
stated, or would have resolved on some other career. The year passed, but his
re-election was again refused. At first this troubled him but little. He had
learned to regard the 'subsidy' of his admirers as his right. It was due from
the rich to the philosopher ; and the philosopher could the more effectually use
his powers if all material anxieties were taken from him. This, however, was
by no means the light in which the case was seen in England. Mr. Grote sent
an additional six hundred francs, but a renewal of the subsidy was declined.
He was dreadfully exasperated. I remember hearing him speak of the refusal
as if some unworthy treachery had been practised on him. I tried to explain
as delicately as I could what I conceived to be the point of view of his friends
who declined to be his bankers; but he had so entirely wrought himself into
the persuasion that the refusal was a moral dereliction, and that no excuse
could be offered for men who had wealth withholding a slight portion of it from
thinkers, whose lives were of importance to the world, that I saw it was useless. He had a fixed idea on the subject, and it may be seen expressed in
haughty terms in his letter to Mr. Mill. If there is much to be said (and I
think there is) in favour of his idea of the duty of the rich towards thinkers
whose aims they approve, there is also not a little to be said on the other side,
and not a little blame attributable to his manner of urging his claims. He
chose to assume a '*haute magistrature morale*,' which others would not recognise. He professed to speak solely as a philosopher, but showed too much personal preoccupation. It is sad to hear that the result of this was a coolness on
the part of Mr. Mill, and the cessation of a correspondence which he had valued,
and to which Comte himself attached great value (as appears in one of his
letters to me inquiring into the cause of the silence, and showing anxiety on
the subject)" (pp. 398, 399).

After 1842 a radical change took place which marks a period of immense importance in the history of Positivism. In his *Politique Positiviste*, and his *Catechisme*, he sets himself to arrange individual and social life according to his own fancy. Many of those who look upon his *Philosophie* as one of the noblest works ever written, abandon him in his *Politique* and *Catechisme*. Among such Positivists are Mr. John Mill, Mr. Grote, Mr. Lewes, M. Littré. Others again place the *Politique* and *Catechisme* far before the *Philosophie*. M. Littré, in order to justify his desertion of the master after 1842, insinuates that the works written after that date are vitiated, owing to a second attack of insanity, which he supposes then took place. If this argument be admitted, it is plain that not even the *Philosophie* is entitled to any regard. For, beyond all doubt, it was published after a fit of insanity so serious and protracted as to have at one time almost forbidden the hope of recovery. In 1852 he published the *Catechisme Positiviste*. Dr. Robinet, his physician, has sketched the routine of his daily life in these his latter years :—

" He rose at five in the morning, prayed, meditated, and wrote till seven in the evening, with brief intervals for his two meals. Every day he read a chapter from the *Imitation of Christ*, and a canto of Dante. Homer also was frequently re-read. Poetry was his sole relaxation, now that he could no longer indulge his passion for the opera. From seven to nine (and on Sundays in the afternoon) he received visits especially from working men, among whom he found disciples. On Wednesday afternoon he visited the grave of Madame de Vaux. At ten he again prayed and went to bed. The hour of prayer was to him an hour of mystic and exquisite expansion. Nothing could be simpler than his meals : breakfast consisted only of milk ; dinner was more substantial, but rigorously limited. At the close of dinner he daily replaced dessert by a piece of dry bread, which he ate slowly, meditating on the numerous poor who were unable to procure even that means of nourishment in return for their work " (pp. 406-7).

The *Synthèse Subjective* he did not live to finish. He died on the 5th of September, 1857, at the age of sixty.

The system elaborated by M. Comte has been developed by many disciples. Among these M. Littré holds the chief place. Convinced that theology and royalism are fast disappearing from our age; that supernaturalism is but an idle hypothesis ; that the mental regimen, half-theological, half-metaphysical, to which the present generations are subjected, is full of contradictions ; that Catholicity is an antiquated and effete creed ; this writer has set himself the task, says M. Sainte-Beuve, of endeavouring " to set humanity free from illusions, from vague disputes, from vain solutions, from deceitful idols and powers." The illusions, the existence of which in the world M. Littré deplores, are simply a belief in Providence and in a Creator ; the solutions and disputes regard the origin and destination of things ; the

20

powers and idols stand for the Living Personal God. "Each one may be allowed to represent such matters to himself as he likes; there is nothing to hinder the man who finds a pleasure in doing so from dreaming upon that past and that future" (*Paroles de Philosophie Positive*, p. 33).

M. Littré is the author of a translation of Strauss's *Life of Christ*, and of several works on Positivism, such as *Paroles de Philosophie Positive; Conservatisme, Revolution, et Positivisme; Auguste Comte et le Positivisme.* He is also editor of a new edition of Comte's works. It will still probably be fresh in the memory of many of our readers how successfully Mgr. Dupanloup exposed the horrors these books contain.[*]

Close upon M. Littré comes the well-known Ernest Renan. As the former is the legislator, so the latter is the poet of Positivism. His *Life of Jesus* may be taken as a sample of the working of Positivism in our days. The principle on which the investigation into the origin of Christianity is therein conducted is avowedly the Positive principle that an immutable material law governs all things, history as well as matter. Hence miracles must be excluded, and hence such portions of the Gospels as contain mention of miracles are quietly set aside by the author. Add to this an art of criticism the most capricious and wanton that can well be imagined, and who will be surprised at his grotesque and blasphemous account of the Divine Author of our religion?

MM. Taine, Havet, and About likewise belong to the Positivist school, and, in particular, to the literary branch of it. The following texts, literally translated from the works of these writers, will enable the reader to judge of their teaching: "There is no free being superior to man;" "it is man who creates God;" "God is but a fiction of the imagination;" "humanity is the supreme existence and the only Providence."[†]

And yet, in the face of such texts as these, Comte's followers are indignant that he and they should be called atheists. In one sense, and in one sense only, they are not atheists. In what sense? In as much as atheism professes to explain the origin and destination of the universe, while the Positivists refuse to consider the question at all. Their highest authority tells us that, "even considered under the purely scientific aspect, atheism only constitutes a very imperfect emancipation, since it tends to prolong indefinitely the metaphysical stage by its ceaseless pursuit of new solutions of theological problems, instead of pushing aside all such problems as essentially inaccessible."[‡]

---

[*] Mgr. Dupanloup, *Avertissement aux Pères de famille.*
[†] Guthlin, *Les Doctrines Positivistes en France*, p. 13.
[‡] *Discourse on the ensemble of Positivism.*

We now pass to what touches us more nearly, namely, the Positivist school in England.

The enormous spread of infidelity in England may be measured by the extent of infidel literature there published. The supply, especially in such matters as this, is created and regulated by the demand. Of Combe's *Constitution of Man*, a work of materialistic tendency, and based on a denial of Providence, more than eighty thousand copies issued from the English press. The total annual issue of immoral publications amounts to twenty-nine millions. In 1851 the purely infidel press in London issued more than twelve millions of publications; the issues of avowed atheism during the same period being more than six hundred and fifty thousand. All this is exclusive of newspapers.*

We need not say how much Rationalism in its critical aspect has gained ground in the country whose Established Church has supplied the writers of the *Essays and Reviews*. But Positivism, in particular, has struck root far and wide in the English mind. Dr. Tulloch† tells us that "Positivism, within the last quarter of a century, has become an active and even fashionable mode of thought, and nowhere more so than among certain literary and intellectual circles in England. So far as it is a philosophising, it is adapted to the common understanding, and falls in fitly with the scientific and social tendencies of the time; while it has received a noted impulse from certain English writers of great ability." As far back as 1838 it was noticed by Sir David Brewster in the *Edinburgh Review*. Miss Harriet Martineau condensed into two English volumes the six volumes of the course, adding from her own stores some spiteful remarks against theologians. But, of all others, Mr. Lewes became the apostle of Positivism in England. His literary labours have been numerous and varied. He began with *Ranthorpe*, a novel (1845); between 1845 and 1857 he devoted himself chiefly to criticism on history and art; a *Life of Robespierre*, an essay on the Spanish drama of Vega and Calderon; an exposition of Comte's *Positive Philosophy* in Bohn's scientific series; a biographical history of Philosophy, and a life of Goëthe. Since 1857 he has edited Johnson's *Chemistry of Common Life*, and published the *Physiology of Common Life*, *Sea-side Studies*, and *Studies of Animal Life*. Nearly a year ago he commenced to edit the *Fortnightly Review*, in which, from time to time, papers in favour of Positivism occur.

Fellow-worker with Mr. Lewes is Marian Evans, better

---

* *Infidelity: its Aspects, Causes, and Agencies.* By Thomas Pearson.
† *The Christ of the Gospels, &c.* By John Tulloch, D.D.

known under the name of George Eliot. In 1846, imitating the examples of Littré and Renan, she contributed her share of labour towards destroying faith in Christianity by translating Strauss's *Life of Christ*, and (in 1853) Feuerbach's *Essence of Christianity*. Besides these works, she published in the *Westminster Review* theological articles animated by the same principles. Under the name of George Eliot she rose to an eminent position among novelists by her *Scenes from Clerical Life, Adam Bede*, and other works. As to the moral and religious purpose of her works it is not necessary to say much. When her early works, published under the name of George Eliot, first became famous, various conjectures were hazarded by critics as to the probable author. One critic* dwelt upon the testimony she unconsciously bore to the truth of Catholicism, and on the way in which she brought home to the conscience the doctrine of the Personality of God. Against this we have to say that there is no one doctrine which she denies more thoroughly than that there exists a personal God. Her views of religion are those of Goëthe, who has been well described as a man of deep religious sentiments, with complete scepticism on most religious doctrines. With her, faith is an illusion; doctrines and creeds are but names for sentiments, useful only to turn "feelings into energies;" the substance of all religions is the same. And yet she speaks as if she had faith in Christianity. And in this, says the reviewer above cited, she is not dishonest. For, although to the Positivist religious doctrines are only impressions on the imagination, not corresponding with any reality in the universe, still they are necessary to enable man to turn his feelings into energies. Hence the Positivist can enter into the feelings of others, and to these others speak like believers in Christianity. A writer in the *Westminster Review* has said of her that she apparently regards creeds "as being only shells of different shape and colour, enclosing the fruit of the religious spirit common to the human race; or as so many mental structures, which in his successive metamorphoses man forms and afterwards casts off."

It is but fair, however, to observe that Mr. Lewes does not altogether share the religious views of M. Comte. First, because in framing his religious system, Comte abandoned the historical method, which had guided him in his philosophical system, and went upon a purely speculative basis. Next, because he made his religion into a system. He introduced a new Grand Etre, a new Bible, a new Catholic Church, a new calendar, a

---

* For these details concerning Mr. Lewes and Miss Evans see *Home and Foreign Review*, No. vi., 1863, *George Eliot's Novels*.

new priesthood, new sacraments, a new spiritual power, a new temporal power. At this point Mr. Lewes, to whom religion and system are incompatible terms, freed himself from his teaching; and at this point he came under the influence of Goëthe.

Mr. John Stuart Mill, in his *System of Logic*, speaks in high praise of M. Comte's fundamental law of the progress of human knowledge.* This generalised law appears to him to have

" That high degree of scientific evidence which is derived from the concurrence of the indications of history with the probabilities derived from the constitution of the human mind. Nor could it be easily conceived, from the mere enunciation of such a proposition, what a flood of light it lets in upon the whole course of history ; when its consequences are traced, by connecting with each of the three states of human intellect which it distinguishes, and with each successive modification of these three states, the correlative condition of other social phenomena. But whatever decision competent judges may pronounce on the results arrived at by any individual inquirer, the method now characterised is that in which the derivative laws of social order and of social law must be sought."

In an elaborate exposition of the *Positive Philosophy* recently reprinted from the *Westminster Review*, Mr. Mill, although differing from M. Comte's system in many and important points, nevertheless adheres to it in the main. Finally, Positivism has at length made its appearance in Ireland. Its formulas have been heard in Trinity College, and, we deeply regret to say, from Catholic lips. It is a painful sign of the times to see a Catholic gentleman join without scruple in the praise which has been heaped on Positivism by so many who have made shipwreck of their Christian faith. But we have said enough for the present of the literature of Positivism ; the system itself deserves more lengthened notice.

II.

Having glanced at the literature of Positivism, it is now time to proceed to examine the system itself. First of all, it may be asked, is Positivism a growth altogether new ? or is it rather an offshoot from philosophical systems which have already appeared in the world ? and if its connection with theories long since familiar can be established, how much of their characteristics does it retain? and what has it added from its own stores ?

Positivism belongs of right to the sensational philosophy, and preserves the leading features of its parent school. The primary elements of all our knowledge are three in number, and philosophical systems† differ one from the other according as

* Vol. ii., p. 518, 4th ed., 1856.
† See Morell's *History of Modern Philosophy*, 2nd ed., vol. i., p. 63.

they hold up one or the other of these three as the chief or sole
element whence our ideas are derived.   The three elements are:
(1) the idea of our own individual existence; (2) the idea of
nature, of things that are not ourselves ; and (3) the idea of the
Absolute or Eternal.   The system which takes for its basis the
first of these dwells especially upon those striking facts of our
consciousness which are our sensations, through which, as through
a channel, comes much of the materials of our thought.   Thus
was formed the school of Sensationalism, represented by the
French encyclopædists, and, in his tendency, by Locke. Others,
again, concentrate attention on the inherent powers of the individual mind, upon which they make the external world to
depend, subordinating the objective to the subjective, and hence
the system of Idealism of Berkeley and Fichte. Those who bring
into prominence the idea of the Absolute, the Eternal, Pure
Being, merge the world of phenomena and the phases of our
own consciousness in the depths of Being *per se*, and subject and
object being thus absorbed, we have the Pantheism of Spinosa,
Schelling, and others.   Sensationalism, Idealism, and Pantheism
represent, therefore, the main currents of the philosophical tendencies which have moved mankind.

The Modern Sensationalism received its impetus from Bacon, in
whose system of analysis outward observation held the chief
place, the importance of abstract ideas being made to yield to
that of the study of external phenomena. In the inductive
philosophy experience was made the principal part. Not that
the Baconian spirit was so wedded to empirical research as to
leave no place for metaphysical analysis.   On the contrary, by
endeavouring to point out a *philosophia prima*, and by calling
upon its followers to seek out the *forms* of things, its influence
on speculative philosophy was not altogether to the disadvantage
of the latter.

The principle of experience was thus established as the leading principle of modern philosophy.   Hobbes developed it still
farther, so as to make sensation the real basis of every mental
operation, sole originator of ideas, and sole test of truth. Now,
through sensation we can perceive only matter ; hence, he concludes, matter is the only reality.   Hence scientific investigation
was reduced by him to the *doctrine of bodies*, that is, of their
existence and *changes*.   The doctrine of bodies includes " the
knowledge of all phenomena, in relation to their probable causes,
and of all possible causes as known from their observed effects."
In the heat of the controversies, excited by the philosophy of
Hobbes, John Locke became convinced that the disputants were
travelling by a wrong road ; that the first thing to be done was,
not to analyse things or doctrines to their simplest elements,

but to investigate the faculties of the mind, in order to see what objects lie within its reach, and what beyond it. Hence the famous *Essay on the Human Understanding*. We cannot here stay to show how this work leads to materialism. Enough for our present purpose to show to what use Locke's principles, without his materialism, have been put in the hands of a school of thinkers of our own day. This modern school attempts to show, by metaphysical analysis, "that every notion springs from the senses as the original channels through which the whole material of thought has been supplied." The leader of this school is Mr. James Mill, in his *Analysis of the Phenomena of the Human Mind*. Mr. John Stuart Mill, although he does not pledge himself to any metaphysical system, also belongs to this school.

In this sketch of the sensational school of philosophy there are some broad and deeply marked lines which it will be of importance to point out more carefully to the reader. From the fundamental idea, that the sensations are the basis of our knowledge, it was easy to pass, once the analytic method was established, to an exaggerated estimate of the value of outward observation of phenomena. This state of mind, acted on by Locke's doctrine concerning the proper limits of the intellectual faculties, ever tended more and more to confine scientific investigation to the bare existence of phenomena. All these features are to be recognised again in the Positive Philosophy, which we shall now proceed to set forth.

M. Comte begins by taking a comprehensive survey of the state of the intellectual world as represented in European civilisation. He finds human knowledge to be in an utterly disjointed state. Conflicting systems of philosophy divide the schools; contradictory religions are multiplied in the churches. What one philosophy or religion asserts is refuted by another. A twofold cause of this intellectual confusion presents itself to his thoughts. "The human mind may be searching for truth beyond the legitimate region of its actual knowledge; or it may not take a sufficiently comprehensive view of that truth which really does lie within its grasp." A true philosophy which would supply a remedy to so painful a disorder should, therefore, effect two things. First, it should define accurately the limits within which the mind may legitimately exercise itself in the search for truth; and, secondly, it should give unity to science, by pointing out a secure pathway by which the elevation of a universal philosophy may be reached. The Positive Philosophy undertakes this double task. It endeavours, in the first place, to discard for ever from among the objects of thought all that regards the essential nature of things, their causes, either efficient or final, all speculation as to their origin or destination. " We have no knowledge of anything but phenomena ; and our knowledge of phenomena is relative, not absolute. We know not the essence, nor the real mode of production, of any fact, but only its relations to other facts in the way of succession or of similitude. These relations are constant, that is, always the same in the same circumstances. The constant resemblances which link phenomena together, and the consequent sequences which unite them as antecedent and consequent, are termed their laws. The laws of phenomena are all we know respecting them. Their essential nature, and their ultimate causes, either efficient or final, are unknown and inscrutable to us."*

This golden rule has not been always grasped by the human mind. On the contrary, M. Comte assures us, as a matter of history, that two other methods of philosophising, antagonistic to his method and to each other, have successively swayed humanity, as well in the aggregate as in individuals. The law of progress thus embraces three distinct stages, called by him respectively the Theological, the Metaphysical, and the Positive. Mr. Mill believes that these terms, especially in the English language, are not quite suited to the purpose, as they excite ideas other than those intended. Hence, instead of the Theological he would prefer to speak of the Personal or Volitional explanation of nature ; instead of the Metaphysical, the Abstractional or Ontological ; instead of the Positive, the Phenomenal or Experiential.

In the Theological stage the mind regards the phenomena of the universe as operations of divinities. First, each object is looked upon as animated. Next, each entire class of objects or events is believed to be under the superintendence of an invisible being. Finally, the multitude of divinities is merged in a single God, who made the world, and guides it either by his continued action, or by specially interfering from time to time.

In the Metaphysical stage phenomena are accounted for by being ascribed not to volitions, but to realised abstractions. Instead of the Dryads presiding over trees, every plant is now supposed to have a vegetative soul. These various forces at last terminate in the universal idea of Nature, which, though regarded as impersonal, is supposed as acting in a sort of motion : as when we say, Nature abhors a *vacuum*.

In the Positive stage, finally, the palpable facts of the phenomena are alone attended to with the view of discovering the laws of their co-existence and succession. Every other question concerning them is ignored.

* J. S. Mill, *Auguste Comte and Positivism*, p. 6.

Every single science which can occupy the human mind must invariably pass through this triple stage, from the theological, through the metaphysical, into the positive. This last is destined, says Mr. Mill (p. 12), finally to prevail, by the universal recognition that all phenomena, without exception, are governed by invariable laws, with which no volitions, either natural or supernatural, interfere. But the different branches of knowledge do not pass from one of those stages to the other equally and at the same time. Some sciences are more advanced than others. Thus astronomy, physics, and chemistry have already arrived at the positive stage, whereas physiology, or biology, is only at the metaphysical; while the whole science of humanity (sociology) is yet in its earliest stage, being hampered with the false idea of a Providence and a God. M. Comte's division of the sciences deserves more praise than anything else he has achieved. The sciences are not independent one of the other, but are so arranged that each depends upon a preceding one less complex than itself, whose laws it takes up with an addition of its own, and then sends on to the science next in order. Thus, the truths of Number are true of all things, and depend only on their own laws; therefore the science of Number (arithmetic and algebra) may be stated without any reference to any other science. On this principle M. Comte has arranged the sciences in a series, each term of which is an advance beyond the term preceding it, the phenomena belonging to it being determined by a more numerous combination of laws: 1st, Mathematics (Number, Geometry, Mechanics); 2nd, Astronomy; 3rd, Physics; 4th, Chemistry; 5th, Biology; 6th, Sociology, or the Social Science, the phenomena of which depend on the truths of all the other sciences. Thus all the sciences are co-ordinated; thus the entire edifice rises by degrees to its last and noblest stage, the science of man. Thus the experimental study of facts, and facts only, is made the secure and solid pathway to universal philosophy.

Before we pass on to consider Positivism from the religious point of view (for to its religious bearings we intend to confine our remarks) it may be well to observe that Comte's system can make no honest claim to whatever credit belongs to the inductive philosophy. Bacon's "mission," says Dr. Newman,* was the increase of physical enjoyment and social comfort ; and most wonderfully, most awfully, has he fulfilled his conception and his design. Almost day by day have we fresh and fresh shoots and buds and blossoms, which are to ripen into fruit on that magical tree of knowledge which he planted, and to which none

* Discourses on University Education, Disc. iv., p. 192.

of us, perhaps, except the very poor, but owes, if not his present life, at least his daily food, his health, and general well-being. He was the divinely provided minister of temporal blessings, to all of us so great that, whatever I am forced to think of him as a man, I have not the heart, from mere gratitude, to speak of him severely. And, in spite of the tendencies of his philosophy, which are, as we see at this day, to depreciate or to trample on theology, he has himself, in his writings, gone out of his way, as if with a prophetic misgiving of those tendencies, to insist on it as the instrument of that beneficent Father who,* when He came on earth in visible form, took on Himself first and most prominently the office of assuaging the bodily wounds of human nature. Now, Positivism completely discards this providential mission of knowledge, and altogether refuses to admit into its circle the idea of God. Besides, the inductive philosophy admits *a priori* axioms, and speaks of a *Philosophia Prima;* Positivism rejects them: the former includes our inner consciousness among the subjects to which its principles may be applied; the latter limits its observation to outward facts. Bacon, after observation, seeks to discover the *natures* of things; Comte holds all investigation into the essences of things to be useless and impossible. Systems, which are kept apart by differences so deep-rooted and so large, can have little affinity one with the other.

Again, the law of intellectual progress laid down by M. Comte, as consisting of the triple stage, theological, metaphysical, and positive, fills an important place in his system. According to him, every branch of science must invariably pass through these stages in succession. What is to be said of this law?

We shall find, upon analysis, that this law, as expressed by M. Comte, includes two statements: first, that every science which can occupy the intellect, has invariably passed, or must necessarily pass, through the theological, metaphysical, and positive stages; second, that the metaphysical stage supplants the theological, and in turn is supplanted by the positive. Neither of these statements can be established by induction from the history of the sciences. Which of the sciences exhibits this triple stage of progress? M. Comte replies at once by naming astronomy. But, admitting for a moment that his theory is borne out by the history of astronomy, what other science has commenced with the theological stage? Dr. Whewell† shows

---

* " Atque illud insuper enixe rogamus ne humana divinis officiant; neve ex reservatione viarum sensus, et accensiono majoris luminis naturalis, aliquid incredulitatis et noctis, animis nostris erga divina mysteria oboriatur," etc. *Pref. Instaur. Magn.*

†*Macmillan's Magazine, Comte and Positivism,* March, 1866.

that Physics has not, and quotes Adam Smith's saying, that there was never a god of weight. Nor did chemistry begin with a theological stage, although it, too, had a theological or mythological period, but that period was *not* its first. In the ages of alchemy, the substances on which chemists operated were personified in a most remarkable and lively manner. "Gold was the *king* of metals," says Dr. Whewell (p. 354), "silver the *queen*. An object much aimed at was to obtain the *regulus*, the metallic young one of the more imperfect metals." So, also, astronomy arrived among the Greeks at a precision which conferred on its discoveries a value so lasting, that even to-day they form part of the science, and yet long afterwards the period of astrology came on. If the law were accurate, it must follow that the theological stage has long since been superseded in the case of very many of the sciences; for M. Comte himself admits that the crowning science of sociology is the most backward of all, for the very reason that it is still in the theological stage. Now, in this case, the early ages ought to be the only religious ages, or the most religious ages. This, however, is far from being the case. Leaving out of consideration a few so-called philosophers, who are not more numerous now than ever, the entire human race with one accord admits the existence of a Supreme Being, even although some nations outrage his majesty by giving to false gods the homage which the true and Living God alone can claim. M. Comte asserts, moreover, that even in individual minds this triple stage may be observed: in our childhood we refer everything to God; in our youth, to metaphysical abstractions; in our riper years we advance to Positivism. This may be true of M. Comte, who, as we have seen, shook off all religion almost with his boyhood; but is it true of those great minds who, while they were kings of science, were at the same time, according to their own views, the most religious of men? Of such men Newton may be taken as a type.

We admit, however, that in some of the natural sciences men attributed in the beginning to God functions which, after investigation, had been traced to natural causes. Thus, in early times men believed the heavenly bodies to be gods, or to be guided by gods. But at this stage science had not begun at all; it was but the preliminary to science.

Nor is it true to say that, as a science progresses, the metaphysical supplants the theological, to be in turn supplanted by the positive stage. What we have already observed of astronomy and chemistry is a proof of this. But Dr. Whewell does not hesitate to assert that there is no science in which this pretended succession of a metaphysical and a positive stage can be pointed out. "There is no science in which the discovery of laws of phenomena, when once begun, has been carried on independently of discussions concerning ideas, which must be called *metaphysical*, if anything be so called. There is no science in which the expression of the laws of phenomena can at this time dispense with ideas which have acquired their place in science in virtue of metaphysical considerations. There is no science in which the most active disquisitions concerning ideas did not come *after*, not *before*, the first discovery of the laws of phenomena. This may be exemplified in all sciences which have made any progress. Kepler's discoveries would never have been made but for his metaphysical notions. And again, those discoveries of the laws of phenomena did not lead immediately to Newton's theory, *because* a century of metaphysical discussion was requisite as a preparation" (p. 354).

The truth is that all three stages may and do co-exist in such proportions as are determined by the peculiar nature of each several science. The sphere of each becomes more accurately defined as the science progresses; but the most accurate positive knowledge of the laws of co-existence and sequence of phenomena can never clash with the natural tendency of the human mind to refer these phenomena to their causes, and to seek beyond all secondary causes a primary and first cause upon which all depends. It is wise to observe accurately and patiently what is passing in the world around us; it is wise to seek, as far as we can, the nature and causes of what we observe; but it is wisest to trace every finite contingent being to the First Cause, the God who created all things.

THE IRISH CARDINAL.

IN the Consistory of the 22nd June our Holy Father, Pope Pius the Ninth, conferred upon the Archbishop of Dublin the honour of the Cardinalate. In this event the Irish Church has a legitimate subject of great joy. The entire Catholic Church on earth, to use St. Augustine's words, is like a pilgrim whose pathway lies between the persecutions of the world and the consolations of heaven; but for the Catholic Church of Ireland, during several centuries, the persecutions have far outnumbered the consolations. To-day, however, we salute with gladness the beginning of a happier period ; and in the creation of an Irish Cardinal we recognise the sure pledge of its approach.

To form a correct estimate of the value of an honour conferred upon another, we should take into account the character of him who confers it, the measure of honour bestowed, and the order of merit of which it is the acknowledgment. Considered under each of these respects, the honour conferred upon the Irish Church, in the person of Cardinal Cullen, will be found so remarkable as to justify us in regarding it as one of the happiest events in the later history of our Church.

The creation of an Irish Cardinal is exclusively the work of Pius the Ninth himself. It is not necessary in this place to lay stress upon the sublime dignity of the Roman Pontiff, nor to speak of the power he exercises over the entire earth. When we have said that he is the Vicar of Christ, the Centre of Unity, the Head of the Church, we have said all we need to say. But it should not be forgotten that there is hardly one of the titles and offices of honour now in existence in Europe which does not derive, directly or indirectly, from the Roman Pontiff. He has been at all times for the civilised world the chief fountain of honour. How truly honoured then is he whom the Roman Pontiff delights to honour ! And how singularly honoured when, of all the long line of Roman Pontiffs, it is Pius the Ninth who delights to honour him ! Between Pius the Ninth and every form of baseness, and of meanness, and of wrong, there exists uncompromising hostility. Between Pius the Ninth and all that is noble and truthful, and loyal, and holy, there is closest sympathy. Of all living men, not one loves justice and hates iniquity with greater energy than Pius the Ninth. It is, then, a legitimate source of gratification to Irish Catholics that a Roman Pontiff, and that Pontiff Pius the Ninth, should bestow upon their mother Church so signal a mark of his esteem.

But it is even more than a mark of esteem. It is a solemn act of recognition on the Sovereign Pontiff's part of the loyal devotion ever exhibited by Ireland to that chair, which is the centre of unity in the Church. From the Synod of St. Patrick to the Synod of Thurles an intense, unswerving devotion to St. Peter's successor has been the distinguishing mark of the Irish Church. Not now for the first time has this devotion been recognised by the Holy See, but now for the first time with so splendid a requital.

The Cardinalate is the highest honour in the gift even of the Roman Pontiff, who is the most august ruler in the world. Its functions are the noblest that man can be called upon to discharge, namely, to take part with the Vicar of Christ in the government of the Universal Church. Its purple makes those who wear it the equals of kings. The flower of the human race, the men who were conspicuous above all others for singular gifts of sanctity and learning, are upon the roll of the Cardinals of the Holy Roman Church. And what in the present case enhances the honour is the character of the time in which it has been conferred. The war which the gates of hell incessantly wage against the Church was never more deadly than at present. It is no longer this or that part of the House of God, but the entire Christian revelation which is assailed. Persistent efforts are being made all over the world to uproot the very foundations of religion; in the intellectual order, by means of a philosophy which makes the Christian demonstration impossible; in the social order, by sharply separating secular from religious education, and refusing to admit the Church's rights in matters of teaching; and in an especial manner by destroying the temporal independence of the Roman Pontiff, who is the rock on which Christianity is built. From his watch-tower on the walls of the city of God Pius the Ninth beholds these assaults, and gathers around him a sacred band of the most devoted, the ablest, and most prudent among the prelates of the Church. If the Cardinalate be at all times and under every circumstances an honour beyond the honours of earth, how much more brilliant does it become when it is at once the place of honour and the post of responsibility and danger!

Of the personal merits of Cardinal Cullen we may not venture, for obvious reasons, to speak of at any length in these pages. That we owe, in a great measure, to those merits the honours conferred upon the Irish Church in his person is plain from the language of the allocution itself. We are at full liberty, however to speak of the merits he has now acquired in the eyes of his countrymen as the man who has restored Catholic Ireland to her place in the public opinion of the world, as one among the Catholic nations of the earth. For several centuries our history has been a uniform recital of incessant efforts towards contradictory solutions of the question: shall Ireland continue to exist as a Catholic nation? On the one hand, to destroy our Catholic nationality were arrayed a thousand forms of brute force, cruel laws, and state-craft, while to defend it we had but heroic faith and heroic patience. It was a modern rendering of the unequal battle of old, between the mighty who came with sword and shield and spear against those whose only weapon was the name of the Lord of Hosts. Those who have watched the conflict from close at hand have long since seen upon what side the victory has remained. In spite of all the power of her foes, Ireland has preserved her Catholic nationality distinct and entire. That she remains a Catholic nation is now admitted even by Protestant publicists, whose ingenuity is every day more and more tasked to invent philosophic theories by which to explain away the fact which they cannot deny. But the creation of an Irish Cardinal is a public acknowledgment in face of the world that Ireland has been victorious in her arduous struggle. It is the world's verdict that the weak has vanquished the strong, that every attempt to rob her of her faith has been a shameful failure, and that, as a Catholic nation, Ireland is worthy to have one of her sons seated as her representative in the Sacred College of Cardinals.

And, as if to make this testimony the more eloquent, it is not a little remarkable that the church which has been assigned to the new Cardinal as his title is the very spot, of all others, on which the past and present of Ireland may best be contrasted. The Church of San Pietro, in Montorio, is the last resting-place of Prince Hugh O'Neill, and of Eugene Mathews, Archbishop of Dublin. The cloisters of the adjoining convent were often trodden by the feet of Fr. Luke Wadding, who, before St. Isidore's was built, lived at San Pietro, and there commenced his great work. These three men are worthiest types of the three best glories of Catholic Ireland ; of the princely valour, of the priestly zeal, and of the sacred learning which have ever been the characteristics of her sons. During a struggle of three hundred years, valour, and zeal, and learning were lavishly expended in the glorious cause of Ireland's Catholic nationality, and for that crime prince, and bishop, and scholar were driven to find an exile's grave in a foreign land. But at length the just God, in whom they trusted when oppressed, has been mindful of his great mercy. From their very ashes He has caused to spring a throne upon which an Irish Cardinal—at once prince, bishop, and scholar—is the living proof that at length their cause is triumphant.

Nor does the glory of the Irish Church, thus triumphant to-day, pale before the glories of the Irish Church of past ages. If, in the days of persecution, her scattered children went weeping from their home, with their tears they cast the seed of the faith ; and now coming, they come with joy, carrying their sheaves of the new churches they have founded. In America, in Australia, in Africa, in Asia, in the missions watered by Irish sweat and Irish blood, the name of the Irish Cardinal will be honoured and blessed by millions of his race. Their interests shall be his care, their spiritual welfare his solicitude. And not least among the merits of Cardinal Cullen do we account it, that through him it has been given to the Irish exiles dispersed over the world to find close to the throne of the Sovereign Pontiff a powerful protector, whose prudence will guide them in their doubt, whose lips will plead for them in their distress, and whose heart will ever turn towards them in love, as a father ever turns in love towards his children.

THE LAST THIRTY YEARS IN THE ENGLISH CHURCH.*

THE history of the inner life of a soul which has been carried along by the Catholic movement till it has touched the very threshold of the Church, and which yet refuses either to enter the Church or to relapse into Protestantism, is a history which at the present time commands attention. Unfortunately it is the history of too many. When we consider how widespread has been the movement towards Catholicism, and how deeply in all ranks of life men's hearts have been stirred, it is plain that the handful, so to speak, which has been gathered into the Church is by no means an adequate result of the mighty influences that have been outpoured upon the land. What is the nature of the obstacle that has hindered so much good? What manner of reasoning is that which suspends so many souls between Anglicanism and the Catholic Church, so that they, while they depart from the one, refuse to enter the other?

Some answer to this question may be gathered from an autobiography of which we desire to give in this place some account to our readers. It is headed *The last thirty years in the English Church*, and is presented to the public as an essay in the form of a narrative.† Though it chronicles the experiences of a single individual only, this narrative is nevertheless the history of an entire, and that a numerous class: of those, namely, who ever seek a middle term between Protestantism and Catholicism. With some of those who joined the movement the Protestant influences were preponderant, and those fell away into

---

* Since this essay was written the Rev. Mr. Shipley has been received into the Catholic Church.

† *Essays on Questions of the Day.* By various writers. Edited by the Rev. Orby Shipley, M.A. London, 1866. Longmans.

rationalism. With others the Catholic influences were victorious, and those, again, were gathered into the Church. But the
great remaining body, yielding exclusively to the action of
neither, passed first from Evangelical Protestantism to Anglicanism as to a *via media* between the Reformation and Rome,
and, having been dislodged from Anglicanism, are now taking
refuge in Unionism as a second *via media* between Anglicanism
and Rome. Thus the history of the Catholic movement in England presents two distinct periods, each remarkable for a *via
media* of its own: the first, starting from Protestantism, and
stopping short of the Church in Anglicanism; the second, starting from Anglicanism, and stopping short of the Church in
Unionism. What the *Tracts* were for the first period, the
Eirenicon is in some measure for the second. In the first, the
Catholic Church in England was looked upon as a schism; in
the second, she is looked upon as a sister. It is of the thirty
years within which this startling change has been effected that
the writer of this autobiography treats. She is the daughter of
an English clergyman, and, in what she tells us of her early
training, we have a fair sketch of the Evangelical Protestantism
she was led to abandon. The attainment of respectability with
the due performance of the social duties of life, certain specified
devotional exercises and the subdual of sin in the soul, formed
the standard of Evangelical perfection in that day. The Evangelicals held by Episcopacy rather as a matter of good order
than as a divinely instituted authority; supernatural grace, as
tied to sacerdotal acts, they were inclined to repudiate. Among
the Evangelicals of this school our authoress was brought up.
The theology of the works put into her hands at home was unmitigatedly bad, and full of Nestorian heresy. She studied,
with more than usual attention, various works denouncing Roman
Catholic and Greek idolaters. And yet, strange to say, the first
great desire she felt was to receive the Sacrament. Urged by
this desire, she not only remained, of her own accord, for the
additional service at Church, but also at home used often to
practise acts of spiritual communion, though at that time she
had never heard of the practice. Once she attempted a kind of
examination of conscience, but soon gave up the attempt in despair, having been told it was an impossibility, "that there was
not a moment or an action of our lives that was not full of sin."
About the same time she first heard of the Oxford tracts, and
great was her wonder to hear the clergy who came to see her
father so earnest and at times so angry about them. Arthur
Willis, a pupil of her father's, and who is still a distinguished
leader of the movement, became infected with the new views.
" There was much low-voiced speaking and sad condemnation

21

going on, not, however, shared to any great degree by my father,
from which I could at first only gather that there was a terrible
Dr. Pusey, and a no less terrible Mr. Newman, putting forth
sadly wicked things, and that my father's dear pupil, Arthur
Willis, was departing from the teaching of his early days. Besides Willis, another member of the family plunged into a fierce
partisanship of the tracts, and this gave occasion to much childish
controversial zeal. "I well remember sitting on a clergyman's
knee and abusing the Pope in terms for which I ought to have
had my ears boxed, but which were thought rather amusing."
This bigoted prejudice ruled her soul until she was about the
age of thirteen. At that date three events occurred which led
to a great change in her opinions. First, she read the tracts,
and found that they were not so wicked as she had been led to
expect; secondly, she heard her first choral service at Westminster Abbey; and thirdly, she had a visit from some cousins
rather older than herself who were under the influence of the
movement. They had wonderful arguments on the subject in
their little way, and our authoress always got the worst of them.
She also began to learn that the superstition ascribed to Roman
Catholics and Puseyites was not invariably true. "It was some-
where about this time, too, that I first read with, and was startled
by, the expression, 'God died for man,' and I perceived that up
to that time I had never really believed in our Lord's divinity
at all." Confirmation, the Communion that followed, the use of
Wilberforce's *Eucharistica* as an altar manual, and, above all, the
third volume of Dr. Pusey's *Plain Sermons*, helped principally
to dislodge her unfounded early prejudices. "The last-named
work brought definitely before me the duty of self-denial in
things lawful, and of fasting and mortification. Then every day
increased the desire to have the advice of some priest. Confession had never entered my head; but to be helped and counselled
was becoming almost a necessity. . . . I held the English Church
to be the only uncorrupt branch of the Church, and supposed
myself bound to accept every word of her formularies." Acquaintance with Roman Catholics, the study of church architecture and restoration, interior trials, and the example of devout
friends, gave an importance to the notion of confession, which increased day by day. At last, after much struggling, she resolved,
in the autumn of 1849, to make a confession to Mr. Willis,
now a married clergyman, and accordingly she spoke to him
about it:

"He quite agreed that confession would do me a great deal of good, but
decidedly declined to hear me himself. Confessions, he thought, should not be
made to intimate friends; but, if I liked, he would write for me to a priest he
knew in London, and get him to undertake my case. I had not contemplated

this, but there was no drawing back ; and in a short space I had a letter from this gentleman, enclosing a book of directions for self-examination, which made me perceive that I had hastily concluded myself to be ready. I had not the most distant idea how a confession was made, and was too shy even to ask Mr. Willis much about it. I had a month for final preparation, and went to meet Mr. Goodwin, for the first time, in London, at the beginning of Advent. None of my relations had the least idea of my intentions except one, who raised some doubts in my mind about acting without the sanction of my parents. But they did not much weigh with me. I was then no longer a child ; we had always been allowed a considerable measure of independence ; and I felt, too, that the interests at stake were beyond any human interference, and that I alone could be accountable for my own soul. To have felt compelled to go to confession, in direct contravention of parental commands, was a conceivable possibility, but one to be avoided at all risks. I do not think I felt much apprehension then at the thought of the act itself beyond ordinary nervousness. I believed I knew what my own part of it would be, and what I should have to say. So I went to meet my confessor, at the appointed time, in his large, dreary, London church ; and, after a short conversation in the vestry, he took me into the building, and left me for a while, according to the custom then in existence there, kneeling at the altar rail, until he returned in his surplice, and, after a few prayers, took his place by my side. My confession occupied nearly six hours on two successive days, so long a time being necessary, in consequence of the imperfect preparation which, in my ignorance, I had supposed to be sufficient. Years have passed since then—days and weeks of severe suffering, mental and bodily, but never anything that can be compared to those hours, and the weeks that followed them, and I know that I never can pass through anything worse on the earth side of the grave. My own history was comparatively soon told, and freely ; but Mr. Goodwin was experienced enough to see that neither conscience nor memory had been fully roused. I think he was more severe than he would have been if he had not mistaken ignorance and nervous terror for obstinacy or evasion ; but, notwithstanding, I have never since met his equal as a confessor, or ceased to be grateful for all he did for me.

" It was a terrible but most necessary hour of self-revelation, and showed me the evil of my life, as the preparatory self-examination had, strangely enough, completely failed to show it me. We think that when the life is investigated, and memory taxed to its utmost, then the inner self stands completely revealed, and that the recital to another can add nothing to the knowledge of the past. Many persons think so, and that their sins confessed in secret to God are fully confessed. I believe it to be a most fatal mistake ; and that, brought up with a superficial knowledge of sin, as all Protestants are, the conscience of a person who has never been to confession, probably has never, and never will be, fully investigated. ' Fully,' after all, means but imperfectly, even when confession is over ; but yet I feel sure that the guilt of individual acts, and still more the relative proportion of sins to one another, and to the whole spiritual life, can be known in no other way. And this accounts for the mass of careless, unspiritual Anglicans who neglect confession, and who avoid great sins, but never seem to make real progress in holy living. I, at all events, found out the mischief of my life then, undeveloped as my views were at that time of the Sacrament of Penance. I looked upon the priest as a commissioned minister ; and I did not see that it was our Lord Himself to whom I was confessing, and who was speaking to me ; nor did I see, as I have seen since, that the confessor's words are not his own, but that he is under the control of One who regulates them in a way of which the priest himself is generally unconscious. I had gone to confession thinking myself rather a good sort of young person on the whole, though I had none of the ideas popularly attributed to Catholics, that my own doings were of the least value in the sight of God ; but only that He had mercifully preserved me from great sins, and that his holiness would be accepted instead of mine. I went home with very different ideas of myself ; wretched enough, but with a feeling of having been rescued from the brink of a precipice.

" The scene of the confession itself I could not venture to recall. It was months before I could let my thoughts return to it ; and even now I cannot dwell upon it without the shrinking with which, in after life, men recall a severe surgical operation, although they may also feel, as I feel, a deep thankfulness for its results."

From the manner in which, in this extract, "Anglicans" are contrasted with " Protestants," and distinguished from them as one form of religion is distinguished from another, the reader may learn how completely the writer was already changed from an Evangelical Protestant into an Anglican Catholic. The time was now at hand when she was to be brought face to face with events and arguments, the force of which was to overthrow the whole fabric of the Anglican theory.

The events of the year 1850 were necessarily a source of disquiet to such as were under the influence of the Catholic movement. The Gorham judgment brought numberless anxieties and difficulties to their minds. It was on this occasion that the possibility of leaving the English Church first came before the writer. In vain she sought to lean upon her trusted adviser, Mr. Goodwin ; every time she visited him she found him more and more hopeless. In May he informed her that he found no Church open to him but the Roman, although he intended to wait until everything should have been tried.   " His view of the case was, that the Church of England had given up to the State or Civil Power that jurisdiction over doctrine which was committed to the Church's own exclusive keeping by our Lord Himself, and so he felt that he must leave her."   But he would not sanction his penitent's attending any Catholic service, or taking any step until all hope should finally be over. But for this advice she declares that unquestionably she would have become a Roman Catholic then. In obedience to it, she declined an opportunity of conversing with Dr. Newman, and when she had actually set out from home to the nearest Roman Catholic chapel, intending to consult the priest, this very advice caused her to return. However, she had an interview with "a distinguished preacher and confessor in our own communion," to whom she made known her state, and what an awful step she felt leaving the Church to be. *He was at that time, although no one knew it, meditating secession himself*. She declined to comply with his wish, that she should write out a statement of her difficulties to be laid before Dr. Pusey, and circumstances prevented her from meeting him again.

Thus thrown on her own resources, she set herself to read and to think. She did not conceal her difficulties from her friends, nor what she thought would be the probable result. At length Mr. Willis came to the rescue, and urged upon her that "a Church, because it could not meet in synod, but which, if it did meet, would assuredly pronounce against heresy, could not be considered heretical." This did not reach her difficulties, which now turned upon the entire question of the Royal Supremacy in the Church, and its permitted spiritual usurpations. She began to read Roman Catholic books, and even then came to the conclusion which Dr. Pusey has expressed in his *Eirenicon*, that the truth of the Tridentine doctrine by no means proved the falsity of that of the English Church. Prayer to the saints soon followed, and she perceived that the veneration of the Blessed Virgin to a certain extent really exalted our Divine Lord, by showing the dignity attached to everything connected with the Incarnation, and that Protestants misunderstand it because they practically degrade Him to the level of a saint, and then, of course, are shocked at any human creature being compared with Him.

The question of the Royal Supremacy still occupied her attention. As investigation went on, it appeared to her that the spiritual supremacy of the crown was brought about by no intentional act of the English Church. "It was a claim made, indeed, or so I then understood, by the sovereign, but rejected by the Church, and only slowly and surreptitiously assumed as time went on, and ignorance prevailed, and convocation was silenced." Besides, even if what was alleged about the supremacy was true, she judged that it did not affect the English succession nor the vitality of the Church.

"These were terrible months, and every day brought its contrary expressions, and its almost conclusion in both directions. I could only pray earnestly for light; but for a long time every fresh leading seemed to point the same way. There was the fear always present with me that any resolution to stay contentedly in the English Church would be the result of the preponderance of earthly motives. They were all, even to religious predilection, on one side ; and I loved the Anglican service far more than I do now. I remember attending one of the best choral services then in London, and feeling most bitterly that I must lose all share in that beloved ritual if I seceded. The incumbent of the church, I believe, did his best to give me an opportunity of opening my mind to him, but I could not avail myself of it. I have often been sorry that he should have died without my ever being able to tell him how grateful I felt to him. The crisis came, I think, one night when, after a long vigil, I fell asleep, and had a vivid and enticing dream of all that might, if I chose, be mine. I remember half-waking to a very different reality, signing myself with the cross, and making an act of renunciation of it all, if God should call. The next day came the first gleam of light. By degrees the question resolved itself for me into a belief that 'the English Church is still a part of the Catholic Church, unless she sinned sufficiently at the Reformation to justify Rome in cutting her off; and there, for a time, I thought the subject of investigation lay. I never regarded the severance of the two communions as the act of the English Church herself. History was against this view ; but I thought there might be a foundation for the charges of Protestant heresy which were brought against her.

"There was a tone of argument current at that time which accused the

English Church of intentionally making her formularies ambiguous to admit heretics; but it seemed to me then, when I came to inquire, and does still seem, that the cordial acceptance of the former Liturgy, in which the language on the disputed points was decisive, is a proof that the Church meant her words to be understood in no Protestant sense. And so, I think, by degrees my doubts sank down into a fear, whether I was not disregarding the leadings of the Holy Spirit, by not following one whose advice had been so blessed to me, and whether I was not allowing earthly motives to weigh down and overbalance the pleadings of a higher call. About this time I received decisive orders from my father that I was to go to Mr. Goodwin no more. I wrote to him at once and told him so. He sent me an affectionate farewell, begging me to do nothing on impulse, and reminding me that the truth would bear any amount of investigation; but also not to resist the leadings of the Holy Spirit, and to set eternity before me in all my decisions. I parted from him with great sorrow; but I felt that it was no doing of my own, and that there could be no shadow of reason for disobedience to this parental command, as I was not cut off from confession itself. I never again heard from him, and missed him when I afterwards called. He entered the Roman Catholic Church some months afterwards, and died in that communion a few years ago. I think this separation virtually disposed of one difficulty, but still the other remained.

"Almost a necessary consequence of my at length deciding that I had no ground for quitting the Anglican communion was a marriage engagement. For a time it seemed as if it would be almost well to resign this, with mutual consent, as a test of sincerity. I consulted one whose advice Catholics in our days have always been accustomed to look upon with great reverence, and received a careful answer. He told me that, believing me right in remaining in the English communion, he could not advise as though it were doubtful. He thought 'it hardly possible that earthly motives could have changed my whole way of viewing the relations of the English and Roman Churches imperceptibly;' and he believed 'that I had been carried away for the time by the general disquiet, and by argument on one side, and that when this impression had subsided I should see things as before.' Looking back at this distance of time, I think he was right. To a Roman it would, of course, appear that I had a decided call into the true Church, and allowed myself to reject it for earthly reasons. Certainly every year of reading and reflection since, while it has removed many prejudices, and awakened more and more strongly my reverence for the Roman Church, and taught me the great beauty of her services, does not lead me for one moment to think the grounds upon which I then contemplated leaving the English communion otherwise than entirely mistaken. Had the Roman Church been the only true one, and had I then entered her fold, I must still have felt now that I came to a right decision from a falsified view of facts. Whether renunciation of the worldly advantages gained by my decision might not have been the higher course is another matter; and I do not suppose that in this world I shall ever resolve the question, in itself now a useless one. I know that the path I chose, which I trusted would have led to an active life of special devotion to God's work, has carried me into regions of suffering and desolation, perhaps lower, perhaps higher, than those to which I aspired. I was directed to pray for serious illness if what I had done in this matter was not in accordance with the will of God, and I have never been well since; but I would not part with one day's suffering now. It is not till we emerge from our entangled path on to the mountain-top that we can see wheter it is higher than the eminence we had intended to ascend. But that it has been *better* for me, whether higher or lower, I doubt nothing; and I know now that services offered as mine were offered, and accompanied with so much evil, could never have been accepted. But I knew nothing of this then; and the life to which I had always looked forward seemed about to be realised. A difficulty arose, happily only temporary, about the Sacrament of Penance, as administered by the priest who was to become my confessor. It is one of the many instances in which I felt that, if temptation had not been mercifully withdrawn, I should probably have been led to compromise my principles."

At this point ends the struggle between Anglicanism and Catholicism; she definitely made up her mind that she had no sound reason for quitting the Anglican communion, and that the grounds upon which she had for a moment contemplated leaving it were not otherwise than entirely mistaken. And yet she admits that day by day her reverence for Rome grew greater and greater, and that the authority of a divinely guided Church appeared to her absolutely necessary to save men from rationalism.

How came it to pass, then, that notwithstanding all this, she clung, and still clings to Anglicanism? The reason is, that the Anglicanism to which she is now attached is quite different from the Anglicanism to which she had been attached before the trials and doubts of 1850. She has found the *via media* between Anglicanism and Rome, and she has found it in Unionism :

"It will be said that I have recorded progressive phases of faith which can have but one termination, and that sooner or later I shall submit to the Roman Catholic Church. I think not. So far as I understand my own mental history, it becomes less and less likely, although for years I have continued to see more plainly, what Dr. Pusey has startled many by declaring, 'that there is nothing in the Council of Trent which could not be explained satisfactorily to us if it were explained *authoritatively.*' I believe, too, that rightly understood, they are, in the main, truer statements than our own. But with this comes also the deepening conviction that the claims of the Papal Supremacy have no foundation whatever, and that to confine the true Church of God within the limits of the Roman obedience alone is in reality an absurdity. . . . To my own mind secessions to Rome in this country could scarcely have received a more damaging blow than the publication of Dr. Newman's *Apologia*. Had I been wavering, I think the thoughtful reading of that book would have decided me to remain in the English Church. It showed me how completely he misconceived the very nature of the Catholic Church while he was among us ; and it showed almost startlingly the progress of the Catholic faith among us since his departure. It is his sectarian notion of an Anglican Church which I once, with most of my contemporaries, believed in ; and it is one which Unionists soon lose. We acknowledge no doctrines as binding but those of the Universal Church ; and if it can be distinctly proved that anything in the English formularies is contrary to them, we say, and without any doubt of our position, that the English formularies are wrong."

It is impossible to peruse this remarkable narrative without experiencing a lively feeling of sympathy with the writer. The details she communicates are told with a quiet simplicity which is attractive; her remarks not unfrequently exhibit proof of considerable ability; and throughout the entire history there breathes an air of devotion, especially towards our Lord in the Blessed Sacrament, which cannot fail to be very affecting. We cannot say, however, that the essay has thrown any new light upon the theology of the questions at issue between Anglicans and Catholics. The reasoning by which the writer quieted the very serious doubts that harassed her mind, owing to the events of 1850, is to us simply incomprehensible. We have quoted in full her own account of it, that our readers may see upon what slender grounds many resist the call given them by God and their conscience to enter the true Church. An overwhelming array of substantial arguments had presented themselves to her mind to urge her to become a Catholic. As far as doctrine was concerned, she was ready to accept the teaching of the Council of Trent as, in the main, truer than the teaching of the Anglican Church. She admits that "the plain sense of the Bible tells much more for the peculiarities of the Roman Catholic faith than against them." She once wrote "that there are abuses, but nothing that can be called error, in the Church of Rome. As to Rome cutting us off, she had provocation enough to do so." She saw the holiest and best among Anglican clergymen—her own spiritual directors, whose advice had been blessed to her— so much shaken by the same doubts that oppressed her own soul that they left the Anglican communion at the cost of dreadful sacrifices. She was filled with an ardent longing for the Blessed Sacrament, which longing could not be gratified in the English Church, where she deplored a suspension of the daily sacrifice that was "to her almost the most serious departure from duty of which a church and priesthood can be capable." Then came the whole question of the royal supremacy in the Church : the question of the validity of Anglican orders, which Rome has always refused to acknowledge, and without which the Sacrament of Penance and the Eucharistic Sacrifice must cease to exist. And, as against all these reasons for becoming a Catholic what had she to oppose ? A belief "that the English Church is still part of the Catholic Church, unless she sinned sufficiently at the Reformation to justify Rome in cutting her off." This belief involved two statements : first, that the severance between the Churches was not the act of England, but of Rome ; and, secondly, that the English Church did not at the Reformation fall into heresy. She admits she saw that history was against the first statement. As to the second, the acceptance of the former liturgy by the English Church was proof enough for her that the English Church meant her formularies to be understood in no Protestant sense. It is to us surprising in the extreme how a keen-witted and conscientious woman could build, upon this unsteady reasoning, a resolution upon the character of which she knew her peace and salvation mainly to depend.

But although it neither suggests nor disposes of any solid

arguments affecting the controversy with Anglicans, the narrative affords matter for some observations which may not be without interest.

It will, perhaps, have come upon many like a surprise to learn that Nestorianism has so largely infected the Anglican Establishment. Our writer tells that the books put into her hands in her early youth were unmitigatedly bad in their theology, and full of Nestorian heresy. Besides, she says that " Protestants practically degrade our Lord to the level of a saint ;" and again, that they " do not hesitate to ask our Lord to pray for them," which is pure Nestorianism.

This capital error is at the root of the universal prejudice entertained by Protestants against the worship and invocation of our Blessed Lady and of the saints : since in their minds our Lord stands on the level of a saint, " of course they are shocked at any human creature being compared with Him." In another place we are told that Protestants are taught from their earliest years to speak to no one beyond this world except to God the Father and our Blessed Lord, with a few rare addresses to God the Holy Ghost. They grow up with a notion, most difficult to eradicate, that speaking to any other invisible being is an act of worship; they have an idea that to speak, for instance, to St. Paul, and ask his prayers, is an act of worship ; and, with the same lamentable confusion of idea in another direction, they do not hesitate to ask our Blessed Lord to pray for them. It is very important, in dealing with Protestants, to remember this temper of their minds. The more we reflect upon it the more clearly do we understand the wisdom of the course which Dr. Newman has taken in labouring to impress upon Anglicans that the Roman Catholic Church " allows no saint, not even the Blessed Virgin herself, to come between the soul and its Creator." It serves also to explain why Protestants feel it so difficult to take in the infinite difference between the intercession of Christ and the intercession we ask from the saints.

Considerable light is also thrown by the writer upon the character and prospects of the union movement in England. From what we learn of that movement in these pages, the sovereign wisdom of the Holy See, in forbidding Catholics to take any share in it, is abundantly justified. First of all, the union movement aims at preventing individual conversions by holding out hopes of corporate union. " Secession," writes our authoress, " proves itself a failure in individual cases, and can only be justified by a conviction that there exist no sacraments or priesthood in the English Church. And so we labour on, drawing nearer to union with Rome, but receding further from absorption into her existence as the only reality." The Catholic, therefore, who

favours the movement lends his sanction to the delusion that
the English Church is in possession of a priesthood and of the
sacraments which depend upon a priesthood.   He also favours a
movement the avowed working of which is to make men recede
further from submission to the Church of Rome as the only one
true Church, for this is the only possible union.   This co-operation on the part of Catholics, no matter how they may intend it
to be understood, is practically understood by unionists to be an
admission on the part of Catholics of the existence of Anglicanism
as a church.   " Nothing at first could have appeared more hopeless [than the union movement], for Roman Catholics considered
it a necessary part of their faith to deny our existence as a
church, and therefore would not admit even the possibility of a
reunion with a nonentity."   Of the baneful effects of the union
movement we have a signal example in the life we have just
described.   And yet the writer declares that she is but *one of*
thousands who underwent, and are still undergoing, the same
change, with slightly differing external circumstances, but with
the same inner features.   Thus thousands are kept away from
the Church through the false peace which unionism brings :
thousands who are ready to accept the doctrines of the Council
of Trent, who frequent confession, who would fain live in the
presence of the Blessed Sacrament, who crowd to the sacrifice of
the Mass, who venerate and invoke Mary and the saints, who
detest the Protestant name, and glory in calling themselves
Catholics.   Between them and the Catholic Church there is now
only a single barrier, but it is one which the union movement
will not allow to be removed—that barrier is the doctrine of
the supremacy of the see of St. Peter.   " The claims of the
Papal supremacy have no foundation whatever ; and to confine
the true Church of God within the limits of the Roman obedience
alone is in reality an absurdity.   It can only co-exist, it seems
to me, with ignorance of other nations and their churches."
Would that the amiable writer were satisfied to abide by the
decision which other nations and other churches in every age
have really given to the question which asks, by what sign is
the only true Catholic Church to be known ?   There has been
but one test of Catholicity known at any time in the Church,
and that test was communion with the See of St. Peter at Rome.
St. Cyprian, on behalf of the African Church, speaks of communion with Pope Cornelius as equivalent to communion with
the Catholic Church.   St. Ambrose gives the rule in use at
Milan, when he tells us that when men wished to learn if a
bishop were a Catholic, they asked if he were in communion
with the Roman see.   In the name of the nations and churches
of the East, the oriental bishops promised to Pope Hormisdas

that for the future "no mention should be made during the sacred mysteries of the names of those who were separated from the communion of the Catholic Church, that is to say, of those not agreeing with the Apostolic See;" and even the Arians learned to speak of the Catholics as Romans: "the men of our religion," says St. Gregory of Tours, "they commonly style Romans." How far was St. Augustine from thinking it an absurdity to confine the faith of the true Catholic Church of God to the limits of the Roman obedience, when he declared the Arian heresy to be manifestly anti-Catholic, for this reason, because it would not hold the faith of Rome.*

THE FIRST BISHOP OF NEWFOUNDLAND.

To Ireland may be safely applied what St. Gregory Nazianzen said of the Constantinople of the fourth century, that nations from the east and from the west look to her as to the common centre and emporium of their faith. From her both eastern and western churches have borrowed, and daily borrow, the seeds of Catholic doctrine, and, by doing so, themselves become churches. Ireland is the link that connects them with the churches founded by the apostles, and by supplying proof that they are the offspring of these churches enables them to make good their claim to apostolicity.† Among the new churches of the western world not one, perhaps, owes so much to Ireland as the church of Newfoundland, not one reflects more credit upon its parent church,

---

* " Cognosceris jam quæ sis, omnibus palam facta et qualis sis. *Non crederis veram fidem tenere Catholicæ, quæ fidem doces non esse servandam Romanam*."—Ap. Mai. Nov. Bib. PP. t. 1., p. 273, Serm. cxx. n. 13.

† "Apostoli . . . in orbem profecti eamdem doctrinam ejusdem fidei nationibus promulgaverunt et proinde ecclesias apud unamquamque civitatem condiderunt, a quibus traducem fidei et semina doctrinæ ceteræ exinde ecclesiæ mutuatæ sunt et quotidie mutuantur ut ecclesiæ fiant; ac per hoc et ipsæ apostolicæ deputantur ut soboles apostolicarum ecclesiarum."—Tertullian, *De Præscript.*, c. xx.

and not one acknowledges its obligations with more generous affection. "History," writes the present eloquent Bishop of St. John's, "as well as faith, teaches us that man can do nothing of himself, that human power, energy, talents, or wealth are of no avail unless God wills that a thing should come to pass. 'Unless the Lord buildeth the house, in vain do they labour,' the Psalmist says, 'who build it?' The history of the Catholic Church in Newfoundland most strikingly shows this. Twice under the most favourable auspices was the Catholic Church planted in this island : twice it failed to take root. Sir George Calvert, in Ferryland, intended this country, and particularly in this province of Avalon, to be a city of refuge to his co-religionists. What the Puritans did in New England, he intended, though with more enlightened and Christian sentiments, to accomplish in Newfoundland. The Catholic glories of ancient Verulam were to be renewed here, and the ancient British faith of Avalon and Glastonbury was to flourish with renewed vigour. All ended in disappointment, and the English branch of the Catholic Church never took root. The most powerful monarch of Europe, Louis XIV., justly called Louis the Grand, established, as he thought, Catholicity firmly in Placentia, founded a convent of Franciscans, the apostles of the New World, and laid, as he imagined, the foundations of our faith broad and deep. Again a failure—the lily of France never throve on the soil, and, with the departure of the last French governor, the Catholic faith died away. The very churches were transferred to the professors of another creed. Well, the Irish labourers came out to earn a subsistence by braving the dangers of the ocean; they were not of the class of men who generally succeeded in establishing a church. Their faith, bitterly persecuted in their own country, was strictly prohibited in Newfoundland —the house where Mass was said was burned down by orders of the Government—they had not wealth, nor education, nor any of those human gifts which would give them influence in the land ; still the hidden seed germinated, liberty of conscience was granted, they were grudgingly allowed to raise an humble wooden chapel here and there—the successor of St. Peter looks to this impoverished portion of his flock, and gives them a pastor in the person of Dr. O'Donnell—the weakly plant, trampled on, cut down whenever it showed itself, now begins to throw out vigorous shoots, and we see at present, thank God, that it flourishes like a tree planted by the running water. This is the work of God (mind, of God alone), and it is wonderful in our eyes. Calvert failed. Louis failed; but the poor persecuted Irish fisherman succeeded, and the proud monument of his or

his children's faith—the cathedral—crowns the culminating point of the capital of the island."*
We are not now concerned with the attempts made by Sir George Calvert and by the French to establish the Catholic Church in Newfoundland. We propose to supply from original documents a more detailed account of the labours of Dr. O'Donnell and the early Irish missionaries by whom he was assisted.
As late as 1784 religious toleration was unknown upon the island. On the 24th of October that year a proclamation was published whereby liberty of conscience was allowed to all persons in Newfoundland, and the free exercise of such modes of religious worship as are not prohibited by law. It was in this year that Dr. O'Donnell, the founder and father of the Church in Newfoundland, landed in the island. "Born in 1737," says Dr. Mullock, "in Tipperary, he spent a large portion of his life in the Irish Franciscan Convent of Prague, in Bohemia, afterwards as superior of the Franciscans in Waterford, and subsequently provincial of that Order in Ireland. He was the first regular authorised missioner in Newfoundland after it became a purely British settlement."
The first letter we find from him is dated from St. John's, November 10, 1787, and is addressed to Dr. Troy, then recently promoted to the archiepiscopal see of Dublin. It is not the first which passed between the correspondents, but it is the earliest that has been preserved:

" St. John's, November 10, 1787.

" I have been honoured with your letter, and am happy in joining all ranks of people in congratulating you on your promotion; this agreeable piece of news, together with its truly pleasing circumstances, has been communicated to me by Dr. Caulfield, who honours me with his correspondence.
"'I want two clergymen more, one to the southward, and another to northward of this place, who, by their contiguity to the small harbours, will be able to enforce obedience to lawful authority. I send for Father John Phelan of Waterford, and a Father M'Cormac of St. Isidore's, who, I am informed, is a man of morals and powerful abilities; he wrote to me and offered himself for this mission. He has made three public acts in the *Sapientia Romana ;* in default of him, a Father Yore, who likewise offered himself, of your Grace's diocese, if a man who can be recommended for irreproachable conduct and ability, will be to me very acceptable. Wishing you many happy returns of the season, I've the honour to remain, with unfeigned esteem and profound gratitude, your Grace's devoted humble servant,

" BROTHER JAMES O'DONEL."

---

* *Two Lectures on Newfoundland*, by the Right Rev. Dr. Mullock. New York, 1860.

From a letter dated November 16, 1788, we extract a passage which illustrates the position of Catholics at that time. A letter of accusation against Father O'Donnell was presented to the Surrogate:

"This letter was not only read in the courthouse, where the Surrogate publicly denounced Pope, Popery, priests, and priestcraft, and in an ecstasy blessed his happy constitution that was cleanly purged from such knavery, but also carried about this town by him and his officers, to the great satisfaction of those who envied our large congregation, stately chapel, and the esteem I have been heretofore held in by the governor. This Surrogate, by name Pellu, of French extraction, closed his surrogation to the admiral with the modest request that the priests should be turned out of the country; that circular letters should be sent to all the magistrates, if any more priests arrived, to ship them off immediately; and that no priests should be left but where there was a garrison to keep them in awe. When I heard this I waited on the secretary, who told me that the admiral had made up his mind, and adopted the measures of his favourite, Captain Pellu. I leave your Grace to judge with what depression of spirits and anguish of mind I returned from the garrison; however, I drew up my defence in writing, waited on the governor, who most politely received me, entirely changed his opinion, and assured me that he came to this country with a great regard and esteem for me, as his friend, Admiral Campbell, so often spoke respectfully of my name to him, and that from what he could personally observe in my conduct, that he quitted the island with the same good opinion of me.

"I am truly a son of persecution and child of affliction since I came to this country. However, I could not suffer in a better cause, nor be more sincere in any protestation, than in assuring your Grace that I remain with profound regard and respectful esteem your Grace's most obliged, devoted, and humble servant,

"BROTHER JAMES O'DONEL."

Dr. Mullock remarks, "that were it not for the certainty that religion was permanently fixed in the island, the Irish settlers, who formed the bulk of the population of St. John's and the south of the island, would not have remained here. We have rather an interesting proof of this in a letter written by Governor Milbank to Dr. O'Donnell, before his consecration as bishop, in answer to an application made by him to His Excellency for leave to build a chapel in one of the out-ports. Here is the document, and written, mark you, six years after the proclamation of freedom of religious worship: 'The Governor acquaints Mr. O'Donnell that, so far from being disposed to allow of an increase of places of religious worship for the Roman Catholics of the island, he very seriously intends, next year, to lay those established already under particular restrictions. Mr. O'Donnell must be aware that it is not the interest of Great Britain to encourage people to winter in Newfoundland, and he cannot be ignorant that many of the lower order who could now stay, would, if it were not for the convenience with which they obtain absolution here, go home for it at least once in two or three years; and the governor has been misinformed if Mr. O'Donnell,

instead of advising their return to Ireland, does not rather en-
courage them to winter in this country. On board the Salisbury,
St. John's, Nov. 2, 1790.'"
Father O'Donnell writes on the subject as follows:—

"*December* 6, 1790.
" MY LORD.
" I have been honoured with your esteemed letters both for myself and
Father Ewer, and have likewise received the Cardinal's letter. Our very
numerous and increasing congregations have brought the watchful eye of the
enemies of our profession upon us, as you'll find by the enclosed answer to a
very proper memorial, drawn up and signed by the Catholics of Ferryland, for
leave to build a chapel in that district. You see, my lord, how precarious our
situation is ; but the great God is all sufficient to blow off this impending storm.
However, as human means are not to be neglected, I wrote to Father Callenan
in Cork, and requested he'd use his influence on Mr. O'Leary to apply to some
member of the Privy Council to prevent those prejudicial restrictions. Here is
a wide field for him to display his powerful abilities in favour of religion.
Criminals of all kinds are allowed the unreserved privilege of a clergyman in
the gloomy recesses of the deepest dungeons, and why not an industrious, laborious set of men, who are inured to the hardships of the sea, and ready upon
any emergency to serve his majesty ? The toleration hitherto granted is rather
an encouragement to them to emigrate than a discouragement, as the governor's
monitor supposes, for many of those hardy fellows would never obtain their
parents' consent to cross the seas, if they had not the consoling prospect of the
presence of a clergyman in case of death or sickness. Moreover, the ingredients
that make up the sacrament, the Sacrament of Penance and the pre-requisites
for *absolution*, are not of such easy digestion to a set of fishermen as to induce
them to *go home for it at least once* in two or three years. I really look upon
those intended restrictions as a breach of public faith. It seems they have a
mind to adopt what they often heretofore upbraided us with, *nulla fides ser-
vanda est cum Catholicis*. Admiral Campbell sent a circular letter to all the
justices of the peace in this island, in those very words : ' You are to allow all
people inhabiting this island a free exercise of all such modes of religious worship as are not prohibited by law, pursuant to the king's instruction to me,' &c.
The enclosed is the diction of C. P., of whom I spoke so much in my Latin
letter last year, who, by the many changes and promotions of the navy, has
been unexpectedly appointed the admiral's captain this year, and has great influence over him. I had not the least opportunity of reasoning with the governor, as I only received the enclosed about an hour before he sailed. 'Tis true
he can act as he likes in this place, as he is king, priest, and prophet of the
island. The reason of this prerogative is that the country is not supposed by
law to be inhabited except in summer. In case of war, I believe none of us can
subsist, as the servants upon whom alone we depend will be all pressed and
obliged to become either sailors or soldiers. This is far a more miserable year
with the wretched inhabitants of this island than the last."

"*December* 8, 1791.
" The Governor most faithfully adhered to his promise of representing the
Catholic clergy of this island as encouragers of the people's remaining during
the winter in this country, contrary to the interest and intention of Government ; but in this even he has not succeeded according to his mistaken zeal, as
Providence guided the steps of a Mr. Reeves to this country, who has been
appointed Judge Advocate for the island. This truly good and benevolent man
would not suffer me even to expostulate with the Governor on his foul misrepre-
sentation, as he assured me the state of the Catholic Church should remain un-
molested here, and so it happened. Thus the great God has in his own good

time dispersed all those heavy clouds that threatened our ruin from every quarter, and caused the sun of peace to shine upon us once more. Now, as most of the penal laws in England have been repealed, and the free exercise of our holy religion has been left uncramped by three admirals, it is to be supposed we shall never more be molested by governors; from this favourable prospect I wish to have another missionary. Be pleased, therefore, to send me one of my own Order for the districts of St. Mary and Trepassy; it is absolutely necessary he should speak Irish, and it is indifferent to me what province he is of."

" St. John's, December 8, 1792.

" My Lord,

"I've been honoured with your esteemed letter of 22nd of April, together with the enclosed faculties from Rome, and can't but gratefully return you thanks for your condescension in stooping to execute such commissions as I generally trouble you with. We have had the public papers here up to the 26th of September, which teem with most horrid accounts of the savage barbarity and inhuman cruelty of the Jacobin Club in Paris. I hope, for the honour of the human race in general, they are exaggerated; however, though the Almighty has permitted them to despatch, I hope to a better life, thousands of the most loyal, virtuous, and resolute of the laity, and crowds of the flower of their clergy, He has likewise made the Duke of Brunswick his executioner to scourge and punish them in their turn. I left that great general in our last accounts near Chalons, and I hope you have found him long since in yours in the heart of Paris, severely chastising the guilty, and clemently pardoning the innocent. I am exceedingly concerned to hear of the rapid progress of infidelity in your parts, especially as it always springs from corruption and immorality. The unhappy French have been sunk into the lowest lees of deism those many years past, and you well know that no man ever became a deist because he had a better wit than others, but because he had a more corrupt will, nor because he reasoned better, but because he lived worse. Our present Governor and the Judge Advocate have made very solemn professions of friendship to me : the former returned me public thanks at his own table for the unremitting pains I have taken those eight years in keeping the people amenable to the law; and, on being told he overrated my slender endeavours, he said he was too well informed to think so. You may judge he had not this information from his predecessor. Mr. Cross, of Bridge-street in your city, with whom I correspond, has sent me all the pamphlets that had been printed in Dublin relative to the claim of the Catholics on Government for their right of franchise. I am sorry they disagreed so much among themselves, but am happy to find that you have been so judiciously fortunate as to please both parties.

" We are now at perfect ease, and restored to the same degree of respect that we enjoyed for the three first years of our residence here. May the Almighty preserve your Grace in good health and spirits for many years for his own glory, the good of his holy religion, and salvation of his people. These are the sentiments wherewith I've the honour to remain, your Grace's most devoted, humble, and obliged servant,

" BROTHER JAMES O'DONEL.

" December 27, 1793.

" My Lord,

"I've been honoured with your Grace's kind message and acceptable pamphlet through the hands of Mr. Bolan. I was the more anxious to see this pastoral letter, as I found some ungenerous and very undeserved strictures thrown out against it in the public papers. It was in those times of infidelity, when Catholics scarcely retain anything belonging to their profession but the bare name, a most seasonable production, orthodox, bold, masterly, and replete with erudition, and, without flattery to the author, I think it proves him a man of undaunted zeal and very extensive reading. May God continue him life and health to rise up on all such occasions in defence of God's cause. Time-serving writers stretched their condescending reasons to the very boundaries of the Catholic faith, and the laity, finding themselves standing on such narrow premises, would soon step over them if not timely apprised of their danger by men of weight and authority in the Church. Our affairs in this mission wear a most pleasing aspect. The Governor continues his friendship to me with great warmth. I was the only landsman who dined with him on the eve of his departure aboard his elegant ship, where I had the pleasure to hear him declare, in the presence of five captains of frigates, that the Catholics were the best subjects his majesty had. I am sorry we have no longer lease than one year more of him.

" We have had 300 French prisoners here during the summer. Their officers were at liberty, and, I must own, I did not like to see them coming every Sunday to my chapel with large emblems of infidelity and rebellion plastered on their hats. It was much more pleasing to see three companies of our volunteers, headed by their Protestant officers, with fifes and drums, coming to the chapel to be instructed in the duties of religion and loyalty."

Dr. O'Donnell's appointment as bishop is thus alluded to by Dr. Mullock : " Dr. O'Donnell was at first only prefect apostolic, that is, a priest exercising episcopal jurisdiction, and generally having, like the prefect apostolic of St. Peter's, the right of giving confirmation, which, as we see by the practice of the Greek Catholic Church, is not essentially an episcopal sacrament, if I may call it so. The importance of the population now required episcopal superintendence. The Sovereign Pontiff, to whom is committed the care of all churches, saw that Newfoundland was destined to become the home of a fixed population, not the summer residence of a floating one. Accordingly, in 1796, on the 5th of January, the great Pontiff, Pius the Sixth, the confessor as well as doctor of the faith, appointed Dr. O'Donnell Vicar Apostolic of Newfoundland, and Bishop of Thyatira *in partibus*, and he was consecrated in Quebec on the 21st of September the same year. Thus was the foundation of the Catholic Church solidly laid, and, we hope, for ever."

The following admirable petition to the Holy Father refers to this subject :—

BEATISSIME PATER,

Cum inter multa, eaque praeclara facinora, quae felicissimum Sanctitatis Vestrae Pontificatum illustrant, atque exornant, illud haud minimum sit, quod fideles orthodoxos Americae septentrionalis incolas, paucis ab hinc annis, mirum in modum consolatus sit, fidemque simul Catholicam amplius dilataverit, valdeque consolidaverit per providam institutionem primi illius regionis Episcopi Reverendissimi nimirum D. Joannis Carroll, Episcopi Baltimorensis ; Nos infrascripti tali exempli, tantaque benignitate animati, nomine nostro, omniumque Catholici nominis incolarum Insulae *Terrae Novae* nuncupatae, provoluti ad pedes Sanctitatis Vestrae humillime deprecamur quatenus clementer dignetur in Episcopum instituere, cum titulo in partibus, et in Vicarium Apostolicum, praeclarum et dignissimum Praefectum Missionis nostrae, R. P. Jacobum Ludovicum O'Donel ordinis Fratrum Minorum de Observantia. Hoc siquidem facto illud proculdubio consequetur, ut, et maximum ipsi religioni emolumentum, ingens nobis solatium, atque perenne Sanctitati Vestrae decus sit accessurum. Super-

22

vacaneum porro fore arbitramur, Sanctitati Vestræ recensere quam utile nobis foret, in tanta locorum distantia, Pastorem apud nos habere Episcopali·Charactere insignitum, qui munia Episcopalia pro fidelium consolatione possit obire. Sicut et consulto omittimus elogium meritorum præclarissimi Viri a nobis commendati; quippe cum ejus eximiæ, et singulares Virtutes compertissime jampridem evaserint S. Congregationi de Propaganda Fide. Quare de summa clementia, ac pastorali sollicitudine Sanctitatis Vestræ confisi, in osculo pedum beatorum prosternimur, Apostolicam benedictionem implorantes.

Datum ex Insula Terræ Novæ, Die vigesimo Novembris, A.D. 1794.

Fr. Edmundus Bourke, Ord. Prædicatorum Missionarius Districtus Placentiæ.

Fr. Thos. Ewer, Ord. Min. Strictioris Observantiæ Missionarius Districtus Ferryland.

Fr. Patritius Phelan, Ord. Min. Strictioris Observantiæ Missionariu Districtus de Harbourgrace.

Gulielmus Coman, Generosus Incola S. Joannis.

Dav. Duggin, Generosus Incola S. Joannis.

Henricus Shea, Generosus Incola S. Joannis.

Lucas Maddock, Generosus Incola S. Joannis.

Joannes Wall, Generosus Incola S. Joannis.

Timotheus Ryan, Generosus Incola S. Joannis.

Joannes Bulger, Generosus Incola S. Joannis.

Michael Mara, Generosus Incola S. Joannis.

Jacobus Power, Generosus Incola S. Joannis.

Martinus Delany, Generosus Incola S. Joannis.

Patricius Power, Generosus Incola S. Joannis.

Gulielmus Mullowney, Generosus Incola Districtus de Harbourgrace.

Joannes Quarry, Generosus Incola Districtus de Harbourgrace.

Demetrius Hartery, Generosus Incola Districtus de Harbourgrace.

Jacobus Shortall, Generosus Incola Districtus de Ferryland.

Joannes Coady, Generosus Incola Districtus de Ferryland.

Joannes Power, Generosus Incola pro se aliisque Districtus de Magna Placentia.

Joannes Kearney, Generosus Incola pro se aliisque Districtus de Parva Placentia.

Dr. O'Donnell writes as follows on 25th November, 1794:—

"*St. John's, November* 25, 1794.

" MY LORD,

"I've been honoured with your much esteemed letters of the 18th of March and 19th of July. The former reached me only the 27th of last October, as the vessel in which that and Mr. Cross's bundle were packed up had been captured by the French, but was recaptured in a few days by an English frigate. This was a very fortunate circumstance, as the sacred oils would be probably abused by those infidels, who would make no scruple of using them with their soups or salad. Though they plundered the vessel of many valuable articles, they left the books, beads, and sacred oils untouched, as such articles are now in no demand among them.

"I was never more astonished than at your friendly interference in promoting me to a dignity which I neither deserved, desired, nor ever expected, and for which I know myself to be entirely unfit. This *nolo episcopari* is not, upon my word, in the least feigned ; for, among many other disqualifications and inconveniences, it would subject me to voyages I am hardly able to undertake. I went to Ferryland, only fourteen leagues from this place, last June, was blown off to sea for three days and three nights; during the nights we could not distinguish the froth of the sea, which ran mountains high, from the broken ice with which we were entirely surrounded. I am now in the fifty-sixth year of my age, and consequently will not be long able to bear the great hardships and fatigues of this mission. It would suit me much better to spend the short remainder of my life in retirement than to undertake a burthen to be dreaded by a more learned head and more sanctified shoulders than mine. However, as your Grace has carried the matter so far, I will not mulishly oppose your most zealous and friendly intentions. To this I am urged very pressingly by all my fellow-labourers in this vineyard. I will, then, follow your friendly directions, and for ever retain a grateful memory of the honour you have done me by stooping, in the midst of your great hurry of business and anxiety of mind, to write me so friendly, warm, and affectionate a letter, which I deem a greater favour and honour than any dignified rank you could place me in.

" I am much obliged to you for the pastoral instructions, of which I can now spare one for each of the clergymen of this island, as I had two before.

" I am glad to find the Bishop of Cloyne reaching the hand of fellowship to the Catholic clergy—*tempora mutantur*—and more rejoiced to find him pay you the high compliment of describing you as the ablest divine among the Irish bishops. The London clergyman has done himself honour, and your cause a vast deal of justice, by clearly refuting the Inquirer's malicious strictures : his weapons must be better edged with logic, reason, and information before he can prove your pastoral instructions inconsistent with your declaration in the Catholic committee, or lessen the great esteem and veneration wherein you are held by all the members of the Catholic Church who either read your instructions or are acquainted with your zeal and abilities.

"Should Mr. Concannon succeed in your and his friendly undertaking, as there is no safety in crossing the western ocean in those times, Baltimore would be a more eligible place for my errand than Quebec. However, if there may be a war with America, my journey thither would be impracticable. I shall be much obliged to you for instructions how to act, or whether I should write to Rome upon that occasion.

" I am afraid this letter will not reach your kingdom, as all our first fleet bound for the foreign markets had been taken near the Western Islands. This destructive war has ruined this part of the New World.

" May the great God continue and prolong your life and health for his own honour and glory and the good of his holy Church. This shall be the fervent prayer of your Grace's

" Most obliged, grateful, and devoted humble servant,
" Br. JAMES O'DONEL."

The following letter from Rev. Mr. Ewer, or Yore, brother of the late respected Vicar-General of Dublin, will be read with interest :—

" *September* 20, 1796.
" MOST REV. DOCTOR,

" The happy fruit of your labour in the establishment and support of our mission, the blessings daily arising from your continued protection, and the warmest attachment to so great a patron, must render this occasion of addressing you invaluable to me. In the absence of our most reverend superior, who has honoured me with his care, I feel it my duty to communicate the general satisfaction on his late promotion, and acquaint you with the happy change in the sentiments of a people who, not long since, burned the houses where Mass was said or priests were sheltered.

" On the Rev. Mr. O'Donel's departure for Quebec, the colonel, then our chief commander, and officers, military and navy, presented him with most polite and flattering addresses, expressive of their best wishes to his person and cause.

" I am equally happy to inform you of the progress of religion, particularly in my own district. I have completed an elegant chapel, with a convenient dwelling, at Ferryland, all at my own expense, except ten pounds, which the poor people of that harbour subscribed last year. The many fruitless attempts of Methodist Preachers have been successfully baffled, and there is now but one of that sect in the districts of Ferryland and Trepassey, and even his family became Catholic this year. The Protestants, likewise, lose ground, and their minister was obliged to decamp, notwithstanding his seventy pounds a year from the society. Their feelings at such an event are easily conceived ; but as he was a generous, well-bred man, we always lived in friendship and parted in peace. The place is exceeding poor from a failure in the fishery, containing near 2,500 people, unequally divided in ten different harbours in the space of about seventy miles. The necessary labours attending that district begin to bear heavy on me, and I was attacked last year with violent rheumatisms, but now, thanks to God, am perfectly restored.

" We valued ourselves on being in so peaceable a part of the world, until some days ago the general calamity of a destructive war reached us. The 8th instant nine French men-of-war hove in sight—one eighty gun ship, six seventy-fours, and two frigates. The 10th they bore down on the harbour to attack. The wind not answering them to enter, and discovering our strong and well-manned fortifications, they thought proper to sheer off, and steered for Bay-bulls, seven leagues distant. There they harboured, and in two days consumed it to ashes, burning and sinking all the vessels and boats they could meet ; but, fortunately, on heaving up their anchors, when bound to sea, the flagship cast the wrong way, was near wrecking another of equal force and going ashore, which, we suppose, has deterred them from entering any other harbour. These ten days past they hovered off our coast, apparently going to enter every place as they passed and repassed. The stores and houses were all emptied. Ships and vessels of all kind were loaded and sent off, and the poor inhabitants fled to the woods. We were informed last Sunday that the fleet was seen fifteen leagues to the westward of the island. It consists of fifteen sail. Nine appeared here, eleven in other parts of the island, and three on the banks. They are commanded by Admiral Richery, have no troops aboard, and manned mostly with young boys, without shoes or stockings. They carried away with them every person they could catch, except one man whom they let go. A vessel which arrived here last Sunday left Quebec the 5th instant. Mr. O'Donel was not then arrived. They sailed from this six weeks before. He went north to avoid the enemy. It's generally a long passage, and those who are used to it are not apprehensive of danger. We wait with anxiety to hear from him, and hope God will restore him to us and his people. This port is just now opened, and I return in the morning to my own distressed flock, whose afflictions I feel severely. They were very good to me in my absence, and secured everything that belonged to me.

" Most Rev Doctor,

" I am, with the greatest esteem,

" Your most devoted, most humble

" And obedient servant,

" BR. THOMAS EWER."

A Copy of the Address of the Protestant Inhabitants and Merchants of St. John's to the Rev. Mr. O'Donel.

" REV. SIR,

" As we understand that you shortly intend to make a voyage to the Continent of America, permit us to take this opportunity of assuring you of our good and sincere wishes for your safety and happy return, and how sensible we are of the many obligations we lie under for your very steady and indefatigable perseverance in attending to and regulating with such address the morals of much the greater part of this community, the salutary effects of which have been sufficiently obvious. We are no strangers to the many difficulties with which you have, from time to time, been obliged to encounter, even at the risk of your life, in regularly visiting the different outposts within your reach, and in performing with cheerfulness and alacrity those functions from whence have arisen so many advantages to the inhabitants of this island.

"That you may long be able to fulfil with your wonted zeal and attention the many duties of the honourable office you now hold is the unfeigned wish of,

"Rev. sir,

"Your most obedient servants."

We have not been able to find any letters from Dr. O'Donnell later than the date of his consecration. His labours as bishop are thus described by Dr. Mullock: "In the meantime Dr. O'Donnell was labouring in his arduous mission; he had obtained leave from the local government to take a piece of land at a lease of ninety-nine years, and begun the old chapel, which was very small at first. He made several visitations to the outports of the island, encouraging, as far as he could, education; we believe he was guilty of the charge made against him by Governor Milbank, of encouraging the Irish to winter in the country, and we feel no doubt but that he gave them absolution when they applied for it, and even more frequently than every second or third year, as accused by the worthy governor. During Dr. O'Donnell's episcopacy the population was almost all Irish, English, or Scotch. The Catholic district of St. John's, for it could not be called a parish, comprised the south shore of Conception Bay, and the south shore as far as La Manche toward Ferryland, and still the marriages were, on an average, only about seventeen or eighteen a year among the Catholic population; now the average of the same district gives about two hundred and sixty marriages. Both Protestants and Catholics complained at that time of the spread of infidel opinions in this country. Paine's *Age of Reason*, denying all revelation, was very extensively read, trade was most flourishing, money abundant, and vice of all kinds prevalent. Protestant ministers in the principal towns, St. John's, Harbour Grace, Trinity, and Ferryland, took charge of their own people; priests were stationed wherever there was adequate support for them, when the bishop could procure their services. The Protestant clergy combated infidelity principally by means of the publications of the Tract Society, but the Catholic always trusts more to the living word than to the dead letter. The mission was a laborious and rude one, and, accordingly, Dr. O'Donnell, in the seventieth year of his age, resigned his charge to younger hands, in the person of Dr. Lambert, and sought repose in his native land, where he died four years afterwards, and was buried in the old parish chapel of Clonmel; he had fought the good fight in days of darkness, of danger, and of difficulty, and we hope he received the crown of justice."

In a letter written June 9th, 1807, by Dr. Lambert to Archbishop Troy, we find mention made of Dr. O'Donnell's departure from the island:

" St. John's, Newfoundland, June 9th, 1807.

"MOST REVEREND AND MOST HONOURED LORD,

"I was honoured with your Grace's much esteemed favour of the 28th of March last, about the middle of May, together with the holy oils, for which kindness and condescension deign to accept my best and most grateful acknowledgments. As your Grace is of opinion that I need not scruple to consecrate them with one priest, when no other can be had, I shall in future be no more troublesome to any other prelate for them. Indeed that was my own opinion before, but I allowed myself to be overruled by Dr. O'Donel, who thought otherwise. I have since that received some from Dr. Ryan, and this day more from Dr. Plessis, Bishop of Quebec, so that at present there is no scarcity of oils in Newfoundland. Dr. Plessis complains much of the labour of his diocese, which, he says, it would take him six entire years to visit. He has lately consecrated a coadjutor, who resides now at Montreal, and has petitioned Rome lately for another who (he intends) should reside on the coast of the Gulf of St. Lawrence. He presses me very seriously to accept of another part of it, that is, New Brunswick and Nova Scotia. But, I assure your Grace, I think I have too much sailing round the coasts of Newfoundland without going across to the Continent. However, before I give him a definite answer, I would be. glad to have your Grace's opinion of the business.

"At the time your Grace's letter arrived here I was in Conception Bay, visiting Father Ewer's district, which I had the happiness of finding in as good order as could possibly be expected in so large a range of coast. I cruised about twenty-one leagues of the coast of it, and confirmed almost four hundred children.

"Doctor O'Donel intends going home with a convoy that is expected to sail about the middle of next month. Bristol or Bath he intends making the place of his future residence.

"The pamphlet your Grace was so good as to send me *vid* Halifax has not as yet arrived, neither has the letter.

"I fear I have trespassed on your Grace's patience, and shall therefore conclude, with profound respect and veneration, your Grace's most devoted and most humble servant,

"BR. PATRICK LAMBERT.

"P. S.—The name of the diocese *in partibus* is called in my Bull *Ecclesiœ Chytrensis*, situated in the island of Cyprus, and suffragan to the archdiocese of *Salamina*."

" St. John's, Newfoundland, October 15th, 1810.

"MOST DEAR AND MOST HONOURED LORD,

"About three weeks ago I had the pleasure of receiving your Grace's kind letter of October 1st, conveying the melancholy news of the death of my ever esteemed friend, the Right Rev. Dr. Concannon. May God give him the rewards of those who love and serve Him. His life was innocence and purity itself, and I firmly hope he now sees God in his glory. I had some expectations of seeing him on this side of the grave. Dr. Cheverns, Bishop of Boston, had exhorted from me a promise to pay him a visit there next spring, and it was chiefly from a hope of seeing Dr. Concannon I did promise. But God has disposed otherwise; his blessed will be done. I am sorry, indeed, that the situation of our common father is such as to deprive the Church of his superintending vigilance and care. Worthless and insignificant as I am, I had hopes he would have provided a person more fit than myself for the toils of this truly laborious mission. An All-Ruling Providence regulates matters differently from my short-sighted views, and will, I hope, give me submission and resignation. If I can regulate and arrange matters here to my satisfaction, I intend to take a trip across the Atlantic next summer to try if 1 can prevail on some of those young missionaries that your Grace tells me are now on their way home, to come out with me here to this *land of milk and honey* to enjoy the sweets of it.

"My health is but middling, though at present, thank God, something better than usual. Last September I got a fall off a tree that lay across the path, as I was returning from the district of Ferryland, where I had been for the purpose of confirmation, by which I broke some of my ribs; they are now, I hope, healed, at least are not very troublesome.

" Sir John T. Duckworth, our governor, showed me much civility and politeness during his stay here. I dined three or four times with him, and he did me the honour of dining once at my table, and seemed happy and pleased.

" I congratulate your Grace on the accession of your coadjutor; though not personally acquainted with him, I have long known his character, which was everything good. I request your Grace will condescend to present him my humble respects and felicitations.

" I am happy to find that Dr. Plessis has at length received your Grace's letters. He is a most worthy and zealous prelate, and warmly attached to the Irish prelacy. He prays me to forward to your Grace the enclosed packet. In imitation of him, I have issued nearly similar orders with regard to his Holiness. The vessel that is to convey this is ready to sail. I must, therefore, conclude. Wishing your Grace many happy returns of the approaching solemnities, I remain, with profound respect, your Grace's most devoted and most obedient humble servant,

" PATRICK LAMBERT."

From these letters we can gather that the Church which he had founded with so much toil was now firmly established and self-sustaining. But even with this signal success before their eyes few could have anticipated the bright future in store for the Church of Newfoundland. Its trials under Dr. O'Donnell were great indeed, but yet not so great as the splendid triumph which the piety and ability of the present bishop, Dr. Mullock, have achieved for it in our own day.

THE WEAKNESS OF ENGLISH PROTESTANTISM.

AMONG the many questions of the day which continually engage
the attention of thoughtful men, none are more important, more
complex, or more delicate than those upon which the Church
and the world come in contact.   Any conscientious effort towards
the solution of such questions deserves the careful consideration
of all who have at heart the true interests of mankind.   Of
course there is and can be no other solution than the Catholic
one.   One and the same God is the author of society and the
founder of the Church, and as He helps the weakness of nature
by the aid of grace, so He has placed in the Catholic Church
full relief for the wants of civil society.   The experience of the
last three hundred years has proved, beyond a doubt, that Protestantism has completely failed, not only as a religion, but as a
moral power able to influence men.   In waging war against
Catholic principles and institutions, it has shattered the channels
through which the Church was wont to pour its health-bestow-
ing waters over the world; it has retarded the advance of true
civilisation, and has developed an unhealthy growth of perverse
systems, under the baneful shadow of which modern society
languishes and is sick at heart.

It is only by a return to Catholic principles that the evils
which afflict our modern period can be effectually remedied.
Restricting our view to that phase of Protestantism which prevails in these countries, and with the sight of which it is our
painful lot to be daily afflicted, it is not difficult to perceive that
the absolute necessity of such return is becoming every day more
and more felt by the more candid Protestants themselves.   The
existence of this feeling is the most eloquent justification of
Catholicity which can be desired.   When a man retraces his
steps to gather with a respectful hand what before he had contemptuously trampled in the mire; when he raises to the place
of honour what before he had insultingly degraded; when he
turns for advice and aid to the physician he had just cast out of
doors, his second action is more than a simple retractation of his
first; it is more than an apology; it is an unimpeachable testimony to the real excellence of what he had formerly contemned.
Hence, the testimony of Protestants to the failure of Protestantism, their expressions of regret for what they lost when they
lost Catholicity, their earnest turning once more towards Catholic institutions, are among the best tributes to the glory of our

Holy Mother the Church. They are especially valuable in this country, where the insolence of Protestant ascendency makes itself felt in so many different quarters and in so many different ways. Among those Protestants whom the accident of conquest has placed in the upper ranks of a Catholic people, Protestantism is the light of the world and the salt of the earth, Catholicism a name for all that is degraded and pernicious in society. What will they say, however, when they find the best and most earnest members of the Anglican Church declare that it is only by drawing nearer to the despised principles of Catholicism that the Establishment can hope to escape condemnation?

Such a declaration, accompanied by substantial proof of what it advances, is contained in a collection of essays lately published by some clergymen of the Anglican Church. The testimony of these gentlemen is above suspicion, their words have all the authority which a long and intimate acquaintance with the subject of their remarks and their own personal integrity must be acknowledged to confer.

One of the essays has for its title *The Missionary Aspect of Ritualism*. In this essay the Rev. Richard F. Littledale incidentally shows how powerless to move the masses the Church of England has become. The true idea of an effective Church, in his opinion, is that it should not merely be fully capable of adaptation to the habits of all climates and nations, but that in each nation it should meet the wants of all classes of society and all types of mind. This ideal, he admits, will not always be fully realised; but in proportion as approximation is made to it, will the vital power of the Church be. "Tested by any such standard, three of the great sections within the English Church utterly fail, and are branded as class-religions with no faculty for general absorption."

The three sections just referred to are the great Evangelical school, the school more appropriately than courteously called High and Dry, and the Broad Church, the peculiar characteristics of each of which are too well known to need any mention here. The first, according to our essayist, has never approved itself, hardly speaking to the highest or lowest strata of society. The former it has alienated by its deficiency of culture; the latter by merely subjective character; so that, even if it did not exhibit patent marks of irrevocable decay, it could at best rank only as a creed for the lower middle class. Therefore, it can have no message for two-thirds of those with whom it professes to deal.

The second class, though adorned by many learned, amiable, and devout persons, has never been a real spiritual power in the country. It failed to reach the class on which the Evangelicals

seized; any influence it may have had with the poor is due
solely to the weight of pressure exerted by the squirearchy (its
main strength) in rural districts; in towns it had not even this
to show.

The third section is the least missionary of all. The Broad
Churchman has not reached, nor tried to reach, the poor. More
familiar with the library than with the parish, doing all with
reference to intellect at the price of neglecting the imagination
and the affections, " he might, perhaps, succeed in establishing
a sect of cultivated Christian philosophers, a porch or an academy
of the learned; but he must break down when trying to deal
with those terrible forms of moral and physical evil with which
society is beset. The bland tolerance of our new academy, the
graceful stoicism of our modern peripatetics, however well they
may sit on a courteous gentleman in the repose of his study, or
in genial intercourse with those of his own rank and cultivation,
are but poor help by the dying-bed of a cancer patient, by the
side of a betrayed and deserted woman tempted to despair and
suicide, by the remorseless agonies of a sinner in his first thoughts
of repentance, by the cloudy perplexities of one who begins to
think that the universe is without God " (p. 32).

"All the sections of the English Church, save one," continues
our candid essayist, "have stood their trial, and failed. The
High and Dry, from the beginning of George the Third's reign,
the Evangelicals from the French Revolution, the Latitudinarians in their first period, from William the Third to George the
Second inclusively, and in their second stage from the accession
of George the Fourth to the present day, have severally tried to
include all classes within their ranks, and have in no wise succeeded " (p. 35).

The only hope, then, which Anglicans can have of being an
effective Church is bound up with the Tractarian party. And
wherefore? Because of all others in the Church of England
the Tractarians alone have recognised the principle that the
worship of God should be accompanied by religious ceremonies.
That is to say, every shade of opinion and every combination of
party in the Reformed Church of England has been fairly tested
as a working religion, and has failed, precisely because it was
Protestant, and in the very points in which Protestantism is
opposed to Catholicism; whereas its only success has been where,
departing from Protestant, it has returned to the Catholic principles it had rejected, and in proportion to its approximation to
the Catholic Church has been its success.

Wherever Ritualism has been given a fair trial the result is
that the proportion of men present in church is exceptionally
large, and that all ranks are represented in the congregations.

The reasoning by which the essayist accounts for and justifies this success is worthy of being mentioned here, and will serve as a defence of the Catholic principles regarding the employment of sacred ceremonies in public worship :—

"One of the great practical strides made in the education of the humbler classes of late years has been the introduction of what are called object lessons, wherein, instead of reading and committing to memory by rote on account, for example, of the qualities of caoutchouc, a piece of India-rubber is shown to the class, and subjected to various tests, by which its elastic, inflammable, detergent, and other powers are easily explained and made part of the domain of the understanding, instead of being a mere dead weight in the memory : and such lessons are amongst the most popular in every national school.

"Ritualism is the object lesson of religion; and how popular it is can be said only by those who have seen its working amongst a poor population in towns. It affords a common ground where high and low can meet, for there are certain cravings for the beautiful common to both which are certainly not gratified by the ordinary Sunday routine. . . .

"It may be argued that good and vigorous preaching will fill the cravings of the imagination, and make the employment of material stimuli superfluous, if not mischievous. But good preaching is amongst the rarest of good things, rarer even than good acting, because it requires a wider range of physical and mental gifts. . . .

"And here again a lesson may be learnt from one of the least pleasant forms of ordinary life. There is no institution so widely and universally popular amongst the London poor as the gin palace. Given the craving for drink, and it would seem that an additional inducement would be needful to lure customers across the threshold, and to retain them as long as possible on the premises. Yet it is not so. . . . Internal decoration, abundant polished metal and vivid colour, with plenty of bright light, is found to pay, and to induce people to stay on drinking, just because everything is so pretty and cheerful to the eye, and so unlike the squalid discomfort of their own sordid homes. Many landlords have found even all this insufficient without the additional attraction of music. . . . If, then, painting, light, and music are found necessary adjuncts in a trade which has already enlisted on its side one of the strongest of human passions, it is the merest besotted folly to reject their assistance when endeavouring to persuade men to accept and voluntarily seek an article for which they have never learnt to care, even if they are not actively hostile to it—to wit, Religion " (p. 39).

Of the Protestant Church in Ireland he says it need not be insisted on how completely it has broken down in dealing with the Roman Catholic population :

"It is enough to say that, even if the reports of the proselytising societies were as true as they are unscrupulously mendacious, the results would be a very poor return for three centuries of monopoly." ·

Of the Protestant missions he tells :

"It is needless to dwell on the pitiful history of respectable Anglican missions to the heathen, or on the more boastful but not more useful efforts of the sects. The names of India and New Zealand are enough to exhaust the one subject ; and that of Jamaica will suffice for the other. In every case a purely subjective religion, fatally weighted with the most anti-missionary and anti-Christian of dogmas—the Lutheran doctrine of Justification—has been offered to men who needed to be taught by externals to rise gradually into the conception of spiritual life; and with rejection of these externals came too often practical disbelief in the verities they are meant to typify " (p. 49).

So much concerning the Anglican Church as a body. Let us now see what the essayists have to say touching the condition of each of the two great classes that compose that body, namely, the clergy and the laity.

Speaking of the clergy, the bishops naturally come first. What is the account given of the Protestant bishops of these countries by the very men who look up to them as their spiritual heads?

In the essay *On the Revival of Religious Confraternities*, the Rev. S. Baring Gould, M.A., after alluding to the earnest desire felt by the more Catholic portion of the clergy to work more and better than at present for the salvation of the souls which are daily perishing around them, asks the question : " What will the bishops do when the long pent-up desire bursts into actual work ?" The answer follows close upon the question :

"The episcopal boot is so accustomed to descend on every spark of vitality in the stubble of the Establishment, that perhaps it will follow precedent, . . . and stamp out all this zeal for God and the Church" (p. 106).

And again :

" There is danger looming in the Church horizon likely to precipitate the formation of Religious Confraternities. We mean the threatened attempt to interfere with the liberties of the English Church on the part of the Government, to compromise its orthodoxy by privy council decisions, and to curtail its ritual, thereby striking a blow at its doctrine. What line will be pursued by the prelates of the English Church is uncertain; but their policy has of late been one of oppression to the Catholic party, and we can hardly calculate on their support to any great extent. Courage in the cause of God and the Church is at present not the distinguishing characteristic of her dignitaries; and it may be questioned whether, when a bill is introduced for the altering of the vestments of the priesthood, the episcopal mitre should not be abolished also, as antiquated, to make way for the more appropriate symbol of the white feather. If there is to be a struggle between the Church and the State, we can hardly expect to find champions on the side of God's household in those who owe their position and the enjoyment of their emoluments to the State " (p. 107).

And again :

" The Anglican prelates have so diligently accumulated straws to break the camel's back, that the poor beast will kick over the load, and decline to submit his back to other burden than that laid on him by Providence, his own hump.   The Catholic clergy,* whilst readily acknowledging the essential necessity of an Episcopacy for the perpetuation of the ministry and the confirmation of the baptised, if much further exasperated, will perhaps deny the

---

* The Tractarians.

divine right of the bishops to hinder work for Christ and the salvation of souls " (p. 108).

In days long since passed the English Church gave to the world and to heaven men like St. Thomas of Canterbury, William of Wykeham, and Fisher of Rochester, who died or toiled for the liberty and instruction of the ministers of Christ's Church. To-day it can only show "white-feathered" cowards, recreant defenders of religion, "hinderers of work for Christ and for the salvation of souls," slaves who permit the civil power to compromise the orthodoxy of the Church. What potent poison has worked this awful change ? The Protestant substitution of the supremacy of the sovereign in lieu of that of the Holy See. It is perfectly true that we can hardly expect to find champions on the side of God's household in those who owe their position and emoluments to the State ; and it is equally true that we owe this state of affairs to the principles of the Reformation.

After the bishops follow the inferior clergy. We find scattered over these essays much important information concerning the education, the method of life, and pastoral efficiency of the ministers of the Anglican Church.

And, first of all, the supply of clergy is falling off as the demand increases. Government offices having been thrown open, the number of candidates for holy orders from the universities has sensibly decreased. The vacuum has been partially filled with men from the Theological Colleges. But, generally speaking, the education which is there imparted is by no means satisfactory :

"We are acquainted with several excellent young men of the middle class who have been under prolonged training for the ministry, by a course of French, English, history, geography, and the use of the globes, chemistry, the classic languages, drilling and fencing, the evidences of Christianity, linear and perspective drawing, the Thirty-nine Articles, and Butler's Analogy ; yet there is hardly an individual among them who could be trusted to preach on any one of the articles of the Apostles' Creed without the certainty of his stumbling into heresy through sheer ignorance. If men of all classes are to be taught theology, it must be ground into them, as you grind A B C into a child. But the practice of our universities and theological colleges seems to have been to educate the candidates for the ministry in every ' ology' under the sun, except the one ' ology' which is required more especially of them, and that theology. Ninety-nine chances to a hundred if the men search it out for themselves : they are more likely to indulge their hearers with the thin gruel of their own excogitations than retail to them the solid and sound meal of apostolic and patristic doctrine " (p. 97).

A clergy thus educated must needs be unfit for the duties of the ecclesiastical state. The poor man's heart closes up against such a church parson " in his gloomy suit of black and spotless white cravat, dashing past in a pony chaise with his daughters to the squire's croquet party." Thousands and tens of thousands remain whom the instruction delivered in the parish church never reaches. Great masses of scarcely educated, half-civilised men and women teem in all the large towns, without a God in this world. For this afflicting state of affairs also our essayist has a remedy to propose. His remedy he believes to be the only one which can reach the depths of the spiritual misery of the population, which is in the hands of Anglicanism, and it is the revival of religious confraternities. Blessed be God! at the very moment when the infidel party all over Catholic Europe has raised a heavy hand to chase from their convents and monasteries the humble friars and religious, a cry is raised from the heart of Protestant England, calling out for the despised institutions as the only hope of her neglected populations. At a season when the so-called liberal press rings with ribald abuse of these persecuted men, when they are reviled as the type of idleness and ignorance, when they are cursed as a vile remnant of the superstition of past ages, and regarded as a blot to be wiped out from modern civilisation, a Protestant clergyman is found in busy, wealthy, constitutional, modern England, to praise them as the benefactors of their kind. We make no apology for inserting the following passage, describing the action of the Church in the Middle Ages :—

"Then, as now, there was a dearth of educated clergy; and how did the Church meet the difficulty? She founded religious orders. She gathered together under one roof men of all ranks and grades, and trained them in self-denial, in self-control, in the art of winning souls, in the art of preaching. Having educated them, she sent them forth through the length and breadth of the land to occupy the pulpits of the parish churches, or to stand up on the wayside hedge, or on the steps of the market-cross, and appeal to those who would not come to the house of God to hear. Was there a savour of heresy in the wind? North and south, east and west, flew these bare-footed, serge-frocked champions of orthodoxy, and, in rude language, with argument telling home and forcible, they taught the people the right, and prepared them to combat the wrong.

"All these men, remember, were first trained themselves, first grounded themselves in doctrine, first primed themselves with arguments, and educated in the art of extempore speaking, and then were sent abroad to retail to tens of thousands what they had learned themselves in the seclusion of the cloister. Specimens of the sermons of these men abound. The press of the fifteenth, six-teenth, and seventeenth centuries teemed with their productions, and it is impossible to deny the extraordinary power they possessed. Every quality requisite to the formation of a popular preacher to the lower classes was found in them. They were full of unction ; they excelled in descriptive power ; their arguments were telling, if not always logically conclusive ; their illustrations were pointed, and their style full of fire, . . . and the people heard them gladly.

"Everywhere did the preaching friar attract a crowd. He was a man who knew what hunger was, and what it was to be pinched with cold. The poor man was aware of this, and recognised a brother. If you sound a note on a one-stringed instrument, the corresponding string vibrates on another. So is it with the human heart, and especially with the notes of suffering. God Incarnate, by becoming a Man of Sorrows and acquainted with grief, vibrated a chord in the great human heart which will quiver through eternity. As with the Master, so with the follower. The key to the success of Christianity is in the pangs of its Founder; the preacher of the Gospel now, if he is to reach the broken-hearted and the poor and the oppressed, must have been consecrated by the hand of suffering laid on himself. The poor man's heart responds to the heart of him who has suffered poverty; and therefore of old he loved the friar" (p. 104).

One of the broad features that distinguish the Protestant clergy from the Catholic, and one which, in Ireland at least, is frequently insisted on, is that the former eschews celibacy and inclines to the estate of matrimony. This fact of their marriage necessarily colours the entire life of that clergy. In an essay on *Clerical Celibacy*, the Rev. James Edward Vaux gives us some information as to how a married clergy attends to the things that are of its calling. We say nothing of that portion of their life which precedes their marriage, nor of "the flirting and fortune-hunting clergymen," nor of the circumstance that "a clerical lover is, generally speaking, more graciously received both by parents and daughters than a lay one." We leave it to our reader's judgment to decide how far all this fits young men for the serious duties of their state. We prefer to come at once to the influence their married life exerts upon their ministrations. We who remember the charge delivered to his clergy in the cholera time by the late Protestant Archbishop of Dublin have little reason to be surprised at the "by no means unknown instances in which married priests have avoided infected houses and fever-stricken patients through fear of conveying disease to the little ones at the parsonage" (p. 171). Nor are we surprised to hear that "the temptation to give up that time to wife and children which would otherwise be devoted to such works as night schools, confirmation, communion, and Bible classes, to say nothing of theological reading, is not a small one. As a practical illustration of this, I may mention that, whilst writing this portion of my essay, I had a visit from a most hard-working country incumbent, who gave it as one of his chief reasons for discontinuing the Sunday evening service in his parish church, that it occupied the time and exhausted the energies which he thought right to devote to the religious instruction of his family at home" (p. 171). Now, if a most hard-working man has been led to neglect his parish for his family, what must the case be when the incumbent is negligent or worldly? But even this would not be quite so intolerable if, at least, the family which was the object of such preference were largely benefited by the instructions of which they rob the poor. But is it the normal condition of clergymen's families to be well regulated? "Is not the reverse," asks Rev. Mr. Vaux, "notoriously the case? Without venturing to criticise the daughters at the manse, I may fairly say a word or two about the sons. Let anyone pick out the half-dozen most ill-conducted boys in the public school that he was at, or a similar number of the fastest men, in rather a low direction, that he was acquainted with at the university, and the chances are that a large proportion belonged to those families which are supposed to exercise so much beneficial influence in their respective parishes by their personal example" (p. 172).

If a married clergy, by the fact of their marriage, fail in the spiritual charge of their parishes, and even of their own families, what must be the amount of the failure when they attempt the labours of the foreign missions? When a youthful Catholic resolves to devote himself to the glorious work of the propagation of the faith he deems it an indispensable preparation to spend many years in an institution like our own noble one of All Hallows, where, under the guidance of zealous and skilful ecclesiastics, he is trained in self-denial, in sacred learning, and, above all, in the science of the saints. The sum of his training, however, is this: that he should leave father, and mother, and kindred, and home, and country, and that with a heart freed from every bond that can tie him to himself or to the world, he should go forth to preach the Gospel to every creature. Compare with this the statement made concerning the Protestant missionary by Mr. Vaux, that, "with many, a wife is regarded as well nigh indispensable by one who is about to engage in this peculiar branch of the church's work." The arguments adduced in support of this opinion will be found, when examined, to amount to little more than this, that a missionary is more comfortable with a wife than without one! In one of the Anglican missions, where the bishop was almost alone among the heathen and half-heathen tribes whom he was trying to convert, he was deprived of the aid of three missionaries simultaneously from this cause alone:—

"Two clergymen in England, who had promised their personal aid, withdrew from their engagements because the ladies to whom they had become affianced in the interval, very naturally objected to such uninviting expatriation; while the third, who had gone out as a married man, was compelled to return to the old country because, after the experience of a year or two, the new one did not prove agreeable to his wife" (p. 174).

For all the shortcomings of the Protestant clergy the essayist proposes as a remedy that very clerical celibacy which the Reformers were the first to shake off, and which the Catholic Church has ever held, and still holds, in honour.

We have but scanty space left to touch on the condition of the people, and we must confine our remarks to a single point. This point, however, is so serious, and gives rise to considerations so appalling, that we may well dispense with any other. The Rev. Henry Humble has contributed to the volume before us an essay on *Infanticide : Its Cause and Cure*. Omitting to dwell on the horrible scandal and sin of such places of wholesale murder as have been recently exposed at Torquay, and which, we are told, exist in many other towns, this writer presents the following fearful sketch of the prevalence of child murder in England:—

"Thus bundles are left lying about the streets which people will not touch, lest the too familiar object, a dead body, should be revealed, perchance with a pitch plaster over its mouth, or a woman's garter round its throat. Thus, too, the metropolitan canal boats are impeded, as they are tracked along, by the number of drowned infants with which they come in contact, and the land is becoming defiled by the blood of her innocents. We are told by Dr. Lankester that there are 12,000 women in London to whom the crime of child-murder may be attributed. In other words, that one in every thirty women (I presume between fifteen and forty-five) is a murderess" (p. 57).

In the way of prevention and cure, special appliances, through the efforts of religious and of associated societies, are recommended. It is remarkable that the institutions which he thus recommends are almost in every instance such as owe their existence to the Catholic Church. Thus, orphanages and juvenile reformatories for the young, religious guilds or confraternities, and houses presided over by religious for those in danger, retreats for the betrayed, and penitentiaries for the openly vicious. But above all other means our essayist has confidence in the sacrament of Penance:—

"I have done little more than take for granted throughout habitual resort to confession. The high morality of Ireland is owing, in great part, to this habit; and the low tone of morals in Scotland is, I fear, to be greatly attributed to the impossibility of having recourse to a sacramental ordinance so specially adapted by our most loving Lord to strengthen those who are secretly tempted to sin. It will rest with the clergy everywhere to recommend this practice" (p. 68).

We have thus followed the earnest authors of these essays over each part of the ground covered by the Protestant Church in this country considered as a moral power in the world. From the statement of these men, by no means wedded to the cause of the Roman Catholic Church, we have seen that, considered as a corporate body, in her clergy and in her people, the Protestant Church offers a striking example of impotence and decay. That decay, we have seen, has set in precisely in the parts which are markedly Protestant, as having been substituted for Catholic ones of an opposite character. And, finally, we have heard from the midst of the Anglican clergy themselves the cry go forth to stand once more upon the ancient ways, and to return to the

23

principles which, in their madness, they had abandoned. And thus the wisdom of God's Church is justified in her children; not only in those of them who have remained faithful in their obedience to her, but even in the prodigals who, leaving her, went afar off, and there devoured their substance.

———

DANGEROUS READING.

WE cannot better describe the use and the abuse of the art of printing than by employing the language of two illustrious Roman Pontiffs, who ruled the Church, the one at the commencement of Protestantism, the other in our own day, when the deadly effects of that heresy have reached their development. Leo the Tenth, in the tenth session of the Council of Lateran, declares that the "art of printing has been happily and usefully invented for the glory of God, for the increase of the faith, and for the diffusion of the sciences."

This was in the first days of the Reformation. During the three hundred years that followed, Protestantism arrogated to itself unchecked power over the press, which it declared to be a creation peculiarly its own, and, at the end of that period, Gregory the Sixteenth thus describes the result: " We are filled with horror in seeing what monstrous doctrines, or rather what prodigies of error, we are inundated with through that deluge of books, of pamphlets, and of works of all kinds, the lamentable inroad of which has spread a curse upon the face of the earth." *

This testimony of the Pontiff is borne out by every man who has the interests of religion and the welfare of modern society at heart. We shall mention two facts which must impress even the most careless. In France a commission appointed by the Government some years ago to investigate the results of the system of book-hawking (*colportage*), in its official report addressed to the Minister of the Interior, declared that of the nine millions

* Encycl. *Mirari vos.*

of works which that system scattered broadcast among the popu-
lace, "eight-ninths, that is to say, eight millions, were books
more or less immoral." *

In England we know, on undisputed authority, that infidel
and immoral literature is a most widespread evil. Of Combe's
Constitution of Man, a work of materialistic tendency, and based
on a denial of Providence, more than eighty thousand copies
issued from the English press. The total annual issue of immoral publications amounts to twenty-nine millions. In 1851,
the purely infidel press in London issued more than twelve millions of publications; the issues of avowed atheism being more
than six hundred and fifty thousand. All this is exclusive of
newspapers.†

Now, as the literatures of France and England divide between them the attention of the entire world, this luxuriance of
infidel and immoral publications in the two countries is an argument from which we may safely conclude that the evils deplored
by the Pontiff are almost co-extensive with what is called modern
civilisation.

This multiplication of bad books is one of the most deadly
plagues of modern society. Men's minds have become so fascinated by the glories of the boasted liberty of the press, so im-
patient of all control, especially in the matter of reading, so
negligent of the precautions suggested by the commonest prudence, that the pernicious influences exercised by this noxious
literature are telling on every side. The spirit of faith is
weakened; Christian purity of conscience is sullied; serious and
solid studies are in no esteem; *the whole head is sick, the whole
heart is sad.*

An evil so crying as this, and fraught with such consequences
to the religious and social condition of our country, imperatively
demands a remedy. It is not in our power to propose a remedy
which should meet all the exigencies of the case; but, at least,
we can remind Catholic readers of what their duty requires from
them in this matter. We say to them, therefore, that they are
not free to roam at will through the world of books, reading
whatever they please, no matter how pernicious to their faith or
morals; but, on the contrary, they are bound to subject their
reading to a wholesome discipline, steadfastly refusing to themselves and to those under their charge, not only such books as
are positively hurtful, but even such as are dangerous.

Authority and reason unite in recommending this rule. Even
Paganism in its least corrupt form felt and acknowledged this
truth, that the true object of reading was to instruct, not to

---

* *Moniteur*, 8th April, 1853.　　† *I. E. Record*, vol. ii., p. 270.

pervert. Their libraries bore the noble inscription of *treasure-houses of remedies for the soul*. The Jews were naturally still more jealous of all that could injure the faith or morals of God's chosen people. Eusebius tells us that the holy king Ezechias committed to the flames certain works ascribed to Solomon, fearing lest the people should, by their perusal, be seduced to idolatry. Even the Holy Scriptures themselves were not placed indiscriminately in the hands of all; young persons, until they reached the age of thirty, according to St. Jerome, or twenty-five, according to St. Gregory Nazianzen, were not allowed to read Genesis, certain chapters of Ezechiel, and the Canticle of Canticles.

The early Christians were still more remarkable for the caution with which they avoided dangerous books. Of this we have a notable example recorded in the *Acts of the Apostles*,[*] how many of those who had followed curious things, brought all their books together, and burnt them before all; and so many or so valuable were the bad books thus consumed that, the price of them being computed, the money was found to be fifty thousand pieces of silver. Nor did this spirit decay as time progressed. When heretics were converted to the faith they were not received into the Church except upon the condition of giving publicly to the flames the suspected books of which they were in possession. The General Council (second) of Constantinople, and the General Council (second) of Nice, issued one common anathema against heretics and their books.

In the early part of the fifth century Pope Anastasius condemned Origen, his doctrines, and his books, the reading of which he forbade to the faithful. In 446, Pope Leo the Great made search in every direction for the books of the Manichæans, and succeeded in destroying a large quantity of them; and, in the following year, the same Pontiff wrote to the bishops of Spain, exhorting them to destroy the books of the Priscillianists. It is not necessary to dwell here upon the enactments made to the same effect on this subject by later Pontiffs; and no one can be ignorant how anxiously they have endeavoured to restrain the unbridled licence of the corrupt press. Suffice it to say that, as concerning bad books, the Catholic Church has a clearly defined policy of her own, and that it is her manifest wish that her children should reject with firmness not merely such books as are condemned by name, but also those the tone of which is likely to injure faith or morals.

Our present purpose dispenses us from the obligation of entering upon a defence of the legislation, such as we have

---

[*] *Acts*, xix. 19.

described it, adopted by the Church in the matter of bad books. Addressing ourselves to Catholics, we have no need to justify the principles on which that legislation is based, for no well-instructed Catholic will think of calling them in question. But herein lies the difficulty, that whereas Catholics readily admit the necessity of stringent rules in matter of such reading as really endangers faith or morals, they are not so easily convinced that in their own proper case such danger exists. Hence, professional men have little or no difficulty in taking as their instructors historians, whose books are coloured with anti-Catholic prejudices, and who give the most distorted views of the action of the Church upon the world. Hence, writers on jurisprudence, whose first principles are wholly incompatible with the very charter of the Church's existence, are allowed to form the minds of young Catholic students. In making choice of authors on mental and social philosophy especially, it appears to.be quite forgotten that the Church both possesses and exercises the right of judging philosophical systems. The writer of these lines has had an opportunity of witnessing the result of this forgetfulness. He has heard it seriously maintained by young Catholics, otherwise exemplary, that the Church not only ought never to pass judgment upon philosophy, but ought to tolerate the errors of philosophy, leaving it to correct itself; and that philosophy is to be treated of without taking any account of supernatural revelation : and yet these very propositions have been condemned [nn. xi., xiv.] in the Syllabus. Besides, it very generally happens that Catholics are constant readers of some one or other of the periodicals which judge of passing events, or of new books, from a point of view altogether anti-Catholic ; and when they find these oracles, day after day, occupied in proclaiming the merits of some new work of science or of fiction, which has reached the dignity of being called the book of the season, they become so eagerly curious to read it as seldom to stop to consider whether they are justified in doing so or not. And thus it happens that, while in theory they rightly admit the force of the obligation which imposes caution in the choice of books, they practically disregard it, not, indeed, through contempt, but because they cannot bring themselves to believe that in their case there is any considerable danger incurred by indiscriminate reading.

This secure confidence in their own invulnerability is the source of most serious evils, and it is a confidence as rash as it is dangerous.

No doubt there are a few minds which have but little to fear from the artifices with which error seeks to recommend itself under the double attraction of specious argument and elegant

style. Such minds are remarkable alike for singular vigour and
for ripe judgment; thoroughly disciplined to accurate reasoning;
rich in large stores of information; grounded in knowledge as
well of the object as of the motives of faith; and for whom religion is a living power to control the will, as well as a system
of doctrine to enlighten the intellect. Such minds as these will
be able to unravel the most intricate sophism, to detect the confusion of ideas, and to correct false statements of fact; while
for all the tricks of style under which the poison lies hid they
will feel but contempt or disgust. But men blessed with such
minds are few indeed, and even these few may not venture with
safety on the dangerous voyage through strange seas of thought.
The ablest among them have acknowledged that, after reading
some pages of works in which error was conveyed with treacherous skill under the most graceful forms, they were conscious of
feeling ill at ease, and of a bad impression of an indefinitely
unsettling character, which, if not shaken off at once by a
vigorous effort, threatened to sap the foundation of their strongest
convictions. If these impressions were frequently repeated, as
would naturally happen in cases where such books are habitually
or often read, the danger of the most alarming consequences is
but too apparent.

But the great bulk of readers at present cannot lay claim to
the possession of intellectual gifts of a high order. In the first
place, their religious knowledge is very limited. It is astonish-
ing to find how ignorant of the teaching of the Catholic Church,
on many most important points, is the mass of what is called the
reading public. No doubt they are Catholics, and love and cherish
their faith; but of the reasonable grounds on which that faith
rests—of the solid motives that confirm it—of the harmony and
symmetry of its parts, they have but scantiest knowledge. In
the next place, they have had little or no training of mind, their
understanding is not robust enough to deal with solid matter,
nor their judgment disciplined to separate the true from the
false. Again, they are incapable of serious mental exertion, and
averse from all that imposes the labour of thought. They are
mere passive recipients of what they read, surrendering their
minds to the action of the thoughts of others, without ever
challenging the claims which those others have upon them for
the allegiance they are so slavishly ready to yield. Add to this
that the human mind, under any circumstances, is more tenacious
of an objection than of the reply; more sensitive to a difficulty
than to the solution; and that, owing to the peculiar circumstances of this country, the current literature is a very hot-bed
of difficulties and objections against the Catholic faith. Every
quarter, every month, every fortnight, every week brings out a

crop of reviews and magazines which supply millions with matter for reading, and in these periodicals you will find the Church perpetually calumniated, her doctrines and her history falsified, her moderation qualified as irreconcileable antagonism to all that modern progress has won for humanity, her claim to control thought and science misrepresented and derided. You will find religious indifferentism praised to the skies, and the dogmatic principle condemned as tyranny. And whoever makes a careful examination will find underlying all this, and working up through it, an erroneous philosophy which, by its false doctrine of causes, saps the demonstration of that central truth, the existence of God.

Under conditions such as we have described, the results of indiscriminate reading cannot be other than pernicious. The weak must yield to the strong. Generally speaking, the effect of the bad impressions, reiterated again and again, upon the mind of a Catholic who habitually reads, without restraint or antidote, what is called the literature of the day, will be to bring about a divorce between his faith and his reason. He will cling to his faith, but his adherence to it will be the work more of sentiment or of habit than of conviction. And when the fortunes of his life place him in occasions of temptation, when the wild strength of the passions finds no check upon them save that of a creed which is but half believed in, it requires little knowledge of man's heart to foretel the melancholy result.

But whatever we may suppose to be the probable issue of the battle, no one has the right to tempt the dangers that attend the combat. Faith, no doubt, is a gift of God; but God exacts from us for its preservation a faithful correspondence on our part. Who can tell how far he may go without endangering that precious gift? Woe to us if by rash curiosity to know what may be urged against the doctrines of the Church, or by imprudent dallying with difficulties which we are not prepared to meet, we imperil our secure possession of that priceless blessing which ought to be dearer to us than life.

Now, from what we have said, it follows that indiscriminate reading of the books which go to make up the literature of the day, will, if practised as a habit, infallibly lead to such danger in a greater or less degree.

We are quite prepared, however, to find that not all will agree with us on this point. It will be said that in this age of ours a person of intelligence ought to be familiar with the arguments adduced on both sides of every important question. If not, he will speedily be left behind by the progress of the times, and be unable to keep pace with his fellowmen, who read everything.

But, we ask, do you really and conscientiously carry out your golden rule of studying the arguments on both sides of the question ? In virtue of your rule, you have read, let us suppose, Renan's *Life of Christ*, or Barlow's *Eternal Punishment*, in order to know what is urged against Catholic doctrine on subjects of such importance. But did you read what the learned have written on the other side ? Did you read, for example, the late revered Primate Dixon's *Introduction to the Holy Scriptures*, where the authenticity and veracity of the Bible is proved beyond doubt, and the ground thus cut away from beneath the feet of those unbelieving writers ? Or, perhaps, you habitually read some able Protestant periodical which deals in controversy, or occupies itself with comments on the struggle going on at home and abroad between the Church and her enemies. But do you also read the Catholic side of each of the questions under discussion ? Do you make it your business to study attentively all the arguments which Catholic theologians have brought to the defence of the truth ? If you do (and, as a Catholic, you will naturally begin with Catholic works) you will have little time and less inclination to read the opposite errors. For, besides that, the grace of faith will fill you with joyful confidence in the truth you possess, you will find that Catholic writers are in the habit of giving full answers to all objections. Besides, in such cases, even the material time for such studies would be wanting to you. We fear much, however, that this desire to know both sides of the question in practice becomes little else than an excuse for reading remarkable works written to advocate what is false. And even if you were willing to carry out conscientiously this rule of reading books on both sides the danger attending it would forbid its use, save under exceptional circumstances. To be for ever receiving impressions unfavourable to the Church ; to be constantly reading false statements of fact concerning her doctrines and her acts ; to witness the incessant sneers and derision with which her holiest things are received ; to bring one's self to listen to daily charges against her as being in opposition to all that is free and generous in the modern world, and yet not to bear away any injury, is altogether morally impossible. *Gutta cavat lapidem.* It is vain to quote your past experience ; how the freshness of your faith has never faded ; and how whilst, as you admit, thousands fell around you on the right hand and on the left, the evil came not near unto you. The soul is not always conscious of the wounds she receives in this struggle ; it is only when trial and temptation come on, and when she has to exert her best strength to repel them, that she finds to her cost how, like Samson, she has been robbed of her vigour while she slept.

Thus far we have spoken only of dangers to faith; but there is another and universal danger to be feared from indiscriminate reading: we mean dangers to good morals. There are books which, with shameless audacity, describe in plain language the most infamous scenes of vice; there are others which, with greater refinement, but not less malice, paint them half disguised in the most attractive colours. But, in either case, their universal theme is the exaltation of the worst passions of the heart of man at the expense of virtue and modesty and Christian self-denial. There can surely be no doubt but that literature such as this should be abhorred by everyone. We cannot neglect, however, to say one word concerning that passion for works of fiction, even though not in themselves objectionable, which has seized upon the world, and which has struck roots far and wide among the young. It must not be thought that we condemn works of imagination as such. The mind has its flower-garden as well as its corn-fields to be cultivated, and the best and holiest have not been indifferent to the charms of literature. What we condemn is the habit of giving one's self up to the reading of books of this class exclusively, or almost to the exclusion of more serious studies. Such a habit exercises the worst effects on the heart and upon the mind. The constant perusal of works of fiction unduly develops the imagination at the expense of the reasoning powers, thus disturbing that order of the faculties which nature has established. Besides, it extinguishes all taste for serious studies, especially for the study of history, and where laborious habits of patient and steady work are thus neglected, the mind loses its vigour, and the whole character, dwarfed by the want of healthy exercise, becomes puerile and feeble. The same disastrous effects, though in a minor degree, are the result of newspaper reading, when carried to the excess for which our age is so remarkable. How many are there, both young and old, whose reading alternates between novels and newspapers, newspapers and novels! And what can be expected from minds fed upon such garbage! The best faculties of the understanding—judgment, attention, memory, comprehension—become so depressed and weakened by this desultory reading of trifles that they are no longer able to brace themselves to any high effort worthy of the rational soul of man.

From what we have said, it is evidently the duty of all to exercise great prudence in the choice of books. Two practical rules of great importance may be laid down to guide us in this matter. First, the necessary should go before the useful, the useful before the amusing. Second, we should deny ourselves all such books as are noxious or dangerous, and we should exercise great restraint on ourselves with regard to such as, though indifferent in themselves, are nevertheless easily abused. We should have moral strength enough to resist the tide of public opinion when it would draw us to read some new book remarkable for its novel theories against faith or sound philosophy, or famous for the enchanting pictures it gives of a life forbidden to Christian souls. Nor should we fail to express, in presence of others, our feelings on such a subject. One quiet display of contempt against the idol of the perverse fashion of the day may be the means of freeing others, especially the young, from a thraldom as dangerous as it is unreasonable.*

DR. WHATELY AND THE NATIONAL SYSTEM OF EDUCATION IN IRELAND.

1. WE do not undertake in this paper to set before our readers a complete portrait of the late Protestant Archbishop of Dublin. Of his private life, described as by his latest biographer,† and of his peculiar place in the literature of the age, we shall say nothing in this place. "As to Dr. Whately," writes Dr. Newman in the *Apologia*, "I owe him a great deal. He was a man of generous and warm heart. He was particularly loyal to his friends." On the whole, he was a man of more than ordinary powers, and the circumstances of the time furnished him with peculiar opportunities of employing those powers on matters very closely connected with the interests of Ireland. The Protestant Archbishop of Dublin, ordinarily speaking, is little able to influence the march of public events; he must be satisfied with "wearing lawn sleeves, and being called your Grace," being conscious, at the same time, that the Catholic archbishop is looked upon as the real ruler of the people. But Dr. Whately's connection with the National Board of Education, and the office assigned to him of composing the books which were to form the

* On this whole subject see Zaccaria, *Storia polemica delle probizione dei libri*; and an excellent article in the July number of the *Etudes*.

† *Life and Correspondence of R. Whately, D.D.*, by E. Jane Whately. Two volumes. London, 1866.

minds of the youth of the country at a very critical period, invest his history with particular importance. What manner of man was this who assumed to himself the grave responsibility of writing the books that were to instruct a nation ?   What use did he make of the boundless influence thus placed in his hands ? What result did he propose to himself to achieve ?   In the case of any country this would form an interesting subject of inquiry ; but to Irish Catholics it is one of the last importance. For, should it appear on examination that the object of his labours was to imbue with his own errors the tender Catholic minds which had been given to him in charge ; should it appear that, under pretence of being educated, the youth of Ireland were to be weaned from the Catholic religion, then the Catholics of Ireland have a right to feel indignant that they should have been thus wantonly betrayed.   Such a discovery would also justify them in their distrust of any fresh plan of education proceeding from a similar source, and in their demands for such safeguards as should render it impossible for the Education System ever again to become an instrument of proselytism.

2. In a pastoral published in the year 1853, on occasion of the threatened legislation against convents, which legislation was recommended by Dr. Whately, Cardinal Cullen used these words :—

" We can now form a just estimate of the character of a man who for many years has been insidiously at work to have the management of the education of the country in his hands ; we can understand with what feelings he dictated the works that were destined to form the minds of our children.   Had he been able to form the National System to the image and likeness of his own works, and to infuse into it the spirit that pervades them, without suspecting his in-tentions, we may say that scepticism, rationalism, and infidelity would have been the poisoned fruits we should have gathered from it.   Time will tell whether any seeds of these baneful productions have been cast into the soil. But, as far as we can see, though there is much to be regretted, we have reason to be thankful to a bountiful Providence for having preserved the germ of faith uninjured amongst us ; and we cannot but feel grateful to all those who, whether officially connected or not with the Protestant dignitary just mentioned, in the management of the education of the country, have laboured to keep things in their proper channel, and, as far as in them lay—for their position must have been one of great difficulty, having to contend with a personage whose autho-rity was of great weight until his opinions became known—to give fair play to all, and not to allow anyone to invade the just rights of others " (pp. 22, 23).

These grave charges were much commented on at the time they were uttered, and since, and were ascribed by many to a spirit of narrow-minded and uncharitable bigotry.   Confident in the truth of his assertions, the cardinal appealed to the verdict of time to tell whether or not the attempt had been made to use the National System of Education as a means of sowing in the virgin soil of the youthful Catholic intellect of Ireland the seeds of pernicious doctrines. That verdict has now been delivered. The charges alleged by Cardinal Cullen against Dr. Whately in connection with the National System have been fully confirmed, and confirmed by Dr. Whately himself. The documents contained in the recent biography of the late Protestant Archbishop of Dublin, published by one to whom his honour and fame are naturally most dear, are such as to throw a new light upon the history of the National System, and to help Catholics to a right appreciation of its character. One and all, these documents constitute a signal justification of the action taken by the Catholic bishops in this most important matter. That action was the natural result of their conviction of the truth of the accusations contained in the pastoral mentioned above, and these accusations have now been substantiated by the guilty person himself. *Habemus confitentem reum.*

3. If it be true, first, that Dr. Whately was aware from the very beginning that the National System was founded to supply secular instruction only, without any Scriptural instruction; that, secondly, notwithstanding this, he succeeded in having himself constituted the source from which Scriptural instruction was to be dispensed throughout all Ireland; and if, thirdly, he deliberately and advisedly framed that Scriptural instruction in such a way as that it would destroy the Catholic religion in the minds of the scholars, then it must be admitted that the pastoral, far from being narrow-minded, was most sagacious; far from being uncharitable, was strictly just. Now, it is remarkable that each of these three points is abundantly proved from Dr. Whately's own letters, and from the testimony of his own most intimate friends.

4. And, first of all, Dr. Whately was well aware that Lord Stanley, in founding the National, did not intend to offer to the Irish people any education beyond a secular one. "Six years ago or more," he writes, in 1838, to Dr. Arnold, who had written to ask some questions in reference to the then newly-founded London University, "I should have been rather inclined to doubt the possibility of having any instruction, or any examination in Christian Scriptures, that all various denominations might possibly partake of. *When Lord Stanley formed the Education Board he had no such thought.* . . . But had the plan gone no further than Lord Stanley *at first proposed and expected,* I should not have considered it as furnishing education, but only a portion of education; and I should have been glad to furnish even a small part of that portion if no more could have been admitted" (vol. i., pp. 408, 410).

5. Upon a board founded to give a secular education exclusively, and accepted by Catholic Ireland only on that under-

standing, Dr. Whately accepted a place. Did he, in his new position, loyally carry out Lord Stanley's express intentions as to the exclusively secular character of the training? or did he work for years to have the management of the education in his own hands, so that he might to the secular add Scriptural instruction? His daughter tells us that he entered on the undertaking with the most earnest desire of extending the blessings, at least, of civilisation and intellectual culture, and, as far as he thought practicable, *Scriptural Knowledge* likewise, among his adopted countrymen of all creeds. It was mainly through his instrumentality that a considerable portion of the Scriptures—a work of his own on the Evidences of Christianity, and a volume of Sacred Poetry—were introduced. For years he laboured diligently to carry out the system in its integrity; and it was only when, as it appeared to him, the system had been infringed by the withdrawal of those books, that he withdrew from a work he could no longer conscientiously carry on (pp. 138, 139, vol. i.).

In the letter to Dr. Arnold, from which we have quoted above, he thus describes the issue of his exertions:—

" The result, however, was complete success. All the efforts to raise jealousy in reference to the Scripture extracts have, within the schools themselves, totally failed. They are read with delight and profit by almost all the children; and I and other Protestants, as Bishop Stanley knows, have examined children of all denominations, without knowing to which each child belonged, raising no jealousy, and finding them better taught in Scripture than most gentlefolks' children " (vol. i., p. 401).

Nothing could exceed the solicitude with which he laboured at this task. The *Easy Lessons on Christian Evidences* was the darling of Dr. Whately's heart. The allusions made to it in his papers are remarkably numerous. In 1837, he mentions, with great exultation, that a great number of Roman Catholics are now beginning to read the *Evidences*. In 1839 he transmitted the sum of twenty-one pounds to the Pastor Fabre, at Lausanne, whose wife had translated the work into French, and remarks that his own daughter had begun a translation of the text into French and also into Italian. He himself, he writes, laboured more at the style of that little tract than at that of any volume he ever published. The whole was subjected to the most careful revision of friends, and written over three or four times. In 1840, in a letter to the Bishop of Norwich, he again alludes to the French and Italian versions, and adds, " perhaps your son can learn whether any could be usefully conveyed to the Greek islands." In 1845, writing to Bishop Copleston, he speaks of a proposed Welsh translation, and of one in Romaic, which had lately been forwarded to him from Smyrna. He lived to see the work translated into fourteen or fifteen languages.

6. We now come to the third point, which is the most important of all. With what feelings did he dictate the works that were destined to form the minds of the Catholic children of Ireland? We reply that he deliberately intended, under the excuse of educating them, to destroy their belief in the doctrines of the Catholic Church.

Among Dr. Whately's friends no one was more valued by him than William Nassau Senior. Whenever Mr. Senior was away from home, he was accustomed to keep a journal, and to this habit we are indebted for the preservation of some interesting conversations between Dr. Whately and himself on occasion of a visit he paid the archbishop at Redesdale in the autumn of 1852. He had asked Dr. Whately's opinion of the causes that had wrought so many conversions, as they were called, to Protestantism at that period. Among other things, which we may afterwards refer to, his friend replied :

"The great instrument of conversion, however, is the diffusion of Scriptural education. Archbishop Murray and I agreed in desiring large portions of the Bible to be read in our National Schools : but we agreed in this because we disagreed as to its probable results. He believed that they would be favourable to Romanism ; I believed that they would be favourable to Protestantism, and I feel confident that I was right.

"For twenty years large extracts from the New Testament have been read in the majority of the National Schools far more diligently than that book is read in ordinary Protestant places of education.

"The Irish, too, are more anxious to obtain knowledge than the English. When, on the Queen's visit, she asked for a holiday in the National Schools, the children submitted to that compliment being paid to her, but they considered themselves as making a sacrifice. The consequence is that the majority of the Irish people, between the ages of twenty and thirty, are better acquainted with the New Testament than the majority of the English are.

"Though the priest may still, perhaps, denounce the Bible collectively as a book dangerous to the laity, he cannot safely object to the Scripture extracts which are read to children with the sanction of the prelates of his own Church. . . . But those extracts contain so much that is inconsistent with the whole spirit of Romanism, that it is difficult to suppose that a person well acquainted with them can be a thorough-going Roman Catholic. The principles on which that Church is constructed, the duty of uninquiring, unreasoning submission to its authority, renders any doubt fatal. A man who is commanded not to think for himself, if he finds that he cannot avoid doing so, is unavoidably led to question the reasonableness of the command. And when he finds that the Church, which claims a right to think for him, has preached doctrines, some of which are inconsistent, and others are opposed to what he has read in the Gospels, his trust in its infallibility, the foundation on which its whole system is built, is at an end.

"Such I believe to be the process by which the minds of a large portion of the Roman Catholics have been prepared, and are now being prepared, for the reception of Protestant doctrines. The education supplied by the National Board is gradually undermining the vast fabric of the Irish Roman Catholic Church.

"Two things are necessary on the part of the Government. One is, that it adhere resolutely, not only in its measures, but in its appointments, in the selection of bishops, as well as in making parliamentary grants to the system of mixed education. The other is, that it affords to the converts the legal protection to which every subject of the Queen is entitled, but which all her subjects do not obtain in Ireland : some of the persecutions to which they are exposed are beyond the reach of the law."

And on another day, during the same visit, he said, on the subject of the Education Board :

"I believe, as I said the other day, that mixed education is gradually enlightening the mass of the people, *and that, if we give it up, we give up the only hope of weaning the Irish from the abuses of Popery. But I cannot venture openly to profess this opinion. I cannot openly support the Education Board as an instrument of conversion. I have to fight its battle with one hand, and that my best, tied behind me.*

" One of the difficulties," he continued, "in working the mixed system arises from the difference in character of the parties who have to work it. Much is necessarily left to their honour. If the patron or the master chooses to violate the rules of the Board, he may often do so without detection. Our inspectors are too few to exercise more than a partial superintendence, and too ill-paid to be always trustworthy. Now, I must say that Protestants more strongly feel, or at least observe more faithfully, the obligation of honour and of promises than the Roman Catholics. The more zealous Protestants keep aloof from the system of mixed education because it ties their hands. They cannot, without a breach of faith, teach in our schools their own peculiar doctrines ; or, rather, they can teach them only at particular times and to particular classes ; they naturally wish to make them a part of the ordinary instruction ; they support, therefore, only schools of their own, where their hands are free.

" The zealous Roman Catholics are less scrupulous : their hands are free everywhere. With all its defects, however—and many of those defects would be remedied by a grant not so grossly inadequate as that which it now receives —we must adhere to the system of mixed education.

" The control which it gives to us is not perfect, but it is very great. It secures the diffusion of an amount of secular and religious instruction such as Ireland never enjoyed before its institution, and certainly would not enjoy if it were to be overthrown ; and it prevents the diffusion of an amount of superstition, bigotry, intolerance, and religious animosity, I really believe, more extensive and more furious than any that we have yet encountered."

And, in a letter to Mr. Lewis, dated September 20th, 1853 :

" Those who regard man as a very consistent being, and accordingly look on any instance to the contrary as a kind of prodigy, may well wonder at a Roman Catholic sanctioning a work on evidences. . . . But when you talk of wonders, what more strange than to find men of mature age, and who were supposed to possess common sense and common honesty, and to have some regard for their character, talking about the fitness or unfitness of such-and-such a book for Roman Catholics, as if that had anything to do with the question. The book was (whether wisely or unwisely) deliberately sanctioned for fifteen years by the highest Roman Catholic authorities ; and to say that now they have changed their minds, and may fairly prohibit that book and that whole course of study to those who do not object to it, and many of whom were invited and induced by the bait of such books to place schools under the Board—this is like saying that if a man thinks he has made an imprudent marriage he is entitled to a divorce " (vol. ii., p. 292).

From these extracts it plainly follows that Dr. Whately

deliberately and with forethought availed himself of the National system as an engine to pervert the religious belief of the poor children who were handed over to his care, and that he did this not openly or avowedly, but, to use the cardinal's language, "insidiously." What can be more insidious than to say, " I cannot openly support the Board as an instrument of conversion, but I will do my utmost to make it such, while I recommend it on other grounds to the too credulous Irish Catholics ?"

7. And here we must notice a painful inconsistency between the public reasons assigned by Dr. Whately for his retirement from the Board, and his private principles as described by himself. For above twenty-one years did he manage to conduct the National Education on the plan above described. But, in 1853, his *Lessons on the Evidences,* the object of his most tender solicitude— the work which he had caused to be translated into some fourteen languages—and which had cost him more labour than his most voluminous works, was rejected by those ungrateful Irish Catholic children for whose enlightenment it had been composed. His retirement from the Education Board followed quickly upon the resolution passed by that body to the effect that the *Scripture Lessons* and the *Evidences of Christianity* were to be no longer used in the National Schools. The motives which Dr. Whately assigned for the step he took in withdrawing from the Board have been long before the public, and especially with that portion of it which had been induced to adhere to the National System of Education by the bait of such books as were just condemned. But until to-day the public had not the opportunity of comparing Dr. Whately's dignified protest against breaking faith with others, with Dr. Whately's candid admission to Mr. Senior, that secretly he used " the Education Board as an instrument of conversion," although "he could not openly support it as such." As far back as 1853* the public heard him say :

"I fully concur in the general proposition that the Commissioners are not wrong in prohibiting the use, at the time of combined instruction, of a religious book which Roman Catholics believe to be inconsistent with the doctrines of their Church."

But till to-day the public has not had an opportunity of comparing that statement with the following :

"I believe that mixed education is gradually enlightening the mass of the people, and that if we give it up we give up the only hope of weaning the Irish from the abuses of Popery" (p. 266, vol. ii.).

---

* Letter to the Lord Lieutenant, July 26, 1853, p. 284.

A man whose public and private utterances are thus contradictory ought surely to be the last to censure others for a breach of good faith.

8. Besides, his arguments as against the Board which excluded his books can be most effectively retorted against himself. Dr. Whately, according to an admirer,* was pre-eminently a man of "major premises," and where his readers dissent from his conclusions it is, in the majority of cases, in the *minor* premise that the difference will be found. In words that non-logicians will understand, his general principle is almost always true, while, in his application of it to particular cases, there may be now and then something to question. This criticism is not unjust, and we shall avail ourselves of it in the matter on hand of Dr. Whately's. The major premise indictment against the Commissioners runs thus :—

> "When some books or some rules have been deliberately sanctioned by the unanimous voice of the Commissioners, and have been for many years appealed to in vindication of the system, and as a ground on which co-operation was invited and obtained, if afterwards this decision is reversed and this sanction withdrawn, such a gross breach of faith could not fail to deprive for ever the Commissioners, and all other public men who may be parties to it, of all public confidence and of all just claim to it." †

This general principle is true and very accurately stated by the Archbishop ; but, as Mr. Dickinson warns us, in the application of it to the particular case, there is much to question. The minor premise, which contains the application, is this :—

> "The Board has passed a measure (*i. e.* the prohibition of the archbishop's books) which I have protested against as an unjustifiable breach of faith with the public ;‡ and, moreover, it is a gross injustice towards the many hundred patrons of schools who were invited and induced to place them under the Board on the strength of an implied promise, fully understood by all parties, and acted on for twenty-one years."§

Instead of Dr. Whately's minor premise let us substitute one from Cardinal Cullen's letter of 15th December, 1860 : ||

> "When Lord Stanley first proposed the mixed system, Catholics were solemnly assured that under it their children would be free from the remotest danger of proselytism, and it was understood that the action of the Government should be restricted to the giving of aid to schools, and to inspection as to the application of the funds and the literary progress of the children. But those flattering promises have not been realised. The safeguards laid down by Lord Stanley have been gradually withdrawn ; Catholic children are now publicly

---

* Rev. Hercules Dickinson, vol. ii. appendix, p. 433.
† Letter to the Lord Lieutenant, July 5th, 1853.
‡ *Ibid.*, July 21st, 1853.   § *Ibid.*, July 26th, 1853.
|| Mr. Fitzpatrick's *Memoirs of Archbishop Whately*, vol. ii., p. 174.

24

receiving instruction from Protestant teachers; books replete with an anti-Catholic spirit, and compiled from Protestant sources, under the direction of a dignitary of the Protestant establishment, the author of a work entitled *Errors of Romanism*, have been published at the public expense, and introduced into the schools for the use of Catholic children."

Every single statement contained in this minor premise has been endorsed by Dr. Whately himself, as we have seen above.[*] He admits Lord Stanley's original plan to have been such as the Cardinal describes it; he admits that this plan has not been realised;[†] he admits that Catholic children received religious instruction from Protestant teachers;[‡] he admits that the books composed by himself for the use of Catholic children were replete with anti-Catholic spirit.[§]   The conclusion may be drawn in his own words: therefore " this gross breach of faith cannot fail to deprive the Commissioners, and all other public men who may be parties to it, of all public confidence and of all just claim to it."   Since, then, Dr. Whately, as his daughter assures us, was "mainly instrumental" in engrafting religious instruction upon a system which had been founded and accepted on the very condition that it should give none other than secular instruction, Dr. Whately, by his own principles, was justly deprived of all public confidence and of all reasonable claim to it; and the act of the Commissioners, so far from being a breach of public faith, was in some degree an act of reparation of a breach of public faith.

9. The following extracts furnish the reader with some account of his feelings towards Catholics, and especially towards the Catholic clergy.   His explanation of the so-called Irish conversions is thus given in Mr. Senior's diary :—

" The Archbishop is president of the Society for Protecting the Rights of Conscience. For some time a considerable conversion to Protestantism has been going on in Ireland. The converts are to be numbered by thousands, not by hundreds.

" I asked to what these conversions were to be attributed ?   What were the causes which had suddenly opened men's minds to arguments which had been addressed to them for years without success ?

" 'The causes,' said the Archbishop, 'must be numerous; it is not probable that I am acquainted with them all, or that I assign to those which occur to me their relative importance ; . . . but I will tell you all that I know or conjecture, and I will also tell you what opinions are current.   Many persons think that it is owing to the general diffusion of Bibles, Testaments, and prayer-books, by the societies instituted for those purposes.   But those societies have been at work for many years, and the conversions on the present scale are recent. Others believe, or profess to believe, that the conversions are purchased.   This is the explanation given by the Roman Catholics.   An old woman went to one of my clergy, and said : ' I am come to surrender to your reverence, and I want the leg of mutton and the blanket.'

---

* See above, § 4.   † § 4.   ‡ § 5.   § Sec. 6.

"'What leg of mutton and blanket?' said the clergyman; 'I have scarcely enough of either for myself and my family, and certainly none to give. Who could have put such nonsense into your head?'

"'Why, sir,' she said, 'Father Sullivan told us that the converts got each a leg of mutton and a blanket, and, as I am famished and starving with cold, I thought that God would forgive me for getting them.'

"'But our society has for months been challenging those who spread this calumny to prove it. We circulate queries, asking for evidence, that rewards or inducements have been held out, directly or indirectly, to persons who prove themselves converts. Not only has no case been substantiated, no case has been even brought forward. Instead of being bribed, the converts, until they are numerous enough in any district to protect one another, are oppressed by all the persecution that can be inflicted in a lawless country by an unscrupulous priesthood, hounding on a ferocious peasantry. Another explanation is, that it is owing to the conduct of the priests during the O'Brien rebellion. The priests, it is said, lost their popularity by exciting the people and then deserting them. The fact is true, but it is not enough to account for conversions in many parts of Ireland which were not agitated by that movement.

"'Another theory is, that it is mainly owing to the different conduct of the Protestant and Roman Catholic clergy during the famine.* The Protestant clergy literally shared their bread, or rather their meal, with their parishioners without the least sectarian distinction; they devoted all their time, all their energy, all their health, and all that the Poor Law left them of their small revenues to those who were starving around them. Their wives and daughters passed their days in soup kitchens and meal rations.

"'The Roman Catholic clergy were not sparing of their persons : they lived, and a great many of them died, among the sick ; but the habit of that clergy is never to give ; there is a division of labour between them and the laity—they take faith, and the laity good works, at least as far as almsgiving is a good work. A great part of them, indeed, during the famine, had nothing to give; they starved with their flocks when their flocks ceased to pay dues. But others had means of their own, and many of those who took part in the distribution of the Government money, or of the English subscriptions, helped themselves out of the funds which passed through their hands to what they considered to be the amount due to them from the people. But no part of their revenues, however obtained, found its way to the poor. Their incomes were spent during the famine as they were spent before it, and as they are now spent, on themselves, or hoarded till they could be employed in large subscriptions to chapels or convents. And this was not the worst. In many cases they refused to those who could not, or who would not, pay for them, the sacraments of their Church. In ordinary times this may be excusable ; a clergy unendowed and unsalaried must be supported by voluntary contributions or by dues. In so poor a country as Ireland voluntary contributions cannot be relied on. The priest might often starve if he did not exact his dues ; and, as he has no legal rights, his only mode of exacting them is to make their payment the condition on which his ministrations are performed. But, during the famine, payment was obviously impossible. When, under such circumstances, the sacraments which the priest affirmed to be necessary passports to heaven, were refused, the people could not avoid inferring either that the priest let men sink into eternal torment to avoid a little trouble to himself, or that absolution or extreme unction could not be essential to salvation.

"'I believe that this explanation is not without its truth, and that the influence of the Roman Catholic clergy has been weakened by the contrast of their conduct to that of ours. But I am inclined to attach more importance to the

---

* To appreciate better the injustice of this account of the Catholic clergy the reader ought to call to mind that Dr. Whately publicly announced to his clergy that, lest they should carry " the infection to their own families, they were under no obligation to attend persons dying of contagious diseases."

acquisition by the Protestant clergy of the Irish language. Until within a few years Protestant doctrines had never been preached in Irish. The rude inhabitants of the remote districts in Munster and Connaught believed that English was the language of heretics, and Irish that of saints. The devil, they said, cannot speak Irish.

" ' About ten years ago, on my first visitation, after the province of Cashel had been put under my care, I asked all the clergy what proportion of their parishioners spoke nothing but Irish. In many cases the proportion was very large. 'And do you speak Irish?' I asked. 'No, my lord.' ' I am very sorry to hear it,' I replied. 'Oh,' the clergyman always said, 'all the Protestants speak English.' 'That is just what I should have expected,' I replied ; ' under the circumstances of the case, it would be strange indeed if any who speak only Irish were Protestants.' This sort of dialogue became much rarer on my second triennial visitation, and at my last there was scarcely any occasion for it. There are now very few of my clergy who cannot make themselves understood by all their parishioners, and I am told that the effect of this vernacular preaching is very great.' "

His own theory was that the conversions were the work of the National System of Education. We have given his words above in n. 6.

HIS OPINION ABOUT MAYNOOTH.

" ' Would you support,' I asked, ' Maynooth ?'
" ' I am not sure,' answered the Archbishop, ' that its original institution was wise. Mr. Pitt thought that the young priests were taught disaffection and anti-Anglicanism at Douai, and he created for their education the most disaffected and the most anti-English establishment in Europe ; but having got it, we must keep it. While the grant was annual it might have been discontinued ; now that it is permanent, to withdraw or even to diminish it would be spoliation. It would be gross abuse of the preponderance in Parliament of the British members. We have no more right to deprive the Irish Roman Catholics, against their will, of the provision which we have made for the education of their clergy, than they would have, if they were numerically superior, to pass an act for the sale of the colleges and the estates of Oxford and Cambridge, and the application of the produce in the reduction of the National Debt.'
" ' And yet,' I said, ' you concurred in wishing the act to be extended to Ireland.'
" ' What I concurred in,' said the Archbishop, ' was not in wishing that such an act should be passed for the British Islands, for I utterly disapprove of it ; but in wishing that it should not be passed for England alone. I believed the act, if general, to be a great evil, but a still greater evil if confined to England. It was saying to the English Roman Catholics : You are weak and loyal, therefore we trample on you ; to the Irish : You are strong and rebellious, therefore we leave you alone.' "

HIS OPINION OF IRISH MEDICAL MEN.

" ' You remember,' said the Archbishop, ' our concocting a paper on the Trades' Unions, which have destroyed the commerce and the principal manufactures and handicrafts of Dublin, and force us to import almost everything except poplins and porter, which drive ships from Dublin Bay to be repaired in Liverpool, and have rendered our canals useless.'
" Well, the medical men of Dublin are almost outdoing in narrow-mindedness, selfishness, and tyranny the ignorant weavers and carpenters. They have made an ordinance that no fellow or licentiate of the Royal College of Surgeons

shall pretend, or profess, to cure diseases by the deception called 'homœopathy,' or the practice called 'mesmerism,' or by any other form of 'quackery,' and that no fellow or licentiate of the college shall consult with, meet, advise, direct, or assist any such person engaged in such deceptions or practices, or in any system of practice considered derogatory or dishonourable by the physicians or surgeons. In the spirit of this ordinance a surgeon refused to attend me unless I would promise to give up homœopathy" (vol. ii., 405).

RITUALISM.

WE propose in this paper to furnish our readers with some account of the present Ritualistic movement in England. The vigour exhibited by that movement, the searching influence it now exerts throughout a society hitherto sealed against it, and the character of the results it has already produced, combine not unreasonably to gather around it a large share of public interest.

A plain recital of facts will be the best help we can give our readers towards forming a correct judgment of the nature of this remarkable religious movement in the Anglican Church, of its extent, and of its bearing on the spread of the Catholic faith in England. To understand the Ritualism of to-day we must bear in mind its connection with the so-called Tractarian teachings of 1833. Coleridge has said that the metaphysics of one generation become the ethics of the next. By a similar process of development the doctrinal teaching of the early Oxford movement has found a visible exponent in the ceremonial worship of the present year. And herein lies the true importance of Ritualism, that it is the fruit of matured conviction on points of doctrine, and not merely "a busy looking-up of mediæval millinery," as the *Contemporary Review* would have us believe.

For some time past the religious and even the secular press has teemed with narratives of the doings to be witnessed in the churches of the Ritualists. The various details thus supplied are brought to a focus in a remarkable report* drawn up by a

* For a knowledge of this report we are indebted to the *Etudes*, etc., No. 47, November, 1866, p. 396.

minister, and addressed to an Anglican bishop desirous of forming an accurate notion of the extent of Ritualism and of the
practices common among its adherents. This report has been
examined by three converts from Anglicanism, and by them has
been declared to be rather under than over the mark. The
gentleman who drew up the report is one who for fourteen years
has been intimately and extensively connected with the movement of which he gives so interesting a description, and he
pledges himself that in his description he has not advanced a
single statement of the truth of which he has not had personal
experience.

He first describes the devotional exercises most affected by
the laity who have been won by the new movement. The
favourite prayer-books of laymen are a very accurate index of
the character of the devotions of those who use them. The book
chiefly in use and most highly approved of is the *Churchman's
Guide to Faith and Piety*, which may be considered as the model
of the others. This manual contains morning and evening
prayers, with the examination of conscience; devotions for the
festivals of saints; instructions for the receiving of the Holy
Eucharist and for assisting at the Holy Mysteries; and in these
instructions the doctrine of the real presence and of the Eucharistic Sacrifice is expressed in the plainest possible language.
The book also prescribes prayers for the faithful departed. Two
large editions of this work have already appeared. More than
four thousand copies of a smaller book of the same kind, called
the *Little Prayer-Book*, have been sold within the last two years.
Other books breathing likewise a high Catholic tone are extensively circulated. Many are specially devoted to the Eucharist,
and of one of these, *The Altar Manual*, thousands of copies have
been sold. Others treat of sacramental confession, such as
Pardon through the Precious Blood; others aim at propagating
some particular devotion, such as towards the Passion of Our
Lord.

The following are extracts from the *Little Prayer-Book :—**

"At the words, This is My body, this is My blood, you must believe that
the bread and wine become *the real body and blood with the soul and Godhead of
Jesus Christ.* Bow down your heart and body in *deepest adoration* when the
priest says these awful words, and worship your Saviour then verily and indeed
present on his altar (p. 18).

"The following prayer is offered up: 'Look down, O Holy Father, upon the
sacrifice of Thy well-beloved Son, *which is now presented by Thy priest on earth,*
and which He Himself is offering to Thee in heaven, and for the sake of this

---

* Rev. R. P. Blakeney, p. 37. Discussion between Rev. J. Hunt and the
Rev. R. P. Blakeney, at Clifton (April 17, 1866), on the Ritualism of the Church
of England.

mighty sacrifice grant me (here name your special intention). Remember also for good all for whom I ought to pray. Bless my parents, my friends, my priest, and the whole Catholic Church, and may all the dead in Christ receive light and peace.' Then the prayer is offered up, ' Blood of Christ, inebriate me.' And the Litany of the sacrament contains the following petitions:

" ' Most high and adorable Sacrament, have mercy on us.'

" ' Most holy of all sacrifices, have mercy on us.'

" ' True propitiation for the living and the dead, have mercy on us.'

" ' Most wonderful of all miracles, have mercy on us.'

" ' *Viaticum* of them that die in the Lord, have mercy on us.'

" ' By Thy precious blood, which Thou has left us on our altars, deliver us, O Lord.'

" ' That it would please Thee to strengthen and fortify us with this heavenly viaticum at the hour of death. We beseech Thee,' &c. (p. 22).

" For going to communion the following direction is given : ' Be most careful to receive into your mouth all, even the smallest portion of the most holy Sacrament, since one crumb or drop of it is worth more than the world itself ' (p. 40).

" This is an act of adoration. ' O Lord Jesus Christ, with the Angels and Archangels, with Thy holy Mother and all Saints, I worship and adore Thee, true God and true man, truly present in the most holy Sacrament of the altar ' (p. 43).

" After consecration the following prayer is offered : ' With grateful hearts we now call to mind, O Lord, the sacred mysteries of Thy passion and death, Thy resurrection and ascension. Here is Thy body that was broken, Thy blood that was shed for us, of which these outward signs are but the figures, and yet in reality contain the substance. Now we truly offer to Thee, O Lord, that pure and holy victim which Thou hast been pleased to give us, of which all other sacrifices were but types and figures.' The *Directorium Anglicanum* contains the following passage : ' After the words, " This is My body, which is given for you," the *hostia* should be placed on the paten, and the celebrant with his assistants should reverently genuflect. Then rising, the celebrant should at once elevate IT with the first finger and thumb of both hands, FOR THE WORSHIP OF THE FAITHFUL, while he is saying, " Do this in remembrance of Me." ' The following cautels are given : ' After the consecration. in passing before the Blessed Sacrament, the server will be specially careful to genuflect with the greatest reverence.' ' He should remember that the vessels have touched Christ, that the sacred vestments have been very near to him.' Again, ' As the *corporal* is the linen cloth on which has been laid the Lord's body, the Church orders the washing of it with a minute and pious care.' ' The corporal may not be touched after use by laics without especial permission ; nor must it ever be washed after use in domestic vessels until it has been first washed by a clerk in holy orders, when it may be touched by laics again.'

" Even private Mass is introduced, though the Church directs that there shall be a convenient number present. The editor of the *Directorium Anglicanum* shows *how* private Mass may be celebrated. He says, ' This need not practically even prevent celebration, at least on Sundays and festivals ; for even if the people withdraw after the prayer for the Church, if the oblation has been made, as of course it will have been, the service must go on. Much more should *absent sick persons*, who will, of course, communicate spiritually, be counted in.'

" Further, amongst the cautels the following are given : ' But if the chalice have dropped upon the altar, the drop must be sucked up, and the priest must do penance for three days.' If the drop of ' *blood* ' penetrate to the second linen cloth he is to do penance four days ; if to the third cloth, nine days ; if to the fourth, twenty days ; and the cloths are to be washed three times over a chalice, and the ablution to be reserved with the relics."

Another class of books of devotion is intended for the use of the clergy. The *Priests' Prayer-Book* (of which three editions

have been already exhausted) contains devotional exercises based
on the pre-Reformation liturgy, and most clearly setting forth
the Real Presence, the Eucharistic Sacrifice, and prayers for the
dead.   It likewise contains most minute instructions on the
method of hearing sacramental confessions.

The nature of the case renders it difficult to have a strictly
accurate statistic account of those who habitually frequent confession.   Our informant, who is ever beset by the fear of falling
into any exaggeration, declares the numbers of those who habitually frequent " the sacred tribunal" to amount to many thousands.   " I myself," says he, " have known priests to pass the
whole night in hearing confessions in the church before the
great festivals.   The method of confession does not differ in any
important particular from that generally in use in the churches
of the West.   The priest is seated, wearing a surplice with a
black or violet stole.   The penitent kneels by his side, almost
always before a crucifix, or at least before a cross.   After receiving the priest's blessing, he commences a formula which
corresponds to the *Confiteor* of the Latin Church.   When he
has recited one-half of this formula he confesses his sins, and
generally venial sins as well as mortal, and then completes the
formula.   The priest then gives him advice, and pronounces the
absolution after the form prescribed in the Book of Common
Prayer at the visitation of the sick.   The penitent is then dis-
missed with a blessing.   This is the method almost universally
followed.   Sometimes, however, the priest practises some acts of
devotion before and after the confession " (p. 404).

There are two schools of Ritualism which, however, as far as
results are concerned, differ but little from one another.   One
seeks to restore the ancient national liturgy of the Anglican
Church, as it exists in the Sarum Missal and Ritual ; the other
prefers the actual usages of the Roman Church, and relies upon
the decisions of the Roman Congregation of Rites.

The use of hymns is very common.   A collection of hymns,
containing the principal hymns of the Breviary, named *Hymns
Ancient and Modern*, has been sold to the extent of one million
and a-half copies.   The Gregorian tones have been re-established
for the psalms.   In some churches the celebrant wears a cope
on festivals, and incenses the altar during the *Magnificat*.   An
Appendix to the Hymnale noted has lately been published, to serve
as a directory to arrange the hymns for the offices both according to the Roman and to the Sarum use.

As an illustration of the advance made by the advanced
party in hymnology, we may quote the *Lyra Eucharistica*, containing hymns and verses on the Holy Communion, edited a
few years ago by the Rev. Orby Shipley.   In this book nothing,

it is maintained, has been printed which is not in accordance
with the teaching of the Church of England on the Eucharist.
The hymns have been arranged according to a five-fold division,
and treat respectively of the Preparation, the Oblation, the Consecration, the Communion, and the Thanksgiving. In the part
entitled the Consecration the majority of the hymns are from
ancient or mediæval sources. Among them we find beautiful
translations of the *Lauda Sion Salvatorem*, the *Pange lingua
gloriosi Corporis*, and the *Adoro te devote, latens Deitas* of St.
Thomas of Aquin; also of the *Anima Christi*, of the *Ave!
Christi corpus verum*, of the *Salve! Sancta Caro Dei* (twelfth
century), and of many other Catholic Eucharistic hymns, to
which are added several original pieces of similar character.
We insert one translation from the part entitled Oblation, which
will have its interest for our readers, namely, the late Rev. J.
M. Neale's translation of the ancient Irish hymn, *Sancti Venite*,
from the Antiphonarium of Bangor:

A COMMUNION HYMN OF THE SEVENTH CENTURY.[*]

Sancti venite, Corpus Christi sumite.

Draw nigh, and take the Body of the Lord,
And drink the Holy Blood for you outpoured.

Saved by that Body, hallowed by that Blood,
Whereby refreshed, we render thanks to God.

Salvation's Giver, Christ the Only Son,
By that his cross and Blood the victory won.

Offered was He for greatest and for least,
Himself the Victim, and Himself the Priest.

Victims were offered by the law of old,
That, in a type, celestial mysteries told.

He, Ransomer from death, and light from shade,
Giveth his holy Grace his saints to aid.

Approach ye, then, with faithful hearts sincere,
And take the safeguard of salvation here.

He that in this world rules his saints, and shields,
To all believers Life Eternal yields.

With Heavenly Bread makes them that hunger whole,
Gives Living Waters to the thirsty soul.

Alpha and Omega, to Whom shall bow
All nations at the Doom, is with us now.

---

[*] Our readers will observe that the third verse of the hymn is wanting in
this version. That verse will be found in the *Irish Ecclesiastical Record* for
December, 1866, p. 164.

The change introduced by the movement displays itself
above all in the celebration of the Eucharist. It is hard to find
in England a diocese in which the use of the full set of sacred
vestments for priests has not been more or less fully restored in
the parochial churches. In some dioceses you will find only a
parish here and there in this condition; in others, a dozen, or
even more; in one or two dioceses the restoration is still more
general. In large and wealthy churches the celebrant is attended
by a deacon and sub-deacon fully robed. In a few churches
there are also other ministers—acolytes, thurifers, &c. Lighted
candles on the altar during the rite are still more common even
than the vestments. During the celebration of the Eucharist
the celebrant and his assistants observe with more or less exact-
ness the gestures and postures prescribed by the rubrics of the
Missal. The use of incense obtains in many churches in the
form fixed by the same authority.

At solemn celebration it is usual in many churches to begin
with the singing of the *Introit*, according to the Sarum or Roman
Missal. The responses, *Credo*, Offertory, *Sanctus*, *Gloria in Ex-
celsis*, and *Agnus Dei*, during the priest's communion, are sung
in very many churches, and according to the ancient notation.
The antependium is changed to match the colour prescribed for
the day. The people are taught to assist at the celebration of
the Eucharist, not only as partakers of the sacrament, but also
as assisting at the sacrifice. The practice of inserting in the
Anglican rite prayers from the Ordinary and Canon of the Mass
is favoured by many. Thus the *Judica*, the *Confiteor*, the formula of the Offertory, the *Unde et Memores*, the prayers before
and after the Communion, have been added to what the Anglican
rubrics prescribe.

The extent to which the usage of vestments has spread may
best be gathered from the fact that at the Religious Art Exhibition, held at York this year, the vestments actually employed
in the various Anglican churches, and sent to the exhibition,
were valued at ten thousand pounds sterling. About one hundred
churches took part in the exhibition. Some of the vestments
were of extraordinary magnificence. One chasuble was valued
at two hundred and twenty pounds sterling, and this solely for
the material and the embroidery. The pastoral cross of the late
Bishop Cotton of Calcutta, and three other episcopal crosses, a
cloth of gold mitre, and two copes belonging to the Bishop of
Dunedin, were among the objects most admired at this exhibition.

The use of crucifixes and images, especially of those of Our
Lady with the Divine Infant in her arms, is also widespread.
Many clergymen bless objects of devotion, such as sacred medals,

small crucifixes, and crosses, at the request of members of their congregation. They do not refuse to bless holy water.

So much for the character of the Ritualistic movement : let us now examine how far it has spread in the Anglican Church.

The recent French translation of Dr. Newman's *Apologia* contains, among some notes which are not in the original, a sketch of the state of parties in the Establishment.* "In our own day," says Dr. Newman, "it contains three strong parties, revivals respectively of the three principles of religion, which, from the first, in one shape or other, have exhibited themselves in its history, the Catholic, the Protestant, and the Sceptical, each of them, it is hardly necessary to say, fiercely opposed to the other two. First, the Apostolical or Tractarian party, which at present goes further in the direction of Catholicism than at any former time, or under any former manifestation ; so much so that, in the instance of its more advanced adherents, it may be said to differ in nothing from Catholics, except in the doctrine of the Pope's supremacy. This school arose in the seventeenth century, in the court of James the First and Charles the First; it was almost extinguished by the principles of Locke, and by the accession of William the Third and of the House of Hanover. Its principles were silently taught and handed down through the eighteenth century by the non-jurors, a sect of learned and zealous men who split off from the Church of England, with an episcopal succession, when they were called on to take the oath of allegiance to William the Third; and it has revived in our own day in a large and spreading party in the Church of England, by means of that movement, commenced in the *Tracts for the Times* (hence called Tractarian), of which so much is said in the present volume.

"Secondly, the Evangelical party, which is the life of the Bible societies through the world, and of most of the Protestant missionary societies. It began in the Puritans, towards the close of Elizabeth's reign; it was well-nigh cast out of the Church of England at the restoration of Charles the Second, in 1660. It took refuge among the dissenters, and was gradually expiring when it was revived by means of Whitfield and Wesley, both Anglican clergymen, who founded the influential sect of the Methodists. At the same time that they formed a sect external to the Established Church, they exerted an important influence in that Church itself, and developed in it the Evangelical party, who are at present far the most powerful of the three schools we are engaged in enumerating.

* For this sketch in the original English we are indebted to our excellent contemporary, *The Month*, No. xxx., December, 1866, p. 623.

" Thirdly, the Liberal party, in former centuries called by the less honourable name of Latitudinarian. It rose out of the quasi-Catholic or court party of Charles the First's reign, and was fostered and spread by the introduction into England of the principles of Grotius and of the Arminians of Holland. . . . It took the part of the revolution of 1688, and stood by the Whigs, by William the Third, and by the House of Hanover. The genius of its principles is adverse to display or proselytism : . . . it has not numbered many followers till the last ten years, when, irritated by the Tractarians taking advantage of the conversion to Rome of some of their principal men, and aided by the importation into England of German literature, it has suddenly come forward on the public stage, and has propagated itself with such wondrous rapidity among the educated classes that it would seem as if in the next generation the religious world will be divided between Deists and Catholics. Indeed its principles and modes of reasoning do not stop even at Deism.

" If the Anglican communion simply consisted of these three parties it could not endure. It would be broken up by its internal dissensions. But there is a far larger party in it than these three theological parties which, created by, and availing itself of, the legal status of the Church, its endowments and its fabrics of worship, is the ballast and bond of union of the whole. This is the party of order, or the Conservatives, or, as hitherto they have been called, the Tories. It is not a religious party ; not that it does not include a large number of religious men in its ranks, but that its principles and watchwords are political, or at least ecclesiastical, rather than theological. Its members are not Tractarians, nor Evangelicals, nor Liberals ; or if they are, they are so in a very mild and inoffensive form ; for in the eyes of the world their chief characteristic is that of being advocates of *an* Establishment and of *the* Establishment ; and they are more eager that there should be a national Church than careful what that national Church professes. . . . They constitute the mass of the Church : especially the clergy throughout the country, bishops, deans, chapters, *curés*, have ever been distinguished by their Toryism. . . . This large body of men, the true representatives of that good sense for which England is, for good and evil, so famous, look, for the most part, with suspicion on all theology and theological practices ; and in particular on the three which have already been described. In the seventeenth century they opposed the Puritans ; at the end of that century they opposed the Latitudinarians ; in the middle of the eighteenth they opposed the Methodists and Evangelicals ; and in our own time they were first strong against the Tractarians, and now against Liberals."

With this admirable map of the Establishment spread out before us it will be easy for us to estimate the extent of the settlement already effected by the Ritualists, and to forecast with some degree of accuracy the future fortunes of the party. At the first glance it is evident that Ritualism is as yet far, very far, from being universal in the Establishment. It is rejected by the Evangelicals; it is rejected by the Latitudinarians; it is rejected by the great Conservative party in the Church. Now, of the three religious parties in the Establishment, Dr. Newman declares the Evangelicals to be at present far the most powerful; the Latitudinarians to be wonderfully rapid in propagating their views among the educated classes; and the Conservatives to look with suspicion on all theology and all theological practices. We have thus almost the entire territory of Anglicanism closed against the Ritualistic movement. We cannot, therefore, bring ourselves to believe that its triumph will be either speedy or easily won. It has to make its way against an opposition of the most formidable character. We believe, however, that the success it has hitherto had promises still greater successes for the future. Men do not fight against shadows; and when we see all parties in the Establishment leagued against the Ritualists we have a convincing proof that the influence of the latter is becoming a real power among the people. And, while the obnoxious doctrines and practices are attacked, it is remarkable that they are described not as if declining towards extinction, but as "spreading with portentous vigour and ubiquity." "If Ritualism be allowed *a locus standi*," says Dr. Blakeney, "it will strive on till it attain ascendency." "The immediate result, wherever Ritualism has been given a fair trial, is, that the proportion of men present in the church is exceptionally large, and that all ranks of society are represented in the congregations, instead of delegates from one, or at most two, sections being found. . . . . But the most remarkable fact is the flocking in of Dissenters, and of the members of the small tradesman class in general, from which the ranks of Dissent have been hitherto recruited." * "What is the result," asks Rev. J. Hunt,† "where they have been introduced? Why, that thousands of the poor, who have lived forty or fifty years without going to the house of God, have flocked to those teachers, and have become intelligent and understanding worshippers." Thus foes and friends alike render testimony that the movement possesses a power which helps to support it against the serious opposition which has started up against it. The reception accorded to the *Eirenicon*, and to-day the keen interest excited by Dr. Pusey's letters on Confession,

---

* *The Church and the World*, Essay IX., p. 242.   † *Discussion*, p. 31.

are fresh evidence that, despite of enormous hostility, the Ritualistic school occupies a very prominent position in the thoughts of the British public.

It is now time to inquire how this movement is likely to effect the conversion of England to the Catholic faith. Are we, as Catholics, to rejoice at seeing the commotion which is taking place in the field of dry bones, as at the beginning of a miraculous resuscitation, or are we to regard it as a fresh instance of that unrest which ever pursues those who, outside the Church, are tossed about by every wind of doctrine? Are they airs from heaven or blasts from hell that are just now stirring so many hearts to their lowest depths?

One result at least of Ritualism we must deplore as an unmixed evil, whatever else of good the movement, as a whole, may effect. In itself an unreal delusion, it helps to keep individual souls apart from the Catholic Church by supplying them with an illusive enjoyment of the religious blessings they have learned to long for, and of which they have found Protestantism completely bare. "Secession,"* writes one who has experienced the full effects of Ritualism, "can only be justified by a conviction that there exist no sacraments or priesthood in the Anglican Church. . . . Had I left the English Church in 1850, and learnt in the Roman the blessedness of the Real Presence, as I have since learnt it at our altars, I should of course have ascribed it to the possession of the reality, instead of the shadow, whereas it only depended on a faith which I have attained with advancing years in my own communion." Now, it is precisely this conviction that there exist no sacraments or priesthood in the Anglican Church, which Ritualism effectively repels. It gathers its followers round an altar at which a counterfeit priest, clothed in sacrificial vestments, offers up with solemn rite the awful sacrifice; its tabernacles are made, in the eyes of its votaries, to glow with what they fondly believe to be the Real Presence; every ornament of grace with which God has adorned his Spouse, the Catholic Church, is copied with almost painful accuracy, until the soul that had begun to yearn after its mother the Church is cheated into the belief that it already reposes upon her breast, while, alas! it is yet in the arms of a stranger. Ritualism realises to the full St. Cyprian's description of the devil's work through heresy: "Those whom he cannot detain in the blindness of the old way he compasses and deceives by misleading them on their new journey. He snatches men from out the Church itself, and while they think themselves come to the light, and escaped from the night of this world, he secretly

* *The Church and the World*, Essay II., p. 40.

gathers fresh shadows upon them; so that standing neither with
the Gospel of Christ, nor with his ordinances, nor with his law,
they yet call themselves Christians, walking among darkness,
and thinking that they have light; while the foe flatters and
misleads, transforms himself, according to the word of the
Apostle, into *an angel of light*, and garbs his ministers like
ministers of righteousness; these are the maintainers of night
for day, of death for salvation, giving despair while they proffer
hope, faithlessness clothed as faith, Antichrist made the means
of Christ, that, by putting false things under the appearance of
true, they may with subtlety impede the truth." *

To our minds nothing can purge Ritualism of this its original
sin, that it tends, too often successfully, to lull the fears of those
just awakened from Protestantism, and to fill them with a
treacherous confidence.

But, though in itself a delusion, and fatal to individuals, the
Ritualistic movement, taken as a whole, is not without some
accidental advantages. In the first place, it is a justification of
the Catholic doctrine touching external ceremonies, and a practical retractation of the views adopted in this matter at the so-
called Reformation. It is the assertion of the principle that
rites and ceremonies are the natural complement of a written
liturgy, and that without them the masses of the people cannot
be held faithful to religion. The Anglican establishment
abolished the stately and elaborate ritual of the Catholic ages,
and the result has been that many millions of the English people
never set their foot within a church. We may mention here
that even in Ireland the necessity of a closer adherence to ritual
observances is beginning to make itself felt among Protestants.
No fragment of Protestantism has been, or is, more decidedly
hostile to Ritualism than that composed of the Protestants who
are settled in Ireland. What is the result? It is notorious
that the Protestant clergy, even those of the highest degree, do
not receive from their flocks that respect, nor enjoy that social
consideration which their position would seem to justify and
even to require. Besides, this Irish Establishment, for the support of which such large sums are iniquitously misspent, has
failed not only to Protestantise the Catholic population of the
country, but, according to recent admissions, even to keep the
few members it originally claimed. A dangerous leakage into
dissent has set in not only among the laity, but even among the
clergy of the Irish Establishment. So serious has been the
defection that to counteract and check it there has been formed
in Dublin during the present year an association entitled the

* St. Cyprian, *De Unitate Ecclesiæ*, Ox. trans., p. 133.

Irish Church Society, the objects of which are: "To combine
Churchmen generally, with a view to defend and maintain unimpaired the doctrine and discipline of the Church of Ireland, as
laid down in the Book of Common Prayer and in the other
authorised formularies of the Church, and to promote loyal
adherence to the spirit and letter of the Prayer-Book." *

Like the English, the Irish Protestant Church decried the
Catholic doctrine on ceremonies, and now its own children

---

* Among the considerations set forth to show the need of such an association
the following are worthy of notice :—

" The spread of dissent and of dissenting principles. Whatever may be the
case as regards the alleged decline, between the years 1834 and 1861, in the
number of Protestant Dissenters in Ireland, there can be little doubt that in
several quarters dissent has, since the latter of those two years, been gaining
ground. The recent erection in the metropolis of several places for dissenting
worship is an indication that here, at least, Dissenters have been increasing in
numbers.* Then there is the propagation in some parts of the country of the
tenets of that sect whose most distinguishing peculiarities appear to be the rejection of an ordained ministry, the admission to preach and minister of any
persons possessed of natural gifts, and professing to be called by the Spirit, and
the lay administration of the sacraments. Again, certain laymen of our own
communion, taking upon themselves the office of preachers, have been going
about inculcating loose views regarding the nature of the Christian ministry, as
well as teaching upon other important points doctrines equally at variance with
those of the church to which they profess to belong. It has been alleged that
in the places where this lay preaching is most common, it has resulted in some
members of our church being led away to join the ,sect alluded to ; just as in
the metropolis too many professed church people have deserted their own
churches for the sake of joining in dissenting worship and listening to the more
exciting spiritual exhortations of self-constituted, and sometimes uneducated,
teachers.

" Even if the particulars above stated were to leave any doubt of the necessity for the formation of such a society as the present, there is ample ground for
such a course in the fact of the lamentably small acquaintance with the contents
of their own prayer-book, and with many of the doctrines and authorised practices of their church, possessed by Churchmen generally in Ireland. Hence the
unhappy ignorance of the distinctive character of the church in relation to dissent, which so often manifests itself, especially in the apparently slight sense
entertained of the evils and unjustifiable nature of schism, and which has led
not only to a habit of regarding the Church's teaching and that of the Protestant sects as being almost identical, and to the not uncommon practice of uniting with Dissenters for religious objects, but even to the open secession to
dissent of some who once were numbered among our clergy.† The formation of
the society at the present moment is, in one other important respect, especially
seasonable. Notwithstanding the spread of dissent above alluded to, there has
been for some time past a perceptible growth of attachment to church principles
within the bosom of the Irish Church. This incipient change in the state of
things both furnishes a reason for the society's appearance at this particular
time, and, for the future, affords its principal ground of hope."

* During the past six or seven years, while not a single additional church has been erected
within the city of Dublin (the new Molyneux Asylum Church being without the boundaries), at
least five places for dissenting worship have been either rebuilt or newly opened. Of these some
are capable of holding 1,000 persons ; the largest of them, Merrion Hall, in fact, accommodating
about 4,000.

† In illustration of these statements it may be mentioned that some clergymen of our church
took part in the " religious exercises" at the opening of Merrion Hall ; and that other of her
ordained ministers, forsaking our communion, have within the present year been acting in this
city as Dissenting ministers.

desert its churches to run after the wild earnestness of the Ana-baptists and of the Plymouth Brethren. Both establishments have sown the wind, and must perforce be satisfied to reap the whirlwind.

As a specimen of the reasoning whereby the Ritualists justify their conduct, we insert the following passage from Mr. Hunt's speech at the discussion quoted above :—

"And now I will explain to you the reasons why we wish to introduce them, and why we consider them to be expedient. The first reason which I give is this: that they are so useful—nay, that they are absolutely necessary for the purpose of public instruction. I have been much engaged in educational pursuits in the course of my life. Now, I appeal to anyone in the room who has had any experience in education, whether demonstration—open demonstra-tion—by the means of black-board and chalk, or some other such appliance, is not absolutely necessary, in order to impress the idea which you wish to con-vey on the mind of the pupil? And so it has been the experience of everyone who has restored Ritual that their congregations have learned more of the nature of that Blessed Sacrifice at the altar in a few celebrations by the use of these adjuncts than they have all their lives long without them.

"I know that in putting this matter before an intellectual meeting like the present I labour under a disadvantage, because the absence of these aids is not so *keenly* felt as it is by less educated people ; but come with me into my little country village, and go into any of the villages in Somersetshire, and examine the people as to their knowledge of the doctrine of the Sacrament, and you will find a sad deficiency. But what is the result where they have been introduced? Why, that thousands of the poor, who have lived for forty or fifty years with-out going to the house of God, have flocked to those teachers, and have become intelligent and understanding worshippers. And if it were for the purpose of instructing the mind alone, I say that all the persecution—the bitter, grievous persecution that we have undergone in establishing Ritual, and which, even yet, may be more visibly exhibited—would be but as dust in the balance com-pared with the advantages which are likely to arise.

"And then, Ritual gives people A TRUE NOTION OF WORSHIP. Ask any ordi-nary Protestant what is the nature of worship? It is 'to go and hear this preacher or that preacher.' The sermon stands first in the minds of the people ; and, whatever his creed, the most eloquent preacher will always get the largest attendance. I don't care whether he be Methodist, Independent, or Baptist, or professed Churchman, the eloquent preacher will always 'draw' a congrega-tion. But people must be taught that there is another part of religion besides the subjective, namely, the objective ; that the first duty of going to church is not to 'get good,' not to instruct our own minds, but to celebrate an august Act of Worship to the Ruler of the skies.

"Again, Ritual is *a mighty help to devotion*."

Again, it may, perhaps, be reckoned among the advantages of Ritualism that it familiarises men's minds with forgotten forms of Catholic worship, and thereby disposes them, however indirectly for a more ready reception of the Catholic religion. We are far from attaching weight to ceremonies that are merely external ; but, as we have already remarked, Ritualism is not all external : its ceremonies are the expression of doctrines For example, in the discussion from which we have so often quoted, the following is the proposition maintained by the Rev. J. Hunt :—

> "That the Eucharistic Vestments, Incense, and at least two lights on the altar at the time of the Holy Sacrifice (commonly called the Mass) can be defended by Scripture, Antiquity, the Law of the Church of England, and the rule of expediency."

So also Dr. Newman declares of the party, that it "at present goes further in the direction of Catholicism than at any former time, or under any former manifestation: so much so that, in the instance of its more advanced adherents, it may be said to differ in nothing from Catholics except in the doctrine of the Pope's supremacy." And again, speaking of the rapid diffusion of the Latitudinarian party, he says that "it would seem as if in the next generation the religious world will be divided between Deists and Catholics." Hence, the progress of Ritualism appears likely to render men's minds more and more disposed to embrace Catholic doctrine.

Finally, we are convinced that, at length, Ritualism will place thousands of men face to face with two great questions, upon the solution of which they shall be led to feel that the security of their position depends. Those questions are, the Supremacy of the Roman Pontiff, and the validity of Anglican orders. The more keenly they have been taught to appreciate the privilege of being children of the Church, the more ardent their love for everything Catholic, the less satisfied shall they become with any theory which leaves their claim to those blessings doubtful. The greater their devotion to the Blessed Sacrament and to the Holy Sacrifice the more jealous shall they become of all doubt upon the validity of the orders of those through whose ministry they receive what they so truly prize. Hence Ritualism must, in the long run, provoke on those two points the examination it now tends to stifle, and from such an examination conscientiously conducted the best and most lasting effects may fairly be expected.

A QUARREL AMONG FREEMASONS.

A YEAR ago the Grand Orient of Brussels convoked delegates from the different Masonic Lodges of Belgium to celebrate, after their fashion, a funeral service in honour of the late King of the Belgians, Leopold the First. That monarch had been in his youth an accepted Mason, but for several years before he became king had ceased to take any part in the workings of the order. The Masonic temple was suitably adorned on occasion of this funeral service, and among the other ornaments was to be seen an inscription, which read thus: " *L'âme, emanée de Dieu, est immortelle.*" The soul, emanating from God, is immortal. This inscription, because it supposes the existence of God and of an immortal soul, gave great scandal to many of the Freemasons, and amongst others to those of Louvain, who, in the following letter addressed to the Grand Master, thus expressed their feelings of displeasure. The letter is dated the 17th day of the first month,* 5866 :—

" DEAR AND ILLUSTRIOUS BROTHER,

" At the funeral ceremony celebrated at the Grand Orient of Belgium in memory of B. Leopold, King of the Belgians, Chev— K— D—, all the brethren might have read the following sentence, which was placed in a conspicuous part of the building :—

' *The soul, emanating from God, is immortal.*'

" Now, whereas freethinking has been admitted as their fundamental principle by the Belgian lodges in 1864 ;
" And whereas the admission of this principle imposes the greatest toleration for the opinions of all Masons ;
" And whereas the Grand Orient, by erecting only the inscription, ' The soul, emanating from God, is immortal,' has formally departed from the respect due to the convictions of the brothers who do not admit spiritualistic doctrines ;
" The Lodge *Constancy*, Orient of Louvain, earnestly protests against the attack made by the Grand Orient on the principles of free judgment and of toleration, which are the bases of Belgian Masonry."

This letter was signed by fifteen members. On receipt of the letter the Grand Committee of the Grand Orient met to deliberate on the matter. The National Grand Master, J. Van Schoor, sent a formal reply to the Louvain Lodge. The reply deals with the form of the complaint and with its matter. He declared to the members of that Lodge

* *Revue Catholique,* Dec. 1866, p. 732.

that, as regards the form of their complaint, "it is evident both from the spirit of obedience which has inspired the Constitution of the Grand Orient of Belgium, and from the text of the rules of that great Masonic body, that the Lodge *Constancy* had overstepped its rights and forgotten its duty by sending in a protest to the Grand Orient, and by adopting the imperious and decretorial tone in which its missive was conceived." He added that the publication of such a protest "constitutes a direct infringement of the obligations contracted on oath by all Masons, and the Grand Orient cannot censure too much, nor stringently enough repress, this neglect of the most solemn of all Masonic duties."

So much for the form of the complaint. As for its matter, the Grand Master first reminds them that already, in 1837, by the first article of the general statutes of the order, "the Orient disengaged the National Masonic body from all dogma, whether religious or philosophical." Next, he reproaches the Louvain Lodge for not having paid attention to the following words addressed by the Grand Orient to all the lodges of his obedience on the 17th day of the 9th month, 5865 :—

"Since our Order is an association of men who know how to exercise their own free will, never forget that it is not our business to establish a body of doctrines in religion or in philosophy to which our brethren should be obliged to conform. Our temples should be but vast centres of light, where, all opinions being freely expressed, the Masons may be enabled to choose the matter of their own convictions. . . . The Grand Orient prescribes no dogma ; in our lodges the Materialist, the Positivist, the Pantheist, can live side by side with the Spiritualist. If the principle of the immortality of the soul appears in the rituals or in the formularies ; if the idea of God is found there under the name of the Great Architect of the Universe, it is because these are the traditions of the Order ; but the Grand Orient has never imposed or proclaimed a dogma on any of these points."

The Louvain Lodge, indignant at this letter, replied :—

"In our opinion, Free-mason means free-thinker. All philosophical doctrines not opposed to morals or public order ought to have liberty in the Order. In Masonry we admit the Atheist, the Spiritualist, the Positivist, and even the Catholic, if you like it. Is not Masonry universal toleration itself, the mother who receives with equal love all the children of the great human family, provided that they practise fraternal faith ?

"Such, too, is the opinion of our brothers the *Philadelphi* of London, in their manifesto of the 5th May last, which we have already communicated to you. They say : 'Hence it is, dear brothers, that we ought all to endeavour to make our respective lodges and the profane world (that is, society) understand that, in order to labour for the general welfare, there is no need to bear the stamp of any sect, of any Church, of any philosophical system, or the belly-band (*sous-ventrière*) of any Government whatsoever.'"

On the 7th of November last this same Lodge of the *Philadelphi* of the Orient of London came to a resolution which deserves to be noticed here in connection with the protest of the Louvain Lodge. Up to that date the official documents and rituals of the Lodge had the inscription, "To the glory of the Great Architect of the Universe." It was resolved, on the occasion referred to, that for the future that inscription should be omitted, and the following substituted in its stead : " In the name of Reason and of Universal Brotherhood." After coming to this decision, they received, with unanimous applause, the following manifesto addressed to them by the Lodge at Liege :—

"We have unanimously and with great satisfaction accepted the proposal of affiliation contained in your fraternal manifesto of 30th August, 1866. We enclose herewith the extract relating to this Masonic alliance. . . . The relations existing between the various Lodges of the world have been hitherto too much confined to narrow limits of fraternal courtesy. Almost always they stopped at exchanges of compliments and promises of friendship. Does Freemasonry require no more ? We think it does.

" Reciprocal affiliations such as you propose to us, by establishing continual communications between the different Lodges, will supply the close bond of union which is now wanting. Our forces, instead of travelling as before at hazard by various routes, will now be concentrated, and become a united force of immense power. The distrust and sluggishness that still keep us in evil will disappear. The ardour of some will arouse the sloth of others; each one of us, knowing that he is supported by his brothers, will show himself more firm, and our onward steps, no longer halting, will become vigorous and energetic.

"All our united strength is not too much to combat the errors which still rule the world, and to enable us to reach the good we propose to attain, namely :

" To withdraw humanity from the yoke of priests ;

" To substitute science instead of faith ;

" To substitute instead of the pompous hopes of heavenly rewards for good done, the austere joys of a satisfied conscience ;

" To banish from the mind the vain idea of a future life, and the fetichism of a Providence which is ready to succour every misery ;

" To put down brute force ;

" To humble the pride of riches and privileges ;

" To transform the charity that degrades the poor into a care for the poor's rights which exalts them ;

" To equalise the intellects of men by means of instruction ; their fortunes, by the due equilibrium of salaries ; their privileges, by laws which respect all alike ;

" To make justice seen and felt, instead of merely promising it to a darkened world.

" Such are our aims, such also are yours. The undertaking is vast, worthy of all our enthusiasm and our ardour, but full of obstacles. You have understood that by a combined onset we shall succeed in removing them ; we thank you, and we are with you."

From these extracts we may gather some important information concerning Freemasonry in the religious point of view.

1. The Masons are everywhere hostile to the religious orders of the Catholic Church, and incessantly declaim against the obedience which is exacted from their professed members. And yet we learn from the Grand Master's letter that every Mason

binds himself by oath to be obedient to his superiors. Now, in the case of the religious orders, the limits of the superior's power are clearly and definitely confined within a certain range, whereas the Mason binds himself to receive with blind obedience the commands laid upon him by an irresponsible and unknown authority on which no check exists.

2. The Freemasons are loud in their denunciations of what they call the slavery of the press as existing in Catholic countries, where a public censorship is established and exercised. And yet, from the Grand Orient's letter, we learn that the publication of their protest by the Lodge *Constancy* was a violation of one of the most solemn and strongest of the Masonic obligations. Thus the Freemasons practise in their own case without any authority what they denounce as wicked when put in practice by the divine authority of the Church.

3. The fundamental principle of Freemasons is, by their own admission, free-thinking.

4. The formula about the Great Architect of the Universe and the immortality of the soul has been now formally declared to be an empty phrase, and as in no way asserting the existence of God or of a spiritual soul. Masonry is therefore in itself atheistic and materialistic.

5. The Masonic body aims at the reconstruction of society. The civilisation it would introduce is anti-Christian; the principles it instils are anti-Christian. By its own avowal, it labours to efface all idea of God, of the soul, of a future life, of Providence, and of a revealed religion. It is endeavouring to introduce an anti-Christian civilisation which is akin to Socialism. It intends to abolish property, to destroy inequalities in rank, to do away with Christian charity towards the poor.

6. It is not correct to say that Freemasonry in England is free from these impious and destructive tendencies; that it is merely a benevolent society, the sole aim of which is mutual help and innocent festivity. The *Philadelphi* of London share the views and join in the labours of the most rapid among the Continental Lodges. And because the famous motto of their society spoke of God, they have cancelled it, and for their gods they have chosen Reason and Fraternity.

7. Is it any wonder, then, that it is forbidden to a Catholic to be a Freemason?

THE RIGHT TO EDUCATE: TO WHOM DOES IT BELONG?

1.—*The question stated.*

EVERY child that is born into this world is born with one great, undeniable, pressing need, that of education both physical and moral. Limiting our view for the present to the need of moral education as distinguished from physical, we are taught by our reason that the Author of man's being must have made certain provision through which that want is to be adequately met. At its birth the child is member of two natural societies, of which one is large and one small: the former being civil society, the latter the society of the family. Each of these societies is governed by its own proper authority, and a question at once arises as to which of these authorities has God confided the right of education. Have the parents the exclusive right of educating their children? Or does that right exclusively belong to the State? Or is it a joint right to be exercised by both in common? And how are the claims of the Church to be adjusted with the established claims of either? Few questions are more momentous than this, since on its solution depends the welfare not only of individuals and in the spiritual order, but of nations and in the civil order itself. We propose in this paper to answer it, and to show what parts in the work of education belong respectively to the parents, to the Church, and to the State.

2.—*Proofs that education is a parental right.*

Several philosophers who do not pretend to be statesmen, and many statesmen who have no claim to be philosophers, have asserted that education, being a public function, is placed under the control of the civil power. Among others, M. Cousin* declares roundly that the State has the right of conferring (or of withholding) permission to teach, since teaching is not one of the domestic natural rights, but a power belonging to the public and to society. We hold, on the contrary, that education is not a function of the State, but an inalienable office of the parents.

* *Debats,* 4th March, 1844.

This is proved, first, from the natural indissolubility of marriage; secondly, from the relations established by nature between parent and child; and, thirdly, from the common consent of writers on morals. And, first, from the fact that nature wishes the marriage bond to be indissoluble. Even the most cynical philosophers have recognised in the marriage contract certain elements of perpetual indissolubility, and have acknowledged with Bentham that the perpetuity of the marriage bond is in accordance with nature, suited to the wants and circumstances of families, and more generally favourable to the individual. Now, what manner of wants are those to meet which marriage should be, even by the admission of such men, naturally indissoluble? Principally the education of the children, which, if the marriage contract were to be broken at caprice, would be rendered altogether impossible, since in such an hypothesis the children would become castaways abandoned at hazard. If, therefore, nature has made marriage indissoluble precisely because otherwise the education of the offspring would be neglected, nature has given to the parents the right of educating that offspring. And not only has it given the right, but it has imposed the duty; and a right which is bound up with a duty is altogether inalienable.

In the next place, see how carefully and beautifully the Divine Author of Nature has provided for the discharge of the parental duty and right of education. The most powerful natural motives combine to make the parent fit to educate, and the child apt to receive education. Paternal love, the most abidingly tender of all the natural affections, the consciousness that the peace and honour of his family and the support of his own hoary age depend upon the training given to his children, are strong impulses to urge a father to discharge faithfully what the law of nature teaches him to be a sacred duty. On the children's part, nature has left them absolutely at the power of their parents, and as in the beginning they are actually incapable of action or thought of their own, so they are taught first by instinct, and later by duty, to render full obedience to their parents, and not only to obey, but to obey with implicit confidence and love. Thus the perfect discharge of the great work of education has been hedged in and secured by the strongest impulses that can sway the human heart, by love, duty, and interest. Now, if the right of educating their children did not belong to the parents, all this exquisite economy, this wonderful adaptation of means to an end, would be aimless and wasted. And hence, finally, moral writers who, even on grounds of natural morality, inculcate on the young the duty of obedience to their teachers, are accustomed to assign as a motive for such obedience that the teacher stands in the place of a parent, and that he is the parent's representative. Education, therefore, remains a domestic function, even where many parents provide, at their own expense and care, a teacher to whose care they confide their little ones.

3.—*The Catholic Church possesses educational rights on two grounds.*

On merely natural grounds, then, we conclude that the education of children belongs of right to the parents. The Church recognises these rights of the parent in their fullest extent, and as guardian of all rights, but more especially of natural ones, she has ever protected parents in the exercise of their legitimate authority. Her principles and practice in this matter are admirably illustrated in the following instance.* In the thirteenth century, when the temporal power and influence of the Popes was at their highest, when the brightest diadems in Europe paled before the glory of the tiara, when Innocent the Third, and Gregory the Seventh, and Boniface the Eighth, ruled the world from the chair of St. Peter, it was proposed by some that the infant children of Mahometans and Jews should be forcibly separated from their parents, baptised and educated as Catholics, to the great increase of the Church and the salvation of souls. This proposal met with a determined opposition from St. Thomas of Aquin, who urged that such was not the usage of the Catholic Church. There had been, he argued, many most powerful Catholic sovereigns, such as Constantine and Theodosius, who had many saintly prelates like Sylvester and Ambrose to advise them, and such men as these would not have neglected to recommend the proposed plan had it been conformable to reason. But it is not conformable to reason. It is even repugnant to natural justice. For nature has made the child a thing belonging to the father, and has decreed that, until it attain to the use of reason, it should remain under the father's care. Hence it would be contrary to natural justice that the child, before he has the use of reason, should be withdrawn from the parents' care, or anything done in his regard against his parents' will. But when he begins to have the use of his free will he begins to be his own, and is able to consult for himself in whatever concerns the divine or natural law, and then he is to be led to the faith, not by violence, but by persuasion.† It is on these parental rights that the Church rests, in great

* Taparelli, *Esame critico*, etc., Part I., p. 399.
† S. Thom. ii. 2, *Quæst.* x., act. xii.

part, her propagation among men by means of infant baptism. The law of nature makes the child, as it were, an instrument, so regulated by the father's intelligence that it thinks with the father's thought and wills with the father's will. Now, a Catholic parent, by the very fact that he professes to be a Catholic, publicly and solemnly acknowledges before his fellow-men his conviction of two cardinal truths. He acknowledges, first, that he feels it to be his consciencious duty to submit to the Catholic Church as to the infallible teacher of truth; he acknowledges, secondly, that to belong to the Catholic Church is the sole means of salvation. By virtue of the first of these principles he acknowledges his obligation to follow the guidance of the Church in whatever things concern the possession of the truth and the preservation of the faith; by virtue of the second he admits his obligation to place within her, as within an ark of salvation, all those whose interests are dear to his heart and who have been confided to his care. Hence, love no less than duty leads him to hand over his infant treasure to that divine society which he calls by the endearing name of his Holy Mother the Catholic Church. And what that Church refuses to do in the case of unwilling infidels she does in the case of Catholic parents; and, gladly accepting the child that is offered to her, she regenerates him with water and the Holy Ghost, and incorporates him with her supernatural society.

Over the education of the Catholic child thus incorporated with her the Church can claim, on two distinct grounds, a right to exercise control. First, because she is the divinely appointed guide to truth, and appointed as such by the parents, whom, therefore, she can direct as to the manner in which they are to educate their children so as to discharge their duty faithfully in the sight of God; secondly, because the child itself has been *legitimately* admitted to the society of the faithful, and has become one of those whom she has to guide to salvation, whom she has to instruct in the truth and to warn against every error.

4.—*Nature and extent of the educational rights of the Church.*

The right of the Church in the matter of education, the charter by which it enjoys those rights, and the extent and limits of the same, are so admirably set forth in two documents issued by ecclesiastical authority in Ireland, that we cannot serve our present purpose better than by reproducing portions of them here. Our first extract shall be from the synodical address of the Fathers of the Council of Thurles :—

"As rulers of the Church of Christ, chief pastors of his flock, rigorously responsible to the Prince of Pastors for every soul committed to our charge, it forms, as is obvious, our first and paramount duty to attend to the pastures in which they feed, the doctrine with which they are nourished. . . . It is, we feel assured, unnecessary to observe to you that, of all modes of propagating error, education is the most subtle and dangerous, furnishing as it does the aliment by which the social body is sustained, which circulates through every vein, and reaches every member ; and that, if this aliment should prove to be corrupt or deleterious, it will not fail to carry moral disease and death to the entire system. Hence the awful obligations we are under, at the peril of our souls, of watching over the education of the people whom God has entrusted to our charge" (pp. 6, 7).

Our second extract shall be from the letter addressed by Cardinal Cullen to the Catholic clergy of the archdiocese of Armagh in 1850 :—

"The right which we enjoy, and the obligation under which we are placed, of attending to the education of youth, are derived from the divine commission by which we exercise our spiritual ministry. This commission, which was given to the Apostles and their successors in the following words, ' Going, therefore, teach ye all nations, baptising them in the name of the Father, and of the Son, and of the Holy Ghost, teaching them to observe all things whatsoever I have commanded you: and behold I am with you all days, even to the consummation of the world' (Matt. xxviii. 19, 20), evidently inculcates the duty of teaching all the dogmas of faith as well as all the principles of morality. Whatever regards the nature, attributes, and moral government of the Deity, as well as whatever concerns the conscience of man in his individual capacity or numerous social relations, all this is directly contained in the divine commission. But the subjects thus indicated must have a direct or indirect connection with the various departments of human knowledge, and the exercise of the divine commission must consequently extend to the supervision and control of every system of education proposed or instituted for the children of the Catholic Church, lest in any particular department of knowledge they should be infected with errors or opinions at variance with their faith ; so that the divine commission given to the Apostles implies a positive duty, imposed exclusively on them, to teach all divine truth, and, if I may say so, a negative duty or right to impede the teaching and to resist the propagation of every error opposed to heavenly revelation.

"This right of inspection and control, whenever there is question of the faithful committed to our charge, belongs pre-eminently, as you are all well aware, to the episcopal body, according to the words of the Apostle, ' Take heed to yourselves and to the whole flock, wherein the Holy Ghost hath placed you bishops, to rule the Church of God, which He hath purchased with his own blood' (Acts, xx.). When the education of the children of one diocese is in question the matter is within the jurisdiction of the Ordinary of that diocese. When many dioceses and provinces are concerned, then the question is not to be decided by any particular bishop, but by all the prelates of these provinces, or, when they disagree, by the supreme authority of the Roman Pontiff. To resign such a right, to shrink from the duty it involves, to suffer the little ones of Jesus Christ to be torn from the maternal bosom of the Church and delivered up to the hands of unprincipled or irresponsible teachers, or to be imbued with erroneous doctrines, would be to prove false to the divine commission we have received, to abandon to the wolf, like the hireling pastor, the flock committed to our trust, and to dishonour the glorious ministry with which we are invested by a treachery as cruel as it would be unprincipled" (pp. 6, 7).

5.—*The civil power, as such, has no right to educate.*

From all we have said we may draw the following conclusions : first, that the right to educate is primarily a parental right, the exercise of which, in case of Catholic parents and Catholic children, has been placed by God under the control of the Catholic Church. Secondly, that the Church, in virtue of her divine commission to teach all nations, has a positive right to teach truth, and a negative one to resist the teaching of error, and that this double right is indefeasible and independent of all earthly power. Thirdly, as a logical consequence of the two former, that the civil power has *not* received the right to educate ; that education is not a civil but a domestic function ; and that, far from interfering with the educational rights of parents, the State is bound to protect them in the peaceful enjoyment of those rights. This truth was fully apprehended by the ancient Romans in the best period of Roman society. " The State presumed not to pass the threshold of the Roman father with any educational code in his hand, though it did, at a later period, attempt to expel that novel system imported from captive Greece, which gradually changed the face of Roman life." *

6.—*But it ought to lend material assistance to those who have the right to educate.*

But although the State has no right to take upon itself the office of educator, it is not therefore debarred from all share in the noble work of instructing the people. It must, however, be content to take the place of an assistant, and not that of a principal agent in this work. It is competent for it to assist the parents by providing them with help to exercise with greater ease and efficacy the charge which God has imposed upon them concerning the education of their children. It is a proof of high social perfection in a country, when the civil power fosters with genial care the growth of sound knowledge, especially such as the peculiar circumstances of time, place, and persons seem to require in the people. Elementary schools for the masses, middle schools for the more adult, and a higher, or even the highest, training for the few who can aspire to profit by it, are precious gifts which the State can bring to aid in the enlightenment of a people. It is one of the natural functions of a government to promote the advancement of learning and to provide its

* Professor Ornsby " On the History of Roman Education," *Atlantis*, vol. iv., p. 2.

citizens with the means of instruction. But since it is certain
that the State can interfere in education only as a helper of those
naturally charged with educating the young, its first duty in a
community of mixed religions is that of rigorous impartiality
with regard to the various churches. Let us suppose that, instead of preserving this impartiality, the State employed all its
educational machinery to Protestantise the Catholic body, or to
Catholicise the Protestant children, or to sap the religious faith
of both, and it will be at once apparent how great is the injustice it would commit. The sole claim it has to interfere in
education is that it may help parents to educate their children
according to their conscientious convictions ; and yet, instead of
helping, it would, in the case supposed, do its best to hinder this
result. Such a course of proceeding can be justified only on
the supposition that to *help* and to *hinder* mean the same thing.
This spirit of impartiality between the various religions of the
community is the animating principle of the Prussian state-
educational system.* Starting from the axiom, that for the
education of youth adequate provision must be made by public
schools, it goes on to declare that in the management of the
public schools the confessional (*i.e.* denominational) relations
must be kept in view as much as possible. This principle of
denominational education is fully carried out in all the details
of the system of public instruction.

*7.— These principles violated by a twofold form of educational
monopoly established by modern Governments.*

A far different spirit, however, has obtained and still obtains
in many countries of Europe. In these the Government, not
satisfied to be merely an assistant in the work of educating the
people, has more or less openly arrogated educational functions
to itself, and has so arrogated them as to concentrate in its own
hands the monopoly of instruction. This educational monopoly
has presented itself under two forms. One form is that of a
direct monopoly where all individuals and corporations other
than those licensed *ad hoc* by the State, are prohibited from dis-
pensing knowledge and from teaching at all. In this form the
State simply displaces all other influences to make room for its
own. The other is that of an indirect monopoly, where the
Government makes it impossible for young men *otherwise qualified* to attain to offices of emolument and influence, or makes it

* See *Letter to Most Rev. Archbishop Cullen on the actual state of Education
in Prussia*. Duffy, 1859.

difficult for them to reach the learned professions without first taking degrees, which can be granted only by favoured institutions of the State. In this form it does not directly displace other educational bodies, but enters upon a rivalry with them which it makes altogether unequal by the display of immensely powerful advantages on its own side. It is plain that this form also has all the defects of a monopoly.

8.—*Three classes of motives which have led Governments to monopolise education.*

Before we pass on to point out the defects of some State systems of education it is worth while to delay for a moment to consider the motives which in modern times have influenced Governments to make the work of instructing the people their own peculiar province.

We shall not be guilty of the injustice of saying that these motives have been in every instance unworthy or interested. There have been statesmen, no doubt, who undertook the work of education from a sincere conviction that thereby they were consulting for the best interests of the people under their care. They were acting, according to their lights, under the influence of the traditions that had come down to them from better times. Love for the poor and zeal for their instruction were the leading features of the old Catholic society, and the long years that have elapsed since the so-called Reformation have not been able to obliterate altogether from men's hearts the blessed traces of these virtues. But their good intentions did not guarantee these estimable men from falling into mistakes of the most serious character.

Apart from these philanthropic views, the springs of the modern systems of education have been either simply statecraft or the teachings of that unhappy spirit of naturalism which is the characteristic feature of the age. Modern Governments are, if possible, still more jealous than were the old-fashioned ones of any influence which could cripple their own liberty of action or interfere with their peculiar views. The gigantic power wielded by whoever has the control of the education of a whole nation was a prize too well calculated to dazzle and fascinate them. They saw that, once possessed of this power, they would be enabled to remove the obstacles that stood in the way of their policy, and to lessen the difficulties of the problem which the governing of a community of mixed religions is sure to present. By its help they would be able to mould according to their fancy the intellects of the rising generation, and thus to secure for their own political views a sure support in no long future.   This was one of the ideas conceived and carried out by the first Napoleon, and it bears the mark of his bold and unscrupulous genius.

But the true parent of false systems of education is the modern spirit of naturalism.   By naturalism we understand that cast of thought or bias of reasoning which leads men to exclude altogether, or at least to restrict within limits as narrow as possible, the influence of supernatural revelation upon the practices and institutions of social life.   This habit of mind does not quarrel with revealed doctrines as such as long as they remain in the regions of abstract speculation.   But as soon as they are proclaimed to be the one immutable standard to which all the details of life, whether of individuals or of societies, are to be made conformable, it takes alarm at once, and in the name of liberty puts forth all its strength to crush what it calls fanaticism and priestcraft.   This is not the place to sketch the origin and growth of naturalism by tracing it back to Protestantism.   Nor is it the place to show how it has led to the secularisation of politics, of science, of political economy, and of the marriage contract, all of which have been gradually divorced from the direct action of religion.   It is enough to point out here that it is to its influence we owe the attempts made almost everywhere to exclude the Catholic Church from the work of education, or at least to admit her to a share in that work only upon terms which, while they degrade her and the Divine Religion of which she is the teacher, practically serve to counteract the slender influence she is in theory allowed to exercise in the schools.   It is, we are convinced, impossible to appreciate correctly the mixed system of education without taking into account the parallel process of secularisation which to-day is taking place in so many other matters.   Let anyone take up the Syllabus of 8th December, 1864, and examine the nature of the principal errors of the age as therein described.   He will find underlying each of the ten heads to which these errors are reduced one fundamental, all-pervading principle, viz., that all supernatural action of God and of God's Church is to be banished from the world of thought and of action.   The secularisation of education is not, therefore, to be judged alone.   It is but part of the bitter produce of a poisonous tree ; and no matter how fair it may be made to appear when some cunning hand offers it for the acceptance of an unwary people, it is enough to look at the stalk whence it issued, and at the deadly fruits that cluster by its side, to be quickly convinced that it is a gift fatal to whosoever will use it.   The bad tree will, perforce, produce evil fruits.

9.—*Government system of education for Ireland is an unjust monopoly.*

But whatever may be the motives that have led Governments to monopolise education, directly or indirectly, whether they are moved thereto by philanthropy, or by statecraft, or by naturalism, one thing at least is certain, that all such monopoly is unjust, because it is based on the unjust usurpation of parental and ecclesiastical rights. This deadly sin of its origin taints with poison the entire system of State education.

We now proceed to consider somewhat more fully the form of State education with which in our day and country we have to deal. Besides the radical injustice above described on which it is based, the system of education imposed by the State upon Ireland has two capital defects, in that it is a monopoly, and in that it is mixed.

That it is a monopoly, especially as far as university education is concerned,* has been well shown in an able paper by Monsignore Woodlock, Rector of the Catholic University in Ireland. Of the two universities recognised by law in this country, Trinity College is undeniably and exclusively Protestant. "As a matter of fact, its governing body, consisting of the provost and senior fellows, are *all* members of the Church as by law established, and, with two exceptions, are Protestant clergymen. The other fellows and the scholars on the foundation are likewise Protestants ; and thus in a city where, of a population of 254,000, only 58,000 are Protestants (of all denominations), and in a country in which only 11.8 per cent. of the inhabitants are members of the Established Church. . . . . What wonder that Catholics should consider it a hardship to be forced, if they wish to get university education near home, to seek it in an institution from whose dignities and management they are excluded, in which an antagonistic creed is always put forward ostentatiously in a position of superiority, while the faith of their fathers, if it be not contemned and scoffed at, is systematically treated with silent indifference, or with supercilious patronage ? What wonder that Catholics being declared by Act of Parliament 'freemen,' in every way equal to their Protestant fellow-countrymen, should be unwilling to continue begging as a favour, at the gates of such an institution, for the academical honours and distinctions to which they are entitled as a right ? It is absurd that in the metropolis of a free

* "University Education in Ireland," *Irish Ecclesiastical Record*, vol. i., pp. 24-26.

country, containing inhabitants of various religions, a handful of clergymen of one denomination should pretend to a monopoly of university education—should hold in their hands the keys of knowledge, doling it out as they please, and obliging even those whose faith they denounce as idolatry and superstition, to send their sons to their schools ? Would such a system be allowed in any other country ? Would a few Catholic priests be allowed, even for one hour, to monopolise the university education of Protestant England ?''

So glaringly intolerable was this monopoly that the Queen's University was established to remedy the evil. But here again the Government chose to proceed on the false principle that education is a proper function of the State. The entire scheme of the Queen's Colleges was based on the exclusion of the Catholic Church, and concentrated to an unprecedented degree in the hands of the civil ruler the influences that were to educate this Catholic nation. The system was condemned by the highest authority on earth, and in consequence, as far as Catholics are concerned, the monopoly of university education is as rigid and comprehensive as ever. " We have," says the Rector, " a total of 6,360 Catholic youths receiving a superior education in Ireland. Few, if any, of the Catholic institutions to which these pupils belong look with favour on the existing universities. On the other hand, none of these youths ought to be excluded from university education on account of conscientious objections; and yet by far the greater number are practically excluded at present."

This would be enough to prove that the system is a monopoly. But there is still more. Although the penal laws that inflicted forfeiture of all property on whosoever was educated at a Catholic school have been erased from the statute-book, there yet remain penalties to be incurred by those who, for motives of conscience, cannot avail themselves of the advantages offered by Trinity College and by the Queen's Colleges. Such persons suffer for conscience' sake these disabilities : they are delayed in their course to a profession one or two years longer than the graduates of the favoured institutions, they are obliged to attend additional lectures and to pay extra fees, irrespectively of their proficiency in literature and science, or in law. Besides which the wide stream of Government patronage flows through the universities. It cannot, therefore, be denied that the system protected by such penalties as those is other than a monopoly.

10.—Educational monopoly dangerous to the State.

This monopoly is full of danger to the State itself, and full

of evil consequences to the people who are made to suffer it.
We here consider it especially as it is developed in the colleges
where the Government appoints the professors, determines either
immediately or mediately the curriculum of studies, at pleasure
omitting this branch and extending that, and even stooping to
such minute details as to designate the authors whose works it
would gladly see in the students' hands. By its means the
Government gathers together a band of professors, men of ability
and learning and energy, and to their hands it seeks to commit
the youthful intellects of the nation. What security has the
Government that the power which it has erected and set in
motion may not be turned against itself ? No doubt, in the
beginning things may go right : the educational machine will
obey for a time every touch of the master's hand ; but what is
there to hinder revolutionary principles from being introduced
by degrees into the teaching of the professors, who have full
control over the minds of the pupils ? What is to prevent a
State university from becoming the mother of the wildest and
most insane anarchical doctrines ? Is the philosophy of the day
so sound that in the hands of an unscrupulous professor it may
not readily be used as a weapon to slay the faith of his scholars
even in the existence of God, which faith is the basis of all
moral law and moral order ? Are the social theories now in
vogue so free from the revolutionary taint that it would be idle
to fear the spread of insubordination to authority ? Is there no
danger that statesmen may lack either the time, or the vigilance,
or the ability to detect these evils on their first appearance ? or
that they may not find it possible to check their growth when
once they begin to develop themselves ?

We have had in our own times a striking proof of this danger
born of university monopoly. From 1830 to 1848 the university monopoly was in full force in France. No career was open
to him who was not possessed of a degree, and no degree was
to be procured save in the condition of having made the course
of rhetoric and of philosophy in a State college. For eighteen
years the flower of the French youth was delivered up, bound
hand and foot, to the teaching of the university professors; and
the men who now write and teach and govern in France were
formed in the mould and saturated with the philosophy then
taught in the halls of the State colleges. The late M. Cousin
during all that time was the master mind that ruled and domi-
neered the university, and through the university all the schools
in France, except a few humble Catholic establishments. He
forced his eclecticism upon the minds of the youth ; he compelled them to think as he thought, and to speak as he spoke,
because otherwise they could never proceed to their degree.

What has been the result ?   Let Mgr. Dupanloup's late work,
l'Athéisme et le Péril Social, tell us what it has been.   First, a
widespread atheism, not merely speculative, but carried out in
practice to the subversion of all morality, of all order : an
atheism which has put on new and horrid shapes that never
before had been seen on the earth ; an atheism which, as the
illustrious Bishop of Orleans has shown on the authority of its
own professors, is the consort of socialism, and aims at the overthrow of society.   If France is to-day restless and uneasy as
those are who live over a slumbering volcano, if each morrow
may bring to pass the most startling changes in her social state,
if her Government is in daily fear lest the reins be plucked from
its hands, it is due, beyond all doubt, to the university monopoly
which has moulded the present generation.

Again, the monopoly of education will be a perpetual source
of irritation against the Government.   Many persons who are
placed high enough to disregard the advantages offered by the
State system will save their children from the pernicious effects
of that system by sending them abroad for their education.
Many others not so fortunate will surrender their children, but
with fear and trembling, with uneasy conscience, and, if the
truth be told, with irritation against the power which demands
from them a sacrifice which costs them so dearly.   But the vast
majority of Catholic parents, who prize their own rights and
appreciate their own responsibility as parents, who listen .to the
voice of the Church and love the souls of their children, will
never, never rest under the disabilities which they are made to
suffer for being faithful to their conscience and their duty.
And, above all, the whole influence of the Catholic Church will
be arrayed against the State education.   She never can, and
never will, submit to a tyranny which would rob her children of
their faith, and herself of her children.   The civil power may
afflict her, and persecute her, and fetter her, but it can never
subdue her.   As long as this unjust thing remains, so long will
she use every lawful means in her power against it.   Is it wise,
is it prudent for a Government wantonly and gratuitously to
provoke a contest which experience tells will never end as long
as there is a bishop left in the Church—a contest in which the
best friends of religion, and subordination, and conscience, and
morality will infallibly be arrayed against it ?   To provoke such
a contest is to court sooner or later a defeat.   To come off victorious for a while over the Church is one of those successes
which are even more hurtful than defeats ; for it is a victory
won over that power which alone can make men obedient to
their rulers for conscience' sake.   And when men have once unlearned the duty of conscientious obedience to authority the

framework of society can be kept together only by the iron hands of brute force.

Nor is this monopoly less dangerous for the people. For it is an attempt against their liberties far more aggressive and threatening than a standing army. It is an attempt to take prisoner the national intellect, and to mould it at will upon doctrines prepared and calculated to procure support for the political views of the captors. Under the pretext of freeing education from the bars and bonds placed on it by the Church, and in the name of intellectual liberty, modern progress would make slaves even of the very souls of the young. No doctrines shall be taught save those pleasing to the civil Government; as in the case of the National School books in Ireland, the very name of their country must never be allowed to fall under the scholar's eye; to them the glorious memories of the past must never be mentioned; for them the saints and sages, the priests and kings of their fathers, the heroic morals of every supernatural and natural virtue that can make a people blessed and noble, must disappear from the pages of history. What slavery can be more degrading than this ? what chains more galling ? and what can be more unjust ? Justice demands that the burdens imposed on a people should bear a proportion to the advantages to be derived by them in return. And yet, when a Government monopolises education, it compels the citizen to contribute to support a system which is directly calculated to enslave him, and to teach doctrines subversive of all he holds dear in religion. So that, besides paying his quota towards the support of a system which is hostile to his faith and principles, he is compelled to incur fresh expense to provide for his children an education conformable to his conscience and his feelings. By the common verdict of mankind, the Irish Church Establishment is a monstrous injustice, because the Irish Catholic is compelled to support the minister of a religion which his conscience condemns, and in addition feels bound to contribute towards the maintenance of the clergy of his own Church. And, if this be an injustice, can it be just to insist that a people should pay for an education which their conscience condemns, and at the same time expend their means in providing for their children such instruction as they can approve of ?

11.—*History of the theory of mixed Education.*

The plan which would separate secular instruction from religious training is completely foreign to the idea of education as conceivable by the Catholic Church at all periods of her history. What education ought to be, according to the Catholic idea, shall best be learned by an examination of the Church's teaching on the subject; and of this teaching we shall give samples from the early, middle, and later periods of her history.

It was the teaching of the early Church which guided the studies of St. Gregory and St. Basil under circumstances of peculiar difficulty. The method followed by these two great saints admirably illustrates the two leading features of the Catholic idea of education, namely, love of liberal learning in its widest breadth, engrafted upon love of religion. They devoted themselves with enthusiasm to the study of the entire circle of the sciences as known in their day. "In the whole of grammar," says the biographer of St. Gregory, "nothing escaped them, not the knowledge of metres, nor the flights and figures of poetry, nor history's store, nor the accurate strictness of legal pleading. They devoted themselves to rhetoric in such manner as to cull out and collect all that it had elegant in language, while they shunned its insincerity and proneness to lie. In philosophy, both moral and speculative, not satisfied with such proficiency as might raise them far above the unlearned, they mastered it in such fulness as became teachers and doctors of highest degree. In the study of music they aimed at making their own whatever of ancient grace they could find in it, whereby they might restrain the passion of anger, and soften rude and violent feelings; but whatever in it tended to voluptuousness they banished to the theatres. They learned likewise numerical computation and geometry, and, like new Moseses and Daniels, the place and movements of the constellations; but in such wise as not to be so much led by them as to lead, according to Holy Writ, every intellect into captivity in obedience to Christ; for this they held to be the highest wisdom's beauty and safeguard." *

The canons of the synod of Mar-Timotheus, and the collection of Syriac canons published by Cardinal Mai,† afford a clear insight into the practice of the Eastern Churches; and although the synod belongs to the thirteenth century, the canons declare the earliest Christian traditions of the East. Among what the synod styles the " canons of the apostles and of the ancients established in the synods of the West and of the East, and which are to be guarded as the apple of their eye by all rulers of churches," we find the following injunction : " Besides, let them (the bishops) lay upon the faithful the charge of our Lord's

---

* Vit. S. Greg. Nazian., Opp., t. I.   Paris, 1842, p. 131 seq.
† Mai, *Scriptt. vett.*, tom. x.

word, that they hand over their children to be educated in the fear of God, which is the foundation of Christianity, and let them recall to their minds the advice of the heavenly apostle, ' Fathers, provoke not your children to anger, but educate them in the discipline and learning of our Lord.' Let them (the bishops) know likewise that every church in which there are no pupils is like a barren woman who hath no children, and that, according as learning is increased, so is faith strengthened and enriched, and wherever ignorance prevails, there the fear of God is lessened and Christianity is weakened. Let us, therefore, honour the doctrine of our Lord more than our own life; and whosoever shall have neglected these things shall be Christ's enemy, and castaway from Holy Church." And the canon law of the Syrians* prescribes as follows : " Let every bishop first appoint a master where there is none, and let him make a list of the children who are fit to receive education, and let him command their parents to lead them to school even against their will. But if they be orphans or poor let the Church support them. And if the Church be poor let the Church procurator make every Sunday a collection from the faithful towards their support. And let the master's salary be paid in part by the Church and in part by the children's parents."

So far for the early and middle periods of Church history. It would be a superfluous labour to accumulate similar authorities of recent date. But we cannot refrain from inserting in this place an extract from the constitution in which Leo the Twelfth, 28th August, 1824, regulated the system of education in the States of the Church :

"Having before our eyes the lessons which Divine Wisdom teaches to all, and sets forth to those walking in the way of salvation in these words: 'My mouth shall meditate truth, and my lips shall hate wickedness,' we acknowledge it to be part of our apostolic office to employ every diligence to the end that the teachers not only of sacred learning, but of the human sciences and of the liberal arts, and also the educators of youth, shall steadfastly held and fulfil the same, and earnestly labour to impress them on the minds of their scholars. For upon this depends as well the progress of religion as the welfare of the commonwealth. . . . Sixtus the Fifth learnedly and prudently observes that the knowledge of letters, the liberal education and training of youth in public schools, if united with piety, confer great benefits upon the Christian commonwealth, for cities and kingdoms are then excellently administered when men of wisdom and intelligence hold the reins." And after quoting, as

* Mai, l. cit.

proof that science should be based on religion, the saying of St. Augustine in his epistle to Volusianus, "what disputes, what productions of any philosophers, what laws of any states can be at all compared to the two precepts on which Christ declares the whole law and the prophets to depend : Thou shalt love the Lord thy God with thy whole heart, and with thy whole soul, and with thy whole mind, and thou shalt love thy neighbour as thyself ?" the Pontiff goes on to show that this close union with religion, far from being hurtful to the sciences, is contrariwise an advantage to their real progress. "In truth," says he, "that most brilliant light of the Church (Augustine) does not mean to banish from the schools the natural sciences, nor is he opposed to the exercises of the liberal arts, which he himself possessed in singular fulness ; but he rightly wished to admonish both masters and scholars, that all these branches of learning, if they be good and in accordance with reason and religion, derive their origin from God, and to God, the fountain and end of wisdom, are to be referred. And he teaches, moreover, that we ought to despise the very obstinate contradictions of certain pseudo-philosophers, and of men following the prudence of the flesh, who think, or would have others think, that the doctrine of Christ does not conduce to the advantage of the commonwealth, because they wish the commonwealth to stand not so much by the firmness of virtue as by the impunity of vice."

From these documents it is easy to form a clear notion of the idea that has ever prevailed of education in the Catholic Church. The pastors of the Church look upon the work of educating the young as a sacred duty incumbent upon themselves as guardians of the faith, and to which they are bound to devote their personal attention. They are foes to ignorance, which they believe to be hostile to the best interests of religion. Specially commissioned as they have been to teach revealed truth to men, they have also extended their fostering care over the natural truths that form at once the preamble to faith and the noblest inheritance of the human family. Nor is their care of the natural sciences narrow or partial ; there is not a single branch of the encyclopædia of human learning which they would forbid or mutilate. The universities created by the Church aptly express the breadth and largeness of the Catholic idea of education, in their very name of *Studium Generale*, or home of universal learning.

But, in the mind of the Church, this lusty vigour of intellectual life, the growth of which she loves to contemplate, has need of being wisely trained, lest, in the very wantonness of its youthful strength, it inflict damage upon itself, and thereby injure that high supernatural life to which it has been called, and of which the vivifying principle is Christian faith. And yet, when the Church speaks of controlling this vigour of intellect, the only controlling force she would employ is the influence of Truth. As truth cannot clash with truth, and as God has placed on earth an infallible teacher of the truths that are revealed, the Church requires that reason, which is fallible, should not follow after doctrines which contradict infallible truth. Hence, if we may borrow an expression used by Julian the Apostate, she baptises in Christianity the ear and the tongue of those who teach and of those who are taught. The Catholic idea of education thus weds together in happiest union Faith and Science, and what God has joined through her she forbids anyone to put asunder.

This happy union of religion and science continued to bless Europe and the world until the so-called Reformation sought rudely to destroy it. It has long been one of the commonplaces of the anti-Christian press to inculcate on the public mind that while the Catholic Church has ever been the foe of science, and a perpetual obstacle to its expansion, Protestantism has emancipated human reason, and restored to it that freedom which is its birthright. We have seen how false this theory is, in as far as it describes the relations between Catholicism and science ; we shall now see that it is just as false in the statements it makes to the credit of Protestantism.

We would in this matter make a distinction between primitive Protestantism and Protestantism in its later developments. Both stages have this in common, that they separated science from religion. But they differ from one another in this, that primitive Protestantism sacrificed science to the supposed interests of religion, and Protestantism of later years sacrificed religion to the supposed interests of science. It would be hard to decide which of these errors has proved the more fatal to society. Far from having restored to the human intellect its legitimate empire, Protestantism has inflicted upon it the most serious injury, and would have succeeded in ruining it irreparably but for the incessant labours of the Church in counteracting its pernicious influence.

The influence exerted by early Protestantism upon learning has been twofold,* by reason, namely, of its positive and of its negative teaching. According to its positive teaching,† human reason, if not completely extinguished, exists only in a most degraded condition. Luther held that " fallen man no longer possesses even the mere natural faculty to understand God and

---

* Laforet, *Pourquoi l'on ne croit pas.* 2nd edition, pp. 85-108.
† Moehler, *Symbol.*, vol i., cap. 2, sec. vii., p. 80, Robertson's trans.

his holy will, and, in conformity to that knowledge, to direct his own will. In one word, the faculty of knowledge and will, inasmuch as it has reference to divine things, or (if we prefer the expression) the rational aptitude, is denied to the mere natural man—the man as born of Adam." And in the *Solida Declaratio*, drawn up in 1517, which is conceived in the spirit of Luther's original doctrines,* we read: "In other external things, and in the things of this world which are subject to reason, some portion of intellect, powers and faculties, is still left to man, although it is but a miserable remnant, and even this, little as it is, has been so infected and contaminated by the hereditary disease that God abominates it." Hence proceeds Luther's savage violence against human reason and philosophy, and the time-honoured seats of learning where both were held in honour. We select a few passages among the many collected from his writings by Dr. Döllinger :†

"But if the Christian revelation evidently rejects flesh and blood, that is to say, *human reason*, and all that proceeds from man, . . . it clearly follows that all this cannot be other than lies and darkness. And yet the high schools, those schools of the devil, are for ever parading their *natural lights*, and boasting of them as if they were not only useful, but even indispensable for the setting forth of Christian truth; from all which it is now perfectly proved that *these schools are an invention of the devil*, destined to obscure Christianity, if not to overthrow it completely, as they are really about to do." Again, he declared that the four soldiers who crucified our Saviour were but the symbolical representatives of the universities with their four faculties. In his explanation of the Epistle to the Galatians he teaches that faith ought to trample reason under foot, or, as he expresses it, ought to *strangle the beast*. And in his last sermon at Wittemberg he says: "Reason is the spouse of the devil, a prostitute, . . . who should be trampled under foot, herself and her wisdom." And Clichtovaeus (*de Miss. Sacrif.*, c. 29) tells us that he called Christian schools Sodoms and Gomorrahs and sinks of all wickedness. Nor was he alone, nor the first among the Reformers to utter these sentiments. Already Pope Martin the Fifth had condemned the following proposition, which was defended by John Wickliff: "Universities, places of study, colleges, degrees and masterships in the same, have been introduced by vain paganism; they are of as much service to the Church as the devil is." (Art. xxix.)

This teaching soon produced its natural results. In many

De Peccat. Orig., sec. x., p. 614.
† *La Reforme, son developpement interieur*, etc., tom. i., p. 450.

places where the Reformation succeeded in securing a hold schools and academies were suppressed. "At Wittemberg," says Dr. Döllinger,[*] "the preachers, George Mohr and Gabriel Didymus, both zealous Lutherans, proclaimed from the pulpit that the study of the sciences was not only useless, but even pernicious, and that one could not do better than destroy academies and schools. The result of this preaching was that the Wittemberg schoolhouse was changed into a baker's shop. The same took place in the whole of the duchy of Anspach." Protestant magistrates, alarmed at the abandonment and the ruin of the schools, addressed a petition to the Margrave of Brandenburg, in which they say, "should this state of things continue we are likely to fall into such a state of barbarism, that in a short time nothing will be more difficult than to find a good preacher and an able lawyer." [†]

Nor were the results of the Reformation in Denmark, Norway, and Sweden less fatal to the interests of learning. In 1594, the senate of Copenhagen addressed a circular to the bishops of the realm to recommend measures to guard against the ruin of studies, "which, it could not be denied, was imminent." "There were no longer schools in the villages," says Dr. Döllinger, "and even in the towns the lower as well as the higher schools were, throughout the whole of the sixteenth century, in a state of complete decay." In Sweden the same decadence of learning followed the introduction of the reformed religion. This is shown by two letters of Gustavus Wasa, addressed, in 1533 and 1540, to his subjects in Upsal, Westeras, and the provinces of Upland and Sudermania : " We ourselves are convinced, and we wish to make known to you, that the schools throughout the towns of our kingdom are in a deplorable state of decay, to such a degree that where there were formerly three hundred students there are now hardly fifty. And in a great many parishes the schools are completely deserted, from which very great injury must undoubtedly accrue to this kingdom. Now this state of things has come to pass chiefly because you, good people, neglect to instruct your children as you formerly used to do, and because you no longer wish to assist poor scholars as you ought to do, and as your fathers and ancestors have done. And besides, we no longer have any but a very small number of subjects who devote themselves to study, and even those who would wish to do so are soon compelled to renounce their intentions through want of means and of support from you." [‡]

In the letters of Erasmus we have additional proofs of the hostility of early Protestantism to letters. "When you profess,

* Loc. cit., p. 400.   † *Ibid.*, p. 401.   ‡ Döllinger, p. 664.

as Luther does, that the philosophy of Aristotle, that is to say, the entire philosophical system founded on Aristotle's principles, is nothing else than the work of Satan; when, like Luther, you look upon all speculative science in general as an error and a sin; when, like Farell, you openly and on all occasions treat every kind of human knowledge as a conception of hell and the devil, how can you expect that such principles can produce aught but contempt for study, and the predominance of greedy and sensual passions? Has it not been publicly taught at Strasbourg and elsewhere that it was contrary to the spirit of the Gospel to misspend time either in studying the ancient languages, except the Hebrew, or in mastering any other branch of human learning?" *

Is it not plain from all this that the positive teaching of Protestantism has been fatal to letters? And was not Erasmus perfectly correct in his pithy estimate of the influence of the Reformation upon literature when he said, " *Ubicunque regnat Lutheranismus, ibi litterarum est interitus?*"

The negative teaching of Protestantism consisted chiefly in the denial of all authority in the matter of religion. Everyone has the right to judge for himself, with the Bible for his sole guide, his judgment being completely unfettered by any external authority. This principle pointed straight towards rationalism from the very beginning, and its tendencies were still further developed owing to the weakening of religious feeling which the Reformation had produced throughout Europe. The leaders of the infidel party soon concentrated their influence on the schools of Europe, having correctly judged that by seizing upon the education of the young they could mould the rising generation to their own views. They deliberately aimed at taking into their own hands the entire system of education, from the complete training of the royal prince down to the first rudiments taught to the village child. Voltaire tells us that by means of a conspiracy of philosophers the Prince of Parma was entrusted to the care of Condillac and Leire. The same philosophers succeeded in preventing any bishop from being appointed to educate the Dauphin; and they induced Catherine the Second of Russia to invite D'Alembert to St. Petersburgh to form the mind of the Imperial Prince.† This spirit has maintained itself with unabated energy till the present day. Scepticism and indifferentism have made, and are daily making, incessant struggles to exclude religion from education. We shall take one example from Germany, where Protestantism has reached its full development.

* *Epist. ad fratres Germaniæ Infer.*, p. 4 ; Colon. 1561.
† Barruel, *Memoires pour servir.*, vol. i., chap. 9.

In the National Assembly at Frankfort, in 1848, the question of education was fully discussed by the deputies. "Chase dogmatism from the school," said M. Pauer (of Neisse), who was chairman of the committee on education; "we require a generation which shall not have felt the influence of the Church, nor yet that of the State. . . . Away with the pretensions of the schools to direct the child; let them allow it to go whither it is led by the breath of life it feels moving within its soul! . . . The school ought not to train the child for any determined end. . . . If the school be subjected to any spiritual authority it cannot attain its object, which is purely human. . . . Hence it is that we must protect the young both against the influence of the Church and against any influence whatsoever of an opinion imposed by the State. . . . The clergyman carries about with him, in his dress, in his looks, in his countenance, a character of restraint which proves him to be unfit for the task of guiding the young to the goal of unrestrained development. . . . What is a teacher? Above all else he is the representative of a feeling emancipated from all control."

On the same occasion, M. Nauwerck, deputy from Berlin, said: "The State alone should make itself master of the whole school: were it to neglect this it would betray its most sacred interests. Were the school to become the domain of the Church, then, gentlemen, we may as well pass a decree to the effect that the sun moves, and that the earth is stationary. For to that we shall be brought at last."

The resolution, in defence of which these speeches were made, was carried by a majority of 316 to 74; and we are thereby enabled to see the separatist doctrines in full practice. M. Eugene Rendu* gives a numerous list of schools regulated according to the new theories. The following is a specimen of the songs which the children are taught to sing in these schools:—

"The Old and the New Church."

"There is a house here below, which is called the house of God. Its domes glitter from afar, and tower above the plains.

"And in that house there lives a dark-robed priest. This priest whispers prayers, and sings at times for the last fifteen hundred years. And when the faithful assemble the priest preaches to them the word which God hath entrusted to him.

"Blessed are they whose life the devil cometh not to tor-

---

* See his interesting work, *De l'Education Populaire dans l'Allemagne du Nord.* Paris: Hachette, 1855.

ment. For he goeth about seeking the *why* and the *how* of everything.

" Blessed is he who hungers and who suffers persecution : he shall one day be filled with the sweet bread of heaven.

" Long did we listen in silence to the priest. But at length we draw our breath ! Blessed be the free light of God.

" The world has been freed from the Church ! In the song of the nightingales, in the starry host, in the infant's smile ;

" In the beauty revealed by the painter's skill, in the heart's dreams of a brighter future, in all these do we feel the spirit of God.

"And each man is the priest of his own religion, the religion of love and of humanity. Adieu to the formulas of decrepit Christianity."

" The hour is come at last," says Carl Grün, " when we may make our own of the result of the philosophy of history ; that result is the enjoyment of this world and the *organisation of the five senses."* This was said of the godless universities : after what we have seen, may we not say the same of the godless village school ?

From this sketch of the history of the principle of mixed education we are fully warranted in concluding, first, that the separation of religion from intellectual training is contrary to Catholic tradition ; and, secondly, that it was first introduced by Protestant fanaticism, and afterwards, though in a different way, maintained by Protestant scepticism ; thirdly, that whereas the Catholic idea of education was most favourable to the interests of learning, the Protestant system has ever tended to depreciate and injure them.

12. *Intrinsic defects of the mixed system.*

To complete our investigation concerning educational rights it only remains for us to consider the intrinsic defects of the mixed system of education. By way of preface, we repeat here that the fundamental principle of the system is that the education it gives shall be *unconnected with Catholic faith and the power of the Church,* and deal with *the knowledge of merely natural things, and only, or at least primarily, the ends of earthly social life.** In face of conflicting religious opinions, it is to incline neither to the right nor to the left, but to pursue with scientific calmness the even tenor of its way, having neither praise nor blame for religious teachings of whatever character they may be. It leaves to its scholars the whole right and duty of choosing

* Syllabus, p. 48.

what they are to believe; and pledges itself that, whatever be the colour of their faith, it shall never be questioned or outraged within the academic halls. It is part of its charter that it shall not teach religion; but it is equally part of the same charter that it shall not interfere with the religious teaching its scholars shall have received from other sources.

This being the case, it is plain that the mixed system con- tradicts its own fundamental principle. By virtue of that prin- ciple it declares that its teaching will not assail any one Catholic truth; and yet the very fact of its existence is a standing denial of one of the most important doctrines the Catholic Church has set forth, namely, that education should ever be united with religion. The Catholic Church has distinctly condemned the doctrine that "Catholics may approve of a system of educating youth unconnected with Catholic faith and the power of the Church, and which regards the knowledge of merely natural things, and only, or at least primarily, the ends of earthly social life."* The mixed system asserts both virtually and explicitly the proposition which the Church thus condemns, and, not satis- fied with mere assertion, recommends it to Catholics with all the weight of its influence. It cannot, then, honestly recommend itself to a Catholic nation, *precisely because* it does not interfere with the Catholic religion.

Next, such a system tends by degrees to banish from society the spirit of Christianity.† In treating of the encyclopædia of human knowledge, the mixed system must follow one of two courses : either it must ignore Christianity altogether, or, taking cognisance of the Christian dispensation as a fact, it must ignore all distinction between its various forms, declining to notice the differences which divide the Christian body. The first of these two methods is the straight road to paganism, and it requires no elaborate proof to show that a system which deliberately ignores Christianity must tend to banish from society the Chris- tian spirit. But although, logically speaking, the mixed system does ignore Christianity (for even Jews and Socinians may be among the pupils), it does not profess to be other than Chris- tian. Rather, it professes to ignore the differences which have separated Christians from the Catholic Church, and have split them, when thus separated, into numerous sects. Its professors

---

* Syllabus, p. 48.

† "Hoc enim modo humana societas vero illo Christiano spiritu sensim pri- vatur, qui unus potest et publici ordinis, tranquillitatisque fundamenta stabi- liter servare, ac verum utilemque civilitatis progressum efficere ac moderari, et ea omnia homnibus præbere subsidia, quæ ad ultimum suum post mortales hujusce vitæ statutem finem assequendum, scilicet ad eternam salutem obtinen- dam sunt necessaria."—Pius IX., *Quum non sine maxima*, 14 July, 1864.

say to their Catholic scholars : we will not assail Catholic truth, and you, for your part, shall not say a word against what you believe to be erroneous ; you are not to refute any of our errors, nor are you to defend any of the truths we have rejected. This method leads straight to indifferentism, and weakens faith. Through it the truth, which is one, is degraded to the level of error, which is various and many-sided. To accord the same privileges to the honest man and to the thief would be to destroy the public sense of probity in the community. To place before the young vice on an equality with virtue would be to blunt their moral sense, and beat down the barriers that restrain their waywardness. And, must it not lead to indifferentism to place before the young truth and falsehood on the same level ? To tell them there is a religion which is true, and yet that it does not affect the great questions that occupy the mind of man any more than if it were false like the other religions from which it is distinguished ? that, as far as their own intellects are con-cerned, they need not be influenced by their religious belief in any appreciable degree ? Nothing but the most cynical in-differentism can result from such even-handed dealing between truth and error. The Catholic student will thus be taught that error has rights as strong as those of the truth, and that the doctrines of the Church are but one set of opinions among many others equally deserving of consideration. He will see the Catholic professor occupy the pulpit which has just been vacated by the Protestant or by the infidel, and all the sharp lines that distinguish truth from error will gradually be effaced. This will be the result in the hypothesis that, in reality, no bias shall be shown either as in favour of or as against any one religion.

But, we are of opinion that this impartiality, however attrac-tive in the abstract, will be found to be impossible in the con-crete. History, jurisprudence, philosophy, cannot be omitted from a course of studies ; and if they be omitted, and the pure sciences only be taught, the very idea of the *studium generale* is destroyed. But if they be retained—and at least philosophy ought for very shame sake be retained—it is absolutely impos-sible to treat of them without setting forth definite views for or against Catholic doctrine. And here we would draw attention to the important fact that as almost every branch of human science has its side upon which it touches religion, so also in almost every branch of human science the Church has erected certain landmarks which are to guide the Catholic who devotes himself to its study. This being the case, the entire question of mixed education is thus placed within a nutshell. If, in teaching the circle of the sciences, any regard is to be had to the Catholic definitions thereupon, then the mixed system becomes Catholic, and the difficulty is at an end. If, on the other hand, such definitions be neglected or set aside, then it is a mockery to say that the Catholic student may safely entrust himself to a system which, while it professes not to assail his religious belief, does, notwithstanding, deliberately upset its teaching. Now, it will perhaps surprise some to find how deep and far-reaching are the definitions published by the Church in matters many of which at the first blush appear to belong to the purely natural region of thought. Thus, in philosophical matters, John the Twenty-first, through Bishop Stephen, pronounced judgment upon the philosophical method employed at Paris by Bentus, the Averröist, and condemned his errors concerning philosophers and philosophy, namely, concerning its object, truth, authority, sources, foundations, its relation to theology, and its position with regard to faith.* Again, concerning the origin of the world, John the Twenty-second asserted its creation in time.† Concerning man himself, Hadrian the First,‡ and Leo the Tenth,§ set forth his composite nature resulting from the union of soul and body, the perfections of either part, the relations of the soul to the body, and its commerce with the same. In the logical order, Clement the Sixth asserted against Nicholas de Ultricuria, that the human intellect was able to acquire certain knowledge of things either through natural appearances as by the external senses, or by deduction from other things; he declared, moreover, the nature and character of certitude, its object, its principles, and in an especial manner the certitude of the natural order of cause and effect. In ethics, Pius the Fifth, Gregory the Thirteenth, and Urban the Eighth,‖ condemning the heresy of Baius, asserted the existence of the natural moral law; the morality of acts done in accordance with it; the distinction of both these from the supernatural order; and the very foundation and condition of the moral order itself. Alexander the Eighth, Innocent the Tenth, Alexander the Seventh, Clement the Eleventh, defended, against the Reformers and the Jansenists, the existence of freewill, the qualities of which they carefully explained.¶ Urban the Fifth asserted the right of property** against Soulechat,

---

* Denzinger. Enchirid. Symbol, Ed. 3, No. 390, sqq.
† Propp. 1, 2, damnat. 1329, ap. Denzinger.
‡ Concil. Rom. an. 794, ap. Denzinger.
§ In Bulla "Apostol. Regiminis."
‖ Propp. 22, 25, 34, 36, 37, 38, 46, 50.
¶ Ap. Denzinger.
** Denzing., p. 1, 30.

the justice of commerce, of contracts in general, and of several contracts in particular; the order of justice in compensation,* restitution, satisfaction, and self-defence; the authority of judges, of oaths, of the public power. In the social order, Martin the Fifth† proclaimed the authority of temporal rules; Leo the Tenth, the right and justice of war; Alexander the Seventh, the legislative power of the civil ruler. From all this it results that there are threads of Catholic doctrine closely and variously interwoven with the several sciences that go to make up the material of human thought, and that to take no account of their teaching is to treat these sciences after a fashion which may or may not be scientific, but which decidedly cannot be recommended to Catholics as perfectly consistent with their religious belief, and in no way sinning against their conscientious obligations.

But it will, perhaps, be urged that no matter what may be the theories advanced in scientific matters by their professors, the students are still at liberty to reject them should they be found to be in contradiction with a given religious teaching. This is a gross abuse of terms. The intellect has lost its freedom whenever truth becomes inaccessible to it; and this is verified in our case. It is morally impossible for a callow youth, or for a school, to contend long and successfully against the influences exerted upon their minds by an able and eloquent professor, who naturally recommends, with all his power, the doctrines he himself has seen fit to adopt.

SOME EVENTS OF THE CENTENARY OF SS. PETER AND PAUL.

WE have been requested from many quarters to give a chronicle of the chief events of the festival celebrated in Rome on the Centenary of the Holy Apostles. We undertake the task to-day with diffidence; we will not, however, attempt to give a full description of this great feast, but will be content to describe some of the leading features which characterised it and endeared it for ever to the hearts of the Catholic world.

* Innocent the Eleventh, Prop. 37. † Prop. 30 Huss.

27

It was towards the close of December, 1866, that a circular was addressed from Rome to the bishops of the whole Church, acquainting them with the desire of his Holiness that the approaching eighteenth centenary commemoration of the triumph of the Princes of the Apostles should be celebrated with special pomp and solemnity. This was the third time that, during the present pontificate, the voice of Peter had gone forth inviting the pastors of the fold to assemble around his throne. In 1854, it was to offer a peerless wreath of earthly glory to the holy Mother of God; in 1862, it was to add new names to the lists of our triumphant brethren, as our intercessors in the heavenly court; and now, in 1867, it was to pay a special tribute of devotedness and reverence to the first Vicar of Christ.

Viewed in the light of human policy, this circular of the Holy Father was little less than folly. It was in that very month of December that the last of the French troops should take their departure from the Eternal City. The enemies of Rome, the revolutionists and anarchists of the whole world, were clapping their hands with joy that the moment of their triumph had come. The Papal Government had no longer foreign bayonets for its support, and it should now soon feel the vengeance of its oppressed subjects. Indeed for years the Protestant and infidel press of Europe had sought to decry the government of the Holy See, and to describe the temporal power of Pope Pius the Ninth as resting on a volcano, which, as soon as the French troops were withdrawn, would burst forth in all its violence. Nevertheless, these troops were withdrawn, and still Rome continued tranquil; nay, more, its peace and tranquillity and the harmony of its citizens went on increasing every day; and, despite the efforts of all the secret organisations and open enemies who left no means untried to accomplish its overthrow, the temporal sceptre of Pope Pius was found to rule over faithful subjects, and to hold the love and affection of his people.

The bishops of the Catholic universe heeded not the human dictates which the circumstances of the times would seem to suggest, but listened with joy to the words of the Vicar of Christ. His circular contained no command, no summons to assist at the approaching festival; still its simple invitation found an echo in the hearts of all the faithful, and the bishops of the Church, from north to south, and from east to west, were seen preparing for their pilgrimage to the shrines of Rome. And to many of the aged pastors of Christ's fold how insuperable should be the difficulties which this journey would involve! Yet faith and affection for the Holy See sufficed to overcome every difficulty. From the remotest points of the earth's wide range venerable men were seen converging to the tombs of the Apostles, and representatives of every language, race, government, and clime, pastors of every eastern as well as western rite, were hastening to Rome to offer at the foot of the Papal throne the united homage of the Catholic universe.

In the month of May, and the first weeks of June, the preparatory consistories were held; but as yet few bishops had arrived. It was only on the 20th of June, the feast of Corpus Christi, that the citizens of Rome began fully to realise how imposing would be the representation of the episcopate on the centenary of their great patrons. The procession of the Blessed Sacrament on Corpus Christi day in Rome is always one of the most glorious ceremonies in this city of wonders: but this year the presence of three hundred bishops redoubled its usual splendour, and many of those who had journeyed from the most distant climes were heard to declare, as they witnessed the solemn scene, that even by that day alone all the toil and suffering of their journey had been well repaid. Each hour now brought new prelates to the Seven Hills: every train was crowded, not only with bishops from every country under the sun, but with hundreds of their clergy, and with thousands of their faithful flocks. The Church of the United States, though so lately weeping over the sad results of civil discord, sent twenty-three bishops to this spiritual feast. One of them, the Archbishop of San Francisco, had journeyed full 8,000 miles to pay this tribute of his loyalty to Christ's Vicar. A representative of the British colonies undertook a still longer journey from Vancouver's Island, though he was detained by illness almost in sight of the promised land, and could not complete his pilgrimage. From France sixty-three cardinals, archbishops, and bishops hastened to represent that Catholic nation; Belgium and Holland, and our sister island, also sent their bishops; Austria, though suffering from sad and unforeseen disasters, and though many of her prelates were detained at home by the coronation of their sovereign as King of Hungary, had at least ten bishops to speak in her name; even Poland, and the equally afflicted kingdom of Italy, had their representatives; but noble Catholic Spain, so maligned and misrepresented by the hireling writers of the day, surpassed every other Government in the spirit which she displayed. Her bishops and clergy assembled in the cathedral of Barcelona to implore the divine blessing on their journey. From the church they proceeded in procession to the war-frigate which had been placed at their disposal, for Spain, alone among the Governments of the world, wished that its clergy should not be allowed to incur any expense during this Roman pilgrimage; the standard of the Madonna was unfurled on the quarter-deck, and, as they weighed anchor, the sweet hymn invoking the benign protection of the Immaculate Virgin was intoned, and the thousands of faithful on the shore re-echoed in alternate choirs the *Ave Maris Stella*. The number of bishops from the east recalled to mind the early glories of Antioch and Alexandria. Of the Armenian rite alone there were eighteen bishops, besides two or three mitred abbots; the Syriac, and Maronite, and Coptic, and Chaldean Churches had also many of their pastors: and some of these had arduous journeys to perform, riding upon their camels for twenty days or more, and guarding themselves at the same time against the prowling Bedouins, before they arrived at the Mediterranean coast, or came within reach of any of our modern travelling facilities. The Greek Church, slowly awakening from its dreary lethargy, and the Roumenian, Melchite, and Slavonic rites had also their representatives. The distant Australia sent two Irish prelates, the bishops of Melbourne and Adelaide, to the common centre of Catholic faith. Even China, for the first time, sent one of her missionary bishops to speak her language in the councils of the Church. This was the Vicar-Apostolic of Nankin. He has published a short narrative of his journey to Rome, and we will give a short extract from it. "I was in the depths of China," he writes, "when on the 7th of March I received the pontifical letter addressed to the bishops of the universe. My resolution was at once taken, and on the 23rd of the same month I began my pilgrimage, accompanied by the prayers and sympathy of all my confreres and of all my flock. . . . What could not fail to excite the warmest emotions in my breast was the eager enthusiasm displayed by the Catholics at every station where we stopped. At Hong-Kong, at Saigon, at Singapore, at Point-de-Galle, &c., the local missionaries with many of the faithful flocked around the vessel to salute me, and to pray me to convey to the Holy Father the expression of their devoted reverence, and to bear back to them the Apostolic benediction; and these testimonies of filial sympathy were multiplied as I approached the happy end of my journey." And as it was with this great missionary, so, too, was it with the other bishops: assembling around the tomb of the Apostles, they not only represented their own reverence and devotedness, but they expressed, moreover, the unswerving loyalty and attachment of their widely scattered flocks, clergy alike and laity, to the sacred centre of unity and faith.

From our own dear island fifteen bishops went on this holy errand: they were, the Cardinal Archbishop of Dublin, the Archbishop of Cashel, the Bishops of Down and Connor, Meath, Clogher, Kilmore, Cork, Cloyne, Ross, Limerick, Elphin, and Galway, the Coadjutor of Killaloe, together with the Most Rev.

Dr. Whelan and the Most Rev. Dr. Brady. And yet these were not the only bishops who represented Ireland in the episcopal assembly. There was, in fact, no quarter of the globe that did not send some son of Erin among its representatives to Rome. We have already mentioned the bishops from Australia; from India came Dr. Fennelly, Bishop of Madras; from Grahamstown in South Africa, Dr. Moran; from Glasgow, Dr. Lynch; from Newfoundland, Dr. Mullock; to say nothing of the many whose sees are in the United States of America.

But we must return to our narrative of events. The 21st of June commemorated the election of Pius the Ninth to the Papal throne, and the chapel of the Sistine was crowded by those who wished to render thanks to God for having granted so worthy a successor in the chair of Peter in these perilous times. On that day the devotion of the pilgrims again guided them to the church where the relics of the Angelic Saint Aloysius are enshrined. How beautiful is the sanctuary of the saint, with its countless lustres, its jaspar pillars, its silver lilies, its altar inlaid with precious stones, and, above all, its marble relievo, in which the saint seems as an angel from heaven to repay with heavenly blessings the homage which he receives from the crowds of youth who are grouped below.

The 23rd of June witnessed another glorious feast. The church known as the *Madonna of the Angels* was designed by Michael Angelo in the very central hall of the colossal baths of Diocletian, but, left unfinished by that master mind, was restored and adorned by the munificence of Pius the Ninth; it was on this day to be solemnly consecrated to the service of God. In the era of Diocletian's persecution forty-thousand Christians had been put to death for the faith in that very spot: and how they must have exulted on their heavenly thrones to-day to see that they cemented by their blood a temple dedicated to the living God with such solemnity, under the invocation of the martyrs' Queen.

The 24th, in memory of St. John, is a joyous holiday; and the cathedral of Rome, *Omnium Ecclesiarum Mater et Caput,* puts forth all its grandeur, presents upon its altars all its sacred treasures, and throws wide its portals to receive within its vast aisles the pilgrims, pastors, and faithful from every clime.

The 25th his Holiness wished to admit to special audience the priests who, emulating the devotedness of their chief pastors, had flocked to the Holy City. The hall of Consistories, it was supposed, would be large enough to contain all who had come to Rome, and yet in little more than half an hour so crowded had it become, even to the very steps of the throne, that thousands had to be refused admission. The address made on this occasion by his Holiness was, indeed, the exhortation of a father to loved and cherished sons : it expressed the consolation which he experienced in their being present at this family feast ; it contained, too, sweet words of spiritual exhortation, and granted many favours and blessings for their respective flocks. No sooner had the address ended than the " *Salvum fac Pontificem et Regem Pium*" burst forth from the crowded hall ; chanted by twelve thousand well-trained voices it produced a wonderful effect, and seldom did the vaults of St. Peter's re-echo an anthem of more heartfelt feeling and filial affection.

On the 26th all the bishops were invited to assemble in the Sistine, and the Holy Father, filled with emotion, delivered to them the allocution to which the whole world was looking forward with listless eagerness. Sublime were the inspirations of the Vicar of Christ in this discourse, sublime the picture of the unity and vitality which in that assembly Christ's Church displayed. How all the heretical communions of the world dwindle into insignificance compared with the august scene of the Sistine Chapel ! A leading Protestant organ a few days ago did not hesitate to write : "The Christian world has outgrown the borders of Europe, and the churches of to-day make up a society which no single head on earth could correct or control." So it is, indeed, in the Anglican Church. But ask the assembled bishops of the 26th of June whether unity is impossible in a world-wide communion : they will tell you that the Church of God is necessarily one from pole to pole ; that communions whose extent is bounded by territorial limits cannot be the true fold of Christ ; that the light of faith is one, whether in Africa, or Asia, or America, or Europe, and that one is here below its centre—one the divinely constituted depositary and guardian of heavenly truth. The enemies of the Papacy had long declared that its vitality was extinct, and that its influence belonged to times which had passed away. Yet in that solemn assembly the Popedom stands before us in the full freshness of its vigour and youth. It recalls its past teaching, reveals its sorrows and its triumphs, and announces an approaching *Ecumenical Council*, the mere name of which awakens a thrill of joy throughout the universe. Even the very assailants of Rome on this occasion were forced to pronounce with unwilling lips its eulogy, and to yield their testimony to the undying life and supernatural energy of the Vicar of Christ. It is thus that the infidel *Diritto* of Florence writes :

" The Sovereign Pontiff is right, and we are but poor silly fools and idle declaimers. We spend our breath in crying out against the Church, and fill the air with boasts of what we are going to do against it. Meantime an aged Pope proves himself superior to us. He holds himself erect, and walks firmly along his path. From Rome we hear a voice solemn and resolute, a voice whose very accents make us respect the dignity of man. From the mystical centre of Catholicism rises a sweet harmony which draws all men towards it; but from the chambers of our united Italy there rises not one sound, one thought worthy of the new life which fate has bestowed on us, or worthy of sustaining a moment's comparison with the voice of Rome. We must confess it to our shame, Rome sets us a noble example of love and faith; shows us how to fight and how to conquer. From that old enemy we may learn much; if we despise that example we shall be beaten beyond hope of recovery. The Papacy is there to show us the strength of its system: it stands before us a model of constancy and prudence."

On the morning of the 27th the everyday recurring festive solemnities seemed to be suspended whilst the Irish bishops gathered together in St. Agatha's to offer their prayers for one of the brightest ornaments of our Church that had been summoned to his reward. The Bishop of Ardagh had intended to be in Rome for this great festival, but Providence had otherwise decreed; and as soon as the sad news of his demise reached his brother prelates they resolved to offer to his memory a solemn tribute of their esteem and love. At an early hour on the 27th a pontifical High Mass was offered up for his repose, and all the Irish bishops assisted in their robes around the mournful catafalque.

A few hours later a long line of carriages was seen moving towards the Vatican, bearing our own many bishops and priests to a special audience with his Holiness. This was the occasion on which the offering of the Peter's Pence were presented from most of our dioceses. Pio Nono had for each one a few words of affection and emotion, and many of these venerable prelates burst into tears as they kissed the hand of the Vicar of Christ.

On the 28th the first vespers were solemnly chanted, ushering in the great festival of the following day. In the evening, whilst the horizon still retained the gorgeous colours of an Italian sunset, the colonnade and cupola of St. Peter's seemed transformed into one mass of light, dazzling with its magic splendour, and bringing out in all its grandeur and proportions that noblest monument of human genius; and thousands there were who, contemplating it on that night, instinctively repeated the words of the poet:

> . . . . " But, thou
> Of temples old and altars new
> Standest alone, with nothing like to thee" . . .

The crowds who filled the streets and elevated quarters did not conceal their admiration as witnessing this grand spectacle of which many of them had so often dreamt far away beyond

the Alps or the Atlantic.   And yet it was not from foreign
climes alone that these crowds had come; there were humbler
multitudes from Frascati and Cora, and every city or village
within a range of fifty miles; many, too, from still more distant
towns, who slept around the portico that night to secure their
post at the earliest hour on the following day.

And now the morning of the long-wished-for 29th of June
has dawned, a day that shall mark an era in the history of the
Church.   The eyes of three hundred millions of Catholics
throughout the universe are this day turned to Rome.   It is the
feast of the chief patrons of this city of God: still more, it is
the great jubilee feast of the triumph of the first Vicar of Christ,
a feast common alike to all the pastors and faithful of God's
fold; and as if it did not suffice that the Church militant should
thus exult in all its members, the Church triumphant, too, should
have its share in this great festival, and new crowns are offered
to its saints, new heroes of faith receive the honours of the altar.
Well, indeed, did the clergy of the Church intone that day the
Decora lux œternitatis, thus beautifully paraphrased for the occasion by the Oratorian, Father Caswall:

> " Bathed in eternity's all-beauteous beam,
>   And opening into heaven a path sublime,
> Welcome the golden day which heralds in
>   The apostolic chiefs, whose glory fills all time !
>
> Peter and Paul, the Fathers of great Rome,
>   Now sitting in the senate of the skies !
> One by the cross, the other by the sword,
>   Sent to their thrones on high, and life's eternal prize !
>
> O happy Rome ! whom that most glorious blood
>   For ever consecrates, while ages flow,
> Thou thus empurpled art more beautiful
>   Than all that doth appear most beautiful below."

From the first dawn of the aurora the holy sacrifice was
offered up on the thousand altars of Rome, for permission had
been granted by the Cardinal Vicar that at two o'clock A.M.
Mass might begin.   Already, at six in the morning, every
street was filled with a busy crowd, and wave after wave passed
through the immense Piazza, rushing towards St. Peter's.   The
cloudless heavens presented the brightest azure of the Italian
sky.   The Zouaves and other troops in their gala uniforms were
stationed at intervals, and the military bands contributed their
festive tunes.   The windows of every house wore their gay
festoons and banners; and, with all this, the rich equipages of
the nobility and dignitaries of the Church, the crimson tapestry
hanging from many a balcony, the Papal banners floating over

the Ponte S. Angelo, the curious costumes of the peasantry, the varied attire of foreigners from every country under the sun, the smile that beamed on every countenance, presented such a joyous scene as even the artist's imagination could not surpass.

But it was on entering the church of St. Peter's that the hearts of the hundred thousand pilgrims beat with delight, as a new scene of majestic grandeur and unrivalled splendour was opened to their gaze. The beauty, the sumptuousness, the imposing appearance of the interior of St. Peter's on that day surpasses all power of description. Eight thousand lustres hanging as festoons, corresponding harmoniously with the architecture of the Church, and forty thousand wax lights arranged in the most brilliant devices, realised to the mind all that we have read of Paradise. "The taste displayed in the decoration," writes the correspondent of the *Times*, "is much more pure and simple than that which was shown in 1862, at the last great canonisation. The effort has been made to give effect of colour, and this has been done so as to bring out in bolder relief the architectural ornaments. The general effect was rich and gorgeous in the extreme. Richer still it became when, about seven o'clock, the *servitori* began to light the great wax tapers which hung suspended in festoons between the arches under the colossal statues. Twenty-five thousand tapers were thus soon made to shed their light upon the building, giving to the crimson tapestry a deeper hue, now that all daylight had been excluded, and lending increased brilliancy to the gilding. Sometimes a puff of wind blew aside a curtain, and then down streamed on one particular spot a sunbeam so bright and unexpected that it seemed like a flash of lightning, startling those around as if danger were near. Grander, however, than all else in the way of light was a colossal inverted cross formed of prisms of glass, which had been sought for far and wide. Above it were the keys, gigantic in their proportion, and formed of the same material, while above them still was suspended an enormous tiara of coloured glass. Hanging, as did these brilliant symbols, in the centre of the nave, and flashing and glittering with direct and reflected light, the spectacle was indescribably beautiful."

Such is the church of St. Peter's that no number of individuals assembled there seems possible to make a crowd. Sixty thousand persons can move about with ease in it, and yet on this occasion it seemed not a whit too large for the immense assembly.

A little after six o'clock the procession began to move from the Sistine Chapel. Two hours it took to pass along the *Scala*

Regia, and through the colonnade of Bernini, to the portals of St. Peter's. The religious communities, the chapters of the Basilicas, the members of the Papal household, all took part in this grand procession. Immediately before the Baldacchino, under which his Holiness was borne in *sedia gestatoria*, were carried large banners representing some scenes from the lives of the saints who were about to be canonised. The moment the Holy Father himself appeared the immense crowd, unable to restrain their feelings, burst forth into the most deafening and unanimous applause. It is said that this is the first time in Roman annals that such an ovation was offered to a Pope whilst performing a religious ceremony. On the present occasion it was beyond control, such was the unbounded enthusiasm of the people. Many ladies and gentlemen were seen to shed tears, and to wave their handkerchiefs, literally convulsed with emotion that showed the intensity of their feelings. Pius the Ninth meantime was calm and composed, and as he passed along blessed the heaving multitudes with a sweetness and placid look that made him appear conscious of what was passing around him.

It was precisely nine when the Pope entered the Church. The cardinals and bishops walked immediately before him two-by-two. Their silvery white mitres, the rich copes, which were red in honour of the martyrs, the oriental vestments, with diadems sparkling with diamonds and collars rigid with gold, presented a grand spectacle. All, accompanied by their chaplains, carried torches, and recited the litanies as they went along. As the bishops approached the altar they took off their mitres, and then arranged themselves at either side around the throne. There was no distinction of country or rite or costume: the patriarchs, archbishops, and bishops of every country were blended together, and seniority of consecration was the only precedence in their respective ranks. The silver trumpets as usual announced the entrance of the Pontiff, and sweeter notes it is impossible to conceive. As the great Pius was borne along through the gorgeous scene he seemed filled with emotion. Leaving his chair and ascending the throne, he stood for several minutes absorbed in thought. And how many thoughts must have rushed to his mind as he reflected on the duties and responsibilities of the successor of the Fisherman of Galilee, and how many emotions must have moved his heart as he gazed on the five hundred bishops, representatives of the whole Church of Christ, who there stood around him, all of whom wished to honour him as heir and vicar of the apostle whose relics were enshrined beneath the glorious altar, and whose centenary they now celebrated! But what shall I say of the emotions that filled the souls of those who gazed on him as he stood entranced, of those who had travelled so far in obedience to the voice of Pius, and were ready to sacrifice their lives in devotedness to him as head of the Church and Vicar of Christ? How many of them will have echoed in their heart the sentiments so beautifully expressed by an illustrious pilgrim when he exclaimed:

"Behold the successor of Peter, the head of the Catholic body, the mouth-piece of the Church, ever living, ever conveying its teachings to the universe; the centre of faith and of Christian unity ; the source of light and truth created by the hand of God to illumine the world ; this infirm old man, this feeble priest, is the immovable basis of a divine edifice, against which the powers of darkness shall ever rage in vain, the corner-stone on which stands the city of God here below. Behold the earthly head around which are grouped so many glorious memories of the past, the hopes of the present, nay, the very blessings marked out in the counsels of Eternal Wisdom for the future of our fallen race. Prince of priests, father of fathers, heir of the Apostles: greater than Abraham in patriarchal power, than Melchisedech in priesthood, than Moses in authority, than Samuel in jurisdiction : in a word, pastor of the pastors, leader of the leaders of the spiritual army, cardinal point of all the churches, key of the arch of Catholic unity, impregnable citadel of the children of God !"

The ceremony of canonisation proceeded as usual. Before pronouncing the solemn decree, the Holy Father twice invited the bishops and the faithful to unite with him in prayer to obtain the light and guidance of heaven. The first time, the *Litany of the Saints* was chanted by two Papal choristers, the vast multitude in the church responding as with the voice of many waters. The second time, the *Veni Creator Spiritus* was intoned by his Holiness ; and when at length the decree was published, the silver trumpets announced the glad tidings, the cannon roared from St. Angelo's, and for an hour all the bells of the churches and religious houses of Rome conveyed with their joyous peals the happy announcement to the faithful. The Pope now intoned the *Te Deum*, and, oh ! how grandly it rose and died away as it was sung by the choir, and was then responded to in alternate strophes by the thousands upon thousands of voices throughout the vast edifice ! None who were present can ever forget the solemn chant of that glorious hymn : it seemed, as it swelled through the mighty dome of St. Peter's, as if the voice of every people and every tongue had united to bless the Lord in unison with his earthly Vicar.

As soon as the ceremony of canonisation had been concluded High Mass was celebrated, the Holy Father himself being celebrant. After the Gospel, notwithstanding the fatigue of the preceding ceremonies, he addressed a homily to the assembled bishops, beautiful and happy in its sentiments, as ever are the words of Pio Nono. During the offertory the usual symbolical gifts were made to his Holiness by the promoters of each cause of canonisation: and, as these offerings were borne to the throne, the *Tu es Petrus* was sung, composed expressly for the occasion by the well-known master, Mustafa. Three distinct choirs were formed to give effect to this composition. The Papal choir, in its full numbers, was directed by Mustafa ; a second choir, composed of four hundred voices, was placed in the cupola above ; whilst a third choir, with three hundred chosen amateur singers, took its position at the end of the church, over the central entrance. "Such delicious music," writes the *Times* correspondent, "surely was never heard, as the dulcet tones floated in a series of echoes through the vast building, first rising from earth in a full body of sound, then gradually diminishing in power, though not in distinctness, and then softly breaking forth as though they were angels' whispers." The Papal choir at the altar began this anthem expressive of the prerogatives of St. Peter ; the choir at the entrance, representing the faithful *urbis et orbis*, repeated the joyous chant; and it was echoed from the cupola as if by the choirs of angels. All three then united in one grand burst of harmony, as if Rome, and the whole Church, and heaven itself, wished in unison to proclaim the exalted dignity and royalties of the Prince of the Apostles. At the concluding words, *non prævalebunt*, the effect was peculiarly striking. It was like the echo of his voice who first pronounced these words, now repeated by all his creatures confident in its unfailing effect.

The morning ceremonies did not end till two o'clock, P.M., and yet many of the faithful crowd still lingered in the aisles, feasting their devotion at some special shrine, and closing with vespers that great festival. At night the *girandola*, or fireworks, on the Pincian Hill, far exceeding their usual brilliancy, crowned the enjoyment of St. Peter's day, filling with delight and astonishment the crowds that had gathered from the uttermost bounds of the earth.

June the 30th the festive celebrations were renewed at the church of St. Paul outside the walls. This church is one of the richest of Christendom in its marbles and decorations; and lit up to-day by countless chandeliers and wax-lights beautifully arranged about its nave, nothing could surpass the brilliancy and splendour of the scene ; to whatever side you turned some new feature of the decorations presented itself, and new vistas of wondrous beauty were opened to the view. The Holy Father and many of the bishops assisted at the solemn Mass : and its music and ceremonies, and everything even to the minutest details, contributed to make this commemoration of St. Paul a worthy rival of the preceding day's festivities.

On the 1st of July the bishops again assembled at the Sistine

Chapel to present their reply to the address which was made to them by his Holiness. This reply was worthy of the pastors of the Church of Christ. We need not repeat it, for it is well known to our readers. The bishops congratulate his Holiness on the happy celebration of the centenary feast at which they had assisted; they declare their union with him as Vicar of Christ and successor of St. Peter; they share his joy in the triumph of the Church in so many countries; and they at the same time divide his afflictions and sorrows at the trials to which it is elsewhere exposed; in his teaching they recognise the voice of Him whose office it was to *confirm his brethren;* and they look forward with joy to the future œcumenical council, that it may check the indifferentism of the age, and draw closer the bonds of unity in discipline as well as faith, thus to combat with more energy against the enemies of God.

And now we may chronicle a few of those ideas which the events of this great centenary have awakened in reflecting minds.

1. Never did the pastors of the Church assemble around their Head more free from the cumbrous trammellings of State control, and more independent in the exercise of their sacred ministry. The lesson of preceding centuries had been repeated in our own times, reminding the pastors of the fold how secular princes too often, whilst assuming to protect, only seek to undermine and bind captive the Church of God; and hence it was that, conscious that the true liberty of their sacred ministry was guaranteed by listening to the voice of Peter and by following the guidance of him on whom the Church is built, the bishops of the universe corresponded with ardour to the invitation of Pius, and hastened to offer to him such a testimony of filial homage as was never surpassed in the annals of the Church, and filled with terror the enemies of our holy faith.

2. Whilst the centenary was celebrated in Rome, another great festive holiday was kept in Paris: thus the Exhibition Palace and St. Peter's—the Church and the world—were placed in contrast; each presented its distinctive features and attracted the gaze and attention of the universe. Paris as well as Rome awarded its laurel crowns: in the one, the efforts of human genius were eulogised, and earthly progress merited the prize; in the other, the practice of virtue was commended, and the heroism of sanctity was proposed as a model for imitation; in the one, the human or earthly order alone was deemed worthy of praise; in the other, the supernatural or spiritual order ruled supreme. And yet, even in an earthly point of view, how puny

were the efforts of the world compared with those of the Church
of God; and how many votaries of human reason abandoned
the temple of mere material industry to enjoy with pure
delight the achievements of manly genius elevated and inspired
by faith !

3. There was also a civil government, which, during the
celebration of the centenary, forced itself upon the public gaze
in contrast with the city of Rome. The kingdom of Italy was
a prey to revolution in all its provinces, and by its secret emis-
saries, as well as by its diplomatic agents, sought to extend the
same revolutionary system to the walls of Rome. And what
were the fruits of the revolutionary triumph throughout Italy ?
Despite the many promises of peace and plenty, penury is now
found to knock at every door; taxes overwhelm alike the gentry
and the peasantry; insecurity of property and life deadens the
energies of the whole population ; whilst religion is fettered in
every member, freemasonry and heresy boast of the impunity
which they enjoy; and though libertinism is free from all
restraint, true liberty is extinct. How striking is the contrast
which the maligned city of Rome presents! Like the Ark in
the Deluge, it alone enjoys security and peace, whilst death and
desolation reign around. Pius the Ninth refused to sacrifice to
State diplomacy the principles of justice and religion, and
whilst his enemies are now despised throughout the world even
by their former friends, he by his firmness conciliated the love,
esteem, and veneration of the universe, and, during the glorious
centenary which we have been describing, the bishops of the
whole world, bearing on their brow the aureola of sanctity and
zeal and science, offered to him the voluntary tribute of their
homage, not only as the Vicar of Christ, but also as the ruler
of the patrimony of St. Peter. The revolutionary agents were
compelled to report to their patrons in Florence that it was impossible to act on the people of Rome ; and throughout the
whole period of this glorious celebration tranquillity, peace, concord, prosperity, and plenty smiled benignly on the subjects of
the Holy See.

THE REVIVAL OF ATHEISM.

IT cannot be denied that within the last twenty years the monster of Atheism has wrought and is daily working fearful ravages in the heart of Europe. This statement will, no doubt, startle some of our readers, who have been taught to believe that the spirit of the *Encyclopædia* has been long since extinguished. But, startling as it may be, it is nevertheless strictly true, and whoever will compare the two testimonies we subjoin can no longer refuse to believe it. In the year 1844 some French writers united to publish a dictionary of the philosophical sciences. In the preface to that work we read: "Atheism has well nigh completely disappeared from philosophy; the progress of a sound psychology will render its return for ever impossible." Be it remembered that the group of philosophers who made this statement were not men whose predilections for Christianity might incline them to take for granted a decay of Atheism which they hoped for; on the contrary, they belonged to the school which aimed at making Christianity a religion of purely rational doctrines, translating it into a philosophical system based upon belief in God. They admitted the existence of a personal Deity, distinct from the world, infinitely perfect; they maintained the spirituality, the liberty, and the immortality of the soul; they acknowledged a moral law absolute and unchangeable, and an essential difference between good and evil. But they refused to allow the existence of the supernatural. Twenty years after the publication of the lines quoted above, the heirs of the traditions of the same spiritual school found themselves compelled to hold a very different language. In 1864, M. Janet, professor of philosophy in the Paris Faculty of Letters, made the following avowal: "It is idle to conceal it, the spiritualist school is undergoing a dangerous crisis. If it were only a school of philosophy that is at stake it would not matter so much; but there is question of more than a school: there is question of an idea, the idea of spiritualism. This idea is now threatened by a wave the most dangerous that has appeared since the *Encyclopædia*, and, should it perish, the liberty and dignity of the human soul will be swept away along with it." What a sad change between the utterance of 1844 and that of 1864! At the former date the idea of God shone out in all its brilliancy on the world of thought, and no cloud was there to cast a shadow upon philosophy, then joyous in its hope that it was never more to suffer darkness. But in twenty short years the clouds had arisen and overspread the firmament, blotting out the light of God, and gathering a tempest which threatens to ruin all that we possess of free and exalted and truthful. The *Revue Medicale* thus pithily describes the result of the change wrought in twenty years: "Materialism has seized upon modern science. Its teaching is that there is no God in the world, as there is no soul in man."[*]

These testimonies regard France alone. But the storm rages fearfully over a surface far larger than the plains of France. Almost all the countries of Europe have been subjugated to the same scourge, and the idea of God is everywhere in danger. And it must everywhere be borne in mind that the Atheism of the present day is not merely a speculative doctrine, but one which aims distinctly at practical results. It proposes to itself to achieve a universal reform, and to achieve it not only without God and without religion, but against God and against religion. Nor does it allow a single field of human energy to escape its deadly influences. In philosophy it aims at leaving the reason without God; in the physical sciences it would make no account of his power or of his presence in nature; from education it would banish religion and all traces of it; in morals it would free the passions from the yoke of his law; in politics, it would reconstruct society on revolutionary principles of the wildest character. "In view of such a state of things," says Mgr. Dupanloup,[†] speaking of France, "I know nothing fraught with more danger to the clergy, and to Christians, and to all honest men, than not to know, not to appreciate, or to be indifferent to such a state of things as this."[‡] Impressed with the wisdom of this observation, we propose to do briefly for several countries of Europe what the Bishop of Orleans has done for France, and, taking a rapid glance at each, to point out in them to our readers the traces of the modern revival of Atheism.

Let us begin with France. The schools of Atheism in France are classified by Mgr. Dupanloup under three heads: Positivism, Pantheism, and Materialism. Of the Positive system we have before spoken at some length, and shall, probably, have occasion to speak again. Of all the others, it is the system

---

[*] 15th February, 1866.
[†] *L'Atheisme et le Peril Social*, p. 63.
[‡] For the facts here stated we are indebted to Mgr. Laforet's *Pourquoi l'On ne croit pas*, Louvain, 1866, second edition; and M. Naville's *The Heavenly Father*. MacMillan, 1865.

from which, in this country, we have at present the most to fear, and indications of its spread in Irish anti-Catholic Universities are multiplying themselves daily with an ominous rapidity. It is enough here to point out in M. Vacherot an atheist whose arguments lead straight to Positivism. In a work of twelve hundred pages, published by this writer,* he maintains the thesis that God does not exist. And on what grounds? He lays down as a first principle that reality and perfection mutually exclude one another; therefore, to say of God that He is perfect is to affirm that He does not exist. Hence arises the dilemma: if God is perfect, He does not exist; if God exists, He is not perfect. Therefore, concludes M. Vacherot, the respect we owe to God forbids us to believe in Him. This extravagant system becomes tangible by taking another shape. Perfection exists not in reality, but only in our thoughts. The human mind is, therefore, the summit of the universe, since by the law of progress the world is ever tending towards perfection which is only in the thought of man. It is the human mind, therefore, that we must adore. This conclusion leaves us at the very threshold of Positivism.

Pantheism is the deification of the universe. The idea of God is not directly destroyed, but transformed, and lost in the transformation. God is no longer the Eternal and Almighty Personal Creator, " but the unconscious principle, the substance of things, the whole. The universe alone exists ; above it there is nothing ; but the universe is infinite, eternal, divine." Pantheism was introduced into France by M. Cousin, founder of the eclectic school, who, as far back as 1817, had visited the leaders of the German philosophical movement. For many years before his death M. Cousin emphatically repudiated this doctrine, and the most distinguished among his disciples have kept aloof from it. But Pierre Leroux openly defends Pantheism in his work, *De Humanité;* and, according to Mgr. Laforet, De Lammenais attempted to reconcile it with Christianity in his work, *Esquisse d'une philosophie.* The Bishop of Orleans quotes largely from E. Renan to prove that he is a Pantheist.

Materialism refuses to recognise anything as real which does not come under the experience of the senses. Mgr. Dupanloup quotes from its organs in France passages of the most revolting brutality. *La libre Pensée, La Revue du Progrès* are specially remarkable among the number of these organs. When we take into account the activity of the press employed to propagate Atheism under this triple form ; when we reflect on the prodigious activity and unscrupulousness of its apostles, and on

* *La Métaphysique et la Science*, 2 tom. October, 1858.

the appalling ruin their success is but too surely calculated to work, we cannot but fear for the future of France.

Crossing the Rhine and entering into Germany, we find ourselves at once face to face with the many-sided results of the teachings of Hegel. It cannot be expected that we could present in these pages an exposition of Hegel's system. The mists and clouds in which this philosopher has wrapped up his meaning have hitherto successfully baffled the most patient and keen-witted analysts of speculative doctrines, and have led to the most opposite interpretations. Some have deduced from Hegel's writings a system of Christian theology, whilst others have detected in it a system of undisguised Atheism. It is said that shortly before his death the philosopher himself summed up the results of his teaching in these words: " I have only had one disciple who has understood me, and he has misunderstood me." But if we fail in attempting a scientific exposition of Hegelianism, we have abundant materials from which to estimate the character of the influence it has exercised upon the popular mind. It has been understood as simply meaning the deification of man. The famous Henri Heine wrote, in 1850, to the *Augsburg Gazette :* " I begin to feel that I am not precisely a biped deity, as Professor Hegel declared to me that I was twenty-five years ago." The universe, according to Hegel, is explained by an idea, which is ever in process of developing itself. This development is necessary, and hence everything in the world is necessary, and therefore legitimate. Hence the laws of thought and of conscience are not more necessary or legitimate than the desires of the flesh. Hence there is no law to bind man, no power to govern him : he is a law and a god unto himself.

This popular appreciation of Hegel's doctrines soon passed from the regions of theory to those of practice. In 1845 it was remarked that certain secret societies composed of Germans were in the habit of holding meetings on Swiss soil with the object of working a revolution in Germany. The basis of this movement was Atheism. One of the principal agents wrote as follows: " The idea of God is the keystone of the arch of a tottering civilisation ; let us destroy it. The true road to liberty, to equality, and to happiness is Atheism. No safety on earth as long as man holds on by a thread to heaven. Let us teach man that there is no other God than himself, that he is the alpha and omega of all things, the superior being, and the most real reality."

These revolutionary principles, paraded in all their shameless audacity before the German governments and peoples, aroused a feeling of indignation which has powerfully helped to weaken the influence of Pantheism. But, unfortunately, Materialism has stepped in to take the vacant place. Germany is in these days the principal centre of Materialism. Feuerbach, Max Sterner, Arnold Ruge, Vogt, Moleschott, L. Büchner, and others reject whatever passes the limits of experience: God, the moral law, the immortality of the soul, all the general principles which are at once the light and the rule of human reason. Moleschott's book (*Krieslauf des Lebens*), "The Circular Course of Life," first published in 1852, has had four editions in ten years; Büchner's "Force and Matter" (*Kraft und Stoff*), which appeared in 1856, has had in five years seven editions, and has been translated into French by Gamper. Thus Germany presents almost the same elements of Atheism that we have observed in France, namely, Pantheism and Materialism, although in different combinations. In Germany also they have assumed, besides the speculative, a political form.

Turn we now to England, whose literature is the food upon which so many millions of Catholic minds are fed. England has the unenviable distinction of having been the birthplace of that monster of modern infidelity, the traces of whose ravages in various lands we are now following. As far back as 1624, Lord Herbert of Cherbury reduced Deism to a system, and defended it. Hobbes, Toland, Shaftesbury, Bolingbroke, and others powerfully contributed to its diffusion. Bolingbroke was Voltaire's master. An eloquent French writer, M. Villemain, thus describes the connection between the English and French schools of infidelity :* " There is not a single one of the daring arguments used by French philosophy in the eighteenth century, which is not to be found in the English school at the beginning of that century. Bolingbroke summed up that school in himself. In the midst of the profligacy of his youth, amid his important public duties under Queen Anne, and in his exile, he ever devoted himself with incessant ardour to the acquisition of learning hostile to Christianity. This curious erudition charmed and surprised Voltaire in the interviews he had with Bolingbroke in Touraine. There, instead of that libertine scepticism which had been his earlier school, he found an infidelity which was well informed, polyglot, and recommended by the authority of a scholar and a statesman. It is easy to understand how the brilliancy of that erudition, the confidence of that bold scepticism, the essence of irreligion which breathed from so many books then perused by Voltaire, must have exercised upon him an influence incalculably powerful." Diderot, after Voltaire, the most active infidel of the eighteenth century, drew from

* *Cours de Litterature Française*, Ve leçon.

English sources his earliest philosophical inspirations, and
with D'Alembert, his fellow-editor of the Encyclopædia, placed
on the title-page of that storehouse of impiety the name of
Francis Bacon.   Locke was to Rousseau almost all that Bolingbroke was to Voltaire.   The English people are styled by Germans a double people on account of the strange contrasts they
present.   They are at once stirred by a strong spirit of piety
and by a terrible spirit of irreligion.   In our own day the contrast has become much more deeply marked, and the lines between both more sharply defined.   The religious spirit is
gradually approximating to the Catholic Church, while the
irreligious energy is concentrating itself in the purely pagan
systems of Positivism, German Rationalism, and Secularism.
We have elsewhere sketched the state of infidelity in England.   John Stuart Mill, Miss Martineau, the so-called George
Eliot, Lewes, and several others, are at once popular writers,
whose works are read by tens of thousands, and the apostles of
Positivism.   The political changes wrought within the past
year in the English constitution, and which constitute a revolution of supassing importance, all the more serious because, like
the tide that rises silently, it has covered the land almost without noise, are destined to place political power in the hands of
those who compose the lower stratum of society.   It is right at
such a moment to make some account of the theories of Secularism, which, as an organised system, has gained no slight
hold upon the English working classes.   Practically, it aims at
the overthrow of the existing political order.   Its doctrines are
thus set forth by its chief, Mr. Holyoak: "All that concerns
the origin and end of things, God and the immortal soul, is
absolutely impenetrable for the human mind.   The existence of
God, in particular must be referred to the number of abstract
questions, with the ticket *not determined*.   It is probable, however, that the Nature which we know, must be the God whom
we inquire after.   What is called Atheism is found *in suspension*
in our theory."*   The moral of this reasoning is that men
should put aside all thoughts relating to another world, and
manage to live as advantageously as possible in this present life.
Hence the name of Secularism.   The organs of the body are or
were *The Secular World, The National Reformer, The Secular
Advocate*.   Its means of action are open-air speeches and assemblies for lectures and debates.   In London there were, three
years ago, five of these lecture-rooms.   The programme in one
of these hall for every Sunday includes a discourse at eleven
o'clock, a debate at three o'clock, and a lecture at seven o'clock.

* Ap. Pearson, *Infidelity, etc.*, p. 316.

Liverpool, Manchester, Birmingham, Glasgow, and Edinburgh are the chief centres of operation.

From these facts it is plain that Atheism in England is reproducing itself under features identical to those which mark its appearance in France and Germany. It shows itself at both extremes of society—among the learned, the polished, the favourite novelist, the philosophical oracle, as well as among the rough-handed mechanics who crowd the large manufacturing towns. Besides, it means work: it aims at practical consequences; and it has now opened for it a door through which it may enter upon the stage of public affairs, and make its voice heard and its hand felt in the management of the country.

We have barely time to take a rapid glance at other European countries. Belgium could not escape the contagion of French impiety. Ahrens has planted Pantheism in the University of Brussels. At present M. Tiberghien, scholar and successor of Ahrens in the chair of Philosophy, is teaching Pantheism to the students of the same University.

Italy has not been altogether exempt from the plague; although the See of St. Peter, which God has planted in its midst, has been powerful for the healing of the nation. It seems like a visitation that those who employed even unlawful means to drive out the German stranger from the fair plains of Italy, should themselves have fallen under the most disgraceful slavery of German-born errors. We shall say nothing of Gioberti, nor shall we delay·to inquire how far his philosophy was coloured by that of the detested Germans. But it is a fact that Hegelianism has been installed in the University of Naples; that the scepticism of Ferrari finds followers; that the writings of Ausoni Franchi, formerly a journalist at Turin, and now a professor at Milan, are unmistakably Atheistic. It is needless to say that, from sources such as these, and from the teachings of the secret societies, have proceeded the recent ravings of Garibaldi and of those of whom he is the working spokesman.

That these theories are current in Holland results from M. Naville's testimony, and from a book published last year in Holland, mentioned by Mgr. Dupanloup, which has for inscription: *Extinctis diis, extincto Deo, successit Humanitas.* Of the Russian empire it may be said that the young nobles, and the university students in general, are imbued with irreligious principles. M. Herzen has published, under the pseudonym of Iscander, a work, " *From the other shore,*" in which the worst features of Atheism are manifest. His influence in Russia is described as very great. Besides native works, the leading

Materialist and Atheist publications of foreign countries have been translated into Russian, and widely diffused throughout the country. It is especially noticeable that the universities— those centres of thought—are the citadels of these pernicious principles.

We have now reviewed the appearances of Atheism that at present manifest themselves in so many countries of Europe. No right-thinking man can contemplate without horror the sad spectacle of a world which, while it flatters itself on being more enlightened than at any period of the past, has lost its chief good in losing the knowledge, and fear, and love of God. No Christian heart but must feel sore at the thought that so many young men, who represent the hope of the future, are turning away from Him who alone is the Way, the Truth, and the Life. Besides, in presence of a plague so universally prevalent, it is impossible to escape a painful sense of danger impending even over countries which, like our own Catholic Ireland, have, through God's grace, been preserved intact in the faith once de- livered to the saints. We shall not delay here to urge the general causes which involve the youth of our country in peril. The literature they read which carries to their minds the seeds of error ; the secret societies which, spread like a net-work over Europe, lay snares for their unwary feet ; the company and conversation of freethinkers, with whom society abounds ; the fascination of a licentious, and the sophistry of a sceptical press ; the lack of intellectual and moral vigour, which stamp an age enslaved to sensual impressions ; all these go to make up a complex danger, which, although general, it would be the height of temerity to despise. But when we consider the special cir- cumstances of our time, and the conditions under which the rising generation of Irish Catholics, that is to say, the first generation of emancipated Irish Catholics, is to be educated, the danger becomes more imminent, and the need of precautions more imperative. We deliberately assert that almost all the conditions calculated directly to foster a spirit of infidelity in the young are to be found in the system of education, and especially of university education, which it is attempted to force upon the Catholics of this country.

What, in fact are the causes of infidelity ? Infidelity, ac- cording to St. Thomas, " like faith, exists in the intellect as in its immediate subject, but in the will as in its first motive." And again : " It is contempt on the part of the will that causes the intellect to dissent, and in this dissent infidelity essentially consists ; whence it comes that the cause of infidelity is in the will, although the infidelity itself is in the intellect." The causes of infidelity reside, therefore, in the intellect, or in the will, or in the combined action of both. On the part of the intellect two causes may be specified, one, the perversion of the intellect by the principles of a false philosophy, which destroy faith by rendering the Christian demonstration impossible; the other, a gross ignorance of the doctrines of Christianity. In a system of education which refuses to the Church any part in the selection of professors, and reserves that office exclusively to the civil government, what security is there that the youth who frequent the philosophical schools may not be trained to believe in those monstrous systems which, as we have seen, now prevail in so many universities? What warrant have we that the arguments which prove the existence of God may not be decried in the name of philosophy, and thus the entire foundation of a reasonable faith thoroughly sapped? What force is there strong enough to repel the advancing march of that Positivism which has already gained a footing in our Irish universities, and before which faith in Christ disappears? The Christian demonstration rests upon the motives of credibility; but of what value does such demonstration become to those who have been taught to deny the possibility of the supernatural and of the miraculous? And is not the air thick with philosophical systems, which, if once rooted in the minds of the young, will make for them evermore a perpetual divorce between their reason and the faith they have received from their fathers? And will faith thus weakened resist the shock of the assaults of the passions?

The other intellectual cause of infidelity is ignorance of the doctrines of the Catholic Church. How many lose the faith almost solely because they are ignorant of what the Church teaches! Of how many may it be said with truth that they blaspheme what they know not! And yet the very essence of the mixed system of education is, that this ignorance shall be maintained! To tolerate ignorance of religion would be a defect grave enough to counterbalance many advantages in other respects, but to make such ignorance the very law of a system of education is altogether monstrous. And how frequently does a half-acquaintance with Catholic dogmas give rise to difficulties which can be solved only by a fuller knowledge of the same, and of the bearing of one tenet upon another. And yet, the mixed system sternly denies the advantage of this higher knowledge. To the intellectual dangers which the mixed sytem tends directly to strengthen, we ought to add the moral dangers inseparable from the mixing together of young men of different religions and of no religion. Youth is the season of pleasure; and what check save the grace of God, obtained in answer to humble prayer and through the sacraments,

can bridle the riotous impulses of its wayward passions ? " We
know not," says Bergier,* speaking of the infidels of the last
century, " what these men are, whether they are alive or dead,
fellow-countrymen or strangers ; we wish to describe them only
according to their writings ; we attack books, not men ; and
limiting ourselves to this irrefragable proof, we maintain that
libertinism and the passions are the true causes of incredulity."
But, even if, through some fortunate circumstances which may
happen to exist in spite of the mixed system, gross libertinism
be happily absent, nevertheless the absence of the religious
element in education will infallibly produce a generation of
young men full of levity, dissipated, worldly-minded, weak in
character, and indifferent to the practices of religion.   Men
such as these are not fitted to resist the attacks of that spirit of
infidelity which, as we have seen, is sending its poisoned breath
over Europe ; and we shall be false to our most solemn duty if
we spare any effort that may be necessary to save the young
men of our country, the children of Catholic martyrs, from its
baneful influence.

CHURCH QUESTIONS IN THE THIRD CENTURY.

In the growth of the great Christian Society of the Church
may be traced successive stages analogous to those which mark
the development of civil society from its simplest elements into
its highest form of completeness.   The earliest factors of society
are individuals ; these unite and form families ; the union of
families makes the town ; many towns with their territories
constitute the State.   So it is, likewise, in the growth of the
Church.   The earliest factors were separate individuals, to
whose conscience the Gospel triumphantly appealed ; from these
early converts came Christian families; and these, as they
multiplied in numbers, in wealth, and in social standing, prepared the way for the great change which took place under

Constantine when the Religion of Him whom Roman soldiers had put to a cruel death, became the religion of the sovereign of the Roman world.   It will be readily admitted that each one of these successive stages of growth presented to those who rule the Church difficulties of its own, and problems of government, the conditions of which varied with the varying adjuncts of the occasion.   But of all other periods those were most fertile of intricate combinations, which marked the transition from one stage of growth to another.   At the critical periods of change it became especially difficult to maintain in harmony the various component parts of any whole, excited as they are, and put in motion by the forces that are working the change itself.   It is in such extremity that the skilful pilot is seen. And while, in the strain caused by such a crisis, weak societies perish, the vital energy of robust societies is exhibited in all its strength.   In the critical epochs of Church history it is always the Roman Pontiff who appears in the hour of danger. Through him the conflicting claims of the old and of the new order of things are adjusted ; his voice, speaking with authority, calms all disputes ; his wisdom, heaven-sent for such end, suggests precautions which conjure away the growing danger; and it becomes plain to all that, through him, as visible head of the Church, the Eternal and Invisible Head rules and guides his faithful on earth.

Such a crisis as we have been describing took place early in the third century, and recent discussions among the learned have served to invest its history with an exceptional interest. It was for the Church the period which prepared her transition from the condition of a quasi-domestic society to that of a mighty public corporation, placed in fullest light of day, including within its circle men of all ranks, from the imperial ruler down to the vilest slave who fretted away his life in the dark places of Roman palaces.   Tertullian's well-known words* give an idea of the expansion of the Church at that time.   From being hostile to Christianity, he says, men " become Christians, to wit, from conviction, and begin to hate what they were, and to profess what they hated, and are as numerous as indeed we are publicly declared to be.   Men cry out that the State is beset, that the Christians are in their fields, in their forts, in their islands.   They mourn, as if for a great loss, that every sex, age, condition, and now even rank itself, is going over to this sect."   And yet, numerous as they were, or rather precisely because from their numbers they attracted so much attention, they were subjected to persecution, and that from various

* Apol. i. 1.

quarters. " As many as are strangers to it (Christian truth), so many are its foes: and the Jews, indeed, appropriately from their rivalry, the soldiers from their violence, even they of our own household from nature. Each day are we beset, each day betrayed ; in our very meetings and assemblies are we mostly surprised." *   The persecution put in motion by Septimius Severus lasted down to the year 211. From that year till the death of Pope Zephyrinus, in 218, and even during the five years of the pontificate of Callistus, his successor, the Church enjoyed considerable calm. But the period of persecution handed down to the period of peace many troublesome questions, which remained after the persecution had ceased, as the angry chafing of the sea waves remains after a storm on the deep. The care of the material interests of a large community naturally brought the rulers of the Church into contact with the civil powers, and this contact often involved them in serious difficulties, and demanded on their part a constant exercise of Christian prudence. Again, it was necessary to heal in the time of peace the wounds that had been inflicted in the discipline of the Church, especially in connection with the clergy, during the persecutions. From the several heresies already in dissolution, many persons were finding their way back to Catholic unity, and they were so to be received as that neither the discipline of the Church should suffer, nor yet the path to union be made unnecessarily difficult for them. In the midst of various and shifting shades of error, the light of Catholic faith was to be kept pure and brilliant. The existence of slavery, involving so many difficulties, was also a fruitful source of problems, each of which required most careful consideration. These and other questions called for solution especially in the pontificate of St. Callistus, and we have abundant materials at hand to enable us to study in some detail the method of government followed by that illustrious Pope. It is not our intention in this paper to enter fully into the merits of each of the questions described as having been submitted for judgment to St. Callistus. Nor do we address ourselves to institute a defence of that Pontiff. We propose to ourselves a more limited range of subject. We purpose rather to consider the Church questions of that time in as far as they throw light upon the position of the Roman Pontiff, and are proofs of his supremacy in the government of the entire Church.

The literature of the Callistian period of history has of late years received many additions, and it is right that we should briefly describe it before entering upon our subject. In 1842

* Apol. ii., 7.

a MS.* now famous under the name *Philosophoumenon*, was brought to France from a monastery on Mount Athos, and in 1851 was published at Oxford by Emmanuel Miller.† In this work the author undertakes to refute all heresies, and lays down as a principle admitted by all, that the Holy Scriptures, with the traditions of the holy fathers, is the rule of Christian faith. This principle he applies to all heresies, and shows that, instead of coming from Scripture and tradition, they come from pagan philosophy, from profane mysteries, or from astrology. In his fourth book he shows that the miracles appealed to by the heretics are to be attributed to magic. In the next five books he refers all known heresies to a profane origin; and in reciting the several heresies he follows no order of time. Last but one comes the Callistians, so styled by him as being followers of Pope St. Callistus. In the tenth and last book he sums up all he had said before, and exhorts the whole world to hold true doctrine.

The charges brought by the author of the *Philosophoumena* against Pope Callistus are such as could not fail to attract attention from both the friends and foes of the Catholic Church. Here was a contemporary of that Pontiff who deliberately accused him of having corrupted the true faith, and of having tampered with the purity of ecclesiastical discipline. The book itself was published as the work of Origen; the German Jacobi was the first to attribute it to a Latin writer, who, he thought, was no other than Hippolytus. Bunsen ‡ agreed with Jacobi as to the author, but differed from him, by holding that it was the identical refutation of heresies ascribed by Photius to Hippolytus, whereas Jacobi held that this latter was a work altogether distinct. Canon Wordsworth § defended the views of Jacobi. About this time a fresh theory as to the author's name was started in England, according to which Caius, a contemporary of Pope Zephyrinus, was the writer of the book. This theory found an able defender in Fessler at Tubingen. Soon after a distinguished Irish scholar, Dr. Cruise, brought

* This MS. is now in the Paris Library (No. 464), and is of the fourteenth century. It is a copy from a very old original, and has on the last page the inscription: Χερσί Μιχαὴλ ἥϊε βίβλος τελίθει γραφεῖσα. (*This book was written by the hand of Michael.*)

† *Origenis Philosophoumena sive omnium hæresium refutatio e codice Parisino nunc primum edidit*, Emmanuel Miller: Oxonii, 1851. A second edition appeared at Göttingen in 1859 from Professors Duncker and Schneidwin; and a third at Paris, from Dr. Cruice, the late Bishop of Marseilles. Both these later editions are furnished with notes and critical corrections of the text, which in the MS. itself is full of inaccuracies.

‡ *Hippolytus and his age :* London, 1852.

§ *St. Hippolytus and the Church of Rome in the earlier part of the third century.* London, 1853.

forward an array of reasons why the book should be ascribed to Tertullian.* He did not, however conceal the grave difficulties that exist against this view, which, indeed, had been first proposed by Abbe Jallabert at Paris.† Döllinger, who attributes the work to Hippolytus, has examined in detail the charges it contains against St. Callistus, and abundantly refutes them. Father Torquato Armellini, S.J.,‡ is inclined to make Novatian the author. The Abbé Le Hir, of St. Sulpice, accepts Hippolytus as the author, § but ascribes the work to him prior to his conversion to the Catholic faith. As late as June, 1865, Albert Reville, in the *Revue des Deux Mondes*, brought forward once more as against the Catholic Church, the revelations contained in the *Philosophoumena*, and against him that the illustrious Sulpician took the field. Finally, the Cav. De Rossi has brought to bear on the subject, his marvellous knowledge of Christian antiquities, and in the *Bulletino di Archeologia Christiana* for the year 1866, has devoted himself to the defence of St. Callistus. Even among Catholics, the opinion which would make St. Hippolytus (before his conversion, and while still attached to Novationism) the author of this book, prevails very generally. De Rossi is certainly inclined to attribute it to Tertullian, and this in face of serious difficulties. But on all sides it is admitted that the work is an authentic production of the third century.

The writer, whoever he may have been, betrays the most bitter hostility towards Callistus. His charges against that Pontiff are twofold. One set of accusations is levelled against his personal qualities, another against his public life. We have now to deal only with the latter. Touching the former, we shall merely observe that Callistus was born a slave at Rome. His master, who was a Christian, was named Carpophorus, and De Rossi publishes a sepulchral inscription bearing his name, and fully agreeing with all that is known concerning him. Carpophorus held some post in the palace of the emperor. He confided to his slave a considerable sum of money, wherewith the latter was to trade as a banker. Callistus opened his bank, and so high was the reputation of his master among the faithful that the poor, and especially the widows, placed in his hands large sums of their money. But the bank failed, and Callistus fled from his master's resentment. Car-

---

Etudes sur de nouveaux documents historiques empruntes a l'ouvrage recemment decouvert des Philosophumena. Paris, 1853.

† *Etudes critiques sur le livre des Philosophoumena.* Paris, 1853.

‡ *De prisca refutatione hereseon, Origenis nomine Philosophumenon titulo recens vulgata, commentarius.* Romæ, 1862.

§ *Le Pape St. Calliste et les Philosophumena,* in the *Etudes, etc.* Oct., Nov. 1865.

pophorus pursued him, and, having come up with him at Ostia, condemned him to the punishment of turning a mill. After some time the Christians obtained his release, from this degrading and laborious task, and Callistus went to the synagogue to demand his money from the Jews, who had probably been the cause of his ruin. His visit to the synagogue, and his violence therein, aroused the anger of the Jews, who, after having maltreated him in his person, brought him before the prefect, Fuscianus, accused him as being a Christian, and charged him with having violently disturbed their assembly which was permitted by the law. In vain Carpophorus claimed his slave. The prefect sentenced Callistus to be scourged, and then to be sent to labour in the mines of Sardinia. There he toiled in company with many illustrious confessors of the true faith, until Marcia, consort of Commodus the emperor, a woman most friendly to the Christians, if not herself a Christian, obtained from the sovereign the liberation of them all. On the list of confessors drawn up by Pope Victor for Marcia, the name of Callistus was not, indeed, to be found; but through the intervention of Marcia's commissioner he, too, obtained his liberty together with his companions. On his return to Rome, he was sent by Pope Victor to Antium, where he was admitted into the ranks of the clergy. On the death of Pope Victor, Zephyrinus, who succeeded to St. Peter's chair, summoned Callistus to Rome. According to the writer of the *Philosophoumena*, the new Pope allowed himself to be guided in all things by his deacon, Callistus, in whose hands he placed the government of the clergy and the management of all the important affairs of the Church. It is especially mentioned that the Pontiff placed him over the great cemetery still known by his name. When we consider that the clergy and people had a large share in the election of persons to discharge the higher offices among the clergy, it will be plain that the virtues of Callistus must have won for him the esteem of all. Upon the death of Zephyrinus in 218, Callistus, who had been for eighteen years his principal adviser, was chosen to fill his place. His pontificate lasted but for five years, his death by martyrdom being recorded in the year 223.

We may now proceed to consider the charges brought against Callistus, and examine what light they throw upon the position accorded at that period to the Roman Pontiff.

As we said above, the acts upon which these charges are grounded were demanded by the peculiar circumstances of the time, and by the state of the Church at that period. The multitude of the faithful of every rank, led as a natural consequence to many unequal marriages, which were null in the eyes of the civil law. Was the Church to declare them null, or rather accept them as in accordance with the natural and Christian law ?

Again, in so large a body of believers, those who fell into sin after baptism could not be very few, considering the corrupt atmosphere they were compelled to live in, and the persecution to which the were frequently subject. Nor would there be wanting accusations against bishops, priests, and deacons. Besides, a general movement was urging on towards the Church many schismatics and heretics. How were these cases to be dealt with ? Was the stern, unbending rigour of discipline to be increased, even at the risk of keeping souls out of the Church, lest the faithful should be contaminated ? or was mercy to be shown to the weak but repentant sinner ? The great bulk of the faithful were converts from polytheism, and found some difficulty in comprehending the doctrinal exposition of the Trinity set forth against the heresy of Sabellius ; and how was this embarrassment to be overcome ? Callistus took steps to answer each and all these questions, and his decisions are the subject of the bitter attack of his enemy. Let us examine them one by one.

The author of the *Philosophoumena* accuses Callistus as being guilty of "*impious iniquity, and a teacher of lust and murder.*" Mr. Reville thus develops the charge : "Did he not go as far as to allow patrician ladies to live in concubinage with slaves or men of inferior condition, in cases where, being without husbands (of their own rank), and unwilling to lose their dignity by marrying beneath them, they had no other way of indulging their passions ? The consequence was that women, Christians by profession, were seen to follow the infamous example of pagan nations, and by causing abortion, endeavoured to conceal the results of their shameful weakness. These are the terrible charges which Hippolytus fears not to launch against Callistus. The charges are terrible, indeed, but like many other charges brought against the popes, they are nothing else than a distorted account of what in itself is lawful and just. The text states no more than this that Callistus gave permission to ladies of noble rank, who were still young and unmarried, and who did not wish to fall from their position by publicly marrying an inferior, to marry (as we should now say *morganatically*) a slave or freedman, although such a marriage was declared null and void by the civil law. Under Marcus Aurelius and Commodus, that is a few years prior to the pontificate of Callistus, a decree of the senate was passed to the effect that the widows or daughters of senators should lose their rank as *clarissima femina* or *puella*, in case they should contract marriage with a man not of senatorial rank. Such unions were, however, legitimate. But, on the contrary, unions between *clarissimæ* and slaves or freedmen were declared null and void, and being considered by the law *tanquam non essent*, did not entail on the lady the loss of her high social position. The text, therefore, speaks of the case of ladies of senatorial rank who preferred to a legal marriage with a knight or a plebeian, which would entail on them the loss of their title of nobility, a marriage with a slave or freedman, which, invalid in the eyes of the law, was nevertheless valid according to conscience and before the Church. This being the substance of the accusation, what blame can be attached to Callistus? Let it be borne in mind that the number of converts among senatorial families was exceedingly large, and that it was very difficult for the ladies of such families to find Christian husbands of their own rank, and that to contract legal marriages with persons inferior in rank to their own, was to incur the loss of their dignity. This civil disability, coupled with the difficulty of finding Christian husbands of senatorial rank, was a strong inducement to the Christian *clarissimæ* to intermarry with pagan senators. It was in order to lessen the pressure of this temptation that Callistus allowed them to con-tract, before the Church, marriage with Christian slaves or freedmen, or even *ingenui* of rank inferior to them, while in the eyes of the law such marriage was not recognised as valid, or was never contracted at all. Nor was there anything shocking or repulsive to Christian feeling in those close unions with slaves. "We make no difference," says Lactantius,[*] "between slaves and masters: we give to each other the name of brother, because we believe that we are all equal." And Cav. De Rossi declares that among the many thousand sepulchral inscriptions in the catacombs, he has hardly found a single one which has certain mention of a *servus*, and very rarely one to make mention of a *libertus;* whereas of pagan inscriptions of the same period you can hardly read ten without finding frequent mention of slaves and freedmen. So far, then, from having substantiated his terrible charges against Callistus, the writer has but supplied us with an important fact to prove that in the earliest ages the Church took no account of the matrimonial impediments created by the civil law, but on the contrary claimed to herself entire power over the marriage of Christians. What more striking argument could we have against the propositions 68 and 69, condemned by Pius the Ninth in the *Syllabus:* "The Church has not the power of establishing diriment impediments of marriage, but such a power belongs to the civil

---

[*] *Divin. Instit.* v. 14, 15.

authority, by which existing impediments are to be removed. In the dark ages the Church began to establish diriment impediments, not by her own right, but using a power borrowed from the State."

We learn from the *Philosophoumena* that at the close of the second century the Church had and exercised power over the impediments of matrimony, and that St. Callistus, the sixteenth successor of St Peter, held as clearly as Pius the Ninth, the two hundred and fifty-ninth Pope, that the civil authority has not power to establish such impediments. And so far is it from being true that it was only in the middle ages that the Church began to establish diriment impediments in virtue of a power borrowed from the State, that about one hundred years after the death of St. John the Evangelist, she deliberately set aside laws passed by the State concerning matrimony.

"It was little more than a century after the death of the beloved disciple," writes Cæsar Cantù,* "when the common suffrage of the Church placed at the head of Christendom a slave who had worked at turning a mill-stone, and who, under the name of St. Callistus, became one of the most illustrious of the Popes. What a revolution ! The whole world is divided into two camps; on one side power, wealth, liberty; on the other, slavery, oppression, misery; it is only in the Christian Church that all classes and all conditions are brought near to each other; she alone possesses the highest moral authority that has ever appeared on the earth, and she confides it to a slave; and this slave, become Pontiff, pursues the work of the emancipation, and of the brotherhood of nations. Whilst the Lex Julie and the Lex Papie declare null and void the marriage of a member of a senatorial family with a person of inferior rank, Callistus proclaims that the patrician and the slave have received from God the same duties, that God will judge both with equal rigour, and will never allow pride to sunder a union consecrated by Himself."

It is unnecessary to remark that if some women, led away by the prevailing corruption of the pagan world in which they lived, abused the permission granted them by the Church, such abuse cannot be justly charged upon the Roman Pontiff.

The next accusation we shall examine is that according to which Callistus was guilty of "*being the first who was indulgent with men in what concerns voluptuousness, saying that he forgave sins to all.*" By this plenary remission of sin, Callistus, according to his adversary, gave men full license to indulge

* *La Reforme in Italie*, Discors. I.

in sinful pleasures forbidden by Christ to his disciples. The reader will remark that Callistus is not here accused of absolving sinners without exacting from them the proof of penance, which would have been most wrong, but of holding that the Church has power to forgive all sins without distinction. In this the author shows himself a Montanist, and a believer in the doctrine laid down by Tertullian after he had joined the sect. The Montanists held that the sinner who was guilty of grave crimes should be irrevocably excluded from the sacraments, and from sharing in the sacrifice of the Church even in his last hour. On the contrary, the Catholic Church, ever a tender mother, set before her sinful children the second plank after shipwreck, the sacrament of penance, in which stains contracted after baptism might be wiped away. This was the doctrine of Tertullian himself before his apostasy from the Church. But why is it said that Callistus was "the first" to claim and to exercise the power of forgiving all sins without distinction? According to some, Callistus modified in some degree the rigour of the penitential discipline imposed upon a certain class of penitents, namely, by admitting them to communion and to peace with the Church during their lives, whereas according to the former discipline they could have obtained this favour only at their death. This point is admirably illustrated by Cav. De Rossi. According to others Callistus made no change in the ancient discipline, but opposed his authority against the rigorous severity of some African bishops, of whom St. Cyprian soon after affirmed that they excluded adulterers altogether from penance : *in totum penitentiæ locum contra adulteria clauserant. Ep.* 52. It is not unlikely that the unfortunate sinners treated thus harshly by their own pastors, appealed to the tribunal of the Roman Pontiff. What is certain is, a "decree, and that a peremptory one" (*decretum et quidem peremptorium*), came, as Tertullian complains, from Rome, from the "Sovereign Pontiff, the Bishop of Bishops" (*Pontifex Maximus, Episcopus Episcoporum*), to whom the angry Montanists attribute those words: "I remit to those who have done penance the crime of adultery and of fornication" (*Ego et mœchinæ et fornicationis delicta penitentia functis dimitto*). This language is almost identical with the charges brought by his adversary against Callistus; and it is expressly stated by him that Callistus was "the first" to use this language. From this it would follow that the famous decree which excited the anger of Tertullian was this very decree of Callistus with which we are engaged, and not a decree of Zephyrinus, as was generally supposed hitherto.

We have, therefore, in this second charge of the author of
29

the *Philosophoumena*, a luminous proof of the Catholic doctrine concerning the sacrament of penance, and an illustration of the power of the Roman Pontiff over other Bishops, inasmuch as the exercise of that jurisdiction is compared by an heretical writer to the act of one who is Bishop of Bishops and Sovereign Pontiff.

Another charge against Callistus is, " *that if any of the clergy had contracted marriage he allowed him to remain in the clergy as if he had not sinned.*" To such cases the Pontiff was wont, according to his accuser, to apply the parable of the cockle, of the ark of Noah, and such like, which he interpreted of sinners in the Church. This accusation supplies us with an excellent argument for the apostolic origin of the celibacy of the clergy. It is plain from it that in the beginning of the third century it was considered a sin for one belonging to the higher orders of the clergy either to contract marriage or to make use of marriage before ordination, for the word γαμεῖν is capable of both these interpretations ; and, whatever may have been the precise nature of the Callistian decree which, when maliciously distorted, gave rise to the accusation now under our consideration, it is plain that Callistus himself considered the marriage of clergymen to be sinful : else, why apply to their case the parable of the cockle, of the ark of Noah, which held both the clean and the unclean, all of which he interpreted of sinners in the Church ? De Rossi thinks that allusion is made here to the use of marriage contracted before ordination, which is still tolerated by the Oriental Church. Some cases of this may have occurred during the pontificate of Callistus, and although the Pope acknowledged them to be an abuse, yet he thought it prudent to tolerate them through fear of greater evil, until the time should come in which it should be safe to abolish them entirely. It is well worthy of attention that the author of the *Philosophoumena* does not speak of those abuses as occurring in the Roman Church. On the contrary, he uses the phrase "under him," which he had used in another place in speaking of those bishops who repeated the baptism given by heretics, and who were Oriental prelates. What a clear idea does this give of the supremacy of the Roman Pontiff, in that the abuses committed in the far East were laid to his charge, as if he were responsible for their existence and maintenance ! Such an accusation, far from doing an injury to Callistus, is a splendid homage rendered to the supremacy of the Apostolic See.

The most serious charge of all is that which would represent Callistus as a teacher of false doctrine concerning the Trinity. It is asserted that before the death of Zephyrinus,

Callistus defended the Catholic dogma when in presence of the Catholics, the Noetian doctrine before the Noetians; but, that after the death of Zephyrinus, he promulgated a novel doctrine partly Theodotian and partly Sabellian. But the writer here betrays himself. He adds, that all, with the exception of himself, agreed with Callistus : that the teaching introduced by Callistus continued ever after in the Roman Church, and that it was spread over all the earth. Now, we have an authentic exposition of the faith defended in Rome towards the second half of the third century concerning the Trinity. Dionysius the Pope sent to Dionysius of Alexandria a statement of the faith of the Roman Church on the points raised by the Sabellian controversy, and that faith is the faith afterwards defined at the Council of Nice. If then the doctrine of Callistus remained in the Roman Church, and became universal, it must have been the very faith of the Nicene Fathers.

This is not the place to enter upon a minute examination of the various formulas which the author recites. We shall rather ask our readers to make some reflection upon the results that followed the teaching of Pope Callistus. The writer admits that, as soon as Callistus published a statement of his doctrine, all men adopted his teachings as their own, and this throughout all the world. Besides, he mentions that those who thus followed the teaching of the Roman Pontiff.claimed for that reason to be "the Catholic Church," thereby furnishing an additional proof that the union with Rome in faith was the *tessera* of Catholicity. Again, it is plain that long before the Council of Nice the doctrine of the consubstantiality of the Son was already clearly held in the Roman Church, and through her all throughout the Christian world. On other points, too, the teaching of Rome marked out the path which was afterwards followed in their decisions by the Nicene Fathers. In the second century, Rome had prohibited the celebration of Easter on the same day with the Jews. In the third, Rome proscribed the severity of the Novatians, and the repetition of baptism administered by heretics. And, when the great council assembled in the fourth century, it condemned the Quartodecimans and the Novatians, and declared baptism to be valid, irrespective of the faith of the minister. "At each point," says the learned M. Le Hir, "St. Ambrose's saying was verified by anticipation : *ubi Petrus, ibi Ecclesia.*"

We conclude by bringing together the various details we have touched on in this notice of the questions that stirred men's minds in the Church at the close of the second and the beginning of the third century. Such details present us with an interesting picture of the Catholic Church of that remote age. We find it to have been then as now the congregation of the faithful professing one and the same faith, in obedience to the Bishop of Rome as earthly head of the entire Church. Its hierarchy of bishops, priests, and deacons was as fully defined then as now. Its clergy were unmarried, and even heretics thought the marriage of the clergy to be a sin. Marriage was looked upon as a sacrament, and as such completely under the control of the Church, which claimed and used power over matrimonial impediments, holding as valid marriages which the civil power had declared null and void. The sacrament of penance was in honour and in use, and those who had stained their baptismal innocence sorrowfully submitted their sins to the priests of the Church, who, in virtue of their divine commission, loosed them from even the most grievous offences. Among the faithful the distinction of rank was forgotten ; there was neither slave nor freeman, but all were brothers in Christ. And the ruler and guide of the entire body was the Roman Pontiff, who sat in the chair of Peter. Was there question in the Eastern Churches of re-baptising those baptised by heretics ? it was laid to his charge, because being done "under him," he was responsible for it. Did the African bishops show an excessive severity in admitting poor sinners to the sacraments ? It was the Pope who, as Bishop of Bishops and Pastor of Pastors, sent them a "peremptory edict" which commanded mercy towards the penitent, and who thereby abated their rigour. Was there question of the true faith in the Trinity ? The Roman Pontiff condemns Sabellius, and sends to Alexandria a statement of the faith of the Roman Church to be held by all. And all received the teaching of the Pontiff ; his doctrine became the formula of each Church, and the faithful styled themselves "the Catholic Church" because they agreed in faith with the Bishop of Rome.

Is not the Catholic Church, like its Divine Founder Himself, the same yesterday, to-day, and for ever ?

THE BISHOP OF ORLEANS ON THE NEXT GENERAL COUNCIL.*

ONCE again have we looked upon our amiable and august Pontiff; and, on the festival of the great Apostles, in that vast Basilica which has become all of a sudden too small for the immense crowd, pilgrims from the entire Christian world, have beheld five hundred Catholic bishops around him, whilst, in the midst of the most splendid pomp religion could display, his voice raised to the glory of the saints some of the lowly children of the Church. It was in the midst of the emotions awakened by that great festival of the Centenary of St. Peter and of the Canonisation, and in that assembly of the bishops of the universe, that the voice of St. Peter's successor has suddenly spoken to the world a word that has not been heard there for three centuries, and has announced one of those great parliaments of the Universal Church—a General Council.

What! an œcumenical council in the days we live in; at the close of this century, so agitated and so storm-beaten, about which men ask, how will it end? is it to set in tempest, or will it herald the dawn of a better time? A Council, that thing so grand and so rare! Perhaps it is to preside over the birth of a new world.

But, whatever the future may be, the idea is a grand one, and when I consider what a General Council is, what advantages the Church has ever reaped from it in moments of peril, and what she may hope from it to-day; when I reflect upon the obstacles which seem to arise from the advanced age of the Roman Pontiff, and the dangers that threaten the Holy See; when, notwithstanding, I behold this aged man, now almost eighty years old, raise himself above vulgar solicitudes, and with generous trust in the God who inspires him, undertake without fear a work so great and so laborious, I cannot but think and say: This is an inspiration from on high! this way of viewing things, this courage, this hope, are clearly heaven-sent, and God will bless them.

* From the *Lettre de Mgr. l'Evêque d'Orleans au clergé et aux fidèles de son Diocese, a l'occasion des Fêtes de Rome et pour lui announcer le futur Concile Œcumenical.*

But what are General Councils, so rare and so decisive in the Church? Whence come their great authority and their supreme influence? It is right and necessary, my brethren, to tell you of these things, that your piety may be enlightened, and your faith have clear and precise notions on a subject of so much importance.

General Councils are, as I have said, the solemn parliaments of Catholicism, the general assemblies of the teaching Church. The Pope convokes all the bishops of the universe, and from all parts of the earth they come, representing, with the Pope, who is their head, and who presides over them, all the churches of the world. And the Holy Spirit is there in those sacred meetings, speaking by lips of those men, to whom it has been said : "*As my Father hath sent me, so do I send you. Go teach all nations, teaching them what I have taught you, and behold,* in your great mission as divine teachers, *I am with you all days, even to the consummation of the world !*"

In these divine words of Jesus Christ we have the charter of the doctrinal infallibility of the Church, and, consequently, of General Councils, which, in the language of Bellarmine, of Fenelon, of Bossuet, and of all theologians, are representations of the Universal Church. Hence it is that the decisions of General Councils have always terminated controversies and fixed the faith of the Church. Those who were surprised twelve years ago that the Church should define a dogma, did not know then that it is the Church's mission on earth to DEFINE, that is to say, not to create, but to affirm, to proclaim the dogma, and thereby fix the symbol and maintain immovable the unity of the faith.

Even in the days of the Apostles, the Church was assembled in Jerusalem, and it was in a veritable General Council, such as the times permitted, that the Apostolic College decided the question of the legal observances, and freed Christendom from the yoke of the Mosaic laws.

From the Council of Nicæa to the Council of Trent, whenever Christendom was threatened by any great danger to faith or morals, or when reforms in discipline became necessary, the Pope convened the Bishops of the East and West, placed himself at their head, in person or by his legates, and the Council decided the question in dispute, or passed those general laws of discipline which constitute the statute law of the Church.

Thus, when the subtleties of Arius and of the Greek mind came to trouble the Church's simple faith in the divinity of the Word, and to sap the very basis of Christianity, the bishops, with the legates of Pope St. Sylvester at their head, assembled at Nicæa, and each of them bearing witness to the tradition of his own Church, and of the Universal Church, the Word was declared consubstantial, and we sing to-day, and we shall still sing for ever more, under every sky, the immortal *credo* of the Nicene Fathers.

In the same way, the errors raised after Arius, touching the great and fundamental mysteries of the Trinity and the Incarnation, by Macedonius, Nestorius, and Eutyches, fell before the general faith proclaimed in the famous Councils of Constantinople, where St. Damasus's legates presided ; of Ephesus, where the Mother of our Lord was proclaimed by St. Cyril and all the Fathers of the Council, amidst the rejoicings of the whole world, to be the Mother of God ; and of Chalcedon, where the Fathers cried out that Peter spoke by Leo. Immortal councils ! to which Pope St. Gregory the Great paid reverence as to the four Gospels. And, in very truth, they proclaimed the same faith as the Gospels, and their oracles, too, were inspired by the Holy Spirit.

After the eighth general council, in 869, two centuries elapse without general councils ; but they are the two darkest and most painful centuries in history. In the twelfth and thirteenth centuries the world beheld a new development of . Christian life. How often did the great Popes of these ages recognise the necessity of having recourse to these general assemblies of Catholicism in order to decide with more effect and authority the questions then under discussion in the Church, and to protect at one time the faith, in danger from scholastic subtlety, or from old heresies once more springing up in the dark under new names ; at another, the liberty of the Church, oppressed by secular violence, as in the Investitures; or again, the purity of discipline violated by interior abuses not less disastrous, and which the Church, who never dreads reform because she has the divine power of self-reformation, felt that she should extirpate. This was the object of the four general councils of Lateran, and of the two of Lyons, in the twelfth and thirteenth centuries.

At the close of the twelfth century, Pope Alexander the Third thus expresses himself in the Bull by which he convoked the third council of Lateran : " We observe in the Church of God many things to be corrected. Therefore, to reform what has need of reform, and to promulgate what will advance the salvation of the faithful, we have resolved to summon from different parts the men of the Church, to the end that in accordance with the tradition of the Fathers such measures as the good of the Church requires may be resolved upon and authorised by the concourse of a large number. Particular decisions would not, perhaps, have so much weight." He then indicates the date and place of the council, and adds : "Helped by the grace of the Holy Spirit, let us unite our efforts, and all together, like one man, let us lift on our shoulders the ark of God."

In the following century the great Pope, Innocent the Third, in convoking the fourth council of Latern for 1st November, 1215, used similar language in the Bull *Vineam Domini Sabaoth :* "The vineyard of the Lord of Hosts is now assailed by wild beasts, who seek to destroy it." And then, after drawing a lively picture of the evils of the period, the Pope added that, after serious consideration and much counsel with his brethren the bishops and other prudent men upon the wants of the time, he had come to the conclusion that "general measures for the good of the Church being called for, he had resolved to convoke, according to the old custom, a general council." And then, putting the whole Church in motion to prepare for the coming council, the Pontiff adds : "We have, therefore charged prudent men in the different provinces to investigate whatever ought to be submitted for correction to our apostolic authority." Then recommending all to prepare for the council, he says : "Examine, then, by yourselves, or by help of prudent men, all that seems to require correction or reform, and carefully note it, to submit it in due course to the examination of the council. For the greater the dangers, the more urgent the need of powerful remedies."

And when, on the threshold of modern times, Protestantism had rent the Church as it had never been rent before, what did Paul the Third consider to be the best measure in that supreme crisis ? Again the General Council. "It is," said the Pope, "the remedy in greatest perils :" and he convened that immortal Council of Trent, which, in spite of the opposition it had to contend with, has cast so brilliant a light upon all the dogmas that Protestantism sought to obscure, and has been for the Church the starting-point of one of the greatest movements of Christian life which have ever been produced.

Since the Council of Trent, that is for the last three centuries, the world has seen no general council ; and yet, during that period events of immense importance, the philosophism of the eighteenth century, the French Revolution, the rationalism of our own day, besides changes in the political, social, and religious order, deeper than even those of the sixteenth century, have come to pass in the world, and render the convocation of a general council more necessary than, perhaps, at any other time. It is manifest, and the searching eye of St. Peter's successor has seen it, that we have at this day a state of feeling, of habits, of society, in a word, an entire condition of things, so novel and without parallel in history, as to render it indispensably necessary that the Church should thoroughly probe it with all her divine lights, and with the experience of all her bishops, assisted by the Holy Spirit, under the presidency and direction of the Sovereign Pontiff.

What an immense stride infidelity has made since the sixteenth century! What a fall has been that of Protestantism into rationalism, and from rationalism into all the wanderings which we every day behold : the denial of God, of the soul, of the life to come, of reason as well as of faith, of all truths, in fine, which are the basis of all religion, of all morality, and of all society : and this in the name of modern science, so painfully and so unjustly invoked at the present hour on behalf of atheism, pantheism, and materialism!

On the other hand, what complicated, delicate, and deep problems have been raised by modern doctrines, political and economical, and above all by very serious social questions, and carried throughout by the press—the press, that formidable power of modern times, which our fathers knew not! And concerning each of these problems, what confusion of ideas, what errors, what sophisms, what unhappy mistakes! What a mingling of truth and falsehood, of good and evil in the theories of the day; and what uncertainty in men's minds as to the real bearing of Catholic teaching on these theories, and to the necessary or possible attitude of the Church to the present state of society! How truly important it is to cast fullest light upon each of these points for all men of good will, to sunder between the true and the false, the good and the bad, to separate the precious from the vile, as the Scripture says; and how it is worthy of the Sovereign Pontiff to convoke for this purpose the bishops of all countries who are in daily contact, or in unceasing warfare, with the ideas which are to be cleared up, condemned, or extolled!

And, as touching the inner and outer life of the Church how many questions of capital interest will have to be studied by the Bishops in Council, as well concerning the necessary development of sacred learning in all its branches, seeing that the defence of Christianity and theology have bearings on all the sciences, as also concerning ecclesiastical law, which may, perhaps, be modified in some of its earlier decisions, as also in what concerns discipline, the pastoral ministry, and works of zeal : works which are the labour and the honour of that Christian priesthood, secular or regular, which is devoted to the triple apostleship of truth, of charity, and of holiness. The Holy

Father has, therefore announced a General Council, and in what calm and noble words :

"We have long entertained a project, which circumstances have made known to several of the venerable brethren, and to which we hope to give effect as soon as the desired occasion shall arrive ; namely, to hold a sacred Œcumenical and General Council of all the bishops of the Catholic world, in which, with the help of God, by union of deliberate and careful counsel, such wholesome remedies may be applied as are needed, especially by the many evils weighing upon the Church The result of this, as we greatly hope, will be that the light of Catholic truth will dissipate the darkness of error in which men's souls are wrapt, and shed abroad its salutary beams, so that by the aid of Divine grace, they may discern and follow the true way of righteousness and salvation. As a further result, the Church invincible 'as an army set in array,' will beat back the hostile efforts of her enemies, break their onset, and in her triumph over them will extend and uphold the reign of Jesus Christ over the length and breadth of the earth."

And, in a second allocution to the Bishops, returning upon this great idea, the Holy Father has lovingly congratulated us on

"That common desire of a General Council, and because we all judged it to be not only extremely useful at present (*penitile*), but even necessary (*necessarium*). The divine power of the Church, added he, is then especially potent, when the bishops convoked by the Sovereign Pontiff, and presided over by him, assemble in the name of the Lord to treat of the affairs of the Church."

It is, in truth, in a general council that the power and majesty of the Church are beheld in all their vigour. It is there that she appears truly, as the Holy Father describes her, like an army set in array, when, with Peter at her head, with her bishops ranged around the chair of truth, with Jesus Christ, her invisible Head, in her midst, and with the Spirit of Holiness and Light shedding His influence upon the assembly, she proclaims the truth, she confounds error, she scatters that deceitful science that lifts itself up against the science of God ; and when after having given light to the intellect, she endeavours to enkindle charity in the heart, and prepare the way for peace-making, for union, for returns to harmony. Such is the beautiful and noble design of the Holy Father.

And what adds to the grandeur of the undertaking is the Pontiff's courage and faith, and his magnanimous hope. No labour deters his fresh old age or his great soul. And what are years to him who has the future for his own ? The Pope never dies. And what matter about the threats of the angry revolution ? Against this Peter, against this rock, the waves shall be broken for evermore.

No doubt the enterprise is as bold as it is noble. For, after all, is not the Pope hemmed in by fire and sword ? And, no matter how great the honour, the devotion, and the bravery of that noble pontifical army which we have seen applauded by the people of Rome, and by the Catholic pilgrims of the universe, can it do everything ? Besides, in the midst of so much covetousness, so much meanness, and so much violence, what will become to-morrow of Europe and of the peace of the world ? And yet, it is in this state of things, and amid such perils, that the Pope, with a calm and sure glance around and towards the future, has said : "The Holy See is threatened ; the world is troubled, uncertain, restless : no matter ; the Church will achieve its task ;" and, addressing himself to his brethren, and to his sons, the bishops of the entire world : " Come," he says, "I await you, and here, at Rome, we will work together for the salvation of the world."

At this announcement of a General Council, the bishops, moved by the magnitude of the undertaking and by the august calmness of the Pontiff, were filled with a sudden joy ; and, blessing God for the incalculable blessings which such a design promised for the future, they replied :

" It is with an extensive joy of soul that we have heard from your lips the profound design you have in contemplation in the midst of so many present perils of convoking a general council, ' *the most powerful remedy that can be employed*,' said your predecessor Paul the Third, '*in the greatest perils of the Christian world*.' May God prosper this design which He himself has inspired, and may the men of our day, *so weak in faith, ever seeking and never finding the truth, carried about by every wind of doctrine*, find at least in this holy Council a new and favourable opportunity of drawing near the holy Church which is the pillar and whole ground of truth ; may they come to know the true faith, the source of salvation, and to reject the errors that are leading them to their ruin, and may this general assembly of the Catholic Episcopate become, with God's help, and the prayers of the Immaculate Virgin Mary, a great work of unity, of sanctification, and of peace-making, which will procure for the Church a new splendour and a new triumph for God's Kingdom."

The Council will then be held, and held at Rome, and the Holy Father, in his reply, has announced that, to satisfy the general desire, it shall be opened on the glorious festival of the Immaculate Conception of Mary.

By aid of the modern easy means of locomotion, the bishops will assemble in large numbers, and from regions more remote and various than in any council held in past times. At Trent there were three hundred Bishops, and yesterday, at Rome, we were five hundred. At Chalcedon, which was the largest of the ancient councils, there were six hundred, but they were almost all Orientals. At the coming council you will have the East and the South and the North, the three continents of the Old

World and the two Americas, with the bishops of the Indies, of China, and from the most remote isles of the ocean; in such wise as that this senate of the Catholic Church, composed of the aged men who rule all the Churches of the world, under every latitude and beneath every sky, shall be the most complete representation of the Church which has ever been seen.

And where could we hope to find an assembly to be compared to that of these men, of these Bishops? Gathered from every spot of earth, they will represent not only the Church; they also will be, by their experience and learning, by their gravity and their virtues, the worthiest representatives of the human race itself, and even from the mere human point of view, assuredly the highest moral authority which exists upon the earth. Who can foresee how much light and truth such an assembly, so mature in deliberation, so authoritative in judgment, shall pour out upon the world, together with a powerful and fruitful impulse to virtue?

I have seen the bishops of the various parts of Europe congratulate each other, and consider the future Council as the grandest and happiest effort the Church can make to enlighten minds and soften hearts, to bring back sincere souls now led astray by error or by fatal mistakes, to do good to society as well as to the Church.

I have seen the bishops of the two Americas already salute the great stream of Catholic life which this direct and prolonged communication with the Holy See and with the bishops of the old continents cannot but put in motion both in the young and in the old churches of the New World.

I have seen the Oriental bishops especially glowing with a holy hope; already they seem to behold the old Christian Churches of the East once more animated by the breath of life breathed upon them by the Council. And this is not their only hope. Already, for some time past, a secret travail is taking place in the depths of the East; the separated Churches have begun to feel what their misfortunes ought to have long since brought home to them, that in cutting themselves off from unity they have cut themselves off from the principle of life, and that there is no second birth for them until they return to the Chair of Peter, to the Mother and Mistress of all the Churches. This feeling, very lively in some, is as yet confused in others; and who can tell how much a Council may foster it, and what a splendid lesson it may teach the Oriental Churches against the schism which has been so fatal to them. Oh! if it were given to the Council of the nineteenth century to accomplish at Rome the work

that was once essayed at Florence; and if our age, saddened by so many sorrows, were destined to behold this great
restoration!

And shall I here tell all my hopes? Protestantism, as everyone knows, is stricken with a malady inherent in its very principle, which on one side impels it, as Bossuet foretold and we
ourselves are witnesses, towards rationalism the most anti-
Christian, and on the other side tears and dissolves it by countless divisions. Such Protestants as are yet Christians struggle
in vain against the torrent that carries them along : they feel
the need of unity, and are searching for what is its necessary
principle. We know that especially in England many sincere
men are in this state of mind, and sigh after union. Is it then
presumption to think that this great spectacle of living unity,
speaking in a council of the Universal Church, will bring light
to their eyes, and that there, perhaps, their final difficulties shall
disappear before a simple and luminous exposition of the true
faith? May God hear our prayers, and do you, our separated
brethren, come at length and throw yourselves into our arms
open, now three centuries, to receive you! And is this all we
hope for? No. At this moment, when all the churches of the
world, represented by five hundred bishops, surround our common Father, there is one endeared to us among all, by its fidelity,
its heroism, and its sorrows, which we do not see here. O
beloved Church of Poland, in vain have we sought for even one
of your bishops, that we might kiss his hand as we would the hand
of a martyr. Not one of them was there. And why? Are they
in those regions of exile from which no one ever returns?
Was it feared that they might move with too much sorrow the
gentle Pontiff, by letting him see the evils which thou art suffering? But who is there under the sun who knows not the sad
history? Oh! when will they cease their cruel attempts to tear
thee bleeding from the bosom of the Roman Church, thy mother,
O Poland, as well as ours! At least when the council comes,
may thy bishops too be there, by our side, to labour with us for
the coming of God's Kingdom in the world, and for the, sometimes tardy, triumphs of truth and justice!

To dissipate, then, the errors of the day, to throw the clear
light of Christian tradition and of Catholic learning upon the
great questions at present obscured by such thick darkness ; to
rekindle in the bosom of the Church the glowing fire of charity
and devotedness, to bring into action all its living strength and
send a new breath of holy life from one extremity of this great
body to the other; to remove the grounds of discord and of separation by clearing up what is obscure, and by correcting mis-

apprehensions, and thereby to prepare the way happily for many· a return to unity : to achieve, in one word, a great work of enlightenment and of peace-making—who would not applaud such an effort of the Catholic Church? And is there any government, any statesman worthy of the name, not to say liberal, but sensible and honest, who could take the least umbrage at it, or raise up obstacles to hinder it?

No! I call the conscience of the world to witness : when, in an age like ours, afflicted by so many errors, and menaced by so many storms, the Church holds a Council, that is to say, when the Church sets herself to bring into the world a larger stock of truth and charity and holiness, she is not conspiring against anyone or against anything, but against evil ; she is engaged in a work which affects society as much as it affects Catholicism ; she is toiling for governments and for nations as well as for herself ; on behalf of peace, of universal concord ; to strenghten the foundation of the social order, which is shaken ; for the world's true progress ; and all rulers and nations should bless her for her work.

In the name, then, of the interests of Europe and of the world, as well as of the interest of Catholicism, in the name of modern principles as well as of every right, let the Church be allowed to come together and deliberate, and hold her Council in all liberty and security here at Rome, in her own seat, in the centre of peace and of glory ; and even if, which God forbid! even if those evils we would avert should fall upon the world, even if the errors of the day, giving birth to the calamities they are big with, should once again throw the nations into the bloody conflicts of revolutions and of wars, it would be well that governments and nations should keep the Church in peace, in the midst of the tempests of the world, under their common protectorate, in order that there might be on the earth at least one spot reserved where aged men gathered from all parts of the world may together seek in sacred learning, in meditation, and in prayer, far from the passions of men, those better lights which the world needs, and which alone will bring those who are now divided to understand each other, and to enter once more through the truth to justice and to peace.

O gentle and sainted Pontiff! with those enlightened eyes of the heart of which Scripture speaks, you have discovered the true remedy for the evils of the day, and with that power and courage which you hide beneath your meekness and your sweetness, you had confidence enough in God and man to undertake this most laborious but mighty work, which may result in the peaceful triumph of the Church, and the salvation of this century; may you be blessed for it for ever! Did you not already bear upon your venerable brow the triple aureola of your labours, your virtues, and your sorrows, this alone would have been enough to win for you for evermore the world's grateful admiration; and we trust neither God nor men will fail you. Henceforth, from this hour, the future council will occupy the whole Church with labour and with prayer, and will fill all hearts with a holy hope; and in this mighty work, which completes all you have already done for God and for our souls, God has, perhaps, reserved the consolation and the crown of your long and glorious Pontificate!

A VISIT TO THE ARAN-MORE OF ST. ENDA.

On a summer's day, some fourteen hundred years ago, St. Enda of Aran, as his ancient life tells us, knelt by the shore of the harbour where Lough Corrib joins the sea, to ask a blessing on the fishermen who then plied their craft in Galway Bay.* On a summer's day in the present year, from the very spot where our saint had prayed, we set sail to visit, in love and reverence, the remote Aran, which his virtues had changed from a Pagan isle into Aran of the Saints. And as the faint breeze bore us slowly over the waters that lay almost motionless in the summer calm, we gazed with admiration upon a scene which, at least in its larger outlines, was but little changed since St. Enda and his pilgrim band had first looked upon it. Before us there lay stretched out the same expanse of sea, fringed on one side by the dark plains of Iar-Connaught, along which the eye travelled from the white cliffs of Barna to where the Connemara mountains, in soft blue masses, stood out in fantastic clusters against the sky. On the other side ran the Clare coastline, now retreating before the deep-sea inlets, and now breasting the Atlantic with bold promontories like that of gloomy Black-Head, or with gigantic cliffs like those of Mohir. And as the day closed, and we watched the evening breeze steal out from land, crisping the water into wavelets that presently rippled against the vessel's

* Colgan, Acta SS., p. 709, n. 25.

side; and as we saw the golden glory of the sunset flush with
indescribable loveliness, earth, and sea, and sky, we thought
how often in bygone days, the view of Aran rising, as we then
saw it, out of the sunlit waves, had brought joy to the pilgrim
who was journeying to find rest upon its rocky shore:

> "And as I view the line of light that plays
>   Along the smooth waves, towards the burning west,
> I long to tread that golden path of rays,
>   And think 'twill lead to some bright isle of rest."

It was some such thoughts as these that stirred St. Enda's
heart when he cried out that Aran was to be the place of his
resurrection, where, in his flesh, he was to look upon the face
of his God; it was through some such feeling that St. Columba,
after lavishing upon the Aran of his soul every term of endear-
ment, crowned at length his praise by calling it the "Rome of
the pilgrim."*

The Aran Isles are three in number, named respectively,
Inishmore (the large island), Inishmain (the middle island), and
Inisheen (the eastern island). The eastern island is the smallest
of the three, and is about two and a-half miles long; the middle
island is three miles long; the largest is about nine miles in
length, and twenty-four in circumference. The entire group
contains about 11,288 acres, of which only 742 are productive.
Geologically considered, the islands belong to the upper division
of carboniferous limestone. Mention is made of Aran at a very
early period of Irish history. The most authoritative of our
ancient Irish MSS. relate that after the great battle of Moytura,
on the shores of Loughs Corrib and Mask, in which the Fir-
bolgs or Belgae, after four days' fighting, were defeated by the
Tuatha de Dannan, a portion of the Belgae crossed over to
Aran, where as in an impregnable stronghold, they established
themselves about the beginning of the Christian era. One of
their leaders was Engus Mac Uathmore, after whom the great
fort or dun on Inishmore was named. About the year of our
Lord 480, the island was inhabited by infidels from Corcomroe,
the adjacent part of Clare. About that date, St. Enda received
the island by the donation of Engus, King of Munster, whose
wife, Darenia, was St. Enda's own sister. The pagans were
converted to Christianity, or quitted the island, which, under
St. Enda, soon became one of the great Christian sanctuaries of
the west of Europe. The Annals of the Four Masters tell of a
great conflagration at Aran in the year 1020, and of the devas-
tation wrought there by the Normans or Danes in the year 1081.

* See infra, St. Columba's "Farewell to Aran."

At a later period it was held by the O'Briens, the head of whom, commonly called Mac Teige O'Brien, kept his residence at Aircin or Arkin, on the great island. The O'Briens were expelled in their turn by the O'Flahertys, who, again, were dispossessed by Queen Elizabeth, under whom the castle of Airkin was erected in 1587, on the site of the residence of the O'Briens. Elizabeth gave the island to John Ransom, from whose hands it passed into the possession of Sir Robert Lynch, of Galway. In Cromwell's time this castle was pulled down, and a strong fort erected in its place, of which fort we shall have occasion to speak further on. In December, 1650, 700 of the Irish landed here in boats, flying from defeat on the main land, and were speedily followed by 1,300 of the English foot, with a battery. The Irish surrendered, and Sir R. Lynch having been declared a traitor, Erasmus Smith became owner of Aran. This crafty undertaker disposed of his interest to the Butlers, one of whom, in 1662, was created Earl of Aran; from the Butlers the islands passed through the Fitzpatricks to the Digbys,* who are the present owners.

The present inhabitants, about 3,400 in number, mainly belong to the race that inhabit the south-western parts of Ireland. In their character they exhibit the beautiful results of the action of the Catholic religion upon a stock gifted with fine intellect and great sensibility, under circumstances which allow that religion to exercise, without hindrance, its blessed influence. Their simple Catholic faith, so pure, so tender, and so fervent, is crowned in them with the crown of good works. They are a courteous, handsome, and amiable people, with a refinement of manner and a delicacy of sentiment, which surprised and delighted us. Their high intelligence, their good-natured readiness to oblige; the total absence of the greed of gain, no less than their erect and graceful carriage, marked them out as something of which we had not before seen the like. We bear cheerful witness to the accuracy of the following account of their social state given by Dr. Petrie:†

"I had heard so much of the virtues of the Aran islanders, of their primitive simplicity, their ingenuous manners, and their singular hospitality, that I could not help doubting the truth of a picture so pleasing and romantic, and felt anxious to ascertain, by personal observation, how far it might be real. . . . Collectively, the inhabitants of the Aran Islands may be said to exhibit the virtues of the Irish character with, perhaps, as little intermixture of its vices as the lot of humanity will permit.

* See Ordnance Survey MSS., R.I.A., Lib., Galway, vol. iii., to which we are much indebted, especially for details of measurement.
† Stokes's " Life of Petrie," pp. 49-50.

"They are a brave and hardy race, industrious and enterprising; as is sufficiently evinced, not only by the daily increasing number of their fishing vessels, the barren rocks which they are covering with soil, and making productive, but still more by the frequency of their emigration from their beloved country and friends to a distant wilderness, led solely by the hope that their indefatigable labour may be employed there to the greater ultimate benefit of their families.

"They are simple and innocent, but also thoughtful and intelligent, credulous, and in matters of faith, what persons of a different creed would call superstitious. . . . . Lying and drinking—the vices which Arthur Young considers as appertaining to the Irish character—form, at least, no part of it in Aran, for happily their common poverty holds out less temptation to the one or opportunity for the other.

"I do not mean to say that they are rigidly temperate, or that instances of excess, followed by the usual Irish consequences of broken heads, do not occasionally occur: such could not be expected when their convivial temperament, and dangerous and laborious occupations are remembered. They never swear, and they have a high sense of decency and propriety, honour and justice. In appearance they are healthy, comely, and prepossessing; in their dress (with few exceptions), clean and comfortable; in manner serious, yet cheerful, and easily excited to gaiety; frank and familiar in conversation, and to strangers polite and respectful; but at the same time wholly free from servile adulation. They are communicative, but not too loquacious; inquisitive after information, but delicate in seeking it, and grateful for its communication.

"If the inhabitants of the Aran Islands could be considered as a fair specimen of the ancient and present wild Irish—the veriest savages in the globe, as the learned Pinkerton calls them—those whom chance has led to their hospitable shores, to admire their simple virtues, would be likely to regret that the blessings of civilisation had ever been extended to any portion of this very wretched country."

Though poor, the Araners are not exposed to crushing want. The perennial harvest of the sea supplies these hardy fishermen with abundance of food; their untiring industry covers the barren rock with a scanty crop; their cattle are eagerly sought after in the markets of the mainland, and we believe that still, as in O'Flaherty's time, the young men are accustomed to go down, with ropes tied about them, into the caves of the cliffs to kill the wild birds that love to make their home therein.* Nor is the samphire-gatherer's perilous trade unknown to them. In addition, they export great quantities of kelp, to be used in the manufacture of iodine.

We landed on Inishmore, at the little village of Kilronan, about thirty miles distant from Galway, and, after some rest, set out towards the south-west coast to visit the wonderful fort of Engus. Having gained the low hill that commands the village, we halted to contemplate the weird and dun landscape that surrounded us. It was a landscape peculiar to Aran. The island falls from the south-west, facing east and north; and from the vantage-ground on which we stood, the eye traversed

* O'Flaherty's "Iar Connaught," p. 69.

fields upon fields of bare, dark-gray rocks, which now rose into
hills, now sank into valleys, according to the action of the force
that had originally upheaved the island itself.

> " But here, above, around, below,
>   On mountain or in glen,
>   No tree, nor shrub, nor plant, nor flower,
>   Nor aught of vegetative power,
>   The weary eye may ken;
>   For all is rocks at random thrown,
>   Bleak waves, bare crags, and banks of stone."

The ground was covered with rocks, not scattered and disjointed as they occur elsewhere, but spreading into immense
sheets and tables of stone, sometimes sixty feet broad, as smooth
as polished marble, and giving out beneath the tread a sonorous
metallic ring.   In some places these slabs rise tier upon tier,
stone overlapping stone with a precise regularity of mass and
form, which reminded you of masonry cunningly piled by giant
hands.   Winding in and out, in a thousand mazes, a thread of
fresh green herbage could, on closer inspection, be traced along
the hill side, up-springing where the natural cleavage of the
rocks had left deep fissures, now and then widening into a patch
of verdure, in which wild flowers of every hue bloomed in
luxuriance against the gray crag.   Frequent enclosures of loose
stones crossed each other in and out in almost countless ridges,
until it seemed as if both rocks and verdure were covered with
an iron network of most irregular pattern.

The fertile portion of the island lies in the valley to the
left of the road leading from Kilronan, and in it the principal
religious establishments were erected.   We passed a group of
Araners engaged in gathering the harvest, by the simple process
of tearing up the corn by the root.   On either side of the road
we remarked, at irregular intervals, monuments raised to the
memory of the dead.   They stood sometimes singly, sometimes
in groups, almost in each case surmounted by the cross, and
consisting of a square pile of masonry, about seven feet in height.
A rude cornice, about half-way from the top, divided them into
two portions, the upper of which bore a tablet, having inscribed
upon it a prayer for the soul of the departed one, to whose
memory the pile had been raised.   How touching is the solicitude thus displayed by those good Catholics to procure prayers
for the souls of their beloved dead !   The bodies of the deceased
were interred in the far-off cemeteries, where the saints repose—
ad sanctos—as the sepulchral slabs in the Roman catacombs
express it; but as these outlying places were remote from the
centres of the population, and seldom visited by men, the loving
Catholic instincts of the people suggested the erection of these

monuments of prayer by the wayside, that all who passed by
might bestow on the faithful departed the suffrages of their
charity.

Leaving the road at a point where a sudden fault in the dark
rocks allows the waves to wash a narrow strip of beach covered
with sand of pearly whiteness, we crossed the fields towards the
hill upon which Dun Engus stands. On reaching the south-
west coast, we descended through an opening in the tall cliffs,
down to the water-line, where the Atlantic was surging heavily
against the solid rock. What a scene lay before us! On the
one hand the cliffs rose sheer from the water with surfaces
seamed, and scarred, and torn by the tremendous violence of the
billows driven in upon them by centuries of winter tempests.
At our feet the waves were breaking on the lowest shelf of rock,
leaving uncovered (it was low tide) a hard ledge honeycombed
by the water into countless cavities, some deep, where lived the
richly-coloured sea-anemones and other wonders of the shore,
others shallow, from which we gathered handfuls of salt, extracted
from the brine by the fierce heat of the sun. On the right, a
sudden turn brought us to where the rocks rose into a noble
arch (which recalled forcibly to our mind one of the arches in
the Temple of Peace in the Roman Forum), spanning a polished
pavement, in the middle of which a pool of water azure blue,
carried from the sea through subterranean conduits, rose and
fell within a basin, hewn, as if by hands, in the living rock.
On climbing the almost vertical escarpment at the opening of
this grotto we found a second ledge of rock some thirty feet in
breadth, over which, at high water, the waves rush to dash
themselves against a still higher range of precipitous cliffs. On
the summit of this range the soft grass grows to the very brink.
This height commands a sea prospect which is said to be one of
the noblest in the world. The vast Atlantic stretching illimitably
towards the south and west, the extensive coasts of Kerry and
Clare, with headlands and lofty mountains, and islands far off
in sight, must be seen in the calm, bright sunshine, as we saw
them, in order to form any idea of the sublimity and beauty of
the view.

Crowning the cliff, where it rises precipitously from the sea
some three hundred and two feet, stands the fort of Dun Engus,
the finest specimen of a barbaric fortress now existing in Europe,
or perhaps in the world. We approached it, not from the land
side, but by a route skirting the edge of the cliff, and we shall
endeavour to describe each portion of it in the order in which it
actually fell under our notice. First, we came upon a dry stone
wall, an irregular ellipse in form, which, in its entire circuit
from cliff to cliff, encloses a space of about eleven acres. This

wall is very much injured, and is the outermost of the three walls which protected the fort. It was built in two divisions, after a fashion which we shall describe in treating of the two inner walls. At a considerable distance from this outermost wall we came upon an army of white sharp-pointed stones, set slopewise in the earth, reaching all round breast high, save where a narrow avenue was left. This belt runs all round the second wall from cliff to cliff, and is in some places thirty feet broad. It fully answers the purpose of an *abbatis* or the *chevaux de frise* of modern fortifications, and must have proved a most formidable defence. No assailing party could possibly approach the second rampart, except through the avenue, without having its ranks broken and disordered by its thick and intricate piles of rock. Between the *chevaux de frise* and the second rampart there is a fragment of another wall, about seven feet in height, and covering only about one-tenth part of the second interior line of defence. This second interior defence consists of a cyclopean wall surrounding the fort itself at irregular distances, being about thirty-two feet distant from it at the western side, near the cliff, and about forty-two on the north-western side. It is about six feet thick and twelve high, and, like the outermost wall, is built in two concentric divisions. Within this second rampart the space to the central fortification is clear. The central fortification consists of an immense oval wall, composed of three distinct walls built up against each other, like the several coats of an onion, which arrangement occurs also in the two outermost enclosures, and in the other fortresses of the same kind in Aran and elsewhere. At first it is difficult to understand why the walls were constructed thus in layers and not in solid masses. But this peculiarity is explained by the principle on which these fortresses are constructed, which is thus described by Mr. Ferguson, as exemplified in the Staigue fort in Kerry:— " Within the (enclosure), at about six feet from the surface, the thickness of the wall is diminished by one-third, so as to leave a' circular ledge, or *terre-pleine*, of five or six feet in width, projecting all round. This ledge is reached by flights of stairs on the inner face of the wall. At a height of five or six feet higher another contraction of the thickness of the rampart takes place, leaving a like ridge, or shelf of masonry, approached in like manner by steps from the former, and serving as a kind of *banquette** to the parapet formed by the remaining height of the parapet. An arrangement in the building, exhibiting a good

---

* *Banquette*, in modern fortification, is a little raised way or footbank, running along the inside of a parapet, on which the musketeers stand to fire upon the enemy, in the moat or covered way.—*Encyc.*

deal of military contrivance, is made subservient to the formation of these internal stages. Instead of building the rampart in bulk, and starting with a fresh face of masonry above each ledge, the Fir-Volg builders have, in every case, built their rampart from the foundation in as many concentric independent walls as they designed to have *banquettes;* so that if an enemy should succeed in breaching the external envelope, he would find immediately behind it a new face of masonry, instead of the easily-disturbed loose interior of a dry stone wall."*

The greatest height of this triple wall at present is about eighteen feet; the inner division of the wall is about three feet thick; the second or central, about five; and the external about four; giving in all a total thickness of about twelve feet. The height of the inner division at present is not more than seven feet. The entire central fort from the north side of the ring to the cliff measures one hundred and fifty feet, and along the cliff, from wall to wall, west to east, one hundred and forty feet. On the north-west side of the ring there is a passage leading from the inside into the thickness of the wall, about five feet in width, and four feet high from the bottom to the roof, where it is covered by large stones, placed horizontally. This was probably an apartment for the use of some of the garrison. A sloping roof, round the inner wall, would easily supply shelter for a large number of men.

The door to the keep is in the north-eastern side, and is nearly perfect, resembling in its form that of the earlier churches. It is so much blocked up by the loose stones which have fallen from the walls that we were compelled to enter on our hands and knees. The traces of stairs are still to be distinguished amid the ruin that has been brought upon the walls by the winter blasts, and by the hand of man. The course of the *banquette,* especially along a portion of the eastern side, may be quite plainly discerned.

The stones of which the walls are built are large and small, the large being employed in the outside, the small within. In no instance did we observe huge blocks like those employed in the so-called Cyclopean walls throughout Italy, such as we have admired in the walls of the ancient Tusculum. Indeed, in some of the Christian temples on the island we found blocks much larger than any we could perceive in the ramparts of the Pagan Dun.

Standing on the square blocks of stone which occupy portion of the area of the central fort, we looked in vain for some proof that the fort had originally been a complete oval. Nor have we

* *Dublin University Magazine,* January, 1853, pp. 92-93.

been convinced by any reasoning that has since come in our way that it ever was oval. It is true that the Aran islands and other places in Ireland exhibit frequent instances of round or oval fortresses of the class to which Dun Engus belongs, a near example being that of Dun Connor, on the middle island, which measures from north to south no less than two hundred and twenty-seven feet. But it was difficult for one standing on the brow of the cliff, and scanning the small extent of the change made on the coast-line around him within the historical period, to believe that some hundred and fifty feet of the living solid rock had been eaten away by the action of the waves. Nor do we attach much weight to the argument that unless we admit the fortress to have been oval it would have been left defenceless for a space of above a hundred feet. Surely, a sheer cliff rising from the sea to the height of three hundred and two feet was a defence enough against any force that could be brought up against it in those days. Ledwich, who in his *Antiquities* describes Dun Engus as a monkish *mandra*, furnishes a print in which not only is the oval completed, but the modern houses of the monks are seen rising over the rampart, which in turn is shaded by tall and leafy trees, while in the foreground a group of religious are walking down a rocky pathway, ornamented with large wooden crosses ! These wonders are, we need hardly say, entirely the product of his imagination. Wooden houses in Aran are as rare as leafy trees among its barren rocks ; and how rare these are there is little need to tell. And yet for years Ledwich has thus impudently imposed upon the credulity of his readers by a mendacious print, which he absolutely invented to sustain a foolish story advanced by him concerning St. Enda. It is consoling, however, to reflect that the ancient glories of our Catholic island no longer form the exclusive domain of writers like this charlatan, whose ignorance was equalled only by his insolent attacks upon all that is dear to the heart of a Christian Irishman.

And now quitting these proud fortresses, where the pagan monarch paraded his fierce strength, let us visit the lowly places wherein Christian humility taught St. Enda, himself a king's son, to lead a life hidden with Christ in God.

St. Enda, whose name is written in Irish, Einne and Ende, and in Latin, Endeus and Enna, was born in Louth about the middle of the fifth century, and was the only son of. Conall, King of Oriel, whose territories included the modern counties of Louth, Monaghan, Armagh, and Fermanagh. Three of his sisters, Fanchea, Lochinia, and Carecha, were nuns, and Darenia, the fourth sister, was wife of Engus, King of Cashel, whose death is placed by the Four Masters in the year 489. On the

death of his father, the youthful Enda was chosen to succeed
him as head of the men of Oriel. The warlike spirit of the
times took strong hold of the young prince's heart, and we find
him at an early period of his life captivated by the love of glory,
and eager to show by his military prowess that he was worthy
of the royal race from which he had sprung, and of the throne
which he filled. His holy sister Fanchea was incessant in her
exertions to win for God her brother's heart, which, with all its
defects, she knew to be chivalrous and pure. For a time her
words of warning and entreaty remained without result; but
the season of grace came soon. Enda had asked from his sister
in marriage one of the royal maidens who were receiving their
education in the convent which she ruled. Fanchea communicated his request to the maiden: "Make thou thy choice,
whether wilt thou love Him whom I love, or this earthly bride-
groom?" "Whom thou lovest," was the girl's sweet reply,
"Him also will I love." She died soon after, and gave her soul
to God, the spouse whom she had chosen.

"The holy virgin," says the ancient Life, "covered the face
of the dead girl with a veil, and going again to Enda said to
him: 'Young man, come and see the maiden whom thou
lovest.' Then Enda with the virgin entered the chamber where
was the dead girl, and the holy virgin, uncovering the face of
the lifeless maiden, said to him: 'Now look upon the face
of her whom thou didst love.' And Enda cried out: 'Alas!
she is fair no longer, but ghastly white.' 'So also shalt thy
face be,' replied the holy virgin. And then St. Fanchea dis-
coursed to him of the pains of hell and of the joys of heaven,
until the young man's tears began to flow. Oh! the wondrous
mercy of God in the conversion of this man to the true faith!
for even as he changed the haughty Saul into the humble Paul,
so out of this worldly prince did he make a spiritual and a holy
teacher and pastor of his people. For having heard the words
of the holy virgin, despising the vanities of the world, he took
the monk's habit and tonsure, and what the tonsure signified he
fulfilled by his actions."[*]

After having founded a monastery in his native place, St.
Enda is said to have proceeded to Rosnat or Abba, in Britain,
where he remained for some time under the spiritual direction
of St. Mansenus or Manchan. Thence, according to the above-
mentioned life, he went to Rome, where "attentively studying
the examples of the saints, and preparing himself in everything
for the order of priesthood, having at length been ordained

* (Vita S. Endæi, auctore Augustino Magradin, apud Colgan, Acta SS.,
p. 705.)

priest, he was pleasing to the most high God." He built a monastery called *Laetinum*, or *the Place of Joy*: and rightly so called, adds the Life, " because therein the command of loving God and our neighbour was most faithfully carried out."

Returning to Ireland, he landed at Drogheda, and built several churches on either side of the river Boyne. He then proceeded southwards to visit his brother-in law, Engus, King of Munster, from whom he asked the island of Aran, that he might dwell thereon. The king was first unwilling to comply with his request: not because he was ungenerous, but because he had learned from St. Patrick " not to offer to the Lord his God any lands save such as were good and fertile, and easy of access."* But St. Enda declared that Aran was to be the place of his resurrection; and at length the king made an offering of the island " to God and St Enda," asking in return the blessing of the saint.

Having thus obtained possession of what he rightly deemed a place of singular retirement, and well suited for the rigours of a penitential life, St. Enda returned to his brethren and con-ducted them in safety to the island, which was then inhabited by Pagans from the adjacent coast of Clare. He divided the island into ten parts, and built thereon ten monasteries, each under the rule of its proper superior. He chose a place for his own residence on the eastern coast, and there erected a monastery, the name and site of which is preserved to this day in the little village of Kil-eany (Kill-Enda), about a mile from Kilronan. One-half of the island was assigned to this monastery.

Then began the blessed days, when the sweet odour of penance ascended to heaven from the angelic band of monks who, under the severe rule of St. Enda, made Aran a burning light of sanctity for centuries in western Europe. " The virginal Saint from Anan Island," as Marianus O'Gorman styles St. Enda, was to them a model of all the virtues of the religious life, but above all he excelled in the exercise of penitential mortifications. St. Cuimin of Connor tells us that—

> " Enda loved glorious mortification
> In Aran—triumphant virtue !
> A narrow dungeon of flinty stone,
> To bring the people to heaven."

" Aran," says Froude,† " is no better than a wild rock. It is strewed over with the ruins which may still be seen of the old hermitages ; and at their best they could have been but such places as sheep would huddle under in a storm, and shiver in

---

* Acta SS.. loco. cit.　　　　　　　　　† Short Studies, vol. ii., page 216.

the cold and wet which would pierce through the chinks of the walls. . . . Yes; there on that wet soil, with that dripping roof above them, was the chosen home of these poor men. Through winter frost, through rain and storm, through summer sunshine, generation after generation of them, there they lived and prayed, and at last lay down and died."

These miracles of penance were the first and immediate results of St. Enda's work in Aran.

It was in his life that these holy men had daily before them the personal realisation of all they were striving after : he taught them to cherish the flinty dungeon and the dripping cave for love of the hard manger, and the harder cross; he bade them dwell amid the discomforts and dreariness of their island home, because in the tabernacles of sinners the blessed majesty of God was daily outraged by the crimes of men. Through him they came to know the gift of God, and who He was who spoke with them in their solitude ; whose converse made eloquent for them the silence of the night, and whose angels peopled their lonely island with visions of heavenly beauty. " Trust to one who has had experience," his life said to them, as St. Bernard said to the monks of Citeaux : " you will find something far greater in the woods than you will find in books. Stones and trees will teach you that which you will never learn from masters. Think you not you can suck honey from the rock, and oil from the flinty rock ? Do not the mountains drop sweetness, the hills run with milk and honey, and the valleys stand thick with corn ?"* We cannot, indeed, describe the details of his daily life, for they have been hidden from human view, as it is becoming that such secrets of the Heavenly King should be hidden. But there yet survives the voice of one of those who lived with him in Aran, and in the ideal of an abbot which St. Carthage sets before us we undoubtedly find reproduced the traits which distinguished the Abbot of Aranmore, from whom St. Carthage first learned to serve God in the religious life. St. Enda was his first model of the " patience, humility, prayer, fast, and cheerful abstinence; of the steadiness, modesty, calmness that are due from a leader of religious men, whose office it is to teach in all truth, unity, forgiveness, purity, rectitude in all that is moral; whose chief works are the constant preaching of the Gospel for the instruction of all persons, and the sacrifice of the Body of the great Lord upon the holy altar."† It was on Aranmore, and in St. Enda, that he first beheld at the altar of God that pattern priest after whose example he thus warns all priests :—

* St. Bernard, Ep. 106.
† " Rule of St. Carthage," *Irish Ecclesiastical Record*, vol. i., p. 117.

> " When you come in to the Mass—
> It is a noble office—
> Let there be penitence of heart, shedding of tears,
> And throwing up of hands.
> There shall be no permanent love in thy heart
> But the love of God alone :
> For pure is the body thou receivest.
> Purely must thou go to receive it."[*]

This angelic life did St. Enda live upon Aran in the midst of his children until he reached a venerable old age.

The fame of St. Enda's austere holiness, and of the angelical life which so many were leading in Aran under his guidance, soon spread far and wide throughout the land. The sweet odour of Christ, diffused from the lonely island in the Atlantic, penetrated to every part of Ireland, and wherever it reached its gracious message stirred with joy the hearts of the noblest and best among the servants of God. It told them of a spot where men led a life of higher sanctity and of more thorough severance from fleshy ties than was known elsewhere ; and to souls hungering and thirsting after perfection, to hear of the spiritual treasures stored up in Aran was to long for the wings of the dove to fly thither, to be made happy sharers in its graces. Hence, soon the Galway fishermen, whom St. Enda had blessed, found day after day their *corachs* crowded with strangers— religious men, of meek eye and gentle face—seeking to cross over to the island ; and so frequently was the journey made that the words of the prophet seemed verified, and even in that trackless sea " a path and a way was there, and it was called the holy way."[†] The pilgrims were men of every period of life, some, in the spring of their youth, flying from the pleasures that wooed their senses, and the earthly loves that laid snares for their hearts ; others in the vigour of healthful manhood ; and others aged and infirm, who came to close in religious peace the remnant of their days, which at their best they had accounted as few and evil. And thus Aran gradually came to be as the writer of the life of St. Kieran of Clonmacnoise describes it, the home of a multitude of holy men, and the sanctuary where repose the relics of countless saints, whose names are known only to the Almighty God.[‡] " Great indeed is that island," exclaims another ancient writer, " and it is the land of the saints, for no one, save God alone, knows how many holy men lie buried therein."[§]

---

[*] Loc. cit., p. 118.   [†] Isaias xxxv. 71.

[‡] " In qua multitudo sanctorum virorum manet, et innumerabiles sancti, omnibus incogniti nisi soli Deo Omnipotenti, ibi jacent." Colgan, Acta SS.

[§] " Magna est illa insula, et est terra sanctorum ; quia nemo scit numerum sanctorum qui sepulti sunt ibi, nisi solus Deus." Vita S. Albei. Colgan, Acta SS.

But, although it is not possible to learn the names of all the saints who were formed to holiness by St. Enda in Aran, our ancient records have preserved the names of a few at least out of that blessed multitude. Among them we find almost every name of note that appears in the second part of the well-known list of the saints of Ireland, drawn up by some author who flourished not later than the middle of the eighth century, and, in addition to these, many others of great celebrity who are not included in that catalogue. This second order of saints lasted from about the middle of the sixth to the beginning of the seventh century.

The history of these men is the history of St. Enda's work on Aran.

First among St. Enda's disciples must be ranked St. Kieran, the founder of Clonmacnoise, who has been styled by Alcuin the glory of the Irish race. St. Kieran came to Aran in his youth, and for seven years lived faithfully in the service of God, under the direction of St. Enda. His youth and strength fitted him in an especial manner for the active duties, which were by no means inconsiderable in so large a community, and in a place where the toil spent on an ungrateful soil was so scantily repaid. "During these seven years," says the ancient life of our saint,* "Kieran so diligently discharged the duties of grinding the corn that grain in quantity sufficient to make a heap never was found in the granary of the island." Upon these humble labours the light of the future greatness of the founder of Clonmacnoise was allowed to shine in visions. St. Kieran had a vision, which he faithfully narrated to his master, St. Enda. He dreamed that on the bank of a great river, which is called the Shannon, he saw a mighty tree laden with leaves and fruits, which covered with its shade the entire island of Erin. This dream he narrated to St. Enda, who said, "The tree laden with fruit thou art thyself, for thou shalt be great before God and man, and shalt bring forth sweetest fruits of good works, and shalt be honoured throughout all Ireland. Proceed, therefore, at once, and in obedience to the will of God, build thou there a monastery." Upon this St. Kieran prepared himself for the building of the monastery of Clonmacnoise. His first step was to receive the priesthood. But he could not bring himself to sever the happy ties that bound him to his abbot. He still longed to be under his guidance, and when recommending himself to the prayers of his brethren he said to St. Enda, in the presence of all, "O father, take me and my charge under thy protection, that all my disciples may be thine likewise." "Not so," answered Enda,

* Colgan, Vita S. End., p. 709.

"for it is not the will of God that you should all live under my care in this scanty island; but to thee, for thine admirable humility and perfect charity will Christ the Lord grant the half of Ireland as the portion of thine inheritance." And when they had thus spoken a cross was set up in the place in sign of the brotherhood they had contracted between themselves and those who were to come after them; and they said: "Whosoever in after times shall break the loving bond of this our brotherhood shall not have share in our love on earth, nor in our company in heaven."

The love which St. Enda bore towards his holy pupil for his many and wonderful virtues made their parting singularly painful to them both. For a time the holy abbot felt as if the angels of God were leaving Aran with Kieran, and he could find no relief for his anguish but in prayer. The sternness of religious discipline had not crushed but chastened the tenderness of an affectionate disposition in St. Enda any more than in St. Bernard, whose writings are the truest expression of the best feelings of the religious heart. And as St. Bernard deplored the loss of his brother Gerard, in whom the active and contemplative virtues were admirably united, so might St. Enda have spoken of Kieran. "Whom now shall I consult in doubtful matters? Who will bear my burdens? His wise and gentle speech saved me from secular conversation, and gave me to the silence which I loved. O diligent man! O faithful friend! He plunged himself in cares that I might be spared them, but in this he sought not for his own advantage, for he expected (such was his humility) more profit from my leisure than from his own. Who more strict than he in the preservation of discipline? Who more stern in the chastening of his body? Who more rapt or more sublime in contemplation?"*

The last hours spent by St. Kieran on Aran, as described in the ancient life of St. Enda, are full of touching incidents, which reveal the tender and simple affectionateness of those mortified religious.

The entire community of the island shared the sorrow that had come on their venerable abbot. When the moment of departure was at hand, and the boat that was to bear him from Aran was spreading its sails to the breeze, Kieran came slowly down to the shore, walking between St. Enda and St. Finnian, and followed by the entire brotherhood. His tears flowed fast as he moved along, and those who accompanied him mingled their tears with his. Peter de Blois, when leaving the Abbey of Croyland to return to his own country, stayed his steps seven

* St. Bernard, Serm. in mort. Gerardi. Op. tom. 1, Col. 1354.

times to look back and contemplate once again the place where
he had been so happy ; so, too, did Kieran's gaze linger with
tenderness upon the dark hills of Aran and on the oratories
where he had learned to love God, and to feel how good and
joyous a thing it is to dwell with brethren whose hearts are at
one with each other in God. And when the shore was reached,
again he knelt to ask his father's blessing ; and, entering the
boat, was carried away from the Aran that he was never to see
again. The monastic group stayed for a while on the rocks to
follow with longing eyes the barque that was bearing from them
him they loved ; and when at length, bending their steps home-
wards, they had gone some distance from the shore, St. Enda's
tears once more began to flow. " O my brethren," cried he,
" good reason have I to weep, for this day has our island lost
the flower and strength of religious observance." What was
loss to Aran, however, was gain to Clonmacnoise, and through
Clonmacnoise to the entire Irish Church, to which the venerable
monastery on the Shannon was the source of so many blessings
and of so much glory. Those who admire it even now in its ruins
should not forget that its splendours are reflected back upon the
rocky Aran, where St. Enda formed the spirit of its founder,
and fostered with his blessing the work he had undertaken to
accomplish.

St. Kieran died at Clonmacnoise in the year 549, in the
prime of life, having governed his monastery for the short space
of a single year.

Next among the saints of Aran comes St. Brendan.[*] The
life of this illustrious saint narrates " how the man of God went
westward with fourteen brethren to a certain island called Aran,
where dwelt St. Enda with his brethren. With these the
servant of God, Brendan, remained for three days and three
nights, after which, having received the blessing of St. Enda
and of his holy monks, he set out with his companions for
Kerry." This visit of St. Brendan to Aran has been described
by one of our poets[†] as follows :—

> " Hearing how blessed Enda lived apart,
>   Amid the sacred cares of Aran-Mor;
> And how, beneath his eye, spread like a chart,
>   Lay all the isles of that remoteet shore ;
> And how he had collected in his mind
>   All that was known to man of the old sea :
> I left the hill of miracles behind,
>   And sailed from out the shallow sandy Léigh.

[*] In codice Insulensi. See Colgan, p. 712.
[†] *The Bell-Founder and other Poems*, by D. F. Mac Carthy, p. 180, sqq.

" Again I sailed, and crossed the stormy sound
    That lies beneath Binn-Aite's rocky height,
And there, upon the shore, the saint I found
    Waiting my coming through the tardy night.
He led me to his home beside the wave,
    Where, with his monks, the pious father dwelled ;
And to my listening ear he freely gave
    The sacred knowledge that his bosom held.

" When I proclaimed the project that I nursed,
    How 'twas for this that I his blessing sought,
An irrepressible cry of joy outburst
    From his pure lips, that blessed me for the thought.
He said that *he*, too, had in visions strayed
    O'er the untrack'd ocean's billowing foam ;
Bid me have hope, that God would give me aid,
    And bring me safe back to my native home.

" Thus, having sought for knowledge and for strength,
    For the unheard-of voyage that I planned,
I left these myriad isles, and turned at length
    Southward my barque, and sought my native land.
There I made all things ready, day by day :
    The wicker-boat, with ox-skins cover'd o'er,
Chose the good monks, companions of my way,
    And waited for the wind to leave the shore."

St. Finnian of Moville is also mentioned in the Ancient Life*
of our saint as one of St. Enda's disciples at Aran. This
remarkable man was first placed under the care of St. Colman
of Dromore, who flourished about the year 510. It is expressly
mentioned in the life just quoted that it was from Aran he set
out on his pilgrimage to Rome. This was probably his first
visit to the Apostolic See. Being of an active temperament, he
there devoted himself with great ardour for several years to the
study of the ecclesiastical and apostolical traditions. He then
returned to Ireland, after having received the pontifical benediction, and carrying with him a rich store of relics of the
saints given him by the Pope, and the penitential canons, which
in his biographer's time were still called *the canons of St. Finnian*. He also brought to Ireland the earliest copy of the
Hieronymian translation of the Gospel : a treasure of such value
in the estimation of his ecclesiastical contemporaries that the
records of the period very frequently refer to St. Finnian's
Gospels.

In 540 he founded the great monastery of Moville, where
St. Columba spent portion of his youth. After labouring with
energy for many years in Ireland, St. Finnian returned to Italy,
where, according to the best authorities, he was made Bishop of
Lucca, in Tuscany, in which church he is venerated under the

* Colgan, Act. SS., p. 708.

name of St. Frigidian, or Fridian.   The Italian annals give
588 as the year of his death; the annals of Ulster and Tiger-
nach, 589.

The Irish life of St. Columbkille makes mention of the
sojourn of that great saint on Aran.   The traditions still current
on the island confirm this statement.   The deep love of St.
Columba for Aran, the sorrow with which he quitted its shores
for Iona, the spiritual excellences which he had therein discovered, are expressed with singular warmth of religious feeling
in a poem written by him on his departure, of which Mr. Aubrey
De Vere* has given the following spirited version:—

I.

" Farewell to Aran Isle, farewell !
    I steer for Hy ; my heart is sore:
The breakers burst, the billows swell,
    'Twixt Aran Isle and Alba's shore.

II.

" Thus spoke the Son of God, ' Depart ! '
    O Aran Isle, God's will be done !
By angels thronged this hour thou art ;
    I sit within my barque alone.

III.

" O Modan, well for thee the while !
    Fair falls thy lot, and well art thou !
Thy seat is set in Aran Isle :
    Eastward to Alba turns my prow.

IV.

" O Aran, sun of all the west !
    My heart is thine ! As sweet to close
Our dying eyes in thee as rest
    Where Peter and where Paul repose.

V.

" O Aran, sun of all the west !
    My heart in thee its grave hath found.
He walks in regions of the blest
    The man that hears thy church-bells sound.

VI.

" O Aran blest ! O Aran blest!
    Accursed the man that loves not thee !
The dead man cradled in thy breast—
    No demon scares him—well is he.

---

* De Vere's *Irish Odes and other Poems*, pp. 274, 275.

VII.

" Each Sunday Gabriel from on high
  (For so did Christ the Lord ordain)
Thy Masses comes to sanctify,
  With fifty angels in his train.

VIII.

" Each Monday Michael issues forth
    To bless anew each sacred fane :
Each Tuesday cometh Raphael,
    To bless pure hearth and golden grain.

IX.

" Each Wednesday cometh Uriel,
    Each Thursday Sariel, fresh from God ;
Each Friday cometh Ramael
    To bless thy stones and bless thy sod.

X.

" Each Saturday comes Mary,
    Comes Babe on arm, 'mid heavenly hosts !
O ! Aran ! near to heaven is he
    That hears God's angels bless thy coasts !"

The stanzas which in the original Irish correspond to the
fourth verse of Mr. De Vere's translation have been rendered
as follows by Dr. O'Donovan, who remarks that O'Flanagan's
translation is here defective.

" The Son of the King—Oh ! the Son of the living God,
    It is he who sent me to Iona ;
  It is he who gave to Enna——great the prosperity,
    Arran, the Rome of the pilgrims.
  Aran, thou sun—Oh ! Aran, thou sun !
    My affection lies with thee westward ;
  Alike to be under her pure earth interred,
    As under the earth of Peter and Paul."

The ancient life of St. Enda also reckons among the inhabitants of Aran St. Finnian the elder, the founder of the great
school of Clonard, who died in the second half of the sixth
century ; St. Jarlath, the founder of the See of Tuam ; St. Mac
Creiche, of the race of the men of Corcomroe, who were in
possession of Aran when St. Enda first went thither.   The
Martyrology of Donegal makes mention of St. Guigneus ; the
Martyrology of Aengus adds St Papeus, St. Kevin of Glendalough, St. Carthage of Lismore, St. Lonan Kerr, St. Nechatus
or Nechanus, and St. Libeus, brother of St. Enda.   In the midst
of this holy brotherhood St. Enda died in 540 or 542.
    Among the saints to whom, as we shall soon see, churches
were dedicated on the island, we find St. Benignus of Armagh,

who also most probably resided in Aran, and St. Caradoc, or Carantoc, whose name recalls his British origin. These two men may fairly be taken as representatives of the native and foreign elements which at that period went to make up the Irish Church. It is remarkable to find that on Aran, which seems to have been a common centre for the saints of the second order, these two elements are found in harmony, and most closely connected with each other. These facts contrast strangely with what we read in a late writer, that "the second order of saints do not appear to have had any connection with Armagh or the institutions of St. Patrick," and that "they were connected with the British Church, and not with the Church of St. Patrick."[*] The history of Aran and of its monuments forbids these attempts to disparage the unity of the ancient Irish Church.

The sight of Aran peopled by this host of saints forcibly recalls to mind that other island, where, in an age of wild and fierce passions, the arts of peace, religious learning, and the highest Christian virtues found a sanctuary. At the beginning of the sixth century Aran may with truth be styled the Lerins of the northern seas. True, its bare flags and cold gray landscape contrast sadly with "the gushing streams, the green meadows, the luxuriant wealth of vines, the fair valleys, and the fragrant scents which," according to St. Eucherius, "made Lerins the paradise of those who dwelled thereon."[†] However, its very wilderness did but make it richer in those attractions so well described by St. Ambrose, which made the outlying islands so dear to the religious men of that time.[‡] They loved those islands, "which, as a necklace of pearls, God has set upon the bosom of the sea, and in which those who would fly from the irregular pleasures of the world may find a refuge wherein to practise austerity and save themselves from the snares of this life. The sea that enfolds them becomes, as it were, a veil to hide from mortal eye their deeds of penance; it aids them to acquire perfect continence; it feeds grave and sober thought; it has the secret of peace, and repels all the fierce passions of earth. In it these faithful and pious men find incentives to devotion. The mysterious sound of the billows calls for the answering sound of sacred psalmody; and the peaceful voices of holy men, mingled with the gentle murmur of the waves breaking softly on the shore, rise in unison to the heavens." It must have been one of these men, whose island home had shut out all the sights of earth save that of the altar, of the sea, and of the wild birds disporting along the sunny shore, who, in

* Todd's St. Patrick, pp. 95-96.
† S. Eucherius de laude Eremi, 442.
‡ *Hexaemeron*, lib. 3, c. 5.

an ancient Irish treatise* on the Mass vestments, warns the priest that his "heart should be chaste and shining, and his mind like the foam of the wave, or the chalk on the gable of an oratory, or like the colour of the swan in sunshine—that is, without any particle of sin, great or small, resting in his heart."

At Aran, too, as at Lerins, while men sought after eternal happiness, they found that earthly happiness, pure and without alloy, was poured into their hearts. In their religious brotherhood they met with the hundredfold return which God has promised to those who make sacrifices for Him. Oh! how joyous was the life of that blessed company of the saints of Aran, where the nobly-born Enda and Kevin proved their kingly descent by the regal fulness of their virtues as well as by the grace and dignity of their manners; where Columba could gratify his scholarly passion for fair manuscripts, and Kieran find fresh treasures of ecclesiastical lore to acquire; where Brendan could learn all that man knew of the ocean and its mysteries, and Mochuda evermore delight in the sacred harmonies that first had won his young heart to the religion of Christ; where the highest form of Oriental asceticism was happily united with the fire of the active energy of the West. No wonder that Kieran wept to leave the beloved shore! No wonder that through the farewell wail of the exiled Columba there runs such an intensity of almost passionate sorrow that a thousand years have not been able to efface it!

Thus far we have endeavoured to give a faint outline of the result of the spiritual labours of St. Enda. It is now time to describe the material traces of his presence which came under our observation at Aran. And first as to the churches.

Dr. Malachy Keely, Archbishop of Tuam—a man distinguished for his zeal in religion, and endowed with every virtue—compiled in 1645, or shortly before, a description of the churches then existing in Aran, which has been preserved by Colgan. The following is his list of churches in Aranmore :—

1. The parish church, commonly called *Kill-Enda*, lies in the county of Galway, and half-barony of Aran, and in it St. Endeus, or St. Enna, is venerated as patron on the 21st of March.

2. The church called *Teglach-Enda*, to which is annexed a cemetery, wherein is the sepulchre of St. Endeus, with one hundred and twenty-seven other sepulchres, wherein none but saints were ever buried.

3. The church called *Tempull Mac Longa*, dedicated to St.

* Curry's Lectures on the MS. Materials of Irish History, vol. i., p. 376.

Mac Longius, is situated near the parish church, which is called
sometimes *Kill-Enda*—that is, the cella or cell of St. Endeus—
and sometimes *Tempull mor Enda*, or the great church of
Endeus.

4. The church called *Tempull Mic Canonn*, near the aforesaid
parish church.

5. The church called of St. Mary, not far from the same
parish church.

6. The church which is named *Tempull Benain*, or the temple
of St. Benignus.

7. The church called *Mainistir Connachtach*, that is, the
Connaught Monastery, in place of which, being afterwards
demolished, was built a chapel to St. Kieran.

8. The church called *Kill-na-manach*, that is, the church or
cell of the monks, which was dedicated to St. Cathradochus, or
Caradoc, the monk, surnamed *Garbh*, or the rough.

9. The church *Tempull Assurnuidhe* (or, perhaps, Esserninus),
and this church is held in the greatest veneration among the
islanders.

10. The church called *Tempull an cheathruir aluinn*, or the
church of the four beautiful (saints), who were SS. Fursey,
Brendan of Birr, Conall, and Berchann, whose bodies are also
said to be buried in the same tomb, lying in the cemetery of the
same church.

11. The church called *Tempull-mic-Duach*, or the church of
St. Mac Duagh (who is also called Colmanus, surnamed Mac
Duagh), which is a handsome church dedicated to that saint.

12. The handsome and formerly parochial church, called
Tempull Breccain, or the church of Brecan, in which also his
feast is celebrated on the 22nd of May.

13. The church near the aforesaid church of St. Brecan,
which is commonly called *Tempull a Phuill*.

Several of these edifices have long since perished, and of
those yet remaining, some, as not being immediately connected
with St. Enda, do not come within the scope of this paper. For
this reason we make no mention of the ecclesiastical establishment of St. Brecan,* with its seven churches, and its inscribed
stones marking the graves of St. Brecan, of the seven Roman
strangers, and of the monks. But among the buildings visited
by us which directly concern our present purpose we were fortunate in meeting with samples of almost every class of the
ecclesiastical structures in use among our Christian forefathers
in Ireland. We found within short distance of St. Enda's tomb

---

* Petrie's Inquiry into the origin and uses of the Round Towers of Ireland,
p. 139.

what we may safely style representative specimens of the primitive Irish churches, as well as those known as *daimhliags*, as
of those called *duirteachs*; the remains of a round tower, and
several early stone houses of divers kinds. Before we conduct
our reader through those variously interesting remains, we ask
his attention to Dr. Petrie's* description of the architectural
peculiarities of the primitive Irish churches, which description
we here present in a condensed form.

The ancient Irish churches are almost invariably of small
size, being usually not more than sixty feet in length. In their
general form they closely follow that of the Roman basilica, and
they are even called by this name in the oldest writers; but
they never present the semicircular apsis at the east end so usual
in Roman churches, and the smaller churches are merely simple
oblong quadrangles. In addition to this quadrangle the larger
churches present a second oblong of smaller dimensions extending to the east, and constituting the chancel or sanctuary,
in which the altar was placed, and which is connected with the
nave by a triumphal arch of semicircular form. These churches
have rarely more than a single entrance, which is placed in the
centre of the west end; and they are very imperfectly lighted
by small windows splaying inwards, which do not appear to
have been even glazed. The chancel has usually two or three
windows, one of which is always in the centre of the east wall,
and another in the south wall; the windows in the nave are also
usually placed in the south wall, and rarely exceed two in number.
The windows are frequently triangular headed, but more usually
arched semicircularly, while the doorway, on the contrary, is
almost universally covered by a horizontal lintel, consisting of a
single stone. In all cases the sides of the doorways and windows
incline, like the doorways in the oldest cyclopean buildings, to
which they bear a striking resemblance. The doorways and
windows rarely exhibit ornaments of any kind. The walls are
generally formed of very large polygonal stones, carefully adjusted to each other both on the inner and outer faces, while
their interior is filled up with rubble and grouting. In the
smaller churches the roof was frequently formed of stone, but
in the larger ones always of wood, covered with shingles, straw,
or reeds. These larger churches are designated in Irish writings
by the names *damhliag* or stone church, *tempull* (*templum*) *eccles,*
regles (*ecclesia*), and sometimes *baslie* (*basilica*). The smaller
churches or oratories were called *duirteachs*, and in the beginning were for the most part, as the etymology denotes, *houses
of oak*, although the Tripartite Life of St. Patrick makes men-

* Petrie's Inquiry into the origin and uses of the Round Towers of Ireland, p. 139.

tion of a stone oratory at Armagh coeval with St. Patrick himself. The average dimensions of the *duirteachs* was about fifteen feet in length, and ten in breadth, interior measurement. In the general plan of this class of buildings there was an equal uniformity. They had a single doorway, always placed in the centre of the west wall, and lighted by a single window placed in the centre of the east wall, and a stone altar beneath this window. It can scarcely be questioned that this class of buildings was originally erected for the private devotion of the founders exclusively; for in the immediate vicinity of such oratories we usually find not only the cells which served as habitations for the founders, but also the tombs in which they were interred.

We found a beautiful specimen of the class of larger churches here described in Tempull-Mac-Duagh, at Kilmurvey. It has the nave and chancel which characterise the first-mentioned species of the Tempulls. The nave is little more than eighteen feet long by fourteen broad, and the chancel nearly sixteen feet long by eleven broad. The stones of the walls are of immense size, and the entire building has a sombre, severe look. The doorway is a remarkable instance of the cyclopean door, and resembles the doorway of the Cathedral Church of Kilmacduagh erected for St. Colman Macduagh by his kinsman Guaire Aidhne, King of Connaught, about the year 610. It is five feet six inches in height, two feet in width at the top, and two feet three inches at the bottom. The lintel is of granite, and measures five feet six inches in length, one foot six inches in height, and extends the entire thickness of the wall, which is two feet six inches.*

Our chief interest, however, was naturally centred in the group of buildings which exist at Killeany, and consist of the church of St. Benignus, the church of St. Enda, the round tower of St. Enda, and the stone houses in its immediate vicinity. Our readers will have remarked that the first six churches named in Dr. Keely's list all stood near each other, and to the north of the present village of Killeany. Out of the six four have almost entirely disappeared, namely, *Kill-Enda*, called also *Tempull-mor-Enda*, or the great church of Enda; *Tempull-mac-Longa*, *Tempull-mic-Canonn*, and the church of St. Mary. They were demolished by the unholy hands of the invaders for the sake of the materials which they supplied to build the castle of Arkin. So all-devouring time, says O'Flaherty †—

"Diruit, edificat, mutat quadrata rotundis."

---

* For an engraving of this doorway, see Petrie's *Round Towers*, p. 174.
† Iar Connaught, p. 82.

The church known as Teglach Enda still exists on the shore ; it is in good preservation, and is a fine specimen of the single church without chancel. It is twenty-four feet in length and fourteen in breadth. All the walls now standing are by no means of an equal antiquity. The eastern gable and part of the northern side wall are the only parts belonging to St. Enda's time, the remainder of the building being the work of a later period. The eastern gable is built of large stones like those at Tempull-Mac-Duagh, cemented with excellent mortar, one of the stones extending almost the entire breadth of the gable. The window in the eastern gable is one foot seven inches high and eight broad on the outside, and on the inside two feet three inches high, and one foot two inches at the top, widening, however, at the bottom to one foot eight inches. The doorway is placed in the northern wall, and is about two feet broad and five high. It is in the modern pointed style, and cannot be more than five hundred years old. There is a narrow window in this northern wall of about three feet in height, of the same age as the doorway. Beneath this window, on the outside of the edifice, we found inserted in the wall a beautiful sepulchral slab inscribed, *or do Scandlain, a prayer for Scanlan*, which, however, was clearly not *in situ*, since the lines ran not parallel but at right angles with the ground. It was, probably, one of the many sepulchral slabs belonging to the cemetery which surrounds the church, and was employed by the restorers of the building, just as the sepulchral slabs of the Roman Catacombs are sometimes found in the walls of the oratories erected at a later date over the entrances to the cemeteries, or over the spot where some illustrious martyr reposed below. We do not know who this Scanlan was, but in the list of saints of the family to which St. Enda belonged we find mention made of a Scanlan who was father of Flann Febhla, Archbishop of Armagh. Around the church spreads the cemetery, now almost completely covered up by the sands, in which the body of St. Enda, and those of one hundred and fifty other saints, are interred. Between this cemetery and the castle of Arkin we found some remains of masonry buried in the sands, which had left uncovered what seemed to be the lintel of the doorway of one of the primitive buildings. Probably it was portion of one of the four churches mentioned by Dr. Keely, and which had been destroyed.

A little beyond this point, in the street of the village of Killeany, we entered a narrow road leading up the hill at the foot of which this ruined castle still frowns on the sea, and soon reached a small well sunk deep in the ground, known to the natives as the Friar's Well. It was the well that served the fathers of a Franciscan monastery which was built, Ware says,[*] in the year 1485, probably by the O'Briens, on the slope of the hill just under the round tower of St. Enda. This establishment also was demolished by the barbarians for the sake of its building materials. It was easy for us, however, to trace its site by the lines formed by the foundations of the walls; and the base of a large stone cross, with portion of the cross itself, were found lying in the middle of a field on which the building once stood. The walls of loose stone on the roadside were here festooned by thick and verdant shoots of the hop plant, which spread in great luxuriance around. This shrub is not found elsewhere in the island. It and the ruined cross and a few shapeless walls are all that survive to tell where once stood garden and cloister of the Franciscan monastery.

A little higher up, on the hillside, we came to St. Enda's well and altar, the latter surmounted by a rude cross, and betraying by its clumsiness the work of a modern hand. St. Enda's well, and indeed all the other wells we saw in the island, are carefully protected by the Araners, the scarcity of water rendering the possession of a well almost as precious to them as it was to the Eastern shepherds in the days of Rebecca. At a short distance to the left of the well stands the remnant of the round tower of St. Enda. Once its height was worthy of the cluster of sacred temples which stood within the circle traversed by the shadow it projected in the changing hours, but now it is little more than thirteen feet high. An aged man who joined our group told us that in St. Enda's time the Mass was not commenced in any of the churches of the island until the bell from St. Enda's tower announced that St. Enda himself had taken his place at the altar in his own church. There have been many theories propounded concerning the uses of the round towers less satisfactory than this of the simple Araner. The contrast between the masonry of the round tower and that of the pagan forts is very remarkable. The round tower was built of chiselled stones, bound together with cement; the pagan fortress of stones not dressed by the hand, and put together without mortar. No one who has had an opportunity of comparing both can ever be persuaded that they are the work of the same period or of the same builders.

Ascending the hill where it rises to the south-west behind the tower, we reached the exquisitely beautiful *duirteach* known as *Tempull Benain*, or temple of St. Benignus, pupil of St. Patrick and Archbishop of Armagh, which crowned the highest point of the hill above us, and stood out with its sharp lines clearly defined against the sky. This church is erroneously called Temple Mionnain. It lies north and south, a peculiarity which distinguishes it from the other churches of these primitive ages, which, as a rule, lie east and west. A solitary arched window in the eastern wall, where the altar stood, gave admittance to the light through an opening a little more than a foot high and a foot broad. The doorway is in the north gable, and commands an enchanting prospect over Casla Bay. It is six feet three inches in height, and one foot three inches broad at top, while, like the cyclopean doors, it widens at bottom to a width of two feet. The original height of the side-walls was seven feet four inches; the northern gable rose to the height of seventeen feet, but is now only fifteen feet high. In the western wall there is one large stone, in size four feet by four, and eleven inches in thickness. Tempull Benain measures on the outside only fifteen feet one inch in length, and eleven feet three inches in breadth. The roof has totally disappeared, but was evidently a stone roof like that on the building known as St. Kevin's house, at Glendalough. Dr. O'Donovan, who, in company with Dr. Petrie, examined all the churches in Aran, and to whose accuracy we owe those details of measurement, unhesitatingly declares this church of St. Benain to be an erection coeval with St. Benignus himself. It is well known that this saint has always been the object of great devotion in the West on account of his apostolic labours in that portion of Ireland.

And here, before leaving this part of our subject, we wish to quote Dr. Petrie's eloquent remarks on the primitive churches of our land, and what are especially applicable to those on Aran. "That they have little in them," says the learned man,[*] "to interest the mind or attract regard as works of art it would be childish to deny; yet, in their symmetrical simplicity—their dimly-lighted nave, entered by its central west doorway, and terminated on the other side by its chancel arch, affording to the devout worshipper an unimpeded view of that brighter sanctuary in which were celebrated the divine mysteries which afforded him consolation in this world and hope in the next—in the total absence of everything which could distract his attention—there is an expression of fitness to their purpose too often wanting in modern temples of the highest pretensions; as the artless strains sung to the Creator, which, we may believe, were daily hymned in those unadorned temples, were calculated, from their very simplicity and artlessness, to awaken feelings of deep devotion, which the gorgeous

---

[*] Round Towers, pp. 188, 189.

artificial music of the modern cathedral but too rarely excites, even in minds most predisposed to feel its influences and appreciate its refinement. In short, these ancient temples are just humble, unadorned structures, as we might expect them to have been; but, even if they were found to exhibit less of that expression of congruity and fitness, and more of that humbleness so characteristic of a religion not made for the rich, but for the poor and lowly, that mind is but little to be envied which could look with apathy on the remains of national structures so venerable for their antiquity, and so interesting as being raised in honour of the Creator in the simplest ages of Christianity."

But where, it may be asked, did all these religious men live? How were they sheltered from the Atlantic tempests of which the first fury was necessarily spent on the beetling cliffs of Aran? How were they protected from the wintry cold and from the rain?

Let not our readers expect, in answer to this question, a description of any vast structure sufficient for the adequate accommodation of communities as large as those that were housed in the stately monasteries of the middle ages. In Aran, as elsewhere in Ireland, the early monastic establishments were composed* of separate cells for the abbot, monks, and clergy, while the houses required for the accommodation of strangers, the kitchen, &c., were all separate edifices, surrounded by a cashel or circular wall, and forming a kind of monastery or ecclesiastical town, like those of the early Christians in the East, and known among the Egyptians by the name of *Laura*. The *Laura* herein differed from the *Coenobium*, that the latter was but one habitation where the monks lived in common, whereas the former consisted of many cells divided from each other. Such groups of cells are frequently mentioned in the Lives of the Irish Saints.†

These structures, it is fair to assume, were formed of the materials within easy reach of the builders, and consequently, in many parts of Ireland, of perishable materials, such as wood and clay. For this reason few vestiges of them remain in the northern and eastern portions of the island. But in the west and south many such buildings yet survive, and of these we found interesting specimens in Aranmore. "There," writes O'Flaherty, ‡ "they have *cloghauns*, a kind of building of stones laid one upon another, which are brought to a roof,

---

* Round Towers, p. 416.

† Bollandists, Act. SS. Maii, tom. 3, in Life of St. Mochuda or Carthage of Lismore.

‡ Op. cit. p. 68.

without any manner of mortar to cement them, some of which cabins will hold forty men on their floor, so ancient that nobody knows how long ago any of them was made. Scarcity of wood and store of fit stones, without peradventure, found out the first invention." These houses are of a circular or oval form, having dome roofs, constructed without a knowledge of the principle of the arch, and without the use of cement. They are formed upon the model left by the pagan Firbolg and Tuatha de Danaan tribes, as is obvious from the resemblance they bear to the pagan circular stone forts. One remarkable difference between the houses of the pagan and Christian periods is, that whereas the former are round internally and externally, the latter, though externally round, are occasionally quadrangular in the interior, as if the quadrangular form of the churches had been adopted also for the houses of ecclesiastics. Whole villages of these houses exist on Aran-more.*

The neighbouring island of Ardillaun still exhibits the Laura, founded by St. Fechin, in the seventh century, which is one of the most interesting and best preserved anchoretical establishments in Ireland, or perhaps in Europe.† On the crest of the hill, on which Tempull Benain stands, about thirteen feet to the north-west of the sacred edifice, there was a *cloughaun*, partly under the ground, ten feet in length, and five feet four inches in breadth; the doorway was more than two feet broad, and the walls three feet thick. O'Donovan, who describes it,‡ is of opinion that it was probably the house of St. Benignus himself. Our interest was most excited by a cyclopean house, of angular form, which measured from north to south eleven feet eight inches, and six feet ten inches across. It had two doorways, about two feet broad and three thick; and in one of the chambers there was a window. The double door is said to be more common in the Aran *cloghauns* than in these found elsewhere.§ One of the chambers in this house measures four feet nine inches in length, and four feet in breadth. The entire structure has suffered much from exposure. In addition to these separate cells, Dr. Petrie discovered on Aran-More the ruins of a building which would have been large enough to serve the purpose of a refectory. It is situated near the churches of St. Colman Mac Duach, at Kilmurvey, and is an oval structure, without cement, of fifty by thirty-seven feet, external measurement, with a wall of six

* Proceedings of R. I. Academy, vol. x., p. 25.
† Ibid., pp. 551-555.
‡ Ordnance Survey, MSS.
§ Proceedings R. I. Academy, vol. x., p. 555.

feet in thickness.   But it is now full time to bring our wanderings to a close.

With the permission of the excellent and hospitable priest who has charge of the island we resolved, on the last morning of our stay on Aran, to celebrate Mass in the ruined church of Teglach-Enda, where in the year 540 or 542 St. Enda was interred, and where likewise repose the relics of a countless army of white-robed saints.   The morning was bright and clear, and as we traversed the road skirting the shore from Kilronan to Killeany the dark and rigid outlines of the rocks were softened by the touch of the early sunshine.   The inhabitants of Killeany, exulting in the tidings that the Holy Sacrifice was once again to be offered to God near the shrine of their sainted patron, accompanied or followed us to the venerable ruins.   The men, young and old, were clothed in decent black, or in white garments of home-made stuff, with sandals of undressed leather, like those of the peasants of the Abruzzi, laced round their feet; the women were attired in gay scarlet gowns and blue bodices, and all wore a look of remarkable neatness and comfort.   The small roofless church was soon filled to overflowing with a decorous and devout congregation; and as the sands had accumulated to a considerable height on the exterior of the building, those who found no place within were enabled to overtop the high walls on either side, and thus assist at the Sacrifice.   It was plain to us, from what we saw before us, that these churches had not been originally intended to receive even ordinary assemblages of the faithful.

We can never forget the scene of that morning: the pure, bright sand, covering the graves of unknown and unnumbered saints as with a robe of silver tissue, that glistened in the sunshine; the delicate green foliage of the wild plants that rose here and there, as if wrought in embroidery upon the white expanse; on one side the swelling hill crowned with the church of Benignus, and on the other the blue sea, that almost bathed the foundations of the venerable sanctuary itself; the soft, balmy air that hardly stirred the ferns on the old walls; and the fresh, happy, solemn calm that reigned over all.

The temporary altar was set up under the east window, on the site where of old the altar stood; and there, in the midst of the loving and simple faithful, within the walls which had been consecrated some twelve hundred years before, over the very spot of earth where so many of the saints of Ireland lay awaiting their resurrection to glory, the solemn rite of the Christian Sacrifice was performed, and once more, as in the days of which St. Columba wrote, the angels of God came down to worship the Divine Victim in the churches of Aran. And surely not unworthy of the angelic company were the devotion and faith of the humble worshippers around. Throughout the Mass a hush and a silence came upon them, and the only sounds that fell upon the ear was the solemn voice of the priest, or the murmur of the waves breaking on the beach outside; but at the moment of the elevation, when they beheld the pure and holy and unspotted Host raised up for them to heaven, a cry of adoring faith and love went forth from their lips, and every head was bowed to the dust before the Lord.

M. H. Gill and Son, Printers, Dublin.